Lecture Notes in Computer Science   13059

More information about this subseries at http://www.springer.com/series/7410

Qiong Huang · Yu Yu (Eds.)

Provable and Practical Security

15th International Conference, ProvSec 2021
Guangzhou, China, November 5–8, 2021
Proceedings

Editors
Qiong Huang
South China Agricultural University
Guangzhou, China

Yu Yu
Shanghai Jiao Tong University
Shanghai, China

ISSN 0302-9743   ISSN 1611-3349 (electronic)
Lecture Notes in Computer Science
ISBN 978-3-030-90401-2   ISBN 978-3-030-90402-9 (eBook)
https://doi.org/10.1007/978-3-030-90402-9

LNCS Sublibrary: SL4 – Security and Cryptology

This Springer imprint is published by the registered company Springer Nature Switzerland AG
The registered company address is: Gewerbestrasse 11, 6330 Cham, Switzerland

Preface

This volume contains the papers presented at ProvSec 2021 - the 15th International Conference on Provable and Practical Security, held during November 5–8, 2021. Due to the global COVID-19 pandemic, this year we organized ProvSec 2021 as a hybrid conference. Attendees from low-risk areas of mainland China were invited to join the conference offline at Guangzhou, while other attendees were invited to join the conference online. The conference was hosted by the College of Mathematics and Informatics, South China Agricultural University, China.

The first ProvSec conference was held in 2007. Until 2018, ProvSec conferences focused on "Provable Security". Since 2019, "Practical Security" has been added into the theme of the conference to enrich the scope of the conference and to bring together security researchers and practitioners.

This year we received 67 submissions, which were reviewed in a double-blind manner. Each submission was carefully evaluated by three to five reviewers, and then discussed among the Program Committee. Finally, 21 papers were accepted for presentation at the conference. Based on the reviews and votes by Program Committee members, the following paper was given the Best Paper Award:

"Public Key Based Searchable Encryption with Fine-Grained Sender Permission Control", by Zhongming Wang, Biwen Chen, Tao Xiang, Lu Zhou, Hongyang Yan, and Jin Li.

ProvSec 2021 would not have been possible without the contributions of the many volunteers who freely gave their time and expertise. We would like to thank all the 51 Program Committee members from all over the world and the external reviewers for their substantial work in evaluating the papers. We thank the local organizers for their tremendous efforts in successfully organizing this event. Last but not least, we would like to express our gratitude to all invited speakers and all authors who submitted papers to ProvSec 2021.

November 2021

Qiong Huang
Yu Yu

Organization

General Co-chairs

Rongliang Qiu   South China Agricultural University, China
Fangguo Zhang   Sun Yat-sen University, China

Program Co-chairs

Qiong Huang   South China Agricultural University, China
Yu Yu   Shanghai Jiao Tong University, China

Program Committee

Man Ho Au   University of Hong Kong, China
Shi Bai   Florida Atlantic University, USA
Rishiraj Bhattacharyya   NISER, India
Jie Chen   East China Normal University, China
Cheng-Kang Chu   Huawei, Singapore
Chitchanok   University of Adelaide, Australia
Chuengsatiansup Yi Deng   Institute of Information Engineering, Chinese
                                Academy of Sciences, China
Keita Emura   NICT, Japan
Xiong Fan   University of Maryland, USA
Fei Gao   Beijing University of Posts and Telecommunications,
                                China
Junqing Gong   East China Normal University, China
Swee-Huay Heng   Multimedia University, Malaysia
Xinyi Huang   Fujian Normal University, China
Tetsu Iwata   Nagoya University, Japan
David Jao   University of Waterloo, Canada
Sabyasachi Karati   Indian Statistical Institute, Kolkata, India
Shuichi Katsumata   AIST, Japan
Junzuo Lai   Jinan University, China
Jooyoung Lee   KAIST, South Korea
Hyung Tae Lee   Chung-Ang University, South Korea
Yang Li   University of Electro-Communications, Japan
Kaitai Liang   TU Delft, The Netherlands
Changlu Lin   Fujian Normal University, China
Dongxi Liu   CSIRO, Australia
Shengli Liu   Shanghai Jiao Tong University, China
Zhen Liu   Shanghai Jiao Tong University, China

Kirill Morozov	University of North Texas, USA
Khoa Nguyen	Nanyang Technological University, Singapore
Federico Pintore	University of Oxford, UK
Baodong Qin	Xi'an University of Posts and Telecommunications, China
Somindu C. Ramanna	IIT Kharagpur, India
Amin Sakzad	Monash University, Australia
Olivier Sanders	Orange Labs, France
Daniel Slamanig	Austrian Institute of Technology, Austria
Shi-Feng Sun	Monash University, Australia
Willy Susilo	University of Wollongong, Australia
Atsushi Takayasu	NICT, Japan
Viet Cuong Trinh	Hong Duc University, Vietnam
Lei Wang	Shanghai Jiao Tong University, China
Keita Xagawa	NTT, Japan
Yanhong Xu	University of Calgary, Canada
Haiyang Xue	Institute of Information Engineering, Chinese Academy of Sciences, China
Guomin Yang	University of Wollongong, Australia
Rupeng Yang	Hong Kong Polytechnic University, China
Yong Yu	Shaanxi Normal University, China
Yu Yu	Shanghai Jiao Tong University, China
Fangguo Zhang	Sun Yat-sen University, China
Lei Zhang	East China Normal University, China
Liangfeng Zhang	Shanghai Tech University, China
Cong Zuo	Monash University, Australia

Publicity Chair

Hongbo Li	South China Agricultural University, China

Organizing Committee Co-chairs

Sha Ma	South China Agricultural University, China
Ximing Li	South China Agricultural University, China
Cai Zhang	South China Agricultural University, China
Meiyan Xiao	South China Agricultural University, China

External Reviewers

Maxime Buser
Haixia Chen
Valerio Cini
Dung Hoang Duong
Scott Fluhrer
Qingqing Gan
Floyd Johnson
Shangqi Lai
Jiangtao Li
Jianwei Li
Xiaohong Liu

Ji Luo
Tran Ngo
Jianting Ning
Edoardo Persichetti
Christoph Striecks
Erkan Tairi
Shuo Wang
S. J. Yang
Wei-Chuen Yau
Zuoxia Yu
Fei Zhu

Contents

Functional Encryption

Digital Signature

Practical Security Protocols

Searchable Encryption

Public Key Based Searchable Encryption with Fine-Grained Sender Permission Control

Zhongming Wang[1], Biwen Chen[1], Tao Xiang[1]([✉]), Lu Zhou[2], Hongyang Yan[3], and Jin Li[3]

[1] College of Computer Science, Chongqing University, Chongqing, China
`txiang@cqu.edu.cn`
[2] College of Computer Science and Technology, Nanjing University of Aeronautics and Astronautics, Nanjing, China
[3] Institute of Artificial Intelligence and Blockchain, Guangzhou University, Guangzhou, China

Abstract. Public key encryption with keyword searched (PEKS) is a promising cryptographic primitive that realizes keyword search in the ciphertext. Since it can provide flexible access to encrypted data, PEKS has been widely used in various fields, such as Cloud Computing and Internet of Things. Until now, many PEKS schemes with fine-grained access control have been proposed to satisfy the requirements of data sharing. However, most previous work only considered the control of data receiver and ignored the control of data sender. In practice, the malicious data sender might correctly generate ciphertexts containing useless information, which in turn increases the computational burden and communication load for the data receiver.

To address the above problem, we introduce the concept of PEKS with fine-grained sender permission control, named SCPEKS. In SCPEKS, only those ciphertexts containing matching keywords and of which data sender attributes satisfy the authorized receiver policy will be returned to the data receiver. Also, we present a detailed construction of SCPEKS and prove that the instance achieves ciphertext indistinguishability and unforgeability. Moreover, comparisons with other related schemes suggest that the proposed scheme achieves flexible bidirectional access control at the expense of a slightly higher computation and communication cost.

Keywords: Searchable encryption · Access control · Multi-user

1 Introduction

With the development of information technology, more and more digital data has been stored in cloud servers to facilitate data sharing and flexible access. However, since the outsourced data may contain sensitive information and the cloud servers are not completely trusted, data security problem [22] becomes a

© Springer Nature Switzerland AG 2021
Q. Huang and Y. Yu (Eds.): ProvSec 2021, LNCS 13059, pp. 3–18, 2021.
https://doi.org/10.1007/978-3-030-90402-9_1

problem that urgently to be resolved. As a regular way to preserve data privacy, methods of encrypting data before uploading are used to solve the problem.

Although traditional encryption schemes (e.g., AES) can be used to ensure the confidentiality of outsourcing data, they also limit the data utilization such as search operations frequently performed. To solve this question, Song *et al.* [20] introduced the concept of searchable encryption (SE) which allows a user to search some keywords over ciphertexts without decryption. Later, Boneh *et al.* [4] proposed the public key version of searchable encryption, called public key encryption with keyword search (PEKS). Unlike Song's scheme which relies on the shared secret information, PEKS enables the data sender to create a searchable ciphertext with public information including public parameters and public key. This difference allows PEKS to avoid key distribution and key management issues.

Since PEKS was presented, most existing schemes [12,18] model the data sender as an honest entity and only enforce the data receiver access control. In practice, however, the data sender may be malicious and send illegal data for specific reasons such as internal random error or commercial interests. For example, considering denial of service (DoS) attack in normal encryption, in the absence of sender permission control, a data sender who knows other users' public keys can easily launch the cryptographic version of DoS attack against those users. What's worse, attacks from malicious data senders might cause more serious problems in PEKS than normal encryption. In a PEKS system, the cloud server will transmit the encrypted data to the data receiver if the ciphertext matches the trapdoor. Therefore the DoS attack not only consumes the computing power of the data receiver, but also consumes bandwidth of communication between the cloud server and the data receiver.

Although there has been some encryption schemes [1,2,5,6] on access control for both the data sender and the data receiver, the research on PEKS with bidirectional access control is almost blank. Therefore, our investigation started from one questions: how to implement a PEKS scheme which supports bidirectional access control, namely fine-grained access control to both the data sender and the data receiver.

1.1 Contribution

Fortunately, we present a positive answer to the above question by designing a new PEKS scheme with fine-grained sender permission control (SCPEKS). The main contributions of this paper are outlined as follows:

- Sender permission control is introduced into PEKS for the first time. Considering threats from the malicious data sender, we introduce the concept of sender permission control into PEKS and propose a new variant PEKS scheme (SCPEKS) that achieves bidirectional access control.
- A concrete construction of SCPEKS is proposed in this paper. By using the linear secret-sharing scheme and public key tree, we propose an construction of SCPEKS. The instance achieves hierarchical access control on the data receiver and attribute-based access control on the data sender.

- Detailed security and efficiency analysis of SCPEKS is conducted. We formally prove that our construction satisfies ciphertext indistinguishability and unforgeability. And the functional comparison with other related schemes presents the flexibility of SCPEKS. Moreover, the functionality and performance comparisons with other related schemes presents the flexibility and practicality of SCPEKS.

1.2 Organization

The rest of the paper is organized as follows. We introduce the related work in the following section. In Sect. 3, we describe some preliminaries. Then, system model, formal definition and security model are introduced in Sect. 4. In Sect. 5, we give the concrete construction of SCPEKS. In Sect. 6, we give the security proof of our scheme and analysis its performance from functionality and efficiency. Finally, we conclude the paper in Sect. 7.

2 Related Work

Although the original searchable encryption schemes [4,20] solve the problem of data retrieval on encrypted data, the requirement of data sharing on the cloud storage requires that the PEKS schemes can be applied in multi-user environment. To satisfy the requirement, Yang et al. [24] and Huang et al. [10] proposed multi-user searchable encryption which enables multiple receivers to search over ciphertexts sent to a group. Compared to the original schemes, PEKS in multi-user setting achieves a great improvement in data sharing. However, since data stored in the cloud is often shared among users with different permissions, PEKS in multi-user setting requires fine-grained access control.

To support fine-grained access control, Li et al. [12] proposed hierarchical public key encryption with keyword search (HPEKS). In HPEKS, the public key of users form a public key tree from high to low which allows the user with higher access permission to search over ciphertexts sent to users with lower permission. Meanwhile, attribute-based encryption (ABE) [3,7,19], as an efficient approach to deploy fine-grained access control on computer system, has been considered to be combined with searchable encryption. Sun et al. [21] and Zheng et al. [26] proposed attribute-based searchable encryption (ABSE), respectively. And then, a series of works on key-policy ABSE [18,25] and ciphertext-policy ABSE [8,23] have been proposed. Also, some variants of ABSE have been proposed in [14–16].

However, the above works only implement access control for the data receiver, none of them take into account the threat of malicious data sender. Recently, Huang et al. [11] proposed public key authenticated encryption with keyword search (PAEKS) to resist keyword guessing attack from insider adversary. In their scheme, generating a ciphertext requires the secret key of the data sender, and thus the malicious data senders cannot send useless ciphertexts to the data receiver. Subsequently, He et al. [9] proposed certificateless PAEKS which eliminated the influence of key management problem. And then, Li et al. [13] introduced PAEKS into identity based encryption setting. Although PAEKS realizes access control to the data sender, data can only be transmitted from one sender to a single receiver, which limits data sharing in cloud storage.

3   Preliminaries

In this section, the notations and building blocks used in the SCPEKS are described in detail.

3.1   Notations

Let A, B be two strings and $A \parallel B$ denote the concatenation of A and B. For $n \in \mathbb{N}$, we define $[n] = 1, 2, \ldots, n$. Then, we denote the attributes of data sender as att_{snd}, the policy of data receiver to data sender as $\mathbb{R}$, the attributes set of data sender as σ and the number of different attributes as l in this paper. Moreover, if $\mathbb{R}(\sigma) = 1$, which denotes that attributes σ satisfies the policy $\mathbb{R}$. Otherwise, $\mathbb{R}(\sigma) \neq 1$ means that attributes σ does not satisfy the policy $\mathbb{R}$.

3.2   Bilinear Maps

Let $\mathbb{G}$ and $\mathbb{G}_T$ be two cyclic groups of same prime order p and g be a generator of $\mathbb{G}$. A bilinear map $e : \mathbb{G} \times \mathbb{G} \to \mathbb{G}_T$ has the following properties:

- **Bilinearity.** For any $P, Q \in \mathbb{G}$ and $a, b \in \mathbb{Z}_p^*$, the equation $e(g^a, g^b) = e(g, g)^{ab}$ holds.
- **Non-degeneracy.** For any generator $g \in \mathbb{G}$, $e(g, g) \in \mathbb{G}_T$ is a generator of $\mathbb{G}_T$.
- **Computability.** For any $P, Q \in \mathbb{G}$, there is an effective polynomial time algorithm to compute $e(P, Q) \in \mathbb{G}_T$.

3.3   Hardness Assumption

We prove the security of our construction based on Computational Bilinear Diffie-Hellman (Computational BDH) assumption and Decisional Bilinear Diffie-Hellman (Decisional BDH) assumption.

Definition 1 (Computational BDH Assumption). *Let* $e : \mathbb{G} \times \mathbb{G} \to \mathbb{G}_T$ *be a bilinear map. A Computational BDH assumption is that, for any probabilistic polynomial time adversary, given* $(g^a, g^b, g^c) \in \mathbb{G}$, *the probability for adversary to compute* $e(g, g)^{abc}$ *is negligible.*

Definition 2 (Decisional BDH Assumption). *Let* $e : \mathbb{G} \times \mathbb{G} \to \mathbb{G}_T$ *be a bilinear map and* g, h *be two different generators of* $\mathbb{G}$. *A Decisional BDH assumption is that, for any probabilistic polynomial time adversary, given* $g, g^a, g^b, h, h^b, h^c \in \mathbb{G}$, *the probability for the adversary to distinguish* $e(g, h)^{abc}$ *from a random element* $e(g, h)^r \in \mathbb{G}_T$ *is negligible.*

3.4   Linear Secret-Sharing Schemes

Definition 3 (Linear Secret-Sharing Schemes). *Let p be a prime and $\mathcal{S}$ be the universe of attributes. A secret-sharing scheme Π with domain of secrets $\mathbb{Z}_p$ realizing access structure on $\mathcal{S}$ is linear over $\mathbb{Z}_p$ if*

1. *The share of a secret $s \in \mathbb{Z}_p$ for each attribute form a vector over $\mathbb{Z}_p$.*
2. *For each access structure $\mathbb{R}$ on $\mathcal{S}$, there exists a share-generating matrix $M \in \mathbb{Z}_p^{l \times n}$, and a function ρ that labels the rows of M with attributes from $\mathcal{S}$. i.e. $\rho : [l] \to \mathcal{S}$, which satisfies the following: During the generation of shares, we set the column vector $\overrightarrow{x} = (s, r_2, \ldots, r_n)^{\top}$, where $r_2, \ldots, r_n \to \mathbb{Z}_p$. Then the vector of l shares of the secret s according to Π is equal to $M\overrightarrow{x} \in \mathbb{Z}_p^{l \times 1}$. The share $(M\overrightarrow{x})_j$ "belongs" to attribute $\rho(j)$, where $j \in [l]$.*

The pair (M, ρ) will be referred as the policy of the access structure $\mathbb{R}$ in the following sections.

3.5   Public Key Tree (PKTree)

In order to achieve hierarchical access control to the data receiver in PEKS scheme, we take PKTree [12] as the basic build block of SCPEKS. The PKTree (Fig. 1) enables the data receiver with high access permission to search over ciphertext sent to data receivers with lower permission. We recall the details of PKTree below:

- **Setup(1^{λ}):** Input security parameter λ, the algorithm first selects a bilinear pairing $e : \mathbb{G}_1 \times \mathbb{G}_2 \to \mathbb{G}_T$, where the generators of $\mathbb{G}_1, \mathbb{G}_2$ are g, h, and $(\mathbb{G}_1, \mathbb{G}_2, \mathbb{G}_T)$ have the same prime order p. Then, it randomly chooses $k \in \mathbb{Z}_p$ and selects cryptographic hash functions: $H^* : \{0, 1\}^* \to \mathbb{G}_2, H_1 : \{0, 1\}^* \to \mathbb{G}_2, H_2 : \{0, 1\}^* \to \mathbb{Z}_p$. Finally, it sets public parameter as $\mathcal{PP} = \{\mathbb{G}_1, \mathbb{G}_2, \mathbb{G}_T, p, g, h, e, MPK, H^*, H_1, H_2\}$, where the master secret key $MSK = k$ and the master public key $MPK = g^k$. We assume that $\mathcal{PP}$ will be the input of following algorithm implicitly.
- **BuildTree(msk, ID_{Rt}, τ):** Input the master secret key msk, the identity ID_{Rt} of root node and a time stamp τ, the algorithm generates the public/secret keys of the root node Rt as follows:
  - Randomly choose $\varsigma \in \mathbb{Z}_p$ and generate Rt's public parameter $Pub_{Rt} = (pk_{Rt} = g_1^{H_2(sk_{Rt})}, \overline{ID}_{Rt} = (ID_{Rt}, \varsigma))$, where $sk_{Rt} = H_1(\overline{ID}_{Rt})^{msk}$.
  - Generate a signature $\sigma_{0,Rt} = Sig_{msk}(Pub_{Rt}) = (H^*(Pub_{Rt}||\varsigma)^{msk}, \varsigma)$.
  - Set $Node_{Rt} = (Pub_{Rt}, \sigma_{Rt})$ as root of PKTree and upload $Tree = (Node_{Rt}, P_0)$ to the cloud, where P_0 indicating the position of the node.
- **AddNode($Tree, sk_i, ID_j, \tau_j$):** Input the tree $Tree$, the secret key sk_i of $Node_i$, the identity ID_j of $Node_j$ and j-th time stamp τ_j. The algorithm sets $Node_j$ as the child node of $Node_i$ and computes the public/secret keys of $Node_j$ as follows:
  - Randomly choose $\varsigma_j \in \mathbb{Z}_p$ and generate public parameter $Pub_j = (pk_j = g_1^{H_2(sk_j)}, \overline{ID}_j = (ID_j, \varsigma_j))$, where $sk_j = H_1(\overline{ID}_j)^{H_2(sk_i)}$.

- Sign $\overline{ID}_j$ with sk_i and get signature $\sigma_{i,j} = Sig_{sk_i}(Pub_j) = (H^*(Pub_j||\varsigma_j)^{H_2(sk_i)}, \varsigma_j)$.
- Set child node as $Node_j = H^*(Pub_j, \sigma_{i,j})$

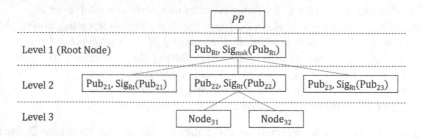

Fig. 1. Structure of PKTree

4   Definition of SCPEKS

In this section, we present the related definitions of SCPEKS, including the system model, formal definition and security requirements.

4.1   System Model

The system model of SCPEKS is shown in Fig. 2. It includes four types of entities: trust authority, data sender, data receiver and cloud server.

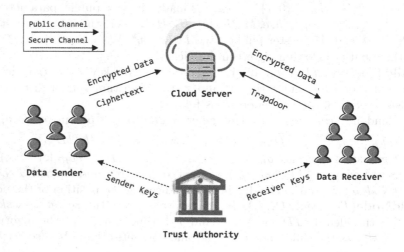

Fig. 2. System model of SCPEKS

- **Trust authority** is responsible for system initialization, the key generation of both data sender and data receiver in the system. After receiving
  the attributes from the data sender, the trust authority will generate and distribute secret keys corresponding to the attributes to the data sender through
  secure channel. In addition, the trust authority will generate the root node
  of PKTree and distribute to the data receiver through secure channel. We
  assume that the trust authority are honest all the time.
- **Data sender** may be honest or malicious. The secret key of data sender is
  corresponding to some attributes and can be verified by the data receiver. In
  the system, the data sender first encrypts keywords to generate the searchable
  ciphertexts by using its secret key and the public key of the data receiver.
  Then, it uploads the searchable ciphertexts to the cloud server along with
  encrypted data.
- **Data receiver** may be honest or malicious. It first generates a legal trapdoor
  containing an access control policy for the data sender using its secret key,
  and then transmits the trapdoor to the cloud server for keyword search.
- **Cloud server** is honest but curious. After receiving the trapdoor from the
  data receiver, it verifies whether the attributes of data sender satisfy the
  access control policy specified by data receiver and tests whether the ciphertext matches the trapdoor. If both conditions are met, it returns the encrypted
  data corresponding to the matching searchable ciphertext to the data receiver.

4.2 Definition of Algorithm

A SCPEKS scheme consists of five algorithms:

- **Setup** (1^λ): The Setup algorithm is run by the trust authority. It takes the
  security parameter 1^λ as input, and then outputs the master public key mpk
  and master secret key msk. We assume that the master public key will be
  used as implicit input in all subsequent algorithms.
- **SkGen** (σ, msk): The SkGen algorithm is run by the trust authority. It takes
  the attributes σ of the data sender as input, and then outputs the data
  sender's secrete key ssk corresponding to the attributes.
- **RkGen** $(sk, ID, \tau, Tree)$: The RkGen algorithm is run by the trust authority
  or a $Node_i$ belonging to the PKTree. It takes secret key sk belongs to the
  $Node_i$ or the trust authority, identity ID of the data receiver or the root
  node, a timestamp τ and PKTree $Tree$ as input, and then generates a pair
  of public and secret key (rsk, rpk) to the data receiver or the root node.
- **Encryption** (w, σ, ssk, rpk): The encryption algorithm is run by the data
  sender. It takes a keyword w, attributes σ, sender's secret key ssk and
  receiver's public key rpk as input, and then outputs the ciphertext Ct of w.
- **Trapdoor** $(w, \mathbb{R}, rsk)$: The trapdoor algorithm is run by the data receiver. It
  takes a keyword w, policy $\mathbb{R}$ and receiver's secret key rsk as input, and then
  outputs the trapdoor $T = (\mathbb{R}, T_w)$.

- **Test** (Ct, T): The test algorithm is run by the cloud server. Takes the input of ciphertext Ct, and the trapdoor T from receiver. It outputs 1 indicating that Ct contains the same keyword with T_w and satisfies policy $\mathbb{R}$ at the same time. If not, it outputs 0.

4.3   Security Model

A secure SCPEKS needs to satisfy both *ciphertext indistinguishability* and *unforgeability*. We give the formal definitions in follows:

Definition 4. *(Ciphertext indistinguishability) A SCPEKS satisfies ciphertext indistinguishability, if there is no polynomial bounded adversary $\mathcal{A}$ has non-negligible advantage against the challenger $\mathcal{C}$ in the following game:*

Ciphertext Indistinguishability Game. The ciphertext indistinguishability game played between the challenger $\mathcal{C}$ and an adversary $\mathcal{A}$ is described as follows:

- **Setup.** Takes input of security parameter 1^λ, the challenger $\mathcal{C}$ generates the master public key mpk and the master secret key msk. $\mathcal{C}$ transmits mpk to $\mathcal{A}$ and keeps msk secretly.
- **Query Phase 1.** After receiving public parameters, the adversary $\mathcal{A}$ makes queries as follows:
  - **SkGen Oracle** $\mathcal{O}_S$: Given sender's attributes σ, the oracle computes and returns the corresponding secret key ssk to $\mathcal{A}$.
  - **RkGen Oracle** $\mathcal{O}_R$: Given secret key sk, identity ID, a timestamp τ and PKTree $Tree$, the oracle computes and returns corresponding secret key rsk and public key rpk to $\mathcal{A}$.
  - **Trapdoor Oracle** $\mathcal{O}_T$: Given a keyword w, the access control policy $\mathbb{R}$ and receiver's public key rpk, the oracle computes and returns trapdoor T corresponding to rpk, w and $\mathbb{R}$ to $\mathcal{A}$.
  - **Encryption Oracle** $\mathcal{O}_E$: Given keyword w, sender's secret key ssk and receiver's public key rpk, the oracle computes and returns corresponding ciphertexts.
- **Challenge.** Once $\mathcal{A}$ decides that **Query Phase 1** is over, it chooses sender's attributes σ^*, receiver's public key rpk^* and keywords $w_0^*, w_1^* \in \mathcal{W}$ which has not appeared in previous query phase and transmits them to $\mathcal{C}$. Then, $\mathcal{C}$ randomly chooses $b \in \{0,1\}$, computes $Ct^* = \mathbf{Encryption}(w_b^*, \sigma^*, ssk_{\sigma^*}, rpk^*)$ and returns it to $\mathcal{A}$.
- **Query Phase 2.** The adversary $\mathcal{A}$ makes queries to challenger $\mathcal{C}$ again. The only constraint is that the queries to $\mathcal{O}_T$ can not be (w_0^*, rpk^*) or (w_1^*, rpk^*).
- **Guess.** Finally, the adversary $\mathcal{A}$ outputs a guess bit $b' \in \{0,1\}$ and wins the game if $b = b'$.

We define the advantage of adversary $\mathcal{A}$ winning the ciphertext indistinguishability game as: $\mathrm{Adv}(\mathcal{A}) = \left| Pr\left[G_{SCPEKS,\mathcal{A}}^{Ind} = 1 \right] - \frac{1}{2} \right|$.

Definition 5. *(Unforgeability) A SCPEKS scheme satisfies unforgeability, if there is no polynomial bounded adversary $\mathcal{A}$ has non-negligible advantage against the challenger $\mathcal{C}$ in the following game:*

Unforgeability Game. The unforgeability game played between the challenger $\mathcal{C}$ and an adversary $\mathcal{A}$ is described as follows:

- **Setup.** Takes input of security parameter 1^λ, the challenger $\mathcal{C}$ generates master public key mpk and master secret key msk. $\mathcal{C}$ transmits mpk to $\mathcal{A}$ and keeps msk by itself.
- **Query Phase.** After receiving the public parameters, the adversary $\mathcal{A}$ makes queries as follows:
  - **SkGen Oracle $\mathcal{O}_S$:** Given attributes σ, the oracle computes and returns the secret key ssk_σ of the data sender. The challenger $\mathcal{C}$ maintains a list $\mathcal{L}_S$ to record all queries about the attributes σ, where the list is empty at the beginning.
  - **RkGen Oracle $\mathcal{O}_R$:** Given secret key sk, identity ID, a timestamp τ and PKTree $Tree$, the oracle computes and returns corresponding secret key rsk and public key rpk to $\mathcal{A}$.
  - **Encryption Oracle $\mathcal{O}_E$:** Given keyword w, sender's secret key ssk and receiver's public key rpk, the oracle computes and returns corresponding ciphertexts. The challenger $\mathcal{C}$ maintains a list $\mathcal{L}_E$ to record all queried ciphertexts Ct, where the list is empty at the beginning.
  - **Trapdoor Oracle $\mathcal{O}_T$:** Given keyword w, policy $\mathbb{R}$ and receiver's public key rpk, the oracle computes and returns trapdoor T corresponding to rpk, w and $\mathbb{R}$ to $\mathcal{A}$.
- **Guess.** After determining that **Query Phase** is over, $\mathcal{A}$ sends the ciphertext Ct^* and the policy $\mathbb{R}^*$ to $\mathcal{C}$. If Verify $(Ct^*, \mathbb{R}^*) = 1$, and $(Ct^*, \mathbb{R}^*)$ satisfies the following requirements: 1. $\forall \sigma \in \mathcal{L}_S, \mathbb{R}^*(\sigma) \neq 1$. 2. $\forall Ct \in \mathcal{L}_E$, Verify $(Ct, \mathbb{R}^*) \neq 1$. Then, the game outputs 1, else outputs 0.

We define the advantage of adversary $\mathcal{A}$ winning the unforgeability game as: $\text{Adv}(\mathcal{A}) = Pr\left[G^{Unf}_{SC\mathcal{PEKS},\mathcal{A}}(\lambda) = 1\right]$.

5 Construction of SCPEKS

In this section, we propose a concrete construction of SCPEKS which supports hierarchical receiver access control and attribute-based sender access control.

Setup (1^λ): Takes input of security parameter 1^λ, the setup algorithm generates two cyclic groups $\mathbb{G}$ and $\mathbb{G}_T$ of prime order $p > 2^\lambda$ with two different generators $g, h \leftarrow \mathbb{G}$ and a bilinear map $e : \mathbb{G} \times \mathbb{G} \to \mathbb{G}_T$. Then, it selects multiple cryptographic hash functions, including $H_1 : att_{snd} \to \mathbb{G}$, $H_2 : \mathbb{G} \to \mathbb{Z}_p^*$, $H_3 : \{0,1\}^* \to \mathbb{G}$, $H_4 : \{0,1\}^* \to \mathbb{Z}_p^*$ and $H_5 : \{0,1\}^* \to \mathbb{G}$. The hash functions H_1, H_3 will be modeled as random oracle in the security proof. Finally, the algorithm randomly chooses $\alpha, \beta \in \mathbb{Z}_p^*$, generates the master secret key $msk = (g^\alpha, \beta)$ and the master public key $mpk = (\mathbb{G}, \mathbb{G}_T, e, p, g, h, g^\beta, e(g,g)^\alpha, H_1, H_2, H_3, H_4, H_5)$.

SkGen (σ, msk): Takes input of attributes of the data sender $\sigma = (\sigma_1, \sigma_2, \ldots, \sigma_l)$ and msk, the algorithm randomly chooses $s \leftarrow \mathbb{Z}_p^*$ and computes the data sender's secret key as $ssk_{1,i} = g^\alpha H_1(\sigma_i)^s$ and $ssk_2 = g^s$, where $i = \{1, \ldots, l\}$.

RkGen $(msk/sk_i, ID_{Rt}/ID_{rcv}, \tau, Tree)$: Depending on whether the algorithm is the first run or not, the two different running processes of the algorithm are described as follows:

- When the algorithm is run for the first time. Takes input of the master secret key msk, identity ID_{Rt} of root node Rt and a timestamp τ. The algorithm runs $PKTree.BuildTree$ $(mpk, msk, ID_{Rt}, \tau)$ to generate the public key pk_{Rt} and the secret key sk_{Rt} for the root node.
- Otherwise, takes input of secret key sk_i of node i in PKTree, identity ID_{rcv} of the data receiver, a timestamp τ and PKTree $Tree$. The algorithm runs $PKTree.AddNode$ $(mpk, Tree, sk_i, ID_{rcv}, \tau)$ to generates the secret key rsk for ID_{rcv} and sets ID_{rcv} as its child note. The public key of ID_{rcv} is compute as $rpk = g^{H_2(rsk)}$.

Encryption (w, σ, ssk, rpk): Takes input of a keyword w, attributes σ, the data sender's secret key ssk and the data receiver's public key rpk, the algorithm randomly chooses $r_1, r_2, r_3 \leftarrow \mathbb{Z}_p^*$ and computes the corresponding ciphertext as follows:

- Computes $C_1 = e(rpk^{r_1 \cdot H_4(w)}, H_3(ID_{rcv}))$, $\quad C_2 = g^{r_1}$, $\quad C_3 = h^{r_1}$.
- Computes $C_4 = ssk_2 \cdot g^{r_2}$, $\quad C_5 = g^{r_3}$.
- For each $i \in [1, l]$, computes $C_{6,i} = ssk_{1,i} \cdot H_1(\sigma_i)^{r_2} \cdot H_5(C_{1-5})^{r_3}$, where C_{1-5} denotes $C_1 \parallel C_2 \parallel C_3 \parallel C_4 \parallel C_5$.

Finally, the encryption algorithm outputs the ciphertext: $Ct = (\sigma, C_1, C_2, C_3, C_4, C_5, C_{6,i})$.

Trapdoor $(w, \mathbb{R}, rsk)$: Takes input of a keyword w to be search, the policy $\mathbb{R}$ specified by receiver and the receiver's secret key rsk, the algorithm randomly chooses $t_1 \leftarrow \mathbb{Z}_p$ and computes $T_1 = h^{t_1} \cdot H_3(ID_{rcv})^{H_2(rsk)H_4(w)}$ and $T_2 = g^{t_1}$. Then, the algorithm outputs a trapdoor $T = (\mathbb{R}, T_w = (T_1, T_2))$ of keyword w.

Test (Ct, T): Takes input of a ciphertext Ct and the trapdoor $T = (\mathbb{R}, T_1, T_2)$. The algorithm parses the policy $\mathbb{R}$ in T as (M, ρ) format: $M \in \mathbb{Z}_p^{l \times n}$ and ρ : $[l] \rightarrow \mathbb{Z}_p^*$. Then it randomly chooses $\overrightarrow{x} = (1, x_2, \ldots, x_n) \leftarrow \mathbb{Z}_p^{n \times 1}$ and computes $\overrightarrow{\lambda} = (\lambda_1, \lambda_2, \ldots, \lambda_l)^\top = M\overrightarrow{x}$. Subsequently, it computes $\{w_i \in \mathbb{Z}_p\}_{i \in I}$ by equation $\sum_{i \in I} w_i \overrightarrow{M_i} = (1, 0, \ldots, 0)$, $I = \{i : \rho(i) \in S\}$. Finally, the algorithm checks whether the following equation holds.

$$C_1 \cdot e(T_2, C_3) \cdot \prod_{i \in I} \left(\frac{e(C_{6,i}, g)}{e(H_1(\sigma_i), C_4) \cdot e(H_5(C_{1-5}), C_5)} \right)^{\lambda_i w_i} = e(g, g)^\alpha \cdot e(C_2, T_1)$$

If the above equation holds which means the ciphertext matches the trapdoor and the attribute set of data sender satisfies the access control policy of data receiver, and the algorithm outputs 1. Otherwise, outputs 0.

6 Security Proof and Experimental Evaluation

In this section, we prove the security of our construction under decisional BDH assumption and computational BDH assumption. And then, we compare our construction with other related schemes in terms of functionality and efficiency.

6.1 Security Proof

Theorem 1. *If there exists a probabilistic polynomial time adversary $\mathcal{A}$ winning the ciphertext indistinguishability game in non-negligible advantage ϵ, then we can construct a probabilistic polynomial time adversary $\mathcal{B}$ that solves Decisional BDH assumption in non-negligible advantage ϵ.*

Proof. In the beginning, $\mathcal{B}$ is given a Decisional BDH instance $(\mathbb{G}, \mathbb{G}_T, e, g,$ $g^a, g^b, h, h^b, h^c, R)$ to distinguish whether R is equal to $e(g, h)^{abc}$ or a random element from $\mathbb{G}_T$. And then, $\mathcal{B}$ plays the game $G_{SCPEKS,\mathcal{A}}^{Ind}$ with adversary $\mathcal{A}$ as follows:

- **Setup phase:** $\mathcal{B}$ randomly chooses $\alpha, \beta \to \mathbb{Z}_p^*$ and selects hash functions $H_{i=1,\ldots,5}$. Then $\mathcal{B}$ sets $mpk = (\mathbb{G}, \mathbb{G}_T, e, p, g, h, g^\beta, e(g,g)^\alpha, H_1, H_2, H_3,$ $H_4, H_5)$ and transmits it to $\mathcal{A}$. Note that H_3 will be programmed as a random oracle.
- **Query phase 1:** $\mathcal{B}$ answers adversary $\mathcal{A}$'s queries in the following way:
  - Hash Oracle $\mathcal{O}_H$: Upon receiving an identity ID, it randomly chooses a random number $r_j \in \mathbb{Z}_p^*$ and outputs $H_3(ID) = (h^c)^{r_j}$.
  - SkGen Oracle $\mathcal{O}_S$: Upon receiving attributes σ_i, it runs SCPEKS. **SkGen**(σ) to generate ssk to $\mathcal{A}$.
  - RkGen Oracle $\mathcal{O}_R$: Upon receiving secret key sk, identity ID, a timestamp τ and PKTree $Tree$. It returns the previous results if ID is queried before. Otherwise, it runs SCPEKS.**RkGen**$(sk, ID, \tau, Tree)$ to generate corresponding $Node$ and secret key to $\mathcal{A}$.
  - Trapdoor Oracle $\mathcal{O}_T$: Upon input receiver's public key rpk, a policy $\mathbb{R}$ and keyword w, it randomly chooses $t_1 \in \mathbb{Z}_p$ and returns $T = (T_w = (T_1, T_2), \mathbb{R})$.
- **Challenge phase:** After $\mathcal{A}$ decides that **Query Phase 1** is over, it chooses an identity ID^* and two keywords $w_0^*, w_1^* \in \mathcal{W}$ which is not appeared in previous query phase to $\mathcal{B}$. $\mathcal{B}$ randomly chooses $b \in \{0, 1\}$ and $r_2, r_3 \leftarrow \mathbb{Z}_p^*$. Then, $\mathcal{B}$ computes Ct^* and $Node^*$ as follows:

$$Node^* = ((g^\alpha, (h^c)^{r_c}), Sig_{sk_i}(Pub^*))$$
$$C_1^* = R^{r_c H_4(w_b^*)}, C_2^* = g^b, C_3^* = h^b$$
$$C_4^* = ssk_2 \cdot g^{r_2}, C_5^* = g^{r_3} \cdot$$
$$C_{6,i}^* = ssk_{1,i} \cdot H_1(\sigma_i)^{r_2} \cdot H_5(C_{1-5})^{r_3}$$

Note that r_c is a random number from the response of $\mathcal{O}_H$ to ID^* in query phase.

- **Query phase 2**: $\mathcal{A}$ issues queries to $\mathcal{B}$ as in Query phase 1, the only constraint is that $\mathcal{A}$ can not query (ID^*, w_0^*) or (ID^*, w_1^*) to the trapdoor oracle $\mathcal{O}_T$.
- **Guess phase**: Finally, the adversary $\mathcal{A}$ outputs a guess bit $b' \in (0,1)$ and wins the game if $b = b'$.

When $\mathcal{A}$ win the ciphertext indistinguishability game, the adversary $\mathcal{B}$ returns $R = e(g, h)^{abc}$ to the Decisional BDH challenger. Otherwise, $\mathcal{B}$ returns R is a randomly chosen element in $\mathbb{G}_T$.

As shown in the construction, the responses of $\mathcal{B}$ are identical to that of the real scheme and there is no abort in the simulation. Thus, $\mathcal{B}$ can solve the decisional BDH assumption in a non-negligible advantage ϵ, since $\mathcal{A}$ can win the ciphertext indistinguishability game in non-negligible advantage ϵ.

Theorem 2. *If there exists a probabilistic polynomial time adversary $\mathcal{A}$ who can win the unforgeability game in non-negligible advantage ϵ, then we could construct probabilistic polynomial time adversary $\mathcal{B}$ who solves the Computational BDH assumption in non-negligible probability ϵ.*

Proof. In the beginning, $\mathcal{B}$ is given a Computational BDH challenge $(\mathbb{G}, \mathbb{G}_T, e, g, g^a, g^b, g^c)$ to compute $e(g,g)^{abc}$. And then, $\mathcal{B}$ plays the game $G_{SCPEKS,\mathcal{A}}^{Unf}$ with adversary $\mathcal{A}$ as follows:

- **Setup phase**: $\mathcal{B}$ initializes the game by setting $mpk = (\mathbb{G}, \mathbb{G}_T, e, p, g^b, h, g^\beta, e(g^a, g^b), H_1, H_2, H_3, H_4, H_5)$. Then, $\mathcal{B}$ transmits mpk to $\mathcal{A}$. Note that H_1 is program as a random oracle in the proof. The master secret key g^α is set as $g^{\frac{a}{b}}$ implicitly in the proof, since $e(g^a, g^b) = e(g^b, g^b)^{\frac{a}{b}}$.
- **Query phase**: $\mathcal{B}$ answers adversary $\mathcal{A}$'s queries in the following way:
  - Hash Oracle $\mathcal{O}_H$: Upon input attribute σ_i, if σ_i is queried before, it returns value from $\mathcal{L}_H$. Else, it computes return value as follows: For $\mathbb{R}(\sigma_i) = 1$, it choose $r = 0$, $r' \in \mathbb{Z}_p$. For $\mathbb{R}(\sigma_i) \neq 1$, it choose $r, r' \in \mathbb{Z}_p$. Finally, it returns $(g^b)^r g^{r'}$ to $\mathcal{A}$ and record $\{\sigma_i, r, r'\}$ in list $\mathcal{L}_H$.
  - SkGen Oracle $\mathcal{O}_S$: Upon input attributes σ_i, it randomly choose $s \in \mathbb{Z}_p$ and compute $ssk_{1i} = g^{b\alpha} \cdot H(\sigma_i)^s = g^a \cdot H(\sigma_i)^s$ $ssk_2 = g^{bs}$.
  - RkGen Oracle $\mathcal{O}_R$: Same as in the ciphertext indistinguishability game.
  - Trapdoor Oracle $\mathcal{O}_T$: Same as in the ciphertext indistinguishability game.
- **Guess phase**: If $\mathcal{A}$ decides that **Query Phase** is over, it outputs the ciphertext Ct^* and one receiver's policy $\mathbb{R}^* = (M, \rho)$. After receiving the ciphertext Ct^*, $\mathcal{B}$ picks $\vec{x} = (c, x_1, \ldots, x_n)^\top \leftarrow \mathbb{Z}_p^{n \times 1}$ and computes $\vec{\lambda} = (\lambda_1, \lambda_2, \ldots, \lambda_l)^\top = M\vec{x}$. Then it computes $\{w_i \in \mathbb{Z}_p\}_{i \in I}$ by the equation $\sum_{i \in I} w_i \vec{M}_i = (1, 0, \ldots, 0)$, $I = \{i : \rho(i) \in S\}$. Finally, $\mathcal{C}$ computes the following equation.

$$\prod_{i \in I} \left(\frac{e(C_{6,i}, g)}{e(H_1(\sigma_i), C_4) \cdot e(H_5(C_{1-5}), C_5)} \right)^{\lambda_i w_i} = e(g,g)^{abc}$$

As shown in the construction, the responses of $\mathcal{B}$ are identical to that of the real scheme and there is no abort in simulation. Thus, $\mathcal{B}$ can solves the computational BDH assumption in a non-negligible advantage ϵ, since $\mathcal{A}$ can win the unforgeability game in non-negligible advantage ϵ.

6.2   Performance Analysis

In this subsection, we analyze the functionality and efficiency of our scheme. From the functionality, we compare features of our scheme with other related PEKS schemes [11–13,23]. From the efficiency, since no other PEKS schemes directly support the feature on fine-grained sender permission control, we modify the dIBAEKS [13] to multi-attributes dIBAEKS (MA-dIBAEKS) by setting access structure to AND gate only and representing attributes with identities.

Table 1. Features comparison with related schemes

	FKS-HPABE [23]	HEPKS [12]	PAEKS [11]	dIBAEKS [13]	Ours
Receiver control	√	√	√	√	√
Sender control	×	×	√	√	√
Fine-grained control	√	√	×	×	√

Table 1 presents the feature comparisons among FKS-HPABE [23], HEPKS [12], PAEKS [11], dIBAEKS [13] and ours. From the comparison, we can see that [12,23] implement fine-grained access control to receiver, but do not support access control to sender. [11,13] and ours implement access control on both sender and receiver side. However, [11,13] only allow one to one data flow and do not support fine-grained access control in the multi-user scenario. Compared with other relevant schemes, our construction not only supports bidirectional access control, but also supports fine-grained access control in the multi-user scenario, which makes it more flexible to be use.

Table 2. Computation cost comparison with MA-dIBAEKS

	MA-dIBAEKS	Ours
SkGen	$(E + H) \times l$	$(l + 1)E + lH$
RkGen	$E + H$	E
Encryption	$(3E + H + 2P) \times l$	$(l + 6)E + (l + 3)H + P$
Trapdoor	$(2E + H + P + M) \times l$	$3E + 3H$
Test	$(2E + 2P + M) \times l$	$(i + 1)H + (2i + 3)P$

Let E denotes the evaluation of exponentiation on $\mathbb{G}$, H denotes the evaluation of hash function and P denotes the evaluation of bilinear pairing. Commonly, l denotes the number of attributes and i denotes the size of set I in both Table 2 and Table 3. Table 2 presents the computation cost of SCPEKS. Since MA-dIBAEKS doesn't support fine-grained access control directly, it needs to generate multiple ciphertexts and trapdoors. The comparison demonstrates that our construction achieves fine-grained access control while maintaining similar or even lower computation costs.

Table 3. Communication cost comparison with MA-dIBAEKS

	MA-dIBAEKS	Ours
Sender's key	$\|\mathbb{G}\| \times l$	$(l+1)\|\mathbb{G}\| + \|\sigma\|$
Receiver's key	$2\|\mathbb{G}\|$	$2\|\mathbb{G}\|$
Ciphertext	$(2\|\mathbb{G}\| + \|\mathbb{G}_T\|) \times l$	$\|\mathbb{G}_T\| + (l+4)\|\mathbb{G}\| + \|\sigma\|$
Trapdoor	$2\|\mathbb{G}\| \times l$	$2\|\mathbb{G}\| + \|\mathbb{R}\|$

We denote the size of element in $\mathbb{G}$, $\mathbb{G}_T$ and sender's attributes set as $\|\mathbb{G}\|, \|\mathbb{G}_T\|$ and $\|\sigma\|$ respectively. Table 3 presents the communication costs of SCPEKS. From the table, our construction achieves more flexible access control while maintaining similar or even lower communication costs.

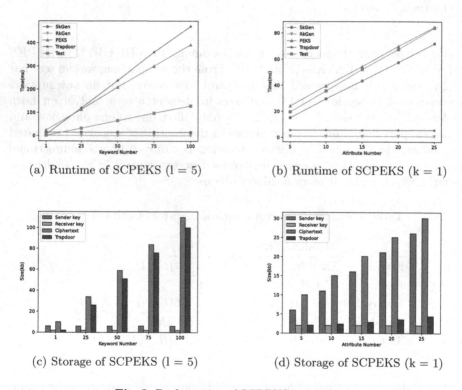

(a) Runtime of SCPEKS (l = 5)

(b) Runtime of SCPEKS (k = 1)

(c) Storage of SCPEKS (l = 5)

(d) Storage of SCPEKS (k = 1)

Fig. 3. Performance of SCPEKS in practice

For experimental analysis, we conduct the simulation of our scheme on PC with 3.8 GHz Intel(R) Core(TM) i5-1135G7 CPU and 16 GB memory. The implementation is based on PBC library [17] with Type A curve (q-bits = 512). We denote the number of attributes and keywords as l and k respectively. The experimental result is present in Fig. 3. Figure 3a and Fig. 3c presents the computation and communication costs that vary with the number of keywords when attribute number is fixed to five. Relatively, Fig. 3b and Fig. 3d presents the computation and communication cost that vary with the number of attributes when keyword number is fixed to one.

7 Conclusion

To address the threats from malicious data senders, in this paper, we present a new PEKS which supports fine-grained access control to data sender. In our construction, an encrypted data can be successfully returned if and only if when data receiver's identities belong to the authentication set and the attribute set of data sender's attributes satisfies the policy specified by data receiver. The security analysis shows that our construction achieves the target security features. Moreover, performance analysis suggests that our construction is efficient in practice.

Acknowledgment. This work was supported by the National Natural Science Foundation of China under Grants 62072062, U20A20176 and 6210070829, and the Natural Science Foundation of Chongqing, China under Grant cstc2019jcyjjqX0026.

References

1. Ateniese, G., Francati, D., Nuñez, D., Venturi, D.: Match me if you can: matchmaking encryption and its applications. J. Cryptol. **34**(3), 1–50 (2021)
2. Badertscher, C., Matt, C., Maurer, U.: Strengthening access control encryption. In: Takagi, T., Peyrin, T. (eds.) ASIACRYPT 2017. LNCS, vol. 10624, pp. 502–532. Springer, Cham (2017). https://doi.org/10.1007/978-3-319-70694-8_18
3. Bethencourt, J., Sahai, A., Waters, B.: Ciphertext-policy attribute-based encryption. In: IEEE Symposium on Security and Privacy, pp. 321–334 (2007)
4. Boneh, D., Di Crescenzo, G., Ostrovsky, R., Persiano, G.: Public key encryption with keyword search. In: Cachin, C., Camenisch, J.L. (eds.) EUROCRYPT 2004. LNCS, vol. 3027, pp. 506–522. Springer, Heidelberg (2004). https://doi.org/10.1007/978-3-540-24676-3_30
5. Damgård, I., Haagh, H., Orlandi, C.: Access control encryption: enforcing information flow with cryptography. In: Hirt, M., Smith, A. (eds.) TCC 2016. LNCS, vol. 9986, pp. 547–576. Springer, Heidelberg (2016). https://doi.org/10.1007/978-3-662-53644-5_21
6. Fuchsbauer, G., Gay, R., Kowalczyk, L., Orlandi, C.: Access control encryption for equality, comparison, and more. In: Fehr, S. (ed.) PKC 2017. LNCS, vol. 10175, pp. 88–118. Springer, Heidelberg (2017). https://doi.org/10.1007/978-3-662-54388-7_4
7. Goyal, V., Pandey, O., Sahai, A., Waters, B.: Attribute-based encryption for fine-grained access control of encrypted data. In: ACM Conference on Computer and Communications Security, pp. 89–98 (2006)
8. Hattori, M., et al.: Ciphertext-Policy delegatable hidden vector encryption and its application to searchable encryption in multi-user setting. In: Chen, L. (ed.) IMACC 2011. LNCS, vol. 7089, pp. 190–209. Springer, Heidelberg (2011). https://doi.org/10.1007/978-3-642-25516-8_12

9. He, D., Ma, M., Zeadally, S., Kumar, N., Liang, K.: Certificateless public key authenticated encryption with keyword search for industrial internet of things. IEEE Trans. Ind. Inform. **14**(8), 3618–3627 (2018)

10. Huang, H., Du, J., Wang, H., Wang, R.: A multi-keyword multi-user searchable encryption scheme based on cloud storage. In: 2016 IEEE Trustcom/BigDataSE/ISPA, pp. 1937–1943 (2016)

11. Huang, Q., Li, H.: An efficient public-key searchable encryption scheme secure against inside keyword guessing attacks. Inf. Sci. **403–404**, 1–14 (2017)

12. Li, H., Huang, Q., Susilo, W.: A secure cloud data sharing protocol for enterprise supporting hierarchical keyword search. IEEE Trans. Dependable Secure Comput. (2020). https://doi.org/10.1109/TDSC.2020.3027611

13. Li, H., Huang, Q., Shen, J., Yang, G., Susilo, W.: Designated-server identity-based authenticated encryption with keyword search for encrypted emails. Inf. Sci. **481**, 330–343 (2019)

14. Liang, K., Su, C., Chen, J., Liu, J.K.: Efficient multi-function data sharing and searching mechanism for cloud-based encrypted data. In: ACM on Asia Conference on Computer and Communications Security, pp. 83–94 (2016)

15. Liang, K., Susilo, W.: Searchable attribute-based mechanism with efficient data sharing for secure cloud storage. IEEE Trans. Inf. Forensics Secur. **10**(9), 1981–1992 (2015)

16. Liu, J.K., Au, M.H., Susilo, W., Liang, K., Lu, R., Srinivasan, B.: Secure sharing and searching for real-time video data in mobile cloud. IEEE Network **29**(2), 46–50 (2015)

17. Lynn, B., et al.: The pairing-based cryptography library. Internet: crypto. stanford. edu/pbc/ (2006). https://crypto.stanford.edu/pbc/

18. Meng, R., Zhou, Y., Ning, J., Liang, K., Han, J., Susilo, W.: An efficient key-policy attribute-based searchable encryption in prime-order groups. In: Okamoto, T., Yu, Y., Au, M.H., Li, Y. (eds.) ProvSec 2017. LNCS, vol. 10592, pp. 39–56. Springer, Cham (2017). https://doi.org/10.1007/978-3-319-68637-0_3

19. Sahai, A., Waters, B.: Fuzzy identity-based encryption. In: Cramer, R. (ed.) EUROCRYPT 2005. LNCS, vol. 3494, pp. 457–473. Springer, Heidelberg (2005). https://doi.org/10.1007/11426639_27

20. Song, D., Wagner, D., Perrig, A.: Practical techniques for searches on encrypted data. In: IEEE Symposium on Security and Privacy, pp. 44–55 (2000)

21. Sun, W., Yu, S., Lou, W., Hou, Y.T., Li, H.: Protecting your right: attribute-based keyword search with fine-grained owner-enforced search authorization in the cloud. In: IEEE INFOCOM, pp. 226–234 (2014)

22. Swinhoe, D.: The 15 biggest data breaches of the 21st century. Website, January 2021. https://www.csoonline.com/article/2130877/the-biggest-data-breaches-of-the-21st-century.html

23. Wang, H., Ning, J., Huang, X., Wei, G., Poh, G.S., Liu, X.: Secure fine-grained encrypted keyword search for e-healthcare cloud. IEEE Trans. Dependable Secure Comput. (2019). https://doi.org/10.1109/TDSC.2019.2916569

24. Yang, Y.: Towards multi-user private keyword search for cloud computing. In: IEEE International Conference on Cloud Computing, pp. 758–759 (2011)

25. Zhao, F., Nishide, T., Sakurai, K.: Multi-user keyword search scheme for secure data sharing with fine-grained access control. In: Kim, H. (ed.) ICISC 2011. LNCS, vol. 7259, pp. 406–418. Springer, Heidelberg (2012). https://doi.org/10.1007/978-3-642-31912-9_27

26. Zheng, Q., Xu, S., Ateniese, G.: Vabks: verifiable attribute-based keyword search over outsourced encrypted data. In: IEEE INFOCOM, pp. 522–530 (2014)

Improved Security Model for Public-Key Authenticated Encryption with Keyword Search

Baodong Qin[1,2,3]([✉]), Hui Cui[4], Xiaokun Zheng[1], and Dong Zheng[1,5]

[1] School of Cyberspace Security, Xi'an University of Posts and Telecommunications,
Xi'an 710121, China
qinbaodong@xupt.edu.cn
[2] State Key Laboratory of Integrated Services Networks, Xidian University,
Xi'an, China
[3] Science and Technology on Communication Security Laboratory,
Chengdu 610041, China
hui.cui@murdoch.edu.au
[4] Discipline of IT, College of Arts, Business, Law and Social Sciences,
Murdoch University, Western Australia, Perth, WA 6150, Australia
zhengdong_xupt@sina.com
[5] Westone Cryptologic Research Center, Beijing 100070, China

Abstract. The motivation of public-key authenticated encryption with keyword search (PAEKS) was to resist against inside keyword guessing attacks. Its security model captures both cipher-keyword indistinguishability (CI-security) and trapdoor indistinguishability (TI-security). Recently, this security model was extended from one-user settings to multi-user settings, or from one cipher-keyword indistinguishability to multiple cipher-keyword indistinguishability, making it more practical. However, none of previous CI-security model for PAEKS scheme captures fully chosen keyword to cipher-keyword (CKC) attacks, in which an attacker may obtain cipher-keywords of any keyword (even a challenge keyword) of his choice. Due to this, the paper introduces an improved CI-security model for PAEKS to capture fully CKC attacks in a multi-user setting, and proves that CI-security against fully CKC attacks implies multiple cipher-keyword indistinguishability. Then, the paper proves that some previous PAEKS schemes cannot achieve CI-security under fully CKC attacks. Next, the paper proposes a new PAEKS scheme and proves its CI-security in the improved security model. Finally, the paper demonstrates its comparable security guarantees and computational efficiency by comparing it with previous PAEKS schemes.

Keywords: Searchable encryption · Keyword guessing attacks · Security model

1 Introduction

With the rapid development of cloud computing technology, more and more organizations and individual have moved their data to cloud server for saving

© Springer Nature Switzerland AG 2021
Q. Huang and Y. Yu (Eds.): ProvSec 2021, LNCS 13059, pp. 19–38, 2021.
https://doi.org/10.1007/978-3-030-90402-9_2

local storage and increasing the convenience of data usage. Due to various reasons, however, cloud data may be compromised and leaked to outsiders [24]. As users' data contains many sensitive information, e.g., identity number, biometric information and electronic medical records, information leakage has become the major obstacle to the popularity of cloud computing. To alleviate the harm caused by data leakage, the data must be encrypted before sending into the cloud storage server.

In the last decades, many prominent cryptographic primitives have been proposed for achieving secure and efficient cloud data usage, such as attribute-based encryption [12], proxy re-encryption [2] and searchable encryption [4,26]. Among these primitives, searchable encryption is a promising one, that allows a remote server to search in the encrypted data on behalf of a client without the knowledge of plaintext data. There are two types of searchable encryption: Symmetric-key Searchable Encryption (SSE) and Public-key Encryption with Keyword Search (PEKS). SSE was firstly proposed by Song, Wagner and Perrig [26] in 2000. It has received extensive attention and research in recent years [10,22,25,30,31]. In SSE, both the keyword ciphertext and trapdoor are computed with the same (secret) key, so it is primarily used for application scenarios of personal cloud data storage. In multi-user setting, PEKS [4] is a good candidate as it allows any user to encrypt keywords for searching by designated searching key holders. However, PEKS schemes are inherently suffer from keyword guessing attacks (KGA), as the consistency of PEKS schemes holds [15]. That is, the adversary can generate a ciphertext of a guessing keyword and then test whether it matches with a search trapdoor. If the number of possible keywords is bounded by polynomial, the adversary can find the keyword hidden in the search trapdoor. Indeed, many PEKS schemes are shown to be insecure against KGAs [5,15,17,20,28,29].

To date, there are many variant of PEKS schemes claimed to be secure against KGAs, such as [3,6,7,9,11,13,14,16,18,19,23,27]. However, most of them are later proven to be insecure and only a handful of constructions can resist against inside keyword guessing attacks. The primitive of Public-key Authenticated Encryption with Keyword Search (PAEKS) was recently proposed by Huang and Li [14] to capture inside keyword guessing attacks. Its security model guarantees two security goals: cipher-keyword indistinguishability (CI-security) and trapdoor indistinguishability (TI-security). Recently, some works found that this security model is not complete, as two important scenarios are not considered: one is the multi-user setting and the other is the multi-cipher-keyword setting. Indeed, Noroozi et al. [18] showed that the PAEKS scheme in [14] is not secure in the multi-user setting, and Qin et al. [23] showed that it is not secure in the multi-cipher-keyword setting. Recently, Pan et al. [21] proposed a security model for both multi-cipher-keyword indistinguishability and multi-trapdoor indistinguishability in one-user settings. But, their PAEKS scheme has a serious security flaw [8]. Though these works devoted to making the security model of PAEKS being more complete, we find that none of their CI-security models resists against fully chosen keyword attacks, in which an attacker is allowed to query cipher-keywords of any keyword of his choice. In fact, in previous CI-security models, the attacker is forbidden to issue a cipher-keyword query for any challenge keyword. This may limit the application of PAEKS schemes in a scenario where multiple files with some common keywords were encrypted.

To solve about issue, this paper proposes an improved CI-security model for a PAEKS scheme. Specifically, the contributions of this paper are as follows:

- We propose an improved CI-security model for PAKES in multi-user settings. The improved security model achieves cipher-keyword indistinguishability against fully chosen keyword to cipher-keyword attacks (shorted as fully CI-security). In a fully CI-security model, an attacker is allowed to request cipher-keyword of any keyword of his choice. We show that fully CI-security implies multiple cipher-keyword indistinguishability.
- We find that all previous CI-security models for PAEKS schemes never considered fully chosen keyword to cipher-keyword attacks. Specifically, some PAEKS schemes are proven to be insecure in the fully-CI security model, and given a tuple of cipher-keywords, there exists an efficient algorithm to determine whether two cipher-keywords encrypt the same keyword.
- We give a new construction of PAEKS scheme in the improved security model. It satisfies fully CI-security under bilinear Diffie-Hellman assumption, and TI-security under oracle Diffie-Hellman assumption. We also analyse its performance and demonstrate its comparable efficiency with previous ones.

The rest of this paper is organized as follows. Section 2 reviews some cryptographic tools that will be used in the paper. Section 3 gives the formal definition of the improved CI-security model for PAEKS. Section 4 anlyzes the security of previous PAEKS schemes in the improved CI-security model. Section 5 describes our new PAEKS scheme and its provable security. Section 6 evaluates efficiency with some related PAEKS schemes. Finally, Sect. 7 concludes the paper.

2 Preliminaries

2.1 Bilinear Map

Let G and G_T be two groups with prime order p and $e : G \times G \to G_T$ be the bilinear map between them. The bilinear map satisfies the following three properties.

- Bilinear: for any $g \in G$ and $x, y \in \mathbb{Z}_p$, we have $e(g^x, g^y) = e(g, g)^{xy}$;
- Non-degenerate: if g is a generator of G, then $e(g, g)$ is a generator of G_T.
- Computable: given $g, h \in G$, there is an efficient algorithm to compute $e(g, h)$.

2.2 Complexity Assumptions

In this section, we introduce some computational problems that are believed to be hard.

BDH: Bilinear Diffie-Hellman Problem. This is the standard computational Diffie-Hellman problem over a bilinear group. Let G be a bilinear group with prime order p, and g be a random generator of G. The *Bilinear Diffie-Hellman* (BDH) problem states that, given g^x, g^y, g^z, where x, y and z are chosen randomly from $\mathbb{Z}_p$, to compute $e(g,g)^{xyz}$. The BDH problem is believed to be hard over a prime order group. Here is the formal definition.

Definition 1 (BDH assumption). *Let G be a bilinear group with prime order p, let g be a random generator of G, and let $\mathcal{A}$ be any PPT adversary. The BDH assumption states that the following advantage of $\mathcal{A}$ is negligible in κ*

$$\mathsf{Adv}_{\mathcal{A}}^{BDH}(\kappa) = Pr[\mathcal{A}(g^x, g^y, g^z) = e(g,g)^{xyz} : x, y, z \leftarrow \mathbb{Z}_p].$$

ODH: Oracle Diffie-Hellman problems. We introduce a new problem, namely *Computational Oracle Diffie-Hellman* (CODH) problem. It is the computational version of the *Decisional Oracle Diffie-Hellman* (DODH) problem, proposed by Abdalla, Bellare and Rogaway [1]. We first recall the DODH problem.

Let G be a group with prime order g and g be a random generator of G. Given g^u, g^v and an oracle $\mathcal{H}_v(\cdot)$, which computes $\mathcal{H}_v(X) = H(X^v)$, the DODH problem aims to distinguish $H(g^{uv})$ from a random $k \in \{0,1\}^{hLen}$, where H is a cryptographic hash function with range $\{0,1\}^{hLen}$. The DODH problem is believed to be hard, as long as the oracle $\mathcal{H}_v$ cannot be queried at g^u.

Definition 2 (DODH assumption [1]). *Let G be a group with prime order p, let g be a random generator of G, let $H : \{0,1\}^* \to \{0,1\}^{hLen}$ be a cryptographic hash function, and let $\mathcal{A}$ be any PPT adversary. The DODH assumption states that the following advantage of $\mathcal{A}$ is negligible in κ*

$$\mathsf{Adv}_{\mathcal{A}}^{DODH}(\kappa) = \left| Pr[\mathcal{A}^{\mathcal{H}_v(\cdot)}(g^u, g^v, H(g^{uv})) = 1] - Pr[\mathcal{A}^{\mathcal{H}_v(\cdot)}(g^u, g^v, k) = 1] \right|$$

where $u, v \leftarrow \mathbb{Z}_p$, $k \leftarrow \{0,1\}^{hLen}$, and $\mathcal{H}_v(X) = H(X^v)$. $\mathcal{A}$ is not allowed to issue a query for $\mathcal{H}_v(g^u)$.

In contrast to distinguish $H(g^{uv})$ from a random value, the CODH problem aims to find the value $H(g^{uv})$ given g^u and g^v. In addition to the oracle $\mathcal{H}_v(X) = H(X^v)$, the CODH problem also give the adversary access to the oracle $\mathcal{H}_u(X) = H(Y^u)$. As long as the adversary does not issue queries for neither $\mathcal{H}_u(g^v)$ nor $\mathcal{H}_v(g^u)$, we believe the CODH problem is hard.

Definition 3 (CODH assumption [1]). *Let G be a group with prime order p, let g be a random generator of G, let $H : \{0,1\}^* \to \{0,1\}^{hLen}$ be a cryptographic hash function, and let $\mathcal{A}$ be any PPT adversary. The CODH assumption states that the following advantage of $\mathcal{A}$ is negligible in κ*

$$\mathsf{Adv}_{\mathcal{A}}^{CODH}(\kappa) = Pr[\mathcal{A}^{\mathcal{H}_u(\cdot), \mathcal{H}_v(\cdot)}(g^u, g^v, H) = H(g^{uv})]$$

where $u, v \leftarrow \mathbb{Z}_p$, $\mathcal{H}_u(X) = H(X^u)$ and $\mathcal{H}_v(X) = H(X^v)$. $\mathcal{A}$ is not allowed to issue queries for $\mathcal{H}_u(g^v)$ and $\mathcal{H}_v(g^u)$.

The following theorem shows that the CODH problem is harder to solve than the DODH problem over bilinear group in the random oracle model. The proof of the theorem can be found in the full version.

Theorem 1. *Let G be a bilinear group with prime order p, let g be a random generator of G, and let H be randomly chosen hash function. Then*

$$\mathsf{Adv}_{\mathcal{B}}^{DODH}(\kappa) \geq \mathsf{Adv}_{\mathcal{A}}^{CODH}(\kappa) - \frac{1}{2^{hLen}}.$$

2.3 The Syntax of PAEKS

A *public-key authenticated encryption with keyword search* (PAEKS) consists of the following six (probabilistic) polynomial-time algorithms:

- $sp \leftarrow \mathsf{Setup}(1^{\kappa})$: This algorithm is performed by a trusted authority so that everyone in the system would trust the generated parameters. It takes as input the security parameter 1^{κ}, and outputs a global system parameter sp.
- $(pk_S, sk_S) \leftarrow \mathsf{SGen}(sp)$: This algorithm is performed by a data sender. It takes as input a system parameter sp, and outputs a pair of keys (pk_S, sk_S).
- $(pk_R, sk_R) \leftarrow \mathsf{RGen}(sp)$: This algorithm is performed by a data receiver. It takes as input a system parameter sp, and outputs a pair of keys (pk_R, sk_R).
- $C_w \leftarrow \mathsf{PAEKS}(sk_S, pk_R, w)$: This algorithm is performed by a data sender. It takes as input his secret key sk_S, a data receiver's public key pk_R and a keyword w, and outputs a ciphertext C_w of the keyword w.
- $T_w \leftarrow \mathsf{Trapdoor}(sk_R, pk_S, w)$: This algorithm is performed by a data receiver. It takes as input his secret key sk_R, a data sender's public key pk_S and a keyword w, and outputs a search trapdoor T_w of the keyword w.
- $0/1 \leftarrow \mathsf{Test}(pk_S, pk_R, T_w, C_{w'})$: This algorithm is performed by the cloud server. It takes as input a data sender's public key pk_S, a data receiver's public key pk_R, a trapdoor T_w of keyword w and a ciphertext $C_{w'}$ of keyword w', and outputs 1 if $w = w'$, and 0 otherwise.

3 Improved CI-Security Model of PAEKS

A semantic security model for PAEKS includes both cipher-keyword indistinguishability (CI-security) and trapdoor indistinguishability (TI-security). Our TI-security model (see Definition 6) is identical to that of [14,18] in multi-user settings. Below, we mainly discuss the difference of CI-security models between ours and previous ones.

Suppose that (pk_S, sk_S) and (pk_R, sk_R) are the key pairs of the attacked data sender and data receiver respectively. In our security models, an adversary may has the following two abilities to attack a PAEKS scheme.

- *Chosen keyword to cipher-keyword* (CKC) attacks: In a CKC attack, the adversary has the ability to obtain cipher-keyword for any keyword, e.g., w, of its choice under a receiver's public key, e.g., pk, specified by the adversary. That is, the adversary will obtain the cipher-keyword $C_w = \mathsf{PAEKS}(sk_S, pk, w)$. Formally, we model CKC attacks by giving the adversary $\mathcal{A}$ access to a cipher-keyword oracle $\mathsf{PAEKS}_{sk_S}(\cdot, \cdot)$, viewed as a "black box"; the adversary can repeatedly submit any keyword w and a (data receiver's) public key pk of its choice to this oracle, and is given in return a cipher-keyword $C_w = \mathsf{PAEKS}(sk_S, pk, w)$.

- *Chosen keyword to trapdoor* (CKT) attacks: In a CKT attack, the adversary has the ability to obtain trapdoor of any keyword, e.g., w, of its choice under a sender's public key, e.g., pk. That is, the adversary will obtain the trapdoor $T_w = \mathsf{Trapdoor}(sk_R, pk, w)$. Similarly, we model CKT attacks by giving the adversary $\mathcal{A}$ access to a trapdoor oracle $\mathsf{Trapdoor}_{sk_R}(\cdot, \cdot)$; the adversary can repeatedly submit any keyword w and a (data sender's) public key pk of its choice to this oracle, and is given in return a trapdoor $T_w = \mathsf{Trapdoor}(sk_R, pk, w)$.

Let w_0^* and w_1^* be two challenge keywords, chosen by the adversary. The adversary's access to the above oracles may be restricted to some trivial queries. For example, in the CI-security model, the adversary will be given a challenge cipher-keyword $C_{w_b^*}$ of one of the two challenge keywords. Clearly, the adversary cannot request trapdoors of the challenge keywords. Otherwise, there is no hope for any PAEKS scheme to satisfy the CI-security. Except the limitation of such trivial trapdoor queries, previous CI-security models still had some other limitations on the cipher-keyword oracle. Especially, the adversary is not allowed to query cipher-keyword oracle with challenge keywords. In our improved CI-security model (see Definition 4), we remove this limitation, and call it fully chosen keyword to cipher-keyword attacks (fully CKC attacks).

Recently, Qin et al. [23] introduced the security notion of multiple cipher-keyword indistinguishability (MCI) to capture the case of multiple encryptions in PAEKS. Specifically, given two tuples of challenge keywords $(w_{0,1}, \ldots, w_{0,n})$ and $(w_{1,1}, \ldots, w_{1,n})$, the MCI-security requests an adversary to distinguish encryptions of one tuple keywords from the other tuple keywords. But, their MCI-security model as well as following up work [21] also did not allow the adversary to query cipher-keyword oracle with any challenge keywords. We will extend our CI-security model from one encryption to multiple encryptions under the fully CKC attacks in multi-user settings (see Definition 5). Actually, our CI-security under fully CKC attacks implies MCI-security as shown Theorem 2.

Table 1 gives an overview of an adversary's abilities in previous CI-security models [9, 14, 18, 21, 23] as well as ours.

In Huang et al.'s security model, "$pk = pk_S \wedge w \neq w_b^*$" means that the adversary can only obtain encryptions of keywords being distinct from w_0^* and w_1^* under the target data receiver's public key pk_R (using the target data sender's secret key sk_S). "$pk = pk_R \wedge w \neq w_b^*$" means that the adversary can only obtain trapdoors of keywords being distinct from w_0^* and w_1^* under the target data sender's public key pk_S (using the target data receiver's secret key sk_R). That is, Huang et al.'s security model only captures the single sender-receiver setting.

Table 1. Restrictions on an adversary's queries in CI-security model. In the table, $b \in \{0,1\}$ and $i \in \{1,\dots,n\}$. The symbol "$\star$" stands for any public key or keyword.

Model	(M)CI-security	
	Cipher-keyword oracle	Trapdoor oracle
Huang et al. [14]	$pk = pk_R \wedge w \neq w_b^*$	$pk = pk_S \wedge w \neq w_b^*$
Noroozi et al. [18]	$(pk, w) \neq (pk_R, w_b^*)$	$(pk, w) \neq (pk_S, w_b^*)$
Chi et al. [9]	$(pk, w) \neq (pk_R, w_b^*)$	$(pk, w) \neq (pk_S, w_b^*)$
Qin et al. [23]	$pk = pk_R \wedge w \neq w_{b,i}^*$	$pk = pk_S \wedge w \neq w_{b,i}^*$
Pan et al. [21]	$pk = pk_R \wedge w \neq w_{b,i}^*$	$pk = pk_S \wedge w \neq w_{b,i}^*$
This paper	$(pk, w) = (\star, \star)$	$(pk, w) \neq (pk_S, w_{b,i}^*)$

In Noroozi et al.'s security model, (pk, w) can be any pairs as long as $(pk, w) \neq (pk_R, w_b^*)$ in the cipher-keyword oracle and $(pk, w) \neq (pk_S, w_b^*)$ in the trapdoor oracle. This indicates that the adversary can not only obtain cipher-keywords and trapdoors between the target data sender and data receiver, but also obtain cipher-keywords generated by other data senders for the target data receiver, and trapdoors generated by other data receivers for the target data sender. This model captures a multi-user setting. Chi et al.'s security model follows from Noroozi et al.'s CI-security model in multi-user settings.

In above three schemes, they did not consider multiple cipher-keyword indistinguishability. The multiple cipher-keyword indistinguishability was previously defined in [23] and [21]. But, both of them did not capture multi-user settings. Our CI-security model not only follows Noroozi et al.'s multi-user security model, but also captures a fully chosen keyword to cipher-keyword attacks, i.e., an adversary can obtain cipher-keyword for any data receiver and any keyword of his choice. Specifically, in addition to challenge cipher-keyword(s), the adversary can still obtain a cipher-keyword of any challenge keyword between the target data sender and the target data receiver via cipher-keyword oracle $\mathsf{PAEKS}_{sk_S}(\cdot, \cdot)$. But, this is not allowed in all other (M)CI-security models.

In next sections, we give a formal definitions of our fully CI-security model and extend it to multiple CI-security model, which are defined through a game played between a challenger and an adversary.

3.1 Fully (M)CI-Security Model

Fully CI-security game: Let $\mathcal{A}$ be an adversary and κ be the security parameter.

- Initialization: The challenger first runs the algorithm $\mathsf{Setup}(1^\kappa)$ to generate the system parameter sp. Then, it runs $\mathsf{SGen}(sp)$ and $\mathsf{RGen}(sp)$ to generate the target data sender's key pairs (pk_S, sk_S) and data receiver's key pairs (pk_R, sk_R) respectively. The challenger gives the system parameter sp and the two public keys pk_S and pk_R to $\mathcal{A}$.

- Phase 1: The adversary may repeatedly and adaptively ask polynomially many queries on the cipher-keyword oracle $\mathsf{PAEKS}_{sk_S}(\cdot, \cdot)$ and the trapdoor oracle $\mathsf{Trapdoor}_{sk_R}(\cdot, \cdot)$.
- Challenge: Once $\mathcal{A}$ finished Phase 1, it outputs two challenge keywords w_0^* and w_1^* with the restriction that (pk_S, w_0^*) and (pk_S, w_1^*) never be queried on the trapdoor oracle by $\mathcal{A}$ in Phase 1. Now, the challenger flips a random coin $b \in \{0, 1\}$ and sends the cipher-keyword $C_{w_b^*} \leftarrow \mathsf{PAEKS}(sk_S, pk_R, w_b^*)$ to $\mathcal{A}$.
- Phase 2: In this phase, the adversary can continue to access the oracles as in phase 1, but cannot access the trapdoor oracle with (pk_R, w_0^*) and (pk_R, w_1^*).
- Guess: Eventually, $\mathcal{A}$ returns a bit $b' \in \{0, 1\}$ as his guess of b and wins the game if $b' = b$.

The advantage of $\mathcal{A}$ in breaking the cipher-keyword indistinguishability of PAEKS is defined as

$$\mathsf{Adv}_{\mathcal{A}}^{CI}(\kappa) = \left| \Pr[b' = b] - \frac{1}{2} \right|.$$

Definition 4 (Fully CI-security). *A PAEKS scheme satisfies cipher-keyword indistinguishability under a fully chosen keyword to cipher-keyword attack and a chosen keyword to trapdoor attack, if for all probabilistic polynomial-time adversaries $\mathcal{A}$, the advantage $\mathsf{Adv}_{\mathcal{A}}^{CI}(\kappa)$ is negligible in κ.*

The definition of MCI-security game is identical to that of CI-security, except that the adversary submits two tuple of challenge keywords $(w_{0,1}^*, w_{0,2}^*, \ldots, w_{0,n}^*)$ and $(w_{1,1}^*, w_{1,2}^*, \ldots, w_{1,n}^*)$, and the challenger randomly selects one tuple to encrypt.

Definition 5 (Fully MCI-security). *A PAEKS scheme is multiple cipher-keywords indistinguishability under a fully chosen keyword to cipher-keyword attack and a chosen keyword to trapdoor attack, if for all probabilistic polynomial-time adversaries $\mathcal{A}$, the advantage $\mathsf{Adv}_{\mathcal{A}}^{MCI}(\kappa)$ is negligible in κ.*

Relations Between Fully CI-Security and Fully MCI-Security. According to the above definitions, if a PAEKS scheme is fully MCI-secure, then it is clearly fully CI-secure as well. Importantly, the converse also holds; that is, fully CI-security implies fully MCI-security. We state the following theorem and give its proof below. The proof of the theorem can be found in the full version.

Theorem 2. *If a PAEKS scheme Π is fully CI-secure, then it is also fully MCI-secure.*

3.2   TI-Security Model

Besides cipher-keyword indistinguishability, a PAEKS scheme should satisfy trapdoor indistinguishability, i.e., a trapdoor of one keyword is indistinguishable from that of another keyword, under reasonable chosen keyword attacks. Next, we recall Noroozi et al.'s TI-security model [19], which is defined in multi-user settings.

TI-Security Game: Let $\mathcal{A}$ be an adversary and κ be the security parameter.

- Initialization: The challenger first runs the algorithm Setup(1^κ) to generate the system parameter sp. Then, it runs SGen(sp) and RGen(sp) to generate the target data sender's key pairs (pk_S, sk_S) and data receiver's key pairs (pk_R, sk_R) respectively. The challenger gives the system parameter sp and the two public keys pk_S and pk_R to $\mathcal{A}$.
- Phase 1: The adversary may repeatedly and adaptively ask polynomially many queries on the cipher-keyword oracle PAEKS$_{sk_S}(\cdot, \cdot)$ and the trapdoor oracle Trapdoor$_{sk_R}(\cdot, \cdot)$.
- Challenge: When $\mathcal{A}$ finished Phase 1, it outputs two challenge keywords w_0^* and w_1^* with the restriction that PAEKS$_{sk_S}(pk_R, w_i^*)$ and Trapdoor$_{sk_R}(pk_S, w_i^*)$ ($i = 0, 1$) have never been queried by $\mathcal{A}$ in Phase 1. Now, the challenger flips a random coin $b \in \{0, 1\}$ and sends the challenge trapdoor $T_{w_b^*} \leftarrow$ Trapdoor(sk_R, pk_S, w_b^*) to $\mathcal{A}$.
- Phase 2: In this phase, the adversary can continue to access the oracles as in phase 1, but cannot access the cipher-keyword oracle PAEKS$_{sk_S}(pk_R, w_i^*)$ and the trapdoor oracle Trapdoor$_{sk_R}(pk_S, w_i^*)$ ($i = 0, 1$).
- Guess: Eventually, $\mathcal{A}$ returns a bit $b' \in \{0, 1\}$ as his guess of b and wins the game if $b' = b$.

The advantage of $\mathcal{A}$ in breaking the trapdoor distinguishability of PAEKS is defined as

$$\mathsf{Adv}_{\mathcal{A}}^{TI}(\kappa) = \left| \Pr[b' = b] - \frac{1}{2} \right|.$$

Definition 6 (Trapdoor indistinguishability). *A PAEKS scheme satisfies trapdoor indistinguishability (TI-security) under a chosen keyword to cipher-keyword attack and a chosen keyword to trapdoor attack, if for all probabilistic polynomial-time adversaries $\mathcal{A}$, the advantage* $\mathsf{Adv}_{\mathcal{A}}^{TI}(\kappa)$ *is negligible in κ.*

4 Security Analysis of Previous PAEKS Schemes

In this section, we analyze the security of previous PAEKS schemes in the fully CI-security model. We first recall Noroozi et al.'s PAEKS scheme [18].

Noroozi et al.'s PAEKS Scheme: It consists of the following algorithms.

- Setup(1^κ): Choose two cyclic group G and G_T of prime order p. Also, choose two random generators $g, h \in G$, and a bilinear pairing $e : G \times G \to G_T$. In addition, choose a secure cryptographic hash function $H : \{0, 1\}^* \to G$. The system parameter is $sp = (G, G_T, p, g, h, e, H)$.
- SGen(sp): Choose a random element $x \in \mathbb{Z}_p$ and set the data sender's key pair as (pk_S, sk_S) = (h^x, x).
- RGen(sp): Choose a random element $y \in \mathbb{Z}_p$ and set the data receiver's key pair as (pk_R, sk_R) = (h^y, y).
- PAEKS(sk_S, pk_R, w): Choose a random $r \in \mathbb{Z}_p$, and compute $c_w^1 = H(w)^{sk_S} \cdot g^r$ and $c_w^2 = (pk_R)^r$. Set $C_w = (c_w^1, c_w^2)$ as the cipher-keyword of keyword w.

- Trapdoor(sk_R, pk_S, w): Compute $T_w = e(H(w)^{sk_R}, pk_S)$ as the search trapdoor of keyword w.
- $0/1 \leftarrow$ Test($pk_S, pk_R, T_w, C_{w'}$): For a cipher-keyword $C_{w'} = (c^1_{w'}, c^2_{w'})$ of keyword w' and a trapdoor T_w of keyword w, verify $e(c^1_{w'}, pk_R) \overset{?}{=} T_w \cdot e(g, c^2_{w'})$. Output 1 if the equation holds, and 0 otherwise.

The above PAEKS scheme is in fact identical to the Huang et al.'s PAEKS scheme, except that some group element g in Huang et al.'s scheme are replaced with another random group element h. Thus, if the group element h in the above scheme is replaced by g, we immediately obtain the PAEKS scheme of [14].

Theorem 3. *The PAEKS schemes of [14, 18] do not satisfy cipher-keyword indistinguishability under a fully chosen keyword to cipher-keyword attack.*

Proof. We now construct an efficient algorithm $\mathcal{A}$ to break the fully CI-security. It works as follows:

In Phase 1 of the fully CI-security game, $\mathcal{A}$ chooses an arbitrary keyword w_0, and queries it to the cipher-keyword oracle $\mathsf{PAEKS}_{sk_S}(pk_R, \cdot)$ to obtain a cipher-keyword $C_{w_0} = (c^1_{w_0}, c^2_{w_0})$ of keyword w_0.

In the challenge phase, $\mathcal{A}$ outputs a pair of challenge keywords $(w^*_0, w^*_1) = (w_0, w_1)$, where w_1 is another keyword chosen by $\mathcal{A}$. When the challenger receives the keywords, it chooses a random bit $b \in \{0, 1\}$, and gives the challenge ciphertext $C_{w^*_b} = (c^1_{w^*_b}, c^2_{w^*_b})$ to $\mathcal{A}$.

In guess phase, $\mathcal{A}$ verifies whether the following equation holds

$$\frac{e(c^1_{w_0}, pk_R)}{e(g, c^2_{w_0})} \overset{?}{=} \frac{e(c^1_{w^*_b}, pk_R)}{e(g, c^2_{w^*_b})}. \tag{1}$$

If so, it outputs $b' = 0$; otherwise $b' = 1$.

Next, we discuss $\mathcal{A}$'s success probability in the above attack. Suppose that the randomness used in cipher-keyword C_{w_0} is r, then $c^1_{w_0} = H(w_0)^{sk_S} \cdot g^r$ and $c^2_{w_0} = (pk_R)^r$. Also, suppose that the randomness is r^* in the challenge cipher-keyword $C_{w^*_b}$, then $c^1_{w^*_b} = H(w^*_b)^{sk_S} \cdot g^{r^*}$ and $c^2_{w^*_b} = (pk_R)^{r^*}$. We have that

$$\frac{e(c^1_{w_0}, pk_R)}{e(g, c^2_{w_0})} = \frac{e(H(w_0)^{sk_S} \cdot g^r, h^{sk_R})}{e(g, (h^{sk_R})^r)} = e(H(w_0), h)^{sk_S \cdot sk_R}$$

and

$$\frac{e(c^1_{w^*_b}, pk_R)}{e(g, c^2_{w^*_b})} = \frac{e(H(w^*_b)^{sk_S} \cdot g^{r^*}, h^{sk_R})}{e(g, (h^{sk_R})^{r^*})} = e(H(w^*_b), h)^{sk_S \cdot sk_R}.$$

Obviously, if $b = 0$, then $w^*_b = w_0$ and the Eq. (1) must hold. If $b = 1$, then $w^*_b \neq w_0$ and the Eq. (1) does not hold, unless the collision $H(w_0) = H(w_1)$ happens. By the collision-resistance of the hash function, $\mathcal{A}$ can successfully guess the random bit b, with overwhelming probability (approximate to 1). Thus, $\mathcal{A}$ breaks the fully CI-security of the NE-PAEKS scheme as well as the HL-PAEKS scheme with non-negligible advantage (approximate to 1/2). $\qquad\square$

Theorem 3 indicates that the two PAEKS schemes in [14,18] cannot resist against fully chosen keyword to cipher-keyword attacks. However, for PAEKS schemes [9,23], we do not know whether they are secure in the fully CI-security model. But, their security proofs did not capture the scenario of fully chosen keyword to cipher-keyword attacks. For Pan et al.'s PAEKS scheme [21], Cheng and Meng [8] recently showed that it was not MCI-secure.

5 New PAEKS Scheme

In this section, we first propose a new PAEKS scheme and then prove its security. The scheme includes the below algorithms:

- Setup(1^κ): The trusted authority first chooses two cyclic group G and G_T with prime order p, a random generator g of group G and a bilinear pairing $e : G \times G \to G_T$. Then, it chooses three hash functions $H_1 : \{0,1\}^* \to G$, $H_2 : G \to \{0,1\}^{\log p}$ and $H_3 : G \to \{0,1\}^{hLen}$, where $hLen$ is the output length of a cryptographic hash function such as SHA-1. The system parameter is $sp = (G, G_T, p, g, e, H_1, H_2, H_3)$.
- SGen(sp): The data sender chooses two random elements $u \in \mathbb{Z}_p$ and sets the key pair to be $pk_S = g^u$ and $sk_S = u$.
- RGen(sp): The data receiver chooses two random elements $x, v \in \mathbb{Z}_p$ and sets the key pair to be $pk_R = (g^x, g^v)$ and $sk_R = (x, v)$.
- PAEKS(sk_S, pk_R, w): The data sender chooses a random element $r \in \mathbb{Z}_p$, and computes $A = g^r$, $B = H_2(e(h^r, g^x))$, where $h = H_1(w||pk_s||pk_R||k)$ and $k = H_3(g^{vu})$. The cipher-keyword of w is $C_w = (A, B)$.
- Trapdoor(sk_R, pk_S, w): The data receiver computes the trapdoor $T_w = h^x$, where $h = H_1(w||pk_s||pk_R||k)$ and $k = H_3(g^{uv})$.
- 0/1 $\leftarrow$ Test($pk_S, pk_R, T_w, C_{w'}$): For a cipher-keyword $C_{w'} = (A, B)$ of keyword w' and a trapdoor T_w of keyword w, the cloud server tests $H_2(e(T_w, A)) \overset{?}{=} B$. If so, it outputs 1, and 0 otherwise.

Correctness of above scheme is easy to follow. We mainly prove its security.

Security Proof. The fully CI-security of the above scheme is stated in Theorem 4.

Theorem 4. *Under the BDH assumption, our PAEKS scheme has cipher-keyword indistinguishability under a fully CKC attack and a CKT attack in random oracle model. Specifically, if there is an adversary $\mathcal{A}$ that can break the fully CI-security of our PAEKS scheme with advantage ϵ, then there is an algorithm $\mathcal{B}$ solving the BDH problem with probability ϵ', such that $\epsilon' \geq \frac{\epsilon}{e \cdot Q_{H_2} \cdot (1 + Q_T)}$, where e is the base of the natural logarithm, and Q_{H_2} and Q_T are the maximum hash queries to H_2 and the maximum trapdoor queries made by $\mathcal{A}$.*

Proof. To prove Theorem 4, we construct an algorithm $\mathcal{B}$ that uses $\mathcal{A}$ as a subroutine. Let G be a bilinear group with prime order p and $e : G \times G \to G_T$ be the bilinear map. $\mathcal{B}$ is given an instance $(g, X = g^x, Y = g^y, Z = g^z) \in G^4$

of the BDH problem, and its goal is to compute $T = e(g,g)^{xyz}$. $\mathcal{B}$ simulates the fully CI-security game for $\mathcal{A}$ as follows.

Initialization. $\mathcal{B}$ chooses the three hash functions H_1, H_2 and H_3 as in the scheme and sets the system parameter as $sp = (G, G_T, p, g, e, H_1, H_2, H_3)$. Then, it chooses a random $u \in \mathbb{Z}_p$ by itself, and sets $pk_S^* = g^u$ as the data sender's public key and $sk_S^* = u$ as the corresponding secret key. Similarly, it chooses a random $v \in \mathbb{Z}_p$ and sets the data receiver's public key to be $pk_R^* = (X, g^v)$ and the corresponding secret key to be $sk_R^* = (x, v)$, here x is known to $\mathcal{B}$. It gives the public keys pk_S^* and pk_R^*, as well as the system parameter sp to $\mathcal{A}$.

Hash Queries. In this proof, H_3 is viewed as a standard cryptographic hash function. Given an input x, $\mathcal{A}$ (and $\mathcal{B}$) can compute $H_3(x)$ by itself. H_1 and H_2 are viewed as random oracles, and work as follows.

- H_1-**queries:** $\mathcal{B}$ maintains a list of tuples $\langle I_i, a_i, c_i, h_i \rangle$, called H_1-list, where $I_i = w_i || pk_S || pk_R || k_i$. When $\mathcal{A}$ makes a query with $I_i = w_i || pk_S || pk_R || k_i$, $\mathcal{B}$ responds as follows:
  - It first checks whether there is a tuple indexed with index I_i in the H_1-list. If so, it returns the corresponding h_i to $\mathcal{A}$.
  - Otherwise, it picks a random coin $c_i \in \{0, 1\}$ such that $\Pr[c_i = 0] = \frac{1}{Q_{H_1}}$.
  - It also chooses a random $a_i \in \mathbb{Z}_p$. If $c_i = 0$, it sets $h_i = Y \cdot g^{a_i}$; if $c_i = 1$, it sets $h_i = g^{a_i}$.
  - Finally, it returns h_i to $\mathcal{A}$ as the hash value of $H_1(I_i)$, and adds $\langle I_i, a_i, c_i, h_i \rangle$ to the H_1-list.
- H_2-**queries:** $\mathcal{B}$ maintains a list of tuples $\langle t_i, V_i \rangle$, called H_2-list. When $\mathcal{A}$ makes a query with $t_i \in G_T$, $\mathcal{B}$ first checks whether there is a tuple indexed with t_i. If so, $\mathcal{B}$ returns the corresponding value V_i. Otherwise, it chooses a random $V_i \in \{0, 1\}^{\log}$. Finally, $\mathcal{B}$ returns V_i to $\mathcal{A}$ as the hash value of $H_2(t_i)$ and adds $\langle t_i, V_i \rangle$ to the H_2-list.

Cipher-Keyword Queries. When $\mathcal{A}$ queries the cipher-keyword oracle with $(pk_R = (pk_{R,1}, pk_{R,2}), w_i) \in G^2 \times \{0, 1\}^*$, algorithm $\mathcal{B}$ first computes $k_i = H_3(pk_{R,2}^u)$. Then, it makes the H_1-queries with $I_i = w_i || pk_S^* || pk_R || k_i$ to obtain an h_i such that $H_1(I_i) = h_i$. Next, it chooses a random $r \in \mathbb{Z}_p$, and computes $A = g^r$ and $t_i = e(h_i, pk_{R,1})^r$. $\mathcal{B}$ makes the H_2-queries with t_i to obtain a V_i such that $H_2(t_i) = V_i$. Finally, $\mathcal{B}$ sets $B = V_i$ and returns the cipher-keyword $C_{w_i} = (A, B)$ to $\mathcal{A}$.

Trapdoor Queries. When $\mathcal{A}$ queries the trapdoor oracle with $(pk_S, w_i) \in G \times \{0, 1\}^*$, $\mathcal{B}$ first computes $k_i = H_3(pk_S^v)$ and then makes the H_1-queries with $I_i = w_i || pk_S || pk_R^* || k_i$ to obtain an h_i such that $H_1(I_i) = h_i$, and the corresponding tuple $\langle I_i, a_i, c_i, h_i \rangle$. If $c_i = 0$, $\mathcal{B}$ aborts the game. Otherwise, it has $h_i = g^{a_i}$ and $\mathcal{B}$ can compute $T_{w_i} = X^{a_i} (= H_1(I_i)^x)$. Finally, $\mathcal{B}$ returns the trapdoor T_{w_i} to $\mathcal{A}$.

Challenge. When $\mathcal{A}$ submits two challenge keywords w_0^* and w_1^*, $\mathcal{B}$ first picks a random coin $b \in \{0, 1\}$. Then, it computes $k^* = H_3(g^{uv})$ and makes the H_1-queries with $I^* = w_b^* || pk_S^* || pk_R^* || k^*$ to obtain the value h^* such that $H_1(I^*) =$

h^*, and the corresponding tuple $\langle I^*, a^*, c^*, h^* \rangle$. If $c^* = 1$, $\mathcal{B}$ aborts the game. Otherwise, $c = 0$ and $h^* = Y \cdot g^{a^*}$. $\mathcal{B}$ picks a random $V^* \in \{0,1\}^{\log p}$ and returns the challenge cipher-keyword $C^* = (Z, V^*)$ to $\mathcal{A}$. This implicitly defines $H_2(t^*) = V^*$ and $t^* = e(H_1(I^*), X)^z = e(g^y \cdot g^{a^*}, g^x)^z = e(g,g)^{xz(y+a^*)}$.

More Queries. $\mathcal{A}$ can continue to issue both cipher-keyword queries and trapdoor queries, except for the restriction that $\mathcal{A}$ cannot request trapdoors for (pk_S^*, w_0^*) and (pk_S^*, w_1^*).

Guess. Finally, $\mathcal{A}$ outputs a bit b' as its guess that C^* is the encryption of keyword $w_{b'}^*$. Meanwhile, $\mathcal{B}$ chooses from H_2-list a random tuple $\langle t, V \rangle$ and outputs $t/e(X, Z)^{a^*}$ as the guess of $e(g,g)^{xyz}$.

At this point, we complete the description of algorithm $\mathcal{B}$. Next, we discuss $\mathcal{B}$'s success probability. First, we explain why $\mathcal{B}$ may succeed in above game. Let $I_0 = w_0^* \| pk_S^* \| pk_R^* \| k^*$ and $I_1 = w_1^* \| pk_S^* \| pk_R^* \| k^*$, where $k^* = H_3(g^{uv})$. Let F be the event that $\mathcal{A}$ issues a query for either $H_2(e(H_1(I_0), X)^z)$ or $H_2(e(H_1(I_1), X)^z)$ in the above simulated game. Next, we prove the following lemma.

Lemma 1. *If adversary $\mathcal{A}$ has advantage ϵ in breaking the fully CI-security of our PAEKS scheme, then $\Pr[F] \geq 2\epsilon/(e \cdot (1 + Q_T))$.*

Proof. Let E_1 and E_2 be the event that $\mathcal{B}$ does not abort during the trapdoor queries and the challenge phase respectively. For $\mathcal{A}$'s i-th trapdoor query (pk_s, w_i), there is a tuple $\langle I_i, a_i, c_i, h_i \rangle$ such that $I_i = w_i \| pk_S \| pk_R^* \| H_3(pk_S^v)$. Since h_i has the same distribution regardless of $c_i = 0$ or $c_i = 1$, c_i is independent of $\mathcal{A}$'s view prior to issuing the query. Therefore, algorithm $\mathcal{B}$ aborts with probability at most $1/(1 + Q_T)$ in this query. Since $\mathcal{A}$ makes at most Q_T trapdoor queries, we have that $\Pr[E_1] = \left(1 - \frac{1}{1+Q_T}\right)^{Q_T} \geq \frac{1}{e}$.

Similarly, in the challenge phase, c^* is independent of $\mathcal{A}$'s view, prior to issuing the challenge cipher-keyword. Therefore, $\Pr[E_2] = \Pr[c^* = 0] = \frac{1}{1+Q_T}$.

Since $\mathcal{A}$ is forbidden to query the trapdoor oracle with (pk_S^*, w_0^*) and (pk_S^*, w_1^*), the two events E_1 and E_2 are independent from each other. Thus, $\Pr[E_1 \wedge E_2] \geq \frac{1}{e \cdot (1+Q_T)}$.

Let E_3 be the event that $\mathcal{A}$ issues a query for either $H_2(e(H_1(I_0^*), X)^z)$ or $H_2(e(H_1(I_1^*), X)^z)$ in the real fully CI-security game. Clearly, if E_3 never occurs, $\mathcal{A}$ has no advantage to guess b. Since, $\Pr[b' = b] = \Pr[b' = b|E_3] \cdot \Pr[E_3] + \Pr[b' = b|\overline{E_3}] \cdot \Pr[\overline{E_3}]$, we have that

$$\Pr[b' = b|\overline{E_3}] \cdot \Pr[\overline{E_3}] \leq \Pr[b' = b] \leq \Pr[E_3] + \frac{1}{2} \cdot \Pr[\overline{E_3}]$$

$$\Rightarrow \frac{1}{2} - \frac{1}{2} \cdot \Pr[E_3] \leq \Pr[b' = b] \leq \frac{1}{2} + \frac{1}{2} \cdot \Pr[E_3]$$

$$\Rightarrow \left| \Pr[b' = b] - \frac{1}{2} \right| \leq \frac{1}{2} \cdot \Pr[E_3].$$

So, $\Pr[E_3] \geq 2 \cdot \epsilon$. Note that, if $\mathcal{B}$ does not abort, it simulates the real fully CI-security game perfectly. Therefore,

$$\Pr[F] = \Pr[F|(E_1 \wedge E_2)] \cdot \Pr[E_1 \wedge E_2] + \Pr[F|\overline{E_1 \wedge E_2}] \cdot \Pr[\overline{E_1 \wedge E_2}]$$

$$\geq \Pr[E_3]\Pr[E_1 \wedge E_2] \geq \frac{2\epsilon}{e(1 + Q_T)}.$$

This completes the proof of Lemma 1.   □

Note that the occurring of event F implies that the H_2-list must include a tuple $\langle t, V \rangle$ with probability $1/2$, such that $t = e(H_1(I_b), X)^z$. Since,

$$t = e(H_1(I_b), X)^z = e(H_1(I^*), X)^z = e(Y \cdot g^{a^*}, X)^z,$$

it follows that $e(g, g)^{xyz} = t/e(X, Z)^{a^*}$, as required.

Finally, recall that $\mathcal{B}$ chooses the correct tuple $\langle t, V \rangle$ with probability $1/Q_{H_2}$. Therefore, $\mathcal{B}$ can successfully break the BDH assumption with probability at least $\Pr[F]/(2 \cdot Q_{H_2})$, i.e.,

$$\epsilon' \geq \frac{\Pr[F]}{2 \cdot Q_{H_2}} \geq \frac{\epsilon}{e \cdot Q_{H_2} \cdot (1 + Q_T)}.$$

This completes the proof of Theorem 4.   □

The TI-security of our scheme is stated in the following theorem.

Theorem 5. *Under the CODH assumption, our PAEKS scheme satisfies trapdoor indistinguishability in the random oracle model. Specifically, if there is an adversary $\mathcal{A}$ that can break the TI-security of our PAEKS scheme with advantage ϵ, then there is a PPT algorithm $\mathcal{B}$ solving the oracle DH problem with probability ϵ', such that $\epsilon' \geq \frac{\epsilon}{Q_{H_1}}$, where Q_{H_1} is the maximum hash queries to H_1 made by $\mathcal{A}$.*

Proof. To prove Theorem 5, we show how to construct an algorithm $\mathcal{B}$ using $\mathcal{A}$ as a subroutine to solve the CODH problem. Let G be a bilinear group with prime order p and a bilinear map $e : G \times G \to G_T$. $\mathcal{B}$ is given an instance $(g, U = g^u, V = g^v, H_3)$ and two oracles $\mathcal{O}_u(X) = H_3(X^u)$ and $\mathcal{O}_v(Y) = H_3(Y^v)$ of the oracle DH problem. It simulates the TI-security game for $\mathcal{A}$ as follows.

Initialization. $\mathcal{B}$ chooses the two hash functions H_1 and H_2 as in the scheme and sets the system parameter as $sp = (G, G_T, p, g, e, H_1, H_2, H_3)$. Then, it sets $pk_S^* = U$ as the data sender's public key and $sk_S^* = u$ as the corresponding secret key (though u is known to $\mathcal{B}$. It also chooses a random $x \in \mathbb{Z}_p$ by itself, and sets $pk_R^* = (g^x, V)$ as the data receiver's public key and $sk_R^* = (x, v)$ as the corresponding secret key, here x is known to $\mathcal{B}$. It gives the public keys pk_S^* and pk_R^*, as well as the system parameter sp to $\mathcal{A}$.

Hash Queries. In this proof, H_2 and H_3 are viewed as normal cryptographic hash functions, but H_1 is viewed as a random oracle, and works as follows.

- H_1-**queries:** $\mathcal{B}$ maintains a list of tuples $\langle I_i, h_i \rangle$, called H_1-list, where $I_i = w_i\|pk_S\|pk_R\|k_i$. When $\mathcal{A}$ makes a query with $I_i = w_i\|pk_S\|pk_R\|k_i$, $\mathcal{B}$ responds by choosing a random $h_i \in G$ and adds $\langle I_i, h_i \rangle$ to the H_1-list. $\mathcal{B}$ may query the H_1 oracle by itself with a special form I_i, in which k_i is the special symbol "$\star$". It denotes the unknown solution $H_3(g^{uv})$ of the oracle DH problem. In this case, $\mathcal{B}$ still picks a random $h_i \in G$ and sets $H(I_i) = h_i$.

Cipher-Keyword Queries. When $\mathcal{A}$ queries the cipher-keyword oracle with $(pk_R = (pk_{R,1}, pk_{R,2}), w_i) \in G^2 \times \{0,1\}^*$, if $pk_{R,2} \neq V$, algorithm $\mathcal{B}$ queries the oracle $\mathcal{O}_u(pk_{R,2})$ to obtain $k_i = H_3(pk_{R,2}^u)$. Otherwise, it sets $k_i = \star$. Then, it makes the H_1-queries with $I_i = w_i\|pk_S^*\|pk_R\|k_i$ to obtain an h_i such that $H_1(I_i) = h_i$. Next, it chooses a random $r \in \mathbb{Z}_p$, and computes $A = g^r$ and $B = H_2(e(h_i, pk_{R,1})^r)$. Finally, $\mathcal{B}$ returns the cipher-keyword $C_{w_i} = (A, B)$ to $\mathcal{A}$.

Trapdoor Queries. When $\mathcal{A}$ queries the trapdoor oracle with $(pk_S, w_i) \in G \times \{0,1\}^*$, if $pk_S \neq U$, $\mathcal{B}$ queries the oracle $\mathcal{O}_v(pk_S)$ to obtain $k_i = H_3(pk_S^v)$. Otherwise, it sets $k_i = \star$. Then, $\mathcal{B}$ makes the H_1-queries with $I_i = w_i\|pk_S\|pk_R^*\|k_i$ to obtain an h_i such that $H_1(I_i) = h_i$. It computes $T_{w_i} = h_i^x$ $(= H_1(I_i)^x)$ and returns it to $\mathcal{A}$.

Challenge. When $\mathcal{A}$ submits two challenge keywords w_0^* and w_1^*, $\mathcal{B}$ first picks a random coin $b \in \{0,1\}$ and then makes the H_1-queries with $I^* = w_b^*\|pk_S^*\|pk_R^*\|\star$ to obtain the value h^* such that $H_1(I^*) = h^*$. It computes the challenge trapdoor $T_{w_b^*} = (h^*)^x$ and returns it to $\mathcal{A}$.

More Queries. $\mathcal{A}$ can continue to issue both cipher-keyword queries and trapdoor queries, except for the restriction that $\mathcal{A}$ cannot request cipher-keyword for (pk_R^*, w_0^*) and (pk_R^*, w_1^*), and request trapdoors for (pk_S^*, w_0^*) and (pk_S^*, w_1^*).

Guess. Finally, $\mathcal{A}$ outputs a bit b' as its guess that $T_{w_b^*}$ is the trapdoor of keyword $w_{b'}^*$. At this point, $\mathcal{B}$ chooses from the H_1-list (excluding those special queries issued by $\mathcal{B}$) a random tuple $\langle I = w\|pk_S\|pk_R\|k, h \rangle$ and outputs the corresponding k as the guess of $H_3(g^{uv})$.

This completes the description of simulated TI-security game. Next, we discuss algorithm $\mathcal{B}$'s success probability in the above game.

Let $I_0 = w_0^*\|pk_S^*\|pk_R^*\|k^*$ and $I_1 = w_1^*\|pk_S^*\|pk_R^*\|k^*$, where $k^* = H_3(g^{uv})$. Since $\mathcal{A}$ cannot issue queries for $\mathsf{PAEKS}_{sk_S^*}(pk_R^*, w_i^*)$ and $\mathsf{Trapdoor}_{sk_R^*}(pk_S^*, w_i^*)$ $(i = 0, 1)$, prior to issuing the challenge trapdoor, the hash value $H_1(I_i)$ is independent of $\mathcal{A}$'s view. In addition, no matter $I^* = I_0$ or $I^* = I_1$, the corresponding hash values have the same distribution. Thus, if $\mathcal{A}$ never issues a query for neither $H_1(I_0)$ nor $H_1(I_1)$, it has no advantage to distinguish the challenge trapdoor. Let E be the event that $\mathcal{A}$ issues a query for either $H_1(I_0)$ or $H_1(I_1)$. We show that if $\mathcal{A}$ has non-negligible advantage ϵ, to distinguish the challenge trapdoor, the event E must occur with non-negligible. Since,

$$\Pr[b' = b] = \Pr[b' = b|E] \cdot \Pr[E] + \Pr[b' = b|\overline{E}] \cdot \Pr[\overline{E}]$$

we have that

$$\Pr[b' = b|\overline{E}] \cdot \Pr[\overline{E}] \leq \Pr[b' = b] \leq \Pr[E] + \frac{1}{2} \cdot \Pr[\overline{E}]$$

$$\Rightarrow \frac{1}{2} - \frac{1}{2} \cdot \Pr[E] \leq \Pr[b' = b] \leq \frac{1}{2} + \frac{1}{2} \cdot \Pr[E]$$

$$\Rightarrow \left|\Pr[b' = b] - \frac{1}{2}\right| \leq \frac{1}{2} \cdot \Pr[E].$$

It follows that $\Pr[E] \geq 2\epsilon$.

Recall that $\mathcal{B}$ chooses the challenge coin b uniformly at random. If the event E indeed occurs, the hash query $I_b = w_b^* \|pk_S^*\|pk_R^*\|H_3(g^{uv})$ will be in the H_1-list with probability at least $1/2$. By randomly choosing from the H_1-list, $\mathcal{B}$ can obtain the correct tuple $\langle I_b, h^* \rangle$ with probability at least $1/Q_{H_1}$. Taking all conditions together, $\mathcal{B}$ finds the solution of the oracle DH instance with probability $\epsilon' \geq \frac{\epsilon}{Q_{H_1}}$, as required in Theorem 5. □

6   Efficiency Evaluation

In this section, we evaluate the efficiency of our PAEKS scheme and compare it with previous PAEKS schemes HL17 [14], NE19 [18], QCH+20 [23], CQZ20 [9] and PL21 [21].

Table 2. Security comparison

Schemes	Fully CI-security	TI-security	Multi-user setting	Assumptions
HL17 [14]	✗	✓	✗	mDLIN and DBDH
NE19 [18]	✗	✓	✓	mDLIN and DBDH
QCH+20 [23]	Unknown	✓	✗	BDH
CQZ20 [9]	Unknown	✓	✓	ODH
PL21 [21]	✗	✓	✗	BDHI
This paper	✓	✓	✓	BDH and CODH

Table 2 summarizes the security guarantees of these PAEKS schemes. In the table, "Fully CI-security" denotes the notion of cipher-keyword indistinguishability against fully chosen keyword to cipher-keyword attacks. "mDLIN", "DBDH" and "BDHI" stand for modified Decision Linear (mDLIN) assumption, Decisional Bilinear Diffie-Hellman (DBDH) assumption and Bilinear Diffie-Hellman Inversion (BDHI) assumption respectively. The other symbols are consistent to the definitions in previous sections. Table 2 shows that only our scheme achieves the fully CI-security in the multi-user setting. Though the schemes of NE19 and CQZ20 both are proven in multi-user setting, none of them was proven to be fully CI-secure. The scheme of QCH+20 and PL21 revisited multiple cipher-keyword indistinguishability for PAEKS, but they still did not allow the adversary to query cipher-keyword oracle with challenge keywords in their CI-security model. In addition, their security proof is given in one-user setting rather than multi-user setting.

Table 3. Efficiency comparison

Schemes	Key generation	Encryption	Trapdoor	Test
HL17 [14]	E_G	$3E_G + H_1$	$E_G + P + H_1$	$2P$
NE19 [18]	E_G	$3E_G + H_1$	$E_G + P + H_1$	$2P$
QCH+20 [23]	E_G	$3E_G + P + H_1$	$2E_G + H_1$	P
CQZ+20 [9]	E_G	$E_G + 3F$	$E_G + 2F$	F
PL21 [21]	E_G	$3E_G + H_1$	$3E_G + P + H_1$	$2P$
This paper	$2E_G$	$3E_G + P + H_1$	$2E_G + H_1$	P

Table 3 demonstrates the number of operations in each algorithm. Suppose that the bilinear map used in each schemes is $e : G \times G \to G_T$. Then, we use "E_G" to denote the operation of exponentiation in group G, and use "P" to denote the pairing operation. "H_1" is the special hash function that maps any string to a group element of G, and "F" is the pseudorandom function. In the table, we ignore some low-cost operations, such as normal hashing. In theory, with the exception of [9], the other schemes almost have the same efficiency. For key generation algorithm, our scheme requires two group exponentiations, while the others requires only one. As the key generation algorithm runs only once for each user, it has very little effect on the whole efficiency. For keyword encryption algorithm, our scheme has almost the same operations as that of QCH+20. The schemes of HL17, NE19 and PL21 may be slightly faster than that of ours, as they did not need pairing operations in the keyword encryption algorithm. For trapdoor generation algorithm, our scheme requires two exponentiations. This is almost optimal among these PAEKS schemes. For test algorithm, ours and QCH+20 requires only a half number of pairings compared with HL17 and NE19. The scheme of CQZ20 is the most efficient one among these five schemes, but it is not fully CI-secure. Ours is the only one that achieves such security.

7 Conclusion

In this paper, we revisited the security model of public-key authenticated encryption (PAEKS), and pointed out a weakness in previous model. Specifically, the cipher-keyword indistinguishability is not fully secure, as it did not allow adversary to query cipher-keyword of challenge keywords. We solved this issue by defining an improved security model for cipher-keyword indistinguishability. The improved security model captures a realistic scenario that multiple cipher-keywords are still indistinguishable. Finally, we proposed a new construction of

PAEKS scheme in this improved security model. The scheme still has comparable efficiency with previous ones. A future work is to study whether it is possible to construct a PAEKS scheme with both fully ciphertext indistinguishability and fully trapdoor indistinguishability.

Acknowledgment. This work is supported by the National Natural Science Foundation of China (grant numbers 61872292 and 62072371), the Key Research and Development Program of Shaanxi (grant number 2020ZDLGY08-04 and 2021ZDLGY06-02), the Basic Research Program of Qinghai Province (grant number 2020-ZJ-701) and the fund of Science and Technology on Communication Security Laboratory (grant number 6142103190101).

References

1. Abdalla, M., Bellare, M., Rogaway, P.: The oracle Diffie-Hellman assumptions and an analysis of DHIES. In: Naccache, D. (ed.) CT-RSA 2001. LNCS, vol. 2020, pp. 143–158. Springer, Heidelberg (2001). https://doi.org/10.1007/3-540-45353-9_12
2. Ateniese, G., Fu, K., Green, M., Hohenberger, S.: Improved proxy re-encryption schemes with applications to secure distributed storage. ACM Trans. Inf. Syst. Secur. **9**(1), 1–30 (2006). https://doi.org/10.1145/1127345.1127346
3. Baek, J., Safavi-Naini, R., Susilo, W.: Public key encryption with keyword search revisited. In: Gervasi, O., Murgante, B., Laganà, A., Taniar, D., Mun, Y., Gavrilova, M.L. (eds.) ICCSA 2008. LNCS, vol. 5072, pp. 1249–1259. Springer, Heidelberg (2008). https://doi.org/10.1007/978-3-540-69839-5_96
4. Boneh, D., Di Crescenzo, G., Ostrovsky, R., Persiano, G.: Public key encryption with keyword search. In: Cachin, C., Camenisch, J.L. (eds.) EUROCRYPT 2004. LNCS, vol. 3027, pp. 506–522. Springer, Heidelberg (2004). https://doi.org/10.1007/978-3-540-24676-3_30
5. Byun, J.W., Rhee, H.S., Park, H.-A., Lee, D.H.: Off-Line keyword guessing attacks on recent keyword search schemes over encrypted data. In: Jonker, W., Petković, M. (eds.) SDM 2006. LNCS, vol. 4165, pp. 75–83. Springer, Heidelberg (2006). https://doi.org/10.1007/11844662_6
6. Chen, R., et al.: Server-aided public key encryption with keyword search. IEEE Trans. Inf. Forensics Secur. **11**(12), 2833–2842 (2016). https://doi.org/10.1109/TIFS.2016.2599293
7. Chen, Y.: SPEKS: secure server-designation public key encryption with keyword search against keyword guessing attacks. Comput. J. **58**(4), 922–933 (2015). https://doi.org/10.1093/comjnl/bxu013
8. Cheng, X., Meng, F.: Security analysis of pan et al.'s "Public-key authenticated encryption with keyword search achieving both multi-ciphertext and multi-trapdoor indistinguishability". J. Syst. Archit. **119**, 102248 (2021)
9. Chi, T., Qin, B., Zheng, D.: An efficient searchable public-key authenticated encryption for cloud-assisted medical Internet of Things. Wirel. Commun. Mob. Comput. **2020**, 8816172:1–8816172:11 (2020). https://doi.org/10.1155/2020/8816172
10. Demertzis, I., Chamani, J.G., Papadopoulos, D., Papamanthou, C.: Dynamic searchable encryption with small client storage. In: 27th Annual Network and Distributed System Security Symposium. NDSS 2020, San Diego, California, USA, 23–26 February 2020. The Internet Society (2020). https://www.ndss-symposium.org/ndss-paper/dynamic-searchable-encryption-with-small-client-storage/

11. Fang, L., Susilo, W., Ge, C., Wang, J.: Public key encryption with keyword search secure against keyword guessing attacks without random oracle. Inf. Sci. **238**, 221–241 (2013). https://doi.org/10.1016/j.ins.2013.03.008

12. Goyal, V., Pandey, O., Sahai, A., Waters, B.: Attribute-based encryption for fine-grained access control of encrypted data. In: Juels, A., Wright, R.N., di Vimercati, S.D.C. (eds.) Proceedings of the 13th ACM Conference on Computer and Communications Security. CCS 2006, pp. 89–98. ACM (2006). http://doi.acm.org/10.1145/1180405.1180418

13. He, D., Ma, M., Zeadally, S., Kumar, N., Liang, K.: Certificateless public key authenticated encryption with keyword search for industrial internet of things. IEEE Trans. Ind. Inform. **14**(8), 3618–3627 (2018). https://doi.org/10.1109/TII.2017.2771382

14. Huang, Q., Li, H.: An efficient public-key searchable encryption scheme secure against inside keyword guessing attacks. Inf. Sci. **403**, 1–14 (2017). https://doi.org/10.1016/j.ins.2017.03.038

15. Jeong, I.R., Kwon, J.O., Hong, D., Lee, D.H.: Constructing PEKS schemes secure against keyword guessing attacks is possible? Comput. Commun. **32**(2), 394–396 (2009). https://doi.org/10.1016/j.comcom.2008.11.018

16. Liu, X., Li, H., Yang, G., Susilo, W., Tonien, J., Huang, Q.: Towards enhanced security for certificateless public-key authenticated encryption with keyword search. In: Steinfeld, R., Yuen, T.H. (eds.) ProvSec 2019. LNCS, vol. 11821, pp. 113–129. Springer, Cham (2019). https://doi.org/10.1007/978-3-030-31919-9_7

17. Lu, Y., Wang, G., Li, J.: Keyword guessing attacks on a public key encryption with keyword search scheme without random oracle and its improvement. Inf. Sci. **479**, 270–276 (2019). https://doi.org/10.1016/j.ins.2018.12.004

18. Noroozi, M., Eslami, Z.: Public key authenticated encryption with keyword search: revisited. IET Inf. Secur. **13**(4), 336–342 (2019). https://doi.org/10.1049/iet-ifs.2018.5315

19. Noroozi, M., Eslami, Z.: Public-key encryption with keyword search: a generic construction secure against online and offline keyword guessing attacks. J. Ambient Intell. Humaniz. Comput. **11**(2), 879–890 (2020). https://doi.org/10.1007/s12652-019-01254-w

20. Noroozi, M., Karoubi, I., Eslami, Z.: Designing a secure designated server identity-based encryption with keyword search scheme: still unsolved. Ann. des Télécommunications **73**(11–12), 769–776 (2018). https://doi.org/10.1007/s12243-018-0653-4

21. Pan, X., Li, F.: Public-key authenticated encryption with keyword search achieving both multi-ciphertext and multi-trapdoor indistinguishability. J. Syst. Archit. **115**, 102075 (2021). https://doi.org/10.1016/j.sysarc.2021.102075

22. Patel, S., Persiano, G., Yeo, K.: Lower bounds for encrypted multi-maps and searchable encryption in the leakage cell probe model. In: Micciancio, D., Ristenpart, T. (eds.) CRYPTO 2020. LNCS, vol. 12170, pp. 433–463. Springer, Cham (2020). https://doi.org/10.1007/978-3-030-56784-2_15

23. Qin, B., Chen, Y., Huang, Q., Liu, X., Zheng, D.: Public-key authenticated encryption with keyword search revisited: security model and constructions. Inf. Sci. **516**, 515–528 (2020). https://doi.org/10.1016/j.ins.2019.12.063

24. Singh, S., Jeong, Y., Park, J.H.: A survey on cloud computing security: issues, threats, and solutions. J. Networks Comput. Appl. **75**, 200–222 (2016). https://doi.org/10.1016/j.jnca.2016.09.002

25. Soleimanian, A., Khazaei, S.: Publicly verifiable searchable symmetric encryption based on efficient cryptographic components. Des. Codes Cryptography **87**(1), 123–147 (2019). https://doi.org/10.1007/s10623-018-0489-y
26. Song, D.X., Wagner, D.A., Perrig, A.: Practical techniques for searches on encrypted data. In: 2000 IEEE Symposium on Security and Privacy, pp. 44–55. IEEE Computer Society (2000). https://doi.org/10.1109/SECPRI.2000.848445
27. Tang, Q., Chen, L.: Public-Key encryption with registered keyword search. In: Martinelli, F., Preneel, B. (eds.) EuroPKI 2009. LNCS, vol. 6391, pp. 163–178. Springer, Heidelberg (2010). https://doi.org/10.1007/978-3-642-16441-5_11
28. Yau, W.-C., Heng, S.-H., Goi, B.-M.: Off-Line keyword guessing attacks on recent public key encryption with keyword search schemes. In: Rong, C., Jaatun, M.G., Sandnes, F.E., Yang, L.T., Ma, J. (eds.) ATC 2008. LNCS, vol. 5060, pp. 100–105. Springer, Heidelberg (2008). https://doi.org/10.1007/978-3-540-69295-9_10
29. Yau, W., Phan, R.C., Heng, S., Goi, B.: Keyword guessing attacks on secure searchable public key encryption schemes with a designated tester. Int. J. Comput. Math. **90**(12), 2581–2587 (2013). https://doi.org/10.1080/00207160.2013.778985
30. Zhang, Z., Wang, J., Wang, Y., Su, Y., Chen, X.: Towards efficient verifiable forward secure searchable symmetric encryption. In: Sako, K., Schneider, S., Ryan, P.Y.A. (eds.) ESORICS 2019. LNCS, vol. 11736, pp. 304–321. Springer, Cham (2019). https://doi.org/10.1007/978-3-030-29962-0_15
31. Zuo, C., Sun, S.-F., Liu, J.K., Shao, J., Pieprzyk, J.: Dynamic searchable symmetric encryption with forward and stronger backward privacy. In: Sako, K., Schneider, S., Ryan, P.Y.A. (eds.) ESORICS 2019. LNCS, vol. 11736, pp. 283–303. Springer, Cham (2019). https://doi.org/10.1007/978-3-030-29962-0_14

Public Key Encryption with Fuzzy Matching

Yuanhao Wang[1], Qiong Huang[1(✉)], Hongbo Li[1], Meiyan Xiao[1],
Jianye Huang[2], and Guomin Yang[2]

[1] College of Mathematics and Informatics, South China Agricultural University,
Guangzhou 510642, Guangdong, China
yuanhao.wang@stu.scau.edu.cn, {qhuang,hongbo,maymayxiao}@scau.edu.cn
[2] Institute of Cybersecurity and Cryptology, School of Computing and Information
Technology, University of Wollongong, Wollongong 2522, Australia
jianye.huang207@uowmail.edu.au, gyang@uow.edu.au

Abstract. The rise of cloud computing is driving the development in various fields and becoming one of the hot topics in recent years. To solve the problem of comparing ciphertexts between different users in cloud storage, Public Key Encryption with Equality Test (PKEET) was proposed. In PKEET, a tester can determine whether two ciphertexts encrypted with different public keys contain the same message without decrypting the ciphertexts. However, PKEET only supports exact matching, which may not be practical when two messages have misspellings, formatting differences, or differences in the data itself. Therefore, to support fuzzy matching, in this paper we propose the concept of Public Key Encryption with Fuzzy Matching (PKEFM), which allows to determine whether the edit distance between two encrypted messages is less than a threshold value. PKEFM can be well applied to support fuzzy data comparison in encrypted e-mail systems or encrypted gene testing. We then modify the scheme to provide the decryption function, and support (encrypted) wildcards in the matching, in order to further improve the generality of PKEFM at the cost of a small amount of extra computation.

Keywords: Cloud computing · Public key encryption · Fuzzy matching · Edit distance · Wildcard

1 Introduction

Cloud computing has been pushing the information field towards a more intensive, large-scale and specialized direction. Being convenient and scalable, it links today's various technologies and resources and has become the current hot topic in the information field. Cloud storage, as one of the core services of cloud

This work is supported by National Natural Science Foundation of China (61872152), the Major Program of Guangdong Basic and Applied Research (2019B030302008), and the Science and Technology Program of Guangzhou (201902010081).

Q. Huang and Y. Yu (Eds.): ProvSec 2021, LNCS 13059, pp. 39–62, 2021.
https://doi.org/10.1007/978-3-030-90402-9_3

computing, provides data backup, data sharing and other services for businesses and individuals [18].

Due to the increasing significance of data, protecting the data stored in the cloud has become an urgent need. Specifically, this includes integrity, confidentiality, and etc. [23]. One way to circumvent these issues while enjoying the convenience of cloud services is to encrypt data before it is uploaded. Cloud servers only store encrypted data and could not decrypted them. Only the trusted or authorized users can decrypt and access the data.

Searchable encryption is used to search over encrypted data for the presence of specific keywords. Symmetric Searchable Encryption (SSE) was first proposed by Song et al. [22]. However, using the same private key for encryption and search in SSE means that the private key has to be shared among users, in order to share data. This way, however, is not convenient enough in a cloud environment. Thus, Boneh et al. proposed Public Key Encryption with Keyword Search (PEKS) [3]. Anyone can share encrypted data to the intended user without the need of negotiating a private key with him in advance.

Although PEKS can search over the ciphertexts stored in the cloud, there are still some limitations. Keyword trapdoors in PEKS are generated using the receiver's private key, and they are used to search for the ciphertexts encrypted under this user's public key. In the encrypted database or the encrypted email system, data of different users is encrypted by their respective public keys, which means the search of all users' ciphertexts cannot be accessed through a single trapdoor. Furthermore, even if a group of users want the tester to compare their data analytically for some reason, for instance, to check encrypted data retrieval or de-duplication, the tester cannot compare the ciphertexts of different users to determine whether they have the same parts in their ciphertexts.

In order to solve the problem above, Yang et al. proposed Public Key Encryption with Equality Test (PKEET) [34]. It allows the tester to determine whether two ciphertexts encrypted with different public keys contain the same message without decryption. Subsequently, many researchers have conducted further research on PKEET in different research directions. For example, in terms of authorization, Tang noted that Yang et al.'s scheme has no authorization mechanism, which means there is a risk that anyone can test on ciphertexts. Thus he proposed the first PKEET scheme that supports authorization [24]. After that, Ma et al. proposed a PKEET-FA scheme that supports multiple types of authorization [16]. For functional extension, Xu et al. proposed a PKEET scheme [33] that can be validated against test results. In terms of security enhancement, Tang proposed a scheme [25] based on dual-server mechanism to prevent *Offline Message Recovery Attacks (OMRA)*, and Wu et al. proposed a scheme [32] based on group mechanism. To address the issues of certificate management, Ma first proposed an Identity-based Encryption with Equality Test (IBEET) scheme [15]. To support more flexible authorization, Attribute-based Encryption with Equality Test (ABEET) schemes were proposed by Zhu et al. [36] and Cui et al. [6].

However, the current PKEET schemes only support exact matching. In other words, even if the messages contained in two users' ciphertexts are only 1-bit different, the test algorithm will output that the messages contained in the two ciphertexts are different.

The reasons for data discrepancies can be divided into two main categories. One is subjective, for users may have spelling errors or formatting differences when entering data. The other is objective and genetic data can serve as a good example, where two related users may have mutations in individual loci of their gene fragments that cannot be guaranteed to be fully consistent. Mutations in individual loci may lead to the uncertainty of ensuring the complete consistency of two related users' gene fragments. In early searchable encryption schemes, if there is any difference between the keyword in the trapdoor and the message contained in the ciphertext, the search scheme would not be able to return the message ciphertext. It is not convenient from a practical application perspective, since the ciphertext returned must contain the exact keyword.

From the perspective of results, schemes that do not support fuzzy matching have more stringent requirements for user input. But from the perspective of convenience and utility, users would want the test algorithm to determine the two messages as "containing similar messages" if the difference between the two messages is small (e.g., the difference is no more than 1 character).

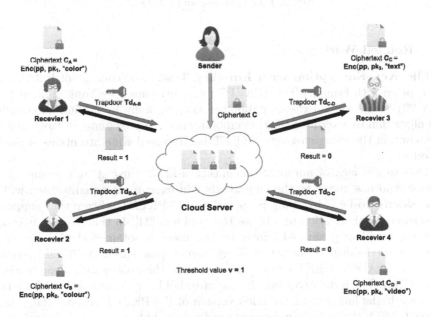

Fig. 1. System model of PKEFM

Therefore, it is of practical significance to design and implement a fuzzy matching scheme for public key ciphertexts. As shown in Fig. 1, the system sets the threshold value as $v = 1$. The sender encrypts the message wiht the receiver's public key and stores it on a cloud server. The receiver generates a trapdoor and sends it to cloud server. Since the ciphertexts of receiver 1 and receiver 2 have a high similarity, that is, the edit distance of the messages contained in their ciphertexts is no more than the threshold value v, the cloud server sends the fuzzy matching result "1" to represent the "similarity" to two receivers. Ciphertext of Receiver 3 and Receiver 4 contain messages with an edit distance greater than the threshold value, so that the cloud server returns "0" for "not similar" to both receivers.

As shown in Fig. 2, the edit distance can be used for fuzzy matching of plaintext. Our scheme calculates the edit distance of ciphertext, so as to realize the fuzzy matching of ciphertext.

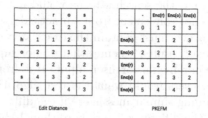

Fig. 2. Edit Distance and PKEFM

1.1 Related Work

Public Key Encryption with Equality Test. The concept of Public Key Encryption with Equality Test (PKEET) was introduced by Yang et al. at CT-RSA 2010 [34], which extends public-key cryptography by adding an equality test algorithm to determine whether ciphertexts encrypted under different public keys contain the same message. PKEET has received wide attentions since its introduction.

Due to the lack of authorization mechanism in Yang et al.'s scheme [34], anyone who has access to the ciphertexts can execute an equality test, which is considered to be risky. Tang proposed an FG-PKEET scheme that supports fine-grained authorization to address this problem [24]. In this scheme, it is not until the trapdoor generated jointly by two users is obtained that the sever is allowed to perform an equality test. Tang then proposed an AoN-PKEET scheme [26] and an ADG-PKEET scheme [25] to refine the authorization mechanism, respectively. The former requires the server to hold trapdoors obtained from two users while the latter is an extended version of FG-PKEET scheme [24], which resists OMRA through a dual-server mechanism, but requires additional computation and communication costs due to the data interaction between the two servers. Ma et al. proposed an PKE-DET scheme [17], which delegates equality test to a third party. In this scheme, only the specified server can perform equality test on ciphertexts. Huang et al. proposed a PKE-AET scheme [9], which supports two types of authorization, namely, allowing the tester to compare all or some specific ciphertexts of a user. Ma et al. designed a PKEET-FA scheme [16], which supports four types of authorization. Xu et al. proposed a V-PKEET scheme [33], which supports two different types of authorization than those in [16] and allows users to verify the result of an equality test. Zhang et al. proposed a PKEET scheme [35] under a specific cryptographic assumption in the standard model. Wang et al. designed a PKAE-DET scheme [30] that resists OMRA without dual-server mechanism. Ling et al. proposed a G-PKEET scheme [14], which resist OMRA through a group mechanism.

To simplify the certificate management of PKEET, Ma proposed the concept of Identity-based Encryption with Equality Test (IBEET) [15], which combines PKEET and IBE. Wu et al. proposed an IBEET scheme [31] that reduces the time-consuming HashToPoint function and effectively improves the execution efficiency of the scheme. Wu et al. designed an IBEET scheme [32] that resists inside adversaries by introducing a grouping mechanism. Qu et al. proposed a certificate free IBEET scheme [21], in which part of the private key is generated by the CA center and the other part is generated by the user locally. Li et al. [11] proposed an IBEET-FA scheme that supports four types of authorization.

To achieve more flexible authorization, Zhu et al. proposed a Key-policy Attribute-based Encryption with Equality Test (KP-ABEET) scheme [36]. Wang et al. designed a Ciphertext Policy Attribute-Based Encryption with Equality Test (CP-ABEET) scheme [28]. Cui et al. designed an outsourced CP-ABEET (OCP-ABEET) scheme [6], which outsources the heavy computation to a third-party. Wang et al. designed and CP-ABEET scheme without random oracles [29]. These studies further expand the application scenarios for PKEET.

Fuzzy Keyword Search. In searchable encryption, Li et al.'s scheme [12] transforms the keywords as a collection of fuzzy keywords with wildcards based on edit distance. Wang et al.'s scheme [27] implements a multi-keyword search based on a locally sensitive hash function and Bloom filter. Instead of treating keywords as collections of fuzzy keywords, the scheme treats each keyword as a bi-gram vector. Fu et al. [7] uses the Porter Stemming Algorithm [20] to ascertain the root of the word, and uses the uni-gram vector to represent the keyword. Li et al. [13] utilizes n-grams for fuzzy keyword search, and takes into account initials and suffixes.

Boneh et al. [4] introduced the notion of *Hidden Vector Encryption* (HVE). When the index I contained in a ciphertext match the index I' contained in the token in all the coordinates where I' is not the wildcard $*$, the search/query algorithm will output 1.

Phuong et al. [19] designed a new fuzzy public key cryptography called Edit Distance Based Encryption (EDE). In this scheme, the sender specifies a message and a threshold value when encrypting. The receiver specifies another message to generate the decryption key. The message can only be successfully decrypted if the edit distance between the two messages is less than the threshold value.

However, we notice that all the schemes above cannot be used to compare the similarity between ciphertexts of two users. How to fulfill the task is an interesting and important problem.

1.2   Our Work

In this paper, we focus on how to implement the fuzzy equality test of ciphertexts encrypted under different public keys efficiently. Concretely, we make the following contributions.

- To support fuzzy matching of ciphertexts, we propose the concept of Public Key Encryption with Fuzzy Matching (PKEFM). A threshold value v is set when the system is initialized. Two users' ciphertexts are stored on a cloud server. When two user-generated trapdoors are obtained, the cloud server can determine whether the edit distance between the two messages contained in the ciphertexts is less than the given threshold value.
- We present a concrete construction of PKEFM and prove its security based on simple mathematical assumptions under the given security models. In the scheme, the tester converts the ciphertexts to ciphertext vectors after obtaining the trapdoor and calculates the edit distance of two ciphertext vectors. During the calculation, the tester gets no further information about the messages contained in the ciphertexts.
- In order to make PKEFM more applicable, we introduce wildcards into PKEFM, and propose the notion of PKEFM with Wildcards (PKEFM-W). We present a concrete construction, in which a user's message can have wildcards. The tester uses an improved edit distance calculation method that supports the calculation of edit distances for ciphertexts containing wildcards.
- We provide a comparison of the proposed schemes in terms of computation cost and communication cost. Furthermore, we implement our schemes. Experiments show that both schemes are efficient.

1.3   Paper Organization

We introduce some preliminaries in Sect. 2. Then we give the definition of PKEFM and its security model in Sect. 3. The concrete construction of PKEFM is given in Sect. 4. We present the concrete construction of PKEFM-W is provided in Sect. 5. In Sect. 6, we implement and compare PKEFM with PKEFM-W. Some applications of PKEFM are presented in Sect. 7. Finally, we conclude the paper in Sect. 8.

2   Preliminaries

2.1   Decisional Diffie-Hellman (DDH) Assumption

Let $\mathbb{G}$ be a group of prime order p, and g be a group generator of $\mathbb{G}$. Given $\{g, g^a, g^b, g^r\}$, where $a, b, r \in \mathbb{Z}_p$, an adversary has only a negligible advantage in distinguishing g^r from $g^{a \cdot b}$ [2].

2.2   Symmetric External Diffie-Hellman (SXDH) Assumption

The DDH problem is hard in both $\mathbb{G}_1$ and $\mathbb{G}_2$, if there does not exist an efficiently computable isomorphism $\psi : \mathbb{G}_1 \rightarrow \mathbb{G}_2$ or $\psi' : \mathbb{G}_2 \rightarrow \mathbb{G}_1$ [1].

2.3   Split Function

In this paper, an n-length message D is treated as a message vector $\overrightarrow{D}$ by the following split function:

$$\mathsf{Split}(D) = \overrightarrow{D} = \langle D_1, D_2, \cdots , D_n \rangle,$$

where each D_i could be a character of the message.

2.4   Edit Distance

Edit Distance proposed by Levenshtein [10] usually refers to the Levenshtein Distance, and it can be used to measure the difference between two messages by counting the minimum number of edit operations that convert one message to another. An edit operation means: adding, decreasing or transforming a character. Obviously, there are many ways to convert, but they do not affect the minimum number of edit operations. Thus, the edit distance between two messages is an invariable.

The schemes proposed in this paper require to calculate the edit distance of two ciphertext vectors, which is computed as follows.

Let $\overrightarrow{X} = \langle X_1, X_2, \cdots , X_n \rangle$, $\overrightarrow{Y} = \langle Y_1, Y_2, \cdots , Y_m \rangle$ be two vectors. $\mathsf{Edt}_{\overrightarrow{X},\overrightarrow{Y}}(i,j)$ denotes the edit distance between the sub-vectors $\langle X_1, X_2, \cdots , X_i \rangle$ $(1 \leq i \leq n)$ and $\langle Y_1, Y_2, \cdots , Y_j \rangle$ $(1 \leq j \leq m)$. The edit distance of $\overrightarrow{X}$ and $\overrightarrow{Y}$ is then $\mathsf{Edt}_{\overrightarrow{X},\overrightarrow{Y}}(n,m)$, computed as follows:

$$\mathsf{Edt}_{\overrightarrow{X},\overrightarrow{Y}}(i,j) = \begin{cases} max(i,j) & , min(i,j) = 0 \\ min \begin{cases} \mathsf{Edt}_{\overrightarrow{X},\overrightarrow{Y}}(i-1,j)+1 \\ \mathsf{Edt}_{\overrightarrow{X},\overrightarrow{Y}}(i,j-1)+1 \\ \mathsf{Edt}_{\overrightarrow{X},\overrightarrow{Y}}(i-1,j-1)+S(X_i,Y_j) \end{cases} & , min(i,j) \neq 0 \end{cases}$$

where if $X_i \neq Y_j$, $S(X_i, Y_j) = 1$, and $S(X_i, Y_j) = 0$ otherwise.

2.5   Similarity Function

The similarity of two messages is based on the edit distance. The higher the similarity is, the more similar the two messages are. Variables n and m are the lengths of message vectors $\overrightarrow{X}$ and $\overrightarrow{Y}$, respectively, and the similarity between vectors $\overrightarrow{X}$ and $\overrightarrow{Y}$ is computed as:

$$\mathsf{Sim}_{\overrightarrow{X},\overrightarrow{Y}} = 1 - \frac{\mathsf{Edt}_{\overrightarrow{X},\overrightarrow{Y}}(n,m)}{max(n,m)}.$$

3 Public Key Encryption with Fuzzy Matching

3.1 Definition

Below we formalize the notion of *Public Key Encryption with Fuzzy Matching (PKEFM)*.

Definition 1 (PKEFM). *A Public Key Encryption with Fuzzy Matching scheme consists of the following probabilistic polynomial-time algorithms:*

- $pp \leftarrow \mathsf{Setup}(1^\lambda)$: *The setup algorithm takes as input 1^λ and outputs the public parameter pp (including the threshold value v).*
- $(pk, sk) \leftarrow \mathsf{KeyGen}(pp)$: *The key generation algorithm takes as input the public parameter pp and outputs a public/private key pair (pk, sk).*
- $C \leftarrow \mathsf{Enc}(pp, pk, D)$: *The encryption algorithm takes as input pp, pk and a message D, and outputs a ciphertext C.*
- $Td \leftarrow \mathsf{Aut}(pp, sk, C, C')$: *The authorization algorithm takes as input pp, sk and two ciphertexts C and C', and outputs a trapdoor Td.*
- $result \leftarrow \mathsf{FMat}(pp, C, C', Td, Td')$: *The fuzzy matching algorithm takes as input pp, two ciphertexts C and C', two corresponding trapdoors Td and Td', and outputs 1 if the similarity of messages contained in C and C' is greater than the threshold value v, and 0 otherwise.*

Definition 2 (Correctness). *A PKEFM scheme is correct if for any two messages D and D' with similarity greater than the threshold value v, the fuzzy matching result equals to 1 with a probability no less than $1 - negl(n)$:*

$$\Pr[\mathsf{FMat}(pp, C, C', Td, Td') = 1] \geq 1 - negl(n),$$

where C, C are the ciphertexts of D and D', respectively, and Td, Td' are two trapdoors corresponding to C and C'

3.2 Security Threats

Regarding the security models for PKEFM, we consider two main types of adversaries.

- Outside adversary: It can obtain the private keys and trapdoors of users, except for the target user. Its goal is to distinguish which of the two messages is contained in the challenge ciphertext.
- Inside adversary: It may be an honest-but-curious server that can get users' trapdoors. Since the message space is small and contains only the characters that make up the message, the adversary who gets the trapdoor corresponding to the challenge ciphertext can traverse the message space and generate ciphertexts to compare with the challenge ciphertext. As a result, the scheme cannot achieve indistinguishability or one-wayness. The goal of the adversary is to determine whether the messages contained in the two given challenge ciphertexts are the same.

We define two games to formalize the security properties, and present the security models in Appendix A.

4   Our PKEFM Scheme

In this part we propose a concrete construction of PKEFM scheme, which makes use of bilinear maps. It works as follows.

- Setup(1^λ): Given a security parameter 1^λ, choose a bilinear map $\hat{e} : \mathbb{G}_1 \times \mathbb{G}_2 \to \mathbb{G}_T$, where $\mathbb{G}_1, \mathbb{G}_2, \mathbb{G}_T$ are multiplicative groups of prime order p. Let g_1 be a generator of $\mathbb{G}_1$ and g_2 be a generator of $\mathbb{G}_2$. Choose an element $k \in \mathbb{G}_1$. Choose three hash functions: $H_1 : \{0,1\}^* \to \mathbb{G}_1$, $H_2 : \mathbb{G}_1 \to \{0,1\}^{l_1}$, $H_3 : \{0,1\}^* \to \mathbb{G}_1$, where l_1 is the representation length of an element of group $\mathbb{G}_1$. Choose a threshold value $v \in (0,1]$. Set and output the system parameter $pp = \{\mathbb{G}_1, \mathbb{G}_2, \mathbb{G}_T, \hat{e}, g_1, g_2, k, v, H_1, H_2, H_3\}$.
- KeyGen(pp): Given the system parameter pp, select two random elements x, y from $\mathbb{Z}_p$. Compute and output a public key $pk = \{pk_1, pk_2\} = \{k^x, g_1{}^y\}$ and a secret key $sk = \{sk_1, sk_2\} = \{x, y\}$.
- Enc(pp, pk, D): Given the system parameter pp, a public key pk and a message D, create the message vector $\overrightarrow{D} = \mathsf{Split}(D) = \langle D_1, D_2, \cdots, D_n \rangle$. Compute a ciphertext C as follows:
  - Select $n + 2$ random elements $\{s, w, r_1, \cdots, r_n\} \in \mathbb{Z}_p^{n+2}$.
  - Compute $C_0 = g_1{}^w$, $C_1 = k^w$, $C_2 = g_2{}^s$.
  - For $1 \le i \le n$, compute:

$$C_{3,i} = g_1{}^{r_i},$$
$$C_{4,i} = H_1(D_i)^s \cdot pk_1{}^w \oplus H_2(pk_2{}^{r_i})$$
$$= H_1(D_i)^s \cdot k^{x \cdot w} \oplus H_2(g_1{}^{y \cdot r_i}).$$

  - Compute $C_5 = H_3(C_0, C_1, C_2, C_{3,1}, \cdots, C_{3,n}, C_{4,1}, \cdots, C_{4,n})^s$.
  - Return $C = \{C_0, C_1, C_2, C_{3,1}, \cdots, C_{3,n}, C_{4,1}, \cdots, C_{4,n}, C_5\}$.
- Aut(pp, sk, C, C'): Given the system parameter pp, a secret key sk and two ciphertexts $C = \{C_0, C_1, C_2, C_{3,1}, \cdots, C_{3,n}, C_{4,1}, \cdots, C_{4,n}, C_5\}$ and $C' = \{C_0', C_1', C_2', C_{3,1}', \cdots, C_{3,m}', C_{4,1}', \cdots, C_{4,m}', C_5'\}$, compute the trapdoor $Td = \{Td_1, Td_2\}$ as follows:

$$Td_1 = \hat{e}(C_1, C_2')^{sk_1} = \hat{e}(k^w, g_2{}^{s'})^x = \hat{e}(k, g_2)^{x \cdot w \cdot s'},$$
$$Td_2 = sk_2 = y.$$

- FMat(pp, C, Td, C', Td'): Given the system parameter pp, two ciphertexts $C = \{C_0, C_1, C_2, C_{3,1}, \cdots, C_{3,n}, C_{4,1}, \cdots, C_{4,n}, C_5\}$ and $C' = \{C_0', C_1', C_2', C_{3,1}', \cdots, C_{3,m}', C_{4,1}', \cdots, C_{4,m}', C_5'\}$, two corresponding trapdoors $Td = \{Td_1, Td_2\}$ and $Td' = \{Td_1', Td_2'\}$, compute as follows:
  - Return 0 if $\hat{e}(C_5, g_2) \ne \hat{e}(H_3(C_0, C_1, C_2, C_{3,1}, \cdots, C_{3,n}, C_{4,1}, \cdots, C_{4,n}), C_2)$ or $\hat{e}(C_5', g_2) \ne \hat{e}(H_3(C_0', C_1', C_2', C_{3,1}', \cdots, C_{3,m}', C_{4,1}', \cdots, C_{4,m}'), C_2')$.
  - For $1 \le i \le n$, compute:

$$T_i = C_{4,i} \oplus H_2(C_{3,i}{}^{Td_2}) = H_1(D_i)^s \cdot k^{x \cdot w},$$
$$L_i = \hat{e}(T_i, C_2') / Td_1 = \hat{e}(H_1(D_i), g_2)^{s \cdot s'}.$$

- Set $\overrightarrow{L} = \langle L_1, L_2, \cdots, L_n \rangle$.
- For $1 \leq j \leq m$, compute:

$$T_j' = C_{4,j}' \oplus H_2(C_{3,j}'^{Td_2'}) = H_1(D_j')^{s'} \cdot k^{x' \cdot w'},$$
$$L_j' = \hat{e}(T_j', C_2)/Td_1' = \hat{e}(H_1(D_j), g_2)^{s \cdot s'}.$$

- Set $\overrightarrow{L'} = \langle L_1', L_2', \cdots, L_m' \rangle$.
- Compute $d = \mathsf{Edt}_{\overrightarrow{L}, \overrightarrow{L'}}(n, m)$.
- If $\mathsf{Sim}_{\overrightarrow{L}, \overrightarrow{L'}} = 1 - \frac{d}{max(n,m)} \geq v$, return 1, and 0 otherwise, where v is the threshold value of the similarity.

The threshold value v determines the similarity of two messages. If v is set to 1, it means that a complete message is required to output 1. The closer v is set to 0, the greater the difference between the two messages. This value can be adjusted according to actual needs.

The correctness of the scheme could be verified straight forward, so we omit the details here.

Security proofs of the scheme are given in Appendix B.

5 Improved Construction Supporting Decryption and Wildcards

5.1 Decryption Algorithm

Decryption algorithm is not considered in the original scheme of PKEFM, because the message can be encrypted through the classical public key encryption scheme. To decrypt a ciphertext in the scheme, consider the following algorithm:

- $\mathsf{Dec}(pp, sk, C)$: Given a ciphertext $C = \{C_0, C_1, C_2, C_{3,1}, \cdots, C_{3,n}, C_{4,1}, \cdots, C_{4,n}, C_5\}$, compute as follows:
  - Let $\mathcal{M}$ be the character set. For all $M_i \in \mathcal{M}$, compute $N_i = \hat{e}(H_1(M_i), C_2) = \hat{e}(H_1(M_i), g_2)^s$.
  - Set $N = \{N_1, \cdots, N_{|\mathcal{M}|}\}$, where $|\mathcal{M}|$ denotes the size of the character set.
  - For $1 \leq j \leq n$, compute:

$$\begin{aligned} E_j &= (C_{4,j} \oplus H_2(C_{3,j}^{sk_2}))/C_1^{sk_1} \\ &= (C_{4,j} \oplus H_2(g_1^{r_j \cdot y}))/k^{w \cdot x} \\ &= H_1(D_j)^s, \\ F_j &= \hat{e}(E_j, g_2) = \hat{e}(H_1(D_j), g_2)^s. \end{aligned}$$

For all $N_i \in N$, if F_j is equal to N_i, output M_i; otherwise, output $\perp$ indicating decryption failure.

In the premise of this scheme, the plaintext space is limited (and small), thus the receiver can compute the plaintext in polynomial time.

5.2 Edit Distance with Encrypted Wildcard

Wildcards can be used to representing character in a message. They mainly include '*' and '?', which represent any number of characters or one character, respectively. (e.g. **scien*** can be used to represent **science** or **scientist**, and **te?t** can be used to represent **test** or **text**, but not **tenet**.) The edit distance mentioned in Sect. 2.4 does not consider wildcards, so it cannot be used to compute the edit distance for two messages with wildcards directly. In order to solve this problem, *edit distance with wildcards* is proposed.

However, this method does not support encrypted wildcards, which is essential in our scenario. Hence, we improve this method and design **Edit Distance with Encrypted Wildcard**. The improved method is as follows.

Let $\overrightarrow{X} = \langle X_1, X_2, \cdots, X_n \rangle$, $\overrightarrow{Y} = \langle Y_1, Y_2, \cdots, Y_m \rangle$ be two ciphertext vectors. $\mathsf{EdtW}_{\overrightarrow{X}, \overrightarrow{Y}}(i, j, E_*, E_?)$ denotes the edit distance between the vectors $\langle X_1, X_2, \cdots, X_i \rangle$ $(1 \le i \le n)$ and $\langle Y_1, Y_2, \cdots, Y_j \rangle$ $(1 \le j \le m)$, where $E_*, E_?$ denotes the encrypted wildcards '*' and '?', respectively. The edit distance of $\overrightarrow{X}$ and $\overrightarrow{Y}$ is then $\mathsf{EdtW}_{\overrightarrow{X}, \overrightarrow{Y}}(n, m, E_*, E_?)$, computed as follows:

$$
\mathsf{EdtW}_{\overrightarrow{X}, \overrightarrow{Y}}(i, j, E_*, E_?) =
\begin{cases}
max(i, j) & , min(i,j) = 0 \\[2ex]
min \begin{cases} \mathsf{EdtW}_{\overrightarrow{X}, \overrightarrow{Y}}(i-1, j, E_*, E_?) + 1 \\ \mathsf{EdtW}_{\overrightarrow{X}, \overrightarrow{Y}}(i, j-1, E_*, E_?) + 1 \\ \mathsf{EdtW}_{\overrightarrow{X}, \overrightarrow{Y}}(i-1, j-1, E_*, E_?) + S(X_i, Y_j) \end{cases} & , \begin{matrix} min(i,j) \ne 0 \\ X_i \ne E_* \end{matrix} \\[4ex]
min \begin{cases} \mathsf{EdtW}_{\overrightarrow{X}, \overrightarrow{Y}}(i-1, j, E_*, E_?) \\ \mathsf{EdtW}_{\overrightarrow{X}, \overrightarrow{Y}}(i, j-1, E_*, E_?) \\ \mathsf{EdtW}_{\overrightarrow{X}, \overrightarrow{Y}}(i-1, j-1, E_*, E_?) \end{cases} & , \begin{matrix} min(i,j) \ne 0 \\ X_i = E_* \end{matrix}
\end{cases}
$$

where if $X_i \ne Y_j$ and $X_i \ne E_?$, $S(X_i, Y_j) = 1$, otherwise, $S(X_i, Y_j) = 0$.

5.3 An Improved Construction Supporting Wildcards

The construction proposed in Sect. 4 does not support wildcards, and thus may lead to inconvenience in practice. Therefore, we improve the original construction to support wildcards. The modified encryption algorithm, decryption algorithm and fuzzy matching algorithm are defined as follows. Other algorithms remain the same.

- $\mathsf{Enc}(pp, pk, D)$: Given the system parameter pp, a public key pk and a message D, create the message vector $\overrightarrow{D} = \mathsf{Split}(D) = \langle D_1, D_2, \cdots, D_n \rangle$. Notice that $D_i (1 \le i \le n)$ can be '*' or '?'. Compute a ciphertext C as follows:
  - Set $D_{n+1} = $ '*' and $D_{n+2} = $ '?'.
  - Select $n + 4$ random elements $\{s, w, r_1, \cdots, r_{n+2}\} \in \mathbb{Z}_p^{n+4}$.
  - Compute $C_0 = g_1{}^w$, $C_1 = k^w$, $C_2 = g_2{}^s$.

- For $1 \leq i \leq n+2$, compute:

$$C_{3,i} = g_1{}^{r_i},$$
$$C_{4,i} = H_1(D_i)^s \cdot pk_1{}^w \oplus H_2(pk_2{}^{r_i})$$
$$= H_1(D_i)^s \cdot k^{x \cdot w} \oplus H_2(g_1{}^{y \cdot r_i}).$$

  - Compute $C_5 = H_3(C_0, C_1, C_2, C_{3,1}, \cdots, C_{3,n+2}, C_{4,1}, \cdots, C_{4,n+2})^s$.
  - Set $\boldsymbol{C} = \{C_0, C_1, C_2, C_{3,1}, \cdots, C_{3,n+2}, C_{4,1}, \cdots, C_{4,n+2}, C_5\}$.
- Aut$(pp, sk, \boldsymbol{C}, \boldsymbol{C}')$: Given the system parameter pp, a secret key sk and two ciphertexts $\boldsymbol{C} = \{C_0, C_1, C_2, C_{3,1}, \cdots, C_{3,n+2}, C_{4,1}, \cdots, C_{4,n+2}, C_5\}$ and $\boldsymbol{C}' = \{C_0', C_1', C_2', C_{3,1}', \cdots, C_{3,m+2}', C_{4,1}', \cdots, C_{4,m+2}', C_5'\}$, compute the trapdoor $Td = \{Td_1, \cdots, Td_4\}$ as follows:

$$Td_1 = \hat{e}(C_1, C_2')^{sk_1} = \hat{e}(k^w, g_2{}^{s'})^x = \hat{e}(k, g_2)^{x \cdot w \cdot s'},$$
$$Td_2 = sk_2 = y,$$
$$E_1 = (C_{4,n+1} \oplus H_2(C_{3,n+1}{}^{sk_2}))/C_1{}^{sk_1}$$
$$= (C_{4,n+1} \oplus H_2(g_1{}^{r_{n+1} \cdot y}))/(k^w)^x = H_1('*')^s,$$
$$E_2 = (C_{4,n+2} \oplus H_2(C_{3,n+2}{}^{sk_2}))/C_1{}^{sk_1}$$
$$= (C_{4,n+2} \oplus H_2(g_1{}^{r_{n+2} \cdot y}))/(k^w)^x = H_1('?')^s,$$
$$Td_3 = \hat{e}(E_1, C_2') = \hat{e}(H('*'), g_2)^{s \cdot s'},$$
$$Td_4 = \hat{e}(E_2, C_2') = \hat{e}(H('?'), g_2)^{s \cdot s'}.$$

- FMat$(pp, \boldsymbol{C}, Td, \boldsymbol{C}', Td')$: Given the system parameter pp, two ciphertexts $\boldsymbol{C} = \{C_0, C_1, C_2, C_{3,1}, \cdots, C_{3,n+2}, C_{4,1}, \cdots, C_{4,n+2}, C_5\}$ and $\boldsymbol{C}' = \{C_0', C_1', C_2', C_{3,1}', \cdots, C_{3,m+2}', C_{4,1}', \cdots, C_{4,m+2}', C_5'\}$, two corresponding trapdoors $Td = \{Td_1, \cdots, Td_4\}$ and $Td' = \{Td_1', \cdots, Td_4'\}$, compute as follows:

  - Return 0 if $\hat{e}(C_5, g_2) \neq \hat{e}(H_3(C_0, C_1, C_2, C_{3,1}, \cdots, C_{4,n+2}), C_2)$ or $\hat{e}(C_5', g_2) \neq \hat{e}(H_3(C_0', C_1', C_2', C_{3,1}', \cdots, C_{3,m+2}', C_{4,1}', \cdots, C_{4,m+2}'), C_2')$ or $Td_3 = Td_3'$ or $Td_4 = Td_4'$.
  - For $1 \leq i \leq n$, compute:

$$T_i = C_{4,i} \oplus H_2(C_{3,i}{}^{Td_2}) = H_1(D_i)^s \cdot k^{x \cdot w},$$
$$L_i = \hat{e}(T_i, C_2')/Td_1 = \hat{e}(H_1(D_i), g_2)^{s \cdot s'}.$$

  - Set $\overrightarrow{L} = \langle L_1, L_2, \cdots, L_n \rangle$.
  - For $1 \leq j \leq m$, compute:

$$T_j' = C_{4,j}' \oplus H_2(C_{3,j}'{}^{Td_2'}) = H_1(D_j')^{s'} \cdot k^{x' \cdot w'},$$
$$L_j' = \hat{e}(T_j', C_2)/Td_1' = \hat{e}(H_1(D_j), g_2)^{s \cdot s'}.$$

  - Set $\overrightarrow{L'} = \langle L_1', L_2', \cdots, L_m' \rangle$.

- Compute $d = \mathsf{EdtW}_{\overrightarrow{L},\overrightarrow{L'}}(n, m, Td_3, Td_4)$.

- If $\mathsf{Sim}_{\overrightarrow{L},\overrightarrow{L'}} = 1 - \frac{d}{max(n,m)} \geq v$, return 1, and 0 otherwise.

The correctness of the scheme could be verified straight forward, so we omit the details here.

5.4 Security Discussion

Compared with the original construction in Sect. 4, the ciphertext requires additional encryption of wildcards '*' and '?'. In addition, the new part in the trapdoor generated by the receiver is related to these two wildcards. However, wildcards '*' and '?' can match any character in plaintext space $\mathcal{M}$, so that the adversary cannot rely on them to distinguish or recover the ciphertext. Therefore, the security of the improved construction remains unchanged.

6 Performance Evaluation

In this section we analyse the computational cost and communication cost of PKEFM scheme and PKEFM-W scheme.

Table 1. Comparison of computation cost

	PKEFM	PKEFM-W
KeyGen	$2Exp$	$2Exp$
Enc	$(3n + 5)Exp$	$(3n + 11)Exp$
Dec	$|\mathcal{M}|P + 2nExp + nP$	$(|\mathcal{M}| + 2)P + 2nExp + nP$
Aut	$Exp + P$	$4Exp + 3P$
FMat	$(2n + 2m + 4)P$	$(2n + 2m + 4)P$

n, m: length of the message M or M'; Exp, P: computation cost of an exponential operation and pairing operation, respectively; $|\mathcal{M}|$: size of the character set.

Table 1 provides a comparison between the computation costs of the two schemes. When running the encryption algorithm in both schemes, some of the elements can be used for multiple times, so the computational cost of these elements are counted only once. The key generation algorithms of the two schemes require the same cost. In order to support wildcards, PKEFM-W scheme has a slightly higher computation cost in the encryption, decryption and authorization. But the increased computation cost is constant, regardless of the message length.

Table 2 shows the comparison of communication costs. After encrypting the message locally, the sender uploads the ciphertext to the cloud server. PKEFM-W scheme has a slightly longer ciphertext length than PKEFM scheme, but due

Table 2. Comparison of communication cost

	PKEFM	PKEFM-W
$|pk|$	$2|\mathbb{G}_1|$	$2|\mathbb{G}_1|$
$|sk|$	$2|\mathbb{Z}_p|$	$2|\mathbb{Z}_p|$
$|C|$	$(2n+3)|\mathbb{G}_1|+|\mathbb{G}_2|$	$(2n+7)|\mathbb{G}_1|+|\mathbb{G}_2|$
$|Td|$	$|\mathbb{G}_T|+|\mathbb{Z}_p|$	$3|\mathbb{G}_T|+|\mathbb{Z}_p|$

n: length of a message M; $|pk|, |sk|, |C|, |Td|$: size of public key, secret key, the ciphertext and trapdoor, respectively; $|\mathbb{G}_1|, |\mathbb{G}_2|, |\mathbb{G}_T|, |\mathbb{Z}_p|$: bit length of a group element in $\mathbb{G}_1, \mathbb{G}_2, \mathbb{G}_T, \mathbb{Z}_p$, respectively.

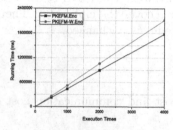

Fig. 3. Comparison of Enc ($n = 10$)

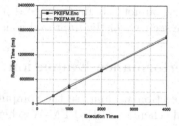

Fig. 4. Comparison of Enc ($n = 100$)

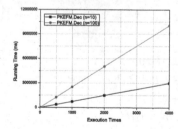

Fig. 5. Comparison of Dec

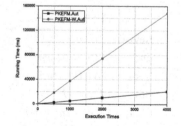

Fig. 6. Comparison of Aut

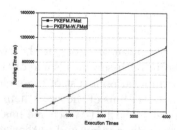

Fig. 7. Comparison of FMat ($n = 10$)

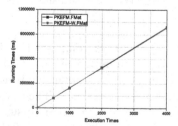

Fig. 8. Comparison of FMat ($n = 100$)

to the fact that the encrypted message M in PKEFM-W scheme is allowed to contain wildcards, an appropriate increase in passphrase length is acceptable. Although the PKEFM scheme has a longer trapdoor length than PKEFM-W scheme, the difference is not significant. The length of the trapdoor is constant, independent of the message length.

To further evaluate the performance of the schemes, we implemented the PKEFM scheme and PKEFM-W scheme based on the JPBC library [5] for comparison. The experiment was run on a host machine with a six-core 2.60 GHz Intel i7-9750H CPU, 8 GB of RAM, Windows 10 operating system.

Figure 3 and Fig. 4 show the computation cost comparison of the encryption algorithm Enc when the message length n is 10 and 100, respectively. PKEFM-W scheme is slightly less efficient than PKEFM scheme because it requires additional encryption of wildcards. However, as the message length n increases, the encryption algorithm efficiency of PKEFM-W scheme gradually approaches that of PKEFM scheme because of the falling proportion of wildcards in the whole ciphertext.

Figure 5 shows the computation cost of the decryption algorithm. The character set needs to be pre-processed before decryption, which requires an invariable time. As the length of the message grows, the percentage of the aforementioned invariable time in the total time spent on decryption decreases. Therefore, the decryption algorithm is more practical if the number of characters that make up the message is small and the message length is long.

Figure 6 shows the computation cost comparison of the two schemes in terms of the authorization algorithm Aut. The PKEFM scheme is more efficient than the PKEFM-W scheme in generating a trapdoor, which requires an additional calculation of two wildcard trapdoors. The time required for trapdoor generation is independent of the length of a ciphertext. The input is only part of the ciphertext. It means that even if the length of the ciphertext is long, it will not increase the time consumption of the authorization algorithm, which works better in practical applications.

Figure 7 and Fig. 8 show the computation cost comparison of the fuzzy matching algorithm for message length n being 10 and 100, respectively. The efficiency of PKEFM scheme is close to that of PKEFM-W scheme. The time spent on fuzzy matching is linearly related to the message length, and the time spent on fuzzy matching will not increase too fast in the case of long messages.

7   Applications

Encrypted Long Message Fuzzy Matching. When a similarity comparison between two confidential documents is required, it can be implemented based on the above scheme. Essentially, there is no need to adjust the scheme. The input D of the encryption algorithm is a text file. The user runs the encryption algorithm to split the text file as a text vector $\overrightarrow{D} = \langle D_1, D_2, \cdots, D_n \rangle$, and D_i as each word in the text file. Then the encryption is performed as described above. The server runs the fuzzy matching algorithm to calculate the similarity between the two files. The edit distance algorithm can be replaced with another similarity calculation algorithm as needed.

BLAST-Based Encrypted DNA Similarity Comparison. BLAST (Basic Local Alignment Search Tool) is an analytical tool for biological sequence databases [8]. It can efficiently perform sequence similarity comparison with sequences in DNA database or protein database.

The sequence entered in the BLAST system and the sequence in the database are in the plain text format. Based on the scheme above, encrypted sequence comparison is feasible. The input D of the encryption algorithm is an DNA or protein sequence and $D_i \in \{A, T, C, G\}$. The tester calculates $\overrightarrow{L}$ and $\overrightarrow{L'}$ according to the fuzzy matching algorithm, and then inputs $\overrightarrow{L}$ and $\overrightarrow{L'}$ into BLAST algorithm for similarity comparison.

8   Conclusion

In order to provide fuzzy matching of ciphertexts from different users, we introduced the concept of Public Key Encryption with Fuzzy Matching (PKEFM). A concrete construction of PKEFM was presented and the security of the scheme is proved under the given security model based on simple assumptions. Considering the use of wildcards in fuzzy matching, we extended PKEFM to support wildcards. It should be noted that in our schemes the tester can know the edit distance between the messages contained in the two ciphertexts, which leads to certain information leakage. How to minimize the information leakage is one of our future works.

A   Security Models

To check the security of PKEFM, consider the following two games:

Game-I: Ciphertext Indistinguishability

Let $\mathcal{A}$ be an outside adversary. Assume that the index t is the target receiver.

1. **Setup**: The challenger $\mathcal{C}$ runs Setup to generate the public parameter pp and runs KeyGen to generate n pairs $\{pk_i, sk_i\}$. It sends pp and all pk_i's to $\mathcal{A}$.
2. **Phase 1**: The adversary $\mathcal{A}$ is allowed to issue the following types of oracle queries in polynomially many times.
   - Key Oracle $\mathcal{O}_K(i)$: Given an index $i \in [1, n]$, it returns the corresponding secret key sk_i.
   - Authorization Oracle $\mathcal{O}_A(i, C, C')$: Given an index $i \in [1, n]$ and two ciphertexts C and C', it returns the corresponding trapdoor Td.

   Specially, t cannot be queried to $\mathcal{O}_K$ and $(t, \cdot, \cdot)$ cannot be queried to $\mathcal{O}_A$.
3. **Challenge**: $\mathcal{A}$ selects two equal-length challenge messages D_0 and D_1 and sends them to $\mathcal{C}$. Then $\mathcal{C}$ selects $\sigma \xleftarrow{R} \{0, 1\}$, and returns $C^* = \mathsf{Enc}(pp, pk_t, D_\sigma)$ to $\mathcal{A}$.

4. **Phase 2**: The same as that in **Phase 1**. In addition, $(\cdot, C^*, \cdot)$ cannot be queried to $\mathcal{O}_A$.
5. **Guess**: $\mathcal{A}$ outputs a guess σ^*. If $\sigma^* = \sigma$, $\mathcal{A}$ wins the game.

We define $\mathcal{A}$'s advantage in Game-I as $\mathrm{Adv}_{\mathcal{A}}^{\mathsf{IND}}(1^\lambda) = |\Pr[\sigma^* = \sigma] - \frac{1}{2}|$.

Definition 3. *A PKEFM scheme satisfies* Ciphertext Indistinguishability *if for any probabilistic polynomial-time outside adversary $\mathcal{A}$, its advantage $\mathrm{Adv}_{\mathcal{A}}^{\mathsf{IND}}(1^\lambda)$ is negligible in the security parameter 1^λ.*

Game-II: Unlinkability

Let $\mathcal{A}$ be an inside adversary. Assume that the indices t and t' are of the target receivers.

1. **Setup**: The challenger $\mathcal{C}$ runs Setup to generate the public parameter pp and runs KeyGen to generate n pairs $\{pk_i, sk_i\}$. It sends pp and all pk_i's to $\mathcal{A}$.
2. **Phase 1**: The adversary $\mathcal{A}$ is allowed to issue the following types of oracle queries in polynomially many times.
   - Key Oracle $\mathcal{O}_K(i)$: Given an index $i \in [1, n]$, it returns the corresponding secret key sk_i.
   - Authorization Oracle $\mathcal{O}_A(i, C, C')$: Given an index $i \in [1, n]$ and two ciphertexts C and C', it returns the corresponding trapdoor Td.

   Specially, t and t' cannot be queried to $\mathcal{O}_K$.
3. **Challenge**: $\mathcal{A}$ selects two equal-length challenge messages D_0, D_1, and sends them to $\mathcal{C}$. Then $\mathcal{C}$ selects $\sigma \overset{R}{\leftarrow} \{0, 1\}$, and returns $C^* = \mathsf{Enc}(pp, pk_t, D_0)$, $C^{**} = \mathsf{Enc}(pp, pk_{t'}, D_\sigma)$ to $\mathcal{A}$.
4. **Phase 2**: The same as that in **Phase 1**. In addition, $(\cdot, C^*, \cdot)$ and $(\cdot, C^{**}, \cdot)$ cannot be queried to $\mathcal{O}_A$.
5. **Guess**: $\mathcal{A}$ outputs a guess σ^*. If $\sigma^* = \sigma$, $\mathcal{A}$ wins the game.

We define $\mathcal{A}$'s advantage in Game-II as $\mathrm{Adv}_{\mathcal{A}}^{\mathsf{Unlink}}(1^\lambda) = |\Pr[\sigma^* = \sigma] - \frac{1}{2}|$.

Definition 4. *A PKEFT scheme satisfies* Unlinkability *if for any probabilistic polynomial-time inside adversary $\mathcal{A}$, its advantage $\mathrm{Adv}_{\mathcal{A}}^{\mathsf{Unlink}}(1^\lambda)$ is negligible in the security parameter 1^λ.*

B   Security Analysis

In this section, we show that our PKEFM scheme is secure under the security models defined in Sect. 3.2.

B.1   Ciphertext Indistinguishability

Theorem 1. *If SXDH assumption holds, our PKEFM scheme above satisfies Ciphertext Indistinguishability against outside adversaries.*

Proof. Let $\mathcal{A}$ be a PPT adversary who has advantage μ to break Ciphertext Indistinguishability of our PKEFM scheme. We build a PPT adversary $\mathcal{C}$ to break SXDH assumption. Given an SXDH instance $\{\mathbb{G}_1, g_1, g_\alpha = g_1{}^\alpha, g_\beta = g_1{}^\beta, Z\}$, where $g_1 \in \mathbb{G}_1, \alpha, \beta \xleftarrow{R} \mathbb{Z}_p$ are unknown, and Z is either $g_1{}^{\alpha \cdot \beta}$ ($b = 1$) or a random element in $\mathbb{G}_1$ ($b = 0$), $\mathcal{C}$ works as follows.

Setup: The challenger $\mathcal{C}$ runs Setup and sets the public parameter $pp = \{\mathbb{G}_1, \mathbb{G}_2, \mathbb{Z}_p, \hat{e}, g_1, g_2, k, v, H_1, H_2, H_3\}$, runs KeyGen to generate n pairs $\{pk_i, sk_i\}$ ($1 \leq i \leq n$) and stores them to the list $L_K\langle pk, sk \rangle$. In particular, $\mathcal{C}$ selects $t \xleftarrow{R} \{1, \cdots, n\}$, sets $pk_t = \{pk_{t,1}, pk_{t,2}\} = \{k^{x_t}, g_\alpha = g_1{}^\alpha\}$, $sk_t = \{sk_{t,1}, sk_{t,2}\} = \{x_t, \alpha\}$, where α is unknown to $\mathcal{C}$. Then $\mathcal{C}$ sends pp and all pk_i's to $\mathcal{A}$.

Phase 1: $\mathcal{A}$ is allowed to issue the following types of oracle queries in polynomially many times. Assume that all the queries would not violate the restrictions.

- Key Oracle $\mathcal{O}_K(i)$: It maintains a list $L_K\langle pk, sk \rangle$ which stores all $\{pk_i, sk_i\}$ ($1 \leq i \leq n$) generated in Setup. Given an index $i \in [1, n]$, it returns the corresponding secret key sk_i.
- Authorization Oracles $\mathcal{O}_A(i, \boldsymbol{C}, \boldsymbol{C}')$: Given an index $i \in [1, n]$ and two ciphertexts $\boldsymbol{C}$ and $\boldsymbol{C}'$, it runs $\mathcal{O}_K$ to get corresponding sk_i, and returns the corresponding trapdoor $Td = \mathsf{Aut}(pp, sk_i, \boldsymbol{C}, \boldsymbol{C}')$.

Challenge: $\mathcal{A}$ selects two equal-length challenging messages D_0 and D_1 and sends them to $\mathcal{C}$. Then $\mathcal{C}$ selects $\sigma \xleftarrow{R} \{0, 1\}$, and computes $\boldsymbol{C}^*$ as follows:

- $\overrightarrow{D}_\sigma = \mathsf{Split}(D_\sigma) = \langle D_{\sigma,1}, \cdots, D_{\sigma,n} \rangle$.
- Select $n + 2$ random elements $\{s_t, w_t, \theta_1, \cdots, \theta_n\} \in \mathbb{Z}_p^{n+2}$.
- Compute $C_0^* = g_1{}^{w_t}, C_1^* = k^{w_t}, C_2^* = g_2{}^{s_t}$.
- For $1 \leq i \leq n$, compute:

$$C_{3,i}^* = (g_\beta)^{\theta_i} = g_1{}^{\beta \cdot \theta_i},$$
$$C_{4,i}^* = H_1(D_{\sigma,i})^{s_t} \cdot pk_{t,1}{}^{w_t} \oplus H_2(Z^{\theta_i})$$
$$= H_1(D_{\sigma,i})^{s_t} \cdot k^{x_t \cdot w_t} \oplus H_2(Z^{\theta_i}).$$

- Compute $C_5^* = H_3(C_0^*, C_1^*, C_2^*, C_{3,1}^*, \cdots, C_{3,n}^*, C_{4,1}^*, \cdots, C_{4,n}^*)^{s_t}$.
- Return $\boldsymbol{C}^* = \{C_0^*, C_1^*, C_2^*, C_{3,1}^*, \cdots, C_{3,n}^*, C_{4,1}^*, \cdots, C_{4,n}^*, C_5^*\}$ to $\mathcal{A}$.

Phase 2: The same as that in **Phase 1**. In addition, $(\cdot, \boldsymbol{C}^*, \cdot)$ can not be queried to $\mathcal{O}_A$. Assume that all the queries would not violate the restrictions.

Guess: $\mathcal{A}$ outputs a guess σ^*. If $\sigma^* = \sigma$, $\mathcal{A}$ wins the game. Then $\mathcal{C}$ outputs $Z = g_1{}^{\alpha \cdot \beta}$ ($b' = 1$) as the guess of the given SXDH instance; otherwise, $\mathcal{C}$ outputs $Z \neq g_1{}^{\alpha \cdot \beta}$ ($b' = 0$).

Consider the game above. If $Z = g_1{}^{\alpha \cdot \beta}$ $(b = 1)$, C^* is a real ciphertext of D_σ, so $\mathcal{A}$ can win the game with probability $\mu + \frac{1}{2}$. If Z is a random element in $\mathbb{G}_1$ $(b = 0)$, then all elements in C^* are random in the view of $\mathcal{A}$, which means C^* hides σ completely. Thus, the probability of $\mathcal{A}$ outputting $\sigma^* = \sigma$ is $\frac{1}{2}$. So the probability that $\mathcal{C}$ breaks SXDH assumption is

$$\Pr[b' = b]$$
$$= (\Pr[b' = 0 \wedge b = 0] + \Pr[b' = 1 \wedge b = 1])$$
$$= (\frac{1}{2} \cdot \frac{1}{2} + \frac{1}{2}(\mu + \frac{1}{2}))$$
$$= \frac{\mu}{2} + \frac{1}{2}.$$

Therefore, if $\mathcal{A}$ can win the game with non-negligible advantage μ, $\mathcal{C}$ can also break the SXDH assumption with non-negligible advantage $\frac{\mu}{2}$. So we have:

$$\mathrm{Adv}_{\mathcal{A}}^{\mathsf{IND}}(1^\lambda) = |\Pr[\sigma^* = \sigma] - \frac{1}{2}| \leq \mathrm{negl}(1^\lambda).$$

This completes the proof of Theorem 1.   ∎

B.2   Unlinkability

Theorem 2. *If SXDH assumption holds, our PKEFM scheme above satisfies Unlinkability against inside adversaries.*

Proof. Let $\mathcal{A}$ be a PPT adversary who has advantage μ to break Unlinkability of our PKEFM scheme. We build a PPT adversary $\mathcal{C}$ to break SXDH assumption. Given an SXDH instance $\{\mathbb{G}_1, g_1, g_\alpha = g_1{}^\alpha, g_\beta = g_1{}^\beta, Z\}$, where $g_1 \in \mathbb{G}_1, \alpha, \beta \xleftarrow{R} \mathbb{Z}_p$ are unknown, and Z is either $g_1{}^{\alpha \cdot \beta}$ $(b = 1)$ or a random element in $\mathbb{G}_1$ $(b = 0)$, $\mathcal{C}$ works as follows.

Setup: The challenger $\mathcal{C}$ runs Setup to generate the public parameter $pp = \{\mathbb{G}_1, \mathbb{G}_2, \mathbb{Z}_p, \hat{e}, g_1, g_2, k = g_\alpha = g_1{}^\alpha, v, H_1, H_2, H_3\}$, runs KeyGen to generate n pairs $\{pk_i, sk_i\}$ $(1 \leq i \leq n)$ and stores them to the list $L_K \langle pk, sk \rangle$. In particular, $\mathcal{C}$ selects $t, t' \xleftarrow{R} \{1, \cdots, n\}$, Then $\mathcal{C}$ sends pp and all pk_i's to $\mathcal{A}$.

Phase 1: $\mathcal{A}$ is allowed to issue the following types of oracle queries in polynomially many times. Assume that all the queries would not violate the restrictions.

– Key Oracle $\mathcal{O}_K(i)$: It maintains a list $L_K \langle pk, sk \rangle$ which stores all $\{pk_i, sk_i\}$ $(1 \leq i \leq n)$ generated in Setup. Given an index $i \in [1, n]$, it returns the corresponding secret key sk_i. Specially, if $i = t$ or $i = t'$, it returns $\bot$ indicating query failure.

- <u>Authorization Oracles</u> $\mathcal{O}_A(i, C, C')$: Given an index $i \in [1, n]$ and two ciphertexts C and C', it runs $\mathcal{O}_K$ to get corresponding sk_i, and returns the corresponding trapdoor $Td = \mathsf{Aut}(pp, sk_i, C, C')$.

Challenge: $\mathcal{A}$ selects two equal-length challenging messages D_0, D_1, and sends them to $\mathcal{C}$. Then $\mathcal{C}$ selects $\sigma \xleftarrow{R} \{0, 1\}$, and computes $C^* = \mathsf{Enc}(pk_t, D_0)$, $C^{**} = \mathsf{Enc}(pk_{t'}, D_\sigma)$ as follows:

- $\overrightarrow{D_0} = \mathsf{Split}(D_0) = \langle D_{0,1}, \cdots, D_{0,n} \rangle$, $\overrightarrow{D_\sigma} = \mathsf{Split}(D_\sigma) = \langle D_{\sigma,1}, \cdots, D_{\sigma,n} \rangle$.
- Get sk_t and $sk_{t'}$ from L_K.
- Select random elements $\{s_t, s_{t'}, r_1, \cdots, r_{2n}, \delta\} \in \mathbb{Z}_p$. Implicitly set $C_0^* = g_\beta = g_1{}^\beta$ and $C_0^{**} = g_\beta{}^\delta = g_1{}^{\beta \cdot \delta}$.
- Compute $C_1^* = Z$, $C_2^* = g_2{}^{s_t}$.
- For $1 \le i \le n$, compute:

$$C_{3,i}^* = g_1{}^{r_i},$$
$$C_{4,i}^* = H_1(D_{0,i})^{s_t} \cdot Z^{sk_{t,1}} \oplus H_2(pk_{t,2}{}^{r_i})$$
$$= H_1(D_{0,i})^{s_t} \cdot Z^{x_t} \oplus H_2(g_1{}^{y_t \cdot r_i}).$$

- Compute $C_5^* = H_3(C_0^*, C_1^*, C_2^*, C_{3,1}^*, \cdots, C_{3,n}^*, C_{4,1}^*, \cdots, C_{4,n}^*)^{s_t}$.
- Set $C^* = \{C_0^*, C_1^*, C_2^*, C_{3,1}^*, \cdots, C_{3,n}^*, C_{4,1}^*, \cdots, C_{4,n}^*, C_5^*\}$.
- Compute $C_1^{**} = Z^\delta$, $C_2^{**} = g_2{}^{s_{t'}}$.
- For $1 \le j \le n$, compute:

$$C_{3,j}^{**} = g_1{}^{r_{n+j}},$$
$$C_{4,j}^{**} = H_1(D_{\sigma,i})^{s_{t'}} \cdot Z^{sk_{t',1} \cdot \delta} \oplus H_2(pk_{t',2}{}^{r_{n+j}})$$
$$= H_1(D_{\sigma,i})^{s_{t'}} \cdot Z^{x_{t'} \cdot \delta} \oplus H_2(g_1{}^{y_{t'} \cdot r_{n+j}}).$$

- Compute $C_5^{**} = H_3(C_0^{**}, C_1^{**}, C_2^{**}, C_{3,1}^{**}, \cdots, C_{3,n}^{**}, C_{4,1}^{**}, \cdots, C_{4,n}^{**})^{s_{t'}}$.
- Set $C^{**} = \{C_0^{**}, C_1^{**}, C_2^{**}, C_{3,1}^{**}, \cdots, C_{3,n}^{**}, C_{4,1}^{**}, \cdots, C_{4,n}^{**}, C_5^{**}\}$.
- Return C^* and C^{**} to $\mathcal{A}$.

Phase 2: The same as that in **Phase 1**. In addition, $(\cdot, C^*, \cdot)$ and $(\cdot, C^{**}, \cdot)$ cannot be queried to $\mathcal{O}_A$. Assume that all the queries would not violate the restrictions.

Guess: $\mathcal{A}$ outputs a guess σ^*. If $\sigma^* = \sigma$, $\mathcal{A}$ wins the game. Then $\mathcal{C}$ outputs $Z = g_1{}^{\alpha \cdot \beta}$ ($b' = 1$) as the guess of the given SXDH instance; otherwise, $\mathcal{C}$ outputs $Z \ne g_1{}^{\alpha \cdot \beta}$ ($b' = 0$).

Consider the game above. The cases that $\mathcal{C}$ aborts the game are described as follows.

- Suppose that $\mathcal{A}$ queried $\hat{C} = \{C_0^{*z}, C_1^{*z}, C_2^{*z}, \hat{C}_{3,1}, \cdots, \hat{C}_{3,n}, \hat{C}_{4,1}, \cdots, \hat{C}_{4,n}, C_5^{*z}\}$, where z is an element in $\mathbb{Z}_p$ (including $1_{\mathbb{Z}_p}$) selected by $\mathcal{A}$, and C_0^{*z}, C_1^*, C_2^*, C_5^* are parts of C^*. If the equation

$$H_3(C_0^*, C_1^*, C_2^*, C_{3,1}^*, \cdots, C_{3,n}^*, C_{4,1}^*, \cdots, C_{4,n}^*)$$
$$= H_3(C_0^{*z}, C_1^{*z}, C_2^{*z}, \hat{C}_{3,1}, \cdots, \hat{C}_{3,n}, \hat{C}_{4,1}, \cdots, \hat{C}_{4,n})$$

holds, which means there exits a hash collision of H_3, $\mathcal{C}$ aborts the game. We define this event by $Event_1$. So we have

$$\Pr[Event_1] \leq \varepsilon_{CR},$$

where ε_{CR} is the probability that $\mathcal{A}$ breaks the collision resistance of H_3.

- Suppose that $\mathcal{A}$ queried $\widetilde{C} = \{C_0^{**z'}, C_1^{**z'}, C_2^{**z'}, \widetilde{C_{3,1}}, \cdots, \widetilde{C_{3,n}}, \widetilde{C_{4,1}}, \cdots, \widetilde{C_{4,n}}, C_5^{**z'}\}$, where z' is an element in $\mathbb{Z}_p$ (including $1_{\mathbb{Z}_p}$) selected by $\mathcal{A}$, and $C_0^{**}, C_1^{**}, C_2^{**}, C_5^{**}$ are parts of C^{**}. If the equation

$$H_3(C_0^{**}, C_1^{**}, C_2^{**}, C_{3,1}^{**}, \cdots, C_{3,n}^{**}, C_{4,1}^{**}, \cdots, C_{4,n}^{**})$$
$$= H_3(C_0^{**z'}, C_1^{**z'}, C_2^{**z'}, \widetilde{C_{3,1}}, \cdots, \widetilde{C_{3,n}}, \widetilde{C_{4,1}}, \cdots, \widetilde{C_{4,n}})$$

holds, which means there exits a hash collision of H_3, $\mathcal{C}$ aborts the game. We define this event by $Event_2$. So we have

$$\Pr[Event_2] \leq \varepsilon_{CR}.$$

Denote by Abort the union of events that $\mathcal{C}$ aborts the game. We have:

$$\Pr[\mathsf{Abort}] = \Pr[Event_1 \vee Event_2] \leq \varepsilon_{CR} + \varepsilon_{CR}.$$

That is

$$\Pr[\neg\mathsf{Abort}] \geq (1 - 2 \cdot \varepsilon_{CR}).$$

Now consider the case that $\mathcal{C}$ does not abort the game. If $Z = g_1^{\alpha \cdot \beta}$ ($b = 1$), C^* is a real ciphertext of D_σ, so $\mathcal{A}$ can win the game with probability $\mu + \frac{1}{2}$. If Z is a random element in $\mathbb{G}_1$, then all elements in C^* are random in the view of $\mathcal{A}$, which means C^* hides σ completely. So the probability of $\mathcal{A}$ outputting $\sigma^* = \sigma$ is $\frac{1}{2}$. In sum, the probability that $\mathcal{C}$ breaks SXDH assumption is

$$
\begin{aligned}
&\Pr[b' = b] \\
&= \Pr[b' = b|\mathsf{Abort}] \cdot \Pr[\mathsf{Abort}] + \Pr[b' = b|\neg\mathsf{Abort}] \cdot \Pr[\neg\mathsf{Abort}] \\
&= \frac{1}{2}(1 - \Pr[\neg\mathsf{Abort}]) + (\Pr[b' = 0|\neg\mathsf{Abort} \wedge b = 0] \\
&\quad + \Pr[b' = 1|\neg\mathsf{Abort} \wedge b = 1]) \cdot \Pr[\neg\mathsf{Abort}] \\
&= \frac{1}{2}(1 - \Pr[\neg\mathsf{Abort}]) + (\frac{1}{2} \cdot \frac{1}{2} + \frac{1}{2}(\mu + \frac{1}{2})) \cdot \Pr[\neg\mathsf{Abort}] \\
&= \frac{\mu}{2} \cdot \Pr[\neg\mathsf{Abort}] + \frac{1}{2}
\end{aligned}
$$

Therefore, if $\mathcal{A}$ can win the game with non-negligible advantage μ, $\mathcal{C}$ can also break the SXDH assumption with non-negligible advantage $\frac{\mu}{2} \cdot (1 - 2 \cdot \varepsilon_{CR})$. So we have:

$$\mathrm{Adv}_{\mathcal{A}}^{\mathsf{Unlink}}(1^{\lambda}) = |\Pr[\sigma^* = \sigma] - \frac{1}{2}| \leq \mathrm{negl}(1^{\lambda}).$$

This completes the proof of Theorem 2.   ∎

References

1. Ateniese, G., Camenisch, J., Hohenberger, S., de Medeiros, B.: Practical group signatures without random oracles. IACR Cryptol. ePrint Arch. **2005**, 385 (2005)
2. Boneh, D.: The Decision Diffie-Hellman problem. In: Buhler, J.P. (ed.) ANTS 1998. LNCS, vol. 1423, pp. 48–63. Springer, Heidelberg (1998). https://doi.org/10.1007/BFb0054851
3. Boneh, D., Di Crescenzo, G., Ostrovsky, R., Persiano, G.: Public key encryption with keyword search. In: Cachin, C., Camenisch, J.L. (eds.) EUROCRYPT 2004. LNCS, vol. 3027, pp. 506–522. Springer, Heidelberg (2004). https://doi.org/10.1007/978-3-540-24676-3_30
4. Boneh, D., Waters, B.: Conjunctive, subset, and range queries on encrypted data. In: Vadhan, S.P. (ed.) TCC 2007. LNCS, vol. 4392, pp. 535–554. Springer, Heidelberg (2007). https://doi.org/10.1007/978-3-540-70936-7_29
5. Caro, A.D., Iovino, V.: jpbc: Java pairing based cryptography. In: Proceedings of the 16th IEEE Symposium on Computers and Communications, ISCC 2011, Kerkyra, Corfu, Greece, pp. 850–855, 28 June–1 July 2011 (2011)
6. Cui, Y., Huang, Q., Huang, J., Li, H., Yang, G.: Outsourced ciphertext-policy attribute-based encryption with equality test. In: Guo, F., Huang, X., Yung, M. (eds.) Inscrypt 2018. LNCS, vol. 11449, pp. 448–467. Springer, Cham (2019). https://doi.org/10.1007/978-3-030-14234-6_24
7. Fu, Z., Wu, X., Guan, C., Sun, X., Ren, K.: Toward efficient multi-keyword fuzzy search over encrypted outsourced data with accuracy improvement. IEEE Trans. Inf. Forensics Secur. **11**(12), 2706–2716 (2016)
8. Gusfield, D.: Algorithms on Strings, Trees, and Sequences: Computer Science and Computational Biology. Cambridge University Press, Cambridge (1997)
9. Huang, K., Tso, R., Chen, Y., Rahman, S.M.M., Almogren, A., Alamri, A.: PKE-AET: public key encryption with authorized equality test. Comput. J. **58**(10), 2686–2697 (2015)
10. Levenshtein, V.I.: Binary codes capable of correcting deletions, insertions, and reversals. Soviet Phys. Dokl. **10**, 707–710 (1965)
11. Li, H., Huang, Q., Ma, S., Shen, J., Susilo, W.: Authorized equality test on identity-based ciphertexts for secret data sharing via cloud storage. IEEE Access **7**, 25409–25421 (2019)
12. Li, J., Wang, Q., Wang, C., Cao, N., Ren, K., Lou, W.: Fuzzy keyword search over encrypted data in cloud computing. In: INFOCOM 2010. 29th IEEE International Conference on Computer Communications, Joint Conference of the IEEE Computer and Communications Societies, 15–19 March 2010, San Diego, CA, USA, pp. 441–445 (2010)
13. Li, J., Wen, M., Wu, K., Lu, K., Li, F., Li, H.: Secure, flexible and high-efficient similarity search over encrypted data in multiple clouds. Peer-to-Peer Networking Appl. **12**(4), 893–911 (2018). https://doi.org/10.1007/s12083-018-0691-8

14. Ling, Y., Ma, S., Huang, Q., Li, X., Ling, Y.: Group public key encryption with equality test against offline message recovery attack. Inf. Sci. **510**, 16–32 (2020)
15. Ma, S.: Identity-based encryption with outsourced equality test in cloud computing. Inf. Sci. **328**, 389–402 (2016)
16. Ma, S., Huang, Q., Zhang, M., Yang, B.: Efficient public key encryption with equality test supporting flexible authorization. IEEE Trans. Inf. Forensics Secur. **10**(3), 458–470 (2015)
17. Ma, S., Zhang, M., Huang, Q., Yang, B.: Public key encryption with delegated equality test in a multi-user setting. Comput. J. **58**(4), 986–1002 (2015)
18. Marston, S., Li, Z., Bandyopadhyay, S., Zhang, J., Ghalsasi, A.: Cloud computing - the business perspective. Decis. Support Syst. **51**(1), 176–189 (2011)
19. Phuong, T.V.X., Yang, G., Susilo, W., Liang, K.: Edit distance based encryption and its application. In: Liu, J.K., Steinfeld, R. (eds.) ACISP 2016. LNCS, vol. 9723, pp. 103–119. Springer, Cham (2016). https://doi.org/10.1007/978-3-319-40367-0_7
20. Porter, M.F.: An algorithm for suffix stripping. Program **14**(3), 130–137 (1980)
21. Qu, H., Yan, Z., Lin, X.J., Zhang, Q., Sun, L.: Certificateless public key encryption with equality test. Inf. Sci. **462**, 76–92 (2018)
22. Song, D.X., Wagner, D.A., Perrig, A.: Practical techniques for searches on encrypted data. In: 2000 IEEE Symposium on Security and Privacy, Berkeley, California, USA, 14–17 May 2000, pp. 44–55 (2000)
23. Subashini, S., Kavitha, V.: A survey on security issues in service delivery models of cloud computing. J. Netw. Comput. Appl. **34**(1), 1–11 (2011)
24. Tang, Q.: Towards public key encryption scheme supporting equality test with fine-grained authorization. In: Parampalli, U., Hawkes, P. (eds.) ACISP 2011. LNCS, vol. 6812, pp. 389–406. Springer, Heidelberg (2011). https://doi.org/10.1007/978-3-642-22497-3_25
25. Tang, Q.: Public key encryption schemes supporting equality test with authorisation of different granularity. IJACT **2**(4), 304–321 (2012)
26. Tang, Q.: Public key encryption supporting plaintext equality test and user-specified authorization. Secur. Commun. Networks 5(12), 1351–1362 (2012)
27. Wang, B., Yu, S., Lou, W., Hou, Y.T.: Privacy-preserving multi-keyword fuzzy search over encrypted data in the cloud. In: 2014 IEEE Conference on Computer Communications, INFOCOM 2014, Toronto, Canada, 27 April–24 May 2014, pp. 2112–2120 (2014)
28. Wang, Q., Peng, L., Xiong, H., Sun, J., Qin, Z.: Ciphertext-policy attribute-based encryption with delegated equality test in cloud computing. IEEE Access **6**, 760–771 (2018)
29. Wang, Y., Cui, Y., Huang, Q., Li, H., Huang, J., Yang, G.: Attribute-based equality test over encrypted data without random oracles. IEEE Access **8**, 32891–32903 (2020)
30. Wang, Y., Huang, Q., Li, H., Huang, J., Yang, G., Susilo, W.: Public key authenticated encryption with designated equality test and its applications in diagnostic related groups. IEEE Access **7**, 135999–136011 (2019)
31. Wu, L., Zhang, Y., Choo, K.R., He, D.: Efficient and secure identity-based encryption scheme with equality test in cloud computing. Future Gener. Comp. Syst. **73**, 22–31 (2017)
32. Wu, T., Ma, S., Mu, Y., Zeng, S.: ID-Based encryption with equality test against insider attack. In: Pieprzyk, J., Suriadi, S. (eds.) ACISP 2017. LNCS, vol. 10342, pp. 168–183. Springer, Cham (2017). https://doi.org/10.1007/978-3-319-60055-0_9

33. Xu, Y., Wang, M., Zhong, H., Cui, J., Liu, L., Franqueira, V.N.L.: Verifiable public key encryption scheme with equality test in 5G networks. IEEE Access **5**, 12702–12713 (2017)
34. Yang, G., Tan, C.H., Huang, Q., Wong, D.S.: Probabilistic public key encryption with equality test. In: Pieprzyk, J. (ed.) CT-RSA 2010. LNCS, vol. 5985, pp. 119–131. Springer, Heidelberg (2010). https://doi.org/10.1007/978-3-642-11925-5_9
35. Zhang, K., Chen, J., Lee, H.T., Qian, H., Wang, H.: Efficient public key encryption with equality test in the standard model. Theor. Comput. Sci. **755**, 65–80 (2019)
36. Zhu, H., Wang, L., Ahmad, H., Niu, X.: Key-policy attribute-based encryption with equality test in cloud computing. IEEE Access **5**, 20428–20439 (2017)

Partitioned Searchable Encryption

Jim Barthel[1], Marc Beunardeau[2], Răzvan Roşie[3], and Rajeev Anand Sahu[1(✉)]

[1] University of Luxembourg, Esch-sur-Alzette, Luxembourg
{jim.barthel,rajeev.sahu}@uni.lu
[2] Nomadic Labs, Paris, France
marc.beunardeau@nomadic-labs.com
[3] JAO Luxembourg, Luxembourg, Luxembourg
rosie@jao.eu

Abstract. Symmetric searchable encryption (SSE) allows to outsource encrypted data to an untrusted server and retain searching capabilities. This is done without impacting the privacy of both the data and the search/update queries. In this work we put forth a new flavour of symmetric searchable encryption (SSE):*Partitioned SSE* is meant to capture the cases where the search rights must be partitioned among multiple individuals. We motivate through compelling examples the practical need for such a notion and discuss instantiations based on functional encryption and trapdoor permutations.

- First we leverage the power of *functional encryption* (FE). Our construction follows the general technique of encrypting the set of keywords and the presumably larger datafiles separately, a keyword acting as a "pointer" to datafiles it belongs to. To improve on the constraint factors (large ciphertext, slow encryption/decryption procedures) that are inherent in FE schemes, the keyword check is done with the help of a Bloom filter – one per datafile: the crux idea is to split the filter into buckets, and encrypt each bucket separately under an FE scheme. Functional keys are given for binary *masks* checking if relevant positions are set to 1 inside the underlying bit-vector of the Bloom filter.
- The second construction we present achieves forward security and stems from the scheme by Bost in CCS'16. We show that a simple tweak of the original construction gives rise to a scheme supporting updates in the partitioned setting. Moreover, the constructions take into account the possibility that some specific users are malicious while declaring their search results.

Keywords: SSE · Functional encryption · Partitioned search · Bloom filter

© Springer Nature Switzerland AG 2021
Q. Huang and Y. Yu (Eds.): ProvSec 2021, LNCS 13059, pp. 63–79, 2021.
https://doi.org/10.1007/978-3-030-90402-9_4

1   Introduction

Searchable encryption [20] is a cryptographic protocol thought to enable its user(s) to perform search queries on encrypted data[1]. In the protocol a set of *keywords* is encrypted and deployed on an untrusted (storage) server. Each keyword originates in some structured *datafile*, which is encrypted separately under a semantic secure symmetric encryption scheme. Ideally, the search operation executed by the client shall work without compromising the privacy of the remaining encrypted data, given that the server has access to the entire history of queries. Speaking about functionality, a client must store some secret information (*key*) that allows to create search tokens corresponding to specific keywords. Tokens are sent to the storage server together with the operation that needs to be executed: *searches* for static schemes, but also *updates* for dynamic schemes. The server uses the tokens to retrieve the index(es) of the encrypted datafile(s) matching the desired keyword(s), but without being able to decrypt the datafile(s) and without learning those keywords. The initial proposals of SSE were designed in a *static* setting where the client cannot perform any *update* on the deployed encrypted data. To address this issue Kamara *et al.* [16] introduced *dynamic SSE* which enables both *searches* and *updates* over the encrypted database. However, update may cause leakage during addition of new (keyword, datafile index) pairs or during the search of a keyword while all the files containing the keyword are deleted. Security against the first case is called *forward privacy* – introduced by Chang and Mitzenmacher [7] and against the second case is referred as *backward privacy* – formalized by Bost et al. [5]. One common issue with the earlier proposals was the search time which was linear in the size of the database. It was until the work of Curtmola *et al.* [9] who put forth the SSE scheme with sublinear search time, in a static setting. The index-based dynamic SSE with sublinear search time was introduced by Kamara *et al.* [15,16]. The current approaches of searchable encryption [4–6] suggest avoiding constructions following from primitives such as fully-homomorphic encryption [10], multi-party computation [23] or oblivious RAM [12]. These are considered non-viable, given their poor practical performance. However, in many settings such techniques can be proven safe as they leak no information on the encrypted data. Consider the case of functional encryption (FE) [3]. A naive but straightforward implementation of searchable encryption consists in issuing functional keys for circuits searching a specific keywords. In the recent years several schemes of SSE have been proposed [17,19] based on different assumptions and targeting advanced properties. Our construction addresses a completely different flavour and unlike the existing schemes has been built using the Bloom filters.

In the existing literature of SSEs, a relevant contribution for our approach is the paper by Goh [11], who proposes a construction – associating an index to each document in a collection – based simply on Bloom filters and pseudorandom functions. Another construction in connection to our results is $\Sigma o\phi o\varsigma$ by Bost [4]

---

[1] For example a doctor wanting to consult all the medical records of patients having diabetes without having to download the entire database.

which is a scheme supporting sublinear search time and achieving forward privacy with improved security guarantees. In essence, the construction avoids the heavy ORAM model while relying solely on the existence of trapdoor permutations. The later Diana and Janus schemes [5] are improvements on this approach.

1.1 Our Results

We introduce a new flavour of symmetric searchable encryption- *partitioned* searchable encryption. More particularly, we propose two constructions of partitioned SSE using the functionalities of a Bloom filter (BF), one from the functional encryption (FE) and one from trapdoor permutations as used in $\Sigma o\phi o\varsigma$.

Partitioned Symmetric Searchable Encryption (PSSE). Imagine a well known governmental agency intercepts the conversation between the president of its country and a foreign leader. Legally, the transcripts of such recordings must be stored on a secure server and access rights must be given to some investigative authority, after which the role of the security agency ends. Following the law, those recordings may only be accessed by some selected committee of the Senate in its plenitude. That is, no single member of the Senate's committee may access the data independently. To address such a problem, the notion of PSSE may be useful. Such protocol consists of three entities: (1) a trusted authority that encrypts data and subsequently deploys them to a storage server[2]; (2) the server that stores the data; (3) the clients that can gain access to data if and only if *all* agree to do so. We also emphasise that in connection to our partitioned SSE a recent work [1] by Ananth *et al.* is much more relevant as it presents a multi-key FHE with one-round decryption. The process of recovering the plaintext(s), taking place in the final step of their construction, is similar to step (3) above. The *multi-client* in [22], which presents a searchable encryption supporting Boolean queries, refers to a group of clients satisfying certain attributes, and not associated to any partition among them. Each client possessing a *search-authorized* private key issued by the data owner can individually perform *search* where the keyword database is encrypted using a CP-ABE. A related problem would consider malicious users: that is, users that misbehave either when inserting or searching for documents. Relative to our previous example, any senator, independent of his/her political opinion must be able to prove that his/her part of the encrypted database DB and search tokens are correctly generated.

We propose multiple instantiations for such a partitioned searching protocol. The first one exploits the power of functional encryption. A naive approach would encrypt the set of keywords, and then issue search tokens for the search function. However, we introduce a novel and more efficient approach for building searchable encryption from FE. Our key insight is the following: given a document D, we store its set of keywords ($\mathbf{w}$) in a Bloom filter, which is built on top of a bitvector $\vec{b}$. We split $\vec{b}$ into buckets and encrypt each bucket independently under a functional encryption scheme. Then, we issue functional keys for circuits that

---

[2] The governmental agency in our case.

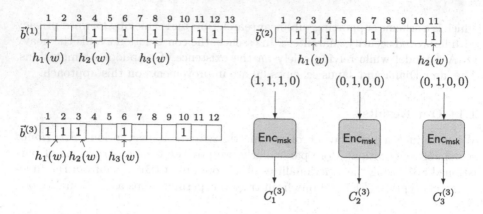

Fig. 1. Each Bloom Filter $\mathsf{BF}^{(i)}$ is associated to a datafile $\mathsf{D}^{(i)}$ (not represented) and consists of a bitvector $\vec{b}^{(i)}$ of size B_i. As seen at the lower right, $\vec{b}^{(3)}$ is split in 3 buckets of size 4, which are encrypted independently under a functional encryption scheme. Thus, the message space supported by the FE scheme consists of 4 bits. Functional keys are issued to check if the j-th bit is set to 1, in order to simulate the membership testing in the Bloom filter specification, as seen in the upper part of the picture.

check if the desired set of bits corresponding to a search query is set to 1. This is illustrated in Fig. 1. The second class of proposed constructions stems from the $\Sigma o\phi o\varsigma$ scheme introduced by Bost in [4]. $\Sigma o\phi o\varsigma$ uses classical primitives, such as simple trapdoor permutations. Whenever a new keyword is inserted, the index of the keyword is *masked* with a pseudorandom value the client is aware of. We achieve a PSSE scheme by distributing such a masked value amongst the participants into the protocol. Concretely, we employ the usage of a Bloom filter to store the index. Then, we split the Bloom filter into buckets, and each party will independently mask a bucket of the Bloom filter. Pictorially, this would correspond to a parallel execution of Bost's protocol. Finally, during the combine (Comb) step, the results of the searches are gathered and the question of a keyword belonging to a document can be settled.

Organization of the Paper. Section 2 introduces the common notations and the definitions we work with in the following parts. Section 3 defines partitioned SSE. In Sect. 4 we introduce the main results of this work: by devising simple PSSE protocols starting from FE and trapdoor permutations, static or supporting updates. Section 5 concludes the contributions.

2   Preliminaries

Mathematical and Algorithmic Conventions. In this work, $\lambda \in \mathbb{N}^*$ stands for the security parameter. We assume λ is implicitly given to all algorithms in the unary representation 1^λ. We consider an algorithm to be equivalent to a Turing machine, and unless stated, we assume that algorithms are randomized. PPT stands for "probabilistic polynomial-time" in the security parameter (rather than the total length of its inputs). Given a randomized algorithm $\mathcal{A}$ we denote the action of running $\mathcal{A}$ on input(s) $(1^\lambda, x_1, \ldots)$ with coins r (sampled uniformly at random) and assigning the output(s) to $(y_1, \ldots)$ by the expression $(y_1, \ldots) \leftarrow_\$ \mathcal{A}(1^\lambda, x_1, \ldots; r)$. We write $\mathcal{A}^{\mathcal{O}}$ for the case that $\mathcal{A}$ is given oracle access to some procedure $\mathcal{O}$. We denote the cardinality of a finite set S by $|S|$ and the action of sampling a uniformly at random element x from X by $x \leftarrow_\$ X$. $[k]$ stands for the set $\{1, \ldots, k\}$. A real-valued function is called negligible if it belong to $O(\lambda^{-\omega(1)})$. We denote the set of all negligible functions by NEGL. Throughout the paper $\perp$ stands for a special error symbol. We use $\|$ to denote concatenation.

2.1 Searchable Encryption

To structure the discussion, we assume a classical *client-server* model, with a client wishing to deploy its data on some untrusted third party; at the same time, the client wants to retain its ability of searching over the encrypted, deployed data. In the first part—the *Setup* phase—the client proceeds as follows with its datafiles $\{D^{(1)}, \ldots, D^{(d)}\}$: (1) extracts all the keywords for each $D^{(i)}$ (let this set of keywords be written in a structure denoted DB); (2) encrypts each $D^{(i)}$ to $ED^{(i)}$, using a semantic-secure symmetric encryption scheme; (3) encrypts the keywords under a scheme that supports searches (let this resulting database of encrypted keywords be denoted as EDB); (4)uploads EDB and the encrypted datafiles on some untrusted storage cloud server.

In the *Search* phase, whenever looking for a datafile corresponding to a specific keyword $\mathbf{w}$ the client should have the ability to identify the datafile(s) $D^{(i)}$ containing $\mathbf{w}$. Then, it will retrieve the encrypted file $ED^{(i)}$ corresponding to $D^{(i)}$ and decrypt it. Our protocols do *not* explicitly mention the last phase consisting of simply downloading and decrypting the datafiles identified as containing the keywords. A rigorous formulation capturing the aforementioned intuition is given below.

Definition 1 (Multi-Keyword SSE). *Let* $D_i \subseteq \{0,1\}^*$ *denote a datafile, for any* $i \in [d]$. *Let* $\mathsf{DB} := \{(i, \mathbf{w}^{(i)})\}_{i \in [d]}$ *denote the set of pairs containing a datafile index* i *and a set of keywords* $\mathbf{w}^{(i)}$. *A static searchable encryption scheme* $\Sigma = (\Sigma.\mathsf{Setup}, \Sigma.\mathsf{Search})$ *consists of a PPT algorithm* $\Sigma.\mathsf{Setup}$ *and a protocol* $\Sigma.\mathsf{Search}$ *between a client and server, such that:*

- $(\mathsf{EDB}, K, \sigma) \leftarrow_\$ \mathsf{Setup}(\mathsf{DB})$: *takes as input the* DB, *encrypts it to obtain* EDB, *and deploys the resulting ciphertext to a server. It returns the key* K *and a state* σ *to the client.*
- $i \leftarrow \mathsf{Search}(\mathsf{EDB}, \sigma, K, \mathbf{w}, \mathsf{I})$: *is a protocol between the client and the server. The client inputs its key* K, *its state* σ, *a search query* $\mathbf{w}$ *which can consist of a single or multiple keywords and an index set* I, *consisting of file indices that should be searched through. In case* I *is absent, we consider it as* $\mathsf{I} = \{1\}$ *meaning the system stores only a single datafile. The server's input is* EDB.

It then returns the index(es) in l that correspond to datafile(s) containing the queried keyword(s).

In addition, we call a symmetric searchable encryption scheme dynamic if there exists a third algorithm:

- EDB′ ← Update(EDB, σ, K, **w**, l, op): the client encrypts a keyword **w** and sends an update query for a specific index set l of datafiles. In case l is absent, we consider it as l = {1} meaning the system stores only a single datafile. The operation op can either be a delete or insert request. Update then returns the updated encrypted database.

We require an SSE scheme to satisfy correctness, meaning that the search protocol must return correct results for every query, except with negligible probability.

Security of SSE. Security of an SSE scheme corresponds to the amount of information a server can gather about the database (file) and the keywords queried. More concretely, it is parametrized by the stateful leakage functions incorporating the leakage of the Setup, Search, Update algorithms. We denote this by a leakage function $\mathcal{L} = \left(\mathcal{L}^{\mathsf{Setup}}, \mathcal{L}^{\mathsf{Search}}, \mathcal{L}^{\mathsf{Update}}\right)$[3]. Security requires that the adversary should not learn more than the outputs of the corresponding leakage function $\mathcal{L}$ after triggering the Setup, Search or Update operations. Of particular interest is the notion of *forward privacy* [21], which ensures that an update query does not leak information on the updated keyword, the server being unable to tell if a particular document leaks the updated keywords.

Forward Privacy: informally, it states that newly updated documents do not leak information about newly added files that match the query. Alternatively, the Update queries do not leak the keyword/file being updated.

Definition 2 (Forward Privacy for SSE). *We say an $\mathcal{L}$-adaptive-secure multi-keyword SSE is forward private if the update leakage function is defined as $\mathcal{L}^{\mathsf{Update}}(\mathsf{op}, \mathsf{in}) := \mathcal{L}'^{\mathsf{Update}}(\mathsf{op}, (f', \mathbf{w}'))$, for operation op with input in where $\mathcal{L}'$ is stateless and the set $(f', \mathbf{w}')$ denotes all updated documents for which the keyword $\mathbf{w}'$ is modified in file f'.*

Security requires that the adversary does not learn more than the outputs of the corresponding leakage function $\mathcal{L}$ after triggering the Setup, Search or Update operations. The corresponding security game is described in Fig. 2.

Definition 3 (Adaptive Security for SSE). *We say a multi-keyword SSE scheme achieves $\mathcal{L}$-adaptive-security if the advantage of any PPT adversary $\mathcal{A}$ in winning the FS − SSE experiment defined in Fig. 2 is negligible. i.e.:* $|\Pr[\mathsf{FS} - \mathsf{SSE}_{\mathsf{SSE}}^{\mathcal{A}}(\lambda) = 1] - \frac{1}{2}| \in \mathrm{NEGL}(\lambda)$.

Definition 4 (Functional Encryption - Public Key Setting). *A functional encryption scheme FE in the public-key setting consists of a quadruple of PPT algorithms (FE.Setup, FE.KDer, FE.Enc, FE.Dec) such that:*

---
[3] For a static scheme $\mathcal{L}^{\mathsf{Update}} := \emptyset$.

$FS - SSE^{\mathcal{A}}_{SSE}(\lambda):$	$PSSE^{\mathcal{A}}_{PSSE}(\lambda, N):$
$b \leftarrow_\$ \{0,1\}$	$b \leftarrow_\$ \{0,1\}$
$DB \leftarrow_\$ \mathcal{A}(1^\lambda)$	$DB \leftarrow_\$ \mathcal{A}(1^\lambda)$
if $b = 0$:	if $b = 0$:
$(EDB, \sigma) \leftarrow_\$ SSE.Setup(1^\lambda)$	$(pp, DB_1, \ldots, DB_N) \leftarrow_\$ PSSE.Setup(1^\lambda, N, DB)$
else:	for $j \leftarrow 1, N$:
$(EDB, \sigma) \leftarrow_\$ \mathcal{S}(\mathcal{L}_{Setup})$	$(pk_j, sk_j) \leftarrow_\$ SSE.ClientSetup(DB_j, j)$
for $q \leftarrow 1, Q$:	else:
if $b = 0$:	$(pp, DB_1, \ldots, DB_N) \leftarrow_\$ \mathcal{S}(\mathcal{L}_{Setup})$
$(op, \mathbf{w}) \leftarrow_\$ \mathcal{A}(EDB, \sigma)$	for $j \leftarrow 1, N$:
if $op =$"Update":	$(pk_j, sk_j) \leftarrow_\$ \mathcal{S}(\mathcal{L}_{ClientSetup})$
$R_q \leftarrow_\$ Update(\sigma, EDB, \mathbf{w})$	for $q \leftarrow 1, Q$:
if $op =$"Search":	$(op, \mathbf{w}) \leftarrow_\$ \mathcal{A}(pp, pk_j, EDB_j), \forall j \in [N]$
$R_q \leftarrow_\$ Search(\sigma, EDB, \mathbf{w})$	if $b = 0$:
if $b = 1$:	if $op =$"Update":
$(op, \mathbf{w}) \leftarrow_\$ \mathcal{A}(EDB, \sigma)$	$R_{q,j} \leftarrow_\$ Update(\sigma, sk_j, j, EDB_j, \mathbf{w}), \forall j \in [N]$
if $op =$"Update":	if $op =$"Search":
$R_q \leftarrow_\$ \mathcal{S}(\sigma, \mathcal{L}_{Update}(\mathbf{w}))$	$R_{q,j} \leftarrow_\$ Search(\sigma, sk_j, j, EDB_j, \mathbf{w}), \forall j \in [N]$
if $op =$"Search":	if $b = 1$:
$R_q \leftarrow_\$ \mathcal{S}(\sigma, \mathcal{L}_{Search}(\mathbf{w}))$	if $op =$"Update":
$b' \leftarrow_\$ \mathcal{A}(\{R_q\}_{q \in [Q]})$	$R_{q,j} \leftarrow_\$ \mathcal{S}(\sigma, j, \mathcal{L}_{Update}(\mathbf{w})), \forall j \in [N]$
return $b = b'$	if $op =$"Search":
	$R_{q,j} \leftarrow_\$ \mathcal{S}(\sigma, j, \mathcal{L}_{Search}(\mathbf{w})), \forall j \in [N]$
	$b' \leftarrow_\$ \mathcal{A}(\{R_{q,j}\}_{q,j})$
	return $b = b'$

Fig. 2. The $FS - SSE$-security defined for a symmetric searchable encryption scheme (left). Simulation-security for a PSSE scheme.

- $(msk, mpk) \leftarrow_\$ FE.Setup(1^\lambda)$: *given the unary representation of the security parameter λ, the setup procedure outputs a pair of master secret/public keys.*
- $sk_f \leftarrow_\$ FE.KDer(msk, f)$: *given the master secret key* msk *and a function f, the (potentially randomized) key-derivation procedure generates a corresponding functional key* sk_f.
- $C \leftarrow_\$ FE.Enc(mpk, M)$: *the randomized encryption procedure encrypts, using the master public key* mpk, *the plaintext M into a ciphertext C.*
- $FE.Dec(C, sk_f)$: *decrypts the ciphertext C using the functional key* sk_f *in order to either learn a valid message $f(M)$ or, in case the decryption procedure fails, a special error symbol $\perp$.*

We say a scheme FE *achieves correctness if $\forall f \in \mathcal{F}_\lambda$, for any $M \in \mathcal{M}$, the following quantity is negligibly close to 1:*

$$\Pr\left[y = f(M) \;\middle|\; \begin{array}{l} (msk, mpk) \leftarrow_\$ FE.Setup(1^\lambda) \wedge sk_f \leftarrow_\$ FE.KDer(msk, f) \wedge \\ C \leftarrow_\$ FE.Enc(mpk, M) \wedge y \leftarrow FE.Dec(C, sk_f) \end{array} \right]$$

2.2   Bloom Filters

Bloom filters (BF), introduced in [2] are *probabilistic* abstract data structures allowing for constant time *searches, insertions* and *deletions*. Thus, they improve over both running time and memory space over the existing approaches using *hash-tables* or different flavours of *tree-based* structures. The core idea behind Bloom filters is to store a representation of a keyword **w** instead of storing **w** itself. To do so, one can imagine an underlying data structure consisting of a bitvector $\vec{b}$ of B bits, that is populated by hashing the inserted strings $\mathbf{w} \in \mathbf{W}$ as depicted in Fig. 3:

- given **w**, compute $i \leftarrow \mathsf{Hash}(\mathbf{w})$, where $\mathsf{Hash} : \{0,1\}^* \rightarrow \{0,\ldots,B-1\}$ denotes a hash function.
- for each hash function outputting an index i, set $\vec{b}_i \leftarrow 1$.

False positives are possible, since b_i can be set to 1 by multiple strings. Still, by controlling the number of hash functions to be used, one can bound the probability of false positives when inserting n elements through γ hash functions:

$$\Pr\left[\exists \mathbf{w} \notin \mathbf{W} \wedge |\mathbf{W}| \geq 1 \wedge \mathsf{BF.Search}(\vec{b},\mathbf{w}) = 1\right] \approx \left(1 - \left(1 - \frac{1}{B}\right)^{\gamma \cdot n}\right)^{\gamma}.$$

Therefore, the optimal number of hash functions is simply: $\gamma \approx \ln(2) \cdot \frac{B}{n}$. Moreover, a technique to reduce the false positive rate in a Bloom filter is discussed in [8] specially with the view of its use in searchable encryption.

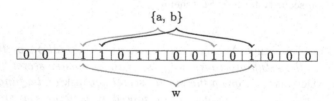

Fig. 3. A depiction of a Bloom filter BF storing elements a, b. Deciding if **w** belongs to BF implies a check over the corresponding positions. In this example **w** is in the set $\{a, b\}$.

Data Representation. Let $\mathsf{D}^{(1)}, \ldots, \mathsf{D}^{(d)}$ be d datafiles, represented in binary. For each $\mathsf{D}^{(i)}$ we instantiate the vector $\mathbf{w}^{(i)} = (\mathbf{w}_1^{(i)}, \ldots \mathbf{w}_{n_i}^{(i)})$, as the vector of keywords, where $\mathbf{w}_t^{(i)}$ denotes the tth keyword belonging to the ith document $\mathsf{D}^{(i)}$. For each $\mathsf{D}^{(i)}$, we instantiate a Bloom filter $\mathsf{BF}^{(i)}$, whose bit-vector $\vec{b}^{(i)}$ can be split into $l^{(i)}$ buckets of equal size $\frac{B_i}{l^{(i)}}$, where B_i denotes the length of $\vec{b}^{(i)}$.

3 Partitioned Symmetric Searchable Encryption

Partitioned symmetric searchable encryption (PSSE) extends the standard definition of SSE in a natural way: the Search algorithm must be post-processed jointly by a group of N users instead of a single one, in order to identify the document(s) with the corresponding keyword(s) by confirming whether a (set of) keyword(s) belongs to some document or not, with sufficient probability[4]. The protocol works by pre-sharing public parameters between the users and then combining the outcome of their results in a similar way to a distributed PRF [18]. As motivated in Sect. 1, certain scenarios benefit from such a setting.

In its simplest setting, a partitioned protocol requires all users to be honest while declaring their outcome, which jointly validates if a keyword belongs or not to some document. We emphasize that a cheater in the group that deliberately changes the result of his/her finding is tantamount to changing the truthfulness of the global outcome. We proceed with a definition and a security notion for the honest model. Our definition encompasses both static and dynamic SSE schemes.

Definition 5 (Partitioned SSE - Honest Setting). *Let N stand for the number of users. Let $\mathsf{D}_i \subseteq \{0,1\}^*$ denote a datafile, for any $i \in [d]$. Let $\mathsf{DB} = \left\{ (i, \mathbf{w}^{(i)}) \right\}_{i \in [d]}$ denote the set of pairs containing a datafile index i and a set of keywords $\mathbf{w}^{(i)}$. An N-party PSSE consists of a tuple of algorithms $\left(\mathsf{PSSE.Setup}, \mathsf{PSSE.ClientSetup}, \mathsf{PSSE.Search}, \mathsf{PSSE.Comb} \right)$ such that:*

- *$(\mathsf{pp}, \mathsf{DB}_1, \ldots, \mathsf{DB}_N) \leftarrow_\$ \mathsf{PSSE.Setup}(1^\lambda, \mathsf{DB}, N)$: is a PPT algorithm that takes as input a database of keywords DB and a number N of users; it extracts the keywords based on which it generates N individual databases denoted DB_j and sends then database DB_j to user j; further auxiliary information may be computed and added to pp (taken as input by all other algorithms).*
- *$(\mathsf{sk}_j, \mathsf{pk}_j) \leftarrow_\$ \mathsf{PSSE.ClientSetup}(\mathsf{DB}_j, j)$: party j samples a private/public key pair $(\mathsf{sk}_j, \mathsf{pk}_j)$. When omitted, the public key is set to $\emptyset$. At this stage, party j encrypts DB_j under pk_j, obtains EDB_j and sends it to the server.*
- *$b_j \leftarrow \mathsf{PSSE.Search}(\mathsf{EDB}, \mathsf{sk}_j, \mathbf{w}, \mathsf{I})$: is a protocol between client j with input its secret key sk_j, and the server with input $\mathsf{EDB} := \cup_{\ell=1}^N \mathsf{EDB}_\ell$. Using sk_j, party j can query for a keyword $\mathbf{w}$ in the datafiles with index in I. A search query can support one or multiple (conjunctions of) keywords. The Server returns to client j a bit b_j indicating if the partial search found $\mathbf{w}$ in any datafile with index in I or not.*
- *$b \leftarrow \mathsf{Comb}(b_1, \ldots, b_N)$: after running the Search procedure, the parties combine their individual outcomes locally without interaction with the server and generate the final outcome of the search query.*

In addition, we say a partitionable symmetric searchable encryption scheme is dynamic if there exists a fifth algorithm:

---

[4] Some of the constructions we propose admit false positives, and therefore we require that correctness holds with a good enough probability, rather than having overwhelming/perfect correctness.

- $(\mathsf{EDB}'_j, \sigma') \leftarrow \mathsf{Update}(\mathsf{EDB}_j, \sigma, \mathsf{sk}_j, \mathsf{l}, \mathbf{w}, \mathsf{op})$: *client j encrypts a keyword $\mathbf{w}$ and sends an update query for a specific datafile index set l. The operation op can be either a delete or insert.*

We require any PSSE scheme to satisfy correctness, in the sense that for any $\mathbf{w} \in \{\mathbf{w}^{(1)}, \ldots, \mathbf{w}^{(d)}\}$, the following quantity is negligibly close to 1:

$$\Pr\left[b \leftarrow \mathsf{Comb}(\{b_j\}) \ \middle| \ \begin{array}{l} \mathsf{pp} \leftarrow_\$ \mathsf{PSSE.Setup}(1^\lambda, \mathsf{DB}, N) \wedge \\ \{(\mathsf{sk}_j, \mathsf{pk}_j) \leftarrow_\$ \mathsf{PSSE.ClientSetup}(\mathsf{DB}_j, j)\}_{j \in [N]} \wedge \\ \{b_j \leftarrow \mathsf{PSSE.Search}(\mathsf{EDB}, \mathsf{sk}_j, \mathbf{w}, \mathsf{l})\}_{j \in [N]} \end{array} \right]$$

A PSSE *scheme is adaptive secure if the advantage of any* PPT *adversary in winning the game in Fig. 2 is negligibly close to 1/2.*

We emphasise that a secret sharing scheme would be an option for combining the individual shares of the parties but it does not allow *searching* over the encrypted database for which a SSE is required. PSSE naturally combines both functionalities.

3.1 Dealing with Malicious Users

Real scenarios are more complex to describe, and often contain entities that are able to actively cheat, in the sense that they may want to change the outcome of a search result. To deal with malicious users we modify Definition 5 by giving the server the possibility to access some verification methods. For example, in our PSSE using FE, the server checks the ciphertexts, and the keys. Let this methods be denoted by $\mathsf{VerCT}, \mathsf{VerKey}$, and we assume they are globally accessible. In such a setting, we enforce ClientSetup to return a public key pk_j for each user. Formally, *correctness* can then be described by requiring the following quantity to be negligibly close to 1:

$$\Pr\left[1 \leftarrow \mathsf{Comb}(\{b_j\}) \ \middle| \ \begin{array}{l} \mathsf{pp} \leftarrow_\$ \mathsf{PSSE.Setup}(1^\lambda, \mathsf{DB}, N) \wedge \\ \{(\mathsf{sk}_j, \mathsf{pk}_j) \leftarrow_\$ \mathsf{PSSE.ClientSetup}(\mathsf{pp}, j)\}_{j \in [N]} \wedge \\ \{b_j \leftarrow \mathsf{PSSE.Search}(\mathsf{pp}, \mathsf{EDB}, K, j, \mathbf{w})\}_{j \in [N]} \wedge \\ \mathsf{VerCT}(\mathsf{pk}_j, \mathsf{EDB}_j) = 1 \wedge \mathsf{VerKey}(\mathsf{pk}_j, K) = 1 \end{array} \right]$$

4 PSSE Instantiations from FE and Trapdoor Permutation Using BF

In this section we present our PSSE constructions from FE and trapdoor permutation using the functionality of Bloom filters.

4.1 A PSSE Scheme from FE

This part introduces a PSSE protocol based on FE and Bloom filters. The scheme discussed stems from the one by Goh [11]. It differs significantly from the new generation of SSE schemes in the sense that a data structure indexed by datafiles is used, as opposed to recent works that use structures indexed by keywords [4,5]. This is somehow natural, in the sense that Bloom filters are meant to store massive datafiles associated to particular documents. It works in two phases: an *offline* setup phase is responsible for generating the required parameters for each Bloom filter and for inserting all document/keyword sets; and an *online* search protocol partitioned between N clients allowing them to recover the indices of the searched elements and to get, through a combine step (Comb), the final result.

The SSE.Setup algorithm instantiates a symmetric encryption scheme SE with key K_{SE} to be used to encrypt the (structured) datafiles. A sufficiently large set of hash functions are also sampled at this stage in order to instantiate the Bloom filters to be used. The Setup, given the database of keywords $DB = \{(i, \mathbf{w}^{(i)})\}_{i \in [d]}$ and the number of users N, proceeds as follows: (1) a set of Bloom filters $BF^{(i)}$, each consisting in a bit-vector $\vec{b}^{(i)}$, is instantiated. For simplicity, we assume the length of each Bloom filter to be B; (2) each keyword $\mathbf{w}_j^{(i)} \in DB$ is inserted into $BF^{(i)}$. Next, the clients proceed as follows: (3) for each Bloom filter $BF^{(i)}$, the underlying bit-vector $\vec{b}^{(i)}$ is split into l buckets. For simplicity we assume[5] that $l = N$; (4) each bucket j in $BF^{(i)}$ is encrypted independently using the mpk_j of some party j. Again, for simplicity we assume a canonical association: bucket j corresponds to party j. During the SSE.ClientSetup phase, each user independently samples a public-key functional encryption scheme supporting inner products: $(msk, mpk) \leftarrow_\$ FE.Setup$. We note that for the purpose of searching, a linear functional encryption scheme suffices. However, more convoluted constructions [13] may support re-encryption queries and thus they may allow insertions. Each user stores its own secret msk_j and publishes its mpk_j. As the scheme is static, each party encrypts its associated chunk of the Bloom filters and sends the resulting ciphertext to the server, which stores them.

On the *client side*, the Search protocol is given a set of query keywords $\mathbf{W}$. For every queried keyword $\mathbf{w} \in \mathbf{W}$, the client j proceeds as follows: first, it determines the places in some bitvector $\mathbf{b}$ that must be set to 1 by the hash functions. Then, each client looks into its allocated chunk: say user j is allocated chunk j. Finally, the client j derives a functional key for the circuit C_f that checks if all required corresponding bits to $\mathbf{W}$ are set to 1 in chunk j. This is done by the functionality CircuitCheckBitsAreOne: for each bucket in some Bloom filter, if some bits are set to 1, then a single circuit-value checker is built. The output of this circuit consists of a single bit. The server is expected to run FE.Dec under these circuits (i.e. apply the functional key) for each bucket:
$$FE.Dec(sk_{f_j}, C_j^{(i)}) = 1 .$$

On the *server side*, the Search protocol will simply evaluate the circuit computing f on the encrypted buckets corresponding to each datafile $D^{(i)}$ and returns $D^{(i)}$ if all decryptions succeed in returning 1 for the buckets corresponding to

---

[5] One can also consider l as a multiple of the number of participants N.

$BF^{(i)}$. As discussed in Sect. 2.2, false positives are possible hence the identification of datafile(s) corresponding to specific keyword(s) is considered with a reasonable probability. Also, if even a single bit in any chunk is not 1 at the desired place then the queried keyword does not correspond to the datafile searched, hence false negative is not possible. Intuitively, the semantic security of FE should guarantee that nothing is leaked on the message apart from $f(M)$.

Our PSSE Construction from FE

Definition 6 (Basic Construction). *Assuming the existence of sub-exponentially semantic-secure FE scheme in the public-key setting, the construction in Fig. 4 is a PSSE scheme for multiple keywords.*

PSSE.Setup(1^λ, DB, N):
for $i \leftarrow 1, d$:
  $BF^{(i)} \leftarrow\$ BF.Setup(1^λ)
  for $j \in 1, N$:
    $BF^{(i)}$.Insert($w_j^{(i)}$)
  $L^{(i)} \leftarrow BF^{(i)}.Split(\vec{b}^{(i)}, N)$
  assert($L^{(i)}$ is a list)
  foreach $x_j^{(i)} \in L^{(i)}$: // $x_j^{(i)}$ is a bucket
    SendClient($j, x_j^{(i)}$)

PSSE.ClientSetup(j, $DB_j = \{x_j^{(1)}, \dots, x_j^{(d)}\}$):
$(msk_j, mpk_j) \leftarrow\$ FE.Setup(1^λ)
for $i \leftarrow 1, d$:
  $C_j^{(i)} \leftarrow\$ FE.Enc($mpk_j, x_j^{(i)}$)
SendServer($C_j^{(1)}, \dots, C_j^{(d)}$)
Store(msk_j, mpk_j)

PSSE.Search():
ClientSide($j, \mathbf{W}$):
BF'.Setup(1^λ)
foreach $w \in \mathbf{W}$:
  BF'.Insert(w)
$x_j \leftarrow BF'$.getChunk(j)
$f_j \leftarrow$ CircuitCheckBitsAreOne(x_j)
$sk_{f_j} \leftarrow\$ FE.KDer(msk_j, f_j)
SendServer(sk_{f_j})

ServerSide(j, mpk_j, sk_{f_j}, I):
$b_j \leftarrow 0$
foreach $i \in I$:
  Parse $(C_1^{(i)}, \dots, C_N^{(i)})$
  $b_j \leftarrow$ (FE.Dec($sk_{f_j}, C_j^{(i)}$) = 1) $\vee$ b_j
SendClient(b_j)

PSSE.Comb($b_1, \dots, b_N$):
return $b_1 \wedge \dots \wedge b_N$

Fig. 4. A PSSE scheme using a functional encryption schemes as an underlying primitive.

Correctness. Assuming a query set $\mathbf{W}$ is to be checked, for each index i (corresponding to the datafile $D^{(i)}$), the client computes the positions of 1s as pointed by some pseudorandom function[6]. Each position will be part of some bucket. The client builds the appropriate circuits to check if the required bits in bucket x are set to 1.

The server uses the functional decryption procedure[7] for each bucket and then for each document. If the FE decryption returns 1 for all positions pointed by the hash functions, then $D^{(i)}$ contains the searched key with high probability.

---

[6] In some sense we want to preserve the idea behind the Bloom filter construction, and work with hash functions having pseudorandom outputs.

[7] Note however that this step is highly parallelizable.

Lemma 1. *If the static* PSSE *in Fig. 4 is built on a semantic secure functional encryption scheme* FE *supporting a bounded number of functional keys, then it is* $PSSE^{\mathcal{A}}_{PSSE}$*-secure (Fig. 2).*

Proof (Lemma 1). We construct the simulator $\mathcal{S}_{PSSE}$ described in Definition 5 using the simulator of the underlying FE scheme. Namely, during the PSSE.Setup procedure, the pp are computed, consisting of the hash functions used to instantiate the Bloom filters, which are then handed to $\mathcal{S}_{PSSE}$, which outputs them. For the ClientSetup case, N $\mathcal{S}_{FE}$ simulators are instantiated, and $\mathcal{S}_{PSSE}$ simply returns as EDB the ciphertexts it receives from the N simulators. During the Search procedure, the leakage function obtained from the functional keys (and the ciphertexts) that are exchanged between the clients and the server, consists only in the FE.Dec(sk_f, C), which is also leaked by the real experiment. Thus, the two settings are indistinguishable. $\square$

We observe that an inner-product FE scheme is sufficient for our purpose. For instance, if a bucket in some bitvector contains m positions set to 1, we issue a functional key for exactly the same bucket and check if its output is m (assuming m is small).

4.2 PSSE from Trapdoor Permutation: PSSE from $\Sigma o\phi o\varsigma$

This section proposes a forward secure SSE scheme supporting a partitioned search amongst N honest users.

$\Sigma o\phi o\varsigma$. The starting point of our proposal is $\Sigma o\phi o\varsigma$ [4]. The construction is keyword-indexed and easy to follow. It uses a master secret key, denoted as K_S to derive a keyword key $K_\mathbf{w}$ for each keyword $\mathbf{w}$ of interest using a PRF:

$$K_\mathbf{w} \leftarrow \mathsf{PRF}(K_S, \mathbf{w}),$$

where $K_\mathbf{w}$ is used in conjunction with some randomly sampled search token ST_0 from the space of admissible tokens $\mathcal{M}$ in order to attain the first insertion of $\mathbf{w}$ in the encrypted database corresponding to some document with index in $\vec{I}$. Then, additional queries will generate new search tokens ST_c. Concretely, the server maintains a table $\mathbf{T}$ with lines corresponding to users and rows corresponding to hash value $\mathsf{Hash}_1(K_\mathbf{w}\|ST_c)$ containing the hidden value $(\mathsf{Hash}_2(K_\mathbf{w}\|ST_c) \oplus \vec{I})$, while the client maintains a table $\mathbf{T}^{(j)}$ saving the relation between search tokens ST_c and $\mathbf{w}$. To insert $\mathbf{w}$ in any new document with index i_c, a new search token ST_c is derived from ST_0. This happens by the means of a trapdoor permutation Π_c:

$$ST_c \leftarrow \Pi_c^{-1}(ST_0)$$

obtained through the repeated application of a pseudorandom permutation PRP.

On the server side, things are remarkably simple. Once the client sends $K_\mathbf{w}$ and some search token ST_c, the server recomputes the hash values $\mathsf{Hash}_1(K_\mathbf{w}\|ST_c)$, $\mathsf{Hash}_2(K_\mathbf{w}\|ST_c)$ and obtains the index. If more than one index has been inserted per keyword $\mathbf{w}$, then all search tokens can be recovered, simply by taking:

$$ST_0 \leftarrow \Pi_c(ST_c)$$

and the previous step is applied. Intuitively, $\Sigma o\phi o\varsigma$ enjoys forward security for the following reason: whenever a new (keyword, index) pair is inserted via the hash function, the server is not able to derive the search token that is used. Thus it can't say which keyword has been inserted, or to which document it belongs to.

A Forward Secure Partitioned SSE Scheme. We aim at having a scheme handling update queries while reaching forward security. The gist of the modifications we make on $\Sigma o\phi o\varsigma$ is to replace the index that identifies the document, with a more convenient data structure – a Bloom filter. Then, we allocate to each party a chunk over the bitvector associated to BF. That is, whenever a keyword is to be inserted at some location, a new Bloom filter is instantiated. Party j will compute independently its search tokens and will XOR the jth chunk of BF. The server will store all these chunks in a 2-dimensional array with rows corresponding to the N possible parties and columns to hashes. Whenever queried by a client for some keyword $\mathbf{w}$, it will identify and return the value of the BF chunk. In the Comb protocol, the parties would be able to recreate the entire BF and check if the words are included or not. For technical reasons, we employ the usage of several hash functions (impersonating random oracles) in order to obtain a joint computation corresponding to the value during the insert and the search phases. An algorithmic description of our scheme can be found in Fig. 5.

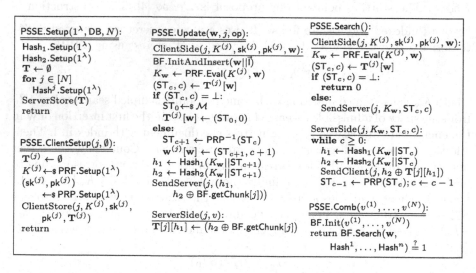

Fig. 5. A construction of forward-private PSSE based on trapdoor permutations.

Forward Security of PSSE. We show the partitioned $\Sigma o\phi o\varsigma$ achieves forward security. To this end, we mainly adapt the proof given by Bost in his paper to our partitioned version in Fig. 5.

Lemma 2 (Forward Security). *Let $\mathcal{S}_S$ denote the simulator used in the forward-security of [4]. The partitioned* SSE *scheme in Fig. 5 achieves partitioned forward security against any* PPT *adversary* $\mathcal{A}$, *as defined in Definition 2 under the advantage* $\mathbf{Adv}_{\Sigma,\mathcal{R}}^{FW}(\lambda) \leq N \cdot \mathbf{Adv}_{\Sigma o \phi o \varsigma, \mathcal{A}}^{FW}(\lambda)$.

Proof (Proof Sketch). Observe that scheme Σ in Fig. 5 can be viewed as N parallel executions of $\Sigma o \phi o \varsigma$. A key difference consists in the indices that are passed by each of the users whenever a keyword is inserted. Naturally, we would like to re-use the already proven forward security in order to attain the same property for our partitioned scheme. In doing so, we proceed using a hybrid argument. A new hybrid game corresponds to simulating the output of the ith client using the simulator put forward by Bost in [4].

Game$_0$: corresponds to the real experiment in the security game $\text{PSSE}_{\text{PSSE}}^{\mathcal{A}}$.

Game$_i$: we use the simulator in [4] to generate the transcript. The distance to the previous game is bounded by the forward security of the scheme in [4].

Game$_N$: is identical to the simulated experiment in Defintion 6.   □

PSSE.Setup(1^λ, DB, N):

Hash$_1$.Setup(1^λ)
Hash$_2$.Setup(1^λ)
$\mathbf{T} \leftarrow \emptyset$
for $j \in [N]$
    Hash^j.Setup(1^λ)
ServerStore($\mathbf{T}$)

PSSE.ClientSetup($j, \emptyset$):

$\mathbf{T}^{(j)} \leftarrow \emptyset$
$(K^{(j)}, \text{vk}^{(j)}) \leftarrow \$ \text{VRF.Setup}(1^\lambda)$
$(\text{sk}^{(j)}, \text{pk}^{(j)}) \leftarrow \$ \text{PRP.Setup}(1^\lambda)$
ClientStore($j, K^{(j)}, \text{sk}^{(j)}, \text{pk}^{(j)}, \mathbf{T}^{(j)}$)

PSSE.Update($\mathbf{w}, j, \text{op}$):

ClientSide($j, K^{(j)}, \text{sk}^{(j)}, \text{pk}^{(j)}, \mathbf{w}$):
BF.Insert($\mathbf{w}||\mathbf{l}$)
$(K_\mathbf{w}, \pi_\mathbf{w}) \leftarrow \text{VRF.Eval}(K^{(j)}, \text{vk}^{(j)}, \mathbf{w})$
$(\text{ST}_c, c) \leftarrow \mathbf{T}^{(j)}[\mathbf{w}]$
if $(\text{ST}_c, c) = \perp$:
    $\text{ST}_0 \leftarrow \mathcal{M}$
else:
    $\text{ST}_{c+1} \leftarrow \text{PRP}^{-1}(\text{ST}_c)$
$\mathbf{T}^{(j)}[\mathbf{w}] \leftarrow (\text{ST}_{c+1}, c+1)$
$h_1 \leftarrow \text{Hash}_1(K_\mathbf{w}||\text{ST}_{c+1})$
$h_2 \leftarrow \text{Hash}_2(K_\mathbf{w}||\text{ST}_{c+1})$
SendServer($h_1, h_2 \oplus$ BF.getChunk[j])

ServerSide(j, v):
$\mathbf{T}[j][h_1] \leftarrow (h_2 \oplus$ BF.getChunk[j])

PSSE.Search():

ClientSide($j, K^{(j)}, \text{sk}^{(j)}, \text{pk}^{(j)}, \mathbf{w}$):
$(K_\mathbf{w}, \pi_\mathbf{w}) \leftarrow \text{VRF.Eval}(K^{(j)}, \text{pk}^{(j)}, \mathbf{w})$
$(\text{ST}_c, c) \leftarrow \mathbf{T}^{(j)}[\mathbf{w}]$
if $(\text{ST}_c, c) = \perp$:
    return 0
else:
    SendServer($j, K_\mathbf{w}, \pi_\mathbf{w}, \text{ST}_c, c$)

ServerSide($j, K_\mathbf{w}, \pi_\mathbf{w}, \text{ST}_c, c$):
while $c > 0$:
    if VRF.Ver($\text{vk}^{(j)}, K_\mathbf{w}, \pi_\mathbf{w}, \mathbf{w}) \neq 1$:
        abort
    $h_1 \leftarrow \text{Hash}_1(K_\mathbf{w}||\text{ST}_c)$
    $h_2 \leftarrow \text{Hash}_2(K_\mathbf{w}, ||\text{ST}_c)$
    SendClient($j, h_2 \oplus \mathbf{T}[j][h_1]$)
    $c \leftarrow c - 1$

PSSE.Comb($v^{(1)}, \ldots, v^{(N)}$):

BF.Init($v^{(1)}, \ldots, v^{(N)}$)
return BF.Search($\mathbf{w}, \text{Hash}^1, \ldots, \text{Hash}^N$) $\stackrel{?}{=} 1$

Fig. 6. A candidate construction of forward-private PSSE based on trapdoor permutations and verifiable random functions (VRFs) for handling malicious users.

4.3 Dealing with Malicious Users

Far more challenging is the scenario that deals with malicious users. A generalization of the preceding scheme may also deal with this additional problem by replacing pseudorandom functions in Fig. 5 by verifiable random functions (VRF). A VRF consists of a setup phase – generating the public parameters, an *evaluation* algorithm – returning an evaluation and a proof for a given input, and a verification algorithm – validating the outcome of the evaluation process. We refer to [14] for the formal definition of VRFs. The verifiability property allows the server to check if a keyword key K_w has been correctly generated by the client and to abort the search otherwise. We present a candidate construction of forward-private PSSE based on trapdoor permutations in Fig. 6.

5 Conclusion

In this work, we proposed a new variant of searchable encryption schemes (SSE). We call it partitioned SSE (PSSE) where datafiles can only be found whenever all search parties give a collective search request. This combines the best parts of searchable encryption and secret sharing. We accompany this new variant with two pragmatic schemes, one based on functional encryption and one on $\Sigma o\phi o\varsigma$. Additionally, we showed how the latter scheme can be used in the presence of malicious users.

Acknowledgements. Jim Barthel was supported in part by the Luxembourg National Research Fund through grant PRIDE15/10621687/SPsquared. The last two authors were supported by ERC Advanced grant CLOUDMAP 787390.

References

1. Ananth, P., Jain, A., Jin, Z., Malavolta, G.: Multi-key fully-homomorphic encryption in the plain model. In: Pass, R., Pietrzak, K. (eds.) TCC 2020. LNCS, vol. 12550, pp. 28–57. Springer, Cham (2020). https://doi.org/10.1007/978-3-030-64375-1_2

2. Bloom, B.H.: Space/time trade-offs in hash coding with allowable errors. Commun. ACM **13**(7), 422–426 (1970)

3. Boneh, D., Sahai, A., Waters, B.: Functional encryption: definitions and challenges. In: Ishai, Y. (ed.) TCC 2011. LNCS, vol. 6597, pp. 253–273. Springer, Heidelberg (2011). https://doi.org/10.1007/978-3-642-19571-6_16

4. Bost, R.: $\Sigma o\phi o\varsigma$: forward secure searchable encryption. In: Weippl, E.R., Katzenbeisser, S., Kruegel, C., Myers, A.C., Halevi, S., (eds.) ACM CCS 16, pp. 1143–1154. ACM Press, October 2016

5. Bost, R., Minaud, B., Ohrimenko,O.: Forward and backward private searchable encryption from constrained cryptographic primitives. In: Thuraisingham, B.M., Evans, D., Malkin, T., Xu, D., (eds.) ACM CCS 17, pp. 1465–1482. ACM Press, October/November 2017

6. Cash, D., et al.: Dynamic searchable encryption in very-large databases: data structures and implementation. In: NDSS 2014. The Internet Society, February 2014

7. Chang, Y.-C., Mitzenmacher, M.: Privacy preserving keyword searches on remote encrypted data. In: Ioannidis, J., Keromytis, A., Yung, M. (eds.) ACNS 2005. LNCS, vol. 3531, pp. 442–455. Springer, Heidelberg (2005). https://doi.org/10.1007/11496137_30

8. Chum, C.S., Zhang, X.: A new bloom filter structure for searchable encryption schemes. In: Proceedings of the Seventh ACM on Conference on Data and Application Security and Privacy, pp. 143–145 (2017)

9. Curtmola, R., Garay, J.A., Kamara, S., Ostrovsky, R.: Searchable symmetric encryption: improved definitions and efficient constructions. In: Juels, A., Wright, R.N., De Capitani di Vimercati, S. (eds.) ACM CCS 06, pp. 79–88. ACM Press, October/November 2006

10. Gentry, C.: Fully homomorphic encryption using ideal lattices. In: Mitzenmacher, M. (ed.) 41st ACM STOC, pp. 169–178. ACM Press, May/June 2009

11. Goh, E.-J.: Secure indexes. Cryptology ePrint Archive, Report 2003/216 (2003). http://eprint.iacr.org/2003/216

12. Goldreich, O., Ostrovsky, R.: Software protection and simulation on oblivious rams. J. ACM (JACM) **43**(3), 431–473 (1996)

13. Goldwasser, S., Kalai, Y.T., Popa, R.A., Vaikuntanathan, V., Zeldovich, N.: Reusable garbled circuits and succinct functional encryption. In: Boneh, D., Roughgarden, T., Feigenbaum, J. (eds.) 45th ACM STOC, pp. 555–564. ACM Press, June 2013

14. Hofheinz, D., Jager, T.: Verifiable random functions from standard assumptions. In: Kushilevitz, E., Malkin, T. (eds.) TCC 2016. LNCS, vol. 9562, pp. 336–362. Springer, Heidelberg (2016). https://doi.org/10.1007/978-3-662-49096-9_14

15. Kamara, S., Papamanthou, C.: Parallel and dynamic searchable symmetric encryption. In: Sadeghi, A.-R. (ed.) FC 2013. LNCS, vol. 7859, pp. 258–274. Springer, Heidelberg (2013). https://doi.org/10.1007/978-3-642-39884-1_22

16. Kamara, S., Papamanthou, C., Roeder, T.: Dynamic searchable symmetric encryption. In: Yu, T., Danezis, G., Gligor, V.D. (eds.) ACM CCS 12, pp. 965–976. ACM Press, October 2012

17. Mishra, P., Poddar, R., Chen, J., Chiesa, A., Popa, R.A.: Oblix: an efficient oblivious search index. In: 2018 IEEE Symposium on Security and Privacy, pp. 279–296. IEEE Computer Society Press, May 2018

18. Naor, M., Pinkas, B., Reingold, O.: Distributed pseudo-random functions and KDCs. In: Stern, J. (ed.) EUROCRYPT 1999. LNCS, vol. 1592, pp. 327–346. Springer, Heidelberg (1999). https://doi.org/10.1007/3-540-48910-X_23

19. Patranabis, S., Mukhopadhyay, D.: Forward and backward private conjunctive searchable symmetric encryption. In: NDSS Symposium 2021 (2021)

20. Song, D.X., Wagner, D., Perrig, A.: Practical techniques for searches on encrypted data. In: 2000 IEEE Symposium on Security and Privacy, pp. 44–55. IEEE Computer Society Press, May 2000

21. Stefanov, E., Papamanthou, C., Shi, E.: Practical dynamic searchable encryption with small leakage. In: NDSS 2014. The Internet Society, February 2014

22. Sun, S.-F., Liu, J.K., Sakzad, A., Steinfeld, R., Yuen, T.H.: An efficient non-interactive multi-client searchable encryption with support for Boolean queries. In: Askoxylakis, I., Ioannidis, S., Katsikas, S., Meadows, C. (eds.) ESORICS 2016. LNCS, vol. 9878, pp. 154–172. Springer, Cham (2016). https://doi.org/10.1007/978-3-319-45744-4_8

23. Yao, A.C.-C.: Protocols for secure computations (extended abstract). In: 23rd FOCS, pp. 160–164. IEEE Computer Society Press, November 1982

Key Exchange and Zero Knowledge Proof

Key Exposure Resistant Group Key Agreement Protocol

Tianqi Zhou[1], Jian Shen[1,2(✉)], Sai Ji[3], Yongjun Ren[1], and Mingwu Zhang[4]

[1] School of Computer and Software, Nanjing University of Information Science and Technology, Nanjing 210044, China
[2] Cyberspace Security Research Center, Peng Cheng Laboratory, Shenzhen 518000, China
[3] Suqian University, Suqian 223800, China
[4] School of Computers, Hubei University of Technology, Wuhan 430068, China

Abstract. With the development of the Internet and computer science, the demand for collaboration over the Internet is constantly increasing. The group key agreement (GKA) protocol has been a desirable candidate for this demand. However, the possibility that some parties in the GKA protocol may be tampered with by the adversary leads to the stronger requirement for the GKA protocol. Thus, in this paper, the key exposure resistant property for the GKA protocol is considered, which is essential for collaborative applications such as smart homes. In particular, the secret sharing scheme is utilized to achieve the key exposure resistant property. Also, in the proposed protocol, the rushing attack can be prevented. Moreover, the group key agreement can be finished in three rounds, which is efficient, specifically for the resource-constrained nodes in smart homes. The security and performance analyses demonstrate the practicality and efficiency of the proposed protocol.

Keywords: Group key agreement protocol · Key exposure · Rushing attack · Secret sharing

1 Introduction

With the development of the Internet and computer science, wireless communication technologies [14] have been improved and perfected. Currently, all kinds of Internet of Things devices [21,23] are connected with the wireless networks, which consists of smart homes [15], smart grids [27] and smart healthcare [16] etc. The above systems integrate advanced technologies in computer networks, electronic engineering and industrial fields to provide a great convenience for

This work is supported by the National Natural Science Foundation of China under Grants No. U1836115, No. 61672295, No. 61922045, the Peng Cheng Laboratory Project of Guangdong Province No. PCL2018KP004, the Postgraduate Research & Practice Innovation Program of Jiangsu Province No. KYCX21_0998, the CICAEET fund, and the PAPD fund.

© Springer Nature Switzerland AG 2021
Q. Huang and Y. Yu (Eds.): ProvSec 2021, LNCS 13059, pp. 83–97, 2021.
https://doi.org/10.1007/978-3-030-90402-9_5

people's lives. In particular, these systems integrate devices by the wireless networks to aggregate, process and generate data. In most cases, devices need to adopt a collaborative approach. For one thing, consisting a system means that devices need to interact with each other. For another thing, it is efficient to process data in a collaborative way.

Note that the wireless networks is vulnerable to the passive and active attacks. The attackers can eavesdrop, modify, intercept and replay message in this opening network environment [24]. Thus, the cryptographic means should be deployed in the wireless networks to offer security guarantees. The group key agreement (GKA) protocol has been a well candidate for this demand. The generated session key can ensure the privacy and authenticity the following communication among the group.

However, the possibility that some parties in the GKA protocol may be tampered with by adversary leads to the stronger requirement for the GKA protocol [25]. Also, some secure issues may derived in the GKA protocol if some parties are malicious. Thus, effective solutions are urgently needed to solve the security problems in the GKA protocol. In addition, the efficiency should be taken into consideration due to the fact that the great majority of devices in the wireless networks is resource constrained. To solve the above mentioned problem, the GKA protocol with key exposure resistant property is proposed. Moreover, in order to adapt to the resource-constrained environment, a basic protocol and an enhanced protocol are designed.

1.1 Our Contributions

- Key exposure resistant for the GKA protocol. In this paper, the key exposure resistant property of the GKA protocol is supported. In particular, the secret sharing scheme is adopted, which guarantee the security of the session key even though some parties' private keys or sensitive information are exposed.
- Rushing attack resistant for the GKA protocol. In this paper, the rushing attack resistant property of the GKA protocol is defined and the enhanced protocol is designed to resist the rushing attack [2]. The rushing attack is launched by some inside malicious parties who try to choose their contributions after the witness of the other parties' contributions. In this way, the malicious parties can decide the final session key previously while the other parties would not be aware of this malicious actions. It is obvious that this action destroys the fairness of the GKA protocol. Thus, by taking advantage of the homomorphic encryption and the delicate design of the enhanced GKA protocol, the rushing attack can be prevented from.
- Fault tolerance property for group key agreement protocol. In the wireless networks, the fault tolerance property should be taken into consideration as the devices and the communication channel are vulnerable. the fault tolerance property ensures the common run of the GKA protocol when some devices are offline or under the deny of service attack. In order to support the fault tolerance property, the fault tolerance mechanism is designed. Note that the fault tolerance mechanism can not only support the fault tolerance property but

also can decrease the communicational and computational overheads during the key agreement phase.

- Efficient and adaptive property for the GKA protocol. The efficiency is the important evaluation indicators for the GKA protocol especially for the resource-constrained wireless networks. Therefore, in this paper a basic GKA protocol with entity authentication is proposed. Furthermore, in order to resist the rushing attack and the key exposure attack, an enhanced GKA protocol is proposed. It is worth noting that two rounds are required in the basic GKA protocol while three rounds are required in the enhanced GKA protocol. In this way, the mode of the key agreement can be selected according to the requirements for safety and efficiency from various applications.

1.2 Organization

The reminder of this paper is organized as follows. In Sect. 2, the related works about the GKA protocol are presented. In Sect. 3, the cryptographical preliminaries are introduced. In Sect. 4, the basic GKA protocol and the enhanced GKA protocol are designed. Section 5 performs the security and the performance analyses. Section 6 draws the conclusion of this paper.

2 Related Works

As an important cryptographic primitive, a large number of key agreement protocols have been proposed. These focus on the security [20] and efficiency [6,17] issues of the key agreement protocol together with various properties ranging from dynamic [28] to collision-resistant [13].

Secret sharing scheme [8,9,19] is the algorithm that distributes a secret to multiparty and reconstructs the secret with the cooperation of some parties. According to the definition and property of the secret sharing scheme, constructing the key distribution scheme seems an intuitive extension of the secret sharing scheme. For example, Chandramowliswaran et al. [5] presented an authenticated group key distribution protocol by employing the Chinese reminder theory [12]. Hu et al. [10] proposed the key distribution scheme for secure cloud storage by using the (2,3) secret sharing scheme. However, the existing key establishment protocols based on the secret sharing scheme can only achieve the key distribution, which implies that the session key is generated by a trusted party and then distributed to the group parties. Also, in these protocols the distribution of the shares should be performed over a secure channel and an honest third party is required to reconstruct the secret.

In [24], Wu et al. a privacy-preserving mutual authentication protocol was proposed. By leveraging the Paillier homomorphic encryption [26] and zero-knowledge proofs [3], the key protection is achieved. Whereas, the key agreement protocol for multiparty with the key exposure resistant property was seldom considered. What is more, the rushing attack in the GKA protocol has been underestimated for a long time.

Algorithm 1. ElGamal encryption algorithm

Input: input the plaintext (M, Enc) or the ciphertext (C, Dec)
Output: output the ciphertext C or the M

Detailed algorithm:
1: **Initialization:**
2: input security parameter l
3: output the cyclic group $\mathbb{G}$ and a generator $g \in \mathbb{G}$
4: **KeyGen:**
5: input $(g, \mathbb{G})$
6: randomly select an element x in Z_q^* and calculate $y = g^x$
7: output the public parameters $(g, \mathbb{G}, y)$ and keep the corresponding private key x private
8: **Encryption:**
9: input a message M $(M \in \mathbb{G})$
10: randomly select an element r in Z_q^* and calculate $C_1 = g^r$ and $C_2 = Y^r M$
11: output the ciphertext $C = (C_1, C_2)$
12: **Decryption:**
13: input the ciphertext $C = (C_1, C_2)$
14: decrypt the ciphertext with the private key x, calculate $M = C_2/(C_1{}^x)$
15: output the plaintext M

---

3   Preliminaries

In this section, the cryptographic preliminaries that are employed in the proposed GKA protocol are presented.

3.1   Homomorphic Encryption

ElGamal Encryption Scheme. Given cyclic multipliative group Z_q^* with order $q - 1$. The ElGamal encryption algorithm [18] is presented as Algorithm 1.

We note that in the proposed GKA protocol, the homomorphic property of the ElGamal encryption algorithm is employed to achieve efficient group key agreement. In particular, the homomorphic property of the ElGamal encryption algorithm is shown as follows.

Given the ElGamal encryption of two messages M_i and M_j, based on the homomorphic property the following Eq. 1 holds.

$$Dec(Enc(M_i) \cdot Enc(M_j)) = Dec(Enc(M_i \cdot M_j)) \tag{1}$$

The security of the ElGamal encryption scheme is ensured suppose that the decisional Diffie-Hellman (DDH) assumption [4] holds, which is formally defined in Definition 1.

Definition 1. *The ElGamal encryption scheme is secure against the chosen-plaintext attacks (IND-CPA), if the advantage $Adv_{\mathcal{A}}^{CPA}(\mathcal{K})$ of the adversary $\mathcal{A}$*

Algorithm 2. Secret sharing algorithm

Input: input the secret s, the number of parties n and the threshold t
Output: output n shares to n parties

Detailed algorithm:
1: **Polynomial construction:**
2: to share the secret s to n parties with threshold t, the dealer selects $t-1$ coefficient $a_1,a_2,a_3,......,a_{t-1}$ at random and constructs the polynomial as

$$f(x) = s + a_1 x + a_2 x^2 + ... + a_{t-1} x^{t-1}$$

3: **Shares generation:**
4: to generate the share to party i, the dealer randomly selects x_i and calculates $y_i = f(x_i)$.
5: **Shares distribution:**
6: the dealer distribute the share (x_i, y_i) to party i in a secure channel or in an encrypted form such that only party i can decrypt.

---

is negligible. In particular, the advantage $Adv_{\mathcal{A}}^{CPA}(\mathcal{K})$ of the adversary $\mathcal{A}$ can be defined as Eq. 2

$$Adv_{\mathcal{A}}^{CPA}(\mathcal{K}) = \left| \Pr\left[Exp_{\Pi,\mathcal{A}}^{CPA}(\mathcal{K}) = 1 \right] - \frac{1}{2} \right| \tag{2}$$

Here, the IND-CPA game can be formally defined as follows. In the IND-CPA game, the ElGamal encryption scheme is the triplet $\Pi = (KeyGen, Enc, Dec)$. At the end of the game, if $b = b'$ returns 1, else returns 0.

$$Exp_{\Pi,\mathcal{A}}^{CPA}(\mathcal{K}):$$
$$(pk, sk) \leftarrow KeyGen(\mathcal{K});$$
$$(M_0, M_1) \leftarrow \mathcal{A}^{Enc_{pk}(\cdot)}(pk);$$
$$b \leftarrow \{0,1\}, C^* = Enc_{pk}(M_b);$$
$$b' \leftarrow \mathcal{A}(pk, C^*).$$

3.2 Secret Sharing Scheme

Secret Sharing Scheme. In the secret sharing scheme [9,22], the dealer selects a secret s and distributes a share to each party in a secure channel. After all parties have received each shares, the collaboration of the group parties can reconstruct the secret. In particular, in order to share the secret to n parties such that the collaboration of at least t parties can reconstruct the secret, the dealer can run Algorithm 1.

After the Algorithm 2, each party obtains his share. According to the definition of the secret sharing scheme, the collaboration of at least t parties can reconstruct the secret s. In particular, these parties together can reconstruct the secret s based on Lagrange interpolation shown in Eq. 3.

$$L(x) = \sum_{j=0}^{t-1} y_j \cdot l_j(x) \tag{3}$$

In Eq. 3, $l_j(x) = \sum_{i=0, i \neq j}^{t} \frac{x - x_i}{x_j - x_i}$.

Note that during the reconstruction phase, an honest third party is required to reconstruct the secret. The security property of the secret sharing scheme guarantees that any collaboration from less t parties can not reconstruct the secret.

3.3   The Group Key Agreement Protocol

The group key agreement protocol can be defined as Definition 2.

Definition 2. *The group key agreement protocol can be defined as* $\prod_{KA} = \{l, N, Init, ConGen, KeyGen\}$. *Where, l is the system security parameter and N is the number of the group.*

- **Init.** *The **Init** algorithm inputs the system security parameter l and the number of the group N. Then, the **Init** algorithm outputs the well-defined group $\mathbb{G}$ for the initialized system with the generator g and each party's public and private key pair (pk_i, sk_i).*
- **ConGen.** *The **ConGen** algorithm inputs the system public parameters and the private key sk_i of each party i. Then, the **ConGen** algorithm outputs the contribution generated by each party.*
- **KeyGen.** *The **KeyGen** algorithm inputs the contribution generated by each party and the private key sk_i of each party i. Then, the **KeyGen** algorithm outputs the session key of the group.*

Generally speaking, for the well-designed GKA protocol, the following properties are satisfactory: 1) entity authentication [1]; 2) key privacy [11]; 3) key confirmation [7].

3.4   Notations

The notations used in this paper are shown in Table 1.

4   The Proposed Protocol

In this section, the GKA protocol is proposed. In order to satisfy the efficient and the adaptive requirement of the wireless networks, a basic GKA protocol with authentication is proposed. After that an enhanced GKA protocol is proposed, which maintains both the key exposure resistant property and the rushing attack resistant property.

Table 1. Notations.

$\mathbb{G}$	The multiplicative cyclic group
g	The generator of $\mathbb{G}$
Z_q^*	The integer set $(1, 2, ..., q-1)$
(sk_i, pk_i)	The signing and verification key pair of party i
(x_i, y_i)	The private and public key pair of party i
$C_{i,j}$	The message sent from i to j in round 1
$\sigma_{i,j}$	The signature on the message sent in round 1
SID	The session identifier
$T_{i,j}, T_c$	The time stamps
$\mathcal{C}_1, \mathcal{C}_2, \mathcal{C}_j$	The aggregated contributions
$\mathcal{K}$	The session key
$sk \in Z_q^*$	The secret of the trusted third party (TTP)
$a_1, a_2, a_3, ..., a_{t-1} \in Z_q^*$	Random coefficients selected by TTP
$f(x)$	The polynomial constructed by TTP
H	The cryptographic one-way hash function

4.1 The Basic Protocol

In the basic GKA protocol, the authenticated and efficient GKA protocol is presented based on the ElGamal encryption. The details of the basic GKA protocol is as follows.

- **Initialization:** Select two large primes p and q, such that $q|(p-1)$. Generate a multiplicative cyclic group $\mathbb{G}$ of order $q-1$ and a generator $g \in \mathbb{G}$. Choose a cryptographic hash function H and set the session identifier SID.
- **Key generation:** Each party selects an element x_i in Z_q^* at random and calculates $y_i = g^{x_i}$. The private and public pair of party is (x_i, y_i).
- **Registration:** Each party i registers at a trust authority and obtains his signing and verification key pair (sk_i, vk_i).
- **Round 1:** In the first round of key agreement, each party i randomly selects his contribution for the session key as $X_i \in \mathbb{G}$. After that for $j = 1...n, (j \neq i)$, party i select a random element $k_{i,j}$ in Z_q^* and calculates $C_{i,j}^1 = g^{k_{i,j}}$ and $C_{i,j}^2 = y_j^{k_{i,j}} \cdot X_i$. Then, party i signs the $C_{i,j} = (C_{i,j}^1, C_{i,j}^2)$, the session identifier SID and the current time stamp $T_{i,j}$ with the signing key $\sigma_{i,j} = Sig_{sk_i}(C_{i,j}, SID, T_{i,j})$. Here, the signature scheme is UMF-unforgeable secure scheme, which consists of three algorithms $\prod = (KeyGen, Sig, Ver)$. After that, party i sends the message $M_{i,j}^1 = (C_{i,j}, \sigma_{i,j}, SID, T_{i,j})$ to each party j, $(j = 1...n, j \neq i)$. Figure 1 illustrates the process in round 1.
- **Round 2:** In the second round of the key agreement, each party j are expected to receive $n-1$ messages $M_{i,j}^1$ from the other $n-1$ parties. Here, $i = 1...n, i \neq j$. When received the message $M_{i,j}^1$, party j first checks the time

	Party 1	Party 2	Party 3	...	Party i	...	Party n	
Party 1	$C_{1,1}$	$C_{1,2}$	$C_{1,3}$	...	$C_{1,i}$	...	$C_{1,n}$	
Party 2	$C_{2,1}$	$C_{2,2}$	$C_{2,3}$	...	$C_{2,i}$	...	$C_{2,n}$	
Party 3	$C_{3,1}$	$C_{3,2}$	$C_{3,3}$	...	$C_{3,i}$	...	$C_{3,n}$	
......								
Party i	$C_{i,1}$	$C_{i,2}$	$C_{i,3}$	...	$C_{i,i}$	...	$C_{i,n}$	Multicast
......								
Party n	$C_{n,1}$	$C_{n,2}$	$C_{n,3}$	...	$C_{n,i}$	...	$C_{n,n}$	

Fig. 1. Multicast in round 1.

stamp $T_{i,j}$. If $T_{i,j} - T_c > \delta$, then party j rejects the message. If $T_{i,j} - T_c < \delta$, party j verifies the message by checking that $Ver_{pk_i}(\sigma_{i,j}, C_{i,j}, SID, T_{i,j}) = 1$. If the message sent by party i is verified, party j calculates the following equations.

$$\mathcal{C}_1 = \prod_{i=1}^{n, i \neq j} C_{i,j}^1 = \prod_{i=1}^{n, i \neq j} g^{k_{i,j}}$$

$$\mathcal{C}_2 = \prod_{i=1}^{n, i \neq j} C_{i,j}^2 = \prod_{i=1}^{n, i \neq j} y_j^{k_{i,j}} \cdot X_i = \prod_{i=1}^{n, i \neq j} g^{x_j k_{i,j}} \cdot X_i$$

Figure 2 illustrates the process in round 2.

	Party 1	Party 2	Party 3	...	Party i	...	Party n
Party 1	$C_{1,1}$	$C_{1,2}$	$C_{1,3}$	...	$C_{1,i}$	...	$C_{1,n}$
Party 2	$C_{2,1}$	$C_{2,2}$	$C_{2,3}$	...	$C_{2,i}$	...	$C_{2,n}$
Party 3	$C_{3,1}$	$C_{3,2}$	$C_{3,3}$	...	$C_{3,i}$	...	$C_{3,n}$
......							
Party i	$C_{i,1}$	$C_{i,2}$	$C_{i,3}$	...	$C_{i,i}$	...	$C_{i,n}$
......							
Party n	$C_{n,1}$	$C_{n,2}$	$C_{n,3}$	...	$C_{n,i}$	...	$C_{n,n}$
					Aggregation		

Fig. 2. Aggregation in round 2.

– **Contributions aggregation:** In the session contributions aggregation phase, each party j in the group can calculate the aggregated contributions with his private key x_j and his own contribution X_j. In particular, party j derives the aggregated contributions by calculating the following equation.

$$\mathcal{C}_j = X_j \cdot \frac{\mathcal{C}_2}{\mathcal{C}_1^{x_j}}$$

– **Session key generation and confirmation:** In order to confirm the aggregated contributions $\mathcal{C}_j$, each party j in the group calculates $V_j^1 = H(\mathcal{C}_j \| SID)$,

$V_j^2 = Sign_{sk_j}(V_j^1 || SID)$ and broadcasts (V_j^1, V_j^2) Finally, if all the V_j^1 ($j = 1...n$) are the same, the session key $\mathcal{K}$ for party j is computed as $\mathcal{K} = H(\mathcal{C}_j)$.

4.2 The Enhanced Protocol

Algorithm 3. Rushing attack on the basic GKA protocol

Input: input the messages sent in round 1 of the basic GKA protocol and the specific selected value X^* from party m
Output: output the session key of the group as $\mathcal{K} = H(X^*)$

Detailed algorithm:
  Initialization:
  party m performs the *Initialization*, the *Key generation* and the *Registration* phases as that defined in the GKA protocol.
  Decision delay :
  in order to perform the rushing attack, the malicious party m will not decide his contribution until all the others have selected and distributed their contributions. In fact, after the observation of all the other parties' contributions, the malicious party m can compute the following equation.

$$\mathcal{C}_1 = \prod_{i=1}^{n, i \neq m} C_{i,m}^1 = \prod_{i=1}^{n, i \neq m} y^{k_{i,m}}$$
$$\mathcal{C}_2 = \prod_{i=1}^{n, i \neq m} C_{i,m}^2 = \prod_{i=1}^{n, i \neq m} y_m^{k_{i,m}} \cdot X_i = \prod_{i=1}^{n, i \neq m} g^{x_m k_{i,m}} \cdot X_i$$

Furthermore, the malicious party m can aggregate all the contributions from all parties except for himself. To do so, he computes

$$\mathcal{C}_m^{par} = \frac{\mathcal{C}_2}{\mathcal{C}_1^{x_m}}$$

  Malicious contribution generation:
  Following by the decision delay phase, the malicious party m generates his contribution X_m as

$$X_m = \frac{X^*}{\mathcal{C}_m^{par}}$$

and distributes it to other parties according to the round 1 defined in the basic GKA protocol.
  Biased session generation:
  After the distribution of the malicious contribution from party m, all parties perform the *Roud 2*, the *Contributions aggregation* and the *Session key generation and confirmation* phases as defined in the basic GKA protocol.

Motivation. In the basic GKA protocol, both the entity authentication and the key agreement are achieve. Also, the generated session key is fresh and the security of this key is based on the IND-CPA secure encryption scheme and the cryptographic one-way hash function. We stress that, in the scenario that all parties behave honest, the basic GKA protocol is secure. For example, in the smart home, all devices are local. These devices are being controlled by the trust authority (i.e. users) and safeguarded by the gateway.

Whereas, the basic GKA protocol still suffers from the rushing attack when some insiders are malicious. Moreover, the private key of the honest parties may be exposed by the adversary. For example, when the devices in smart homes are connected with smart grids, smart healthcare and intelligent transportation systems, some devices are not physically local. As a result, the rushing attack could be launched and the key could be exposed.

The key exposure is intuitive, which means that the private key of the party being exposed owing to careless storage or the control of devices. Whereas, we stress that due to the key exposure is physical, the corresponding countermeasure in cryptography requires delicate design. The method to resist the key exposure is presented in the enhanced GKA protocol. In the following, we demonstrate how to perform the rushing attack on the basic GKA protocol. Algorithm 3 demonstrates the rushing attack, which is performed by party i. In particular, by performing Algorithm 3, party m can independently decide the session key as $\mathcal{K} = H(X^*)$ previously.

By performing Algorithm 3, it can be observed that the final session key $\mathcal{K}$ is decided by the malicious party m previously. In fact, the final session key $\mathcal{K} = H(X^*)$ no matter what contributions are selected by the honest parties in the group. To perform this attack successfully, what the malicious party need to do is only waiting until all others parties distributes their contributions.

The Key Exposure Resistant GKA Protocol. In the key exposure resistant GKA protocol, the secret sharing scheme is employed to resist the rushing attack with the key exposure resistant property. The details of the key exposure resistant GKA protocol is presented as follows.

- **Initialization:** Select two large primes p and q, such that $q|(p-1)$. Generate a multiplicative cyclic group $\mathbb{G}$ of order $q-1$ and a generator $g \in \mathbb{G}$. Choose a cryptographic hash function H and set the session identifier SID.
- **Secret sharing:** In order to resist the key exposure attack, a trusted third party (TTP) is introduced. The public and private key pair of TTP is (PK, SK), in which SK is secure in our system. For a group of n parties who want to agree on a session key with key exposure resistant property, TTP selects a secret $sk \in Z_q^*$ and a threshold t. Then, TTP selects $t-1$ coefficient $a_1, a_2, a_3, ..., a_{t-1} \in Z_q^*$ at random. After that, TTP constructs the polynomial $f(x)$ as

$$f(x) = sk + a_1 x + a_2 x^2 + ... + a_{t-1} x^{t-1}.$$

- **Key generation:** Each party selects an element x_i in Z_q^* at random and calculates $y_i = g^{x_i}$. The private and public pair of party is (x_i, y_i).
- **Registration:** Each party i registers at TTP. TTP generates a secret share sk_i for party i based on the polynomial $f(x)$. Then, TTP sends the share to party i in a secure channel.
- **Round 1:** In the first round of key agreement, each party i randomly selects its contribution as $X_i \in \mathbb{G}$. After that, for $j = 1...n, (j \neq i)$, party i select a random element $k_{i,j}$ in Z_q^* and calculates $C_{i,j}^1 = g^{k_{i,j}}$ and $C_{i,j}^2 = y_j{}^{k_{i,j}} \cdot X_i$. Then, party i generates $C_{i,j} = (C_{i,j}^1, C_{i,j}^2)$ to party $j, (j = 1...n, j \neq i)$. After that, party i aggregates all the $C_{i,j}$ in a vector as

$$V_i = \{C_{i,1}, C_{i,2}, C_{i,3}, ..., C_{i,i-1}, C_{i,i+1}, ..., C_{i,n}\}.$$

Finally, party i encrypts (V_i, sk_i) and sends the encrypted message to TTP.

- **Round 2:** In the second round of the key agreement, TTP first decrypts all the received message to obtain (V_i, sk_i). With the secret shares, TTP recovers the secret sk' by the Lagrange interpolation. Then, TTP checks if the recovered sk' equal to sk. If $sk' = sk$ holds, TTP aggregates the contributory based on the received vector V_i. Figure 3 illustrates the aggregating process. With vector $V_1, V_2, V_3, ..., V_n$, TTP generates $\mathcal{C}^1, \mathcal{C}^2, \mathcal{C}^3, ..., \mathcal{C}^n$ for party 1 to party n. Here, for party j, $\mathcal{C}^j = \{\mathcal{C}_1^j, \mathcal{C}_2^j, \}$ is calculated as follows.

$$\mathcal{C}_1^j = \prod_{i=1}^{n, i \neq j} C_{i,j}^1 = \prod_{i=1}^{n, i \neq j} g^{k_{i,j}}$$

$$\mathcal{C}_2^j = \prod_{i=1}^{n, i \neq j} C_{i,j}^2 = \prod_{i=1}^{n, i \neq j} y_j{}^{k_{i,j}} \cdot X_i = \prod_{i=1}^{n, i \neq j} g^{x_j k_{i,j}} \cdot X_i$$

	Party 1	Party 2	Party 3	...	Party i	...	Party n
V_1	$\perp$	$C_{1,2}$	$C_{1,3}$	...	$C_{1,i}$	...	$C_{1,n}$
V_2	$C_{2,1}$	$\perp$	$C_{2,3}$	...	$C_{2,i}$	...	$C_{2,n}$
V_3	$C_{3,1}$	$C_{3,2}$	$\perp$	...	$C_{3,i}$	...	$C_{3,n}$
			......				
V_i	$C_{i,1}$	$C_{i,2}$	$C_{i,3}$	...	$\perp$	...	$C_{i,n}$
			......				
V_n	$C_{n,1}$	$C_{n,2}$	$C_{n,3}$	...	$C_{n,i}$	...	$\perp$
	$\mathcal{C}^1$	$\mathcal{C}^2$	$\mathcal{C}^i$	...	$\mathcal{C}^2$	...	$\mathcal{C}^n$

Fig. 3. Aggregation at TTP.

- **Round 3:** In round 3, TPA sends the aggregated contributions to the corresponding party. Then, each party j in the group can calculate the aggregated contributions with his private key x_j and his own contribution X_j. In particular, party j derives the aggregated contributions by calculating the following equation.

$$Con_j = X_j \cdot \frac{C_2^j}{(C_1^j)^{x_j}}$$

– **Session key generation and confirmation:** In order to confirm the aggregated contributions C_j, each party j in the group calculates $Ver_j = H(Con_j\|SID)$ and broadcasts Ver_j Finally, if all the Ver_j, $j = 1...n$ are the same, the session key $\mathcal{K}$ for party j is computed as $\mathcal{K} = H(Con_j)$.

5   Security and Performance Analyses

In this section, the security and performance of the proposed GKA protocols are analyzed.

5.1   Security Analysis

– **Session key security.** The privacy of the session key can be ensured if the ElGamal encryption is IND-CPA secure under the DDH assumption. In particular, under the DDH assumption, the ElGamal encryption is IND-CPA secure. Thus, the security of the contributions is preserved. Moreover, the aggregated contributions is secure due to the homomorphic property of the ElGamal encryption.
– **Rushing attack resistant.** By performing the enhanced GKA protocol, each party can generate the session key unbiased. That is because the contributions generated by each party are encrypted and sent to TTP. Without the private key of TTP, no party can learn the other parties' contributions. In this way, the malicious party can not decide the final session key by observing the other parties' contributions.
– **Key exposure resistant.** In the enhanced GKA protocol, if and only if the recovered secret sk' is equal to the secret sk stored in TTP, the session key can be derived. That is because all the contributions are encrypted by the TTP's public key. Only TTP can derive the aggregated contributions for each party. The exposure of some partys' private keys can not reveal any contribution of the other parties. Moreover, the exposure with at most $t - 1$ secret shares can not recover the secret sk due to the security of the secret sharing scheme. Also note that, by introducing the secret sharing scheme, the proposed protocol can support fault tolerance property. That is, if some parties' secret shares are damaged or lost, the group session key can also be derived.

5.2   Performance Analysis

Properties Comparison. The features of the proposed basic GKA protocol and the enhanced GKA protocol are compared with that of in protocol [24].

Table 2 shows the comparison results, which indicates that the enhanced protocol can support multiparty with various properties such as rushing attack resistant and fault tolerance over the other two protocols. In Table 2, the basic GKA protocol and the enhanced GKA protocol are represented as GKA1 and GKA2, respectively.

Table 2. Properties comparison.

Features	GKA1	GKA2	Protocol [24]
Entity authentication	✓	✓	✓
Key confirmation	✓	✓	✓
Key exposure resistant	×	✓	✓
The number of parties	n	n	2
Rushing attack resistant	×	✓	×
Honest third party	×	×	×
Fault tolerance	×	✓	×
Adaptive	×	✓	×
Communicational rounds	2	3	4

6 Conclusion

In this paper, we focus on the security properties of the GKA protocol. By introducing a TTP and employing the secret sharing scheme, the rushing attack in the GKA protocol can be resisted. Moreover, the key exposure attack is resisted due to the security of the secret sharing scheme. It is worth noting that the employment of the homomorphic encryption protects the privacy of contributions and also reduces the computational overhead of parties. Thus making the proposed GKA protocol practical in resource-constrained environment.

References

1. Aghili, S.F., Mala, H., Shojafar, M., Conti, M.: PAKIT: proactive authentication and key agreement protocol for internet of things. In: IEEE INFOCOM 2019 - IEEE Conference on Computer Communications Workshops (INFOCOM WKSHPS), pp. 348–353 (2019). https://doi.org/10.1109/INFCOMW.2019.8845220
2. Bresson, E., Catalano, D.: Constant round authenticated group key agreement via distributed computation. In: Bao, F., Deng, R., Zhou, J. (eds.) PKC 2004. LNCS, vol. 2947, pp. 115–129. Springer, Heidelberg (2004). https://doi.org/10.1007/978-3-540-24632-9_9

3. Bünz, B., Bootle, J., Boneh, D., Poelstra, A., Wuille, P., Maxwell, G.: Bulletproofs: short proofs for confidential transactions and more. In: 2018 IEEE Symposium on Security and Privacy (SP), pp. 315–334 (2018). https://doi.org/10.1109/SP.2018. 00020

4. Cao, Z., Wang, H., Zhao, Y.: AP-PRE: autonomous path proxy re-encryption and its applications. IEEE Trans. Dependable Secure Comput. **16**(5), 833–842 (2019). https://doi.org/10.1109/TDSC.2017.2714166

5. Chandramowliswaran, N., Srinivasan, S., Muralikrishna, P.: Authenticated key distribution using given set of primes for secret sharing. Syst. Sci. Control Eng. **3**(1), 106–112 (2015)

6. Farash, M.S., Attari, M.A.: A provably secure and efficient authentication scheme for access control in mobile pay-TV systems. Multimed. Tools Appl. **75**(1), 405–424 (2016)

7. Fischlin, M., Günther, F., Schmidt, B., Warinschi, B.: Key confirmation in key exchange: a formal treatment and implications for TLS 1.3. In: 2016 IEEE Symposium on Security and Privacy (SP), pp. 452–469 (2016). https://doi.org/10.1109/ SP.2016.34

8. Harn, L.: Comments on'fair (t, n) threshold secret sharing scheme'. IET Inf. Secur. **8**(6), 303–304 (2014)

9. Harn, L., Fuyou, M.: Multilevel threshold secret sharing based on the Chinese remainder theorem. Inf. Process. Lett. **114**(9), 504–509 (2014)

10. Hu, L., Huang, Y., Yang, D., Zhang, Y., Liu, H.: SSeCloud: using secret sharing scheme to secure keys. In: IOP Conference Series: Earth and Environmental Science, vol. 81, p. 012207. IOP Publishing (2017)

11. Jebri, S., Abid, M., Bouallegue, A.: LTKA-AC: lightweight and trusted key agreement based on IBE with anonymous communication. In: 2017 IEEE/ACS 14th International Conference on Computer Systems and Applications (AICCSA), pp. 1293–1298 (2017). https://doi.org/10.1109/AICCSA.2017.27

12. Jia, X., Wang, D., Nie, D., Luo, X., Sun, J.Z.: A new threshold changeable secret sharing scheme based on the Chinese remainder theorem. Inf. Sci. **473**, 13–30 (2019)

13. Khan, M.A., et al.: An efficient and secure certificate-based access control and key agreement scheme for flying ad-hoc networks. IEEE Trans. Veh. Technol. **70**(5), 4839–4851 (2021). https://doi.org/10.1109/TVT.2021.3055895

14. Kibria, M.G., Nguyen, K., Villardi, G.P., Liao, W.S., Ishizu, K., Kojima, F.: A stochastic geometry analysis of multiconnectivity in heterogeneous wireless networks. IEEE Trans. Veh. Technol. **67**(10), 9734–9746 (2018). https://doi.org/10. 1109/TVT.2018.2863280

15. Li, W., Logenthiran, T., Phan, V.T., Woo, W.L.: A novel smart energy theft system (sets) for IoT-based smart home. IEEE Internet Things J. **6**(3), 5531–5539 (2019). https://doi.org/10.1109/JIOT.2019.2903281

16. Liang, J., Qin, Z., Xiao, S., Ou, L., Lin, X.: Efficient and secure decision tree classification for cloud-assisted online diagnosis services. IEEE Trans. Dependable Secure Comput. **18**(4), 1632–1644 (2021). https://doi.org/10.1109/TDSC.2019.2922958

17. Liu, W., Wang, S., Tan, X., Xie, Q., Wang, Q.: Identity-based one round key agreement protocol without bilinear pairings. In: 2015 10th International Conference on P2P, Parallel, Grid, Cloud and Internet Computing (3PGCIC), pp. 470–473. IEEE (2015)

18. Rao, F.Y.: On the security of a variant of ELGamal encryption scheme. IEEE Trans. Dependable Secure Comput. **16**(4), 725–728 (2019). https://doi.org/10. 1109/TDSC.2017.2707085

19. Shamir, A.: How to share a secret. Commun. ACM **22**(11), 612–613 (1979)
20. Shen, J., Zhou, T., He, D., Zhang, Y., Sun, X., Xiang, Y.: Block design-based key agreement for group data sharing in cloud computing. IEEE Trans. Dependable Secure Comput. **16**(6), 996–1010 (2019). https://doi.org/10.1109/TDSC.2017.2725953
21. Shen, J., Zhou, T., Lai, J., Li, P., Moh, S.: Secure and efficient data sharing in dynamic vehicular networks. IEEE Internet Things J. **7**(9), 8208–8217 (2020). https://doi.org/10.1109/JIOT.2020.2985324
22. Srinivasan, A., Vasudevan, P.N.: Leakage resilient secret sharing and applications. In: Boldyreva, A., Micciancio, D. (eds.) CRYPTO 2019. LNCS, vol. 11693, pp. 480–509. Springer, Cham (2019). https://doi.org/10.1007/978-3-030-26951-7_17
23. Wang, C., Huang, R., Shen, J., Liu, J., Vijayakumar, P., Kumar, N.: A novel lightweight authentication protocol for emergency vehicle avoidance in VANETs. IEEE Internet Things J. **8**(18), 14248–14257 (2021). https://doi.org/10.1109/JIOT.2021.3068268
24. Wu, L., Wang, J., Choo, K.K.R., He, D.: Secure key agreement and key protection for mobile device user authentication. IEEE Trans. Inf. Forensics Secur. **14**(2), 319–330 (2018)
25. Xiong, H., Qin, Z.: Revocable and scalable certificateless remote authentication protocol with anonymity for wireless body area networks. IEEE Trans. Inf. Forensics Secur. **10**(7), 1442–1455 (2015). https://doi.org/10.1109/TIFS.2015.2414399
26. Yan, Y., Chen, Z., Varadharajan, V., Hossain, M.J., Town, G.E.: Distributed consensus-based economic dispatch in power grids using the Paillier cryptosystem. IEEE Trans. Smart Grid **12**(4), 3493–3502 (2021). https://doi.org/10.1109/TSG.2021.3063712
27. Yang, H., Zhang, J., Qiu, J., Zhang, S., Lai, M., Dong, Z.Y.: A practical pricing approach to smart grid demand response based on load classification. IEEE Trans. Smart Grid **9**(1), 179–190 (2018). https://doi.org/10.1109/TSG.2016.2547883
28. Zhang, L., Wu, Q., Domingo-Ferrer, J., Qin, B., Dong, Z.: Round-efficient and sender-unrestricted dynamic group key agreement protocol for secure group communications. IEEE Trans. Inf. Forensics Secur. **10**(11), 2352–2364 (2015). https://doi.org/10.1109/TIFS.2015.2447933

NIKE from Affine Determinant Programs

Jim Barthel[1][✉] and Răzvan Roşie[2]

[1] University of Luxembourg, Esch-sur-Alzette, Luxembourg
jim.barthel@uni.lu
[2] JAO, Luxembourg, Luxembourg
rosie@jao.eu

Abstract. A multi-party non-interactive key-exchange (NIKE) scheme enables N users to securely exchange a secret key K in a non-interactive manner. It is well-known that NIKE schemes can be obtained assuming the existence of indistinguishability obfuscation (iO).

In this work, we revisit the original, iO-based, provably-secure NIKE construction by Boneh and Zhandry, aiming to simplify it. The core idea behind our protocol is to replace the functionality of the obfuscator with the one of an affine determinant program (ADP). Although ADPs have been designed with the purpose of attaining indistinguishability obfuscation, such implication is left open for general circuits.

The ingredients enabling to prove the security of our scheme stem into a more careful analysis of the branching programs needed to build ADPs. In particular, we show:

1. An intuitive indistinguishability notion defined for ADPs of puncturable pseudorandom functions (PRFs) is sufficient to prove security for NIKE.
2. A set of simple conditions based on ADP's branching program topology that are sufficient for proving indistinguishability of ADPs. We leave open the question of finding ADPs satisfying them.

Keywords: NIKE · Branching programs · ADP

1 Introduction

Key-exchange [8] is arguably the simplest public-key cryptographic protocol, and probably one of the most used in real world applications. Intriguingly, since its introduction for the case of two parties, and the advances in exchanging keys between three parties [14], few progress has been achieved in obtaining provable, non-interactive key-exchange protocols between multiple parties (at least four for the problem at hand).

In the last decade, it has been shown that the existence of secure advanced cryptographic primitives, such as multilinear maps [9] or indistinguishability obfuscation (iO) [1] would imply the existence of such non-interactive key-exchange protocols [5]. Until recently, the security of the former cryptographic primitives was less understood, and the problem of building NIKE schemes

© Springer Nature Switzerland AG 2021
Q. Huang and Y. Yu (Eds.): ProvSec 2021, LNCS 13059, pp. 98–115, 2021.
https://doi.org/10.1007/978-3-030-90402-9_6

remained open. A stream of recent works [3,11,12] culminated with the break-through result that iO can be obtained from well-understood assumptions [13]. Such results posit the problem of obtaining NIKE in the realizable landscape.

In our work, we propose a new instantiation of the NIKE scheme put forth by Boneh and Zhandry [5], while replacing the circuit to be iO-obfuscated with an affine determinant program [3]. To this end, we proceed with a brief description of the scheme we use, followed by the techniques that allow to plug in the ADP.

1.1 Prior Work on NIKE

NIKE from iO. Boneh and Zhandry [5] put forth a simple NIKE protocol, which can be described as follows: assume that N participants into the protocol have access to a public set of parameters pp. Each participant computes and publishes terms that are designated to the remaining N-1 entities. Finally, each party u, by knowing its own secret key $sk^{(u)}$ as well as the N-1 terms published by other parties, is able to compute the exchanged key.

Concretely, imagine the exchanged key is retrieved as the output of a specific circuit $\mathscr{C}$ applied over the input domain $\{0,1\}^{N \times h'}$ where h' denotes the length of each $sk^{(u)}$. Essentially, $\mathscr{C}$ does two things: (1) performs a check that someone using the circuit is authorized to evaluate the key exchange function; (2) computes the result of a (puncturable) PRF over the joint inputs, then outputs K as an exchanged key (see Fig. 1).

$$
\begin{array}{l}
C_{\mathsf{pPRF.k}}\left(\mathsf{sk}^{(u)}, u, \overline{\mathsf{sk}^{(1)}}, \ldots, \overline{\mathsf{sk}^{(N)}}\right): \\
\hline
\textbf{if } \mathsf{PRG}(\mathsf{sk}^{(u)}) = \overline{\mathsf{sk}^{(u)}}: \\
\quad K \leftarrow \mathsf{pPRF}\left(\mathsf{pPRF.k}, \overline{\mathsf{sk}^{(1)}}\|\ldots\|\overline{\mathsf{sk}^{(N)}}\right) \\
\quad \textbf{return } K \\
\textbf{return } \bot
\end{array}
$$

Fig. 1. Each party u knows its own private key $sk^{(u)}$ and releases $\overline{sk^{(u)}} \leftarrow PRG\left(sk^{(u)}\right)$. On input $u, sk^{(u)}$, and the released values $\left\{\overline{sk^{(v)}}\right\}_{v \in [N]}$, the circuit checks whether $PRG\left(sk^{(u)}\right) = \overline{sk^{(u)}}$, in which case a PRF value is returned.

The verification subroutine of the circuit $\mathscr{C}$ requires to know the pre-image of some PRG value: user u is required to provide $sk^{(u)}$ in order to be checked against the already published $\overline{sk^{(u)}}$, where $\overline{sk^{(u)}} \leftarrow PRG(sk^{(u)})$. If the check passes, evaluate pPRF over all published values and learn

$$
K \leftarrow \mathsf{pPRF.Eval}\left(\mathsf{pPRF.k}, \overline{\mathsf{sk}^{(1)}}\|\ldots\|\overline{\mathsf{sk}^{(N)}}\right).
$$

For the proof, the authors require the PRG to stretch the inputs over a larger output domain, emphasizing that a length-doubling PRG suffices for this task.

The correctness of the scheme follows as all parties evaluate the pPRF in the same point and under the same key. Intuitively, security stems from the necessity to provide a preimage for PRG in order to be able to evaluate pPRF.

1.2   Our Result and Techniques

Our main result is a new instantiation of the multi-partite NIKE protocol proposed in [5]. Our key ingredients are affine determinant programs for puncturable functionalities reaching a natural indistinguishability notion.

Theorem 1 (Informal). *Assuming the existence of secure length-doubling pseudorandom generators, secure puncturable pseudorandom functions in* NC^1, *and indistinguishably-secure affine determinant programs, there exists a secure* NIKE *scheme for N parties.*

As our NIKE construction is close to the one in [5], we begin with the intuition for affine determinant programs (introduced in [3]) for PRFs and then present an overview of our techniques.

Affine Determinant Programs - Setup. The idea behind ADPs is to use branching programs in conjunction with decomposability. Consider a PRF keyed[1] by k and its ith bit restriction PRF^i as a function from $\{0,1\}^{k+n}$ to $\{0,1\}$. Assume the circuit representation of PRF^i is $\mathscr{C}^i$ and that it belongs to NC^1 (this is the class we are interested in). We can infer that its branching program has polynomial size [6]. For each $\mathscr{C}^i$, let $\mathbf{G}^i_{k||\text{input}}$ denote the adjacency matrix[2] of its branching program BP^i. Following known techniques [10], we slightly post-process this adjacency matrix of BP^i, by removing its first column and last row, in order to obtain $\overline{\mathbf{G}}^i_{k||\text{input}}$. Then, we left/right multiply it with random binary invertible matrices $\mathbf{L}^i, \mathbf{R}^i$. The resulting matrix $\mathbf{T}^i_{k||\text{input}}$ satisfies: $\det \underbrace{\left(\mathbf{L}^i \cdot \overline{\mathbf{G}}^i_{k||\text{input}} \cdot \mathbf{R}^i \right)}_{\mathbf{T}^i_{k||\text{input}}} = BP^i(k||\text{input}) = \mathscr{C}^i_k(\text{input})$, where "det"

denotes the determinant over $\mathbb{F}_2$. The *crux* idea is to decompose *each entry* (u,v) of $\mathbf{L}^i \cdot \overline{\mathbf{G}}^i_{k||\text{input}} \cdot \mathbf{R}^i$ into sums of input_j-dependent monomials:

$$\mathbf{T}^i_{u,v,k||\text{input}} \leftarrow \mathbf{T}^i_{u,v,k} + \mathbf{T}^i_{u,v,\text{input}_1} + \cdots + \mathbf{T}^i_{u,v,\text{input}_n}, \tag{1}$$

where each $\mathbf{T}^i_{u,v,\vec{0}_j}, \mathbf{T}^i_{u,v,\vec{1}_j}$ is a sum of degree-three monomials of the form: $l_\alpha \cdot g_\beta \cdot r_\gamma$. Oversimplified, to enable the simulation of $\mathbf{T}^i_{u,v,k||\text{input}}$ in Eq. (1), we reveal all pairs $\{\mathbf{T}^i_{u,v,\vec{0}_j}, \mathbf{T}^i_{u,v,\vec{1}_j}\}$, as depicted in Fig. 2.

---

[1] The length of the key is k.

[2] The structure of adjacency matrix is settled by both k and input, a fact reflected in the notation $\mathbf{G}^i_{k||\text{input}}$.

Fig. 2. An element $\mathbf{T}^i_{u,v,\mathsf{k}}$ is provided for the bits of the key k, while elements $\mathbf{T}^i_{u,v,\mathsf{input}_j}$ correspond to the bits in the binary decomposition of the message. We assume $\mathsf{input} = (0, 1, \ldots, 0, 0)$, meaning that the coloured encodings $\{\mathbf{T}^i_{u,v,\bar{0}_1}, \mathbf{T}^i_{u,v,\bar{1}_2}, \ldots, \mathbf{T}^i_{u,v,\bar{0}_{|\mathsf{input}|-1}}, \mathbf{T}^i_{u,v,\bar{0}_{|\mathsf{input}|}}\}$ are selected and added to $\mathbf{T}^i_{u,v,\mathsf{k}}$.

The setup of the ADP proceeds by generating the branching programs of each boolean function PRF^i and the corresponding adjacency matrices. Then, it samples the invertible matrices $\mathbf{L}^i, \mathbf{R}^i$ to obtain the set:

$$\{\mathbf{T}^i_{u,v,\mathsf{k}}, \mathbf{T}^i_{u,v,\mathsf{input}_1}, \ldots, \mathbf{T}^i_{u,v,\mathsf{input}_n}\}$$

These values are published, for all i and for all entries (u, v) and constitute the *affine determinant program* corresponding to the keyed function PRF.

Affine Determinant Programs - Evaluation. Running the ADP.Eval is straightforward. Given the input message $\mathsf{input} := (\mathsf{input}_1, \ldots, \mathsf{input}_n)$, a first step reconstructs $\mathbf{T}^i_{u,v,\mathsf{k}\|\mathsf{input}} \leftarrow \mathbf{T}^i_{u,v,\mathsf{k}} + \mathbf{T}^i_{u,v,\mathsf{input}_1} + \cdots + \mathbf{T}^i_{u,v,\mathsf{input}_n}$, by simply selecting the terms corresponding to $\mathsf{input}_1, \ldots, \mathsf{input}_n$. In this way, we recover a value $\mathbf{T}^i_{u,v,\mathsf{k}\|\mathsf{input}}$ corresponding to some position (u, v).

Repeating this reconstruction for every entry (u, v), we recover the desired matrix $\mathbf{T}^i_{\mathsf{k}\|\mathsf{input}}$. Then, ADP.Eval computes the determinant of $\mathbf{T}^i_{\mathsf{k}\|\mathsf{input}}$ and recovers one bit in the output of $\mathscr{C}$. This step is repeated for every output bit i of $\mathscr{C}$. We stress that $\mathbf{T}^i_{\mathsf{k}\|\mathsf{input}} \leftarrow \mathbf{L}^i \cdot \overline{\mathbf{G}}^i_{\mathsf{k}\|\mathsf{input}} \cdot \mathbf{R}^i$, and its determinant is in fact $\mathscr{C}^i_\mathsf{k}(\mathsf{input})$ ($\mathscr{C}$'s i^{th} output bit) where $\overline{\mathbf{G}}^i_{\mathsf{k}\|\mathsf{input}}$ is "close to" the adjacency matrix of BP.

Affine Determinant Programs - Reducing the Size of the Program. The size of ADPs can be improved in the following way: instead of releasing both values $\mathbf{T}^i_{u,v,\bar{0}_j}$ and $\mathbf{T}^i_{u,v,\bar{1}_j}$, we add to $\mathbf{T}^i_{u,v,\mathsf{k}}$ the sum corresponding to the *all-zero* message: $\mathbf{T}^i_{u,v,\mathsf{k}} + \sum_{j=1}^n \mathbf{T}^i_{u,v,\bar{0}_j}$. To ensure correctness, we release the difference terms corresponding to each:

$$\mathbf{T}^i_{\Delta_{u,v,j}} \leftarrow \mathbf{T}^i_{u,v,\bar{1}_j} - \mathbf{T}^i_{u,v,\bar{0}_j}, \tag{2}$$

which can be used to reconstruct the sum in Eq. (1). We stress that a user could always recover the difference of monomial-sums depending on 1 and 0 in position (u, v) if it was given both $\mathbf{T}^i_{u,v,\bar{0}_j}$ and $\mathbf{T}^i_{u,v,\bar{1}_j}$. Informally, by providing the difference, we also reduce the amount of information provided to the adversary.

NIKE from IND-Secure ADPs. We observe that ADPs corresponding to *puncturable* PRFs that enjoy a natural indistinguishability property, suffice for our proof. By indistinguishability, we mean that given two different punctured keys[3] for two different points, which are embedded in two equivalent circuits[4], the ADPs of such circuits are indistinguishable. We are able to prove NIKE security under indistinguishable ADPs only for circuits which have *identical* structure but embed different keys. This latter fact constrains us to use a punctured key in our real NIKE protocol in order to make the proof of Theorem 1 work, as usually pPRF.Eval($\cdot$) and pPRF.PuncEval($\cdot$) have different circuit representations, and ADP indistinguishability will not be achievable.

More interesting than the NIKE proof is the ADP indistinguishability. In the full version we provide a thorough analysis of ADPs' security. To this end, we rewrite ADPs into a form that isolates the differing variables occurring in the BP's adjacency matrices. The lack of standard complexity assumption to work with forces us to investigate the perfect security. Finally, we show that ADPs admitting BP representations having the first line set to $(0, \ldots, 0, 1)$ and where the input dependent nodes occur "after" the sensitive nodes admit perfectly secure ADPs. We leave open the problem of obtaining such BP representation.

Paper Organization. In Sect. 2, we introduce the standard notations to be adopted throughout the paper, followed by the definitions of the primitives that we use as building blocks. Section 3 reviews the construction of randomized encodings from branching programs and introduces the novel concept of augmented branching programs In Sect. 4, we describe our NIKE scheme. Section 5 describes our conditions on circuits and BPs to admit indistinguishably-secure ADPs, while in the full version we provide a detail look into ADPs and prove they achieve indistinguishability.

2   Background

Notations. We denote the security parameter by $\lambda \in \mathbb{N}^*$ and we assume it is implicitly given to all algorithms in the unary representation 1^λ. An algorithm is equivalent to a Turing machine. Algorithms are assumed to be randomized unless stated otherwise; ppt stands for "probabilistic polynomial-time" in the security parameter (rather than the total length of its inputs). Given a randomized algorithm $\mathcal{A}$ we denote the action of running $\mathcal{A}$ on input(s) $(1^\lambda, x_1, \ldots)$ with uniform random coins r and assigning the output(s) to $(y_1, \ldots)$ by $(y_1, \ldots) \leftarrow_{\$} \mathcal{A}(1^\lambda, x_1, \ldots; r)$. When $\mathcal{A}$ is given oracle access to some procedure $\mathcal{O}$, we write $\mathcal{A}^{\mathcal{O}}$. For a finite set S, we denote its cardinality by $|S|$ and the action of sampling a uniformly at random element x from X by $x \leftarrow_{\$} X$. We let bold variables such as $\vec{w}$ represent column vectors. Similarly, bold capitals usually stand for matrices (e.g. $\mathbf{A}$). A subscript $\mathbf{A}_{i,j}$ indicates an entry in the

---

[3] This is a significant difference to [5].

[4] The circuits are equivalent by preventing the evaluation of the pPRF at the punctured points through simple sanity checks.

matrix. We abuse notation and write $\alpha^{(u)}$ to denote that variable α is associated to some entity u. For any variable $k \in \mathbb{N}^*$, we define $[k] := \{1, \ldots, k\}$. A real-valued function $\mathrm{NEGL}(\lambda)$ is negligible if $\mathrm{NEGL}(\lambda) \in \mathcal{O}(\lambda^{-\omega(1)})$. We denote the set of all negligible functions by NEGL. Throughout the paper $\bot$ stands for a special error symbol. We use $\|$ to denote concatenation. For completeness, we recall standard algorithmic and cryptographic primitives to be used. We consider circuits as the prime model of computation for representing (abstract) functions. Unless stated otherwise, we use n to denote the input length of the circuit, s for its size and d for its depth.

2.1 Randomized Encodings

Definition 1 (Randomized Encoding Scheme). *A randomized encoding scheme* RE *for a function* $f : \{0,1\}^n \to \mathcal{Y}$ *consists of a randomness distribution* $\mathcal{R}$, *an encoding function* Encode $: \{0,1\}^n \times \mathcal{R} \to \{0,1\}^\ell$, *and a decoding function* Decode $: \{0,1\}^\ell \to \mathcal{Y}$. *A randomized encoding scheme* RE $:= (\mathcal{R}, \mathsf{Encode}, \mathsf{Decode})$ *should satisfy:*

- **Correctness.** *For any input* $M \in \{0,1\}^n$,

$$\Pr_{R \leftarrow \mathcal{R}}[\mathsf{Decode}(\mathsf{Encode}(M; R)) = \mathscr{C}(M)] = 1.$$

- **Security.** *For all* $M, M' \in \{0,1\}^n$ *with* $\mathscr{C}(M) = \mathscr{C}(M')$, *the distribution of* Encode$(M; R)$ *is identical to the distribution of* Encode$(M'; R)$ *when sampling* $R \leftarrow_{\$} \mathcal{R}$.

The definition of security can be relaxed, just requiring that Encode$(M; R)$ *and* Encode$(M'; R)$ *cannot be effectively distinguished by small circuits. Formally:*

- (s, δ)-**Security.** *For all* $M, M' \in \{0,1\}^n$ *such that* $\mathscr{C}(M) = \mathscr{C}(M')$, *for any circuit* $\mathscr{C} : \{0,1\}^\ell \to \{0,1\}$ *of size at most* s,

$$\Pr_{R \leftarrow_{\$} \mathcal{R}}[\mathscr{C}(\mathsf{Encode}(M; R)) = 1] - \Pr_{R \leftarrow_{\$} \mathcal{R}}[\mathscr{C}(\mathsf{Encode}(M'; R)) = 1] \le \delta.$$

2.2 Multi-party Non-interactive Key-Exchange

Non-interactive key-exchange (multi-partite) is a beautiful problem in cryptography. All known, provably-secure constructions rely on either multilinear maps or iO constructions. NIKE definition follows.

Definition 2. *A non-interactive key-exchange (NIKE) scheme consists in a triple of polynomial-time algorithms* (Setup, Publish, KeyGen) *behaving as follows:*

- pars $\leftarrow_{\$}$ Setup$(1^\lambda, N)$: *given the security parameter* λ *in unary and the number of participant parties* N, *the algorithm generates the public parameters* pars.
- $(\mathsf{pk}^{(u)}, \mathsf{sk}^{(u)}) \leftarrow_{\$}$ Publish(pars, u): *each party* u *of* N *taking part into the protocol derives its own secret and public keys. While* $\mathsf{sk}^{(u)}$ *is kept secret,* $\mathsf{pk}^{(u)}$ *is publicly disclosed.*

- $K \leftarrow_s \mathsf{KeyGen}(\mathsf{pars}, u, \mathsf{sk}^{(u)}, \mathsf{pk}^{(u)}, \mathsf{pk}^{(v \in S)})$: *the key-generation procedure corresponding to party $u \in [N]$ uses its secret key $\mathsf{sk}^{(u)}$ together with the public keys of all participants $v \in [N]$ to derive the common key K.*

The **correctness** requirement states that any two parties u and v must derive the same key K: $\forall (u, v) \in [N] \times [N]$:

$$\Pr \left[K_u = K_v \,\middle|\, \begin{array}{l} K_u \leftarrow_s \mathsf{KeyGen}(\mathsf{pars}, u, \mathsf{sk}^{(u)}, \mathsf{pk}^{(v \in [N])}) \ \wedge \\ K_v \leftarrow_s \mathsf{KeyGen}(\mathsf{pars}, v, \mathsf{sk}^{(v)}, \mathsf{pk}^{(u \in [N])}) \end{array} \right] \in 1 - \mathrm{NEGL}(\lambda).$$

Security: The security experiment we present corresponds to the *static* version of the one presented in [5]. Namely, the advantage of any ppt-bounded adversary in winning the game defined in Fig. 3 (left) is bounded:

$$\mathbf{Adv}_{\mathcal{A}, \mathsf{NIKE}}^{\mathsf{IND-NIKE}}(\lambda) := \left| \Pr \left[1 \leftarrow_s \mathsf{IND} - \mathsf{NIKE}_{\mathsf{NIKE}}^{\mathcal{A}}(\lambda) \right] - \frac{1}{2} \right| \in \mathrm{NEGL}(\lambda).$$

$\mathsf{IND} - \mathsf{NIKE}_{\mathsf{NIKE}}^{\mathcal{A}, N}(\lambda)$:

$b \leftarrow_s \{0, 1\}$
$\mathsf{pp} \leftarrow_s \mathsf{NIKE.Setup}(1^\lambda, N)$
for $u \in [N]$:
$\quad (\mathsf{sk}^{(u)}, \mathsf{pk}^{(u)}) \leftarrow_s \mathsf{NIKE.Publish}(\mathsf{pp}, u)$
$K \leftarrow \mathsf{NIKE.KeyGen}\left(\mathsf{pp}, 1, \mathsf{sk}^{(1)}, \{\mathsf{pk}^{(u)}\}_{u \in [N]}\right)$
if $b = 1$, **then** $K \leftarrow \{0, 1\}^{|K|}$
$b' \leftarrow \mathcal{A}\left(1^\lambda, \mathsf{pp}, K, \{\mathsf{pk}^{(u)}\}_{u \in [N]}\right)$
return $(b' \stackrel{?}{=} b)$

$\mathsf{PRF}_{\mathsf{PRF}}^{\mathcal{A}}(\lambda)$:

$b \leftarrow_s \{0, 1\}$; $\mathsf{L} \leftarrow \emptyset$
$K \leftarrow_s \mathsf{Setup}(1^\lambda)$
$b' \leftarrow_s \mathcal{A}^{\mathsf{Prf}(\cdot)}(1^\lambda)$
return $(b' \stackrel{?}{=} b)$

Proc. $\mathsf{Prf}(M)$:
if $M \in \mathsf{L}$ **then return** $\mathsf{L}[M]$
$Y \leftarrow \mathsf{PRF}(K, M)$
if $b = 0$ **then** $Y \leftarrow_s \{0, 1\}^{|Y|}$
$\mathsf{L} \leftarrow \mathsf{L} \cup \{(M, Y)\}$
return Y

Fig. 3. Games defining the security of pseudorandom functions (right), NIKE (left).

2.3   Affine Determinant Programs

Section 1 provides the intuition behind Affine Determinant Programs. Below, we formalize the notion, as introduced in [3], but postpone the formal construction from randomized encodings of branching programs to Sect. 3.3.

Definition 3 (Affine Determinant Programs). *An affine determinant program consists of two ppt algorithms:*

- Prog $\leftarrow_\$$ ADP.Setup($1^\lambda, \mathscr{C}$): *the* Setup *is a randomized algorithm such that given a circuit description $\mathscr{C}$ of some function $\mathscr{C} : \{0,1\}^n \to \{0,1\}$, output a program* Prog *consisting of $n + 1$ square matrices $\mathbf{T}_i$ over some algebraic structure $\mathfrak{S}$ and having dimensions* poly(n). *The matrices correspond to $\mathscr{C}$.*
- $b \leftarrow$ ADP.Eval(Prog, M): *given the program* Prog *and some input M, return a value b. b is computed as the determinant of the subset sum: $\mathbf{T}_0 + \sum_{i=1}^n \mathbf{T}_i^{M_i}$.*

Correctness: *For all $M \in \{0,1\}^n$, it holds that*

$$\Pr\left[\mathscr{C}(M) = \text{ADP.Eval(Prog}, M) \mid \text{Prog} \leftarrow_\$ \text{ADP.Setup}(1^\lambda, \mathscr{C}) \right] = 1.$$

Security: *We say that a* ADP *scheme is* IND $-$ ADP *secure with respect to a class of circuits $\mathcal{C}_\lambda$, if $\forall (\mathscr{C}_1, \mathscr{C}_2) \in \mathcal{C}_\lambda \times \mathcal{C}_\lambda$ such that $\forall M \in \{0,1\}^\lambda, \mathscr{C}_1(M) = \mathscr{C}_2(M)$ it holds that*

$$\left| \Pr\left[b \leftarrow_\$ \mathcal{A}(1^\lambda, \text{Prog}) \mid b \leftarrow_\$ \{0,1\} \wedge \text{Prog} \leftarrow_\$ \text{ADP.Setup}(1^\lambda, \mathscr{C}_b) \right] - \frac{1}{2} \right| \in \text{NEGL}(\lambda).$$

The security definition above makes clear the link between the security of an iO obfuscator [1] and indistinguishability for ADPs. Trivially, a secure IND $-$ ADP affine determinant program gives rise to an indistinguishability obfuscator for the specific class of circuits.

3 Warm-Up: ADP from Randomized Encodings

3.1 Randomized Encodings via Branching Programs

A branching programs corresponds to a sequential evaluation of a function. Depending on each input bit, a specific branch of a circuit computing the function is followed until a terminal node – 0 or 1 – is reached (we assume we only work with single bit output functions). We highlight that any function $\mathscr{C} : \{0,1\}^n \to \{0,1\}$ in NC^1 admits a polynomial size branching program representation. As a consequence of this fact, any function $\mathscr{C}' : \{0,1\}^n \to \{0,1\}^{n'}$ can be thought of as a concatenation of n' branching programs, each outputting a single bit. In an acclaimed result, Barrington [2] shows that the shorter the depth of the circuit representation of $\mathscr{C}$, the shorter the length of the branching program. In independent results, Ben-Or and Cleve [7] show a matrix-based version of Barrington's proof, where the length of the branching program is *constant* for constant depth circuits.

In this work, we consider $\mathbf{G}_M$ to be the adjacency matrix corresponding to the branching program of some $\mathscr{C} : \{0,1\}^{|M|} \to \{0,1\}$. Let, for technical reasons, the main diagonal be 1s and let each row have at most one extra 1 apart from the 1 appearing on the main diagonal. Let $\overline{\mathbf{G}}_M$ stand for the matrix obtained by removing the first column and the last row of $\mathbf{G}_M$. As shown in

[10], $\mathscr{C}(M) = \det(\overline{\mathbf{G}}_M)$. Furthermore, two matrices $\mathbf{R}_l$ and $\mathbf{R}_r$ (sampled from a designated distribution) exist, such that the following relation holds:

$$\mathbf{R}_l \cdot \overline{\mathbf{G}}_M \cdot \mathbf{R}_r = \left(\begin{array}{c|c} \mathbf{0} & \mathscr{C}(M) \\ \hline \mathbf{I} & \mathbf{0} \end{array}\right) = \begin{pmatrix} 0 & 0 & \ldots & 0 & \mathscr{C}(M) \\ 1 & 0 & \ldots & 0 & 0 \\ 0 & 1 & \ldots & 0 & 0 \\ \vdots & \vdots & & \vdots & \vdots \\ 0 & 0 & \ldots & 1 & 0 \end{pmatrix} = \overline{\mathbf{G}}_{\mathscr{C}(M)} \in \mathrm{GF}(2)^{m \times m}$$

Such a representation of $\mathscr{C}(M)$, as a product of fixed matrices $\mathbf{R}_l$ and $\mathbf{R}_r$ plays a role in the simulation security of the randomized encoding. Concretely, the value $\mathscr{C}(M)$ is given to the simulator, which, in turn, is able to simulate a product of either full-ranked matrices or of rank $m-1$, as enforced by the value of $\mathscr{C}(M)$. Therefore, this representation confers an innate randomized encoding. The decoder in the randomized encoding has to compute the determinant of $\mathbf{R}_l \cdot \overline{\mathbf{G}}_M \cdot \mathbf{R}_r$ and recover the value of $\mathscr{C}(M)$, given that $\mathbf{R}_l, \mathbf{R}_r$ are full ranked matrices. For clarity, $\mathbf{R}_r \in \mathrm{GF}(2)^{m \times m}$ and $\mathbf{R}_l \in \mathrm{GF}(2)^{m \times m}$ have the following forms:

$$\mathbf{R}_r = \begin{pmatrix} 1 & 0 & 0 & \ldots & 0 & \$ \\ 0 & 1 & 0 & \ldots & 0 & \$ \\ \vdots & \vdots & \vdots & & \vdots & \vdots \\ 0 & 0 & 0 & \ldots & 1 & \$ \\ 0 & 0 & 0 & \ldots & 0 & 1 \end{pmatrix}, \quad \mathbf{R}_l = \begin{pmatrix} 1 & \$ & \$ & \ldots & \$ & \$ \\ 0 & 1 & \$ & \ldots & \$ & \$ \\ \vdots & \vdots & \vdots & & \vdots & \vdots \\ 0 & 0 & 0 & \ldots & 1 & \$ \\ 0 & 0 & 0 & \ldots & 0 & 1 \end{pmatrix}.$$

A generalization of the previous observation would use different distributions for $\mathbf{R}_l, \mathbf{R}_r$. To this end, let $\mathbf{L}$ and $\mathbf{R}$ be two matrices sampled uniformly at random from the set of invertible matrices over $\mathrm{GF}(2)^{m \times m}$ (i.e., $\mathbf{R}_l$ and $\mathbf{R}_r$ are full rank). One can express $\mathbf{L} \leftarrow \mathbf{L}' \cdot \mathbf{R}_l$ and $\mathbf{R} \leftarrow \mathbf{R}_r \cdot \mathbf{R}'$. Note that:

$$\mathbf{L} \cdot \overline{\mathbf{G}}_M \cdot \mathbf{R} = (\mathbf{L}' \cdot \mathbf{R}_l) \cdot \overline{\mathbf{G}}_M \cdot (\mathbf{R}_r \cdot \mathbf{R}) = \mathbf{L}' \cdot (\mathbf{R}_l \cdot \overline{\mathbf{G}}_M \cdot \mathbf{R}_r) \cdot \mathbf{R}$$

$$= \mathbf{L}' \cdot \overline{\mathbf{G}}_{\mathscr{C}(M)} \cdot \mathbf{R}' \tag{3}$$

Since $\mathbf{L}'$ and $\mathbf{R}'$ are full-rank matrices, $\det\left(\mathbf{L} \cdot \overline{\mathbf{G}}_M \cdot \mathbf{R}\right) = \det\left(\overline{\mathbf{G}}_M\right) = \mathscr{C}(M)$. On a different note, we can observe that each of the $m \times m$ entries of the resulting matrix $\mathbf{T}_M \leftarrow \mathbf{L} \cdot \overline{\mathbf{G}}_M \cdot \mathbf{R}$, can be expressed as a sum of monomials of degree three. As noted in [10], while "splitting" each entry $\mathbf{T}_{i,j}$ into monomials, no monomial depends on more than one input bit of M. Also, each monomial includes one component from each of $\mathbf{L}$ and $\mathbf{R}$. Put differently, each monomial contains at most one entry from $\overline{\mathbf{G}}_M$, which is M-dependent. We return to such a representation while reaching the proof of our construction.

3.2 Augmenting NC^1 Branching Programs for Keyed Functions

This part will be used exclusively in the proof provided in the full version and readers may skip it for the moment and return to it later. In short, we introduce a method to *augment* a branching program with a set of intermediate nodes without changing the behaviour of the program, having the purpose of isolating "sensitive" variables. We use the terminology introduced in Sect. 3.1. To this end, consider the branching program BP corresponding to some keyed function represented by $\mathscr{C}(k\|M)$; its graph representation consists of two complementary sets of nodes: one containing the nodes depending on the secret (k), and the other ones depending on the input (the message M^5). Assume the secret key k is fixed (embedded in the circuit), a fact that settles the nodes depending on k in BP.

What we mean through an augmented branching program is an extra set of nodes that is to be added to the graph of BP. Let v denote a vertex depending on k and let u be any other vertex such that there is an arc $v \rightarrow u$ in the digraph representation of BP. We introduce an auxiliary node α between v and u. Now, v is no longer directly connected to u, but rather the link becomes $v \rightarrow \alpha \rightarrow u$. We present this pictorially in Fig. 4.

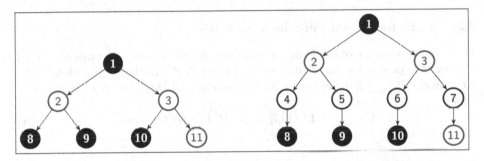

Fig. 4. Left: original branching program. Right: augmented branching program corresponding to $\mathscr{C}$. The auxiliary nodes (4–7) are depicted in blue while red nodes (2,3,11) correspond to nodes settled by the bits of the secret key of the permutation. (Color figure online)

Definition 4 (Augmented Branching Programs for NC^1). *Let* BP *be the branching program corresponding to some circuit $\mathscr{C}_k \in \mathsf{NC}^1$ that embeds k. Let $\mathcal{V}$ denote the set of vertices settled by k. For any vertex $v \in \mathcal{V}$ let u be a vertex such that there exists an arc from v to u. Define the augmented branching program* ABP *by extending the* BP *graph and introducing an intermediate vertex α on the path between any node v depending on k and any child vertex u.*

We show that augmenting a branching program preserves the behaviour (correctness) of the original branching program. It is easy to observe that while working over $\mathbb{F}_2$, computing the determinant is equivalent to computing the permanent [15] of a matrix. To deduce correctness of the output, think at the

---

[5] We assume that any other node (if any) that is input-independent is included in the first set.

determinant as the sum of $m!$ permutations. If there exists a path from the start node to the node that represents 1, then this path, in conjunction with the 1s on the second diagonal will make one of the sums occurring in the development of the permanent be 1.

The size of the augmented branching program ABP is upper-bounded by $3 \times |\mathsf{BP}|$. Assuming the original branching program has $|\mathsf{BP}|$ nodes, each key-dependent node will add two other nodes. Hence the very loose bound of $3 \times |\mathsf{BP}|$.

The main advantage conferred by ABPs is a decoupling of the rows (or columns) in $\mathbf{R}$ (or $\mathbf{L}$) that depend on the sensitive input (k) from the rest of the nodes. More explicitly, when the dependency graph $\mathbf{G}$ is multiplied with $\mathbf{R}$, the lines in $\mathbf{R}$ that are triggered by the nodes depending on k are separated from the lines in $\mathbf{R}$ that are triggered by the message. Similarly, the columns in $\mathbf{L}$ can be split in three independent sets, depending on either k, the message or the auxiliary variables (note the asymmetry to $\mathbf{R}$, where we only split the rows in twain).

3.3   ADPs for Keyed Functions from RE

We turn to the usage of randomized encodings for branching programs described in Sect. 3.1, preserving the goal of instantiating ADPs for keyed functions[6]. We treat each $\mathbf{T}^i_{k||\text{input}}$ independently, as the product of three matrices. Explicitly, this is:

$$\mathbf{T}^i_{k||\text{input}} \leftarrow \mathbf{L}^i \cdot \left(\overline{\mathbf{G}}^i_{k||\text{input}} \cdot \mathbf{R}^i \right), \quad \forall i \in [|\text{input}|] \tag{4}$$

Remark 1. We remind that for the NIKE scheme, the length of input is $N \cdot h$, and we treat each bit $i \in \mu$ of the exchanged key K independently.

ADP.Setup: Using the intuition provided in Sect. 1, we provide an explicit form for:

$$\mathbf{T}^i_{k||\vec{0}} \leftarrow \mathbf{L}^i \cdot \overline{\mathbf{G}}^i_{k||\vec{0}} \cdot \mathbf{R}^i \tag{5}$$

The program Prog^i will consist of $\mathbf{T}^i_{k||\vec{0}}$ as well as the additional set:

$$\left\{ \mathbf{T}^i_{\Delta_j} \leftarrow \mathbf{L}^i \cdot \left(\overline{\mathbf{G}}^i_{k||\vec{1}_j} - \overline{\mathbf{G}}^i_{k||\vec{0}_j} \right) \cdot \mathbf{R}^i \right) \right\}_{j \in [N \cdot h]} \tag{6}$$

for each output bit i.

ADP.Eval : to run Prog^i and recover the output of $\mathscr{C}^i_k(\text{input})$ proceed as follows:

$$\mathscr{C}^i_k(\text{input}) = \det \left(\mathbf{T}^i_k + \sum_{j=1}^{N \cdot h} \text{input}_j \cdot \mathbf{T}^i_{\Delta_j} \right) \tag{7}$$

---

[6] Note that we are mainly interested in ADPs for puncturable PRFs.

4   Multi-party NIKE via ADP

Our NIKE scheme follows from the one in [5]. The main significant difference consists in implementing a puncturable PRFs through affine determinant programs, instead of using the full power of an indistinguishability obfuscator for P/poly[7]. The security analysis follows in Sect. 4.2.

4.1   Our NIKE Scheme

We remind below some useful notations to be used: μ stands for the length of the key to be exchanged, $\mathsf{sk}^{(u)}$ denotes the secret key corresponding to party u having length h, and $\overline{\mathsf{sk}^{(u)}}$ denotes the public key.

Definition 5 (NIKE Scheme for N parties). *Let* $\mathsf{PRG} : \{0,1\}^h \to \{0,1\}^{2h}$ *denote a secure pseudorandom generator, and let* $\mathsf{pPRF} : \{0,1\}^{(N \cdot 2h)+1} \to \{0,1\}^\mu$ *denote a secure puncturable pseudorandom function. Let* $\mathsf{ADP} : \{0,1\}^{N \cdot 2h} \to \{0,1\}$ *denote an affine determinant program reaching indistinguishability. Define a NIKE scheme as follows.*

- $\mathsf{NIKE.Setup}(1^\lambda, N, h, \mu)$: *the* Setup *is given a number of parties* N, *the length* μ *of the exchanged key and the length* h *of each party's secret keys. For each* $i \in [\mu]$, *initiate the public parameters* $\mathsf{pp} \leftarrow \emptyset$. *For each* $i \in [\mu]$, *repeat the following steps:*
  (1) Sample a pPRF *key and puncture it at point* $\mathbf{0}^{N \cdot 2h+1}$:

  $$k_i \leftarrow \mathsf{pPRF.Puncture}(\mathsf{pPRF.KeyGen}(1^\lambda), \mathbf{0}^{N \cdot 2h+1}).$$

  (2) Consider the following circuit $\mathscr{C}^i$:
  (3) Instantiate an ADP from this circuit: $\mathsf{Prog}^i \leftarrow \mathsf{ADP.Setup}(1^\lambda, \mathscr{C}^i_{\mathsf{pPRF}.k_i})$.
  (4) Add to pp *the program* Prog^i: $\mathsf{pp} \leftarrow \mathsf{pp} \cup \mathsf{Prog}^i$. *Publish the public parameters* pp.

- $\mathsf{NIKE.Publish}(\mathsf{pp}, u)$:
  (1) u *samples* $\{\mathsf{sk}_i^{(u)}\}_{i \in [\mu]} \leftarrow_\$ \{0,1\}^h$.
  (2) u *publishes the following value as her public key:* $\overline{\mathsf{sk}_i^{(u)}} \leftarrow \mathsf{PRG}\left(\mathsf{sk}_i^{(u)}\right)$.
  These steps are repeated for all $i \in [\mu]$.

- $\mathsf{NIKE.KeyGen}(\mathsf{pp}, u, \{\mathsf{sk}_i^{(u)}\}_{i \in [\mu]}, \{\mathsf{Prog}^i\}_{i \in [\mu]}, \{\overline{\mathsf{sk}_i^{(v)}}\}_{i \in [\mu], v \in [N]})$:
  (1) Provide to Prog^i *the input* $u, \mathsf{sk}_i^{(u)}, \{\overline{\mathsf{sk}_i^{(v)}}\}_{v \in [N]}$ *and set*

  $$K_i \leftarrow \mathsf{ADP}^i.\mathsf{Eval}\left(\mathsf{Prog}^i, \left(u, \mathsf{sk}_i^{(u)}, \{\overline{\mathsf{sk}_i^{(v)}}\}_{v \in [N]}\right)\right).$$

  Repeat these steps for all $i \in [\mu]$ *(Fig. 5).*

---

[7] An astute reader may notice that, in fact, an iO for NC^1 would suffice here, as we assume the existence of pPRFs in NC^1.

$$\underline{\mathscr{C}^i_{\text{pPRF.k}_i}\left(u, \text{sk}_i^{(u)}, \overline{\text{sk}_i^{(1)}}, \dots, \overline{\text{sk}_i^{(N)}}\right):}$$

$$\textbf{if } \text{PRG}\left(\text{sk}_i^{(u)}\right) = \overline{\text{sk}_i^{(u)}}:$$
$$\quad K \leftarrow \text{pPRF}\left(\text{pPRF.k}_i, 1||\overline{\text{sk}_i^{(1)}}||\dots||\overline{\text{sk}_i^{(N)}}\right)$$
$$\quad \textbf{return } K_i \quad \text{// the } i^{\text{th}} \text{ bit of } K$$
$$\textbf{return } \perp$$

Fig. 5. Note that the pPRF can only be evaluated on half of its input space, as 1 is concatenated to every input. This is a noticeable difference to [5].

Proposition 1. *The construction in Definition 5 is correct.*

Proof (Proposition 1). See full paper.

4.2   Security from IND-Secure ADP

The proof is structured similarly to the one in [5], up to the variation in the usage of ADP. A second notable difference concerns the usage of a punctured PRF key in the real construction: mind the fact that our circuit evaluates the pPRF exclusively in inputs having the first bit set to 1, while the punctured key is punctured under a point having the first bit set to 0. Hence, the pPRF evaluation is always possible. The reason behind embedding a punctured key in the real construction is that we can only prove indistinguishability for ADPs under *identically* structured branching programs. Put differently, it is usually the case that the *normal* and *punctured* evaluation procedures differ for existing pPRFs in NC^1, while we want a unique pPRF.Eval procedure (e.g., [4]).

We also stress that we consider only the static security notion (Definition 5).

Theorem 2. *Let NIKE be the scheme described in Sect. 4.1. Let PRG be a secure pseudorandom generator and pPRF denote a secure puncturable pseudorandom function. Then, the NIKE scheme in Sect. 4.1 is secure according to Definition 5.*

Proof (Theorem 2). The proof follows through a hybrid argument.

Game$_0$: this is the real game, where the adversary is provided either the real exchanged key K or some value sampled uniformly at random.

Game$_{1.0}$: is identical to Game$_0$.

Game$_{1.u}$: in this game, we change the distribution of the published parameters pp; instead of issuing $\overline{\text{sk}^{(u)}}$, as the output of the $\text{PRG}(\text{sk}^{(u)})$, party u samples $\overline{\text{sk}^{(u)}}$ over $\{0,1\}^{2h}$. The distance to the previous game is bounded by the security of the PRG. Most importantly, the newly sampled point is not in the co-domain of the PRG with overwhelming probability, due to the PRG stretch.

$Game_{1.N}$: all public parameters $\overline{sk^{(u)}}$ are sampled uniformly.

$Game_2$: in this game, the original puncturable PRF key is replaced with a new one, which is punctured in the point $1||sk^{(1)}||\ldots sk^{(N)}$. Mind the fact that originally, the key has been punctured in the all-0 point, while the pPRF has been evaluated in an input that always began with 1 (i.e. the evaluation happened for all inputs); for the second case, we note that the PRF will not evaluate over $(\overline{sk^{(1)}}||\ldots||\overline{sk^{(N)}})$ as these points have no pre-image in the PRG domain. This happens thanks to the stretch of the PRG. Therefore, the two circuits are equivalent. The advantage of any adversary in noticing this game hope is negligible, down to the $IND - ADP$ security of our ADP,

In $Game_2$, we can bound the advantage of an adversary in retrieving a bit in the K by the advantage of an adversary in guessing the output of the pPRF in the challenge (punctured) point. Concretely, the pPRF game provides the reduction with a key punctured in the challenge point. This punctured key will be embedded into the circuit. The adversary is also provided with the challenge value the pPRF game provides, which corresponds to either the real NIKE key K (i.e. the real pPRF evaluation) or a uniform value. If the adversary correctly guesses, then it wins the pPRF game. We apply the union bound, and conclude that the advantage of any ppt bounded adversary in winning the $IND - NIKE$ game is upper bounded by:

$$\mathbf{Adv}^{IND-NIKE}_{\mathcal{A},NIKE}(\lambda) \leq \mu \cdot N \cdot \mathbf{Adv}^{prg}_{\mathcal{A}_1,PRG}(\lambda) + \mu \cdot \mathbf{Adv}^{IND-ADP}_{\mathcal{A}_2,ADP}(\lambda) + \mu \cdot \mathbf{Adv}^{puncture}_{\mathcal{A}_3,pPRF}(\lambda) \quad (8)$$

where the right hand side is negligible. $\square$

5   Sufficiency Conditions for IND-Secure ADP

Section 1 provides the intuition behind Affine Determinant Programs. The security definition of ADPs makes clear the link between the security of an iO obfuscator [1] and indistinguishability for ADPs. Trivially, a secure $IND - ADP$ affine determinant program gives rise to an indistinguishability obfuscator for our specific class of circuits.

Furthermore, we can strengthen the security definition in the following sense: for specific classes of functions, it can be the case that $ADP.Setup(1^\lambda, \mathscr{C}_0; R_0) = ADP.Setup(1^\lambda, \mathscr{C}_1; R_1)$. That is, for two equivalent functions, we obtain the same implementation under two different sets of randomness coins, namely R and R'.

Definition 6 (Colliding-Secure ADPs). *We say that two different circuits $\mathscr{C}_0$ and $\mathscr{C}_1$ admit ADP implementations that are colliding-secure if for any R_0, there exists a unique R_1 such that:*

$$ADP.Setup(1^\lambda, \mathscr{C}_0; R_0) = ADP.Setup(1^\lambda, \mathscr{C}_1; R_1).$$

5.1   Admissible Classes of Functions for Matrix-Based ADPs

A relevant theory should link affine determinant programs to existing problems in cryptographic landscape. Such problems are, for instance, multi-party non-interactive key-exchange schemes or indistinguishability obfuscation. The two primitives can be obtained if there exist obfuscation for puncturable pseudorandom functions, as shown by Boneh and Zhandry for the case of NIKE, and by Pass *et al.* for the case of iO (via XiO).

What We Require for Matrix-Based ADPs. Given these observation, our main goal would be to achieve IND − ADP (in fact PS−ADP) branching program-based ADPs for relevant puncturable functions. We state informally the requirements we have over the admissible classes. The requirements are enforced either by the envisioned applications or by the envisioned proof technique.

Requirement 1: The first requirement concerns the depth of circuits. We need circuits to admit branching programs. Thus we need circuits in NC^1.

Requirement 1. *Let $\mathfrak{C}_{d,k+n}$ denote a class of circuits of depth d and input length $k + n$. A necessary condition for $\mathfrak{C}_{d,k+n}$ to admit a matrix-based ADP implementation is*

$$d \in O(\log(k + n)).$$

Requirement 2: Considering that our envisioned applications are built over pseudorandom functions, we are interested in ADPs for keyed functions. Thus we can think at their inputs as concatenation of "k‖input". Our function that is modeled by some circuit can be described as:

$$f : \{0,1\}^{k+n} \to \{0,1\}.$$

Requirement 2. *Let $\mathfrak{C}_{d,k+n}$ denote a class of circuits of depth d and input length n. A necessary condition for $\mathfrak{C}_{d,k+n}$ to admit an PS − ADP-secure implementation is that every $\mathscr{C} \in \mathfrak{C}_{d,k+n}$ models a two input function $\mathscr{C} : \{0,1\}^{k+n} \to \{0,1\}$.*

Requirement 3: We only consider functions that are non-constant under different keys. This requirement is motivated by the need to use invertible matrices in our proof[8]. Formally, the condition becomes:

Requirement 3. *Let $\mathfrak{C}_{d,k+n}$ denote a class of circuits of depth d and input length n. A necessary condition for $\mathfrak{C}_{d,k+n}$ to admit a PS − ADP-secure implementation is that: for every $\mathscr{C} \in \mathfrak{C}_{d,k+n}$ modelling some f, there exists a ppt algorithm $\mathcal{R}$ such that:*

$$\Pr\left[f(\mathsf{k}, \mathsf{input}) = 1 \mid (\mathsf{k}, \mathsf{input}) \leftarrow \mathcal{R}(1^\lambda, f)\right] > \frac{1}{\mathsf{poly}(\lambda = k + n)}.$$

---

[8] We want the function to be puncturable: under two different keys to obtain the same result under multiple points. Ideally, the punctured point will be excluded from the input space.

The condition should be read as: there exists a ppt procedure able to find some key and some input such that $f(\mathsf{k}, \mathsf{input}) = 1$. We **stress** that $\mathcal{R}$ is **not** required to sample uniformly at random the input point, nor the key k.

Requirement 4: In words, we would like to have an efficient procedure $\mathcal{R}$ capable of generating two keys $(\mathsf{k}, \mathsf{k}')$ such that $f(\mathsf{k}, X) = f(\mathsf{k}', X)$. Formally:

Requirement 4. *Let $\mathfrak{C}_{d,k+n}$ denote a class of circuits of depth d and input length n. A necessary condition for $\mathfrak{C}_{d,k+n}$ to admit a $\mathsf{PS} - \mathsf{ADP}$-secure implementation is that: for every $\mathscr{C} \in \mathfrak{C}_{d,k+n}$ modelling some f, there exists a ppt algorithm $\mathcal{R}$ such that $\forall$ input $\in \mathcal{X}$,*

$$\Pr[\mathsf{k} \neq \mathsf{k}' \wedge f(\mathsf{k}, \mathsf{input}) = f(\mathsf{k}', \mathsf{input})|(\mathsf{k}, \mathsf{k}') \leftarrow \mathcal{R}(1^\lambda, \mathscr{C})] > \frac{1}{\mathsf{poly}(k+n)}.$$

Remark 2. $\mathcal{R}$ is not required to sample the keys uniformly at random.

Requirement 5: Another requirement enforced by our security proof in the full version is that the first *line* in matrix $\overline{\mathbf{G}}_{\mathsf{k}||\vec{0}}$ has the form

$$(0, 0, 0, *, *, \ldots, *)$$

From a **high-level** point of view, we can translate this into:

$$f(\mathsf{k}, 0|| * * * *) = 1.$$

An astute reader may observe that for a f fulfilling the constraint above, some branching program can be found such that the first line is not $(0, 0, 0, *, *, \ldots, *)$. However, without loss of generality, we assume this is not the case.

Requirement 5. *Let $\mathfrak{C}_{d,k+n}$ denote a class of circuits of depth d and input length n. A necessary condition for $\mathfrak{C}_{d,k+n}$ to admit a $\mathsf{PS} - \mathsf{ADP}$-secure implementation is that: for every $\mathscr{C} \in \mathfrak{C}_{d,k+n}$ modelling some f, there exists an efficiently computable key k such that:*

$$f(\mathsf{k}, b||\mathsf{input}') := \begin{cases} 1, & if\ b = 0. \\ f(\mathsf{k}, b||\mathsf{input}]), & if\ b = 1 \quad and \quad \forall \mathsf{input}' \in \{0,1\}^{n-1} \end{cases}$$

Requirement 6: Finally, we are left with the ordering of variables. It is necessary that BP nodes depending on inputs have greater order numbers compared to the nodes depending on k. In layman's terms, the nodes depending on input in a branching program are "below" the ones depending on k.

Requirement 6. *Let $\mathfrak{C}_{d,k+n}$ denote a class of circuits of depth d and input length n. A necessary condition for $\mathfrak{C}_{d,k+n}$ to admit an $\mathsf{PS} - \mathsf{ADP}$-secure implementation is that any index of a node depending on input is greater than any index of a node depending on k.*

Definition 7. (Admissible Class for ADPs via Branching Programs).
Let $\mathfrak{C}_{\lambda,d,|k|+n}$ denote a class of circuits, such that $d \in \log(n)$. We call this class admissible if the requirements (1), (2), (3), (4), (5) and (6) stated above hold.

5.2   Our Claim

We state below our claim in terms of the function belonging to the class $\mathfrak{C}_{d,k+n}$ mentioned above. The proof is provided in the full version.

Theorem 3. (IND − ADP **programs for ADP admissible functions**). *Let* $\mathfrak{C}_{d,k+n}$ *denote a class of circuits of depth d and input length n which is admissible according to Definition 7. Then, there exists an* ADP *that reaches* PS − ADP-*security with respect to every single* $\mathscr{C}$ *in the admissible class* $\mathfrak{C}_{d,k+n}$. *Let* pPRF *denote a puncturable* PRF *admitting circuits in* NC^1. *Let* $\mathscr{C}^i$ *denote the circuit described in Sect. 4.1. Let* k *and* k' *be two* pPRF *keys punctured respectively in point* $0||0||\dots||0$ *and in some random point* $1||\$||\dots||\$$. *Then, the distributions of* $ADP^i(\mathscr{C}^i_k)$ *and* $ADP^i(\mathscr{C}^i_{k'})$ *are identical.*

Acknowledgements. Jim Barthel was supported in part by the Luxembourg National Research Fund through grant PRIDE15/10621687/SPsquared. Răzvan Roşie was supported in part by ERC grant CLOUDMAP 787390 and is thankful to Hart Montgomery and Arnab Roy for valuable discussions and ideas.

References

1. Barak, B., et al.: On the (im)possibility of obfuscating programs. In: Kilian, J. (ed.) CRYPTO 2001. LNCS, vol. 2139, pp. 1–18. Springer, Heidelberg (2001). https://doi.org/10.1007/3-540-44647-8_1
2. Barrington, D.A.: Bounded-width polynomial-size branching programs recognize exactly those languages in NC1. J. Comput. Syst. Sci. **38**(1), 150–164 (1989)
3. Bartusek, J., Ishai, Y., Jain, A., Ma, F., Sahai, A., Zhandry, M.: Affine determinant programs: a framework for obfuscation and witness encryption. In: Vidick, T. (ed.) ITCS 2020, vol. 151, pp. 82:1–82:39. LIPIcs, January 2020
4. Boneh, D., Kim, S., Montgomery, H.: Private puncturable PRFs from standard lattice assumptions. In: Coron, J.-S., Nielsen, J.B. (eds.) EUROCRYPT 2017. LNCS, vol. 10210, pp. 415–445. Springer, Cham (2017). https://doi.org/10.1007/978-3-319-56620-7_15
5. Boneh, D., Zhandry, M.: Multiparty key exchange, efficient traitor tracing, and more from indistinguishability obfuscation. In: Garay, J.A., Gennaro, R. (eds.) CRYPTO 2014. LNCS, vol. 8616, pp. 480–499. Springer, Heidelberg (2014). https://doi.org/10.1007/978-3-662-44371-2_27
6. Boyle, E., Gilboa, N., Ishai, Y.: Breaking the circuit size barrier for secure computation under DDH. In: Robshaw, M., Katz, J. (eds.) CRYPTO 2016. LNCS, vol. 9814, pp. 509–539. Springer, Heidelberg (2016). https://doi.org/10.1007/978-3-662-53018-4_19
7. Cleve, R.: Towards optimal simulations of formulas by bounded-width programs. Comput. Complex. **1**(1), 91–105 (1991)
8. Diffie, W., Hellman, M.E.: New directions in cryptography. IEEE Trans. Inf. Theory **22**(6), 644–654 (1976)
9. Garg, S., Gentry, C., Halevi, S.: Candidate multilinear maps from ideal lattices. In: Johansson, T., Nguyen, P.Q. (eds.) EUROCRYPT 2013. LNCS, vol. 7881, pp. 1–17. Springer, Heidelberg (2013). https://doi.org/10.1007/978-3-642-38348-9_1

10. Ishai, Y.: Randomization techniques for secure computation. Secure Multi-party Comput. **10**, 222 (2013)
11. Jain, A., Lin, H., Matt, C., Sahai, A.: How to leverage hardness of constant-degree expanding polynomials over $\mathbb{R}$ to build $i\mathcal{O}$. In: Ishai, Y., Rijmen, V. (eds.) EUROCRYPT 2019. Part I, volume 11476 of LNCS, pp. 251–281. Springer, Heidelberg (2019)
12. Jain, A., Lin, H., Sahai, A.: Simplifying constructions and assumptions for $i\mathcal{O}$. Cryptology ePrint Archive, Report 2019/1252 (2019). https://eprint.iacr.org/2019/1252
13. Jain, A., Lin, H., Sahai, A.: Indistinguishability obfuscation from well-founded assumptions. Cryptology ePrint Archive, Report 2020/1003 (2020). https://eprint.iacr.org/2020/1003
14. Joux, A.: A one round protocol for tripartite Diffie-Hellman. J. Cryptol. **17**(4), 263–276 (2004)
15. Valiant, L.G.: The complexity of computing the permanent. Theoret. Comput. Sci. **8**(2), 189–201 (1979)

OrBit: OR-Proof Identity-Based Identification with Tight Security for (as Low As) 1-Bit Loss

Jason Chia[1(✉)], Ji-Jian Chin[2], and Sook-Chin Yip[1]

[1] Faculty of Engineering, Multimedia University Cyberjaya,
63100 Selangor, Malaysia
1161300548@student.mmu.edu.my, scyip@mmu.edu.my
[2] Faculty of Computing and Informatics, Multimedia University Cyberjaya,
63100 Selangor, Malaysia
jjchin@mmu.edu.my

Abstract. Tightening the security reduction of a cryptosystem involves reducing the advantage of an adversary breaking the cryptosystem to a security assumption as closely as possible. Tighter security on a cryptosystem shows a clearer picture of its security, allowing for a more optimal security parameter at a certain level. In this work, we propose techniques to tighten the security of identity-based identification (IBI) schemes and demonstrate promising new results compared to existing reduction bounds. We show two distinct transformations for tightening security against concurrent attackers via the OR-proof technique of Fujioka et al. to lower security reduction loss. Our proposed techniques produce tighter security guarantees for as low as only a one-bit loss bound, hence the name: OrBit.

Keywords: Identity-based cryptography · Identification protocol · OR-proof · Security reduction · Tight security

1 Identity-Based Identification

Identity-based identification (IBI) is a cryptographic primitive for entity authentication. It operates using an interactive zero-knowledge proof of knowledge on a user's secret key related to an implicitly certified yet meaningful public identity string. For example, in many cases, the social security number or an email address can be used as the public identity string. In contrast to standard identification, where the public key is a random-looking string that requires explicit certification techniques such as X.509 standard certificates, IBI does not require such elaborate and costly implementations. Since the inception of ID-based cryptography, there has been a long line of research on IBI schemes [5,9,11,12,14,16,19,21,22,26,27].

Supported by the Ministry of Higher Education of Malaysia through the Fundamental Research Grant Scheme (FRGS/1/2019/ICT04/MMU/02/5.) and the Multimedia University fund.

Motivation. An IBI scheme is an attractive alternative in scenarios where maintenance of digital certificates (e.g., X.509 standard) is costly. For instance, in a wireless sensor network (WSN) where entity authentication is required, IBI is a suitable alternative to conventional digital signatures because it may be prohibitively expensive to issue a digital certificate to every sensor in large networks. More recent works have even proposed identity-based cryptography as a suitable primitive for landscapes such as internet-of-things (IoT) networks and WSNs [2,15].

In recent literature, there has been an increased focus on having "tight" security for cryptographic schemes [18,24,28]. A scheme can have "tight" security when the reduction loss is a small constant. Reduction loss causes a noticeable efficiency drop in cryptographic schemes. It was observed by Bader et al. [3] that: RSA-based signatures require a 2432-bit RSA modulus when the scheme is tightly secure to achieve a security level of 100-bit. Practically, the actual RSA modulus used must be at least 4000-bit due to a reduction loss of $N \cdot q_s$, where N and q_s denote the number of users and the number of signing queries, respectively. Bellare and Dai also observed this fact in identification schemes, where the loss occurred due to rewinding [4]. For an IBI scheme with a 128-bit desired security level $\epsilon = 2^{-128}$, rewinding forces the security level to drop by half $\epsilon_{ibi} = \sqrt{\epsilon} = 2^{-128/2} = 2^{-64}$. In other words, the key and parameter sizes must be at least doubled to account for reduction loss. Given the recent advancements in tight reductions on standard signatures due to Ng et al. [25] and identification schemes [4], these techniques are also applied to IBI schemes to show tight security reductions.

Our Contribution. In this work, we introduce OrBit, a framework that focuses on minimizing security reduction loss through two transformation techniques. We show improved results to the dual-identity approach of OR-proof techniques by Fujioka et al. [17] using the following 2 different techniques:

1. **OB1** - IMP-CA IBI from OR-proof and trapdoor sampleable relations for "security assumption hardening": We prove that the OR-proof technique can achieve tighter security based on the relationship itself instead of the underlying IBI under passive security when it is used with trapdoor sampleable relations.

2. **OB2** - IMP-CA IBI from OR-proof and 1–2 oblivious transfers (OT) for tight security: We prove that the resulting IBI protocol can achieve tighter security with only 1-bit loss when the OR-proof technique is used with a generic 1–2 OT protocol along with an interactive "multi-base" assumption such as the recently introduced multi-base discrete logarithm (MBDL) assumption. The reduction loss of this method is roughly a factor of 2.

The term "security assumption hardening" is used in OB1 because our result shows that concurrent secure (i.e., IMP-CA) schemes can be proven secure based on a harder problem (i.e., trapdoor sampleable relations) as opposed to the passive security (i.e., IMP-PA) of the IBI schemes. This is desirable because the use of the Reset Lemma [6] on the OR-proof technique causes a square root loss when performing the reduction of IMP-CA to IMP-PA. Subsequently, another round of square root loss occurs when the security of IMP-PA is reduced to the underlying hard assumption. Our method "bypasses" the square root loss on the IMP-CA to IMP-PA reduction by directly reducing to the underlying hard assumption. OB2 requires interactive "multi-base" security assumptions; Each "base" caters to a different user. While the MBDL assumption is less desirable than the more well-known static ones (i.e., discrete logarithm assumption), we demonstrate that it can eliminate the square root loss problem in IBI schemes. In other words, we extend Bellare and Dai's result in identification schemes under passive attacks [4] to the domain of IBI schemes under concurrent attacks.

2   Intuitive View of IBI IMP-CA Security Reduction

It is shown by independently by Kurosawa-Heng and Bellare et al. [5, 21] that IBI can be constructed from digital signature schemes, where the user key is the signature of its identity string by the trust authority. Therefore, it makes sense to consider reducing an IBI impersonator to a digital signature forger for an intuitive understanding. For IMP-PA, the process is simple because the protocol is honest-verifier zero-knowledge, which means it is simulatable. Thus, the forger could create transcripts without knowing any signature. For IMP-CA, the process is complicated by the impersonation queries where the impersonator plays the role of a cheating verifier. The forger is unable to answer challenges from the impersonator without a valid signature. It is traditionally solved through the use of interactive oracles [5, 21, 29], which are used to respond to challenges even without a signature. Another method is to perform OR-proofing: The forger queries the forgery oracle for 1 of the 2 signatures, then uses it to answer impersonation queries. Because OR-proof is witness indistinguishable [17], the impersonator does not know which of the 2 signatures is being used. At the end of the reduction, the forger would then extract the "other" signature from the impersonator and use it as its forgery. Note that if the impersonator used the same signature as the forger (which occurs at probability $1/2$), the reduction would fail[1]. OR-proof is an elegant way to achieve IMP-CA security but is subjected to 2 rounds of square-root losses. To overcome this, we can combine the techniques of Ng et al. [25] together with OR-proof to improve its security because the bit-partitioning technique fits well into how the "1 of the 2" signature approach that OR-proof relies on.

Nevertheless, most IBI schemes still suffer from 1 round of square-root loss due to rewinding of the impersonator to extract the signature. In 2020, Bellare and Dai [4] introduced a new security assumption that removes the need for rewinding on the Schnorr identification scheme. However, both results are only applicable for security under passive attacks. To extend the results into IBI with IMP-CA security, we consider the use of OR-proof. The primary problem in this is the challenge string: The verifier fully controls the challenge but in OR-proof, the verifier sets a "constraint" c, and the prover get to choose 1 of the 2

---

[1] The signature was already queried to the forgery oracle, thus cannot be used as a forgery.

challenges c_0 or c_1 such that $c_0 + c_1 = c$. Even though the prover has no control over the challenge it did not choose, neither does the verifier.

To overcome this, we use 1–2 OT to reveal 1 of the 2 challenges before the commit message is sent, allowing the prover to craft the transcript for the signature that it does not have. The real challenge is then "revealed" after the prover has locked in its commit message. Finally, the verifier reveals its OT secret and allows the prover to decrypt the real challenge to prevent any possible distinguishing attack. The OT scheme is used like a commitment scheme, where we commit encrypted challenges and reveal the secret later to permit decryption. This way, the verifier can control the challenges, and the prover can choose 1 of the challenges before sending its commit message, all without revealing the choice of the prover.

3   Preliminaries

In this work, $a \leftarrow b$ refers to assigning value of b to a, while $a \xleftarrow{\$} S$ refers to uniformly sampling an element a from set S. We borrow most of our notations from the seminal work of Bellare et al. [5]: the notation $S[b] \leftarrow a$ means $I \leftarrow I \cup \{b\}; S \leftarrow S \cup \{a_b\}_{b \in I}$ where I is an index set for S. For an indexed set S, when we write $b \in S$ we actually mean $b \in I$ where I is the index set for S. If A is an algorithm, $A(a_1, ..., a_n : O_1, ..., O_m)$ indicates A is run with input values $a_1, ..., a_n$ and can access to algorithms (or oracles) $O_1, ..., O_m$ while the algorithm is running. If P and V are interactive algorithms, then $(dec, tr) \leftarrow P(.) \leftrightarrow V(.)$ indicates that P and V interact with their respective given inputs and oracles and results in a decision (dec) from V as well as the transcript of the interaction (tr). An interactive algorithm $(M_{out}, st_{i+1}) \leftarrow P(st_i, M_{in})$ is a stateful algorithm which takes in current state information st_i and an input message M_{in} and produces an output message M_{out} along with an updated state st_{i+1}. We view protocols as alternating successive calls to the interactive algorithms P and V respectively.

Definition 1. *An identity-based identification (IBI) scheme is formed by 4 polynomial time algorithms: Master Key Generation* **MKGen**, *User Key Generation* **UKGen**, *Prove* **P** *and Verify* **V**. **P** *and* **V** *are interactive algorithms run by a prover P and a verifier V, respectively. We define the algorithms as follows:*

1. **MKGen:** *Master Key Generation takes in the security parameter 1^k and outputs the master secret key msk and master public key mpk.*
2. **UKGen:** *User Key Generation takes in the master secret key (msk), the master public key (mpk) and an arbitrary string $ID \in \{0,1\}^*$. It then outputs a user key uk corresponding to ID.*
3. **P:** *Prove is an interactive algorithm. Prove takes in public information mpk, the arbitrary string ID and the user key uk and executes a protocol with a party V which runs the Verify algorithm.*

4. **V**: *Verify is an interactive algorithm. Verify takes in public information mpk and the arbitrary string ID and executes a protocol with a party P which runs the Prove algorithm. At the end of the protocol run, outputs **1** if P successfully proves its possession of a uk corresponding to mpk and ID, **0** otherwise.*

We write (dec, tr) $\leftarrow P(mpk, ID, uk) \leftrightarrow V(mpk, ID)$ to denote a protocol execution between prover P and verifier V running the interactive algorithm $\mathbf{P}$ and $\mathbf{V}$, respectively. The decision (dec) of V and the transcript (tr) are the results of the interaction and we say tr is **valid** if dec $= 1$. We call an interactive proof system $(\mathbf{P}, \mathbf{V})$ canonical if the transcript follows a three-move structure in which $\mathbf{P}$ initiates with a uniformly distributed commit message (cm) over the commit message set CM followed by a uniformly distributed challenge message (ch) over the challenge message set CH from $\mathbf{V}$ and finally a response (rs) from $\mathbf{P}$ corresponding to cm and ch. A canonical $(\mathbf{P}, \mathbf{V})$ is non-trivial if the function $2^{-m(k)}$ is negligible in k, where $m(k)$ is the commit message length if $|CM| \geq 2^{m(k)}$.

3.1   Security Model

We adopt the security model of impersonation under concurrent attacks (IMP-CA) when considering the security of IBI schemes. The difference between concurrent and active security is that A can use clones of itself to simultaneously run **PROV** queries against a challenger C. On the other hand, passive security prevents A from playing the role of the cheating verifier and only allows for transcript querying, which is known to be secure if the protocol is honest verifier zero-knowledge [21]. The adversary is also allowed to obtain user keys through the **CORR** oracle. It is obvious that concurrent attackers are the most advanced, and hence IMP-CA is the strongest security model. We adopt the definition of the security of an IBI by Bellare et al. [5] using an experiment $\mathrm{Exp}_{IBI,A}^{IMP\text{-}CA}$ between an adversary A and C shown in Fig. 1.

Definition 2. *Bellare et al. [5], let $IBI = (MKGen, UKGen, P, V)$ be an IBI scheme. For any adversary $A = (CP, CV)$ consisting of a cheating verifier CV and a cheating prover CP, the advantage ϵ_{ibi} of A running at most in time t_{ibi} of attacking the IBI under the security model IMP-CA is:*

$$\epsilon_{ibi} = Pr[Exp_{IBI,A}^{IMP\text{-}CA}(1^k) = 1]$$

An IBI scheme is (q_c, q_h, q_p)-IMP-CA secure if ϵ_{ibi} is negligible for every polynomial-time t_{ibi} A, where q_c, q_h, q_p is the number of corrupt, hash and prove queries respectively.

PROV(ID,s,M_{in})	**CORR**(ID)
1. **if** $ID \in CU \cup AU$ **then return** $\perp$	1. **if** $ID \in CU$ **then return** $\perp$
2. **run INIT**(ID)	2. **run INIT**(ID)
3. $uk \leftarrow LU[ID]$	3. $uk \leftarrow LU[ID]$
4. **if** $(ID,s) \in RU$ **then goto** 8	4. $CU \leftarrow CU \cup ID$
5. $RU \leftarrow RU \cup \{(ID,s)\}$	5. **return** uk
6. initialize random coins ρ for P	**INIT**(ID)
7. $st[ID,s] \leftarrow (mpk,uk,\rho)$	1. **if** $ID \in LU$ **then return** $\perp$
8. $(st[ID,s],M_{out}) \leftarrow P(st[ID,s],M_{in})$	2. $uk \leftarrow UKGen(msk,mpk,ID)$
9. **return** M_{out}	3. $LU[ID] \leftarrow uk$
	4. **return** ID

$\mathrm{Exp}_{IBI,A}^{IMP\text{-}CA}(1^k)$
1. $(msk,mpk) \leftarrow MKGen(1^k)$
2. $LU,CU,AU,RU \leftarrow \emptyset$
3. $(ID^*,st_{CP}) \leftarrow CV(mpk:\textbf{PROV},\textbf{CORR})$
4. $(dec,tr) \leftarrow CP(mpk,ID^*,st_{CP}:\textbf{PROV},\textbf{CORR}) \leftrightarrow V(mpk,ID^*)$
5. **return** dec

Fig. 1. Oracles and subroutines of the IMP-CA experiment. LU - *legal* users, CU - *corrupted* users, AU - *attacked (targeted)* user, RU - *running* user identification processes

3.2   Security Assumptions

We first state the definition of what it means for an advantage ϵ to be "negligible".

Definition 3. *A function* $negl(k)$ *is negligible if* $ncgl(k) = f^{-1}(k)$ *and the function* $f(k)$ *cannot be bounded by any polynomial in* k. *We write* "ϵ *is negligible*" *to imply that* $\epsilon = negl(k)$ *is negligible in the security parameter* k.

The problems described in this section are assumed to be computationally intractable and will be used in proving the security of the schemes derived in this work.

Definition 4. *RSA assumption. Let* (N,e,X) *be an RSA problem instance of length* 1^k *such that* N *is composite of 2 large primes* p,q *and* $X = x^e \bmod N$ *such that* $x \xleftarrow{\$} \mathbb{Z}_N^*$ *and* $ed = 1 \bmod \varphi(N)$ *where* $\varphi(N) = (p-1)(q-1)$. *The advantage* ϵ_{rsa} *of an adversary* A *running in time* t_{rsa} *of breaking the RSA assumption is:*

$$Pr[X^d \bmod N = x \leftarrow A(N,e,X)] = \epsilon_{rsa}$$

The RSA assumption is hard (secure) in $\varphi(N)$ *if* ϵ_{rsa} *is negligible for every polynomial-time* t_{rsa} *A.*

Definition 5. *Co-computational Diffie-Hellman assumption. Let* $\mathbb{G}_1$ *and* $\mathbb{G}_2$ *be multiplicative cyclic groups of prime order* q *generated from a group generator with security parameter* 1^k *as input.* $(g_1,g_2,g_1^a,g_1^b,g_2^a)$ *is a problem instance such that* $a,b \xleftarrow{\$} \mathbb{Z}_q$ *and* g_1,g_2 *are generators in* $\mathbb{G}_1$ *and* $\mathbb{G}_2$, *respectively. The* *advantage* ϵ_{co-cdh} *of an adversary A running in time* t_{co-cdh} *of breaking the co-computational Diffie-Hellman assumption is:*

$$Pr[g_1^{ab} \leftarrow A(g_1, g_2, g_1^a, g_1^b, g_2^a)] = \epsilon_{co-cdh}$$

The co-computational Diffie-Hellman assumption is hard (secure) in $\mathbb{G}_1$ *and* $\mathbb{G}_2$ *if* ϵ_{co-cdh} *is negligible for every polynomial-time* t_{co-cdh} *A.*

To prove the tight security of a scheme, we utilize the new cryptographic assumption known as the multi-base discrete logarithm, which is an interactive assumption due to Bellare and Dai [4]. We adopt the definition of Bellare and Dai for the multi-base discrete logarithm assumption:

Definition 6. *Multi-base discrete logarithm. Suppose* $\mathbb{G}$ *is a cyclic group of prime order* q *with generator* g. *Let* $(g, g^y, g^{x_1}, ... g^{x_n})$ *be a problem instance of length* 1^k *such that* $y, x_1, ..., x_n \xleftarrow{\$} \mathbb{Z}_q$ *and* $dlog(i, W)$ *be a one-time oracle for every* $i = 1, ..., n$ *that returns* w *such that* $W = g^{x_i w}$ *upon invocation. The advantage of* ϵ_{n-mbdl} *of an adversary A running in time* t_{n-mbdl} *of breaking the multi-base discrete logarithm assumption is:*

$$Pr[y \leftarrow A(g^y, g^{x_1}, ... g^{x_n} : dlog)] = \epsilon_{n-mbdl}$$

The multi-base discrete logarithm assumption is hard (secure) in $\mathbb{G}$ *if* ϵ_{n-mbdl} *is negligible for every polynomial-time* t_{n-mbdl} *A.*

The MBDL assumption is parametrized by the number of additional bases supplied on the problem instance n. The weakest form is the 1-MBDL assumption: Given (g, g^y, g^x) with a one-time use dlog oracle on base g^x, compute the dlog of g^y. Likewise, a n-MBDL assumption has n additional bases supplied (i.e., $g^{x_1}, ..., g^{x_n}$), where the dlog oracle similarly can only be used once on each base.

3.3 Homomorphic Trapdoor Sampleable Relations, Honest Verifier Zero Knowledge and 1–2 Oblivious Transfer Protocols

Our definition of homomorphic trapdoor sampleable relations (HTSR) roughly follows Bellare et al. [5], except we include the homomorphic property as a requirement. We also present a brief definition on Honest Verifier Zero Knowledge with Special Soundness (HVZK-SS) and 1–2 oblivious transfer (OT) protocols:

Definition 7. *A relation is a finite set of ordered pairs. The range of a relation* $\mathbf{R}$, *set of images* x *and the set of inverses of* y *are defined respectively, as:*

$$RNG(\mathbf{R}) = \{y : \exists x \ s.t. \ (x, y) \in \mathbf{R}\}$$
$$\mathbf{R}(x) = \{y : (x, y) \in \mathbf{R}\}$$
$$\mathbf{R}^{-1}(y) = \{x : (x, y) \in \mathbf{R}\}$$

A family of homomorphic trapdoor sampleable relation is a triplet of polynomial-time algorithms (i.e., TDG, SMP, INV) such that the following properties are true:

1. *Efficiency: The algorithm TDG takes in 1^k where $k \in \mathbb{N}$ is the security parameter and outputs the description $\langle \mathbf{R} \rangle$ of a relation $\mathbf{R}$ with trapdoor information* **td**.
2. *Sampleability: The output of the SMP algorithm on input $\langle \mathbf{R} \rangle$ is uniformly distributed over $\mathbf{R}$.*
3. *Invertibility: The algorithm INV takes in $\langle \mathbf{R} \rangle$,* **td** *and an element $y \in RNG(\mathbf{R})$ and outputs a random element of $\mathbf{R}^{-1}(y)$.*
4. *One-wayness: For every $\mathbf{R}$ in the family, the probability to correctly invert an element $y \in RNG(\mathbf{R})$ without the trapdoor information* **td** *is negligible.*
5. *Homomorphism: $\mathbf{R}^{-1}(x \cdot y) = \mathbf{R}^{-1}(x) \cdot Y$ where $\mathbf{R}^{-1}(y) = Y$.*

A family of relations is defined as: $\{\mathbf{R} : \exists k, \mathbf{td} \text{ s.t. } (\langle \mathbf{R} \rangle, \mathbf{td}) \in \mathrm{TDG}(1^k)\}$. A family of trapdoor sampleable relations arises naturally from a family of trapdoor one-way permutations. Every member $\mathbf{f}$ in the family of trapdoor one-way permutations corresponds the relation $\mathbf{R}$ consisting of the set of pairs $(x, \mathbf{f}(x))$ for x in the domain of function $\mathbf{f}$.

Definition 8. *A HVZK-SS for $\{\mathbf{R} : \exists k, \mathbf{td} \text{ s.t. } (\langle \mathbf{R} \rangle, \mathbf{td}) \in \mathrm{TDG}(1^k)\}$ is a nontrivial canonical proof system for $(\mathbf{P}, \mathbf{V})$ which satisfies:*

1. *Completeness. If $\mathbf{P}$ knows x s.t. $(x, y) \in \mathbf{R}$, then probability of $\mathbf{V}$ accepting is 1.*
2. *Special Soundness. There exists a polynomial time extractor E to extract x s.t. $(x, y) \in \mathbf{R}$ given two valid transcripts (cm, ch1, rs1), (cm, ch2, rs2) for ch1 $\neq$ ch2.*
3. *Honest Verifier Zero Knowledge. There exist a polynomial time simulator S for valid transcripts with only inputs $(\langle \mathbf{R} \rangle, y)$, such that the transcript is computationally indistinguishable from the distribution of a real conversation honest prover $P(y, x)$ and honest verifier $V(y)$ where $(x, y) \in \mathbf{R}$.*

Definition 9. *Let $OT = (\textbf{Obliv-Send}, \textbf{Obliv-Recv})$ be a 1 out of 2 oblivious transfer protocol with security 1^k, a sender A with 2 messages m_0 and m_1 and a receiver B with a choice bit $b \in \{0, 1\}$. At the end of the protocol, B which runs $\textbf{Obliv-Recv}$ obtains $m_b \leftarrow \textbf{Obliv-Send}(m_0, m_1) \leftrightarrow \textbf{Obliv-Recv}(b)$ from A which runs $\textbf{Obliv-Send}$. An OT protocol has 2 basic properties which must be fulfilled:*

1. *Sender security: B cannot compute the other message $m_{\bar{b}}$ after the interaction except with negligible probability. "B is oblivious to the other message of A".*
2. *Receiver privacy: A cannot distinguish the choice of B, namely the bit b with probability greater than $1/2$. "A is oblivious to the choice bit of B".*

4   OB1: IMP-CA IBI Schemes from OR-Proof and HTSR

In this section, we present our framework to improve tightness of IBI security against active and concurrent attackers using techniques from Ng et al. [25] and Fujioka et al. [17]. The transform requires a HTSR and a HVZK-SS for the relation. Figure 2 shows our transform.

OB1-IBI.MKGen(1^k)

1. $\langle \mathbf{R} \rangle, \mathbf{td} \leftarrow \text{TDG}(1^k)$
2. $(x,X) \leftarrow \text{SMP}(\langle \mathbf{R} \rangle)$
   s.t. $(x,X) \in \langle \mathbf{R} \rangle$
3. **select** $H : \{0,1\}^* \rightarrow \text{RNG}(\langle \mathbf{R} \rangle)$
4. $mpk \leftarrow (\langle \mathbf{R} \rangle, X, H, k)$
5. $msk \leftarrow (\mathbf{td}, x)$
6. **return** (mpk, msk)

OB1-IBI.UKGen(msk,mpk,ID)

1. $b \xleftarrow{\$} \{0,1\}$
2. $u \leftarrow \text{INV}(\langle \mathbf{R} \rangle, \mathbf{td}, H(ID)) \cdot x^b$
   $= \mathbf{R}^{-1}(H(ID)) \cdot x^b$
   $= \mathbf{R}^{-1}(H(ID) \cdot X^b)$
3. $uk \leftarrow (u,b)$
4. **return** uk

OB1-IBI.Protocol(P,V)

$P(mpk,ID,uk)$	$V(mpk,ID)$

$(Y_b, st) \leftarrow \Sigma_{com}(mpk,ID)$

$c_{\bar{b}} \leftarrow \Sigma_{cha}(mpk)$

$(Y_{\bar{b}}, z_{\bar{b}}) \leftarrow \Sigma_{sim}(mpk,ID,c_{\bar{b}}) \xrightarrow{(Y_0,Y_1)}$

$\xleftarrow{\quad c \quad} c \leftarrow \Sigma_{cha}(mpk)$

$c_b \leftarrow c - c_{\bar{b}}$

$z_b \leftarrow \Sigma_{res}(mpk,ID,Y_b,c_b$

$u,st) \xrightarrow{(c_0,z_0,z_1)} c_1 \leftarrow c - c_0$

$\delta_0 \leftarrow \Sigma_{vrf}(mpk,ID,Y_0,c_0,z_0)$

$\delta_1 \leftarrow \Sigma_{vrf}(mpk,ID,Y_1,c_1,z_1)$

return $\delta_0 \wedge \delta_1$

Fig. 2. A framework for enhancing OR-proof on IMP-CA IBI schemes with HTSR. Σ_{com}, Σ_{cha} and Σ_{vrf} are algorithms from the HVZK-SS protocol for the HTSR which generates the commit, challenge and response messages, respectively. Σ_{sim} is the algorithm for honest verifier simulation for the protocol.

Theorem 1. *An IBI scheme resulting from the transform shown in Fig. 2 is $(t_{ibi}, q_c, q_h, q_p, \epsilon_{ibi})$-IMP-CA secure if the underlying one-way HTSR has a HVZK-SS protocol and is $(t_{owtd}, \epsilon_{owtd})$-secure such that*

$$\epsilon_{ibi} \leq \sqrt{2\epsilon_{owtd}} + \frac{1}{n_c}$$

where n_c is the number of possible challenges in which the challenge string $c \leftarrow \Sigma_{cha}(mpk)$ is uniformly distributed.

Proof. Suppose there is an adversary A which $(t_{ibi}, q_c, q_h, q_p, \epsilon_{ibi})$-breaks IMP-CA of an IBI scheme resulting from the framework shown in Fig. 2 in time t_{ibi} with at most q_c CORR queries, q_h HASH queries and q_p PROV queries. We construct a simulator S which can use A to break the one-wayness of the underlying HTSR in time t_{owtd} and with advantage ϵ_{owtd}. S first receives $(\langle \mathbf{R} \rangle, X)$ and security parameter k and must output $\mathbf{R}^{-1}(X) = x$ without knowing the trapdoor td. S sets $mpk \leftarrow (\langle \mathbf{R} \rangle, X, \mathbf{H}, k)$ with $\mathbf{H}$ modelled as the random oracle and starts A as a cheating verifier $CV(mpk : CORR, PROV)$. S initializes the sets $LU, CU, RU, AU \leftarrow \emptyset$ representing *legal users, corrupted users, running users* and *attacked users*, respectively. S answers the queries by CV following the instructions in Fig. 3.

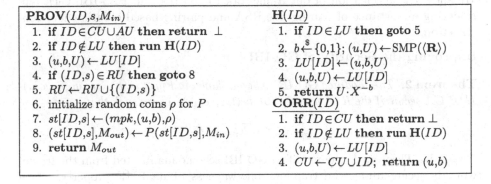

PROV(ID,s,M_{in})	**H(ID)**
1. if $ID \in CU \cup AU$ then return $\perp$	1. if $ID \in LU$ then goto 5
2. if $ID \notin LU$ then run H(ID)	2. $b \xleftarrow{\$} \{0,1\}$; $(u,U) \leftarrow \mathrm{SMP}(\langle \mathbf{R} \rangle)$
3. $(u,b,U) \leftarrow LU[ID]$	3. $LU[ID] \leftarrow (u,b,U)$
4. if $(ID,s) \in RU$ then goto 8	4. $(u,b,U) \leftarrow LU[ID]$
5. $RU \leftarrow RU \cup \{(ID,s)\}$	5. return $U \cdot X^{-b}$
6. initialize random coins ρ for P	**CORR(ID)**
7. $st[ID,s] \leftarrow (mpk,(u,b),\rho)$	1. if $ID \in CU$ then return $\perp$
8. $(st[ID,s],M_{out}) \leftarrow P(st[ID,s],M_{in})$	2. if $ID \notin LU$ then run H(ID)
9. return M_{out}	3. $(u,b,U) \leftarrow LU[ID]$
	4. $CU \leftarrow CU \cup ID$; return (u,b)

Fig. 3. HASH, CORR and PROV are oracles for IMP-CA experiment

The simulations for CORR and PROV are perfect because the user-key u from $\mathbf{H}(ID)$ is the expected user-key for ID due to the random oracle $\mathbf{R}^{-1}(\mathbf{H}(ID)) \cdot x^b = \mathbf{R}^{-1}(U \cdot X^{-b}) \cdot x^b = \mathbf{R}^{-1}(U) = u$. Thus, q_c, q_h and q_p do not affect ϵ_{ibi}. When CV outputs a target identity to impersonate along with state information $(ID^*, st_{CP}) \leftarrow CV(mpk : CORR, PROV)$, S checks if $ID^* \in LU$ and runs $\mathbf{H}(ID^*)$ otherwise. S then sets $AU \leftarrow \{ID^*\}$ and runs A as the cheating prover $CP(mpk, ID^*, st_{CP} : CORR, PROV)$. S interacts with CP and obtains 2 valid transcripts $T = ((Y_0, Y_1), c, (c_0, z_0, z_1))$ and $T' = ((Y_0, Y_1), c', (c'_0, z'_0, z'_1))$ where $c \neq c'$ and $(c_0, z_0, z_1) \neq (c'_0, z'_0, z'_1)$. Following the special soundness property of the protocol, the user secret u^* can be extracted from the 2 transcript T and T'. From then on, S can break the one-wayness of the underlying HTSR if $b^* \neq b$. S would simply return (u^*/u) if $b^* > b$ and $(u^*/u)^{-1}$ if $b > b^*$.

$$\frac{u^*}{u} = \frac{\mathbf{R}^{-1}(\mathbf{H}(ID^*) \cdot X^{b^*})}{\mathbf{R}^{-1}(U)} = \frac{\mathbf{R}^{-1}(U \cdot X^{-b} \cdot X^{b^*})}{\mathbf{R}^{-1}(U)}$$
$$= \mathbf{R}^{-1}(X)^{(b^*-b)} = x^{(b^*-b)}$$

Let event E_1 be the event that S extracts u^* successfully from A and let E_2 be the event in which $b^* \neq b$. By the Reset Lemma [6], we have $Pr[E_1] \leq (\epsilon_{ibi} - \frac{1}{n_c})^2$. $Pr[E_2] = 1/2 + negl(k)$ given that bit b is sampled uniformly and hidden from CV due to the OR-proof. Therefore, the probability of S successfully breaking the one-wayness of the underlying trapdoor assumption is $\epsilon_{owtd} \geq Pr[E_1] \times Pr[E_2] = (\epsilon_{ibi} - \frac{1}{n_c})^2 \times 1/2$ as required. $\qquad\square$

4.1 Application of the Framework

We show the application of our framework to GQ-IBI and BLS-IBI, each representing an instance of pairing-free RSA and pairing-based elliptic curve construction.

Improving the Security of GQ-IBI

Theorem 2. *The modified GQ-IBI scheme shown in Fig. 4 is $(t_{ibi}, q_c, q_h, q_p, \epsilon_{ibi})$-IMP-CA secure if the RSA assumption is $(t_{rsa}, \epsilon_{rsa})$-secure such that*

$$\epsilon_{mgq-ibi} \leq \sqrt{2\epsilon_{rsa}} + 2^{-l(k)}$$

Proof. By Theorem 1, the modified GQ-IBI scheme manifested from the framework is secure under the trapdoor one-wayness of its SMP property, which is exactly the RSA problem: given $(\langle \mathbf{R} \rangle, X) \mapsto ((N, e), X)$, find x such that $X = \mathbf{R}(x) \mapsto X = x^e \bmod N$. $\qquad\square$

4.2 Improving the Security of BLS-IBI

The Boneh-Lynn-Shacham (BLS) IBI scheme was first introduced by Kurosawa and Heng [21] built using the pairing-based BLS signature [8]. We adopt the co-CDH assumption version proposed by Lacharité [23] using Type-3 pairings[2]. Our result is similar to a scheme[3] proposed by Chia and Chin in 2020 [9]. Again, our version is IMP-CA secure and avoids the interactive One-More CDH assumption [7]. Figure 5 shows the HTSR for BLS as well as the modified BLS-IBI scheme.

Theorem 3. *The modified BLS-IBI scheme shown in Fig. 5 is $(t_{ibi}, q_c, q_h, q_p, \epsilon_{ibi})$-IMP-CA secure if the co-CDH assumption is $(t_{co-cdh}, \epsilon_{co-cdh})$-secure such that*

$$\epsilon_{mbls-ibi} \leq \sqrt{2\epsilon_{co-cdh}} + q^{-1}$$

---

[2] BLS signatures was originally designed with Type-1 pairings but its security was compromised by advancements in solving discrete logarithms due to Menezes [1] and Granger [20].

[3] The exposure of user-bit b to the active adversary enables it to always output a bit $b^* = b$ causing the security reduction of [9] to fail. The use of OR-proof fixes the problem and we achieve the same security bound and assumption as theirs.

TSR(RSA-FDH).TDG(1^k)

1. $(N,e),d \leftarrow KG_{rsa}(1^k)$
   s.t. $ed = 1 \bmod \varphi(N)$
2. $\langle \mathbf{R} \rangle \leftarrow (N,e); \mathbf{td} \leftarrow d$
3. **return** $\langle \mathbf{R} \rangle, \mathbf{td}$

TSR(RSA-FDH).SMP($\langle \mathbf{R} \rangle$)

1. $x \leftarrow \mathbb{Z}_N; X \leftarrow x^e$
2. **return** (x,X)

TSR(RSA-FDH).INV($\langle \mathbf{R} \rangle, \mathbf{td}, U$)

1. $u \leftarrow U^d$
2. **return** u

MGQ-IBI.MKGen(1^k)

1. $(N,e),d \leftarrow KG_{rsa}(1^k)$
   s.t. $ed = 1 \bmod \varphi(N)$
2. $x \leftarrow \mathbb{Z}_N; X \leftarrow x^e$
3. **select** $H : \{0,1\}^* \rightarrow \mathbb{Z}_N$
4. $mpk \leftarrow (N,e,X,H,k)$
5. $msk \leftarrow (d,x)$
6. **return** (mpk,msk)

MGQ-IBI.UKGen(msk,mpk,ID)

1. $b \xleftarrow{\$} \{0,1\}$
2. $u \leftarrow (H(ID) \cdot X^b)^d$
3. $uk \leftarrow (u,b)$
4. **return** uk

MGQ-IBI.Protocol(P,V)

$P(mpk,ID,uk)$		$V(mpk,ID)$
$y_b \leftarrow \mathbb{Z}_N$		
$Y_b \leftarrow y_b^e$		
$c_{\bar{b}} \leftarrow \mathbb{Z}_{2^{l(k)}}; z_{\bar{b}} \leftarrow \mathbb{Z}_N$		
$Y_{\bar{b}} \leftarrow z_{\bar{b}}^e(H(ID) \cdot X^b)^{-c_{\bar{b}}}$	$\xrightarrow{(Y_0,Y_1)}$	
$c_b \leftarrow c - c_{\bar{b}}$	$\xleftarrow{\quad c \quad}$	$c \leftarrow \mathbb{Z}_{2^{l(k)}}$
$z_b \leftarrow u^{c_b} y_b$	$\xrightarrow{(c_0,z_0,z_1)}$	$c_1 \leftarrow c - c_0$
		$\delta_0 \leftarrow z_0^e \stackrel{?}{=} Y_0(H(ID) \cdot X^0)^{c_0}$
		$\delta_1 \leftarrow z_1^e \stackrel{?}{=} Y_1(H(ID) \cdot X^1)^{c_1}$
		return $\delta_0 \wedge \delta_1$

Fig. 4. The HTSR for RSA-FDH and the modified GQ-IBI scheme. The scheme is parametrized with prime exponent RSA key generator KG_{rsa} and a super logarithmic challenge length $l : \mathbb{N} \rightarrow \mathbb{N}$ such that $2^{l(k)} < e$ for all $(N,e,d) \in [KG_{rsa}(1^k)]$. Arithmetic operations are performed in group $\mathbb{Z}_n$.

Proof. By Theorem 1, the modified BLS-IBI scheme manifested from the framework is secure under the trapdoor one-wayness of its SMP property, which is exactly the co-CDH problem: given $(\langle \mathbf{R} \rangle, X) \mapsto ((\mathbb{G}_1, \mathbb{G}_2, q, g_1, g_2, g_1^w, g_2^w), X = g_1^x)$, find V such that $V = \mathbf{R}(x) \mapsto V = g_1^{wx}$. $\square$

TSR(BLS).TDG(1^k)

1. $(\mathbb{G}_1,\mathbb{G}_2,e,q,g_1,g_2,g_1^w,g_2^w),w) \leftarrow KG(1^k)$
2. $\langle \mathbf{R} \rangle \leftarrow (\mathbb{G}_1,\mathbb{G}_2,e,q,g_1,g_2,g_1^w,g_2^w)$
3. $\mathrm{td} \leftarrow w$
4. **return** $\langle \mathbf{R} \rangle$,td

TSR(BLS).SMP($\langle \mathbf{R} \rangle$)

1. $x \leftarrow \mathbb{Z}_q$
2. $V \leftarrow g_1^{wx}; X \leftarrow g_1^x$
3. **return** $((x,V),X)$

TSR(BLS).INV($\langle \mathbf{R} \rangle$,td,$U$)

1. $u \leftarrow U^w$
2. **return** u

MBLS-IBI.MKGen(1^k)

1. $(\mathbb{G}_1,\mathbb{G}_2,e,q,g_1,g_2,g_1^w,g_2^w),w) \leftarrow KG(1^k)$
2. $x \leftarrow \mathbb{Z}_q; X \leftarrow g_1^x$
3. select $H:\{0,1\}^* \rightarrow \mathbb{G}_1$
4. $mpk \leftarrow (\mathbb{G}_1,\mathbb{G}_2,e,q,g_1,g_2,g_1^w,g_2^w,X,H,k)$
5. $msk \leftarrow w$
6. **return** (mpk,msk)

MBLS-IBI.UKGen(msk,mpk,ID)

1. $b \xleftarrow{\$} \{0,1\}$
2. $u \leftarrow (H(ID) \cdot X^b)^w$
3. $uk \leftarrow (u,b)$
4. **return** uk

MBLS-IBI.Protocol(P,V)

$P(mpk,ID,uk)$		$V(mpk,ID)$
$y_b \leftarrow \mathbb{Z}_q; Y_b \leftarrow H(ID)^{y_b}$		
$c_{\bar{b}} \leftarrow \mathbb{Z}_q; z_{\bar{b}} \leftarrow \mathbb{G}_1$		
$Y_{\bar{b}} \leftarrow$		
$z_{\bar{b}} \cdot (H(ID) \cdot X^b)^{-c_{\bar{b}}}$	$\xrightarrow{(Y_0,Y_1)}$	
$c_b \leftarrow c - c_{\bar{b}}$	$\xleftarrow{\quad c \quad}$	$c \leftarrow \mathbb{Z}_q$
$z_b \leftarrow (y_b + c_b)u$	$\xrightarrow{(c_0,z_0,z_1)}$	$c_1 \leftarrow c - c_0$
		$\delta_0 \leftarrow e(Y_0 \cdot (H(ID) \cdot X^0)^{c_0}, g_2^w) \overset{?}{=} e(z_0,g_2)$
		$\delta_1 \leftarrow e(Y_1 \cdot (H(ID) \cdot X^1)^{c_1}, g_2^w) \overset{?}{=} e(z_1,g_2)$
		return $\delta_0 \wedge \delta_1$

Fig. 5. The HTSR for BLS and the modified BLS-IBI scheme. $KG(1^k)$ is a pairing generator, where the generated groups $\mathbb{G}_1$ and $\mathbb{G}_2$ are of prime-order q with generators g_1,g_2, respectively. e is a non-degenerate, efficiently computable bilinear map $e:\mathbb{G}_1 \times \mathbb{G}_2 \rightarrow \mathbb{G}_T$ where $\mathbb{G}_T$ is also a group of prime order q.

4.3 Comparison with Existing IBI Frameworks for IMP-CA Security

In 2008, Yang et al. introduced a framework for designing IMP-CA secure IBI schemes. Their transformation requires trapdoor strong one-more relations and a witness dualism proof with special soundness (WD-SS) to achieve security on IMP-CA [29]. Subsequently, in 2012, Fujioka et al. proposed the use of OR-proof in the IBI setting to provide security against IMP-CA attacks. Their results show that the resulting IBI from the OR-proof application has IMP-CA security based on IMP-PA security with a square root reduction loss due to the Reset

Lemma [17]. Table 1 shows the difference between this work and existing IBI frameworks for IMP-CA security, where the security of our work is based on a well studied one-wayness assumption of HTSR with minimal overhead (i.e., an additional bit on uk size and an extra image element of the trapdoor relation on mpk size). Note, in relation to OR-proof, we saved 1 round of square root loss by directly reducing it to the hard problem.

Table 1. Comparison of existing IMP-CA IBI frameworks.

Property	Yang et al. [29]	Fujioka et al. [17]	OB1 (this work)
Security assumption	One-wayness of trapdoor strong one-more relation, $\epsilon_{owtdsom}$	IMP-PA security, ϵ_{imp-pa}	One-wayness of HTSR, ϵ_{owtd}
Security bound	$\sqrt{2\epsilon_{owtdsom}} + 2^{-n_c}$	$\sqrt{2\epsilon_{imp-pa}} + 2^{-n_c}$	$\sqrt{2\epsilon_{owtd}} + 2^{-n_c}$
uk size	$|x|$	$|uk_{ibi}|$	$|x|+1$bit
mpk size	$|\langle \mathbf{R}\rangle|$	$|mpk_{ibi}|$	$|\langle \mathbf{R}\rangle| + |y|$
Protocol bandwidth	$2|y| + 2|cm| + 2|ch| + 2|rs|$	$2|cm| + 2|ch| + 2|rs|$	$2|cm| + 2|ch| + 2|rs|$

5 OB2: Tight IMP-CA IBI Scheme from OR-Proof and 1–2 OT

In this section, we show a further tightening of Schnorr-IBI security bounds under IMP-CA using the MBDL assumption. This process is not trivial because MBDL is only shown to provide tight reduction under passive attacks for the Schnorr Identification scheme. In contrast, we are trying to show security under concurrent attacks. Figure 6 presents an enhanced construction of Schnorr-IBI using a generic 1–2 OT protocol. There are very efficient 1–2 OT protocol constructions which fit our needs such as one by Chou and Orlandi [13], which is based on the Diffie-Hellman key exchange.

Theorem 4. *The OB2 Schnorr-IBI scheme shown in Fig. 6 is $(t_{ibi}, q_c, q_h, q_p, \epsilon_{ibi})$-IMP-CA secure if the 1–2 OT protocol has the properties of Sender security and Receiver privacy and the n-MBDL assumption is $(t_{n-mbdl}, \epsilon_{n-mbdl})$-secure such that*

$$\epsilon_{ibi} \leq 2 \cdot \epsilon_{n-mbdl} + q^{-1}$$

where n is the number of identities queried by the adversary.

Proof. Suppose there exists an adversary A which breaks the OB2 Schnorr-IBI with advantage greater than ϵ_{ibi}, then a simulator S can use A to break the assumption with advantage greater than ϵ_{n-mbdl}. S first receives the challenge $(\mathbb{G}, g, q)$, Z, U_1, ... U_n and has access to the discrete logarithm oracle at most once per base U_i for $i = 1, ..., n$. S generates the msk by randomly sampling $x \xleftarrow{\$} \mathbb{Z}_q$ and computing $X \leftarrow g^x$. S then sets $mpk \leftarrow ((\mathbb{G}, g, q), X, \mathbf{H}, k)$ with $\mathbf{H}$ modelled as a random oracle. S initializes the sets $LU, CU, RU, AU, HL \leftarrow$

OB2-Schnorr-IBI.MKGen(1^k)	OB2-Schnorr-IBI.UKGen(msk,mpk,ID)
1. $(\mathbb{G},q,g) \leftarrow KG_{cyc}(1^k)$	1. $b \xleftarrow{\$} \{0,1\}$
2. $x \xleftarrow{\$} \mathbb{Z}_q; X \leftarrow g^x$	2. $r, w \xleftarrow{\$} \mathbb{Z}_q; R \leftarrow g^r; W \leftarrow g^w$
3. select $H:\{0,1\}^* \to \mathbb{Z}_q$	3. $v \leftarrow H(ID,b,W,X)$
4. $mpk \leftarrow (\mathbb{G},q,g,X,H,k)$	4. $u \leftarrow w+vx$
5. $msk \leftarrow x$	5. $uk \leftarrow (u,v,b,R)$
6. return (mpk,msk)	6. return uk

OB2-Schnorr-IBI.Protocol(P,V)

$P(mpk,ID,uk)$		$V(mpk,ID)$
$W_b \leftarrow g^u X^{-v}; W_{\bar{b}} \leftarrow R$		$c_0, c_1 \xleftarrow{\$} \mathbb{Z}_q$
$y_b, z_{\bar{b}} \xleftarrow{\$} \mathbb{Z}_q; Y_b \leftarrow g^{y_b}$		
$v_{\bar{b}} \leftarrow H(ID,\bar{b},W_{\bar{b}},X)$		
$t_p \xleftarrow{\$} \mathbb{Z}_q$	$\xleftarrow{\quad T_v \quad}$	$t_v \xleftarrow{\$} \mathbb{Z}_q; T_v \leftarrow g^{t_v}$
$T_p \leftarrow T_v^b g^{t_p}$	$\xrightarrow{\quad T_p \quad}$	$s_{v0} \leftarrow H(T_p^{t_v})$
$s_{p\bar{b}} \leftarrow H(T_v^{t_p})$		$s_{v1} \leftarrow H((\frac{T_p}{T_v})^{t_v})$
$c_{\bar{b}} \leftarrow e_{\bar{b}} - s_{p\bar{b}}$	$\xleftarrow{\ (e_0,e_1)\ }$	$e_0 \leftarrow s_{v0}+c_0; e_1 \leftarrow s_{v1}+c_1$
$Y_{\bar{b}} \leftarrow g^{z_{\bar{b}}}(W_{\bar{b}} X^{v_{\bar{b}}})^{-c_{\bar{b}}}$	$\xrightarrow{(Y_0,Y_1,W_0,W_1)}$	
assert $g^{t_v} = T_v$	$\xleftarrow{\quad t_v \quad}$	# Reveal OT secret
$s_{pb} \leftarrow H((T_p T_v^{-b})^{t_v})$		
$c_b \leftarrow e_b - s_{pb}$		
$z_b \leftarrow (y_b+c_b)u$	$\xrightarrow{\ (z_0,z_1)\ }$	for $b=0,1$ do
		$\quad v_b \leftarrow H(ID,b,W_b,X)$
		$\quad \delta_b \leftarrow g^{z_b} \overset{?}{=} Y_b(W_b X^{v_b})^{c_b}$
		return $\delta_0 \wedge \delta_1$

(The steps from T_v exchange down through (e_0,e_1) are bracketed as **OT**.)

Fig. 6. The OB2 Schnorr-IBI scheme using OR-proof and a 1–2 OT protocol.

$\emptyset$ representing *legal users, corrupted users, running users, attacked users* and *hash lists*, respectively. A counter is initialized $i \leftarrow 1$ and the goal of S is to output z such that $Z = g^z \bmod q$. S runs A as the cheating verifier $CV(mpk : CORR, PROV)$ and answers queries by CV following the instructions in Fig. 7.

S trivially simulates the queries perfectly because it has the msk, it can generate at least a valid user key for an ID. The OR-proof hides which of the key S is proving from the view of CV; The interactive proofs of W_0 and W_1 appear equally legitimate. Once CV is ready for impersonation, S obtains $ID^*, st_{CP} \leftarrow CV(mpk : CORR, PROV)$ and checks if $ID^* \in LU$, otherwise runs $\text{INIT}(ID^*)$.

INIT(ID)	PROV(ID,s,M_{in})
1. **if** $ID \in LU$ **then return** $\bot$	1. **if** $ID \in CU \cup AU$ **then return** $\bot$
2. $b \xleftarrow{\$} \{0,1\}$	2. **if** $ID \notin LU$ **then run INIT**(ID)
3. $u, v_b, v_{\bar{b}} \xleftarrow{\$} \mathbb{Z}_q$	3. $(u, v_b, b, R, W, i) \leftarrow LU[ID]$
4. $W \leftarrow g^u X^{-v_b}; R \leftarrow U_i X^{-v_{\bar{b}}}$	4. **if** $(ID,s) \in RU$ **then goto** 8
5. $HL[ID, b, W] \leftarrow v_b$	5. $RU \leftarrow RU \cup \{(ID,s)\}$
6. $HL[ID, \bar{b}, R] \leftarrow v_{\bar{b}}$	6. initialize random coins ρ for P
7. $i \leftarrow i+1$	7. $st[ID,s] \leftarrow (mpk, (u, v_b, b, R), \rho)$
8. $LU[ID] \leftarrow (u, v_b, b, R, W, i)$	8. $(st[ID,s], M_{out}) \leftarrow P(st[ID,s], M_{in})$
9. **return** ID	9. **return** M_{out}

H($h = \{0,1\}^*$)	CORR(ID)
1. **if** $ID \notin LU$ **then run INIT**(ID)	1. **if** $ID \in CU$ **then return** $\bot$
2. **if** $h \in HL$ **then goto** 4	2. **if** $ID \notin LU$ **then run INIT**(ID)
3. $HL[h] = v \xleftarrow{\$} \mathbb{Z}_q$	3. $(u, v_b, b, R, W, i) \leftarrow LU[ID]$
4. $v \leftarrow HL[h]$	4. $CU \leftarrow CU \cup ID$
5. **return** v	5. **return** (u, v_b, b, R)

Fig. 7. CORR and PROV are simulated oracles for the IMP-CA game on the OB2 Schnorr-IBI. The INIT subroutine is only available to S.

S runs A as the cheating prover CP ($mpk, ID^*, st_{CP} : CORR, PROV$) and interacts with A as an honest verifier following Fig. 8. It is apparent that S can successfully extract z such that $g^z \mod q = Z$ if and only if the challenge used by CP for $Y_{\bar{b}}$ is c^*. This event occurs at probability $1/2$, if $c' = c_b$ was chosen by CP during the OT protocol, it will then have to decrypt the encrypted challenge $e_{\bar{b}}$ for $z_{\bar{b}}$ after receiving t_v (See Eq. 1). S has so far only made 1 dlog query on base U_i; S has succeeded in breaking the assumption. Let $\epsilon_{n-mbdl} = P_{sim} \times P_{accept} \times P_{useful}$ be the probability of S outputting z such that z is the discrete log of the target base Z to the multi-base discrete log problem, P_{sim} be the probability of a successful simulation, P_{accept} be the probability that both response z_0 and z_1 are valid responses for impersonation and P_{useful} be the probability that the response obtained from the A is useful in solving the assumption. Clearly, $P_{useful} = Pr[c' = c_b]$ only occurs if the 1–2 OT protocol hides the choice of S when A issues **PROV**($ID = ID^*$) queries[4] while running as CV, which equals to $1/2$ given that b is the result of a random coin toss. We claim $P_{sim} = 1$ because S possesses the msk and can simulate $PROV$ and $CORR$ perfectly. The output of **H** is indistinguishable from the real attack because $v_b, v_{\bar{b}}$ and v are uniformly sampled from $\mathbb{Z}_q$. Given that the IBI protocol is HVZK-SS, we have $P_{accept} \geq \epsilon_{ibi} - q^{-1}$. Thus, we have $\epsilon_{n-mbdl} \geq 1/2(\epsilon_{ibi} - q^{-1})$ as required. $\qquad\square$

---

[4] This is also the reason why R was stored for each user. If R was randomly generated for different **PROV** queries, CV would be able to distinguish b by running **PROV** query on the same ID twice and checking W_0 and W_1.

$$c_{\bar{b}} = e_{\bar{b}} - \mathbf{H}((T_p T_v^{-\bar{b}})^{t_v}) = e_{\bar{b}} - (e_{\bar{b}} - c^*) = c^* \tag{1}$$

5.1 Comparison with Existing Schnorr-Based IBI Schemes

Schnorr-based IBI schemes with IMP-PA can be easily obtained either using the Kurosawa-Heng [21] transform or by Bellare et al.'s transform [5]. IMP-CA security can then be achieved using OR-proof on a IMP-PA Schnorr-based IBI scheme, or through a Schnorr-based signature scheme with strong existential unforgeability (sEUF-CMA) as shown by Yang et al. [29]. However, the instantiations from the existing frameworks are not tight due to the rewinding of CP, and thus being subjected to the square-root loss. Table 2 tabulates existing Schnorr-based IBI schemes along with their security properties and overhead requirements, which clearly shows a tight reduction compared to existing results.

Challenge on $ID^*(CP,S)$

$CP(mpk, ID^*, st_{CP})$		$S(mpk, ID^*)$
		$(u, v_b, b, R, W, i) \leftarrow LU[ID^*]$
		$c_0, c_1 \xleftarrow{\$} \mathbb{Z}_q$
	$\xleftarrow{\quad T_v \quad}$	$t_v \xleftarrow{\$} \mathbb{Z}_q;\ T_v \leftarrow g^{t_v}$
	$\xrightarrow{\quad T_p \quad}$	$s_{v0} \leftarrow H(T_p^{t_v})$
		$s_{v1} \leftarrow H((\frac{T_p}{T_v})^{t_v})$
	$\xleftarrow{\ (e_0, e_1)\ }$	$e_0 \leftarrow s_{v0} + c_0;\ e_1 \leftarrow s_{v1} + c_1$
	$\xrightarrow{(Y_0, Y_1, W_0, W_1)}$	$c^* \leftarrow dlog(i, Z/Y_{\bar{b}})$
	$\xleftarrow{\quad t_v \quad}$	$HL[(T_p T_v^{-\bar{b}})^{t_v}] = e_{\bar{b}} - c^*$
	$\xrightarrow{\ (z_0, z_1)\ }$	$v_{\bar{b}} \leftarrow H(ID, \bar{b}, W_{\bar{b}}, X)$
		$g^{z_{\bar{b}}} \stackrel{?}{=} Y_{\bar{b}}(W_{\bar{b}} X^{v_{\bar{b}}})^{c^*} = Y_{\bar{b}}(U_i)^{c^*} = Z$
		return $z_{\bar{b}}$

Fig. 8. Extracting the discrete log of Z using the cheating prover.

Table 2. Comparison of existing IBI frameworks on security assumption, reduction loss and overhead requirements.

Scheme	Sec.	Reduction bound	$|uk|$	$|mpk|$	Prot. BW
KH-PA [21]	PA	$\sqrt{\epsilon_{ss-euf-cma}} + q^{-1}$	$2\mathbb{Z}_q$	$\mathbb{G}$	$2\mathbb{G} + 2\mathbb{Z}_q$
KH-CA [21]	CA	$\sqrt{\epsilon_{ss-wh}} + q^{-1}$	$2\mathbb{Z}_q$	$\mathbb{G}$	$k(2\mathbb{G} + \mathbb{Z}_q + 1)$
BNN-IBI [5]	CA	$\sqrt{\epsilon_{omdl}} + \sqrt{\epsilon_{ss-euf-cma}} + 2q^{-1}$	$\mathbb{G} + \mathbb{Z}_q$	$\mathbb{G}$	$3\mathbb{G} + 2\mathbb{Z}_q$
KW [29]	CA	$\sqrt{2\epsilon_{kw-seuf-cma}} + q^{-1}$	$2\mathbb{Z}_q$	$3\mathbb{G}$	$8\mathbb{G} + 4\mathbb{Z}_q$
Tan-IBI [26]	CA	$\epsilon_{ddh} + 2(q_c + 1)q^{-1}$	$2\mathbb{Z}_q$	$3\mathbb{G}$	$3\mathbb{G} + 2\mathbb{Z}_q$
OR-proof (on KH-PA) [17]	CA	$\sqrt{2\sqrt{\epsilon_{ss-euf-cma}} + q^{-1}} + q^{-1}$	$2\mathbb{Z}_q$	$\mathbb{G}$	$4\mathbb{G} + 4\mathbb{Z}_q$
Twin [11]	CA	$\sqrt{\epsilon_{dlog}} + q^{-1} + q^{-1}$	$3\mathbb{Z}_q$	$2\mathbb{G}$	$2\mathbb{G} + 3\mathbb{Z}_q$
TNC-IBI [10]	CA	$\epsilon_{dsdh} + (q_c + 1)q^{-1}$	$2\mathbb{Z}_q$	$3\mathbb{G}$	$3\mathbb{G} + 2\mathbb{Z}_q$
OB2 (this work, using OT from [13])	CA	$2\epsilon_{n-mbdl} + q^{-1}$	$\mathbb{G} + 2\mathbb{Z}_q + 1$	$\mathbb{G}$	$6\mathbb{G} + 5\mathbb{Z}_q$

Sec. is short for security, $|uk|$ total user key size, $|mpk|$ total master public key size, Prot. BW for protocol bandwidth (measured per session). PA implies scheme has passive security while CA implies scheme has concurrent security. mpk calculation excludes information for group $\mathbb{G}$, a generator g and order q which are common to all compared schemes. k is the security parameter. Security assumptions are shorthanded as: $\epsilon_{ss-euf-cma}$ EUF-CMA Schnorr Signatures, ϵ_{ss-wh} Schnorr Signatures with witness hiding, ϵ_{omdl} One-More discrete logarithm assumption, $\epsilon_{kw-euf-cma}$ EUF-CMA Katz-Wang Signatures, ϵ_{ddh} Decisional Diffie-Hellman assumption, ϵ_{dsdh} Decisional Square Diffie-Hellman assumption, ϵ_{dlog} Discrete logarithm assumption.

6 Conclusion

In this work, we introduced OrBit, a new way of achieving tight security reduction results in the construction of IMP-CA-secure IBI schemes using the OR-proof in two different flavors. In OB1, our first technique, we showed that by using the OR-proof technique combined with trapdoor sampleable relations, security for the IBI scheme could be reduced directly to the one-wayness trapdoor sampleable relations instead of IMP-PA security [17]. In the second technique, OB2, we explored the possibility of achieving tightness with only a 1-bit loss for a Schnorr-based IBI scheme using the MBDL assumption introduced by Bellare and Dai [4]. While MBDL was initially used for passive-secure proofs, we showed that with a generic 1–2 OT scheme, it is possible to achieve active/concurrent security with tight security.

Acknowledgements. The authors would like to thank the anonymous reviewers for their helpful and critical feedback in the preliminary version of this paper. In addition, the authors acknowledge the Fundamental Research Grant Scheme awarded by the Ministry of Higher Education of Malaysia (FRGS/1/2019/ICT04/MMU/02/5) and the Multimedia University fund.

References

1. Adj, G., Menezes, A., Oliveira, T., Rodríguez-Henríquez, F.: Computing discrete logarithms in f36·137 and f36·163 using magma. In: Arithmetic of Finite Fields: WAIFI 2014, pp. 3–22, 01 2014
2. Andersen, M.P., et al.: WAVE: a decentralized authorization framework with transitive delegation. In: 28th USENIX Security Symposium (USENIX Security 19), Santa Clara, CA, August 2019, pp. 1375–1392. USENIX Association. ISBN 978-1-939133-06-9. https://www.usenix.org/conference/usenixsecurity19/presentation/andersen
3. Bader, C., Jager, T., Li, Y., Schäge, S.: On the impossibility of tight cryptographic reductions. In: Fischlin, M., Coron, J.-S. (eds.) EUROCRYPT 2016. LNCS, vol. 9666, pp. 273–304. Springer, Heidelberg (2016). https://doi.org/10.1007/978-3-662-49896-5_10
4. Bellare, M., Dai, W.: The multi-base discrete logarithm problem: tight reductions and non-rewinding proofs for Schnorr identification and signatures. Cryptology ePrint Archive, Report 2020/416 (2020). https://eprint.iacr.org/2020/416
5. Bellare, M., Namprempre, C., Neven, G.: Security proofs for identity-based identification and signature schemes. In: Cachin, C., Camenisch, J.L. (eds.) EUROCRYPT 2004. LNCS, vol. 3027, pp. 268–286. Springer, Heidelberg (2004). https://doi.org/10.1007/978-3-540-24676-3_17
6. Bellare, M., Palacio, A.: GQ and Schnorr identification schemes: proofs of security against impersonation under active and concurrent attacks. In: Yung, M. (ed.) CRYPTO 2002. LNCS, vol. 2442, pp. 162–177. Springer, Heidelberg (2002). https://doi.org/10.1007/3-540-45708-9_11
7. Boldyreva, A.: Threshold signatures, multisignatures and blind signatures based on the Gap-Diffie-Hellman-group signature scheme. In: Desmedt, Y.G. (ed.) PKC 2003. LNCS, vol. 2567, pp. 31–46. Springer, Heidelberg (2003). https://doi.org/10.1007/3-540-36288-6_3
8. Boneh, D., Lynn, B., Shacham, H.: Short signatures from the weil pairing. In: Boyd, C. (ed.) ASIACRYPT 2001. LNCS, vol. 2248, pp. 514–532. Springer, Heidelberg (2001). https://doi.org/10.1007/3-540-45682-1_30
9. Chia, J., Chin, J.: An identity based-identification scheme with tight security against active and concurrent adversaries. IEEE Access 8, 61711–61725 (2020). https://doi.org/10.1109/ACCESS.2020.2983750
10. Chia, J., Chin, J.-J., Yip, S.-C.: A pairing-free identity-based identification scheme with tight security using modified-Schnorr signatures. Symmetry 13(8) (2021). ISSN 2073-8994. https://doi.org/10.3390/sym13081330. https://www.mdpi.com/2073-8994/13/8/1330
11. Chin, J.-J., Tan, S.-Y., Heng, S.-H., Phan, R.: Twin-Schnorr: a security upgrade for the Schnorr identity-based identification scheme. Scie. World J. 237514(01), 2015 (2015). https://doi.org/10.1155/2015/237514
12. Chin, J.-J., Tan, S.-Y., Heng, S.-H., Phan, R.C.-W.: On the security of a modified beth identity-based identification scheme. Inf. Process. Lett. 113(14–16), 580–583 (2013). https://doi.org/10.1016/j.ipl.2013.04.015
13. Chou, T., Orlandi, C.: The simplest protocol for oblivious transfer. Cryptology ePrint Archive, Report 2015/267 (2015). https://eprint.iacr.org/2015/267
14. Di Crescenzo, G.: On the security of beth's identification schemes against active and concurrent adversaries. In: Mathematical Methods in Computer Science, MMICS 2008, Karlsruhe, Germany, 17–19 December 2008, pp. 1–17 (2008). https://doi.org/10.1007/978-3-540-89994-5_1

15. Emura, K., Takayasu, A., Watanabe, Y.: Efficient identity-based encryption with hierarchical key-insulation from HIBE. Cryptology ePrint Archive, Report 2020/1087 (2020). https://eprint.iacr.org/2020/1087

16. Fiat, A., Shamir, A.: How to prove yourself: practical solutions to identification and signature problems. In: Odlyzko, A.M. (ed.) CRYPTO 1986. LNCS, vol. 263, pp. 186–194. Springer, Heidelberg (1987). https://doi.org/10.1007/3-540-47721-7_12

17. Fujioka, A., Saito, T., Xagawa, K.: Security enhancements by OR-proof in identity-based identification. In: Bao, F., Samarati, P., Zhou, J. (eds.) ACNS 2012. LNCS, vol. 7341, pp. 135–152. Springer, Heidelberg (2012). https://doi.org/10.1007/978-3-642-31284-7_9

18. Fukumitsu, M., Hasegawa, S.: A Galindo-Garcia-like identity-based signature with tight security reduction, revisited. In: 2018 Sixth International Symposium on Computing and Networking (CANDAR), pp. 92–98 (2018). https://doi.org/10.1109/CANDAR.2018.00019

19. Girault, M.: An identity-based identification scheme based on discrete logarithms modulo a composite number. In: Damgård, I.B. (ed.) EUROCRYPT 1990. LNCS, vol. 473, pp. 481–486. Springer, Heidelberg (1991). https://doi.org/10.1007/3-540-46877-3_44

20. Granger, R.: Breaking '128-bit secure' supersingular binary curves, 01 2014

21. Kurosawa, K., Heng, S.-H.: From digital signature to id-based identification/signature. In: Bao, F., Deng, R., Zhou, J. (eds.) PKC 2004. LNCS, vol. 2947, pp. 248–261. Springer, Heidelberg (2004). https://doi.org/10.1007/978-3-540-24632-9_18

22. Kurosawa, K., Heng, S.-H., et al.: Identity-based identification without random oracles. In: Gervasi, O. (ed.) ICCSA 2005. LNCS, vol. 3481, pp. 603–613. Springer, Heidelberg (2005). https://doi.org/10.1007/11424826_64

23. Lacharité, M.-S.: Security of BLS and BGLS signatures in a multi-user setting. Cryptogr. Commun. **10**, 1–18 (2018). https://doi.org/10.1007/s12095-017-0253-6

24. Lee, Y., Park, J.H., Lee, K., Lee, D.H.: Tight security for the generic construction of identity-based signature (in the multi-instance setting). Theoret. Comput. Sci. **847**, 122–133 (2020). ISSN 0304-3975. https://doi.org/10.1016/j.tcs.2020.09.044. https://www.sciencedirect.com/science/article/pii/S0304397520305557

25. Ng, T.-S., Tan, S.-Y., Chin, J.-J.: Improving signature schemes with tight security reductions. In: Heng, S.-H., Lopez, J. (eds.) ISPEC 2019. LNCS, vol. 11879, pp. 273–292. Springer, Cham (2019). https://doi.org/10.1007/978-3-030-34339-2_15

26. Tan, S.-Y., Heng, S.-H., Phan, R.C.-W., Goi, B.-M., et al.: A variant of Schnorr identity-based identification scheme with tight reduction. In: Kim, T. (ed.) FGIT 2011. LNCS, vol. 7105, pp. 361–370. Springer, Heidelberg (2011). https://doi.org/10.1007/978-3-642-27142-7_42

27. Thorncharoensri, P., Susilo, W., Mu, Y.: Identity-based identification scheme secure against concurrent-reset attacks without random oracles. In: Youm, H.Y., Yung, M. (eds.) WISA 2009. LNCS, vol. 5932, pp. 94–108. Springer, Heidelberg (2009). https://doi.org/10.1007/978-3-642-10838-9_8

28. Wu, G., Zhao, Z., Guo, F., Susilo, W., Zhang, F.: On the general construction of tightly secure identity-based signature schemes. Comput. J. **63**(12), 1835–1848 (2020). ISSN 0010-4620. https://doi.org/10.1093/comjnl/bxaa011

29. Yang, G., Chen, J., Wong, D.S., Deng, X., Wang, D.: A new framework for the design and analysis of identity-based identification schemes. Theoret. Comput. Sci. **407**(1), 370–388 (2008). ISSN 0304-3975. https://doi.org/10.1016/j.tcs.2008.07.001

Card-Based Zero-Knowledge Proof Protocols for Graph Problems and Their Computational Model

Daiki Miyahara[1,2](✉) , Hiromichi Haneda[1], and Takaaki Mizuki[1,2](✉)

[1] The University of Electro-Communications, Tokyo, Japan
daiki.miyahara.q4@alumni.tohoku.ac.jp, mizuki+lncs@tohoku.ac.jp
[2] National Institute of Advanced Industrial Science and Technology, Tokyo, Japan

Abstract. Zero-Knowledge Proof (ZKP) is a cryptographic technique that enables a prover to convince a verifier that a given statement is true without revealing any information other than its truth. It is known that ZKP can be realized by physical objects such as a deck of cards; recently, many such "card-based" ZKP protocols for pencil puzzles (such as Sudoku and Numberlink) have been devised. In this paper, we shift our attention to graph theory problems from pencil puzzles: We propose card-based ZKP protocols for the graph 3-coloring problem and the graph isomorphism problem. Similar to most of the existing card-based ZKP protocols, our two protocols have no soundness error. The proposed protocols can be implemented without any technical knowledge, and the principle of zero-knowledge proof is easy to understand. In particular, our protocol for the graph isomorphism problem requires only three shuffles regardless of the sizes of a pair of given graphs. In addition, to deal with our proposed protocols more rigorously, we present a formal framework for card-based ZKP protocols which are non-interactive and have no soundness error.

Keywords: Physical zero-knowledge proof · Card-based cryptography · Graph 3-coloring problem · Graph isomorphism problem

1 Introduction

Suppose that there are two parties, the prover, Peggy, and the verifier, Victor. The prover Peggy has a witness w guaranteeing that a statement x is true, while the verifier Victor does not have it. In this case, a *Zero-Knowledge Proof* (ZKP) protocol, whose concept was devised by Goldwasser et al. in 1989 [9], enables Peggy to convince Victor that the statement x is true without leaking any information about the witness w. Such a ZKP protocol must satisfy the following three conditions.

Completeness. If x is true, then Victor accepts.
Soundness. If x is false, then no matter how Peggy behaves, Victor rejects with an overwhelming probability.

© Springer Nature Switzerland AG 2021
Q. Huang and Y. Yu (Eds.): ProvSec 2021, LNCS 13059, pp. 136–152, 2021.
https://doi.org/10.1007/978-3-030-90402-9_8

Zero-knowledge. No information about w other than the fact that x is true is leaked to Victor.

The probability that Victor accepts even though x is false is called a *soundness error* probability, denoted by δ. If a ZKP protocol having such a probability δ is executed ℓ times, Victor rejects with a probability of $1 - \delta^\ell$. Thus, we can satisfy the soundness condition by repeatedly running such a protocol sufficient times.

Normally, ZKP protocols are implemented on computers and network systems, based on cryptographic primitives, such as public-key cryptography. By contrast, there are *physical* ZKP protocols that do not rely on computers; for example, Gradwohl et al. [10] in 2009 invented the first physical ZKP protocol for Sudoku using a deck of physical cards. This protocol directly verifies a solution of a Sudoku puzzle without reducing it to other NP-complete problems, such as 3SAT. Therefore, a physical ZKP protocol is suitable for visual understanding of the concept of ZKP, as it can be performed with human hands.

It should be noted that because any Boolean circuit can be securely evaluated by card-based cryptography (e.g., [4,14,15,19,21,30]), we can construct a physical ZKP protocol for any 3SAT instance [20].

1.1 Existing Physical ZKP Protocols

Many physical ZKP protocols using a deck of cards have been constructed for Nikoli's pencil puzzles, such as Sudoku [10,24,29], Makaro [3], Slitherlink [16], and Numberlink [26]. These protocols are fun, and their proofs can be easily understood because they were presented using pictures of a deck of cards (as will be seen in Sect. 2).

Going back to history, Goldreich et al. [8] in 1991 proved that, for all languages in NP, there exist ZKP protocols based on cryptographic primitives. In their paper, they also presented a physical ZKP protocol for the 3-coloring problem using boxes having locks to clarify the presentation of their concept. This physical ZKP protocol has a soundness error as will be seen in Sect. 2.3, meaning that the protocol needs to be repeated many times.

1.2 Contribution

In this paper, we shift our attention to *graph theory* problems from pencil puzzles. We propose card-based ZKP protocols for two famous graph problems: the *3-coloring* problem and the *graph isomorphism* problem. Similar to most of the existing card-based ZKP protocols, our two protocols have no soundness error. The proposed protocols can be implemented without any technical knowledge, and the principle of ZKP is easy to understand. In particular, our protocol for the graph isomorphism problem requires only three shuffles regardless of how large a pair of given graphs is.

In addition to constructing the two protocols, we present a formal framework for card-based ZKP protocols which are non-interactive and have no soundness error. Using this proposed framework, we can describe such card-based ZKP protocols in a rigorous way.

We emphasize that this paper is an attempt to connect physical ZKP protocols (in cryptology) and graph theory. Hence, we believe that our work explores new directions of physical ZKP protocols toward graph problems. Constructing efficient ZKP protocols for other famous graph problems is an interesting problem, including the ones in Karp's 21 NP-complete problems [13], as a physical ZKP protocol for the Hamiltonian cycle problem has recently been designed [28].

2   Preliminaries

In this section, we introduce notations of a deck of cards and a shuffling action used in our proposed protocols later. We then introduce the 3-coloring problem and the graph isomorphism problem. We also describe an existing protocol for the 3-coloring problem [8].

2.1   A Deck of Cards

Both of our proposed protocols use a two-colored deck of cards, such as black ♣ and red ♡ cards. In addition, our protocol for the graph isomorphism problem (presented in Sect. 4) uses numbered cards, such as $\boxed{1}\boxed{2}\boxed{3}\cdots$. The backs of all these cards, denoted by $\boxed{?}$, are indistinguishable.

2.2   Pile-Scramble Shuffle

In our construction, we will use a shuffling action called the *pile-scramble shuffle*. This action uniformly shuffles multiple piles of face-down cards at random. More precisely, for some natural number $n\,(\geq 2)$, let $(\mathsf{pile}_1, \mathsf{pile}_2, \ldots, \mathsf{pile}_n)$ denote a sequence of n piles of cards where each pile consists of the same number of cards. Applying a pile-scramble shuffle to such a sequence of piles (denoted by $[\cdot|\ldots|\cdot]$) results in:

$$\begin{bmatrix} \boxed{?} & \boxed{?} & & \boxed{?} \\ \boxed{?} & \boxed{?} & \cdots & \boxed{?} \\ \vdots & \vdots & & \vdots \\ \boxed{?} & \boxed{?} & \cdots & \boxed{?} \\ \mathsf{pile}_1 & \mathsf{pile}_2 & & \mathsf{pile}_n \end{bmatrix} \rightarrow \begin{matrix} \boxed{?} & \boxed{?} & \cdots & \boxed{?} \\ \boxed{?} & \boxed{?} & \cdots & \boxed{?} \\ \vdots & \vdots & & \vdots \\ \boxed{?} & \boxed{?} & \cdots & \boxed{?} \\ \mathsf{pile}_{\pi^{-1}(1)} & \mathsf{pile}_{\pi^{-1}(2)} & & \mathsf{pile}_{\pi^{-1}(n)} \end{matrix},$$

where $\pi \in S_n$ is a random permutation uniformly chosen from the symmetric group of degree n, denoted by S_n. In this case, we regard cards in the same "column" as a pile; thus, the resulting order of cards in each pile does not change. We also consider applying a pile-scramble shuffle "vertically," i.e., cards in the same row are regarded as a pile and all the piles are shuffled.

A pile-scramble shuffle was first used by Ishikawa et al. [12] in 2015. It can be easily implemented by using rubber bands or envelopes to fix each pile of cards and scrambles the piles to randomize the order of them. We assume that, as in the case of usual card games, even if only one player performs a pile-scramble shuffle, nobody (including the executor) can know the resulting order of piles. If some players are skeptical, they may repeat the shuffling action in turn until they are satisfied.

2.3 Known Physical Protocol for 3-Coloring Problem [8]

The *3-coloring* problem is a decision problem to determine whether vertices of a given undirected graph $G = (V, E)$ can be colored with three colors such that every two adjacent vertices are assigned different colors. More precisely, the problem is to determine whether there exists a mapping $\phi : V \rightarrow \{1, 2, 3\}$ such that any edge $(u, v) \in E$ satisfies $\phi(u) \neq \phi(v)$. This problem is known to be NP-complete [6].

Goldreich et al. [8] in 1991 presented a physical ZKP protocol for the 3-coloring problem. It uses boxes each having a lock with a corresponding key, such as safety boxes. Assuming that Peggy knows a correct coloring ϕ but Victor does not, the protocol proceeds as follows.

1. Let n be the number of vertices in a given graph G. Peggy prepares n boxes and assigns a box to each vertex.
2. Peggy assigns three random colors to $\{1, 2, 3\}$ and puts the corresponding color for each vertex into the box without Victor's seeing it. More precisely, Peggy chooses a random permutation $\pi \in S_3$, and for every $u \in V$, Peggy puts $\pi(\phi(u))$ into the box corresponding to u.
3. Victor randomly chooses one edge $(u, v) \in E$ and tells it to Peggy.
4. Peggy sends Victor the keys to the two boxes corresponding to u and v.
5. Victor opens the two boxes using the keys received. If they contain different colors, then Victor continues to the next iteration; otherwise, Victor rejects.

This protocol satisfies the three conditions required for a ZKP protocol. If Peggy has a correct mapping ϕ, then Peggy can always convince Victor because the two boxes corresponding to the two adjacent vertices chosen by Victor never contain the same color, i.e., $\pi(\phi(u)) \neq \pi(\phi(v))$. If Peggy does not have ϕ, then Victor rejects with a probability of at least $1/m$, where m is the number of edges in the given graph G, i.e., this protocol has a soundness error. By repeating this protocol ℓ times, Victor can detect such a malicious prover Peggy with a probability of $1 - (1 - \frac{1}{m})^\ell$. Since Peggy discloses to Victor only the randomly assigned colors of the two adjacent vertices, Victor cannot obtain more information than the fact that the two vertices are colored with different colors.

2.4 Graph Isomorphism Problem

The *graph isomorphism* problem is a decision problem to determine whether two given undirected graphs are isomorphic. More specifically, given two graphs $G_1 = (V_1, E_1)$ and $G_2 = (V_2, E_2)$, the problem is to determine whether there exists a permutation $\pi : V_1 \rightarrow V_2$ such that $(u, v) \in E_1$ if and only if $(\pi(u), \pi(v)) \in E_2$.

It has been believed that the graph isomorphism problem is neither in P nor NP-complete. A quasi-polynomial time algorithm has been reported by Babai [1,11].

3   Card-Based ZKP for 3-Coloring Problem

In this section, we construct a physical ZKP protocol for the 3-coloring problem with no soundness error. As in the existing protocol [8] introduced in Sect. 2.3, our proposed protocol enables the prover, Peggy, to convince the verifier, Victor, that, for a given undirected graph $G = (V, E)$, Peggy has a mapping $\phi : V \to \{1, 2, 3\}$ such that any edge $(u, v) \in E$ satisfies $\phi(u) \neq \phi(v)$ without revealing any information about ϕ.

In our protocol, Peggy first places sequences of cards representing ϕ that she has, and then Peggy and Victor publicly manipulate the sequences for the verification. Thus, after Peggy places the sequences as input, either Peggy or Victor (or even a third party) may manipulate the cards.

The idea behind our proposed protocol is to verify that *every* pair of adjacent vertices is colored with different colors one by one. Our protocol proceeds as follows.

1. Let $V = \{1, 2, \ldots, n\}$. For every vertex $i \in \{1, 2, \ldots, n\}$, Peggy prepares a sequence of face-down cards representing $\phi(i)$ according to the following encoding rule (with one red card and two black cards):[1]

$$\boxed{\heartsuit}\,\boxed{\clubsuit}\,\boxed{\clubsuit} = 1, \quad \boxed{\clubsuit}\,\boxed{\heartsuit}\,\boxed{\clubsuit} = 2, \quad \boxed{\clubsuit}\,\boxed{\clubsuit}\,\boxed{\heartsuit} = 3. \tag{1}$$

Place such n sequences vertically one by one as follows:

$$\boxed{?}\,\boxed{?}\,\boxed{?} = \phi(1)$$
$$\boxed{?}\,\boxed{?}\,\boxed{?} = \phi(2)$$
$$\vdots \quad \vdots \quad \vdots$$
$$\boxed{?}\,\boxed{?}\,\boxed{?} = \phi(n)$$

2. For every edge $(i, j) \in E$, perform the following steps. If Victor does not reject for any edge, then Victor accepts.
   (a) Regarding cards in the same column as a pile, apply a pile-scramble shuffle (horizontally) to the n sequences as follows:

$$\begin{bmatrix} \boxed{?} & \boxed{?} & \boxed{?} \\ \boxed{?} & \boxed{?} & \boxed{?} \\ \vdots & \vdots & \vdots \\ \boxed{?} & \boxed{?} & \boxed{?} \end{bmatrix} \rightarrow \begin{matrix} \boxed{?} & \boxed{?} & \boxed{?} \\ \boxed{?} & \boxed{?} & \boxed{?} \\ \vdots & \vdots & \vdots \\ \boxed{?} & \boxed{?} & \boxed{?} \end{matrix}$$

---

[1] An encoding rule representing a positive integer in this manner was first considered by Shinagawa et al. in 2015 [31].

Let us emphasize that anyone cannot know the resulting order after performing a pile-scramble shuffle.[2]

(b) Reveal all the cards of the i-th and j-th sequences. If the two sequences represent different colors, i.e., the two red cards are revealed to be at different positions, it means that $\phi(i) \neq \phi(j)$, and hence, continue the protocol after turning over the revealed cards; otherwise, Victor rejects. Note that information about the values of $\phi(i)$ and $\phi(j)$ does not leak because a pile-scramble shuffle has been applied to the sequences in the previous step.

Let m be the number of edges in the given graph G. The number of required cards and shuffles for this protocol is $3n$ and m, respectively.

We present a security proof of this protocol in Sect. 6.1. This proof is based on our computational model formalized in Sect. 5.

4   Card-Based ZKP for Graph Isomorphism Problem

In this section, we construct a card-based ZKP protocol for the graph isomorphism problem with no soundness error. Our proposed protocol enables Peggy to convince Victor that for two given undirected graphs $G_1 = (V_1, E_1)$ and $G_2 = (V_2, E_2)$, Peggy has a permutation $\pi : V_1 \to V_2$ (as a witness) such that $(u, v) \in E_1$ if and only if $(\pi(u), \pi(v)) \in E_2$.

4.1   Idea

Assume that Peggy has a correct permutation $\pi \in S_n$ where n denotes the number of vertices in the two given graphs G_1 and G_2. Let $A(G_1)$ and $A(G_2)$ denote their adjacency matrices, respectively. Then, the following equation holds for the permutation matrix P_π corresponding to π [7]:

$$A(G_2) = P_\pi^{\mathrm{T}} A(G_1) P_\pi,$$

where for a row vector e_i in which the i-th element is 1 and the remaining ones are 0, $1 \leq i \leq n$, the permutation matrix P_π is

$$P_\pi = \begin{bmatrix} e_{\pi(1)} \\ \vdots \\ e_{\pi(n)} \end{bmatrix},$$

and P_π^{T} is the transpose. From this equation, it suffices that Peggy and Victor place sequences of face-down cards representing $A(G_1)$, and Peggy having π rearranges the sequences according to the permutation matrix P_π so that the resulting sequences represent $A(G_2)$ (without revealing any information about π).

---

[2] One might think that the resulting order could be easily known because there are only six possibilities. One possible implementation is to put piles of cards into a box or ball whose inside is invisible from outside and then throw it up to randomize the order of them (cf. [32]).

4.2 Description

In our proposed protocol, Peggy first prepares a sequence of face-down cards representing π, and then Peggy and Victor publicly manipulate the sequences for the verification. Our protocol proceeds as follows.

1. Peggy prepares a sequence of face-down numbered cards from $\boxed{1}$ to $\boxed{n}$ representing the inverse permutation $\pi^{-1} \in S_n$ (that she knows as a witness) according to the following encoding:

$$\underbrace{\boxed{?}}_{\pi(1)} \underbrace{\boxed{?}}_{\pi(2)} \cdots \underbrace{\boxed{?}}_{\pi(n)} \quad [\pi^{-1}].$$

This sequence is called the sequence $[\pi^{-1}]$ where the parentheses indicate that all cards in the sequence are face-down.

2. Let $\clubsuit$ represent 0 and $\heartsuit$ represent 1. According to this encoding, place sequences of face-down cards representing the $n \times n$ adjacency matrix of G_1, namely $A(G_1)$. For example, the following 4×4 adjacency matrix is represented using sequences of cards as follows:

$$\begin{pmatrix} 0 & 1 & 1 & 0 \\ 1 & 0 & 1 & 1 \\ 1 & 1 & 0 & 0 \\ 0 & 1 & 0 & 0 \end{pmatrix} \rightarrow \begin{matrix} \clubsuit & \heartsuit & \heartsuit & \clubsuit \\ \heartsuit & \clubsuit & \heartsuit & \heartsuit \\ \heartsuit & \heartsuit & \clubsuit & \clubsuit \\ \clubsuit & \heartsuit & \clubsuit & \clubsuit \end{matrix}.$$

Then, place the sequence of $[\pi^{-1}]$ that Peggy prepared and a sequence of the identity permutation $[\mathsf{id}]$ consisting of $\boxed{1}\boxed{2}\cdots\boxed{n}$ (in this order) on the left side of the matrix $[A(G_1)]$ vertically, as follows:

$$\begin{matrix} \boxed{?} & \boxed{?} & \boxed{?} \cdots \boxed{?} \\ \boxed{?} & \boxed{?} & \boxed{?} \cdots \boxed{?} \\ \vdots & \vdots & \vdots \ddots \vdots \\ \boxed{?} & \boxed{?} & \boxed{?} \cdots \boxed{?} \\ [\mathsf{id}] & [\pi^{-1}] & [A(G_1)] \end{matrix}.$$

Note that the sequence $[\mathsf{id}]$ represents the position of each card in the sequence $[\pi^{-1}]$.

3. Regarding the cards in the same row as a pile, apply a pile-scramble shuffle to the piles as follows:

$$\begin{matrix} \boxed{\boxed{?}\boxed{?}\boxed{?}\cdots\boxed{?}} \\ \vdots \quad \vdots \quad \vdots \ddots \vdots \\ \boxed{\boxed{?}\boxed{?}\boxed{?}\cdots\boxed{?}} \\ [\mathsf{id}]\ [\pi^{-1}]\ [A(G_1)] \end{matrix} \rightarrow \begin{matrix} \boxed{?} & \boxed{?} & \boxed{?}\cdots\boxed{?} \\ \vdots & \vdots & \vdots \ddots \vdots \\ \boxed{?} & \boxed{?} & \boxed{?}\cdots\boxed{?} \\ [r] & [r\pi^{-1}] & [P_r^{\mathsf{T}} A(G_1)] \end{matrix},$$

where $r \in S_n$ is a random permutation generated by applying a pile-scramble shuffle.

4. Reveal the sequence $[r\pi^{-1}]$ to obtain the information about $r\pi^{-1}$. Transform the matrix $[P_r^{T}A(G_1)]$ to $[P_\pi^{T}A(G_1)]$ by sorting the rows of the matrix in ascending order according to $r\pi^{-1}$:

5. Turn over the sequence revealed in the previous step. Then, regarding cards in the same row as a pile, apply a pile-scramble shuffle to the sequences $[r]$ and $[r\pi^{-1}]$ as follows:

   where $r' \subset S_n$ is a random permutation generated by applying a pile-scramble shuffle.

6. Reveal the sequence $[r'r]$. Sort the sequence $[r'r\pi^{-1}]$ in ascending order according to $r'r$. This sorting applies the inverse permutation $(r'r)^{-1}$ to the sequence $[r'r\pi^{-1}]$, and hence, the sequence $[r'r\pi^{-1}]$ becomes a sequence $[\pi^{-1}]$:

7. Horizontally place the sequence $[\pi^{-1}]$ above the matrix $[P_\pi^{T}A(G_1)]$ as follows:

8. Regarding the cards in the same column as a pile, apply a pile-scramble shuffle to the piles:

where $r'' \in S_n$ is a random permutation generated by applying a pile-scramble shuffle.

9. Reveal the sequence $[r''\pi^{-1}]$. Sort the columns of the matrix $[P_\pi^T A(G_1)P_{r''}]$ in ascending order according to $r''\pi^{-1}$ to transform the matrix to $[P_\pi^T A(G_1)P_\pi]$:

$$
\begin{array}{l}
\boxed{?} \cdots \boxed{?} \; [r''\pi^{-1}] \\[4pt]
\boxed{?} \cdots \boxed{?} \\
\;\vdots \;\;\ddots\;\; \vdots \;\; [P_\pi^T A(G_1)P_{r''}] \\
\boxed{?} \cdots \boxed{?}
\end{array}
\;\rightarrow\;
\begin{array}{l}
\boxed{?} \cdots \boxed{?} \\
\;\vdots\;\; \ddots\;\; \vdots\;\; [P_\pi^T A(G_1)P_\pi]\;. \\
\boxed{?} \cdots \boxed{?}
\end{array}
$$

10. Reveal all the cards of the matrix $[P_\pi^T A(G_1)P_\pi]$. If they represent the adjacency matrix of G_2, then Victor accepts; otherwise, Victor rejects.

Let m be the number of edges in the given graphs. The total number of required cards is $n^2 + 2n$, because $2m$ $\boxed{\heartsuit}$s and $(n^2 - 2m)$ $\boxed{\clubsuit}$s are used for representing the adjacency matrix of G_1, and $2n$ numbered cards are used for the sequences of $[\pi^{-1}]$ and $[\mathrm{id}]$. The number of required shuffles is three, which is constant regardless of the size of a pair of given graphs.

We present a security proof of this protocol in Sect. 6.2.

5   Basic Formalization of Card-Based ZKP Protocols

In this section, we give a formalization of card-based ZKP protocols to deal with our proposed protocols more rigorously.

Remember that our two protocols presented in Sects. 3 and 4 are *non-interactive*: After the prover, Peggy, places a hidden sequence of face-down cards at the beginning of each of the protocols according to a witness (that only Peggy knows), the protocol can be executed by *anyone* publicly; for example, it suffices that Peggy does every action while the verifier, Victor, watches all behaviors of Peggy. Note that most of the existing ZKP protocols for pencil puzzles (e.g. [3,17,22,26,27,29]) are also non-interactive.

Thus, this section begins with clarifying the relationship between a witness and a hidden sequence of cards.

5.1   Witness Subsequence

Let $L \subseteq \Sigma^*$ be a language that captures a decision problem (such as the 3-coloring problem and graph isomorphism problem), where Σ is an alphabet. In our setting, Peggy and Victor are given a problem *instance* $x \in L$ such that only Peggy knows a *witness* w of the instance x; w being a witness of x means that, given a pair (x, w), everyone (including Peggy and Victor) can easily confirm that $x \in L$ (say, it can be computed in polynomial time).

For example, given an instance of the graph isomorphism problem, a permutation π which transforms one graph into the other graph serves a witness.

As seen in Sect. 4, Peggy who knows the permutation π is supposed to privately arrange a sequence of face-down cards encoding π:

$$\underbrace{\boxed{?}}_{\pi(1)} \; \underbrace{\boxed{?}}_{\pi(2)} \; \cdots \; \underbrace{\boxed{?}}_{\pi(n)} \quad [\pi^{-1}].$$

Therefore, in general, Peggy and Victor must agree upon a correspondence between a witness and a sequence of cards; we call such a sequence of cards a *witness subsequence*.

Fixing a language L, for an instance $x \in L$, we denote by W_x the set of all witnesses of x. If Peggy knows a witness $w \in W_x$ and she is honest, she should place a witness subsequence correctly (with all cards' faces down); we call it a *correct witness subsequence*. If Peggy does not know any witness, she may place a 'wrong' sequence of cards that follows the 'format' at least; we say a sequence of cards is a *legal witness subsequence* if there exist an instance $y \in L$ and a witness $w' \in W_y$ such that the sequence corresponds to w'. If Peggy is malicious, she may place a random sequence of cards; we call any witness sequence which is not legal an *illegal witness subsequence*.

Let us consider the case where $x \notin L$. If an instance x is clearly outside of L (say, the numbers of edges of G_1 and G_2 are different), Victor would not agree with executing any protocol; therefore, for such an instance, we do not have to construct a protocol. On the other hand, there are instances $x \notin L$ for which we have to construct protocols; define $\check{L} \subseteq \Sigma^* - L$ as

$$\check{L} = \{x \notin L \mid \text{Victor cannot determine if } x \in L\}.$$

If Peggy is malicious, she may present an instance $x \in \check{L}$ to Victor, and place some subsequence to run a protocol (although there is no witness). We call such a subsequence an illegal witness subsequence as well.

Consequently, we are supposed to construct a protocol for every instance in $L \cup \check{L}$.

5.2   Input to Protocol

As seen above, at the beginning of a protocol, Peggy is supposed to prepare a witness subsequence. In addition to the witness subsequence, we need some *helping cards*; for example, our protocol for the graph isomorphism (presented in Sect. 4) uses n^2 black $\boxed{\clubsuit}$ or red $\boxed{\heartsuit}$ cards as well as n numbered cards. These helping cards are placed with their faces up at the beginning of the protocol.

As mentioned, if Peggy is malicious, she may place an illegal witness subsequence. To this end, she may prepare some number of cards stealthily and use them to arrange such an illegal subsequence. Therefore, we have to take into account such stealthy cards (owned by Peggy). Therefore, in addition to the witness subsequence and helping cards, we consider *stealthy cards*: That is, we assume that every input to a protocol consists of these three parts, and that a *deck D* to consider accommodates all these cards.

5.3 Abstract Protocol for ZKP

A card-based protocol itself has been well formalized already [18]. We will slightly adjust the model of protocols by mainly adding a couple of two states, as follows.

First, we review some terms. Let D be a deck containing all cards as mentioned above. We call any element $c \in D$ an atomic card, $\frac{?}{c}$ a face-down card, and $\frac{c}{?}$ a face-up card. Define $\mathsf{top}(\frac{u}{v}) = u$, call

$$\mathsf{top}(\Gamma) = (\mathsf{top}(\alpha_1), \mathsf{top}(\alpha_2), \cdots, \mathsf{top}(\alpha_{|D|}))$$

a visible sequence of a sequence $\Gamma = (\alpha_1, \alpha_2, \ldots, \alpha_{|D|})$, and let Vis^D be the set of all visible sequences from the deck D.

Next, we consider the input to a protocol. As mentioned before, the input consists of three parts: the witness subsequence, helping cards, and stealthy cards. Considering all possible input sequences, we use U to denote the set of all such sequences.

We now consider a state of a protocol. Contrary to the conventional card-based model, we introduce two additional states q_{accept} and q_{reject}. That is, Q is the set of states including the initial state q_0, the accepting state q_{accept}, and the rejecting state q_{reject}. When a protocol terminates with q_{accept}, it means that Victor accepts an input sequence Γ; when it terminates with q_{reject}, it means that Victor rejects.

Based on these definitions and terms, a protocol is defined as follows.

Definition 1. *A card-based protocol P is a 4-tuple $P = (D, U, Q, A)$ that satisfies:*

- *D is a deck.*
- *U is an input set.*
- *Q is a set of states containing q_0, q_{accept}, and q_{reject}.*
- *$A : (Q \backslash \{q_{accept}, q_{reject}\}) \times \mathsf{Vis}^D \to Q \times \mathsf{Action}$ is an action function. Here, Action is a set of all actions consisting of the followings.*
  - *Turning over (turn, T): This action is to turn over cards in the positions specified by $T \subseteq \{1, 2, \cdots, |D|\}$. Thus, this transforms a sequence $\Gamma = (\alpha_1, \alpha_2, \cdots, \alpha_{|D|})$ as follows:*

$$\mathsf{turn}_T(\Gamma) := (\beta_1, \beta_2, \cdots, \beta_{|D|}),$$

such that for $\mathsf{swap}(\frac{u}{v}) := \frac{v}{u}$,

$$\beta_i = \begin{cases} \mathsf{swap}(\alpha_i) & \textit{if } i \in T, \\ \alpha_i & \textit{otherwise.} \end{cases}$$

  - *Permuting (perm, π): This action is applying a permutation $\pi \in S_{|D|}$ to a sequence of cards and transforms $\Gamma = (\alpha_1, \alpha_2, \ldots, \alpha_{|D|})$ as follows:*

$$\mathsf{perm}_\pi(\Gamma) := (\alpha_{\pi^{-1}(1)}, \alpha_{\pi^{-1}(2)}, \cdots, \alpha_{\pi^{-1}(|D|)}).$$

- *Shuffling* (shuf, $\Pi, \mathcal{F}$): *This action is applying a permutation chosen from a permutation set $\Pi \subseteq S_{|D|}$ according to a probability distribution $\mathcal{F}$ on Π. This action transforms $\Gamma = (\alpha_1, \alpha_2, \cdots, \alpha_{|D|})$ as follows:*

$$\mathsf{shuf}_{\Pi, \mathcal{F}}(\Gamma) := \mathsf{perm}_\pi(\Gamma),$$

where $\pi \in \Pi$ is drawn according to $\mathcal{F}$.

A protocol $P = (D, U, Q, A)$ runs as an abstract machine: Staring from the initial state q_0 with some input $\Gamma_0 \in U$, the state and the current sequence change according to the output of the action function. When its state becomes q_{accept} or q_{reject}, the protocol terminates. Considering an execution of the protocol, the tuple of all sequences $(\Gamma_0, \Gamma_1, \cdots, \Gamma_t)$ appeared from the initial state q_0 to the final is called a *sequence trace*. Similarly, $(\mathsf{top}(\Gamma_0), \mathsf{top}(\Gamma_1), \cdots, \mathsf{top}(\Gamma_t))$ is called a *visible sequence trace*.

5.4 Properties of ZKP

Based on the formalization thus far, we formally define a card-based ZKP protocol (collection) that is non-interactive and has no soundness error, as follows.

Definition 2. *Let L be a language, and let $x \in L \cup \check{L}$. We say that a protocol $P_x = (D, U, Q, A)$ is compatible with the instance x if its input set U contains every possible sequence whose prefix is a witness subsequence (corresponding to a witness $w \in W_x$).*[3]

Definition 3. *Let L be a language. Assume that, for every instance $x \in L \cup \check{L}$, we have a protocol P_x compatible with x. We call the set of all these protocols a ZKP protocol collection for L if the following three conditions are met:*

Completeness. *If $x \in L$ and an initial sequence $\Gamma_0 \in U$ for the protocol P_x contains a correct witness subsequence (corresponding to a witness $w \in W_x$), the protocol starting with Γ_0 always terminates with the accepting state q_{accept}.*

Soundness. *If $x \in L$ and an initial sequence Γ_0 for P_x does not contain any correct witness subsequence, the protocol starting with Γ_0 always terminates with the rejecting state q_{reject}. If $x \in \check{L}$, P_x always terminates with q_{reject}.*

Zero-knowledge. *Let $x \in L$, and consider any distribution on input set U of the protocol P_x. For any run of the protocol, the distribution of input and that of the visible sequence trace are stochastically independent.*

6 Proof of ZKP Properties for Our Protocols

In this section, we prove the completeness, soundness, and zero-knowledge of our proposed protocols based on the formalization presented in Sect. 5.

---

[3] All other sequences in U start with illegal witness subsequences.

6.1 3-Coloring Problem

We prove that our ZKP protocol for the 3-coloring problem presented in Sect. 3 satisfies the three conditions.

Theorem 1 (Completeness). *If the input sequence Γ_0 corresponding to ϕ contains a correct witness subsequence, the protocol always terminates with the accepting state q_{accept}.*

Proof. In Step 2(a), we apply a pile-scramble shuffle horizontally to the three piles. Let $\pi \in S_3$ be a random permutation generated by this pile-scramble shuffle. Two sequences that represented $\phi(i)$ and $\phi(j)$ before applying the pile-scramble shuffle become to represent $\pi\phi(i)$ and $\pi\phi(j)$, i.e., the positions of the red cards in the two sequences are $\pi\phi(i)$-th and $\pi\phi(j)$-th, respectively. By revealing the two sequences, we can know whether $\pi\phi(i) = \pi\phi(j)$ (i.e., $\phi(i) = \phi(j)$) or not. Therefore, the protocol always terminates with the accept state q_{accept}. $\square$

Theorem 2 (Soundness). *If the input sequence Γ_0 corresponding to ϕ does not contain any correct witness subsequence, the protocol always terminates with the rejecting state q_{reject}.*

Proof. We consider the case where a sequence placed in Step 1 does not contain a correct witness subsequence. In Step 2(a), we make vertical piles by pile-scramble shuffle. That is, the sequence is placed in such a way that $\psi(u) = \psi(v)$ satisfied in Step 1. When the turn operation (turn, T) is performed in Step 2(b), it is found that $\boxed{\heartsuit}$ is in the same column, resulting in the rejecting state. $\square$

Theorem 3 (Zero-knowledge). *For any run of the protocol, the distribution of input and that of the visible sequence trace are stochastically independent.*

Proof. In Step 2(b), the sequence to be turned over by the operation (turn, T) is randomly selected from the following six patterns:

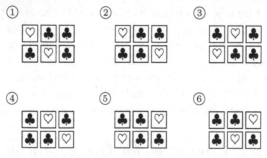

Let $r \in S_3$ be a uniformly randomly generated permutation. This sequence is transformed by (perm, r). Thus, the visible sequence trace of the protocol is uniformly distributed. Therefore, the distribution of input and the visible sequence trace are stochastically independent. $\square$

6.2 Graph Isomorphism Problem

We prove that our ZKP protocol for the graph isomorphism problem presented in Sect. 4 satisfies the three conditions.

Theorem 4 (Completeness). *If the input sequence Γ_0 corresponding to π contains a correct witness subsequence, the protocol always terminates with the accepting state q_{accept}.*

Proof. As shown in Sect. 4.1, there exists a permutation matrix P_π for the adjacency matrices $A(G_1)$ and $A(G_2)$ of two isomorphic graphs G_1 and G_2 as follows:

$$A(G_2) = P_\pi^T A(G_1) P_\pi.$$

In Step 4, $(\text{perm}, (r\pi^{-1})^{-1})$ is equal to computing $P_\pi^T A(G_1)$, and in Step 9, $(\text{perm}, (r''\pi^{-1})^{-1})$ is equal to computing $(P_\pi^T A(G_1)) P_\pi$.

Therefore, the protocol always terminates with q_{accept} in Step 10.   □

Theorem 5 (Soundness). *If the input sequence Γ_0 corresponding to ϕ does not contains any correct witness subsequence, the protocol always terminates with the rejecting state q_{reject}.*

Proof. Consider the case where a witness subsequence placed in Step 1 is not correct but legal. Let π' be a permutation corresponding to that witness subsequence. The card sequences in Steps 3, 4, 8, and 9 is transformed by (perm, π'). As shown in Sect. 4.1, if the permutation matrix $P_{\pi'}$ corresponding to π is used, it is transformed into a sequence corresponding to the graph G_2' instead of the graph G_2 such that

$$A(G_2') = P_{\pi'}^T A(G_1) P_{\pi'}.$$

Thus, when (turn, T) is performed in Step 10, the sequence is different from that of the adjacency matrix in G_2, resulting in the rejecting state. Next, consider the case where a sequence corresponding to an illegal witness subsequence is placed. In this case, when (turn, T) is performed in Step 10, it is found that the sequence does not follow the format of the sequence, resulting in the rejecting state as well.   □

Theorem 6 (Zero-knowledge). *For any run of the protocol, the distribution of input and that of the visible sequence trace are stochastically independent.*

Proof. As seen in Sect. 2.2, pile-scramble shuffles are applied so that random permutations r, r', r'' are generated. The sequence in Steps 3, 5, and 8 is transformed by (perm,r), (perm,r'), and (perm,r''), respectively. Thus, the visible sequence trace of the protocol is uniformly distributed. Therefore, the distribution of input and the visible sequence trace are stochastically independent.   □

7   Conclusion

In this paper, we proposed physical ZKP protocols using a deck of cards for the two major graph problems. Our protocols have no soundness error and they are easy to implement. In particular, it is interesting to note that our ZKP protocol for the graph isomorphism problem requires only three shuffles. Similar to the proposed protocol, we believe that we can propose a card-based ZKP with no soundness error for other graph problems. In addition, we constructed a rigorous definition of a card-based ZKP protocol that is non-interactive and with no soundness error.

As future work, we are interested in the subgraph isomorphism problem[4] and in analyzing computation classes in more details. Furthermore, formalizing interactive card-based ZKP protocols (e.g., [2,5,16,23]) is an important future task. In addition, investigating the relationship between our model and the standard definitions of ZKP in details will be expected.

Acknowledgements. We thank the anonymous referees, whose comments have helped us improve the presentation of the paper. We would like to thank Hideaki Sone for his cooperation in preparing a Japanese draft version at an earlier stage of this work. We would also like to thank Kazumasa Shinagawa for his idea improving a protocol for the 3-coloring problem. The second author is grateful to Haruka Mizuta for helpful discussions at the beginning of this work. This work was supported in part by JSPS KAKENHI Grant Numbers JP19J21153 and JP21K11881.

References

1. Babai, L.: Graph isomorphism in quasipolynomial time. In: ACM Symposium on Theory of Computing, STOC 2016, ACM, New York, pp. 684–697 (2016). https://doi.org/10.1145/2897518.2897542

2. Bultel, X., Dreier, J., Dumas, J.G., Lafourcade, P.: Physical zero-knowledge proofs for Akari, Takuzu, Kakuro and KenKen. In: Demaine, E.D., Grandoni, F. (eds.) Fun with Algorithms, Schloss Dagstuhl, Dagstuhl, LIPIcs, vol. 49, pp. 8:1–8:20 (2016). https://doi.org/10.4230/LIPIcs.FUN.2016.8

3. Bultel, X., et al.: Physical zero-knowledge proof for Makaro. In: Izumi, T., Kuznetsov, P. (eds.) SSS 2018. LNCS, vol. 11201, pp. 111–125. Springer, Cham (2018). https://doi.org/10.1007/978-3-030-03232-6_8

4. Crépeau, C., Kilian, J.: Discreet solitary games. In: Stinson, D.R. (ed.) CRYPTO 1993. LNCS, vol. 773, pp. 319–330. Springer, Heidelberg (1994). https://doi.org/10.1007/3-540-48329-2_27

5. Dumas, J.-G., Lafourcade, P., Miyahara, D., Mizuki, T., Sasaki, T., Sone, H.: Interactive physical zero-knowledge proof for Norinori. In: Du, D.-Z., Duan, Z., Tian, C. (eds.) COCOON 2019. LNCS, vol. 11653, pp. 166–177. Springer, Cham (2019). https://doi.org/10.1007/978-3-030-26176-4_14

---

[4] Very recently, Ruangwises and Itoh [25,28] implied that a card-based ZKP protocol for the Hamiltonian cycle problem can be constructed in a similar way to our protocol for the graph isomorphism problem.

6. Garey, M., Johnson, D., Stockmeyer, L.: Some simplified NP-complete graph problems. Theoret. Comput. Sci. **1**(3), 237–267 (1976). https://doi.org/10.1016/0304-3975(76)90059-1
7. Godsil, C., Royle, G.F.: Algebraic Graph Theory, Graduate Texts in Mathematics, vol. 207. Springer, New York (2001). https://doi.org/10.1007/978-1-4613-0163-9
8. Goldreich, O., Micali, S., Wigderson, A.: Proofs that yield nothing but their validity or all languages in NP have zero-knowledge proof systems. J. ACM **38**(3), 690–728 (1991). https://doi.org/10.1145/116825.116852
9. Goldwasser, S., Micali, S., Rackoff, C.: The knowledge complexity of interactive proof systems. SIAM J. Comput. **18**(1), 186–208 (1989). https://doi.org/10.1137/0218012
10. Gradwohl, R., Naor, M., Pinkas, B., Rothblum, G.N.: Cryptographic and physical zero-knowledge proof systems for solutions of Sudoku puzzles. Theory Comput. Syst. **44**(2), 245–268 (2009). https://doi.org/10.1007/s00224-008-9119-9
11. Grohe, M., Schweitzer, P.: The graph isomorphism problem. Commun. ACM **63**(11), 128–134 (2020). https://doi.org/10.1145/3372123
12. Ishikawa, R., Chida, E., Mizuki, T.: Efficient card-based protocols for generating a hidden random permutation without fixed points. In: Calude, C.S., Dinneen, M.J. (eds.) UCNC 2015. LNCS, vol. 9252, pp. 215–226. Springer, Cham (2015). https://doi.org/10.1007/978-3-319-21819-9_16
13. Karp, R.M.: Reducibility among combinatorial problems. In: Miller, R.E., Thatcher, J.W., Bohlinger, J.D. (eds.) Complexity of Computer Computations, pp. 85–103. Springer, Boston (1972). https://doi.org/10.1007/978-1-4684-2001-2_9
14. Koch, A.: Cryptographic protocols from physical assumptions. Ph.D. thesis, Karlsruhe Institute of Technology (KIT) (2019). https://doi.org/10.5445/IR/1000097756
15. Koch, A., Schrempp, M., Kirsten, M.: Card-based cryptography meets formal verification. New Gener. Comput. **39**(1), 115–158 (2021). https://doi.org/10.1007/s00354-020-00120-0
16. Lafourcade, P., Miyahara, D., Mizuki, T., Robert, L., Sasaki, T., Sone, H.: How to construct physical zero-knowledge proofs for puzzles with a "single loop" condition. Theoret. Comput. Sci. (2021). https://doi.org/10.1016/j.tcs.2021.07.019, in press
17. Miyahara, D., et al.: Card-based ZKP protocols for Takuzu and Juosan. In: Farach-Colton, M., Prencipe, G., Uehara, R. (eds.) Fun with Algorithms, Schloss Dagstuhl, Dagstuhl, LIPIcs, vol. 157, pp. 20:1–20:21 (2020). https://doi.org/10.4230/LIPIcs.FUN.2021.20
18. Mizuki, T., Shizuya, H.: A formalization of card-based cryptographic protocols via abstract machine. Int. J. Inf. Secur. **13**(1), 15–23 (2013). https://doi.org/10.1007/s10207-013-0219-4
19. Mizuki, T., Sone, H.: Six-card secure AND and four-card secure XOR. In: Deng, X., Hopcroft, J.E., Xue, J. (eds.) FAW 2009. LNCS, vol. 5598, pp. 358–369. Springer, Heidelberg (2009). https://doi.org/10.1007/978-3-642-02270-8_36
20. Niemi, V., Renvall, A.: Secure multiparty computations without computers. Theoret. Comput. Sci. **191**(1–2), 173–183 (1998). https://doi.org/10.1016/S0304-3975(97)00107-2
21. Ono, H., Manabe, Y.: Card-based cryptographic logical computations using private operations. New Gener. Comput. **39**(1), 19–40 (2021). https://doi.org/10.1007/s00354-020-00113-z

22. Robert, L., Miyahara, D., Lafourcade, P., Mizuki, T.: Physical zero-knowledge proof for Suguru puzzle. In: Devismes, S., Mittal, N. (eds.) SSS 2020. LNCS, vol. 12514, pp. 235–247. Springer, Cham (2020). https://doi.org/10.1007/978-3-030-64348-5_19

23. Robert, L., Miyahara, D., Lafourcade, P., Mizuki, T.: Interactive physical ZKP for connectivity: applications to Nurikabe and Hitori. In: De Mol, L., Weiermann, A., Manea, F., Fernández-Duque, D. (eds.) CiE 2021. LNCS, vol. 12813, pp. 373–384. Springer, Cham (2021). https://doi.org/10.1007/978-3-030-80049-9_37

24. Ruangwises, S.: Two standard decks of playing cards are sufficient for a ZKP for Sudoku. In: Computing and Combinatorics. LNCS, Springer, Cham (2021, to appear)

25. Ruangwises, S., Itoh, T.: Physical zero-knowledge proof for connected spanning subgraph problem and Bridges puzzle (2020). https://arxiv.org/abs/2011.02313

26. Ruangwises, S., Itoh, T.: Physical zero-knowledge proof for Numberlink puzzle and k vertex-disjoint paths problem. New Gener. Comput. **39**(1), 3–17 (2021). https://doi.org/10.1007/s00354-020-00114-y

27. Ruangwises, S., Itoh, T.: Physical zero-knowledge proof for ripple effect. In: Uehara, R., Hong, S.-H., Nandy, S.C. (eds.) WALCOM 2021. LNCS, vol. 12635, pp. 296–307. Springer, Cham (2021). https://doi.org/10.1007/978-3-030-68211-8_24

28. Ruangwises, S., Itoh, T.: Physical ZKP for connected spanning subgraph: applications to Bridges puzzle and other problems. In: Unconventional Computation and Natural Computation. LNCS, Springer, Cham (2021, to appear)

29. Sasaki, T., Miyahara, D., Mizuki, T., Sone, H.: Efficient card-based zero-knowledge proof for Sudoku. Theoret. Comput. Sci. **839**, 135–142 (2020). https://doi.org/10.1016/j.tcs.2020.05.036

30. Shinagawa, K.: On the construction of easy to perform card-based protocols. Ph.D. thesis, Tokyo Institute of Technology (2020)

31. Shinagawa, K., et al.: Multi-party computation with small shuffle complexity using regular polygon cards. In: Au, M.-H., Miyaji, A. (eds.) ProvSec 2015. LNCS, vol. 9451, pp. 127–146. Springer, Cham (2015). https://doi.org/10.1007/978-3-319-26059-4_7

32. Ueda, I., Miyahara, D., Nishimura, A., Hayashi, Y., Mizuki, T., Sone, H.: Secure implementations of a random bisection cut. Int. J. Inf. Secur. **19**(4), 445–452 (2019). https://doi.org/10.1007/s10207-019-00463-w

Post Quantum Cryptography

Recovery Attack on Bob's Reused Randomness in CRYSTALS-KYBER and SABER

Satoshi Okada[1] and Yuntao Wang[2](✉) (iD)

[1] Graduate School of Information Science and Technology, The University of Tokyo, Tokyo, Japan
okada-satoshi323@g.ecc.u-tokyo.ac.jp
[2] School of Information Science, Japan Advanced Institute of Science and Technology, Nomi, Japan
y-wang@jaist.ac.jp

Abstract. Quantum computing capability outperforms that of the classic computers overwhelmingly, which seriously threatens modern public-key cryptography. For this reason, the National Institute of Standards and Technology (NIST) and several other standards organizations are progressing the standardization for post-quantum cryptography (PQC). There are two contenders among those candidates, CRYSTALS-KYBER and SABER, lattice-based encryption algorithms in the third round finalists of NIST's PQC standardization project. At the current phase, it is important to evaluate their security, which is based on the hardness of the variants of Ring Learning With Errors (Ring-LWE) problem. In ProvSec 2020, Wang et al. introduced a notion of "meta-PK" for Ring-LWE crypto mechanism. They further proposed randomness reuse attacks on NewHope and LAC cryptosystems which meet the meta-PKE model. In their attacks, the encryptor Bob's partial (or even all) randomness can be recovered if it is reused. In this paper, we propose attacks against CRYSTALS-KYBER and SABER crypto schemes by adapting the meta-PKE model and improving Wang et al.'s methods. Then, we show that our proposed attacks cost at most 4, 3, and 4 queries to recover Bob's randomness for any security levels of I (AES-128), III (AES-192), and V (AES-256), respectively in CRYSTALS-KYBER. Simultaneously, no more than 6, 6, and 4 queries are required to recover Bob's secret for security levels I, III, and V in SABER.

Keywords: PQC · Randomness reuse attack · Meta-PKE · CRYSTALS-KYBER · SABER

1 Introduction

The security of current public-key crypto algorithms is commonly based on the difficulty of the large number factorization problem or the discrete logarithm problem. However, it is possible to break these cryptosystems in polynomial time

© Springer Nature Switzerland AG 2021
Q. Huang and Y. Yu (Eds.): ProvSec 2021, LNCS 13059, pp. 155–173, 2021.
https://doi.org/10.1007/978-3-030-90402-9_9

by quantum computers in the near future, due to Shor's quantum algorithm [19] and the rapid development of quantum computing technique. Therefore, it is urgent to develop the quantum-safe crypto algorithms, or academically named by post-quantum cryptography (PQC) in general, to protect against the threat of quantum computers. Several years ago, some international standards organizations such as NIST, ISO, and IETF already started the PQC standardization projects. Among the several categories, lattice-based cryptography is considered as one of the most promising contenders for its reliable security strength, comparative light communication cost, fast performance and excellent adaptation capabilities [1]. Indeed, three of four encryption/KEM algorithms and two of three digital signature schemes are lattice-based candidates in the third round finalists selected and announced by NIST in 2020.

CRYSTALS-KYBER [6] and SABER [7] are two of lattice-based encryption/KEM candidates that progressed to the third round of NIST's PQC standardization project. Specifically, the security of CRYSTALS-KYBER is based on the difficulty of the underlying Ring-LWE problem in the module lattice (i.e. Module-LWE problem) [2]. Similarly, SABER's security depends on the difficulty of the Module-LWR problem, which chooses deterministic errors and consumes less computational resources. Generally, owing to the ring structure, the key size in the Ring-LWE based crypto schemes is smaller than that of the typical LWE based ones. At the current stage, it is crucial to analyze their security carefully to resist malicious attacks.

Recently, it has been common to reuse keys or randomness in network communications in order to improve the performance of the protocols. For instance, TLS 1.3 [18] adopts the pre-shared key (PSK) mode, where the server is allowed to reuse the same secret key (randomness) and public key in intermittent communication with the clients to reduce the procedure of handshakes. Such key reuse mode has the risk of leaking information about a secret key when an adversary has enough chances to send queries to the honest server and get correct responses from it. There are kinds of key reuse attacks on Ring-LWE based crypto schemes. In this paper, we consider the case that the client Bob reuses his randomness, which is used for the encryption process. This attack works as follows: an adversary sends chosen public keys to the server and recovers Bob's partial or entire randomness by observing the returned public key and ciphertext. For example, it is dangerous when the client Bob communicates with an honest server after accessing a malicious one and reusing the same randomness. That is because his ciphertext is easily decrypted by misusing his leaked randomness.

In [21], Wang et al. introduce a meta-PKE construction and show that both NewHope and LAC follow this construction. Then, they observe that the meta-PKE is vulnerable against the randomness reuse attack, and they propose attacks on NewHope [2] and LAC [13], respectively. However, this attack for CRYSTALS-KYBER or SABER has not been proposed so far.

1.1 Our Contributions

The randomness reuse attacks on LAC and NewHope proposed in [21] are not adaptable to CRYSTALS-KYBER and SABER because the encryption processes of the crypto schemes are different. In this paper, we first discuss necessary conditions for the success of attacks against CRYSTALS-KYBER and SABER and present attack methods when the conditions are satisfied. Then, we also propose attack methods for crypto schemes that do not meet that condition. Furthermore, we shows that in CRYSTALS-KYBER, our proposed attack costs at most 4, 3, and 4 queries to recover Bob's randomness for security levels of I (AES-128), III (AES-196), and V (AES-256), respectively. Meanwhile, in SABER, at most 6, 6, and 4 queries are needed for security levels of I, III, and V. Indeed, our proposed algorithms can recover Bob's randomness with 100% success rate. Furthermore, we experimentally verified our proposed attacks. Considering the success rate and the number of queries, the reuse of the randomness is very dangerous and should be strictly avoided. It is notable that CRYSTALS-KYBER and SABER are two of the leading contenders in NIST PQC standardization project, namely, one of them may be applied in some randomness reuse scenarios such as TLS communications in the near future.

Due to the vulnerability of randomness reuse, once the attacker recovered the client's (Bob's) randomness, there is potential risk that the attacker can obtain other parties' symmetric keys issued by the server. Consequently, this work may call attention to relevant countermeasures for such attacks in real-world applications.

1.2 Related Works

There have been a number of key recovery attacks on Ring-LWE [14] based cryptosystems under a key reuse scenario. In general, they are divided into two types: the signal leakage attacks taking advantage of the signal function [5,8,10,12], and key reuse attacks focusing on the final shared key or the ciphertext. Concerning the latter, in ACISP 2018, Ding et al. [9] proposed a general key mismatch attack model for Ring-LWE based key exchange protocol. Subsequently, there are several key mismatch attacks on specific lattice-based cryptographic schemes. For example, attacks on NewHope are proposed in [4,15,16,20]. In 2019, Qin et al. [17] proposed attacks on CRYSTALS-KYBER, and Greuret et al. [11] proposed attacks on LAC in 2020. Furthermore, there is also a key mismatch attack using quantum algorithms proposed by Băetu et al. [3] in 2019. Besides the key mismatch attack on Alice's secrets, there is also a key reuse attack on Bob's randomness by observing his ciphertext. In 2020, Wang et al. [21] proposed such attacks on NewHope and LAC, which are both the ring-LWE based cryptosystems with compressing technique. In this paper, we improve the attacks in [21] and apply them to the Module-LWE based CRYSTALS-KYBER with compressing technique, and the Module-LWR based SABER with bitwise shift operation.

1.3   Roadmap

We recall some preliminaries, including mathematical notations, CRYSTALS-KYBER, SABER, and Wang et al.'s proposition in Sect. 2. Then, we apply Wang et al.'s theorem and propose our key reuse attacks on CRYSTALS-KYBER and SABER in Sect. 3. Finally, we give our experimental results and show how our proposed attack works well in Sect. 4. Finally, we make a conclusion and present some countermeasures against our proposed attack in Sect. 5.

2   Preliminary

In this section, we introduce the algebraic definitions and notations used in this paper. Next, we show each protocol's outline, including several core functions in CRYSTALS-KYBER [6] and SABER [7]. Finally, we explain an important theorem advocated by Wang et al. [21].

2.1   Mathematical Notations

Set $\mathbb{Z}_q$ the integer residue ring modulo q, and $\mathbb{Z}_q[x]$ represents a polynomial ring whose coefficients are sampled from $\mathbb{Z}_q$. $\mathcal{R}_q$ is the quotient ring $\mathbb{Z}_q[x]/(x^n + 1)$. In this paper, bold upper-case letters such as $\mathbf{A}$ represent matrices, and bold lower-case letters such as $\mathbf{b}$ represent vectors. The transpose of matrix $\mathbf{A} \in \mathcal{R}_q^{k \times k}$ is denoted by $\mathbf{A}^T \in \mathcal{R}_q^{k \times k}$. Similarly, the transpose of vector $\mathbf{b} \in \mathcal{R}_q^{k \times 1}$ is denoted by $\mathbf{b}^T \in \mathcal{R}_q^{1 \times k}$. For $a \in \mathcal{R}_q$, $a[i]$ represents ith coefficient of a $\left(a = \sum_{i=0}^{n-1} a[i]x^i\right)$. For $\mathbf{b} \in \mathcal{R}_q^k$, $\mathbf{b}_i$ means ith component of $\mathbf{b}$ ($0 \leq i \leq k-1$). The operation $\lfloor x \rfloor$ on real number x represents the largest integer no larger than x; and $\lfloor x \rceil = \lfloor x + \frac{1}{2} \rfloor$.

For a probability distribution χ, $x \leftarrow \chi$ denotes that polynomial x's coefficients are randomly sampled from χ; and $\mathbf{x} \leftarrow \chi^{k \times 1}$ denotes sampling polynomial vector $\mathbf{x}$ with all coefficients sampled from χ. Given a set S, the notation $x \leftarrow \mathcal{U}(S)$ means selecting x from S uniformly at random.

2.2   CRYSTALS-KYBER [6]

We show the outline of the CRYSTALS-KYBER public key encryption protocol in Fig. 1. Note that the public polynomial matrix $\mathbf{A}$ is shared in advance. B_η is a centered binomial distribution, and its element is sampled by calculating $\sum_{i=1}^{\eta} (b_i - b_i')$ (b_i and b_i' are sampled from $\{0, 1\}$ uniformly at random). CRYSTALS-KYBER consists of the below three steps.

1. Alice first selects a secret key $\mathbf{s}_A$ and an error $\mathbf{e}_A$ from $B_\eta^{k \times 1}$. Then, she calculates the public key $\mathbf{P}_A = \mathbf{A}\mathbf{s}_A + \mathbf{e}_A$ using the previously shared $\mathbf{A}(\in \mathcal{R}_q^{k \times k})$, and sends $\mathbf{P}_A$ to Bob. From the public key $\mathbf{P}_A$ and the previously shared polynomial $\mathbf{A}$, it is difficult to obtain information about the secret key $\mathbf{s}_A$ due to the hardness of Module-LWE problem.

pre-shared key $\mathbf{A} \in \mathcal{R}_q^{k \times k}$	
Alice	Bob

$\mathbf{s}_A, \mathbf{e}_A \leftarrow B_\eta^{k \times 1}$

$\mathbf{P}_A = \mathbf{A}\mathbf{s}_A + \mathbf{e}_A \quad \xrightarrow{\;\mathbf{P}_A\;}$

$\qquad\qquad\qquad\qquad\qquad\qquad \mathbf{s}_B, \mathbf{e}_B \leftarrow B_\eta^{k \times 1}$

$\qquad\qquad\qquad\qquad\qquad\qquad e'_B \leftarrow B_\eta$

$\qquad\qquad\qquad\qquad\qquad\qquad \mathbf{P}_B = \mathbf{A}^T \mathbf{s}_B + \mathbf{e}_B$

$\qquad\qquad\qquad\qquad\qquad\qquad m \leftarrow \mathcal{U}^{256}(\{0,1\})$

$\qquad\qquad\qquad\qquad\qquad\qquad v_B = \mathbf{P}_A^T \mathbf{s}_B + e'_B + \mathrm{Decompress}_q(m, 1)$

$\qquad\qquad\qquad\qquad\qquad\qquad \mathbf{c_1} = \mathrm{Compress}_q(\mathbf{P}_B, d_{\mathbf{P}_B})$

$\mathbf{u}_A = \mathrm{Decompress}_q(\mathbf{c_1}, d_{\mathbf{P}_B}) \quad \xleftarrow{\;c=(\mathbf{c_1}, c_2)\;} \quad c_2 = \mathrm{Compress}_q(v_B, d_{v_B})$

$v_A = \mathrm{Decompress}_q(c_2, d_{v_B})$

$m' = \mathrm{Compress}_q\left(v_A - \mathbf{s}_A^T \mathbf{u}_A, 1\right)$

Fig. 1. A sketch of CRYSTALS-KYBER public key encryption scheme

Table 1. Parameter choices in CRTSTALS-KYBER [6]

	n	k	q	$d_{\mathbf{P}_B}$	d_{v_B}	Security level
Kyber-512	256	2	3329	10	3	I (AES-128)
Kyber-768	256	3	3329	10	4	III (AES-192)
Kyber-1024	256	4	3329	11	5	V (AES-256)

2. After receiving $\mathbf{P_A}$, Bob samples polynomial vectors $\mathbf{s}_B$, $\mathbf{e}_B$ and polynomial e'_B from $B_\eta^{k \times 1}$ and B_η, respectively. Then, he computes the public key $\mathbf{P}_B = \mathbf{A}^T \mathbf{s}_B + \mathbf{e}_B$. Subsequently, he generates m from $\mathcal{U}^{256}(\{0,1\})$ and computes $v_B = \mathbf{P}_A^T \mathbf{s}_B + e'_B + \mathrm{Decompress}_q(m, 1)$. Finally, he compresses $\mathbf{P}_B, v_B$ to $\mathbf{c_1}$, c_2 and sends them to Alice.

3. When Alice receives $(\mathbf{c_1}, c_2)$ from Bob, she decompresses them and get $\mathbf{u_A}$ and v_A. In order to obtain m', she calculates $v_A - \mathbf{s}_A^T \mathbf{u}_A$ using her secret key $\mathbf{s_A}$ and compresses it.

Here, $\mathrm{Compress}_q(a, d)$ and $\mathrm{Decompress}_q(a, d)$ are defined as follows.

Definition 1. *The compression function* $\mathbb{Z}_q \to \mathbb{Z}_{2^d}$:

$$\mathrm{Compress}(a, d)_q = \left\lceil \frac{2^d}{q} \cdot a \right\rfloor \pmod{2^d}$$

Definition 2. *The decompression function* $\mathbb{Z}_{2^d} \to \mathbb{Z}_q$:

$$\mathrm{Decompress}(a, d)_q = \left\lceil \frac{q}{2^d} \cdot a \right\rfloor$$

When these two functions are used with $x \in \mathcal{R}_q$ or $\mathbf{x} \in \mathcal{R}_q^{k \times 1}$, the procedure is applied to each coefficient of them.

We list three parameter sets for KYBER: KYBER-512, KYBER-768, and KYBER-1024 in Table 1.

pre-shared key $\mathbf{A} \in \mathcal{R}_q^{k \times k}$	
Alice	Bob
$\mathbf{s}_A, \mathbf{e}_A \leftarrow \beta_\mu^{k \times 1}$	
$\mathbf{P}_A = ((\mathbf{As}_A + \mathbf{h}) \bmod q) \gg (\epsilon_q - \epsilon_p)$ $\xrightarrow{\mathbf{P}_A}$	$\mathbf{s}_B \leftarrow \beta_\mu^{k \times 1}$ $\mathbf{P}_B = ((\mathbf{As}_B + \mathbf{h}) \bmod q) \gg (\epsilon_q - \epsilon_p)$ $m \leftarrow \mathcal{U}^{256}(\{0,1\})$ $v_B = ((\mathbf{P}_A^T \mathbf{s}_B) \bmod p)$
$v_A = ((\mathbf{P}_B^T \mathbf{s}_A) \bmod p)$ $m' = ((v_A - 2^{\epsilon_p - \epsilon_T} c + h_2) \bmod p) \gg (\epsilon_p - 1)$	$\xleftarrow{(\mathbf{P}_B, c)}$ $c = (v_B + h_1 - 2^{\epsilon_p - 1} m \bmod p) \gg (\epsilon_p - \epsilon_T)$

Fig. 2. A sketch of SABER public key encryption scheme

2.3 SABER [7]

Figure 2 shows the outline of SABER crypto scheme. The polynomial matrix $\mathbf{A}$ is shared in advance. β_μ is a centered distribution with probability mass function $P[x \mid x \leftarrow \beta_\mu] = \frac{\mu!}{(\mu/2+x)!(\mu/2-x)!} 2^{-\mu}$. Thus, the integer sampled from β_μ is in the range $[-\mu/2, \mu/2]$. Different from CRYSTALS-KYBER, SABER uses three constants instead of selecting error polynomials: a constant polynomial $h_1 \in \mathcal{R}_q$ with all coefficients being $2^{\epsilon_q - \epsilon_p - 1}$, a constant vector $\mathbf{h} \in \mathcal{R}_q^{k \times 1}$ whose polynomials are equal to h_1 and a constant polynomial $h_2 \in \mathcal{R}_q$ with all coefficients set to be $\left(2^{\epsilon_p - 2} - 2^{\epsilon_p - \epsilon_T - 1} + 2^{\epsilon_q - \epsilon_p - 1}\right)$. The bitwise shift operations $\ll$ and $\gg$ have the usual meaning when applied to an integer and are extended to polynomials and matrices by applying them coefficient-wise. We list the parameter sets with respect to security levels in Table 2, and review the main procedure of SABER below.

Table 2. Parameter choices in SABER [7]

	n	k	q	p	T	μ	Security
LightSaber	256	2	2^{13}	2^{10}	2^3	10	I (AES-128)
Saber	256	3	2^{13}	2^{10}	2^4	8	III (AES-192)
FireSaber	256	4	2^{13}	2^{10}	2^6	6	V (AES-256)

1. Alice first selects a secret key $\mathbf{s}_A$ from $\beta_\mu^{k \times 1}$. Then, she calculates the public key $\mathbf{P}_A = ((\mathbf{As}_A + \mathbf{h}) \bmod q) \gg (\epsilon_q - \epsilon_p)$ using the previously shared $\mathbf{A}(\in \mathcal{R}_q^{k \times k})$, and sends $\mathbf{P}_A$ to Bob. It is difficult to recover $\mathbf{s}_A$ from $\mathbf{P}_A$ due to the hardness of Module-LWR problem.
2. After receiving $\mathbf{P}_A$, Bob samples $\mathbf{s}_B$ from $\beta_\mu^{k \times 1}$. Then, he computes the public key $\mathbf{P}_B = ((\mathbf{As}_B + \mathbf{h}) \bmod q) \gg (\epsilon_q - \epsilon_p)$. After that, he generates m from $\mathcal{U}^{256}(\{0,1\})$ and computes $v_B = ((\mathbf{P}_A^T \mathbf{s}_B) \bmod p)$. Finally, he calculates c and sends $\mathbf{P}_B$ and c to Alice.
3. When Alice receives $(\mathbf{P}_B, c)$, she calculates $v_A = ((\mathbf{P}_B^T \mathbf{s}_A) \bmod p)$, and obtains $m' = ((v_A - 2^{\epsilon_p - \epsilon_T} c + h_2) \bmod p) \gg (\epsilon_p - 1)$ using v_A.

2.4   Wang et al.'s Proposition

Wang et al. propose the so-called "meta-PKE" construction and show both NewHope and LAC follow this construction. Next, they observe that the ciphertext may reveal the encryptor's randomness information using the feature of meta-PKE if the public key satisfies certain conditions.

In the encryption algorithm adopting meta-PKE construction, there is a key step of

$$V = t \times B + f + Y.$$

B is the public key sent by Alice, V is the ciphertext encoded by Bob, and Y is the plaintext. t and f are randomnesses which are usually sampled from a centered binomial distribution. There Wang et al. proposed the following theorem.

Lemma 1. [21] $t, f, Y \in R_q$, and the coefficients $t[i], f[i]$ are in $\{-D, \ldots, D\}, D \ll q, Y_i \in \{0, \frac{q}{2}\}, i = 1, \ldots, n$. $B \in \mathbb{Z}_q$ and $V = B \times t + f + Y \bmod q$. If $2D + 1 \leq B < q/(4D) - 1$, then V will reveal the values of t, f, Y completely.

Proof. We refer the readers to [21] for a proof of this lemma.

3   Our Proposed Attack

We observe that CRYSTALS-KYBER and SABER also follow meta-PKE construction. Therefore, Lemma 1 can be adapted to these two protocol schemes. However, when an adversary tries to recover Bob's randomness, he can only access the compressed ciphertext (V). Thus, we take this fact into consideration and propose the following Theorem 1 for CRYSTALS-KYBER and Theorem 2 for SABER.

Theorem 1. $t, f, Y \in R_q$, and the coefficients $t[i], f[i]$ are in $\{-D, \ldots, D\}, D \ll q, Y_i \in \{0, \frac{q}{2}\}, i = 1, \ldots, n$. $B \in \mathbb{Z}_q$ and $V = B \times t + f + Y \bmod q$. Let compress function be $\mathtt{Compress} : \mathbb{Z}_q \to \mathbb{Z}_p (q > p)$ and $\mathtt{Compress}(x) = \left\lceil \frac{p}{q} x \right\rfloor$. If $\left\lfloor \frac{p(B-2D)}{q} \right\rfloor = 1$, $\frac{p(\frac{q}{2} - 2DB - 2D)}{q} \geq 1$, and $4D + 2 \leq p$, then $\mathtt{Compress}(V)$ will reveal t and Y completely in attacking CRYSTALS-KYBER schemes.

Proof. Since f is small and has little effect on $\mathtt{Compress}(V)$ and B is constant, V can be regarded as a bivariate function $V(t, Y)$. When $\mathtt{Compress} \circ V$ is injective, t and Y can be completely recovered from $\mathtt{Compress}(V(t, Y))$. Then in the remain of the proof, we just need to show the above three conditions guarantee $\mathtt{Compress} \circ V$ injective. We consider two Vs:

$$V_1 = B_1 \times t_1 + f_1 + Y_1 \bmod q \tag{1}$$
$$V_2 = B_2 \times t_2 + f_2 + Y_2 \bmod q. \tag{2}$$

When t_1 and t_2 are different from each other, the minimum difference between V_1 and V_2 is $B - 2D$. Thus, when the condition $\left\lfloor \frac{p(B-2D)}{q} \right\rfloor = 1$ holds,

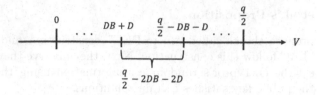

Fig. 3. The minimum difference between V_1 and V_2 when $Y_1 = 0$ and $Y_2 = \frac{q}{2}$.

$\texttt{Compress}(V_1) \neq \texttt{Compress}(V_2)$ and
$\texttt{Compress}(V_1) - \texttt{Compress}(V_2) = 1$. Furthermore, when $Y_1 = 0$ and $Y_2 = \frac{q}{2}$, the minimum difference between V_1 and V_2 is $\frac{q}{2} - 2DB - 2D$ (Fig. 3).
Hence, if $\frac{p(\frac{q}{2} - 2DB - 2D)}{q} \geq 1$, $\texttt{Compress}(V_1) \neq \texttt{Compress}(V_2)$. Additionally, the size of the image of $\texttt{Compress} \circ V$ must be smaller than that of $\mathbb{Z}_p$, i.e. $4D + 2 \leq p$.
In summary, under the three conditions of ① $\left\lfloor \frac{p(B - 2D)}{q} \right\rfloor = 1$, ② $\frac{p(\frac{q}{2} - 2DB - 2D)}{q} \geq 1$, ③ $4D + 2 \leq p$, $\texttt{Compress} \circ V$ is injective and reveals t and Y.

Theorem 2. $t, f, Y \in R_p$, and the coefficients $t[i]$ are in $\{-D, \ldots, D\}$, $D \ll p$, $f[i] = h, h < p$ $Y_i \in \{0, \frac{p}{2}\}, i = 1, \ldots, n$. $B \in \mathbb{Z}_p$, $p = 2^{\epsilon_p}, T = 2^{\epsilon_T}$, and $V = B \times t + f + Y \bmod q$. If $B \gg (\epsilon_p - \epsilon_T) = 1$, $(\frac{p}{2} - 2DB) \gg (\epsilon_p - \epsilon_T) \geq 1$, and $4D + 2 \leq p$, then $V \gg (\epsilon_p - \epsilon_T)$ will reveal t and Y completely in attacking SABER schemes.

Proof. For convenience, we set $\texttt{Compress}$ as $\epsilon_p - \epsilon_T$ bit shift to the right (i.e. $\gg (\epsilon_p - \epsilon_T)$). In this proof, we also show the above three conditions guarantee $\texttt{Compress} \circ V$ injective. We consider two Vs such as (1) and (2). Different from Theorem 1, $f[i]$ is constant. Therefore, when t_1 and t_2 are different from each other, the minimum difference between V_1 and V_2 is B. So if the condition $B \gg (\epsilon_p - \epsilon_T) = 1$ holds, $\texttt{Compress}(V_1) \neq \texttt{Compress}(V_2)$ and
$\texttt{Compress}(V_1) - \texttt{Compress}(V_2) = 1$. Furthermore, when $Y_1 = 0$ and $Y_2 = \frac{p}{2}$, the minimum difference between V_1 and V_2 is $\frac{p}{2} - 2DB$. Due to this, the condition $(\frac{p}{2} - 2DB) \gg (\epsilon_p - \epsilon_T) \geq 1$ realizes $\texttt{Compress}(V_1) \neq \texttt{Compress}(V_2)$. Finally, the size of the image of $\texttt{Compress} \circ V$ must be smaller than that of $\mathbb{Z}_p$, i.e. $4D + 2 \leq p$.

3.1 General Attack Model

In the key reuse attack model, we assume that Bob reuses the same randomness and honestly responds to a number of queries. Namely, an adversary sends freely chosen public keys to Bob and can get the corresponding ciphertexts several times. For convenience, to simulate the behavior of Bob, we build an oracle $\mathcal{O}_k$ (Algorithm 1) and $\mathcal{O}_s$ (Algorithm 4) for CRYSTALS-KYBER and SABER, respectively. Each time the adversary can choose a public key arbitrarily and put it into the oracle. He can get information about s_B by observing the responses.

3.2 Key Reuse Attack on CRYSTALS-KYBER

We build an oracle $\mathcal{O}_k$ in Algorithm 1 for the key reuse attack on CRYSTALS-KYBER. This oracle takes public key $\mathbf{P}_A$ as an input and returns c_2.

Algorithm 1: KYBER_Oracle($\mathbf{P}_A$)

    Input: $\mathbf{P}_A \in \mathcal{R}_q^{k \times 1}$
    Output: $c_2 \in \mathcal{R}_{2^{d_{v_B}}}$
1 $m \leftarrow \mathcal{U}^{256}(\{0,1\})$
2 $e_B' \leftarrow B_\eta$
3 $v_B = \mathbf{P}_A^T s_B + e_B' + \text{Decompress}(m, 1)$
4 $c_2 = \text{Compress}(v_B, d_{v_B})$
5 Return c_2

Attack on Kyber-768 and Kyber-1024. Kyber-768 and Kyber-1024 satisfy Lemma 1 and Theorem 1 when appropriate B is chosen. For example, in Kyber-1024, $D = 2, q = 3329, p = 32$. If we set $B = 109$, the following formulas hold:

$$2D + 1 (= 5) \leq B(= 109) \leq q/4D - 1(\fallingdotseq 416),$$

$$\left\lfloor \frac{p}{q}(B - 2D) \right\rceil = \left\lfloor \frac{32}{3329} \cdot 105 \right\rceil = 1,$$

$$\frac{p}{q}\left(\frac{q}{2} - 2DB - 2D\right) = \frac{32}{3329} \cdot 1224.5 \fallingdotseq 11.7 > 1, \text{and}$$

$$4D + 2 = 10 \leq 32.$$

Therefore, an adversary can recover one polynomial of s_B per query. We show the details of the attack in Algorithm 2.

In this attack, when an adversary wants to recover polynomial s_{Bi} $(0 \leq i \leq k)$, he sets public key $\mathbf{P_A} = [0, \cdots, 0, B, 0, \cdots 0]$ i.e. $\mathbf{P}_{Ai} = B$. Then he sends $\mathbf{P_A}$ to the oracle and obtain ciphertext c_2. We show how the coefficient $c_2[j]$ changes according to the coefficient of s_{Bi} and m in Table 3 for Kyber-768 and Table 4 for Kyber-1024, respectively.

By using these tables, an adversary can recover s_{Bi} (and m simultaneously) completely by observing $c_2[j]$ corresponding to $s_{Bi}[j]$ and $m[j]$. Because he can recover one element of s_B per query, the total cost of this attack is k queries.

Table 3. The behavior of $c_2[j]$ corresponding to $(s_{Bi}[j], m[j])$ when $B = 213$ in Kyber-768

$c_2[j]$ $s_{Bi}[j]$ / $m[j]$	-2	-1	0	1	2
0	14	15	0	1	2
1	6	7	8	9	10

Table 4. The behavior of $c_2[j]$ corresponding to $(\mathbf{s}_{Bi}[j], m[j])$ when $B = 105$ in Kyber-1024

$c_2[j]$ \ $\mathbf{s}_{Bi}[j]$ $m[j]$	-2	-1	0	1	2
0	30	31	0	1	2
1	14	15	16	17	18

Algorithm 2: KYBER_768_1024_Attack()

Output: $\mathbf{s}'_B \in \mathcal{R}_q^{k \times 1}$

1   $B = \lceil \frac{q}{2^{d_{v_B}}} \rceil + 4$

2   **for** $i \leftarrow 0$ **to** k **do**

3     $\mathbf{P_A} = []$

4   **for** $j \leftarrow 0$ **to** k **do**   ▷ Set optimized $\mathbf{P_A}$

5   **if** $j == i$ **then**

6         $\mathbf{P_A}$.append(B)

       else

7         $\mathbf{P_A}$.append(0)

8     $c_2 = \mathcal{O}_k(\mathbf{P_A})$

9   **for** $l \leftarrow 0$ **to** n **do**   ▷ Recover the randomness based on Table 3 or 4

10   **if** $2^{d_{v_B}-1} - \eta \le c_2[l] \le 2^{d_{v_B}-1} + \eta$ **then**

11         $\mathbf{s}'_{Bi}[l] = c_2[l] - 2^{d_{v_B}-1}$

12   **else if** $c_2[l] \le \eta$ **then**

13         $\mathbf{s}'_{Bi}[l] = c_2[l]$

14   **else**

        $\mathbf{s}'_{Bi}[l] = c_2[l] - 2^{d_{v_B}}$

15   **Return** $\mathbf{s}'_B$

Attack on Kyber-512. In contrast, Kyber-512 does not satisfy Theorem 1 ($\because 4D + 2 = 10 > 2^3$). Actually, when the adversary sets $B = 421$, which satisfies $\left\lfloor \frac{p(B-2D)}{q} \right\rfloor = 1$, the relationship between ciphertext c_2 and $(\mathbf{s}_B, m)$ is shown in Table 5.

In this case, when an adversary get $c_2[j] = 6$ or $c_2[j] = 2$, he can not judge whether $\mathbf{s}_{Bi}[j] = 2$ or -2. As a countermeasure, we set one more $B = 631$ and observe how $c_2[j]$ changes in Table 5. It shows that an adversary can recover $\mathbf{s}_{Bi}[j] = 2, -2$ from $c_2[j]$. Consequently, the attack on Kyber-512 works and we show its details in Algorithm 3. In this attack. the adversary can recover all the coefficients of $\mathbf{s}_B$ completely by at most 2k(=4) queries.

Table 5. The behavior of $c_2[j]$ corresponding to $(s_{Bi}[j], m[j])$ when $B = 421, 631$ in Kyber-512

$c_2[j]$ $s_{Bi}[j]$ $m[j]$	421					631				
	-2	-1	0	1	2	-2	-1	0	1	2
0	6	7	0	1	2	5	6	0	2	3
1	2	3	4	5	6	1	2	4	6	7

Algorithm 3: KYBER_512_Attack()

Output: $s'_B \in \mathcal{R}_q^{k \times 1}$

1 $B = 421$
2 **for** $i \leftarrow 0$ **to** k **do**
3 $\quad$ $\mathbf{P_A} = []$
4 $\quad$ **for** $j \leftarrow 0$ **to** k **do**
5 $\quad\quad$ **if** $j == i$ **then**
6 $\quad\quad\quad$ $\mathbf{P_A}$.append(B)
   $\quad\quad$ **else**
7 $\quad\quad\quad$ $\mathbf{P_A}$.append(0)
8 $\quad$ $c_2 = \mathcal{O}_k(\mathbf{P_A})$
9 $\quad$ **for** $l \leftarrow 0$ **to** n **do**
10 $\quad\quad$ **if** $c_2[l] == 2$ or $c_2[l] == 6$ **then**
11 $\quad\quad\quad$ continue
12 $\quad\quad$ **else if** $3 \leq c_2[l] \leq 5$ **then**
13 $\quad\quad\quad$ $s'_{Bi}[l] = c_2[l] - p/2$
14 $\quad\quad$ **else if** $c_2[l] == 0$ or $c_2[l] == 1$ **then**
15 $\quad\quad\quad$ $s'_{Bi}[l] = c_2[l]$
16 $\quad\quad$ **else**
17 $\quad\quad\quad$ $s'_{Bi}[l] = c_2[l] - p$

18 $B = 631$
19 **for** $i \leftarrow 0$ **to** k **do**
20 $\quad$ $\mathbf{P_A} = []$
21 $\quad$ **for** $j \leftarrow 0$ **to** k **do**
22 $\quad\quad$ **if** $j == i$ **then**
23 $\quad\quad\quad$ $\mathbf{P_A}$.append(B)
   $\quad\quad$ **else**
24 $\quad\quad\quad$ $\mathbf{P_A}$.append(0)
25 $\quad$ $c_2 = \mathcal{O}_k(\mathbf{P_A})$
26 $\quad$ **for** $l \leftarrow 0$ **to** n **do**
27 $\quad\quad$ **if** $c_2[l] == 1$ or $c_2[l] == 5$ **then**
28 $\quad\quad\quad$ $s'_{Bi}[l] = -2$
29 $\quad\quad$ **if** $c_2[l] == 3$ or $c_2[l] == 7$ **then**
30 $\quad\quad\quad$ $s'_{Bi}[l] = 2$

31 Return s'_B

3.3 Key Reuse Attack on SABER

In the key reuse attack on SABER, we build oracle $\mathcal{O}_s$ (Algorithm 4). Given $\mathbf{P}_A$, this oracle outputs c.

Algorithm 4: SABER_Oracle($\mathbf{P}_A$)

Input: $\mathbf{P}_A \in \mathcal{R}_q^{k \times 1}$
Output: $c \in \mathcal{R}_T$
1 $m \leftarrow \mathcal{U}^{256}(\{0, 1\})$
2 $v_B = ((\mathbf{P}_A^T s_B) \bmod p)$
3 $c = (v_B + h_1 - 2^{\epsilon_p - 1} m \bmod p) \gg (\epsilon_p - \epsilon_T)$
4 Return c

Attack on FireSaber. FireSaber, whose security level is V, satisfies Theorem 2 when $B = 16$. Therefore, the attack method is almost the same as that for Kyber-768 and Kyber-1024. In this case, the relationship between ciphertext c

---

Algorithm 5: FireSaber_Attack()

Output: $\mathbf{s}'_B \in \mathcal{R}_q^{k \times 1}$

1 $B = 2^{\epsilon_p - \epsilon_T}$
2 **for** $i \leftarrow 0$ **to** k **do**
3 | $\mathbf{P_A} = []$
4 | **for** $j \leftarrow 0$ **to** k **do**
5 | | **if** $j == i$ **then**
6 | | | $\mathbf{P_A}$.append(B)
   | | **else**
7 | | | $\mathbf{P_A}$.append(0)
8 | $c = \mathcal{O}_s(\mathbf{P_A})$
9 | **for** $l \leftarrow 0$ **to** n **do**
10 | | **if** $\frac{T}{2} - \eta \leq c[l] \leq \frac{T}{2} + \eta$ **then**
11 | | | $\mathbf{s}'_{Bi}[l] = c[l] - \frac{T}{2}$
12 | | **else if** $c[l] \leq \eta$ **then**
13 | | | $\mathbf{s}'_{Bi}[l] = c[l]$
14 | | **else**
   | | | $\mathbf{s}'_{Bi}[l] = c[l] - T$

15 Return $\mathbf{s}'_B$

---

and $(\mathbf{s}_B, m)$ is shown in Table 6. From Table 6, we can see that $c[j]$ corresponds to $\mathbf{s}_{Bi}[j]$ one-to-one. Thus, an adversary can recover $\mathbf{s}_B$ with k queries. The detail of this attack is described in Algorithm 5.

Table 6. The behavior of $c[j]$ corresponding to $\mathbf{s}_{Bi}[j]$ and $m[j]$ when $B = 16$ in FireSaber

$c[j]$ \ $\mathbf{s}_{Bi}[j]$ / $m[j]$	-3	-2	-1	0	1	2	3
0	61	62	63	0	1	2	3
1	29	30	31	32	33	34	35

Attack on Saber. Meanwhile, Saber, whose security level is III, does not satisfy Theorem 2. Here we take the similar discussion to that for Kyber-512 in Sect. 3.2. First, we show how $c[j]$ changes according to $m[j]$ and $\mathbf{s}_{Bi}[j]$ in Table 7 when $B = 64$. If $c[j] = 12$ or $c[j] = 4$, an adversary can not judge whether $\mathbf{s}_{Bi}[j] = 4$ or $\mathbf{s}_{Bi}[j] = -4$ only from $c[j]$. Then, we set $B = 96$ and show the relationship between $c[j]$ and $(\mathbf{s}_{Bi}, m)$ in Table 7. It shows that an adversary can judge $\mathbf{s}_{Bi}[j] = -4$ when $c[j] = 10, 2$ and judge $\mathbf{s}_{Bi}[j] = 4$ when $c[j] = 6, 14$ if he knows all the coefficients of $\mathbf{s}_{Bi}$ in $[-3, 3]$. Namely, an adversary first recovers the coefficients $[-3, 3]$ by sending a query with $B = 64$ to the oracle, and next

Table 7. The behavior of $c[j]$ corresponding to $s_{Bi}[j]$ and $m[j]$ when $B = 64, 96$ in Saber

B	64									96								
$c[j]$ \ $s_{Bi}[j]$ / $m[j]$	-4	-3	-2	-1	0	1	2	3	4	-4	-3	-2	-1	0	1	2	3	4
0	12	13	14	15	0	1	2	3	4	10	11	13	14	0	1	3	4	6
1	4	5	6	7	8	9	10	11	12	2	3	5	6	8	9	11	12	14

Algorithm 6: Saber_Attack()

Output: $s'_B \in \mathcal{R}_q^{k \times 1}$

```
 1  B = 64
 2  for i ← 0 to k do
 3      P_A = []
 4      for j ← 0 to k do
 5          if j == i then
 6              P_A.append(B)
            else
 7              P_A.append(0)
 8      c = O_s(P_A)
 9      for l ← 0 to n do
10          if c[l] == 4 or c[l] == 12 then
11              continue
12          else if 5 ≤ c[l] ≤ 11 then
13              s'_Bi[l] = c[l] − T/2
14          else if 0 ≤ c[l] ≤ 3 then
15              s'_Bi[l] = c_2[l]
16          else
17              s'_Bi[l] = c_2[l] − T

18  B = 96
19  for i ← 0 to k do
20      P_A = []
21      for j ← 0 to k do
22          if j == i then
23              P_A.append(B)
            else
24              P_A.append(0)
25      c = O_s(P_A)
26      for l ← 0 to n do
27          if c[l] == 2 or c[l] == 10 then
28              s'_Bi[l] = −4
29          if c[l] == 6 or c[l] == 14 then
30              s'_Bi[l] = 4

31  Return s'_B
```

---

recovers the coefficients in $\{-4, 4\}$ by a query with $B = 96$. As a result, all the coefficients of s_{Bi} in Saber can be recovered by at most 2k(=4) queries. The details of this attack are described in Algorithm 6.

Attack on LightSaber. LightSaber, which has the lowest security level I (AES-128) in SABER, does not satisfy Theorem 2 neither. Actually, when an adversary set $B = 128$ so that $B \gg (\epsilon_p - \epsilon_T) = 1$, the behavior of $c[j]$ is shown in Table 8. There is no pair of $(c[j], m[j])$ which corresponds to $s_{Bi}[j]$. In other words, from Table 8, an adversary can not obtain any information about $s_{Bi}[j]$. Thus, we consider the case $B = 16$ (Table 9). In this case, when $c[j] = 7$ or $c[j] = 3$, $s_{Bi}[j]$ is judged to be negative and when $c[j] = 0$ or $c[j] = 4$, $s_{Bi}[j]$ is non-negative. After he knows whether $s_{Bi}[j]$ is negative or non-negative, he can distinguish the

Table 8. The behavior of $c[j]$ corresponding to $s_{Bi}[j]$ and $m[j]$ when $B = 128$ in LightSaber

$c[j]$ \ $s_{Bi}[j]$ $m[j]$	-5	-4	-3	-2	-1	0	1	2	3	4	5
0	3	4	5	6	7	0	1	2	3	4	5
1	7	0	1	2	3	4	5	6	7	0	1

Table 9. The behavior of $c[j]$ corresponding to $s_{Bi}[j]$ and $m[j]$ when $B = 16, 128, 192$ in LightSaber

B					16							128					192					
$c[j]$ \ $s_{Bi}[j]$ $m[j]$	-5	-4	-3	-2	-1	0	1	2	3	4	5	Refer to Table 8	-5	-4	-3	-2	-1	0	1	2	3	4	5
0	7	7	7	7	7	0	0	0	0	0	0		0	2	3	5	6	0	1	3	4	6	7
1	3	3	3	3	3	4	4	4	4	4	4		4	6	7	1	2	4	5	7	0	2	3

coefficients in $[-4, -2]$ and those in $\{2, 3\}$ from Table 8. Further, to identify the coefficients in $\{-5, -1\}$ or in $\{0, 1, 4, 5\}$, the adversary again set $B = 192$ (Table 9). We summarize the attack on LightSaber by the following three steps.

1. An adversary first sends a query with $B = 16$ and tell whether $s_{Bi}[j]$ is negative or non-negative.
2. He sends a query with $B = 128$ and recover the coefficients in $[-4, -2] \cup \{2, 3\}$.
3. Finally, he recover the coefficients in $\{-5, -1\}$ or $\{0, 1, 4, 5\}$ by a query with $B = 192$.

The details of this attack are shown in Algorithm 7.

4   Experiments

We implement and verify the attack algorithms from Algorithm 1 to 7 by Python3. The experimental results are shown in Table 10. From this table, it is clear that the number of queries necessary for each attack is remarkably small. Furthermore, we plot the relationship between the number of queries and the rate of coefficients recovered in Bob's randomness for each crypto scheme in Appendix A. It is notable that the final success rate of each attack is 100%.

Table 10. The results in each parameter sets of CRYSRALS-KYBER and SABER

Crypto scheme	CRYSTALS-KYBER			SABER		
Parameter set	Kyber-512	Kyber-768	Kyber-1024	LightSaber	Saber	FireSaber
Number of queries	≤ 4	3	4	≤ 6	≤ 6	4

Algorithm 7: LightSaber_Attack()

Output: $\mathbf{s}'_B \in \mathcal{R}_q^{k \times 1}$

```
 1  B = 16
 2  negative_list = []
 3  for i ← 0 to k do
 4      P_A = []
 5      for j ← 0 to k do
 6          if j == i then
 7              P_A.append(B)
            else
 8              P_A.append(0)
 9      c = O_s(P_A)
10      for l ← 0 to n do
11          if c[j] == 7 or c[j] == 3 then
12              negative_list.append(true)
            else
13              negative_list.append(false)

14  B = 128
15  for i ← 0 to k do
16      P_A = []
17      for j ← 0 to k do
18          if j == i then
19              P_A.append(B)
            else
20              P_A.append(0)
21      c = O_s(P_A)
22      for l ← 0 to n do
23          if negative_list[l] then
24              if 4 ≤ c[l] ≤ 6 then
25                  s'_B[l] = c[j] − 8
26              else if 0 ≤ c[l] ≤ 2 then
27                  s'_B[l] = c[j] − 4
28              else
29                  continue
            else
30              if 2 ≤ c[l] ≤ 3 then
31                  s'_B[l] = c[j]
32              else if 6 ≤ c[l] ≤ 7 then
33                  s'_B[l] = c[j] − 4
34              else
35                  continue

36  B = 192
37  for i ← 0 to k do
38      P_A = []
39      for j ← 0 to k do
40          if j == i then
41              P_A.append(B)
            else
42              P_A.append(0)
43      c = O_s(P_A)
44      for l ← 0 to n do
45          if negative_list[l] then
46              if c[l] == 0, 4 then
47                  s'_B[l] = −5
48              else if c[l] == 2, 6 then
49                  s'_B[l] = −1
50              else
51                  continue
            else
52              if c[l] == 0, 4 then
53                  s'_B[l] = 0
54              else if c[l] == −1, 5 then
55                  s'_B[l] = 1
56              else if c[l] == 2, 6 then
57                  s'_B[l] = 4
58              else if c[l] == 3, 7 then
59                  s'_B[l] = 5
60              else
61                  continue

62  Return s'_B
```

5   Conclusion and Discussion

In this paper, we extended Wang et al.'s idea and proposed new theorems and practical attacks on CRYSTALS-KYBER and SABER. The attacks are designed to be optimized for each crypto scheme and each security category. Furthermore, we actually implemented the crypto schemes and attacks and confirmed that our proposed method can recover Bob's randomness completely. We also count the number of queries necessary for each attack. Taking into consideration the success rate and the number of queries, the reuse of randomness is very dangerous and should be strictly avoided.

There is potential risk that the attacker may obtain other parties' symmetric keys issued by the client (Bob) if his randomness variants are leaked in the communication. Consequently, for a more robust real-world applications, we suggest two feasible countermeasures against our attacks as follows: 1. Rejecting any freely chosen queries, 2. Refreshing randomness every time public key are sent. About the first countermeasure, it is easy to check whether sent queries match the forms of those proposed in our attack. However, adversaries can develop our attacks and change the forms of queries. Thus, such signature detection is not suitable. From above discussion, anomaly detection may be better, but one should also consider the problem about false positive and false negative is common with it. The second one is fundamental and more effective to our attack than the first one. However, it should also be considered that the disadvantage of this countermeasure is that there will be an additional load on the server.

Acknowledgement. This work was supported by JSPS KAKENHI Grant Number JP20K23322 and JP21K11751, Japan.

Appendix A
Plots of Experimental Results

We show the relationships between the number of queries and the rate of recovered Bob's randomness from Fig. 4, 5, 6, 7, 8, 9. Figure 4 shows that the whole randomness can be recovered with at most 4 queries (at least 2 queries) in the attack on KYBER-512, and Fig. 5 and 6 show it requires 3 and 4 queries in the attacks on KYBER-768 and KYBER-1024, respectively. Simultaneously, Fig. 7 and 8 show it requires at most 6 queries (at least 4 and 3 queries) to recover the whole randomness in LightSaber and Saber, while just 4 queries is needed in the key recovery attack on FireSaber (Fig. 9).

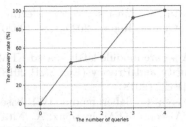

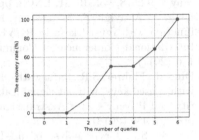

Fig. 4. KYBER-512.

Fig. 5. KYBER-768.

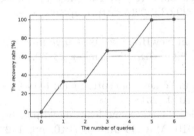

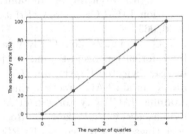

Fig. 6. KYBER-1024.

Fig. 7. LightSaber.

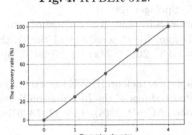

Fig. 8. Saber

Fig. 9. FireSaber

References

1. US Department of Commerce: National Institute of Standards and Technology. Post-Quantum Cryptography (2019). http://csrc.nist.gov/projects/post-quantum-cryptography/
2. Alkim, E., Ducas, L., Pöppelmann, T., Schwabe, P.: Post-quantum key exchange - a new hope. In: Proceedings pf the 25th USENIX Security Symposium, USENIX Security 16, August 10–12 2016, pp. 327–343 (2016)
3. Băetu, C., Durak, F.B., Huguenin-Dumittan, L., Talayhan, A., Vaudenay, S.: Misuse attacks on post-quantum cryptosystems. In: Proceedings of the EUROCRYPT 2019, May 19–23, 2019 , Part II, pp. 747–776 (2019)
4. Bauer, A., Gilbert, H., Renault, G., Rossi, M.: Assessment of the key-reuse resilience of NewHope. In: Proceedings of the The Cryptographers' Track at the RSA Conference 2019 (CT-RSA 2019), March 4–8 2019, pp. 272–292 (2019)

5. Bindel, N., Stebila, D., Veitch, S.: Improved attacks against key reuse in learning with errors key exchange. Cryptology ePrint Archive, Report 2020/1288 (2020). https://eprint.iacr.org/2020/1288

6. Bos, J.W., et al.: CRYSTALS - kyber: a CCA-secure module-lattice-based KEM. In: 2018 IEEE European Symposium on Security and Privacy (EuroS&P 2018), London, UK, April 24–26 2018, pp. 353–367. IEEE (2018)

7. D'Anvers, J., Karmakar, A., Roy, S.S., Vercauteren, F.: Saber: module-IWR based key exchange, CPA-secure encryption and CCA-secure KEM. In: Joux, A., Nitaj, A., Rachidi, T. (eds.) Proceedings of the Progress in Cryptology - AFRICACRYPT 2018–10th International Conference on Cryptology in Africa, Marrakesh, Morocco, May 7–9 2018, vol. 10831, LNCS, pp. 282–305. Springer (2018)

8. Ding, J., Alsayigh, S., Saraswathy, R.V., Fluhrer, S.R., Lin, X.: Leakage of signal function with reused keys in RLWE key exchange. In: Proceedings of the IEEE International Conference on Communications (ICC 2017), May 21–25 2017, pp. 1–6 (2017)

9. Ding, J., Fluhrer, S.R., Saraswathy, R.V.: Complete attack on RLWE key exchange with reused keys, without signal leakage. In: Proceedings of the Information Security and Privacy - 23rd Australasian Conference (ACISP 2018), July 11–13 2018, pp. 467–486 (2018)

10. Fluhrer, S.R.: Cryptanalysis of ring-LWE based key exchange with key share reuse. IACR Cryptology ePrint Archive, 2016:85 (2016). http://eprint.iacr.org/2016/085

11. Greuet, A., Montoya, S., Renault, G.: Attack on LAC key exchange in misuse situation. IACR Cryptology ePrint Archive, 2020:63 (2020). http://eprint.iacr.org/2020/063

12. Liu, C., Zheng, Z., Zou, G.: Key reuse attack on NewHope key exchange protocol. In: Information Security and Cryptology (ICISC 2018), November 28–30, 2018, Revised Selected Papers, pp. 163–176 (2018)

13. Lu, X., et al.: LAC: practical ring-lwe based public-key encryption with byte-level modulus. IACR Cryptol. ePrint Arch. **2018**, 1009 (2018)

14. Lyubashevsky, V., Peikert, C., Regev, O.: On ideal lattices and learning with errors over rings. In: Proceedings EUROCRYPT 2010, May 30–June 3 2010, pp. 1–23 (2010)

15. Okada, S., Wang, Y., Takagi, T.: Improving key mismatch attack on NewHope with fewer queries. In: Liu, J.K., Cui, H. (eds.) ACISP 2020. LNCS, vol. 12248, pp. 505–524. Springer, Cham (2020). https://doi.org/10.1007/978-3-030-55304-3_26

16. Qin, Y., Cheng, C., Ding. J.: A complete and optimized key mismatch attack on NIST candidate newhope. In: Proceedings of the 4th European Symposium on Research in Computer Security (ESORICS 2019), September 23–27 2019, Part II, pp. 504–520 (2019)

17. Cin, Y., Cheng, C., Din, J.: An efficient key mismatch attack on the NIST second round candidate Kyber. IACR Cryptology ePrint Archive. 2019:1343 (2019). http://eprint.iacr.org/2019/1343

18. Rescorla, E.: The transport layer security (TLS) protocol version 1.3. Technical report. http://www.rfc-editor.org/info/rfc8446

19. Shor, P.W.: Polynomial-time algorithms for prime factorization and discrete logarithms on a quantum computer. SIAM J. Comput. **26**(5), 1484–1509 (1997)

20. Vacek, J., Václavek, J.: Key mismatch attack on newhope revisited. IACR Cryptol. ePrint Arch. **2020**, 1389 (2020)
21. Wang, K., Zhang, Z., Jiang, H.: Security of two NIST candidates in the presence of randomness reuse. In: Proceedings of the Provable and Practical Security - 14th International Conference (ProvSec 2020), Singapore, November 29–December 1, 2020, pp. 402–421 (2020)

A Lattice Reduction Algorithm Based on Sublattice BKZ

Jinzheng Cao[1,2], Yanbin Pan[3], and Qingfeng Cheng[1,2(✉)]

[1] Strategic Support Force Information Engineering University, Zhengzhou 450001, China
qingfengc2008@sina.com
[2] State Key Laboratory of Mathematical Engineering and Advanced Computing, Zhengzhou 450001, China
[3] Key Laboratory of Mathematics Mechanization, Academy of Mathematics and Systems Science, Chinese Academy of Sciences, Beijing 100190, China

Abstract. We present m-SubBKZ reduction algorithm that outputs a reduced lattice basis, containing a vector shorter than the original BKZ. The work is based on the properties of sublattices and the Gaussian Heuristic of the full lattice and sublattices. By theoretical analysis and simulation, we suggest a BKZ call on the sublattice is possible to produce a short vector close to the shortest vector in the full lattice. The key idea of our algorithm is to extract multiple sublattices from the preprocessed lattice, restricting the context in which a lattice reduction solver is called. The full basis is then updated with vectors from the reduced basis of each sublattice. The new algorithm improves on the efficiency of the original BKZ algorithm and the BKZ 2.0 variant. We show the experimental results on random lattices to compare the length of vectors produced by our algorithm and original BKZ and BKZ 2.0. On the 180-dimension basis, the m-SubBKZ reaches 47% of the output of BKZ and 46% of BKZ 2.0. The ratio drops with the dimension increasing. The effect is more oblivious with smaller blocks. The results show that the new algorithm is able to produce a shorter vector at a relatively low cost compared with previous algorithms, and the improvements are especially explicit for lattices of high dimensions.

Keywords: Lattice reduction · Shortest vector problem · BKZ algorithm · Sublattice

1 Introduction

1.1 Background

Lattice reduction algorithms serve as an essential part in the analysis of lattice-based cryptography, which may update the standard of public key cryptography, considering that quantum computing is making rapid progress and about to impose a real threat to the current public key schemes at any time. Among

© Springer Nature Switzerland AG 2021
Q. Huang and Y. Yu (Eds.): ProvSec 2021, LNCS 13059, pp. 174–189, 2021.
https://doi.org/10.1007/978-3-030-90402-9_10

the many hard lattice problems, the Shortest Vector Problem (SVP) has been a key stone of the theory. To solve this NP-hard problem, much work has been done to study the cost of lattice reduction algorithms and other algorithms in the hope to solve the SVP. Among them, BKZ [1] and its variants are the most commonly used algorithms for lattice reduction and solving approximate SVP. The BKZ algorithm calls an SVP oracle on blocks. Two implementations of the SVP oracle are lattice enumeration and lattice sieving. In most publicly available implementions of BKZ, enumeration is used as the SVP solver. For lattices of large dimension, enumeration is not the fastest algorithm, as the sieving algorithm [2] has been proved to be of lower time complexity than enumeration asymptotically [3], and the optimized sieving implementation [4] by Lucas et al. has outperformed enumeration-based algorithms in solving the SVP. However, the memory cost of sieving algorithm grows exponentially with the lattice dimension and the cost grows out of our affordability when considering dimensions suggested by lattice-based schemes. On the other hand, BKZ and other enumeration-based algorithms have a memory cost that grows moderately with the dimension. Even if BKZ runs with relatively low efficiency on large lattices and blocks, it still remains a popular tool for preprocessing and for solving approximate SVP.

1.2   Related Work

The first practical lattice reduction algorithm, LLL, was first proposed in 1982 [5] and it is still in use today. In polynomial time the algorithm is able to produce a reasonably short lattice vector, but usually far from the shortest in high dimensions. In 1994, Schnorr and Euchner proposed BKZ, which can be considered as a generalization of LLL, combined with blockwize HKZ reduction [1]. The algorithm has a time complexity of $\beta^{\beta/(2e)}$, but outputs a better lattice basis. While BKZ is the main-stream algorithm for lattice reduction, its behaviour and efficiency are relatively hard to analyze. It is noted in practice that the algorithm usually performs better than the estimation in theory, making it tricky to give an accurate estimation of its output quality.

Most of the studies and improvements on lattice reduction algorithms are concentrated on the running time and the optimization of strategies and parameters [6]. The work of Chen and Nguyen analyzed the behaviour of blockwise reduction by the simulator and showed that the last several tours only have a small impact on the output basis. In their work, a new variant of blockwise reduction algorithm, BKZ 2.0, was proposed [7]. The algorithm employed an early-abort technique, along with other fixes. This variant performs well in practice, and the algorithm has been the most recognized variant of lattice reduction algorithm. In 2016, a version of progressive reduction [8] was proposed, suggesting that reduction algorithm may achieve a better output when the block size is properly updated during iteration. A new enumeration-based reduction algorithm was proposed in 2020 by Albrecht et al., achieving a small Hermite factor with a lower-dimension SVP solver. They suggest a new aspect that the context in which a reduction solver is called may be separated from the block, where the SVP solver is called [9]. Slide reduction is another blockwize reduction algorithm initiated in 2008 by Gamma et al., and recently reviewed in 2020 [6,14]. The algorithm is based on the Mordell's inequality, reaching a rather small approximation factor. But in many practical senarios, BKZ and the BKZ 2.0 are still taken as reduction algorithms.

1.3 Our Contribution

This work is based on analysis of properties of sublattice and improvements on lattice reduction algorithms. As the main contribution, we present a lattice reduction algorithm that outputs a BKZ-reduced basis, containing a vector shorter than the original algorithm, with the same block size.

(1) We focuses on the reduction of sublattice, which denotes a lattice generated by some of the basis vectors of the full lattice. We first analyze the properties of the sublattice, then analyze the behaviour and efficiency of BKZ on sublattice basis compared with on the full basis. The running time of BKZ increases sharply with block size increasing, but the output vectors do not gain an obviously better quality. By the Gaussian Heuristic and experiments on SVP challenge lattices we show that the shortest vector length $\lambda_1(\mathcal{L}_1)$ in a sublattice of dimension $n' = n/2$ can be as long as $1.41\lambda_1(\mathcal{L})$ for dimension $n \leq 130$. Thus, when a sublattice is well reduced, a list of short vectors can be returned. The properties of sublattice suggest the possibility to reach a similar outcome with lower cost by modifying the context, where a BKZ tour runs.

(2) We present the m-SubBKZ algorithm to exploit the properties of sublattice we have found, where m denotes the number of reduction tours. Our method restricts the context of reduction subprocedure to a list of sublattices and employs a progressive technique to accelerate the reduction in the full basis. The algorithm achieves improved efficiency by running SVP reduction on randomly generated sublattices recursively. As the reduction context is restricted to the sublattice, each round has a lower time complexity compared to BKZ.

(3) Finally, we give an experimental illustration of the efficiency of our algorithm. We illustrate the effectiveness of our algorithm by trying to recover a short vector from the basis with the same block size for BKZ, BKZ 2.0 and single round SubBKZ. The block size is 30 for smaller lattices and 60 larger ones. We show the vectors output by different algorithms and the time cost to find the vectors, compared with BKZ and BKZ 2.0. By results, we specify a reasonable improvement achieved by the new algorithm. For the 180 dimension basis, the progressive method reaches 47% of the output of BKZ and 46% of BKZ 2.0. The ratio drops with the dimension increasing. We also compared m-SubBKZ with progressive BKZ, with block size increasing together up to 60. Our algorithm still has the advantage in output and time cost. The results show that the new algorithm is able to produce a shorter vector at a relatively low cost compared with previous algorithms

and the improvements are especially useful in reducing lattice basis of higher dimension.

1.4 Outline

Section 2 will recall the basic definitions about lattice and basis reduction. Details of the sublattice and sublattice and its properties are introduced in Sect. 3. We then present our main work, the SubBKZ algorithm, in Sect. 4. In Sect. 5, we show the efficiency of the new algorithm by experiments to find short vectors and the time cost, with our implementation in python. Finally, we give our conclusion in Sect. 6.

2 Preliminaries

2.1 Lattice

In this part we introduce the basic notions and definitions concerned in the following sections. The definitions about lattice are mostly from literature [4,9]. For more details on lattice, it is recommended to refer to [10].

Definition 1. *Let* $b_1, b_2, \ldots, b_n \in \mathbb{R}^n$ *be a list of linearly independent vectors, we define the basis* $B = [b_1, b_2, \ldots, b_n]$ *and the lattice generated by* B *as* $\mathcal{L}(B) = \{\sum_{i=1}^n x_i b_i : x_i \in \mathbb{Z}\}$.

The determinant of $\mathcal{L}$ is defined as the volume of the fundamental area $det\mathcal{L} = detB$. For a given basis B of lattice $\mathcal{L}$ we define π_i as the projections orthogonal to the span of $b_1, b_2, \ldots, b_i$ and the Gram-Schmidt orthogonalisation as $B^* = [b_1^*, b_2^*, \ldots, b_n^*]$, where $b_i^* = \pi_i(b_i)$. The projected lattice $\mathcal{L}_{[l:r]}$, where $0 \leq l < r \leq n$ is defined as the lattice with basis $B_{[l:r]} = (\pi_l(b_l), \ldots, \pi_l(b_r))$.

Definition 2. *(Sublattice) A sublattice* $\mathcal{L}_1$ *is a sebset of* $\mathcal{L}$, *with basis* $B_1 = [b_{i_1}, b_{i_2}, \ldots, b_{i_m}]$, *where* $i_j \in \{1, 2, \ldots, n\}, m < n$.

We refer to $\mathcal{L}$ as the full lattice compared with the sublattice generated by the submatrix of full basis B.

Most lattice hard problems can be reduced to the shortest vector problem (SVP). SVP is one of the most important problems of lattice-based cryptography. The problem demands to find a non-zero lattice vector of minimal length.

Definition 3. *(Shortest Vector Problem, SVP) Given a basis* B *of a lattice* $\mathcal{L}$, *find a non-zero lattice vector* $v \in \mathcal{L}$ *of minimal length* $\lambda_1(\mathcal{L}) = \min_{0 \neq w \in L} \|w\|$.

In practice, most cryptography schemes only depend on approximate versions of SVP, where we aim to find a vector longer than the shortest vector by a polynomial factor. The problem of finding a non-zero lattice vector of length $\leq \gamma \cdot \det(\mathcal{L})^{1/n}$ is called Hermite-SVP with parameter γ (γ-HSVP).

To analyze lattice reduction algorithms, heuristic assumptions [11] are needed to estimate the determinant (or volume) of a lattice. We will rely on the following Gaussian Heuristic to explain our analysis in the following sections of the work.

Heuristic 1. Let $K \subset \mathbb{R}^n$ be a measurable body, then $|K \cap \mathcal{L}| \approx Vol(K)/\det(\mathcal{L})$. When applying the heuristic to an n-dimension ball of volume $\det(\mathcal{L})$ we obtain that $\lambda_1(\mathcal{L}) \approx \frac{\Gamma(\frac{n}{2}+1)^{\frac{1}{n}} \det(\mathcal{L})^{\frac{1}{n}}}{\sqrt{\pi}} \approx \sqrt{\frac{n}{2\pi e}} \det(\mathcal{L})^{1/n}$. We denote the length as $gh(\mathcal{L})$ or $GH(\mathcal{L})$ in short.

2.2   Lattice Reduction Algorithms

LLL. Given the basis of a lattice $\mathcal{L}$, LLL outputs a basis $\{B = b_1, b_2, \ldots, b_n\}$ with the following statements hold:

(1) $\forall 1 \leq i \leq n, j < i, |\mu_{i,j}| \leq 1/2$.
(2) $\forall 1 \leq i < n, \|\delta b_i^*\|^2 \leq \|\mu_{i+1,i} b_i^* + b_{i+1}^*\|^2$.

We refer to the first statement as size-reduced. LLL is mostly used for reducing lattices of small dimensions. The LLL algorithm has a polynomial time complexity but the quality of output basis is limited.

A lattice basis B is HKZ-reduced when $b_i^* = \lambda_1(\pi_i(\mathcal{L}_{[i:n]}))$, where $i = 1, \ldots, n-1$ and if it is size-reduced. While HKZ algorithm will output the shortest vector in theory, the algorithm calls enumeration without prunning recursively and requires a strongly reduced basis as preprocessed input, making it inefficient in practice. As a relaxation of the condition, the BKZ algorithm reaches a better quality-cost trade-off.

BKZ. BKZ algorithm is commonly used to get a basis better than LLL and with less cost than HKZ. A BKZ-reduced lattice basis B for block size $\beta \geq 2$ satisfies $b_i^* = \lambda_1(\pi_i(\mathcal{L}_{[i:\min(i+\beta,n)]})), i = 1, \ldots, n - 1$. BKZ is based on a relaxation of HKZ reduction and with lower time complexity, although some algorithms such as slide reduction allow better analyses in theory. The BKZ algorithm takes the lattice basis B and block size β as input. In the process BKZ calls an SVP oracle on every projected block of dimension β. The BKZ also calls LLL on the local block $\mathcal{L}_{[i:\min(i+\beta,n)]}$ after the SVP call. The procedure terminates when certain termination condition is fulfilled or the b_i^* don't drop fast enough. When taking an n-dimensional lattice as input, the algorithm outputs a short vector of length $\approx (\beta^{1/2\beta})^n \cdot \det(\mathcal{L})^{1/n}$ in time $\beta^{\beta/(2e)}$. The BKZ algorithm achieves a good balance between the quality of reduced basis and running-time, and is the most commonly used lattice reduction algorithm to analyze the lattice.

Geometric Series Assumption (GSA). To analyze the behaviour of BKZ algorithm and predict the length of the shortest vector in the lattice, the Geometric Series Asumption (GSA) is introduced to describe the quality of a reduced lattice basis.

Heuristic 2. Geometric Series Assumption for a BKZ-reduced basis of lattice $\mathcal{L}$, $\|b_i^*\|/\|b_{i+1}^*\| \approx r, i = 1, \ldots, n - 1$, where $\frac{3}{4} \leq r^{-2} < 1$.

3 Sublattice Reduction

3.1 Determinant of Sublattice

To improve the performance of BKZ-reduction and produce a short vector with lower cost, we reduce the dimension of the context, where the reduction is called. We look into the matter and propose an algorithm that reaches the same Hermite factor with BKZ but requires smaller block size. This can be done by running a BKZ call not on the full lattice, but on a sublattice, generated by $b_1, b_2, \ldots, b_{[n/2]}$. By experimental results we show that for a BKZ-reduced basis, the determinant of a sublattice is about half of the bit length of that of the full lattice. We intend to find a short vector in the sublattice with norm close to the norm of the shortest vector in the full lattice. And the BKZ-reduced basis of the sublattice usually contains a vector close to or shorter than the second or third vector produced by simple BKZ. On each of the sublattices, we run a BKZ oracle to recover a list of short vectors, and use the list to update the basis of the full basis. We analyze the efficiency of the algorithm with experiment data.

To estimate the length of a possible shortest lattice vector, the Gaussian Heuristic is necessary to define the approximate shortest vector problem. As shown by the definition $\lambda_1(\mathcal{L}) \approx \sqrt{\frac{n}{2\pi e}} \det(\mathcal{L})^{1/n}$, the Gaussian Heuristic depends on both the size and the determinant of the lattice. Suppose a sublattice generated by the submatrix B_1 of the given lattice basis, it has a lower dimension by definition, and hopefully will have a smaller determinant. Suppose a lattice $\mathcal{L}$ generated by basis $B = [b_1, b_2, \ldots, b_n]$, and sublattices $\mathcal{L}_1, \mathcal{L}_2$ generated by $B_1 = [b_1, b_2, \ldots, b_{\lfloor n/2 \rfloor}]$ and $B_2 = [b_{\lfloor n/2 \rfloor+1}, b_{\lfloor n/2 \rfloor+2}, \ldots, b_n]$. It follows that $B = [B_1 \ B_2]$,

$$\left|B^T B\right| = \begin{vmatrix} B_1^T B_1 & B_1^T B_2 \\ B_2^T B_1 & B_2^T B_2 \end{vmatrix}. \tag{1}$$

For a random lattice basis B, it is relatively hard to specify a relationship between B_1 and B_2, especially for determinants. Thus, we move on to discuss the situation where B is a reduced basis. To give an estimation to a sublattice we suppose the basis vectors follow the Geometric Series Assumption (GSA) [12].

Theorem 1. (Under GSA). *For the sublattice $\mathcal{L}_1$ of basis $B_1 = [b_1, b_2, \ldots, b_{n/2}]$, $\det(\mathcal{L}_1) = r^{n^2/8} \det \mathcal{L}^{1/2}$.*

Proof. If all vectors of the basis follow the Geometric Series Assumption, then $\det(\mathcal{L}) = \sum_{i=1}^{n} \|b_i^*\| = \|b_1^*\|^n / r^{\frac{n(n-1)}{2}}$. For a BKZ-reduced sublattice $\mathcal{L}_1$, $\|b_1^*\| = r\|b_2^*\| = r^2\|b_3^*\| = \ldots = r^{\lfloor n/2 \rfloor-1}\|b_{\lfloor \frac{n}{2} \rfloor}^*\|$. So we have the formular $\det(\mathcal{L}_1) = \sum_{i=1}^{\lfloor n/2 \rfloor} \|b_i^*\| = \|b_1^*\|^k / r^{1+2+\ldots+(k-1)} = \|b_1^*\|^k / r^{\frac{k(k-1)}{2}}$, where $k = \lfloor n/2 \rfloor$. To simplify the analysis of our analysis, we suppose the n to be even, so $k = n/2$. consider

$$
\begin{aligned}
\det\left(\mathcal{L}_1\right)/\det\left(\mathcal{L}\right)^{1/2} &= \|b_1^*\|^{k-\frac{n}{2}}/r^{\frac{k(k-1)}{2}-\frac{n(n-1)}{4}}\\
&= 1/r^{\frac{n(n-2)-2n(n-1)}{8}}\\
&= 1/r^{-n^2/8}\\
&= r^{n^2/8}.
\end{aligned}
\tag{2}
$$

Therefore, under the Geometric Series Assumption, we can get $\det\left(\mathcal{L}_1\right) = r^{n^2/8}\det\mathcal{L}^{1/2}$. $\qquad\square$

In fact, comparing the lower bound of $\det\left(\mathcal{L}_1\right)$ with $\det\mathcal{L}^{1/2}$, we have

$$
\det\left(\mathcal{L}_1\right)/\det\left(\mathcal{L}\right)^{1/2} = r^{n^2/8} > 1.
\tag{3}
$$

So $\det\left(\mathcal{L}_1\right) > \det\mathcal{L}^{1/2}$.

However, for an actual BKZ-reduced basis, the Geometric Series Assumption may not apply to all the basis vectors, but only the first few vectors instead. To obtain a smaller sublattice, we hope that the determinant of $\mathcal{L}_1$ falls around $\mathcal{L}^{1/2}$. To illustrate this assumption, we verify it with lattices from the SVP challenge site. At least for a smaller basis that is BKZ-reduced, we assume that the determinant of sublattice is around the square root of the full lattice.

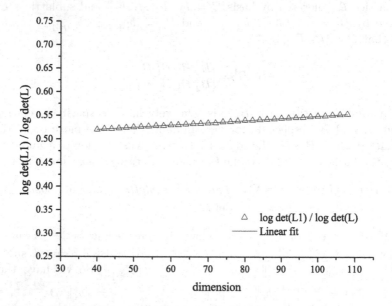

Fig. 1. Determinant of sublattices to the full lattice

Heuristic 3. For a lattice $\mathcal{L}$ of dimension $n(n < 200)$ and its sublattice $\mathcal{L}_1$ of dimension $n/2$, $\log \det(\mathcal{L}_1) = \frac{1}{2} \log \det(\mathcal{L}) + \alpha, \alpha < 1$.

Recall that the Gaussian Heuristic has a more accurate form

$$\mathrm{GH}(\mathcal{L}) = \frac{\Gamma\left(\frac{n}{2} + 1\right)^{\frac{1}{n}} \det(\mathcal{L})^{\frac{1}{n}}}{\sqrt{\pi}}, \tag{4}$$

so the shortest vector in $\mathcal{L}_1$ is estimated to have length $\mathrm{GH}_1 = \frac{\Gamma\left(\frac{n}{4}+1\right)^{\frac{2}{n}} \det(\mathcal{L}_1)^{\frac{2}{n}}}{\sqrt{\pi}}$ and is close to the shortest length of the full $\mathcal{L}$. From the discussion above, we have the approximation $\det(\mathcal{L}_1) \approx \sqrt{\det(\mathcal{L})}$. With the Gamma function and approximation $\Gamma(x) \sim \sqrt{2\pi} e^{-x} x^{x-\frac{1}{2}}$, we get $\Gamma\left(\frac{n}{2}+1\right) \approx \sqrt{2\pi} e^{-\left(\frac{n}{2}+1\right)} \left(\frac{n}{2}+1\right)^{\frac{n}{2}+\frac{1}{2}}$, $\Gamma\left(\frac{n}{4}+1\right) \approx \sqrt{2\pi} e^{-\left(\frac{n}{4}+1\right)} \left(\frac{n}{4}+1\right)^{\frac{n}{4}+\frac{1}{2}}$. Therefore $\Gamma\left(\frac{n}{2}+1\right)^{\frac{1}{n}} \approx \sqrt{2\pi} e^{-\left(\frac{1}{2}+\frac{1}{n}\right)} \left(\frac{n}{2}+1\right)^{\frac{1}{2}+\frac{1}{2n}}$, $\Gamma\left(\frac{n}{4}+1\right)^{\frac{2}{n}} \approx \sqrt{2\pi} e^{-\left(\frac{1}{2}+\frac{2}{n}\right)} \left(\frac{n}{4}+1\right)^{\frac{1}{2}+\frac{1}{n}}$. Then we have the relation

$$\frac{\Gamma\left(\frac{n}{2}+1\right)^{\frac{1}{n}}}{\Gamma\left(\frac{n}{4}+1\right)^{\frac{2}{n}}} \approx e^{\frac{1}{n}} \left[\frac{2(n+2)}{n+4}\right]^{\frac{1}{2}+\frac{1}{n}} \cdot \left(\frac{n}{2}+1\right)^{\frac{1}{2}+\frac{1}{n}}. \tag{5}$$

As a result, the estimated shortest length of sublattice gh_1 is about $\sqrt{2}$ times of gh.

$$\frac{\mathrm{GH}_1}{\mathrm{GH}} \approx \sqrt{2} \cdot \frac{\det(\mathcal{L}_1)^{\frac{1}{n}}}{\sqrt{\det(\mathcal{L})}^{\frac{1}{n}}} = \sqrt{2}. \tag{6}$$

The actual property of the basis is also affected by how much the basis is reduced. Note that not all vectors follow the Geometric Series Assumption and the actual GH may differ from estimation. To look into the fact, we compare the GH of lattice and the sublattice, with the lattice LLL or BKZ preprocessed. Figure 2 shows a comparison between LLL-reduced basis and BKZ-reduced basis. Note that by BKZ-β we denote BKZ reduction with block size β. Compared with the LLL-reduced sublattice basis, the Gaussian Heuristic of a BKZ-reduced sublattice is apparently of smaller value, refrained around the GH of the full lattice, while the GH of LLL-reduced sublattice is relatively hard to predict. By further experiments, it is shown that with a larger block size, the Gaussian Heuristic of the sublattice gets smaller, approaching the original GH of the full lattice.

3.2   Basis Reduction on Sublattice

In this part we try to exploit the findings about properties of the sublattice. We follow the analysis of previous sections, where the dimension of the sublattice is set to be half of the full lattice. From Fig. 2, we note that for a BKZ-reduced basis (dimension ≤ 130), the Gaussian Heuristic for sublattice $\mathcal{L}_1$ satisfies $\lambda_1(\mathcal{L}_1) \leq 1.41\lambda_1(\mathcal{L})$, while the BKZ-reduced basis can provide a vector about 1.15 times

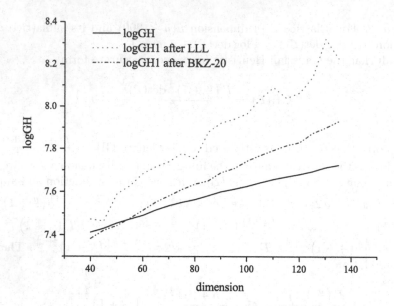

Fig. 2. Gaussian Heuristic of sublattices after reduction

longer than that of $\mathcal{L}$ up to dimension 100. Therefore, we expect to find a vector not too longer than $\lambda_1(\mathcal{L})$ in a sublattice.

BKZ and other enumeration-based reduction algorithms are commonly applied to recover a short vector. And it is observed that the efficiency of the reduction is generally affected by the size of lattice [13]. In most cases the algorithm will cost less time to produce a reduced basis. With the same block size, BKZ will recover a vector with smaller approximate factor than applied to a larger lattice. Thus, we intend to search for the possibility that such a reduction call can return a vector shorter than the vector recovered from the full lattice. To exploit the finding further, it is also possible to use the sublattice vector to update the reduced basis. For example, when a recovered sublattice vector is shorter than one of the first few minima then we can insert the vector into the full basis to change the arrangement of the basis vectors. By this we add some disturbance to the basis and hope to obtain an even better reduced basis by calling BKZ recursively.

4 m-SubBKZ Reduction

4.1   Basic Algorithm

In this section we present our new algorithm of sublattice BKZ reduction. We refer to one BKZ tour and a sublattice SVP call as a round. Suppose a n dimension basis B is given, referred to as full basis. We select the first $n/2$ vectors to form a sublattice basis B_1. The aim of this section is to provide a practical reduction algorithm for large basis. We will test the performance using FPYLLL library.

Algorithm 1: SubBKZ

Input: Basis B, sublattice block b_1, full lattice block b
Output: Reduced basis B
Set list $l = \{\}$;
BKZ-reduce B;
generate sublattice $\mathcal{L}'$;
call BKZ-b_1 reduction over $\mathcal{L}'$;
add reduced $\mathcal{L}'$ basis vectors to l;
insert list to B;
call BKZ-b reduction on B;

A sublattice $\mathcal{L}'$ is generated in the process of the above algorithm. The basis of $\mathcal{L}'$ is chosen from the first $n/2$ basis vector of the full lattice $\mathcal{L}$.

To analyze the algorithm, we assume a sublattice $\mathcal{L}_1$ of dimension $n/2$. Let SubBKZ and BKZ share a same block size β, then a BKZ call and a sublattice reduction has the same time complexity $\beta^{\beta/(2e)}$. Compared with BKZ, which outputs a vector of length $\approx \left(\beta^{1/2\beta}\right)^n \cdot \det\left(\mathcal{L}\right)^{1/n}$, a SubBKZ round on a sublattice will give a vector of norm $\approx \left(\beta^{1/2\beta}\right)^{\frac{n}{2}} \cdot \det\left(\mathcal{L}_1\right)^{2/n} \approx \left(\beta^{1/2\beta}\right)^{\frac{n}{2}} \cdot \sqrt{\det\left(\mathcal{L}_1\right)}^{2/n} = \left(\beta^{1/2\beta}\right)^{\frac{n}{2}} \cdot \det\left(\mathcal{L}\right)^{1/n}$. Therefore, a shorter vector is produced by SubBKZ with the same time complexity. However, the BKZ result in practice may differ from the theory. We will show the experimental results in Sect. 5.

4.2 A Practical SubBKZ Variant

Recursive Short Vector Searching. Recall the estimated determinant of sublattice $\mathcal{L}_1$,

$$\det\left(\mathcal{L}_1\right) = \sum_{i=1}^{\lfloor n/2 \rfloor} \|b_i^*\| \approx \|b_1^*\|^{\frac{n}{2}}/r^{\frac{n(n-1)}{4}}. \tag{7}$$

With BKZ running on the full basis, the value r will see an increase, asymptotically to 1. It is interesting to find that while r is increasing, $\det\left(\mathcal{L}\right)$ drops with it. it follows that the Gaussian Heuristic $GH_1 = \frac{\Gamma\left(\frac{n}{4}+1\right)^{\frac{2}{n}} \det(\mathcal{L}_1)^{\frac{2}{n}}}{\sqrt{\pi}}$ gets smaller with $\det\left(\mathcal{L}_1\right)$ decreasing. Thus, for every round of SubBKZ, it is possible to find a shorter vector in the sublattice. In theory, the recursive sublattice reduction will lead to a much shorter vector when r increases fast enough in every round.

Optimized Algorithm Variant. We exploit the idea by building sublattices for several rounds. In this way, the sublattice short vector search is executed recursively in order to obtain a strongly reduced basis B and a shorter lattice vector. In practice, we set the number of rounds to run and allow the block size on sublattices to increase progressively by each round.

Instead of only one sublattice, it is possible to build two or more sublattices with different basis vectors. The structure of the sublattice reduction suggests the possibility to implement a parallel algorithm. In fact, a list of random sublattices can be generated and reduced to accelerate the reduction. Simply running the parallel BKZ processes will serve our purpose. Here we describe the m-SubBKZ algorithm, where the m denotes the number of tours. In each tour, new sublattices are generated and reduced.

Algorithm 2: m-SubBKZ

   Input: Basis B, block list $P = \{b_1, b_2, \ldots, b_m\}$, full lattice block b
   Output: Reduced basis B
   BKZ-reduce B;
   foreach $b_i \in P$ **do**
     | Round Start:
     | generate sublattice $\mathcal{L}'$;
     | call BKZ-b_i reduction over $\mathcal{L}'$;
     | **foreach** v in *basis of* $\mathcal{L}'$ **do**
     | | **if** $v \notin B$ **then**
     | | | insert v to B
     | | **end**
     | **end**
     | LLL and remove linear dependencies in B;
     | BKZ-b_i reduce B;
     | Round End:
   end
   call BKZ-b reduction on B;

Note that the parameter m denotes the number of "rounds" in the procedure. We refer to the algorithm with parameter m as "m round algorithm". Further, $b_1, b_2, \ldots, b_m$ implies that the blocks for every round can be different, allowing β to increase progressively.

5   Implementation and Experiment

5.1   Implementation Details

In the previous section we give the new lattice reduction algorithm. While we analyze in Sect. 3 that a short vector of length $\approx \sqrt{2}\lambda_1(\mathcal{L})$ can be found in theory, in this section we show the details of the implementation of m-SubBKZ and its performance compared with other algorithms (BKZ and BKZ 2.0).

5.2   Experimental Results

In addition to the disscusion in Sect. 3, we illustrate the efficiency of the new algorithms of this work mainly by experiment data on random lattices. In the experiment, we compare the m-SubBKZ with the original BKZ and BKZ 2.0 to

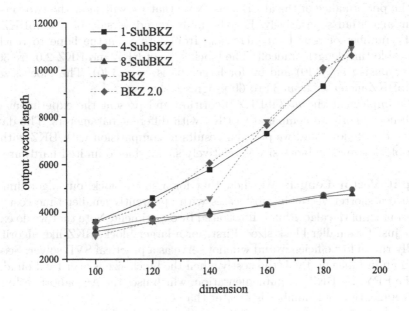

(a) First vector length output by algorithms

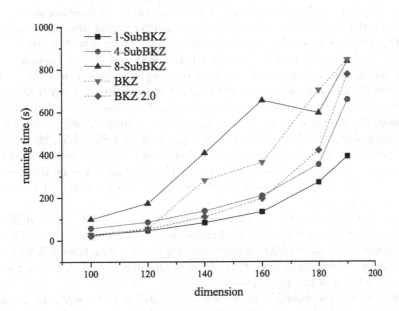

(b) Running time of algorithms

Fig. 3. Experimental results of algorithms

test the performance of the algorithms. Note that we will show the two versions of our algorithm separatively. For the multi-round version of m-SubBKZ, we set the number of rounds m increasing from 1 to 8, in the hope to reach an acceptable time-length tradeoff. The block sizes of BKZ and BKZ 2.0 are 30 for smaller basis ($n \leq 140$) and 60 for larger basis ($n > 140$). The block size for m-SubBKZ increases from 30 to 60 progressively.

We implement the m-SubBKZ algorithm and present the experiment data of the new algorithm compared to BKZ with different parameters. The data is displayed as follows and we plot our results in comparision with BKZ with the same block size. The block size is relatively small, due to limited hardware.

Output Vector Length. We show that for a small block, our algorithm will produce a shorter vector in most cases with apparently smaller time cost. The performance of the algorithm is illustrated by experiment. Note that we do experiment just for smaller block size . First, for a larger block, BKZ-like algorithms usually run in low efficiency and will not serve as a practical SVP solver. Second, to run an instance on PC is too costly when the block size is over the bound. We use the FPYLLL BKZ 2.0 implementation, which uses the Autoabort technique. On everage, the tour number is greater than 6.

For dimensions from 100 to 190, our algorithm is able to achieve a shorter vector than BKZ 2.0. By Table 1 as well as Fig. 3(a), we show that our approach will output a shorter vector than BKZ (and BKZ 2.0) on large-dimension basis. In fact, the simple one-round version of SubBKZ meets the crossing point around 160, while the progressive version outputs a shorter vector after dimension 120.

Intuitively, the algorithm is able to find a shorter vector with larger m. However, by the discussion in Sect. 4.2, the r is required to drop fast enough in every round, which may not always happen. In our implementation, when $m = 4$, the algorithm already outputs a reasonably short vector. However, with $m > 4$, the efficiency of the reduction tends to drop, without big improvements on the output basis. For example, given $m = 8$, the output quality doesn't explicitly gain an improvement, but the time cost is twice as long as 4-SubBKZ. Thus, for the-block size in this paper, the appropriate sterategy is to set $m = 4$. The detailed experimental results are listed in Table 1. The running time of the instances can be found in Table 2. More detailed description of time cost can be found in following paragraphs.

For dimension 100, our approach reaches a length only 93% of what BKZ 2.0 will give. When the size mounts to dimension 180, we have a vector with length 53% shorter than the BKZ 2.0 output and 54% shorter than the BKZ output. By the result, we argue intuitively that the new algorithm reaches a better output on a lattice basis of higher dimension.

We also compare SubBKZ with progressive BKZ in lattices of dimension 140, 160 and 180. After 15 tours with b increasing by 2 every tour starting from 30 (140-dimension) or from 40 (160 and 180-dimension), progressive BKZ reaches norm 5171.9, 5987.9 and 8066.7 respectively. The results are similar to the output of 4-SubBKZ, but takes more tours.

Table 1. First vector length output by algorithms

Dimension	m-SubBKZ			BKZ	BKZ 2.0
	$m = 1$	$m = 4$	$m = 8$	≥ 6 tours	≥ 6 tours
100	3592.0	3323.1	3179.5	2980.6	3566.1
120	4582.8	3728.3	3566.3	3594.1	4298.4
140	5767.9	3868.3	3984.3	4561.8	6046.5
160	7270.8	4304.5	4247.9	7780.8	7624.7
180	9266.0	4676.9	4610.5	9926.2	10038.5
190	11081.8	4903.2	4704.1	10869.7	10568.0

Running Time. By the time cost we illustrate the efficiency of the new algorithm. Table 2 lists the running time of experiments whose output norms are listed in Table 1. When comparing the time cost, we include the whole procedure and the preprocessing cost as well. As shown in Fig. 3(b), with the same block size b, while our algorithm is able to reach a shorter vector than BKZ with the same block size, the running time of one round of new reduction algorithm is still close to that of BKZ in most cases. Further, the progressive-rounds version of the algorithm reaches a vector far shorter than BKZ within twice of the running time of BKZ and BKZ 2.0. This is a acceptable time cost. Especially, the 4-SubBKZ has a lower time cost than BKZ and BKZ 2.0 in dimensions greater than 160. This suggests that at least for smaller blocks, the m-SubBKZ can output a shorter vector with lower cost with appropriate parameters and strategy.

We try to give a empirical explanation about the behaviour of m-SubBKZ. On the one hand our algorithm runs several rounds of sublattice reduction, thus calling BKZ recursively. And the reduction on a smaller scale reduces the computation resources needed. On the other hand, with the sublattice reduction and preprocessing, each BKZ call is cheaper and returns a reduced basis in less time. Therefore, the actual performance is determined by the tradeoff between the scale of sublattices and the number of rounds. Specifically, the running time of 4-rounds version is about 52% of BKZ. This illustrates the efficiency of our algorithm. Interestingly, when m is greater than 4, the algorithm consumes even longer time than BKZ 2.0. Recalling that the running 8 rounds will only slightly improve the output quality, we can conclude that for the current parameters, setting m to 4 is enough to reach a reasonably short vector with lower while requiring less computation resourses than BKZ and BKZ 2.0, especially in higher dimensions.

We observe that the experimental results of different algorithms on lattices of smaller dimensions ($n \leq 100$) are similar. In fact, a smaller basis makes it easier to find the shortest vector with smaller block size, while larger lattices need stronger algorithms and more tours to reach a relatively short vector. To illustrate the efficiency of various algorithms, we show the more obvious difference where higher dimensions are concerned.

Table 2. Running time of algorithms

Dimension	m-SubBKZ			BKZ	BKZ 2.0
	$m = 1$	$m = 4$	$m = 8$	≥ 6 tours	≥ 6 tours
100	26.5 s	57.8 s	100.4 s	28.5 s	21.3 s
120	47.0 s	86.5 s	174.0 s	55.5 s	53.8 s
140	84.1 s	139.1 s	409.7 s	281.5 s	111.6 s
160	134.7 s	209.4 s	654.0 s	364.8 s	196.3 s
180	272.4 s	355.3 s	596.2 s	702.2 s	421.4 s
190	394.2 s	658.1 s	836.7 s	844.3 s	776.37 s

When comparing progressive BKZ with SubBKZ, we still choose dimension 140, 160 and 180. The time cost of progressive BKZ are 133 s, 276 s and 368 s respectively, similar to SubBKZ. Considering the shorter output by SubBKZ, the result illustrates the improved efficiency of our algorithm.

6   Conclusion

In this work, we propose a lattice reduction algorithm based on BKZ. We analyze the fact that a sublattice BKZ call is possible to produce a list of short vectors with lower cost, compared with reduction on the full lattice. Based on analysis, we propose the SubBKZ in the simple form and the progressive form (m-SubBKZ), with different strategies and parameters. The simple algorithm calls a BKZ reduction on a sublattice before running reduction on the full basis. The progressive version of the new algorithm recursively runs a lattice reduction solver on a sublattice basis to ensure a well reduced sublattice, thus improving the quality of the full lattice basis.

The efficiency of the new algorithm is illustrated with experiment results on random lattices, with dimension from 100 to 190. Especially on higher dimensions, the new algorithm is able to produce a vector of 47% the length of BKZ 2.0 output, with running time 85% of BKZ 2.0, illustrating our improved efficiency. Since the sublattice reduction technique proved useful in improving BKZ, it is interesting to investigate how it will perform when combined with sieving and other algorithms.

Acknowledgement. The authors would like to thank the anonymous reviewers for their valuable comments. This work was supported by the National Natural Science Foundation of China (No. 61872449, 62032009) and the National Key Research and Development Program of China (No. 2018YFA0704705).

References

1. Schnorr, C.P., Euchner, M.: Lattice basis reduction: improved practical algorithms and solving subset sum problems. Math. Program. **66**, 181–199 (1994)

2. Nguyen, P.Q., Vidick, T.: Sieve algorithms for the shortest vector problem are practical. J. Math. Cryptol. **2**(2), 181–207 (2008)
3. Micciancio, D., Voulgaris, P.: Faster exponential time algorithms for the shortest vector problem. In: 21st Annual ACM-SIAM Symposium on Discrete Algorithms, pp. 1468–1480. ACM-SIAM, Austin (2010)
4. Ducas, L.: Shortest vector from lattice sieving: A few dimensions for free. In: EUROCRYPT 2018, Part I, LNCS, vol. 10820, pp. 125–145. Springer, Cham (2018). https://doi.org/10.1007/978-3-319-78381-9_5
5. Lenstra, A.K., Lenstra, H.W., Lovász, L.: Factoring polynomials with rational coefficients. Math. Annalen **261**, 515–534 (1982)
6. Aggarwal, D., Li, J., Nguyen, P.Q., Stephens-Davidowitz, N.: Slide reduction, revisited - filling the gaps in SVP approximation. In: Advances in Cryptology - CRYPTO 2020, LNCS, vol. 12171, pp. 274–295. Springer, Cham (2020). https://doi.org/10.1007/978-3-030-56880-1_10
7. Chen, Y., Nguyen, P.Q.: BKZ 2.0: Better lattice security estimates. In: ASIACRYPT 2011, LNCS, vol. 7073, pp. 1–20. Springer, Heidelberg (2011). https://doi.org/10.1007/978-3-642-25385-0_1
8. Aono, Y., Wang, Y., Hayashi, T., Takagi, T.: Improved progressive BKZ algorithms and their precise cost estimation by sharp simulator. In: Advances in Cryptology - EUROCRYPT 2016, LNCS, vol. 9665, pp. 789–819. Springer, Heidelberg (2016). https://doi.org/10.1007/978-3-662-49890-3_30
9. Albrecht, M., Bai, S., Fouque, P.A., Kirchner, P., Stehle, D., Wen, W.: Faster enumeration-based lattice reduction : root hermite factor k1/(2k) time kk/8+o(k). In: Advances in Cryptology - CRYPTO 2020. LNCS, vol. 12171, pp. 186–212. Springer, Cham (2020). https://doi.org/10.1007/978-3-030-56880-1_7
10. Nguyen, P.Q., Vallee, B.: The LLL Algorithm, Survey and Applications, 1st edn. Springer, Heidelberg (2010). https://doi.org/10.1007/978-3-642-02295-1
11. Micciancio, D., Walter, M.: Practical, predictable lattice basis reduction. In: Advances in Cryptology - EUROCRYPT 2016, LNCS, vol. 9665, pp. 820–849. Springer, Heidelberg (2016). https://doi.org/10.1007/978-3-662-49890-3_31
12. Schnorr, C.P.: Lattice reduction by random sampling and birthday methods. In: STACS 2003, LNCS, vol. 2607, pp. 145–156. Springer, Heidelberg (2003). https://doi.org/10.1007/3-540-36494-3_14
13. Guillaume, H., Pujol, X., Stehle, D.: Analyzing blockwise lattice algorithms using dynamical systems. In: Advances in Cryptology - CRYPTO 2011, LNCS, vol. 6841, pp. 447–464. Springer, Heidelberg (2011). https://doi.org/10.1007/978-3-642-22792-9_25
14. Gama, N., Nguyen, P.Q.: Finding short lattice vectors within Mordell's inequality. In: 40th ACM STOC, pp. 207–216. ACM Press, Columbia (2008)
15. The FPLLL development team. FPLLL, a lattice reduction library. https://github.com/fplll/fplll. Accessed 25 May 2021
16. The FPLLL development team. FPyLLL, a Python interface to fplll. https://github.com/fplll/fpylll. Accessed 25 May 2021

On the (M)iNTRU Assumption
in the Integer Case

Jim Barthel[1(✉)], Volker Müller[1], and Răzvan Roşie[2]

[1] University of Luxembourg, Esch-sur-Alzette, Luxembourg
{jim.barthel,volker.muller}@uni.lu
[2] Jao Luxembourg, Luxembourg, Luxembourg
rosie@jao.eu

Abstract. In AsiaCrypt 2019, Genise, Gentry, Halevi, Li and Micciancio put forth two novel and intriguing computational hardness hypotheses: The inhomogeneous NTRU (iNTRU) assumption and its matrix version MiNTRU. In this work, we break the integer case of the iNTRU assumption through elementary lattice reduction, and we describe how the attack might be generalized to polynomial rings and to the low dimensional MiNTRU assumption with small noise.

Keywords: iNTRU · MiNTRU · Cryptanalysis · Lattice reduction

1 Introduction

Security reductions form the core of modern cryptography. Appraised by theorists, but largely ignored by programmers, reductions guarantee that specific attacks captured by some security experiment are infeasible. A reduction has two main components: some construction that needs to be proven secure and some problem that is assumed to be hard – usually denoted by the term *assumption*.

The last cryptographic epoch was synonymous with the raise of post-quantum cryptographic assumptions. Among these, lattice assumptions occupy a central role and today most of the provably secure lattice schemes rely on the *Learning-with-Errors* (LWE) problem, as described in the seminal paper of Regev [16]. A second group of assumptions is based on the NTRU problem, as postulated in [9]. While the former group is reducible to standard average-case assumptions, the latter is not. However, often the latter group offers superior practical performance, and results in this area are preferred for implementations. Besides the traditional definitions, there are a wide set of versions used in different sub-areas of cryptography, not all of them being deeply studied.

In this work, we consider two novel versions of the NTRU assumption from [6]. We show a practical attack against the one-dimensional version and generalize it to the multidimensional version with small dimension or small noise. In particular, our attacks show that both problems can directly be reduced to the *shortest vector problem*.

© Springer Nature Switzerland AG 2021
Q. Huang and Y. Yu (Eds.): ProvSec 2021, LNCS 13059, pp. 190–211, 2021.
https://doi.org/10.1007/978-3-030-90402-9_11

1.1   Contribution 1: Breaking the Integer iNTRU Assumption

The inhomogeneous NTRU (decision) problem (iNTRU) introduced in [6] consists in distinguishing between a random and a synthetically constructed $(\ell+1)$-tuple. The synthetically constructed tuple follows the so-called iNTRU distribution that is obtained in two steps: First, a secret invertible ring element $s \in \mathcal{R}/q\mathcal{R}$ is randomly sampled and small error values e_i stemming from a specific error distribution are determined. Second, the tuple is defined by setting $a_0 := e_0/s \mod q$ and the remaining ℓ entries are fixed by $a_i := (2^{i-1} - e_i)/s \mod q$.

We analyse the integer iNTRU problem (i.e., $\mathcal{R} = \mathbb{Z}$) and develop two elementary lattice based distinguisher. Our key idea consists in replacing a_i by $b_i := 2a_i - a_{i+1} = (-2e_i + e_{i+1})/s \mod q$, making so the entries independent of the blow up term 2^i. This change guarantees the existence of an extremely small vector (smaller than the expected heuristic value) inside well constructed lattices. A vector of this magnitude will not be contained in those lattices if the initial tuple was randomly sampled. Finally, simple lattice reduction spots the difference and even reveals the secret s.

1.2   Contribution 2: Generalizing the One-Dimensional Attack to the MiNTRU Assumption

After introducing the one dimensional version of the inhomogeneous NTRU problem, the authors of [6] generalize it to matrices. The matrix inhomogeneous NTRU (decision) problem (MiNTRU) consists in distinguishing between a randomly sampled and a synthetically constructed matrix. The synthetically constructed matrix is again obtained in two steps: First, a random invertible matrix $\mathbf{S} \in \mathbb{Z}_q^{n \times n}$ is sampled and an error matrix $\mathbf{E} \in \mathbb{Z}_q^{n \times (n(\ell+1))}$ stemming from a specific error distribution is determined. Second, the challenge matrix is defined as $\mathbf{A} := \mathbf{S}^{-1} \times (\mathbf{G} - \mathbf{E}) \mod q$ where $\mathbf{G} = [0|\mathbf{I}|2\mathbf{I}|...|2^{\ell-1}\mathbf{I}]$ is an extended gadget matrix.

We generalize our previous iNTRU distinguisher to the multidimensional case. Again, the method relies on first eliminating the blow up factor 2^{i-1} (hidden in the gadget matrix), but this time even the secret matrix $\mathbf{S}$ will be canceled out, leading to a system of low norm matrices only. From there on, a well constructed lattice reveals again an extremely short vector, which can not be found in case of a random initial matrix. As the involved lattice dimensions are increasing, the output may deviate from the shortest vector, and so the secret will no longer be recovered. Nonetheless, this method has a relatively good success rate if the dimension n is small or if the error distribution for $\mathbf{E}$ is too narrow.

1.3   Disclaimer 1

We highlight that our attacks differ from the one in [12] based on [10].

Our iNTRU attack and its generalization follow standard lattice techniques and do not require advanced sub-lattice constructions. Although the latter may be used to simplify the construction, it is not needed. In particular, we will not get back to the highly useful methods from [10].

We note that besides using a different construction, we also work in a different context than [12]. Indeed, whereas they started from secret Bernoulli matrices $(-1, 0, 1$ entries), we work in a more general context where the secret matrix is sampled completely at random. In addition, our methods allow bypassing far larger entropic noise than their sub-lattice attack, but our approach is still somewhat dependent on the overstretched regime of the iNTRU instantiation.

Unfortunately, compared to their attack, our attacks are less powerful. More precisely, they managed to recover efficiently the secret matrix, thereby breaking the search version of the assumptions. We will be content with attacking the decision version without guarantee of recovering the secret.

Finally, we note that [6] has been updated to bypass the attack from [12] (which was in fact based on a toy example from [6]). In particular, the secret matrix is not a Bernoulli matrix anymore, implying that the size estimate used in [12] does no longer hold, and the final recovering step cannot be applied. We are not aware on how to use their attack on a completely random secret matrix.

1.4   Disclaimer 2

We remark that our attacks are devised for the integer case ($\mathcal{R} = \mathbb{Z}$) only, and that their efficiency for general rings is limited. Albeit they reflect a potential theoretical threat, our constructions are not strong enough to impact the security of recent cryptographic constructions such as [7] or [6] that either use iNTRU with rings of large degree or the MiNTRU with matrices of large dimension. Thereby, our contribution can only be seen as a first indication that the iNTRU (respectively the MiNTRU) assumption is not as hard as other well-known assumptions (like LWE). Further security analyses may be required to develop practical attacks against iNTRU (respectively MiNTRU) based cryptographic protocols.

1.5   Paper Organization

We start with setting the notations in Sect. 2 and continue this section with a reminder about lattices. In Sect. 3, we redefine the iNTRU assumption, and we quickly review its recent use. In Sect. 4 and Sect. 5, we develop two complementary lattice attacks against the one-dimensional integer iNTRU assumption. The first one will only be applicable if a specific invertibility condition is satisfied, and the second attack may be used in the opposite case. We complete our analysis in Sect. 6 with a short description on how to generalize our attacks to the polynomial ring iNTRU assumption and to the low dimensional MiNTRU assumption with low entropic noise. The full version of our paper including a more precise analysis of the MiNTRU assumption, a short comparison of the studied assumptions with the Learning-with-Errors assumption, and fully commented SageMath source codes corresponding to our attacks may be found at http://hdl.handle.net/10993/47990.

2   Preliminaries

2.1   Notations

For a finite set S, we denote its cardinality by $|S|$ and the action of sampling an element x uniformly at random from S is denoted by $x \leftarrow_\$ S$. When another, non-uniform distribution χ over the support set S is used, we abuse the notation and write $x \leftarrow \chi(S)$ or simply $x \leftarrow \chi$ if the support set is clear from context. We denote by $\| \cdot \| := \| \cdot \|_2$ the real Euclidean norm and by $\log := \log_2$ the base 2 logarithm. For an integer $q \geq 2$, we denote by $\mathbb{Z}/q\mathbb{Z}$ the ring of integers modulo q and we represent it using the 0-centered representation $\mathbb{Z}/q\mathbb{Z} = (-q/2, q/2] \cap \mathbb{Z}$. We denote an ordered list of n elements by $(a_1, \ldots, a_n)$. Lowercase variables in **bold** font, such as **a**, usually denote (row) vectors and bold uppercase letters, such as **A**, usually denote matrices.

2.2   Lattice Preliminaries

Lattices. Let $\mathbf{v}_1, \ldots, \mathbf{v}_n \in \mathbb{Z}^m$ be linearly independent row vectors. The row lattice generated by the basis $\mathbf{v}_1, \ldots, \mathbf{v}_n$ is the linear span

$$\Lambda = \mathcal{L}(\mathbf{v}_1, \ldots, \mathbf{v}_n) = \left\{ \sum_{i=1}^n x_i \mathbf{v}_i \mid x_1, \ldots, x_n \in \mathbb{Z} \right\}.$$

We call a matrix **B** a basis matrix of Λ if Λ is generated by the rows of **B**. It is well known that two bases $\mathbf{B}, \mathbf{B}'$ generate the same lattice if and only if there is an unimodular matrix $U \in GL(\mathbb{Z}, n)$ such that $\mathbf{B} = U\mathbf{B}'$. The determinant of a lattice Λ is defined by $\det(\Lambda) = \sqrt{\det(\mathbf{BB}^T)}$ where **B** denotes any basis of Λ. Naturally, this determinant is independent of the chosen basis. The rank (or dimension) of a lattice is the dimension as a vector space of the lattice, and a lattice is full rank if it has maximal rank.

Successive Minima. For $i \in \{1, \ldots, n\}$, we define the ith *successive minimum* of Λ as the smallest $r > 0$ such that Λ contains at least i linearly independent vectors of length bounded by r, $\lambda_i(\Lambda) = \inf\{r \in \mathbb{R}_{>0} : \dim(span(\Lambda \cap B(0,r))) \geq i\}$ where $B(0,r) = \{x \in \mathbb{R}^m : \|x\| \leq r\}$ is the closed ball of radius r around 0. The successive minima are achieved (thus, one may use the minimum instead of the infimum in its definition) and lattice points of norm $\lambda_i(\Lambda)$ are called i-th shortest vectors, but may not be unique. Minkowski's Second Theorem states that for each $1 \leq i \leq n$ the product $\left(\prod_{j=1}^i \lambda_j(\Lambda) \right)^{1/i} \leq \sqrt{\frac{n}{2\pi e}} \det(\Lambda)^{1/n}$.

LLL Reduction. Given $1/4 < \delta < 1$, a lattice basis $\mathbf{v}_1, \ldots, \mathbf{v}_n$ of Λ is LLL reduced with factor δ if the following holds

1. Size reduced: $\left| \frac{\langle \mathbf{v}_i, \mathbf{v}_j^* \rangle}{\langle \mathbf{v}_j^*, \mathbf{v}_j^* \rangle} \right| \leq \frac{1}{2}$ for all $1 \leq j < i < n$;

2. Lovász condition: $\|\mathbf{v}_j^*\|^2 \geq \left(\delta - \left|\frac{\langle \mathbf{v}_j, \mathbf{v}_{j-1}^* \rangle}{\langle \mathbf{v}_{j-1}^*, \mathbf{v}_{j-1}^* \rangle}\right|^2\right) \|\mathbf{v}_{j-1}^*\|^2$ for each $2 \leq j \leq n$;

where $\mathbf{v}_1^*, \ldots, \mathbf{v}_n^*$ denote the Gram-Schmidt orthogonalization of the basis vectors. Traditionally $\delta = 3/4$, but in practice $\delta = 0.99$ is chosen. LLL reduced bases are not unique, but they have many desired properties. Indeed, let $\alpha = \frac{1}{\delta - \frac{1}{4}}$, then

1. $\|\mathbf{v}_j\| \leq \alpha^{\frac{n-1}{2}} \lambda_i(\Lambda)$ for all $1 \leq j \leq i \leq n$;
2. $\det(\Lambda) = \prod_{i=1}^n \|\mathbf{v}_i^*\| \leq \prod_{i=1}^n \|\mathbf{v}_i\| \leq \alpha^{\frac{n(n-1)}{2}} \det(\Lambda)$.

The LLL algorithm [13] outputs a LLL reduced basis of a rank n lattice in $\mathbb{Z}^m$ in time $O(n^5 m \log(K)^3)$ from basis vectors of norm less than K.[1]

Heuristics. The Gaussian Heuristic (see [2] and [5]) yields that for a "random" rank n lattice of "large" dimension, we expect the shortest vector to be of norm $\lambda_1(\Lambda) \simeq \sqrt{\frac{n}{2\pi e}} \det(\Lambda)^{1/n}$. Furthermore, in this case, all the lattice minima can be expected to be of approximately the same size.

Q-ary lattices. If $q\mathbb{Z}^m \subseteq \Lambda \subseteq \mathbb{Z}^m$ for some $q \in \mathbb{Z}_{\geq 2}$, then Λ is called a q-ary lattice. We remark first that, by definition, every q-ary lattice has full rank $n = m$. Secondly, we observe that the lattice minima of a q-ary lattice are upper bounded by $\lambda_i(\Lambda) \leq q$ for all $i \in \{1, \ldots, m\}$. Given any matrix $\mathbf{A} \in (\mathbb{Z}/q\mathbb{Z})^{k \times m}$, we define the two special q-ary lattices $\Lambda_q(\mathbf{A}) = \{\mathbf{y} \in \mathbb{Z}^m | \mathbf{y} = \mathbf{A}^T\mathbf{x}$ mod (q) for some $\mathbf{x} \in \mathbb{Z}^k\}$ and $\Lambda_q^\perp(\mathbf{A}) = \{\mathbf{y} \in \mathbb{Z}^m | \mathbf{A}\mathbf{y} = 0$ mod $(q)\}$. As a matter of fact, any q-ary lattice may be expressed as one of those lattices for some matrix $\mathbf{A} \in (\mathbb{Z}/q\mathbb{Z})^{k \times m}$ and $\det(\Lambda_q(\mathbf{A})) \geq q^{m-k}$ with equality if $\mathbf{A}$ is non-singular. Due to their special structure, q-ary lattices can not be seen as random (as required for the Gaussian heuristic). Nonetheless, [3] states that the Gaussian heuristic appears to hold exceedingly well for such lattices. A bit more precisely, [17, Lemma 2.18] proves that for fixed prime q and $m \geq k$, and for a randomly sampled matrix $\mathbf{A} \in (\mathbb{Z}/q\mathbb{Z})^{k \times m}$, the first lattice minimum is lower bounded by $\min\left\{q, \sqrt{\frac{m}{8\pi e}} q^{\frac{m-k}{m}}\right\}$ with probability greater than $1 - 2^{-m}$. We note that $\sqrt{\frac{m}{8\pi e}} q^{\frac{m-k}{m}}$ corresponds to half the Gaussian heuristic if $\mathbf{A}$ is non-singular.

Our Lattices. Hereinafter, we will use particular q-ary lattices where $\mathbf{A} \in (\mathbb{Z}/q\mathbb{Z})^{1 \times m}$ with a fixed entry equal to 1 and where q is not necessarily a prime. Although, none of the above results perfectly match our setup, we assume that, with noticeable probability, the first lattice minimum satisfies

$$\lambda_1(\Lambda) \geq \min\left\{q, \sqrt{\frac{m}{8\pi e}} q^{\frac{m-1}{m}}\right\}. \tag{H}$$

---

[1] Hereinafter, we will only use the LLL algorithm for lattice reduction. Better results may be achieved using recent results on the BKZ algorithm (see [14]). However, the LLL algorithm suffices for our elementary analysis.

3   The iNTRU Assumption

In this section, we (re-)define the inhomogeneous NTRU (iNTRU) assumption, we describe some variants and outline its use.

3.1   The iNTRU Assumption

The iNTRU problem has initially been introduced in [6, Sect. 4.1] formula (3).

Definition 1 (iNTRU Distribution). *Let $\mathcal{R}$ be a ring, q any modulus, $\ell = \lceil \log(q) \rceil$ and χ be a symmetric error distribution over $\mathcal{R}$ producing with overwhelming probability elements with norm $\ll q$. Define the iNTRU distribution with these parameters to be obtained by the following sampling process*

$$\text{iNTRU} = \left\{ \begin{array}{l} s \leftarrow_s \mathcal{R}/q\mathcal{R} \\ e_i \leftarrow \chi \quad \forall i \in \{0, ..., \ell\} \\ a_0 := e_0/s \mod q \\ a_i := (2^{i-1} - e_i)/s \mod q \quad \forall i \in \{1, ..., \ell\} \end{array} \right\} \tag{1}$$

and denote any such tuple $(a_0, \ldots, a_\ell)$ by iNTRU tuple.

Definition 2 (iNTRU Search Problem.). *Given an iNTRU tuple $(a_0, \ldots, a_\ell)$ and a modulus q, the iNTRU search problem consists in finding the hidden secret s. The iNTRU search assumption predicts that s can only be determined with negligible probability.*

Definition 3 (iNTRU Decision Problem). *Given a tuple $(x_0, \ldots, x_\ell)$ and a modulus q, the iNTRU decision problem consists in distinguishing whether the tuple has been sampled using the iNTRU distribution or the uniform distribution over $\mathcal{R}/q\mathcal{R}$. The iNTRU decision assumption predicts that such a distinction can only be made with negligible probability.*

We highlight that in [6] only the decision variant has been defined. However, in practice, the search variant may be used.

3.2   Further Remarks

Hereinafter, we will point out some particular points of the definitions:

1. The iNTRU definition gives no limitation for the modulus q. Indeed, theoretically $\mathcal{R}/q\mathcal{R}$ might only be a ring and does not need to be a field.
2. If $\mathcal{R} = \mathbb{Z}$, then the underlying error distribution χ may be considered to be the discrete Gaussian distribution with variance $\sigma_\chi = O(\sqrt{q})$ (following a suggestion of [6]).
3. One can define shortened iNTRU tuples by removing the first entries of an iNTRU tuple. Especially, the first entry a_0 is sometimes removed.

3.3 Applications

Currently, the iNTRU assumption has only been used in [7] to develop two ring based short integer solution lattice trapdoors. The pseudorandomness of those trapdoors stems directly from the iNTRU assumption. We will fast revise their construction.

Trapdoors. Intuitively, a trapdoor is some information that allows to invert a function [4]. For instance, if $f_{\mathbf{a}}(\mathbf{x}) := \mathbf{a} \cdot \mathbf{x}^T$, where $\mathbf{a}, \mathbf{x}$ are elements over some polynomial quotient ring $(\mathcal{R}/q\mathcal{R})^m$, then a trapdoor would allow recovering $\mathbf{x}$.

Short Integer Solutions. The *Short Integer Solution* (SIS) problem (see [1] for the original integer case, [15] for the ring based definition, and [11] for the module version) is a standard cryptographic problem which, in the ring version, asks to find, for a given vector $\mathbf{a} \in (\mathcal{R}/q\mathcal{R})^m$ and a bound value $\beta \in \mathbb{R}_{>0}$, a vector $\mathbf{x} \in (\mathcal{R}/q\mathcal{R})^m$ such that $f_{\mathbf{a}}(\mathbf{x}) = \mathbf{a} \cdot \mathbf{x}^T = 0$ and $\|\mathbf{x}\|_\rho < \beta$ for a suitable metric $\| \cdot \|_\rho$.

Usually, this problem is tackled by an elementary trapdoor mechanism. More precisely, assume that it is easy to solve the short integer solution problem for $f_{\mathbf{g}}$ where $\mathbf{g}$ is a known vector called the gadget. Assume further to know a low norm matrix $\mathbf{R}$, called a $\mathbf{g}$-trapdoor, such that $\mathbf{a} \cdot \mathbf{R} = \mathbf{g}$. Then, it is easy to solve the initial short integer solution problem. Indeed, one first samples at random any $\mathbf{x}$ such that $f_{\mathbf{g}}(\mathbf{x}) = 0$ and $\|\mathbf{x}\|_\rho < \beta$ (which is supposedly easy to find). Next, one computes $\mathbf{x}' := \mathbf{R} \cdot \mathbf{x}$ and finally hopes that it still fulfills $\|\mathbf{x}'\|_\rho < \beta$, which, due to the low norm entries of $\mathbf{R}$, generally holds. The preimage construction (i.e., finding $\mathbf{x}$) is commonly based on a discrete Gaussian sampling procedure (see [8] for a broad overview).

Despite their utility, such trapdoors may incorporate a security threat. Indeed, as outlined above, anyone knowing the trapdoor may solve the initial problem. Thereby, a necessary security feature required by such a trapdoor is that it is difficult to be guessed or put another way, it should be pseudorandom. [7] constructs two such trapdoors as follows.

Their Idea. The main idea behind their trapdoors is to use the inherent trapdoor potential of the iNTRU distribution. Concretely, a shortened iNTRU tuple $\mathbf{a} = (a_1, \ldots, a_\ell)$ can be represented as $\mathbf{a} = s^{-1}(\mathbf{g} + \mathbf{e})$ where $\mathbf{g} = (1, 2, 2^2, \ldots, 2^{\ell-1})$ is the gadget vector, $\mathbf{e} = (e_1, \ldots, e_\ell) \hookleftarrow_\$ \chi^\ell$ and $s \in (\mathcal{R}/q\mathcal{R})^\times$ (they even choose $s \leftarrow \chi$). Since $s\mathbf{a} = \mathbf{g} + \mathbf{e} \approx \mathbf{g}$, the secret s is almost a $\mathbf{g}$-trapdoor for $\mathbf{a}$, falling only short of the corresponding error vector $\mathbf{e}$.

Their Trapdoor Generation. Unfortunately, such a direct construction might leak some information on the trapdoor (we omit the details here). To bypass this leakage, the authors suggest replacing the gadget $\mathbf{g}$ by an approximate gadget $\mathbf{f} = (2^j, \ldots, 2^{\ell-1})$ for some $j \in \mathbb{N}_{>1}$ (often $j = \lceil \log(q)/2 \rceil$) and to proceed in the usual way, i.e., $\mathbf{a} = s^{-1}(\mathbf{f} + \mathbf{e})$. The $\mathbf{f}$-trapdoor will then consist in $(s, \mathbf{e})$.

The main difference of their constructions are the preimage sampling processes. These rely on different choices of perturbations and provoke a change in the discrete Gaussian sampling step. We omit the technical details about the procedures, as they will not be affected by what follows.

Pseudorandomness. In the described construction, trapdoor pseudorandomness stems directly from the pseudorandomness of iNTRU tuples. Indeed, if, for given **a** (and implicitly the approximate gadget **f**), one could retrieve the secret s, then one can also find the error tuple **e** and so the desired trapdoor.

3.4 Our Contribution

We are going to prove that neither the decision, nor the search variant of the iNTRU assumption are safe in the integer case $\mathcal{R} = \mathbb{Z}$ and so the iNTRU distribution is not pseudorandom. Independent of the chosen modulus and the exact error distribution, our lattice attacks will distinguish with noticeable probability between random tuples and synthetically constructed ones, and they will retrieve the hidden secret in the latter case.

Our first attack is the natural choice when facing a challenge tuple. It will slightly modify the challenge entries and then construct a lattice. In the presence of a random challenge tuple, the shortest vector of this lattice will follow a specific heuristic (close to the Gaussian heuristic) whereas for a synthetically constructed one, the shortest vector will be far smaller and can be used to retrieve the secret. Unfortunately, the involved transformations include a modular inversion which may not be feasible in some cases, and one may bypass the attack by a suitable construction.

Our second attack can be used in case the first attack does not apply. It follows a similar transformation chain, but does not involve a modular inversion. The basic idea of the attack is the same, but this time the second-shortest vector will be compared to the heuristic. Due to this non-standard approach and an increased complexity, the first attack is preferable in most cases.

Although our attacks are conceived for the integer case, one may generalize them for polynomial rings. Such a generalization however needs to be carried out carefully, as the lattice dimension will increase and limits the applicability of the attack. Thereby, the attack is predicted to work for low degree polynomial rings only.

4 Attacking the iNTRU Assumption - First Approach

In this section, we describe our first lattice attack against the search and decision variant of the iNTRU assumption. We develop the attack for $\mathcal{R} = \mathbb{Z}$ only, but we emphasise that it can be generalized to low degree polynomial rings. Our attack first outlines whether a given tuple stems from the iNTRU distribution and if so it will find the underlying secret s. The development is based on full length challenge tuples but can, through small changes, also be applied to shortened tuples.

4.1   Our First Lattice and Its Properties

Let $(x_0, \ldots, x_\ell)$ be a challenge tuple corresponding either to the uniform or the iNTRU distribution.

Lattice Construction. First, we slightly modify our challenge tuple and set

$$y_0 := x_0 \mod q \quad \text{and} \quad y_i = 2x_i - x_{i+1} \mod q \quad \forall i \in \{1, \ldots, \ell - 1\}. \quad (2)$$

Let $t \in \{0, \ldots, \ell - 1\}$ be an index such that $\gcd(y_t, q) = 1$. If no such index exists, the subsequent development will not work and our second iNTRU attack needs to be used (c.f. Sect. 5)[2]. We set

$$z_i := y_t^{-1} y_i \mod q \quad \forall i \in \{0, \ldots, \ell - 1\} \quad (3)$$

where $z_t = 1$. Then, we define the $\ell \times \ell$ q-ary row lattice:

$$\Lambda = \mathcal{L} \begin{pmatrix} z_0 \ldots z_{t-1} \, 1 \, z_{t+1} \ldots z_{\ell-1} \\ q \ldots 0 \; 0 \; 0 \; \ldots \; 0 \\ \vdots \; \ddots \; \vdots \; \vdots \; \vdots \qquad \vdots \\ 0 \ldots q \; 0 \; 0 \; \ldots \; 0 \\ 0 \ldots 0 \; 0 \; q \; \ldots \; 0 \\ \vdots \qquad \vdots \; \vdots \; \vdots \; \ddots \; \vdots \\ 0 \ldots 0 \; 0 \; 0 \; \ldots \; q \end{pmatrix} \quad (4)$$

4.2   Case of a Random Tuple

Assume that our initial challenge tuple $(x_0, \ldots, x_\ell)$ was sampled uniformly at random. Then, our constructed variables y_i as well as z_i (except $z_t = 1$) will still follow the uniform distribution as they involve only the addition and multiplication of random variables. Thereby, the shortest lattice vector can be expected to follow heuristic H and to satisfy

$$\lambda_1(\Lambda) \geq \min \left\{ q, \sqrt{\frac{\ell}{8\pi e}} q^{\frac{\ell-1}{\ell}} \right\}. \quad (5)$$

4.3   Case of a Synthetic Tuple

Assume next that the initial tuple $(x_0, \ldots, x_\ell)$ has been synthetically constructed following the iNTRU distribution. We will show that in this case the lattice contains a non-trivial short vector being magnitudes smaller than the expected heuristic.

---

[2] For $\mathcal{R} = \mathbb{Z}$ and random $x_0, \ldots, x_\ell$, the probability that our first attack cannot be used is only $\left(1 - \frac{\phi(q)}{q}\right)^\ell$ where ϕ denotes the Euler totient function. In particular, if q is prime our first attack should always work.

First Observation. We recall that a synthetically constructed tuple $(a_0, \ldots, a_\ell)$ following the iNTRU distribution satisfies

$$a_0 = \frac{e_0}{s} \mod q \quad \text{and} \quad a_i = \frac{2^{i-1} - e_i}{s} \mod q \quad \forall i \in \{1, \ldots, \ell\} \quad (6)$$

where $e_0, \ldots, e_\ell$ denote random errors sampled from the symmetric error distribution χ producing with overwhelming probability small elements. Thereby,

$$y_0 = \frac{e_0}{s} \mod q \quad \text{and} \quad y_i = \frac{-2e_i + e_{i+1}}{s} \mod q \quad \forall i \in \{1, \ldots, \ell - 1\} \quad (7)$$

where the numerators are still quite small. More precisely, the numerators follow the distribution χ' where:

1. The mean $\mu_{\chi'}$ of χ' is given by

$$\mu_{\chi'} = -2\mu_\chi + \mu_\chi = 0$$

   where the first equality stems from the distribution properties of sums of random variables as well as the fact that a_i and a_{i+1} follow the same distribution χ, and the second equality comes from the fact that the mean $\mu_\chi = 0$ since χ is a symmetric distribution (i.e., $-\chi = \chi$).
2. The variance $\sigma_{\chi'}$ of χ' is given by

$$\sigma_{\chi'}^2 = 3\sigma_\chi^2$$

   since all three variables follow the distribution χ.

In particular, we conclude that since χ produces with overwhelming probability elements with absolute value $\ll q$, so does χ'. Thereby, the numerators are expected to be quite small when compared to the modulus q.

Second Observation. Continuing to outline the effect of our variable changes leads to the conclusion that

$$z_i = \frac{-2e_i + e_{i+1}}{e_t'} \mod q \quad \forall i \in \{0, \ldots, \ell - 1\} \quad (8)$$

where $e_t' = e_0$ if $t = 0$ and $e_t' = -2e_t + e_{t+1}$ if $t \in \{1, \ldots, \ell - 1\}$. Thus, each z_i is the quotient of two small error elements.

The Shortest Lattice Vector. Interestingly, our two observations imply that our lattice contains the vector

$$\mathbf{v} = (e_0, (-2e_1 + e_2), \ldots, (-2e_{\ell-1} + e_\ell)) \quad (9)$$

obtained by multiplying the first row by e_t' and applying the "modulo q reduction", corresponding to an addition of the respective rows, as often as needed.

We are going to show that this vector will be almost surely smaller than the expected heuristic and the canonically short vectors with a single entry q. To do so, first assume that the error entries are upper bounded by some constant $K > 0$. i.e.,

$$\max\{|e_0|, |-2e_1 + e_2|, \ldots, |-2e_{\ell-1} + e_\ell|\} \leq K. \tag{10}$$

Then, the size of v may be upper bounded by

$$\|\mathbf{v}\|_2 \leq \sqrt{\ell K^2} \leq \sqrt{\ell}\, K. \tag{11}$$

Proposition 1. *If* $\max\{|e_0|, |-2e_1 + e_2|, \ldots, |-2e_{\ell-1} + e_\ell|\} \leq \min\left\{\frac{q}{\sqrt{\ell}}, \frac{1}{\sqrt{8\pi e}}q^{(\ell-1)/\ell}\right\}$, *then the target vector* $\mathbf{v}$ *is shorter than* $\min\left\{q, \sqrt{\frac{\ell}{8\pi e}}q^{\frac{\ell-1}{\ell}}\right\}$.

Proof. Replace K in Eq. (11) with the predicted values and compare.   □

As in practice the error terms are $O(\sqrt{q})$, the size condition is almost always satisfied. For comparison, the probability that a completely randomly sampled ℓ-tuple would be of this size is lower than $\left(\frac{2\sqrt{\ell}K+1}{q}\right)^\ell$, which is rapidly decreasing for small K.

Lattice Reduction. We need to make sure that our target vector v can also be determined. We will show that upon slightly decreasing the upper bound K, we are guaranteed that ordinary LLL reduction returns a vector that is smaller than the expected heuristic. In general, the first LLL reduced vector with factor δ will not be a smallest lattice vector, but only a good approximation of it. More precisely, the first LLL reduced vector $\mathbf{w}_1$ satisfies theoretically $\|\mathbf{w}_1\| \leq \alpha^{\frac{\ell-1}{2}}\lambda_1$ where λ_1 denotes the length of a shortest lattice vector and $\alpha = \frac{1}{\delta - \frac{1}{4}}$. However, in practice, this artificial blowup is barely observed. We note that for increasing δ, the blow-up factor α decreases. For the sake of explicit results, we consider $\delta = \frac{63}{64} < 0.99$ resulting in $\alpha = \frac{64}{47} < \sqrt{2}$. By Eq. (11), we know that $\lambda_1 \leq \|v\|_2 \leq \sqrt{\ell}K$. This implies that

$$\|\mathbf{w}_1\|_2 \leq \alpha^{\frac{\ell-1}{2}}\sqrt{\ell}K \leq 2^{\frac{\ell-1}{4}}\sqrt{\ell}K \leq 2^{\frac{\log(q)}{4}}\sqrt{\ell}K \leq q^{\frac{1}{4}}\sqrt{\ell}K. \tag{12}$$

Proposition 2. *If* $\max\{|e_0|, |-2e_1 + e_2|, \ldots, |-2e_{\ell-1} + e_\ell|\} \leq \min\left\{\frac{q^{3/4}}{\sqrt{\ell}}, \frac{1}{\sqrt{8\pi e}}q^{\frac{3\ell-4}{4\ell}}\right\}$, *then* $\|\mathbf{w}_1\|_2$ *is smaller than* $\min\left\{q, \sqrt{\frac{\ell}{8\pi e}}q^{\frac{\ell-1}{\ell}}\right\}$.

Proof. Replace K in Eq. (12) by the predicted values and compare.   □

As usually $K = O(\sqrt{q})$, we can expect the condition of Proposition 2 to hold in practice. We highlight also that finding another vector of this magnitude is rather improbable, and we can even expect $\mathbf{w}_1 = \pm\mathbf{v}$.

4.4   Conclusion

We conclude that:

1. In case of a random tuple, the first LLL reduced vector can be expected with noticeable probability to be lower bounded by $\min\left\{q, \sqrt{\frac{\ell}{8\pi e}}q^{\frac{\ell-1}{\ell}}\right\}$.

2. In case of a synthetic tuple, the first LLL reduced vector is with high probability smaller than the predicted value $\min\left\{q, \sqrt{\frac{\ell}{8\pi e}}q^{\frac{\ell-1}{\ell}}\right\}$ and we can even expect it to be equal to $\pm\mathbf{v}$ where $\mathbf{v} = (e_0, (-2e_1 + e_2), \ldots, (-2e_{\ell-1} + e_\ell))$ is our target vector.

Hence, we can distinguish with noticeable probability between a randomly sampled tuple and a synthetically constructed one by simply comparing the length of the first LLL reduced vector with $\min\left\{q, \sqrt{\frac{\ell}{8\pi e}}q^{\frac{\ell-1}{\ell}}\right\}$. Furthermore, in case of a synthetically constructed tuple, the first LLL reduced vector is expected to reveal the modified error terms. Choosing the error term in the t-th position e_t', and computing $\frac{e_t'}{y_t}$ mod $q = \pm s$ reveals then the hidden secret s. The corresponding SAGEMATH source codes for our first distinguisher (distinguisher1) can be found in the full version of our article.

Optional Bootstrapping. We note that in the whole development, we never assumed to know the precise error distribution. Indeed, multiple passages could have been formalized and simplified when the error distribution was known (e.g., Discrete Gaussian). Besides retrieving the secret s, our method even allows to retrieve the underlying error distribution. Indeed, upon reception of the secret s, one easily reveals the original error values $e_0, \ldots, e_\ell$. Once the errors have been determined, any bootstrapping method may simulate the whole error distribution.

5   Attacking the iNTRU Assumption - Second Approach

In this section, we describe our second attack against the integer iNTRU assumption. Whereas our first attack is foremost suitable for prime moduli q, it may not be used under unfortunate circumstances, namely if none of the y_i is invertible. This can be easily determined and in the improbable case this happens, one needs to opt for our second attack. Although slightly more challenging and bound on a more restricted success probability, our second attack will work for any initial challenge input. However, due to its increased complexity and unusual approach, the first method should be used if possible.

5.1   Our Second Lattice and Its Properties

Let $(x_0, \ldots, x_\ell)$ be an iNTRU challenge tuple corresponding either to the uniform or the iNTRU distribution.

Lattice Construction. Similar than in our first attack, we modify our challenge tuple by setting

$$y_0 := x_0 \mod q \quad \text{and} \quad y_i = 2x_i - x_{i+1} \mod q \quad \forall i \in \{1, \ldots, \ell - 1\}. \quad (13)$$

But contrary to the first attack, we stop our modifications and directly construct the $(\ell + 1) \times (\ell + 1)$ q^2-ary row lattice:

$$\Lambda = \mathcal{L} \begin{pmatrix} y_0 q & y_1 q & y_2 q & \cdots & y_{\ell-1} q & 1 \\ q^2 & 0 & 0 & \cdots & 0 & 0 \\ 0 & q^2 & 0 & \cdots & 0 & 0 \\ 0 & 0 & q^2 & \cdots & 0 & 0 \\ \vdots & \vdots & \vdots & \ddots & \vdots & \vdots \\ 0 & 0 & 0 & \cdots & q^2 & 0 \end{pmatrix} \quad (14)$$

Predicted Value. Assuming the first row of Λ random, heuristic H yields that

$$\lambda_1(\Lambda) \geq \min \left\{ q^2, \sqrt{\frac{\ell+1}{8\pi e}} q^{\frac{2\ell}{\ell+1}} \right\}. \quad (15)$$

However, here our heuristic needs to be considered with precaution as it only applies to random initial matrices **A** and prime moduli. Especially for our lattice Λ, where both of those conditions are not satisfied, we must pay attention and indeed, our lattice contains a shorter vector. More precisely, our lattice contains the vector $(0, \ldots, 0, q)$ obtained by multiplying the first row by q and then for each $i \in \{0, \ldots, \ell - 1\}$ subtracting y_i times row $i + 1$ from it. Thus, $\lambda_1 \leq q$. Nonetheless, our heuristic is a good indication for the size of the other successive minima and in particular for λ_2 (not to say that it is the only applicable estimation).

5.2   Case of a Random Tuple

Let the initial tuple $(x_0, \ldots, x_\ell)$ be randomly sampled at uniform from $(\mathbb{Z}/q\mathbb{Z})^{\ell+1}$. Then, also the corresponding y_i will follow the uniform distribution and so the first row of our lattice behaves, up to the common factor q and the last entry, almost randomly. We will prove that apart from our trivially short vector $(0, \ldots, 0, q)$, its suitable multiples, and the canonical vectors with a single entry q^2 (if applicable), it is improbable to find another vector smaller than the expected heuristic value.

Lemma 1. *Let $B \leq \frac{q}{2}$ be an integer and $S \subseteq \mathbb{Z}$ be fixed. Choose randomly $r \in \mathbb{Z}/q^2\mathbb{Z}$ and for each $i \in \{0, \ldots \ell - 1\}$, let also $y_i \in \mathbb{Z}/q\mathbb{Z}$ be random. Set*

$$\mathbf{y} = (y_0 q, y_1 q, \ldots, y_{\ell-1} q, 1).$$

Then, the probability that $r \in S$ and the norm of the vector $ry \mod q^2$ is at most Bq is upper bounded by

$$\mathbb{P}\left(\left(\left\| [ry \mod q^2] \right\|_2 \leq Bq\right) \cap (r \in S)\right) \leq \sum_{\substack{\beta_\ell = -Bq \\ \beta_\ell \in S}}^{Bq} \frac{\ell(2\lfloor B/\gcd(\beta_\ell, q)\rfloor + 1)}{q^2} \left(\frac{\gcd(\beta_\ell, q)}{q}\right)^\ell.$$

We note that the computation of $\left\| [ry \mod q^2] \right\|_2$ takes place sequentially and component-wise. More precisely, first ry is computed, then each component is reduced modulo q^2 to its centrally symmetric representative (i.e., the smallest representative in absolute value), and finally the Euclidean norm is taken on the resulting vector as seen over the integers. The proof of Lemma 1 can be found in Appendix A.

To put the previous lemma into context, we point out that if $S = \{kq \mid k \in \mathbb{Z}\}$, then the probability is smaller than $\frac{1}{\sqrt{q}}$ and if $S = (\mathbb{Z}/q^2\mathbb{Z})^\times$ is the set of units, then the probability is smaller than $\frac{\ell}{q^{\ell-1}}$. Although our lattice contains the trivial short vector $(0, \ldots, 0, q)$ and its multiples, the probability of finding a short vector with nonzero entries on the first $\ell - 1$ entries is rapidly decreasing with increasing q. For small bounds B, we expect with a high probability that such a vector will not even exist. In this case, the best possible guess for the size of the second-shortest vector will be $\min\left\{q^2, \sqrt{\frac{\ell+1}{8\pi e}} q^{\frac{2\ell}{\ell+1}}\right\}$.

5.3   Case of a Synthetic Tuple

Assume next that the initial tuple $(x_0, \ldots, x_\ell)$ has been synthetically constructed following the iNTRU distribution. Then, we will prove that apart from our trivially short vector $(0, \ldots, 0, q)$, its multiples and the canonical vectors with a single entry q^2, our lattice contains at least one more linearly independent short vector.

Preliminary Observation. Similar than in our first attack, we note that a tuple $(a_0, \ldots, a_\ell)$ following the iNTRU distribution satisfies

$$a_0 = \frac{e_0}{s} \mod q \quad \text{and} \quad a_i = \frac{2^{i-1} - e_i}{s} \mod q \quad \forall i \in \{1, \ldots, \ell\} \qquad (16)$$

where $e_0, \ldots, e_\ell$ denote random errors sampled from the symmetric error distribution χ producing with overwhelming probability small elements and that

$$y_0 = \frac{e_0}{s} \mod q \quad \text{and} \quad y_i = \frac{-2e_i + e_{i+1}}{s} \mod q \quad \forall i \in \{1, \ldots, \ell - 1\} \quad (17)$$

where the numerators follow the symmetric distribution χ' with $\mu_{\chi'} = 0$ and $\sigma_{\chi'} = \sqrt{3}\sigma_\chi$ and are thus still quite small.

Another Short Vector. Our lattice contains the vector

$$\mathbf{v} = (e_0 q, (-2e_1 + e_2)q, \ldots, (-2e_{\ell-1} + e_\ell)q, s) \tag{18}$$

obtained by multiplying the first row by s and applying the "modulo q^2 reduction", corresponding to an addition of the respective rows, as often as needed. We are going to show that this vector will be almost surely smaller than the expected heuristic. To do so, we first assume that the error entries are upper bounded by some constant $K > 0$. i.e.,

$$\max\{|e_0|, |-2e_1 + e_2|, \ldots, |-2e_{\ell-1} + e_\ell|\} \leq K. \tag{19}$$

Then, the size of v may be upper bounded by

$$\|\mathbf{v}\|_2 \leq \sqrt{\ell K^2 q^2 + s^2} \leq \sqrt{\ell K^2 q^2 + q^2} \leq \sqrt{\ell + 1}\, qK. \tag{20}$$

Whenever K is small enough, this upper bound is smaller than the expected heuristic. That this smallness condition is in general no limitation is shown by the following proposition.

Proposition 3. *If* $\max\{|e_0|, |-2e_1 + e_2|, \ldots, |-2e_{\ell-1} + e_\ell|\} \leq \min\left\{\frac{q}{\sqrt{\ell+1}}, \frac{1}{\sqrt{8\pi e}} q^{\frac{\ell-1}{\ell+1}}\right\}$, *then the target vector* $\mathbf{v}$ *is shorter than* $\min\left\{q^2, \sqrt{\frac{\ell+1}{8\pi e}} q^{\frac{2\ell}{\ell+1}}\right\}$.

Proof. Replace K by the upper bound for max in Eq. (20). □

As usually the error terms are $O(\sqrt{q})$, our target vector $\mathbf{v}$ will almost surely be smaller than the expected heuristic.

Lattice Reduction. Finally, it is time to check whether our target vector v can even be determined using ordinary lattice reduction. Hereinafter, we will only consider LLL reduction. An LLL reduced basis $(\mathbf{w}_1, \ldots, \mathbf{w}_{\ell+1})$ satisfies theoretically $\|\mathbf{w}_i\|_2 \leq \alpha^{\frac{\ell}{2}} \lambda_i$ where λ_i denotes the i-th successive minimum of the lattice and $\alpha = \frac{1}{\delta - \frac{1}{4}}$. For the sake of explicit results, we again consider $\delta = \frac{63}{64} < 0.99$ resulting in $\alpha = \frac{64}{47} < \sqrt{2}$.

Let us concentrate on the first LLL output, namely $\mathbf{w}_1$. We recall that our shortest vector will probably be $\mathbf{v}_0 = (0, ..., 0, q)$.[3] Thus, we assume $\lambda_1 \leq q$. This implies that

$$\|\mathbf{w}_1\|_2 \leq \alpha^{\frac{\ell}{2}} q \leq 2^{\frac{\ell}{4}} q \leq 2^{\frac{\log(q)+1}{4}} q \leq (2q)^{\frac{1}{4}} q.$$

Lemma 1 yields that such a short vector can only be found at random with extremely low probability Thus, it seems improbable that apart from $\mathbf{v}_0$ and its

---

[3] The only possibility for which this would not be the case takes place when $g = \gcd(y_0, \ldots, y_{\ell-1}, q) > 1$ as then $(0, \ldots, 0, \frac{q}{g})$ will be the shortest lattice vector, but this scenario is rather improbable.

multiples, another vector of this magnitude exists, and we expect $\mathbf{w}_1$ to be (a multiple of) $\mathbf{v}_0$.[4]

Next, we consider the second LLL output, namely $\mathbf{w}_2$. Assuming that $\mathbf{w}_1$ is a multiple of $\mathbf{v}_0$, the second LLL output $\mathbf{w}_2$ needs to contain non-zero entries on the first ℓ entries (otherwise it would not be linearly independent from $\mathbf{w}_1$). By Eq. (20), we know that $\|\mathbf{v}\|_2 \le \sqrt{\ell+1}\, qK$ where K denotes the maximal error term and by Proposition 3 we know that our target vector is almost surely smaller than $\min\left\{q^2, \sqrt{\frac{\ell}{8\pi e}} q^{\frac{2\ell}{\ell+1}}\right\}$. If we slightly reduce the upper bound K, we obtain a similar result for $\mathbf{w}_2$.

Proposition 4. *If* $\max\{|e_0|, |-2e_1 + e_2|, \ldots, |-2e_{\ell-1} + e_\ell|\} \le \min\left\{\frac{q^{3/4}}{2^{1/4}\sqrt{\ell+1}}, \right.$ $\left. \frac{1}{2^{3/4}\sqrt{\pi e}} q^{\frac{3\ell-5}{4(\ell+1)}}\right\}$, *then* $\|\mathbf{w}_2\|_2$ *is smaller than* $\min\left\{q^2, \sqrt{\frac{\ell}{8\pi e}} q^{\frac{2\ell}{\ell+1}}\right\}$.

Proof. Let $\max\{|e_0|, |-2e_1 + e_2|, \ldots, |-2e_{\ell-1} + e_\ell|\} \le K$. Then we know that $\|\mathbf{w}_2\|_2 \le \alpha^{\frac{\ell}{2}}\lambda_2 \le \alpha^{\frac{\ell}{2}}\mathbf{v}$. Using again the fact that $\alpha \le \sqrt{2}$ implies $\alpha^{\frac{\ell}{2}} \le (2q)^{\frac{1}{4}}$ and with Eq. (20), we conclude

$$\|\mathbf{w}_2\|_2 \le (2q)^{\frac{1}{4}}\sqrt{\ell+1}\, qK.$$

Replacing K by the claimed upper bounds concludes the proposition.   □

The upper bound for K in Proposition 4 is $O(q^{\frac{3}{4}})$ and as usually $K = O(\sqrt{q})$, we can expect the condition to hold in practice. In comparison, using Lemma 1, we conclude that such a short vector will only be found at random with low probability. Thereby, we can even expect $\mathbf{w}_2 = \pm\mathbf{v}$.

5.4 Conclusion

Our cautious lattice analysis gives rise to multiple conclusions:

1. In case of a random tuple as well as in the case of a synthetically constructed one, the first LLL reduced vector will with overwhelming probability be a multiple of $(0, \ldots, 0, q)$.

2. In case of a random tuple, the second LLL reduced vector can be expected to be lower bounded by $\min\left\{q^2, \sqrt{\frac{\ell}{8\pi e}} q^{\frac{2\ell}{\ell+1}}\right\}$.

3. In case of a synthetic tuple, the second LLL reduced vector is with a high probability smaller than $\min\left\{q^2, \sqrt{\frac{\ell}{8\pi e}} q^{\frac{2\ell}{\ell+1}}\right\}$. Furthermore, we can expect it to be equal to $\pm\mathbf{v}$ where $\mathbf{v} = (e_0 q, (-2e_1 + e_2)q, \ldots, (-2e_{\ell-1} + e_\ell)q, s)$ is our target vector.

---

[4] This conclusion also holds in the case of a random tuple.

Hence, we finally conclude that we can distinguish with noticeable probability between a randomly sampled tuple and a synthetically constructed one by simply comparing the length of the second LLL reduced vector with $\min\left\{q, \sqrt{\frac{\ell}{8\pi e}}q^{\frac{2\ell}{\ell+1}}\right\}$. Furthermore, in case of a synthetically constructed tuple, the last entry of this vector should reveal the secret value s or its negative $-s$. Especially if the initial errors are comparably small with respect to q (e.g., $O(\sqrt{q})$), there is a high chance of revealing the secret. The corresponding SAGE-MATH source codes for our second distinguisher (distinguisher2) can be found in the full version of our article.

Optional Bootstrapping. As in the first attack, we never assumed to know the precise error distribution. Similar to the first attack, after retrieving the secret s, one can extract the original error values $e_0, \ldots, e_\ell$ and use a suitable bootstrapping method to simulate the whole error distribution.

6   Generalizing Our Attacks

Our two lattice attacks against the iNTRU assumption have been conceived for the integer case ($\mathcal{R} = \mathbb{Z}$) only. However, it is not difficult to generalize them.

6.1   iNTRU - The General Case

In, order to generalize our attacks to polynomial rings, one may simply replace the x_i's by the corresponding polynomial values and carry on with the constructions. The corresponding lattices will then contain the corresponding polynomial coefficients. The arising difficulty is that in the presence of degree d polynomials, the lattice dimension will increase by a factor of d as well. This blow-up heavily impacts the detectable error limits in Proposition 2 and Proposition 4 up to the point where only Bernoulli errors would be detectable (i.e. $-1, 0, 1$). To be precise, degree d polynomials would only lead to the theoretical bound $\|\mathbf{w}_1\|_2 \leq q^{\frac{d}{4}}K$ for the first LLL reduced vector in Eq. (12) which, for large d, is not short enough to grant the required upper bound $\|\mathbf{w}_1\|_2 \leq q$. Likewise, for our second distinguisher, the theoretical bound $\|\mathbf{w}_2\|_2 \leq q^2$ will not be fulfilled for large d. As in general LLL performs better in practice than in theory, slightly larger degrees might be achievable, but only the use of stronger reduction algorithms such as BKZ (see [14]) will lead to well-functioning distinguishers.

6.2   MiNTRU

Our attacks can also be generalized to the second assumption introduced in [6], the so called matrix inhomogeneous NTRU (MiNTRU) assumption. The MiNTRU assumption essentially replaces polynomial elements in the iNTRU assumption by integer modular matrices. To be precise, let q be any modulus, $\ell = \lceil \log(q) \rceil$, $m = n(\ell + 1)$, $\mathbf{G} = [0|\mathbf{I}|2\mathbf{I}|...|2^{\ell-1}\mathbf{I}] \in \mathbb{Z}^{n \times m}$ an extended gadget matrix, and χ

a symmetric error distribution over $\mathbb{Z}$ producing with overwhelming probability elements with norm $\ll q$. Then, the MiNTRU distribution with these parameters is obtained by the following sampling process

$$\text{MiNTRU} = \begin{cases} \mathbf{S} \leftarrow \left(\mathbb{Z}_q^{n \times n}\right)_{invertible} \\ \mathbf{E} \leftarrow \chi^{n \times m} \\ \mathbf{A} := \mathbf{S}^{-1} \times (\mathbf{G} - \mathbf{E}) \mod q \end{cases}$$

and the MiNTRU decision problem requires to distinguish this distribution from the random distribution over $\mathbb{Z}_q^{n \times m}$. By decomposing the matrix $\mathbf{A}$ into $(\ell + 1)$ individual $n \times n$ matrices $\mathbf{A}_0, \dots \mathbf{A}_\ell$ such that $\mathbf{A} = [\mathbf{A}_0 | \dots | \mathbf{A}_\ell]$, then setting $\mathbf{Y}_0 := \mathbf{A}_0 \mod q$ and $\mathbf{Y}_i = 2\mathbf{A}_i - \mathbf{A}_{i+1} \mod q$ $\forall i \in \{1, \dots, \ell - 1\}$ and finally computing $\mathbf{Z}_i := \mathbf{Y}_t^{-1} \mathbf{Y}_i \mod q$ $\forall i \in \{0, \dots, \ell - 1\}$ for some invertible matrix $\mathbf{Y}_t$, removes completely the dependence of the gadget matrix $\mathbf{G}$ and ends up in matrices with entries of quotients of small norm error elements only. Thereby, the same strategy as in the iNTRU attack may be mounted against the underlying decision problem. However, once again, the success chance of our attack is strongly affected by the matrix dimensions. Concretely, the generalized attacks will only work for low dimensional matrices or matrices with low entropic noise. A more detailed analysis may be found in the full version of our article.

7   Conclusion

Our simple lattice based distinguishers break with noticeable probability the integer case of the iNTRU assumption. Additionally, their construction yields a theoretical thread for the general iNTRU and the MiNTRU assumption. Nonetheless, this threat is not reflected in practice as the distinguishers don't cope with large dimensions of polynomial rings (iNTRU) or with large matrix dimensions (MiNTRU) as used in recent cryptographic constructions. This work should mainly raise awareness that new hardness hypotheses should be used with caution and questions whether the two studied assumptions can compete with the long-standing Learning-with-Errors (LWE) assumption [16] which does not suffer from the described vulnerability. We emphasize that, if possible, well-known hardness assumptions should be used.

Acknowledgement. Jim Barthel was supported in part by the Luxembourg National Research Fund through grant PRIDE15/10621687/SPsquared. Răzvan Roşie was supported in part by ERC grant CLOUDMAP 787390.

A   Proof of Lemma 1

We observe that by the properties of the Euclidean and the infinity norm, we have

$$\mathbb{P}\left(\left(\left\|[\mathbf{ry} \mod q^2]\right\|_2 \leq Bq\right) \cap (r \in S)\right) \leq \mathbb{P}\left(\left(\max\left\{\left|[\mathbf{ry} \mod q^2]\right|\right\} \leq Bq\right) \cap (r \in S)\right)$$

where the maximum is taken over all the modulo reduced entries of ry. The right expression is equal to

$$\mathbb{P}\left(\left(\bigcap_{i=0}^{\ell-1}\underbrace{(|[ry_iq \mod q^2]| \le Bq)}_{:=C_i}\right) \cap \underbrace{(|[r \mod q^2]| \le Bq)}_{:=C_\ell} \cap (r \in S)\right).$$

Each event $C_0, \ldots, C_{\ell-1}$ in the probability statement can be written as a union of events $C_i = \bigcup_{\beta_i=-Bq}^{Bq}([ry_iq \mod q^2] = \beta_i)$. As this event can only take place whenever β_i is a multiple of q (otherwise, the equality cannot be satisfied), we need only to consider the restricted union of events $\bigcup_{\beta_i=-B}^{B}([ry_iq \mod q^2] = \beta_iq) = \bigcup_{\beta_i=-B}^{B}([ry_i \mod q] = \beta_i)$. Furthermore, $C_\ell = \bigcup_{\beta_\ell=-Bq}^{Bq}([r \mod q^2] = \beta_\ell) = \bigcup_{\beta_\ell=-Bq}^{Bq}(r = \beta_\ell)$ which is restricted to $\beta_\ell \in S$ by the last condition. Thus, our overall probability is equal to

$$\mathbb{P}\left(\left(\bigcap_{i=0}^{\ell-1}\bigcup_{\beta_i=-B}^{B}([ry_i \mod q] = \beta_i)\right) \cap \left(\bigcup_{\substack{\beta_\ell=-Bq \\ \beta_\ell \in S}}^{Bq}(r = \beta_\ell)\right)\right).$$

Reordering the events gives

$$\mathbb{P}\left(\bigcup_{\beta_0=-B}^{B}\cdots\bigcup_{\beta_{\ell-1}=-B}^{B}\bigcup_{\substack{\beta_\ell=-Bq \\ \beta_\ell \in S}}^{Bq}\left(\bigcap_{i=0}^{\ell-1}([ry_i \mod q] = \beta_i) \cap (r = \beta_\ell)\right)\right).$$

As the events are mutually exclusive, this probability is equal to

$$\sum_{\beta_0=-B}^{B}\cdots\sum_{\beta_{\ell-1}=-B}^{B}\sum_{\substack{\beta_\ell=-Bq \\ \beta_\ell \in S}}^{Bq}\mathbb{P}\left(\bigcap_{i=0}^{\ell-1}([ry_i \mod q] = \beta_i) \cap (r = \beta_\ell)\right).$$

Using Bayes' conditional probability rule followed by Euler's rule of interchanging finite sums, this quantity can be rewritten as:

$$\sum_{\beta_0=-B}^{B}\cdots\sum_{\beta_{\ell-1}=-B}^{B}\sum_{\substack{\beta_\ell=-Bq \\ \beta_\ell \in S}}^{Bq}\mathbb{P}(r = \beta_\ell)\,\mathbb{P}\left(\bigcap_{i=0}^{\ell-1}([ry_i \mod q] = \beta_i)\,\middle|\,(r = \beta_\ell)\right)$$

$$= \sum_{\substack{\beta_\ell=-Bq \\ \beta_\ell \in S}}^{Bq}\mathbb{P}(r = \beta_\ell)\sum_{\beta_0=-B}^{B}\cdots\sum_{\beta_{\ell-1}=-B}^{B}\mathbb{P}\left(\bigcap_{i=0}^{\ell-1}([ry_i \mod q] = \beta_i)\,\middle|\,(r = \beta_\ell)\right)$$

Naturally $\mathbb{P}(r = \beta_\ell) = \frac{1}{q^2}$ for any β_ℓ. It remains to investigate the value of the rightmost probability. To do so, we rewrite $\beta_\ell = g_\ell\beta_\ell'$ where $g_\ell = \gcd(\beta_\ell, q)$. Then, for fixed $\beta_0, \ldots, \beta_{\ell-1}, \beta_\ell$:

$$\mathbb{P}\left(\bigcap_{i=0}^{\ell-1}([ry_i \mod q] = \beta_i) \mid (r = \beta_\ell)\right)$$

$$=\mathbb{P}\left(\bigcap_{i=0}^{\ell-1}([\beta_\ell y_i \mod q] = \beta_i)\right)$$

$$=\mathbb{P}\left(\bigcap_{i=0}^{\ell-1}([g_\ell \beta'_\ell y_i \mod q] = \beta_i)\right)$$

The events in this probability will only be satisfiable if β_i is a multiple of g_ℓ, say $\beta_i = \beta'_i g_\ell$. Thus, our cumulative probability rewrites as

$$\sum_{\substack{\beta_\ell=-Bq \\ \beta_\ell \in S}}^{Bq} \frac{1}{q^2} \sum_{\beta'_0=-\lfloor B/g_\ell \rfloor}^{\lfloor B/g_\ell \rfloor} \cdots \sum_{\beta'_{\ell-1}=-\lfloor B/g_\ell \rfloor}^{\lfloor B/g_\ell \rfloor} \mathbb{P}\left(\bigcap_{i=0}^{\ell-1}([g_\ell \beta'_\ell y_i \mod q] = \beta'_i g_\ell)\right)$$

$$=\sum_{\substack{\beta_\ell=-Bq \\ \beta_\ell \in S}}^{Bq} \frac{1}{q^2} \sum_{\beta'_0=-\lfloor B/g_\ell \rfloor}^{\lfloor B/g_\ell \rfloor} \cdots \sum_{\beta'_{\ell-1}=-\lfloor B/g_\ell \rfloor}^{\lfloor B/g_\ell \rfloor} \mathbb{P}\left(\bigcap_{i=0}^{\ell-1}([\beta'_\ell y_i \mod \tfrac{q}{g_\ell}] = \beta'_i)\right)$$

$$=\sum_{\substack{\beta_\ell=-Bq \\ \beta_\ell \in S}}^{Bq} \frac{1}{q^2} \sum_{\beta'_0=-\lfloor B/g_\ell \rfloor}^{\lfloor B/g_\ell \rfloor} \cdots \sum_{\beta'_{\ell-1}=-\lfloor B/g_\ell \rfloor}^{\lfloor B/g_\ell \rfloor} \mathbb{P}\left(\bigcap_{i=0}^{\ell-1}([y_i \mod \tfrac{q}{g_\ell}] = [\beta'_i \beta'^{-1}_\ell \mod \tfrac{q}{g_\ell}])\right)$$

where we used the fact that $g_\ell = \gcd(\beta_\ell, q)$ which implies that β'_ℓ is invertible modulo $\frac{q}{g_\ell}$. It is now clear that the remaining events are independent as they only depend on y_i. Thus

$$\mathbb{P}\left(\bigcap_{i=0}^{\ell-1}([y_i \mod \tfrac{q}{g_\ell}] = [\beta'_i \beta'^{-1}_\ell \mod \tfrac{q}{g_\ell}])\right)$$

$$=\prod_{i=0}^{\ell-1} \mathbb{P}\left([y_i \mod \tfrac{q}{g_\ell}] = [\beta'_i \beta'^{-1}_\ell \mod \tfrac{q}{g_\ell}]\right)$$

$$=\left(\frac{1}{\frac{q}{g_\ell}}\right)^\ell$$

$$=\left(\frac{g_\ell}{q}\right)^\ell.$$

Thereby, the cumulative probability is given by

$$\sum_{\substack{\beta_\ell=-Bq \\ \beta_\ell \in S}}^{Bq} \frac{\ell(2\lfloor B/g_\ell \rfloor + 1)}{q^2} \left(\frac{g_\ell}{q}\right)^\ell.$$

$\square$

References

1. Ajtai, M.: Generating hard instances of lattice problems (extended abstract). In: Proceedings of the Twenty-Eighth Annual ACM Symposium on Theory of Computing (STOC 1996), pp. 99–108, New York, NY, USA. Association for Computing Machinery (1996)
2. Ajtai, M.: Generating random lattices according to the invariant distribution, March 2006
3. Albrecht, M.R., Fitzpatrick, R., Göpfert, F.: On the Efficacy of Solving LWE by Reduction to Unique-SVP. In: Lee, H.-S., Han, D.-G. (eds.) ICISC 2013. LNCS, vol. 8565, pp. 293–310. Springer, Cham (2014). https://doi.org/10.1007/978-3-319-12160-4_18
4. Diffie, W., Hellman, M.E.: New directions in cryptography. IEEE Trans. Inf. Theory **22**(6), 644–654 (1976)
5. Gama, N., Nguyen, P.Q.: Predicting Lattice Reduction. In: Smart, N. (ed.) EUROCRYPT 2008. LNCS, vol. 4965, pp. 31–51. Springer, Heidelberg (2008). https://doi.org/10.1007/978-3-540-78967-3_3
6. Genise, N., Gentry, C., Halevi, S., Li, B., Micciancio, D.: Homomorphic encryption for finite automata. In: Galbraith, S.D., Moriai, S. (eds.) ASIACRYPT 2019. LNCS, vol. 11922, pp. 473–502. Springer, Cham (2019). https://doi.org/10.1007/978-3-030-34621-8_17
7. Genise, N., Li, B.: Gadget-based iNTRU lattice trapdoors. In: Bhargavan, K., Oswald, E., Prabhakaran, M. (eds.) INDOCRYPT 2020. LNCS, vol. 12578, pp. 601–623. Springer, Cham (2020). https://doi.org/10.1007/978-3-030-65277-7_27
8. Gentry, C., Peikert, C., Vaikuntanathan,V.: Trapdoors for hard lattices and new cryptographic constructions. In: Proceedings of the Fortieth Annual ACM Symposium on Theory of Computing (STOC 2008), pp. 197–206, New York, NY, USA. Association for Computing Machinery (2008)
9. Hoffstein, J., Pipher, J., Silverman, J.H.: NTRU: a ring-based public key cryptosystem. In: Buhler, J.P. (ed.) ANTS 1998. LNCS, vol. 1423, pp. 267–288. Springer, Heidelberg (1998). https://doi.org/10.1007/BFb0054868
10. Kirchner, P., Fouque, P.-A.: Revisiting lattice attacks on overstretched NTRU parameters. In: Coron, J.-S., Nielsen, J.B. (eds.) EUROCRYPT 2017. LNCS, vol. 10210, pp. 3–26. Springer, Cham (2017). https://doi.org/10.1007/978-3-319-56620-7_1
11. Langlois, A., Stehlé, D.: Worst-case to average-case reductions for module lattices. Des. Codes Cryptogr. **75**(3), 565–599 (2014). https://doi.org/10.1007/s10623-014-9938-4
12. Lee, C., Wallet, A.: Lattice analysis on mintru problem. Cryptology ePrint Archive, Report 2020/230 (2020). https://ia.cr/2020/230
13. Lenstra, A.K., Lenstra, H., Lovász, L.: Factoring polynomials with rational coefficients. Math. Ann. **261**, 515–534 (1982)
14. Li, J., Nguyen, P.Q.: A complete analysis of the BKZ lattice reduction algorithm. Cryptology ePrint Archive, Report 2020/1237 (2020). https://ia.cr/2020/1237
15. Peikert, C., Rosen, A.: Efficient collision-resistant hashing from worst-case assumptions on cyclic lattices. In: Halevi, S., Rabin, T. (eds.) TCC 2006. LNCS, vol. 3876, pp. 145–166. Springer, Heidelberg (2006). https://doi.org/10.1007/11681878_8

16. Regev, O.: On lattices, learning with errors, random linear codes, and cryptography. In: Proceedings of the Thirty-Seventh Annual ACM Symposium on Theory of Computing (STOC 2005), pp. 84–93, New York, NY, USA. Association for Computing Machinery (2005)
17. Wen, W.: Contributions to the hardness foundations of lattice-based cryptography. Ph.D. thesis. Université de Lyon, Computational Complexity, HAL archives-ouvertes.fr (2018)

Functional Encryption

Verifiable Functional Encryption Using Intel SGX

Tatsuya Suzuki[1]($\boxtimes$), Keita Emura[2], Toshihiro Ohigashi[2,3],
and Kazumasa Omote[1,2]

[1] University of Tsukuba, Tsukuba, Japan
s2030117@s.tsukuba.ac.jp
[2] National Institute of Information and Communications Technology, Koganei, Japan
[3] Tokai University, Tokyo, Japan

Abstract. Most functional encryption schemes implicitly assume that
inputs to decryption algorithms, i.e., secret keys and ciphertexts, are generated honestly. However, they may be tampered by malicious adversaries. Thus, verifiable functional encryption (VFE) was proposed by
Badrinarayanan et al. in ASIACRYPT 2016 where anyone can publicly check the validity of secret keys and ciphertexts. They employed
indistinguishability-based (IND-based) security due to an impossibility
result of simulation-based (SIM-based) VFE even though SIM-based security is more desirable. In this paper, we propose a SIM-based VFE scheme.
To bypass the impossibility result, we introduce a trusted setup assumption. Although it appears to be a strong assumption, we demonstrate that
it is reasonable in a hardware-based construction, e.g., Fisch et al. in ACM
CCS 2017. Our construction is based on a verifiable public-key encryption
scheme (Nieto et al. in SCN 2012), a signature scheme, and a secure hardware scheme, which we refer to as VFE-HW. Finally, we discuss an implementation of VFE-HW using Intel Software Guard Extensions (Intel SGX).

Keywords: Functional encryption · Intel SGX · Verifiability ·
Simulation security

1 Introduction

Functional Encryption: Cloud computing has gained increasing attention since
it supports several functionalities, e.g., data analysis. However, sensitive user data
must be secured, and protected. Thus, since Public-Key Encryption (PKE) only
provides all-or-nothing decryption capabilities, functional encryption [14] has been
proposed. Functional encryption allows clients to flexibly access sensitive data
toward usual "all or nothing" decryption procedure. Briefly, a Trusted Authority
(TA) first generates a master public key mpk and a master secret key msk. A client
sends the information of function P to the TA. Generally, P can enforce sophisticated functions, e.g., access control etc. The TA generates a secret key sk_P using
the msk, and gives it to the client. A plaintext msg is encrypted by the mpk, where
CT is the ciphertext. Finally, the client obtains P(msg) by decrypting CT using sk_P.

© Springer Nature Switzerland AG 2021
Q. Huang and Y. Yu (Eds.): ProvSec 2021, LNCS 13059, pp. 215–240, 2021.
https://doi.org/10.1007/978-3-030-90402-9_12

The security of functional encryption is defined by indistinguishability-based (IND-based) or simulation-based (SIM-based) notions. IND-based security guarantees that no adversary can distinguish which plaintext was encrypted. IND-based functional encryption schemes have been proposed for the class of all (polynomial-sized) functionalities under inefficient assumptions, e.g., multi-linear maps, or indistinguishability obfuscation [15,26,27,38]. Consequently, Abdalla et al. [2] proposed an IND-based functional encryption scheme that supports inner products under simple assumptions, and several works followed this direction [3,4,19,22,23,37]. However, Boneh et al. [14] and O'Neil [34] demonstrated that IND-based functional encryption yields insufficient security. For example, an adversary is allowed to obtain secret keys for a function P selected by the adversary with the restriction $P(msg_0^*) = P(msg_1^*)$ where msg_0^* and msg_1^* are challenge plaintexts with the condition $msg_0^* \neq msg_1^*$. Thus, the class of P remains restricted, e.g., we cannot specify a cryptographic hash function as P due to collision resistance. Thus, SIM-based security is more desirable. Several SIM-based functional encryption schemes [6–8,14,18,34] have been proposed recently. However, several works [6,7,14,18] have shown that achieving SIM-based functional encryption that supports all (polynomial-sized) functionalities is impossible.

Functional Encryption Using Intel SGX: To overcome this impossibility result, Fisch et al. [24] proposed IRON, a SIM-based functional encryption scheme that uses Intel SGX [9,30–32]. Intel SGX is a hardware protection set that protects sensitive data (e.g. medical data) from malicious adversaries by storing them in enclaves generated as isolated spaces in an application. They employed a secure hardware scheme (HW) which modeled Intel SGX.

Briefly, IRON is described as follows. The TA generates a public key pk and a decryption key dk for a PKE scheme, as well as a verification key vk and a signing key sk for a signature scheme (SIG). Then, the TA generates a secret key sk_P, where P is a function for the client. The TA generates a signature of P as a secret key sk_P using sk in a Key Manager Enclave (KME), and sends it to the client. Let CT be the ciphertext of a plaintext msg under pk. In the decryption procedure, if sk_P is a valid signature using vk, CT is decrypted inside an enclave, and $P(msg)$ is output.

Verifiable Functional Encryption: Most functional encryption schemes implicitly assume that inputs to decryption algorithm, i.e., sk_P and CT, are generated honestly according to the algorithmic procedures. However, they may be tampered by malicious adversaries. Badrinarayanan et al. [10] proposed Verifiable Functional Encryption (VFE). With VFE, anyone can publicly check the validity of sk_P and CT. If verification of sk_P and CT passes, the decryption algorithm of VFE correctly outputs $P(msg)$. Badrinarayanan et al. insisted that VFE are useful for some applications, e.g., storing encrypted images [14] and audits [29]. As a drawback, they demonstrated that SIM-based VFE implies the existence of one message zero-knowledge proof systems for **NP** in the plain model. This implication contradicts the impossibility result shown by Goldreich et al. [28]. We emphasize that IRON does not help us to bypass this impossibility

Table 1. Comparison of Verifiable Functional Encryption

	Security	Functionality	Verifiability	Secure HW	Trusted setup
Fisch et al. [24] (Functional Encryption)	SIM-based	Any	Not considered	Yes	Yes[a]
Badrinarayanan et al. [10]	IND-based	Limited	Normal	No	No
Soroush et al. [36]	IND-based	Limited	Normal	No	No
Our VFE scheme	SIM-based	Any	Weak	Yes	Yes

[a]The HW.Setup algorithm in the pre-processing phase is required to be honestly run by the TA.

result. As a result, they employed IND-based security as shown in Table 1. A VFE proposed by Soroush et al. [36], which supports inner products, employs the same IND-based security definition. Thus, no SIM-based VFE has been proposed so far.

Our Contribution: We propose a SIM-based VFE scheme that supports any (polynomial-sized) functionality. To support such functionality, we employ the hardware-based construction given in IRON [24], and, to achieve SIM-based security, we relax the verifiability of the definition given by Badrinarayanan et al. without losing the practicability. Intuitively, we assume that mpk and msk are generated honestly whereas those can be arbitrary values in the definition given by Badrinarayanan et al. Due to this trusted setup assumption, mpk can be considered a common reference string (CRS) in the one message zero-knowledge context [13]. One may think that this trusted setup assumption is unreasonable and too strong in practice. However, this is not the case in the hardware-based construction. We will explain it in detail in Sect. 4.

In addition to provide a security definition that bypasses the impossibility result, we also give a SIM-based VFE construction. The original IRON has supported public verifiability of secret keys (because these are signatures), thus we focus on how to support public verifiability for ciphertexts. Therefore, we employ (publicly) Verifiable PKE (VPKE) [33] proposed by Nieto et al. in addition to the ingredients of IRON (PKE, SIG, and HW). We employ HW as in IRON, thus we refer to proposed system as VFE-HW. Note that publicly executable computations should be run outside of memory-constrained enclaves as much as possible. Simultaneously, as in IRON, ciphertexts input to enclaves require to be non-malleable, and thus the underlying (V)PKE scheme needs to be CCA-secure. Consequently, we modify the definition of VPKE (Sect. 2).

Finally, we give our implementation of the proposed VFE-HW scheme for a cryptographic hash function H as the function P, i.e., the decryption algorithm for a ciphertext of msg outputs H(msg). Due to the nonlinearity of the hash function, the functionality seems hard to be supported by functional encryption with linear computations, e.g., inner products. Moreover, the IND-based VFE scheme does not support the function due to the key generation query restriction. In addition to these theoretical perspectives, it seems meaningful to support this functionality in practice, e.g., a password PW is encrypted and H(PW) can be computed without revealing PW. Here, we employ the Pairing-Based Cryptography (PBC) library [1] to implement the VPKE scheme proposed by Nieto et al. Briefly, the encryption algorithm runs in 0.11845 s, the verification algorithm for ciphertexts runs in 0.12329 s, the verification algorithm for secret keys runs in 0.00057 s, and the decryption algorithm runs in 0.06164 s.

2   Preliminaries

Here, we define PKE, VPKE, SIG, and HW. When x is selected uniformly from set S, we denote this as $x \xleftarrow{\$} S$, and $y \leftarrow A(x)$ represents that y is the output of an algorithm A with an input x.

First, we define PKE as follows. Here, let $\mathcal{M}_{\mathsf{pke}}$ be a plaintext space of PKE. The setup algorithm PKE.KeyGen(1^λ) generates ($\mathsf{pk}_{\mathsf{pke}}, \mathsf{dk}_{\mathsf{pke}}$), the encryption algorithm PKE.Enc($\mathsf{pk}_{\mathsf{pke}}$, msg) outputs CT, and the decryption algorithm PKE.Dec($\mathsf{dk}_{\mathsf{pke}}$, CT) outputs msg or $\perp$. We require that the PKE provides the indistinguishability against chosen ciphertext attack (IND-CCA) security.

Next, we define SIG as follows. Here, let $\mathcal{M}_{\mathsf{sig}}$ be a message space. The key generation algorithm SIG.KeyGen(1^λ) generates ($\mathsf{sk}_{\mathsf{sign}}, \mathsf{vk}_{\mathsf{sign}}$), the signing algorithm SIG.Sign($\mathsf{sk}_{\mathsf{sign}}$, msg) outputs σ, the verification algorithm SIG.Verify($\mathsf{vk}_{\mathsf{sign}}$, msg, σ) outputs 0 or 1. We require that the SIG provides the existential unforgeability against chosen message attack (EUF-CMA) security.

Next, we introduce VPKE as defined by Nieto et al. [33]. VPKE provides public verifiability, where anyone can check the validity of ciphertexts without using any secret value. They defined the decryption algorithm VPKE.Dec using two algorithms, i.e., the verification algorithm VPKE.Ver and the decryption algorithm for converted ciphertext VPKE.Dec'. VPKE.Ver verifies ciphertext CT and converts CT to CT' if CT is valid. VPKE.Dec' decrypts CT', and outputs msg. In this paper, we further decompose VPKE.Ver into two algorithms, i.e., VPKE.Ver and VPKE.Conv, which will be explained later. The verification algorithm VPKE.Ver verifies CT and the conversion algorithm VPKE.Conv converts CT into CT'.

Next, we define VPKE. Here, let $\mathcal{M}_{\mathsf{vpke}}$ be a plaintext space of VPKE.

Definition 1 (Syntax of VPKE).

VPKE.PGen(1^λ): *This public parameter generation algorithm takes the security parameter $\lambda \in \mathbb{N}$ as input, and returns a public parameter* pars.

VPKE.KeyGen(pars): *This key generation algorithm takes* pars *as input, and returns a public key* $\mathsf{pk}_{\mathsf{vpke}}$ *and a secret key* $\mathsf{dk}_{\mathsf{vpke}}$.

VPKE.Enc(pars, $\mathsf{pk}_{\mathsf{vpke},msg}$): *This encryption algorithm takes* pars, $\mathsf{pk}_{\mathsf{vpke}}$ *and a plaintext* msg $\in \mathcal{M}_{\mathsf{vpke}}$ *as input, and returns a ciphertext* CT.

VPKE.Dec(pars, $\mathsf{pk}_{\mathsf{vpke}}, \mathsf{dk}_{\mathsf{vpke}}$, CT): *This decryption algorithm takes* pars, $\mathsf{pk}_{\mathsf{vpke}}$, $\mathsf{dk}_{\mathsf{vpke}}$ *and CT as input, and returns a plaintext* msg *or reject symbol $\perp$. Internally the algorithm runs* VPKE.Ver, VPKE.Conv, *and* VPKE.Dec', *which are defined as follows.*

VPKE.Ver(pars, $\mathsf{pk}_{\mathsf{vpke}}$, CT): *This verification algorithm takes* pars, $\mathsf{pk}_{\mathsf{vpke}}$ *and CT as input, and returns 1 or 0.*

VPKE.Conv(pars, $\mathsf{pk}_\mathsf{vpke}$, CT): *This conversion algorithm takes* pars, $\mathsf{pk}_\mathsf{vpke}$ *and* CT *as input, and returns a ciphertext* CT′.

VPKE.Dec′(pars, $\mathsf{pk}_\mathsf{vpke}$, $\mathsf{dk}_\mathsf{vpke}$, CT′): *This decryption algorithm takes* pars, $\mathsf{pk}_\mathsf{vpke}$, $\mathsf{dk}_\mathsf{vpke}$ *and* CT′ *as input, and returns a plaintext* msg.

Correctness is defined as follows: For all pars $\leftarrow$VPKE.PGen(1^λ), all ($\mathsf{pk}_\mathsf{vpke}$, $\mathsf{dk}_\mathsf{vpke}$) $\leftarrow$ VPKE.KeyGen(pars), all msg $\in \mathcal{M}_\mathsf{vpke}$, VPKE.Dec′(pars, $\mathsf{pk}_\mathsf{vpke}$, $\mathsf{dk}_\mathsf{vpke}$ and VPKE.Conv(pars, $\mathsf{pk}_\mathsf{vpke}$, CT)) = msg holds, where CT $\leftarrow$ VPKE. Enc(pars, $\mathsf{pk}_\mathsf{vpke}$, msg) and VPKE.Ver(pars, $\mathsf{pk}_\mathsf{vpke}$, CT) = 1.

Next, we define strictly non-trivial public verification. Condition 1 requires that the decryption of a ciphertext CT succeeds if and only if its verification outputs 1, and Condition 2 excludes CCA-secure schemes where the decryption algorithm does not output ⊥.

Definition 2 (Strictly Non-Trivial Public Verification). *For any PPT adversary* $\mathcal{A}$ *and the security parameter* $\lambda \in \mathbb{N}$, *let* pars $\leftarrow$ VPKE.PGen(1^λ). *We define the* VPKE.Ver *algorithm is strictly non-trivial public verifiable if (1)* ($\mathsf{pk}_\mathsf{vpke}$, $\mathsf{dk}_\mathsf{vpke}$) $\leftarrow$ VPKE.KeyGen(pars), *and* VPKE.Ver(pars, $\mathsf{pk}_\mathsf{vpke}$, CT) = 0 $\Longleftrightarrow$ VPKE.Dec(pars, $\mathsf{pk}_\mathsf{vpke}$, $\mathsf{dk}_\mathsf{vpke}$, CT) = ⊥ *for all* CT, *and (2) there exists a ciphertext* CT *for which* VPKE.Dec(pars, $\mathsf{pk}_\mathsf{vpke}$, $\mathsf{dk}_\mathsf{vpke}$, CT) = ⊥ *are provided.*

Next, we define IND-CCA [33] as follows.

Definition 3 (IND-CCA). *For any PPT adversary* $\mathcal{A}$ *and the security parameter* $\lambda \in \mathbb{N}$, *we define the experiment* $\mathrm{Exp}_{\mathsf{VPKE},\mathcal{A}}^{\mathrm{IND\text{-}CCA}}(\lambda)$ *as follows. Here,* state *is state information that an adversary* $\mathcal{A}$ *can preserve any information, and* state *is used for transferring state information to the other stage.*

$\mathrm{Exp}_{\mathsf{VPKE},\mathcal{A}}^{\mathrm{IND\text{-}CCA}}(\lambda)$:

    pars $\leftarrow$ VPKE.PGen(1^λ); ($\mathsf{pk}_\mathsf{vpke}$, $\mathsf{dk}_\mathsf{vpke}$) $\leftarrow$ VPKE.KeyGen(pars)

    (msg_0^*, msg_1^*, state) $\leftarrow \mathcal{A}^{\mathsf{VPKE.DEC}}$(find, pars, $\mathsf{pk}_\mathsf{vpke}$)

    msg_0^*, $\mathsf{msg}_1^* \in \mathcal{M}_\mathsf{vpke}$; $|\mathsf{msg}_0^*| = |\mathsf{msg}_1^*|$

    $\mu \xleftarrow{\$} \{0,1\}$; CT* $\leftarrow$ VPKE.Enc(pars, $\mathsf{pk}_\mathsf{vpke}$, msg_μ^*)

    $\mu' \leftarrow \mathcal{A}^{\mathsf{VPKE.DEC}}$(guess, CT*, state)

    If $\mu = \mu'$ then output 1, and 0 otherwise

- VPKE.DEC: *This decryption oracle takes a ciphertext* CT $\neq$ CT* *as input. If* VPKE.Ver(pars, $\mathsf{pk}_\mathsf{vpke}$, CT) = 0, *output* ⊥. *Otherwise, compute* CT′ $\leftarrow$ VPKE.Conv(pars, $\mathsf{pk}_\mathsf{vpke}$, CT), *and return* msg *by running the* VPKE.Dec′(pars, $\mathsf{pk}_\mathsf{vpke}$, $\mathsf{dk}_\mathsf{vpke}$, CT′) *algorithm.*

We say that VPKE is *IND-CCA secure if the advantage* $\mathrm{Adv}_{\mathsf{VPKE},\mathcal{A}}^{\mathrm{IND\text{-}CCA}}(\lambda) :=$ $| \Pr[\mathrm{Exp}_{\mathsf{VPKE},\mathcal{A}}^{\mathrm{IND\text{-}CCA}}(\lambda) = 1] - 1/2 |$ *is negligible for any PPT adversary* $\mathcal{A}$.

For the sake of clarity, we give the Nieto et al. VPKE scheme employed in our implementation in the Appendix A.

Next, we define the secure hardware scheme (HW scheme) [24]. In this paper, the hardware instance HW denotes an oracle that provides the functionalities given in Definition 4. Furthermore, the hardware oracle HW(·) denotes an interaction with other local secure hardware in addition to HW, and the Key Manager oracle KM(·) denotes an interaction with a remote secure hardware over an untrusted channel.

Definition 4 (Syntax of HW Scheme). *A HW scheme for a set of probabilistic programs $\mathcal{Q}$ comprises the following seven algorithms. HW has variables* HW.sk$_{report}$, HW.sk$_{quote}$, *and a table* T. *Here,* HW.sk$_{report}$ *and* HW.sk$_{quote}$ *are leveraged to store keys, and the table* T *is leveraged to manage the internal state of loaded enclave programs.*

- HW.Setup(1^λ): *This hardware setup algorithm takes the security parameter $\lambda \in \mathbb{N}$ as input, and returns a public parameters* params. *This algorithm also generates the secret keys* sk$_{report}$ *and* sk$_{quote}$, *and stores these keys in the* HW.sk$_{report}$ *and* HW.sk$_{quote}$ *valuables respectively.*
- HW.Load(params, Q): *This loading program algorithm takes* params *and a program $Q \in \mathcal{Q}$ as input, and returns a handle* hdl. *Intuitively, this algorithm loads the stateful program into the enclave to be launched. Here,* hdl *is leveraged to identify the enclave running* Q.
- HW.Run(hdl, in): *This running program algorithm takes* hdl *and a symbol* in *as input, and returns* out *corresponding to an enclave running a designated program* Q. *Intuitively, this algorithm runs* Q *at state* T[hdl] *with* in, *and records* out.
- HW.Run&Report$_{sk_{report}}$(hdl, in): *This running program and generating report algorithm, which can be verified by an enclave program on the same hardware platform for a local attestation, takes* hdl *and* in *as input, and returns a report* report := (md$_{hdl}$, tag$_Q$, in, out, mac), *where* md$_{hdl}$ *is a metadata relative enclave,* tag$_Q$ *is a program tag that identifies the program running inside an enclave, and* mac *is a message authentication code produced using* sk$_{report}$ *for* (md$_{hdl}$, tag$_Q$, in, out).
- HW.Run&Quote$_{sk_{quote}}$(hdl, in): *This running program and generating quote algorithm, which can be publicly verified different hardware platform for a remote attestation, takes* hdl *and* in *as input, and returns a quote* quote := (md$_{hdl}$, tag$_Q$, in, out, σ), *where* md$_{hdl}$ *is a metadata relative enclave,* tag$_Q$ *is a program tag that identifies the program running inside an enclave, and σ is a signature produced using* sk$_{quote}$ *for* (md$_{hdl}$, tag$_{Q, in, out}$).
- HW.ReportVerify$_{sk_{report}}$(hdl, report): *This report verification algorithm takes* hdl *and* report *as input, and uses* sk$_{report}$ *to verify* mac. *If* mac *is valid, then the algorithm outputs* 1 *and adds a tuple* (1, report) *to* T[hdl]. *Otherwise, the algorithm outputs* 0 *and adds tuple* (0, report) *to* T[hdl].
- HW.QuoteVerify(params, quote): *This quote verification algorithm, takes* params *and* quote *as input. This algorithm verifies σ. If the verification of σ succeeds, then the algorithm outputs* 1. *Otherwise,* 0 *is output.*

Correctness is defined as follows: HW is correct if the following things hold. For all $Q \in \mathcal{Q}$, in in the input domain of Q and all handles hdl

- Correctness of Run: out = Q(in) if Q is deterministic. More generally, ∃ random coins r (sampled in time and used by Q) such that out = Q(in).
- Correctness of Report and ReportVerify: $\Pr[\text{HW.Report-Verify}_{\text{sk}_{\text{report}}}(\text{hdl},$ report) = 0] = negl(λ)
- Correctness of Quote and QuoteVerify: $\Pr[\text{HW.Quote-Verify}(\text{params}, \text{quote}) = 0] = \text{negl}(\lambda)$.

Next, we define local attestation unforgeability (LOC-ATT-UNF) of HW as follows. This security guarantees that no adversary that does not have $\text{sk}_{\text{report}}$ can produce a valid report.

Definition 5 (LOC-ATT-UNF). *For any PPT adversary $\mathcal{A}$ and the security parameter $\lambda \in \mathbb{N}$, we define the experiment $\text{Exp}_{\text{HW},\mathcal{A}}^{\text{LOC-ATT-UNF}}(\lambda)$ as follows.*

$\text{Exp}_{\text{HW},\mathcal{A}}^{\text{LOC-ATT-UNF}}(\lambda)$:

   $(\text{params}, \text{sk}_{\text{report}}, \text{sk}_{\text{quote}}, \text{state}) \leftarrow \text{HW.Setup}(1^{\lambda})$

   $\text{QUERY} := \emptyset$; $(\text{hdl}^*, \text{report}^*) \leftarrow \mathcal{A}^{\text{HW},\text{HW}(\cdot)}(\text{params})$

   If $\text{HW.ReportVerify}_{\text{sk}_{\text{report}}}(\text{hdl}^*, \text{report}^*) = 1$ *where*

   $\text{report}^* = (\text{md}_{\text{hdl}}^*, \text{tag}_Q^*, \text{in}^*, \text{out}^*, \text{mac}^*)$ *and*

   $(\text{md}_{\text{hdl}}^*, \text{tag}_Q^*, \text{in}^*, \text{out}^*) \notin \text{QUERY}$

   then output 1, and 0 otherwise

- HW: *$\mathcal{A}$ can access the instance as follows.*
  - HW.LOAD: *$\mathcal{A}$ queries the instance as input* params *and* Q, *and the instance returns the handle* hdl *by running the* HW.Load(params, Q) *algorithm.*
  - HW.REPORTVERIFY: *$\mathcal{A}$ queries the instance as input* hdl *and* report, *and the instance returns the result by running the* $\text{HW.ReportVerify}_{\text{sk}_{\text{report}}}(\text{hdl},$ report) *algorithm.*

- HW(·): *$\mathcal{A}$ can access the oracle as follows.*
  - HW.RUN&REPORT : *$\mathcal{A}$ queries the oracle as input* hdl *and* in, *and the oracle returns* report := $(\text{md}_{\text{hdl}}, \text{tag}_Q, \text{in}, \text{out}, \text{mac})$ *by running the* $\text{HW.Run\&Report}_{\text{sk}_{\text{report}}}$ (hdl, in) *algorithm. Finally, the oracle stores* $(\text{md}_{\text{hdl}}, \text{tag}_Q, \text{in}, \text{out})$ *in* QUERY.

We say that HW *is LOC-ATT-UNF secure if the advantage*

$$\text{Adv}_{\text{HW},\mathcal{A}}^{\text{LOC-ATT-UNF}}(\lambda) := \Pr[\text{Exp}_{\text{HW},\mathcal{A}}^{\text{LOC-ATT-UNF}}(\lambda) = 1]$$

is negligible for any PPT adversary $\mathcal{A}$.

Next, we define remote attestation unforgeability (REM-ATT-UNF) of HW as follows. This security guarantees that no adversary that does not have sk_{quote} can produce a valid quote.

Definition 6 (REM-ATT-UNF). *For any PPT adcersary $\mathcal{A}$ and the security parameter $\lambda \in \mathbb{N}$, we define the experiment $\mathrm{Exp}_{\mathsf{HW},\mathcal{A}}^{\mathrm{REM\text{-}ATT\text{-}UNF}}(\lambda)$ as follows.*

$$\mathrm{Exp}_{\mathsf{HW},\mathcal{A}}^{\mathrm{REM\text{-}ATT\text{-}UNF}}(\lambda):$$

    $(\mathsf{params}, \mathsf{sk_{report}}, \mathsf{sk_{quote}}, \mathsf{state}) \leftarrow \mathsf{HW.Setup}(1^\lambda)$

    $\mathsf{QUERY} := \emptyset$; $\mathsf{quote}^* \leftarrow \mathcal{A}^{\mathsf{HW}, \mathsf{KM}(\cdot)}(\mathsf{params})$

    If $\mathsf{HW.QuoteVerify}(\mathsf{params}, \mathsf{quote}) = 1$ *where*

    $\mathsf{quote}^* = (\mathsf{md}_{\mathsf{hdl}}^*, \mathsf{tag}_\mathsf{Q}^*, \mathsf{in}^*, \mathsf{out}^*, \sigma)$ *and*

    $(\mathsf{md}_{\mathsf{hdl}}^*, \mathsf{tag}_\mathsf{Q}^*, \mathsf{in}^*, \mathsf{out}^*) \notin \mathsf{QUERY}$

    then output 1, *and* 0 *otherwise*

- HW: *$\mathcal{A}$ can access the instance as follows.*
  - HW.LOAD: *$\mathcal{A}$ queries the instance as input* params *and* Q, *and the instance returns the handle* hdl *by running the* $\mathsf{HW.Load}(\mathsf{params}, \mathsf{Q})$ *algorithm.*

- KM($\cdot$): *$\mathcal{A}$ can access the oracle as follows.*
  - HW.RUN&QUOTE: *$\mathcal{A}$ queries the oracle as input* hdl *and* in, *and the oracle returns* $\mathsf{quote} := (\mathsf{md}_{\mathsf{hdl}}, \mathsf{tag}_\mathsf{Q}, \mathsf{in}, \mathsf{out}, \sigma)$ *by running the* $\mathsf{HW.Run\&Quote}_{\mathsf{sk_{quote}}}(\mathsf{hdl}, \mathsf{in})$ *algorithm. Finally, the oracle stores* $(\mathsf{md}_{\mathsf{hdl}}, \mathsf{tag}_\mathsf{Q}, \mathsf{in}, \mathsf{out})$ *in* QUERY.

We say that HW *is REM-ATT-UNF secure if the advantage*

$$\mathrm{Adv}_{\mathsf{HW},\mathcal{A}}^{\mathrm{REM\text{-}ATT\text{-}UNF}}(\lambda) := \Pr[\mathrm{Exp}_{\mathsf{HW},\mathcal{A}}^{\mathrm{REM\text{-}ATT\text{-}UNF}}(\lambda) = 1]$$

is negligible for any PPT adversary $\mathcal{A}$.

3   Impossibility Result of VFE

In this section, we recall the impossibility result of VFE shown by Badrinarayanan et al. [10]. We remark that this impossibility is caused by the verifiability of VFE. Thus, they have mentioned that even if the impossibility of SIM-based security given by Agrawal et al. [6] is bypassed, still the impossibility of VFE remains.

Since their VFE syntax is differ from our VFE-HW, first we introduce their syntax as follows. The setup algorithm $\mathsf{VFE.Setup}(1^\lambda)$ generates (mpk, msk), the key-generation algorithm $\mathsf{VFE.KeyGen}(\mathsf{mpk}, \mathsf{msk}, \mathsf{P})$ outputs $\mathsf{sk_P}$, the encryption algorithm $\mathsf{VFE.Enc}(\mathsf{mpk}, \mathsf{msg})$ outputs CT, and the decryption algorithm $\mathsf{VFE.Dec}(\mathsf{mpk}, \mathsf{P}, \mathsf{sk_P}, \mathsf{CT})$ outputs $\mathsf{P}(\mathsf{msg})$ or $\bot$. In addition to these algorithms, VFE supports two verification algorithms. The ciphertext verification algorithm $\mathsf{VFE.VerifyCT}(\mathsf{mpk}, \mathsf{CT})$ outputs 0 or 1, and the secret key verification algorithm $\mathsf{VFE.VerifyK}(\mathsf{mpk}, \mathsf{P}, \mathsf{sk_P})$ outputs 0 or 1.

Next, we introduce verifiability defined by them as follows. The verifiability guarantees that if ciphertexts and secret keys are verified by the respective algorithms then each ciphertext should be associated with a unique message msg, and the decryption result is P(msg). We remark that it holds even under possibly maliciously generated mpk. Let $\mathcal{P}_{\mathsf{VFE}}$ and $\mathcal{M}_{\mathsf{VFE}}$ be a family of function for VFE and a plaintext space of VFE respectively.

Definition 7 (Verifiability). *For all security parameter* $\lambda \in \mathbb{N}$, mpk $\in \{0,1\}^*$, *and all* CT $\in \{0,1\}^*$, *there exists* msg $\in \mathcal{M}_{\mathsf{VFE}}$ *such that for all* P $\in \mathcal{P}_{\mathsf{VFE}}$ *and* $\mathsf{sk_P} \in \{0,1\}^*$, *if* VFE.VerifyCT(mpk, CT) $= 1$ *and* VFE.VerifyK(mpk, P, $\mathsf{sk_P}$) $= 1$, *then* $\Pr[\mathsf{VFE.Dec}(\mathsf{mpk}, \mathsf{P}, \mathsf{sk_P}, \mathsf{CT}) = \mathsf{P(msg)}] = 1$ *holds.*

We further remark that the probability that the VFE.Dec algorithm outputs P(msg) is exactly 1 if CT and $\mathsf{sk_P}$ are valid. Thus, Badrinarayanan et al. assumed that perfect correctness holds (otherwise, a non-uniform malicious authority can sample ciphertexts/keys from the space where it fails to be correct). We note that the probability is exactly 1 yields perfect soundness for all adversaries when a proof system is constructed from VFE.

Next, we describe the impossibility result as follows.

Theorem 1 ([10], **Theorem 3**). *There exists a family of functions, each of which can be represented as a polynomial sized circuit, for which there does not exist any simulation secure verifiable functional encryption scheme.*

To prove the theorem, Badrinarayanan et al. showed that SIM-based VFE implies the existence of one message zero-knowledge proof system for **NP** in the plain model which is known to be impossible. More concretely, let L be a **NP** complete language and R be the relation of L which takes as input a string x and a polynomial sized (in the length of x) witness ω. R(x, ω) outputs 1 if and only if $x \in L$ and ω is its witness. We denote R(x, $\cdot$) for all $x \in \{0,1\}^\lambda$. A one message zero-knowledge proof system $(\mathcal{P}, \mathcal{V})$ for the language L with relation R is constructed from VFE as follows. For (x, ω), the prover $\mathcal{P}$ runs (mpk, msk) $\leftarrow$ VFE.Setup(1^λ) where $\lambda = |x|$, computes CT $\leftarrow$ VFE.Enc(mpk, ω) and $\mathsf{sk}_{\mathsf{R}(x,\cdot)} \leftarrow$ VFE.KeyGen(mpk, msk, R(x, $\cdot$)), and outputs a proof $\pi = $ (mpk, CT, $\mathsf{sk}_{\mathsf{R}(x,\cdot)}$). The verifier $\mathcal{V}$ accepts π if VFE.Dec(mpk, R(x, $\cdot$), $\mathsf{sk}_{\mathsf{R}(x,\cdot)}$, CT) $= 1$. Obviously, the proof system is perfectly complete if the underlying VFE scheme is perfectly correct. Moreover, due to the verifiability property, the system is perfectly sound. Furthermore, since the verifiability holds even for maliciously generated mpk, CT, and sk, no trusted setup is assumed. Due to the SIM-based security, i.e., the existence of the simulator that can produce a ciphertext only from R(x, ω) without knowing ω (here, $1 = $ R(x, ω) in this case), the system provides computational zero knowledge.

To bypass the impossibility result, we introduce the trusted setup where (mpk, msk) is generated honestly, and mpk is considered as a CRS.[1] One may

---

[1] We note that we also relax the condition that the verifiability holds where the probability that the decryption algorithm outputs P(msg) is not exactly 1 (concretely 1-negl(λ)) in our definition. Because the underlying local or remote attestations require non-perfect correctness, this relaxation is reasonable. This relaxation provides the converted proof system to be an argument, i.e., soundness holds only for computationally bounded adversaries.

think that this trusted setup assumption is unreasonable and too strong in practice. However, this is not the case in the hardware-based construction. In our system, mpk and msk are generated by running a setup program, and it is implicitly assumed that the setup program is executed correctly (Q in our scheme). That is, anyone can verify the description of the function. Moreover, we assume that the program is hardcoded as the static data, and is assumed to be not tampered. The remaining is to trust the computer that correctly runs the program, and is widely assumed when cryptographic protocols are implemented. Thus, we claim that the trusted assumption is reasonable, and leave how to remove the assumption without losing the SIM-based security as a future work of this paper.

We remark that even if one message zero-knowledge proof system in the CRS model can be constructed from SIM-based VFE, this does not bypass the impossibility result since the proof system in the plain model implies a proof system in the CRS model. We emphasize that the setup algorithm that generates (mpk, msk) must be run first since other algorithms take mpk or msk as input. Due to this situation, we can bypass the impossibility result of Badrinarayanan et al. since any VFE-based one message zero -knowledge proof system or argument need to run the Setup algorithm first, and then mpk can be seen as a CRS. As mentioned by Barak and Pass [11], one message zero-knowledge proofs and arguments can be constructed in the CRS model (without certain relaxations).

Regarding the CRS model, Badrinarayanan et al. have mentioned that VFE seems to be constructed from a functional encryption scheme with Non-Interactive Zero-Knowledge (NIZK) proof systems. However, the CRS may be maliciously generated and then soundness does not hold. Thus, they gave up for employing NIZK proof systems and employed non-interactive witness indistinguishable proof (NIWI) systems as the ingredients. Since we introduce the trusted setup assumption, we may be able to construct VFE from this direction without employing a HW scheme. However, even then, another impossibility arises [6]. For bypassing the impossibility, we employ a HW scheme.

Random oracles may be employed to avoid introducing the trusted setup assumption. However, as mentioned by Agrawal, Koppula, and Waters [7], there is an impossibility result of SIM-based security in the random oracle model. Thus, we do not further consider the random oracle model in this paper.

4   Definitions of VFE-HW

In this section, we define VFE-HW. Here, let HW be a hardware instance that takes a handle hdl that identifies an enclave. If an algorithm is allowed to access HW, then the algorithm can use the secure hardware functionality given in Definition 4. Let $HW(\cdot)$ (resp. $KM(\cdot)$) be a hardware (resp. a key manager) oracle that takes hdl and an authentication information (Report (resp. Quote) in our construction), interacts with other local enclave specified by hdl, and runs the function contained in the authentication information. Let $\mathcal{P}_{\text{VFE-HW}}$ and $\mathcal{M}_{\text{VFE-HW}}$ be a family of functions for VFE-HW and a plaintext space of VFE-HW respectively.

Definition 8 (Syntax of VFE-HW). *A VFE-HW scheme comprises the following seven algorithms:*

VFE-HW.Setup^{HW}(1^λ): *This setup algorithm takes the security parameter* $\lambda \in \mathbb{N}$ *as input, and returns a master public key* mpk *and a master secret key* msk.

VFE-HW.KeyGen^{HW}(msk, P): *This key generation algorithm takes* msk *and a function* P $\in \mathcal{P}_{\mathsf{VFE-HW}}$ *as input, and returns a secret key* sk$_{\mathsf{P}}$ *for* P.

VFE-HW.Enc(mpk, msg): *This encryption algorithm takes* mpk *and a plaintext* msg $\in$ $\mathcal{M}_{\mathsf{VFE-HW}}$ *as input, and returns a ciphertext* CT.

VFE $-$ HW.DecSetup$^{\mathsf{HW},\mathsf{KM}(\cdot)}$(mpk): *This decryption node setup algorithm takes* mpk *as input, and returns a handle* hdl.

VFE-HW.VerifyCT(mpk, CT): *This ciphertext verification algorithm takes* mpk *and* CT *as input, and returns 1 or 0.*

VFE-HW.VerifyK(mpk, P, sk$_{\mathsf{P}}$): *This secret key verification algorithm takes* mpk, P, *and* sk$_{\mathsf{P}}$ *as input, and returns 1 or 0.*

VFE-HW.Dec$^{\mathsf{HW}(\cdot)}$(mpk, hdl, P, sk$_{\mathsf{P}}$, CT): *This decryption algorithm takes* mpk, hdl, P, sk$_{\mathsf{P}}$, *and* CT *as input, and returns a value* P(msg) *or a reject symbol* $\perp$.

Correctness is defined as follows: For all P $\in \mathcal{P}_{\mathsf{VFE-HW}}$, all (mpk, msk) $\leftarrow$ VFE-HW. Setup^{HW}(1^λ), all sk$_{\mathsf{P}} \leftarrow$ VFE-HW.KeyGen^{HW}(msk, P), all hdl $\leftarrow$ VFE-HW.Dec-Setup$^{\mathsf{HW},\mathsf{KM}(\cdot)}$(mpk), and all msg $\in \mathcal{M}_{\mathsf{VFE-HW}}$, let CT $\leftarrow$ VFE-HW.Enc(mpk, msg), then Pr[VFE-HW.Dec$^{\mathsf{HW}(\cdot)}$(mpk, hdl, sk$_{\mathsf{P}}$, CT) = P(msg)] = $1 - \mathsf{negl}(\lambda)$ holds.

Next we define weak verifiability. We somewhat relax the original verifiability definition, i.e., we employ the trusted setup and the probability of verifiability is not exactly 1 due to the correctness of HW scheme. Thus, we call our definition weak verifiability. Weak verifiability guarantees that if ciphertexts and secret keys are verified by the respective algorithms, then each ciphertext should be associated with a unique message msg, and the decryption result is P(msg). Note that this holds only when mpk is generated honestly and hdl is non-$\perp$.

Definition 9 (Weak Verifiability). *For all security parameters* $\lambda \in \mathbb{N}$, (mpk, msk) $\leftarrow$ VFE-HW.Setup^{HW}(1^λ), *and* hdl $\leftarrow$ VFE-HW.DecSetup$^{\mathsf{HW},\mathsf{KM}(\cdot)}$ (mpk) *where* hdl $\neq \perp$, *and all* CT $\in \{0,1\}^*$, *there exists* msg $\in \mathcal{M}_{\mathsf{VFE-HW}}$ *such that for all* P $\in \mathcal{P}_{\mathsf{VFE-HW}}$ *and* sk$_{\mathsf{P}} \in \{0,1\}^*$, *if* VFE-HW.VerifyCT(mpk, CT) = 1 *and* VFE-HW.VerifyK(mpk, P, sk$_{\mathsf{P}}$) = 1, *then* Pr[VFE-HW.Dec$^{\mathsf{HW}(\cdot)}$ (mpk, hdl, P, sk$_{\mathsf{P}}$, CT) = P(msg)] = $1 - \mathsf{negl}(\lambda)$ *holds.*

Next, we define the simulation security of VFE-HW as follows. This security guarantees that no adversary can distinguish REAL and IDEAL, where REAL represents the actual environment. Note that msk and the challenge plaintext msg* are not explicitly used in IDEAL. Although Semi-adaptive SIM-based functional encryption scheme have been proposed [5,40] where an adversary declares the challenge after obtaining mpk but before issuing secret key queries, our definition does not have such a restriction.

Definition 10 (Simulation security). *For a stateful PPT adversary $\mathcal{A}$, a stateful PPT simulator $\mathcal{S}$ and the security parameter $\lambda \in \mathbb{N}$, we define the real experiment $\mathrm{Exp}_{\mathsf{VFE\text{-}HW}}^{\mathrm{REAL}}(\lambda)$ and the ideal experiment $\mathrm{Exp}_{\mathsf{VFE\text{-}HW}}^{\mathrm{IDEAL}}(\lambda)$ as follows. Here, let $\mathsf{U}_{\mathsf{msg}}(\cdot)$ denote a universal oracle where $\mathsf{U}_{\mathsf{msg}}(\mathsf{P}) = \mathsf{P}(\mathsf{msg})$.*

$\mathrm{Exp}_{\mathsf{VFE\text{-}HW}}^{\mathrm{REAL}}(\lambda)$:

    $(\mathsf{mpk}, \mathsf{msk}) \leftarrow \mathsf{VFE\text{-}HW.Setup}^{\mathsf{HW}}(1^\lambda)$; $\mathsf{msg}^* \leftarrow \mathcal{A}^{\mathsf{VFE\text{-}HW.KeyGen}^{\mathsf{HW}}(\mathsf{msk},\cdot)}(\mathsf{mpk})$

    $\mathsf{CT}^* \leftarrow \mathsf{VFE\text{-}HW.Enc}(\mathsf{mpk}, \mathsf{msg}^*)$; $\alpha \leftarrow \mathcal{A}^{\mathsf{VFE\text{-}HW.KeyGen}^{\mathsf{HW}}(\mathsf{msk},\cdot),\mathsf{HW}(\cdot),\mathsf{KM}(\cdot)}(\mathsf{mpk}, \mathsf{CT}^*)$

    Output (msg^*, α)

– HW: $\mathcal{A}$ *can access the instance as follows.*
    – HW.LOAD: $\mathcal{A}$ *queries the instance as input* params *and* Q, *and the instance returns* hdl *by running the* HW.Load(params, Q) *algorithm.*
    – HW.RUN: $\mathcal{A}$ *queries the instance as input* hdl *and* in, *and the instance returns* out *by running the* HW.Run(hdl, in) *algorithm.*
– VFE-HW.KeyGen^{HW}: $\mathcal{A}$ *queries this key generation oracle as input* msk *and* P. *The oracle accesses* HW.RUN *as input* hdl = msk *and* in = P, *and the oracle returns* sk$_\mathsf{P}$ *as* out *by running the* HW.Run(hdl, in) *algorithm.*
– HW(·): $\mathcal{A}$ *can access* HW.RUN&REPORT *in addition to* HW *as input* hdl *and* in, *and the oracle returns* report *by running the* HW.Run&Report$_{\mathsf{sk}_{\mathsf{report}}}$(hdl, in) *algorithm.*
– KM(·): $\mathcal{A}$ *can access* HW.RUN&QUOTE *as input* hdl *and* in, *and the oracle returns* quote *by running the* HW.Run&Quote$_{\mathsf{sk}_{\mathsf{quote}}}$(hdl, in) *algorithm.*

        $\mathrm{Exp}_{\mathsf{VFE\text{-}HW}}^{\mathrm{IDEAL}}(\lambda)$:

        $\mathsf{mpk} \leftarrow \mathcal{S}(1^\lambda)$; $\mathsf{msg}^* \leftarrow \mathcal{A}^{\mathcal{S}^{(\cdot)}}(\mathsf{mpk})$

        $\mathsf{CT}^* \leftarrow \mathcal{S}^{\mathsf{U}_{\mathsf{msg}}(\cdot)}(1^\lambda, 1^{|\mathsf{msg}^*|})$; $\alpha \leftarrow \mathcal{A}^{\mathcal{S}^{\mathsf{U}_{\mathsf{msg}}(\cdot)}(\cdot)}(\mathsf{mpk}, \mathsf{CT}^*)$

        Output (msg^*, α)

– $\mathcal{S}(\cdot)$: $\mathcal{S}$ *simulates the* HW, VFE-HW.KeyGen^{HW}, HW(·) *and* KM(·) *oracles.*
– $\mathcal{S}^{\mathsf{U}_{\mathsf{msg}}(\cdot)}(\cdot)$: $\mathcal{S}$ *simulates the* HW, *the* VFE-HW.KeyGen^{HW}, *the* HW(·) *and the* KM(·) *oracles. Here, if $\mathcal{A}$ queries this oracle as input* CT* *and* sk$_\mathsf{P}$, $\mathcal{S}$ *outputs* P(msg) *using the universal oracle* $\mathsf{U}_{\mathsf{msg}}(\cdot)$ *that inputs* P *queried in the* VFE-HW.KeyGen^{HW} *oracle.*

If there exists a stateful simulator $\mathcal{S}$ and $\mathrm{Exp}_{\mathsf{VFE\text{-}HW}}^{\mathrm{REAL}}(\lambda)$ and $\mathrm{Exp}_{\mathsf{VFE\text{-}HW}}^{\mathrm{IDEAL}}(\lambda)$ are computationally indistinguishable, then we say that the VFE-HW *scheme is simulation secure against a stateful PPT adversary.*

Remark: Damgård et al. [21] showed a construction of multi-designated verifier signatures from VFE. As the security of underlying VFE (for achieving verifier-identity-based signing), they also introduced a trusted setup where key generations are assumed to be honestly run, and defined ciphertext verifiability.

Although both their ciphertext verifiability and our weak verifiability capture a malicious encryptor, as a difference, their definition is for VFE and our verifiability definition is for VFE-HW where hdl is also assumed to be honestly generated. Moreover, they considered IND-based security only whereas we consider SIM-based security that spreads the class of functionalities as mentioned before.

5 Proposed Scheme

In this section, we describe the proposed VFE-HW scheme. The proposed scheme is constructed from IND-CCA secure and strictly non-trivial public verifiable VPKE, IND-CCA secure PKE, EUF-CMA secure SIG and REM-ATT-UNF, and LOC-ATT-UNF secure HW.

High-Level Description: Essentially, we follow the construction of IRON. IRON has supported public verifiability of secret keys (since these are signatures), we focus on supporting the public verifiability of ciphertexts. Therefore, we replace a PKE scheme in IRON with a VPKE scheme.

In our VFE-HW scheme, the (function) enclave securely executes computations that require secret values, however, its computational power and memory are constrained. Thus, the verification part should be run outside of the enclave, and we employ the public verifiability of VFE. However, the ciphertext is converted if the original VPKE.Ver algorithm is employed. Thus, the converted ciphertext CT′ is decrypted via VPKE.Dec′ in the enclave. Although at least IND-CPA security is guaranteed if VPKE.Dec is replaced with VPKE.Dec′ [33], the underlying VPKE scheme is required to be CCA-secure. Thus, we decompose VPKE.Ver to VPKE.Ver and VPKE.Conv, and run VPKE.Conv inside of the enclave.

We consider the following assumptions in the construction of the VFE-HW. These assumptions are the same as those of IRON (but the last one is implicitly assumed).

- Pre-Processing: The TA and a client need to complete the pre-processing phase before using VFE-HW scheme. In our construction, we consider that a manufacturer setups and initializes the secure hardware. A public parameter is generated by this phase independent of the VFE-HW algorithms, and this parameter is implicitly given to all algorithms.
- Non-Interaction: In VFE-HW, a plaintext is encrypted using a public key of a VPKE scheme, and thus the decryption of the ciphertext requires the corresponding decryption key, which differs from a secret key sk_P. To obtain the decryption key from the KME, we require a one-time hardware setup operation. The VFE-HW.DecSetup$^{HW, KM(\cdot)}$ algorithm interacts with the KME via the KM$(\cdot)$, and the VFE-HW.Dec$^{HW(\cdot)}$ algorithm is non-interactive.
- Trusted Setup: VFE-HW.Setup^{HW} and VFE-HW.DecSetup$^{HW, KM(\cdot)}$ are executed honestly. In short, mpk, msk and hdl are generated honestly.

The proposed scheme is given as follows. First, we describe the programs Q_{KME} (for the KME), Q_{DE} (for a Decryption Enclave DE) and Q_{FE} (for a Function

Enclave FE). Q_{FE} is parameterized by a function P, and thus we denote $Q_{FE}(P)$. Let T be an internal state valuable, $tag_{Q_{DE}}$ be a measurement of Q_{DE} hardcoded in the static data of Q_{KME}, and $tag_{Q_{FE}}(P)$ be a measurement of $Q_{FE}(P)$.

Q_{KME} :

- On input ("init", 1^λ):
  1. Run pars $\leftarrow$ VPKE.PGen(1^λ).
  2. Run $(pk_{vpke}, dk_{vpke}) \leftarrow$ VPKE.KeyGen(pars) and $(sk_{sign}, vk_{sign}) \leftarrow$ SIG.KeyGen(1^λ).
  3. Update T to $(dk_{vpke}, sk_{sign}, vk_{sign})$ and output $(pars, pk_{vpke}, vk_{sign})$.
- On input ("provision", quote, params):
  1. Parse quote $= (md_{hdlDE}, tag_{Q_{DE}}, in, out, \sigma)$. If $tag_{Q_{DE}}$ is not matched to tag hardcoded as static data, then output $\bot$.
  2. Parse in $=$ ("init setup", vk_{sign}) and check if vk_{sign} matches with one in T.
  3. Parse out $= (sid, pk_{ra})$ and run b $\leftarrow$ HW.QuoteVerify(params, quote). If b $= 0$ output $\bot$.
  4. Retrieve dk_{vpke} from T and compute $ct_{dk} = $ PKE.Enc(pk_{ra}, dk_{vpke}) and $\sigma_{dk} = $ SIG.Sign($sk_{sign}, (sid, ct_{dk})$), and output $(sid, ct_{dk}, \sigma_{dk})$.
- On input ("sign", msg): Compute sig $\leftarrow$ SIG.Sign(sk_{sign}, msg) and output sig.

Q_{DE} :

- On input ("init setup", vk_{sign}):
  1. Run $(pk_{ra}, dk_{ra}) \leftarrow$ PKE.KeyGen(1^λ).
  2. Generate a session ID, sid $\leftarrow \{0,1\}^\lambda$.
  3. Update T to $(sid, dk_{ra}, vk_{sign})$ and output (sid, pk_{ra}).
- On input ("complete setup", $pk_{ra}, sid, ct_{dk,\sigma_{dk}}$):
  1. Look up T to obtain the entry $(sid, dk_{ra}, vk_{sign})$. If no entry exists for sid, output $\bot$.
  2. If SIG.Verify($vk_{sign}, (sid, ct_{dk}), \sigma_{dk}$) $= 0$, output $\bot$. Otherwise, run $dk_{vpke} \leftarrow$ PKE.Dec(dk_{ra}, ct_{dk}).
  3. Add the tuple (dk_{vpke}, vk_{sign}) to T.
- On input ("provision", report, sig):
  1. Check to see that the setup has been completed, i.e. T contains the tuple (dk_{vpke}, vk_{sign}). If not, output $\bot$.
  2. Check to see that the report has been verified, i.e. T contains the tuple $(1, report)$. If not, output $\bot$.
  3. Parse report $= (md_{hdlp}, tag_{Q_{FE}}(P), in, out, mac)$ and parse out $= (sid, pk_{la})$.
  4. If SIG.Verify($vk_{sign}, tag_{Q_{FE}(P)}$, sig) $= 0$, then output $\bot$. Otherwise, output $(sid, ct_{key} = $ PKE.Enc(pk_{la}, dk_{vpke})).

$Q_{FE}(P)$:

- On input ("init", sig):
  1. Run $(pk_{la}, dk_{la}) \leftarrow$ PKE.KeyGen(1^λ).
  2. Generate a session ID, sid $\leftarrow \{0,1\}^\lambda$.
  3. Update T to (sid, dk_{la}) and output (sid, pk_{la}).
- On input ("run", pars, params, mpk, $pk_{la}, report_{dk}$, CT):
  1. Parse mpk $= (pk_{vpke}, vk_{sign})$.
  2. Check to see that the report has been verified, i.e. T contains the tuple $(1, report_{dk})$. If not, output $\bot$.
  3. Parse $report_{dk} = (md_{hdlDE}, tag_{Q_{DE}}, in, out, mac)$. Parse out $= (sid, ct_{key})$.
  4. Look up T to obtain the entry (sid, dk_{la}, sk_P). If no entry exists for sid, output $\bot$.

5. Compute $dk_{vpke} \leftarrow PKE.Dec(dk_{l_a}, ct_{key})$.
6. Compute $CT' \leftarrow VPKE.Conv(pars, pk_{vpke}, CT)$.
7. Compute $msg \leftarrow VPKE.Dec'(pars, pk_{vpke}, dk_{vpke}, CT')$.
8. Evaluate P on msg using sk_P and record the output $out := P(msg)$. Output out.

Next, we describe the proposed scheme as follows. Here, without loss of generality, prior to running VFE-HW.Dec, we assume that a ciphertext CT is verified by VFE-HW.VerifyCT, and a secret key sk_P is verified by VFE-HW.VerifyK. Then, CT and sk_P are input to VFE-HW.Dec only when these are valid, and VFE-HW.Dec does not check their validity. This assumption is natural because we consider public verifiability for both CT and sk_P.

Proposed Scheme:

Pre-Processing phase : The trusted authority platform and decryption node run respectively.
    1. Call params $\leftarrow$ HW.Setup(1^λ), and output params.

VFE-HW.Setup^{HW}(1^λ):
    1. Call $hdl_{KME} \leftarrow HW.Load(params, Q_{KME})$.
    2. Call $(pars, pk_{vpke}, vk_{sign}) \leftarrow HW.Run(hdl_{KME}, (\text{"init"}, 1^\lambda))$.
    3. Output $mpk = (pars, pk_{vpke}, vk_{sign})$, $msk = hdl_{KME}$.

VFE-HW.Keygen^{HW}(msk, P):
    1. Parse $msk = hdl_{KME}$.
    2. Compute tag_P by using a function P.
    3. Call $sig \leftarrow HW.Run(hdl_{KME}, (\text{"sign"}, tag_P))$.
    4. Output $sk_P = sig$.

VFE-HW.Enc(mpk, msg):
    1. Parse $mpk = (pars, pk_{vpke}, vk_{sign})$.
    2. Compute $CT \leftarrow VPKE.Enc(pars, pk_{vpke}, msg)$.

VFE-HW.DecSetup$^{HW, KM(\cdot)}$(mpk):
    1. Call $hdl_{DE} \leftarrow HW.Load(params, Q_{DE})$.
    2. Parse $mpk = (pars, pk_{vpke}, vk_{sign})$.
    3. Call $quote \leftarrow HW.Run\&Quote_{sk_{quote}}(hdl_{DE}, (\text{"init setup"}, vk_{sign}))$.
    4. Call KM(quote) which internally run $(sid, ct_{dk}, \sigma_{dk}) \leftarrow HW.Run(hdl_{KME}, (\text{"provision"}, quote, params))$.
    5. Call $HW.Run(hdl_{DE}, (\text{"complete setup"}, pk_{ra}, sid, ct_{dk}, \sigma_{dk}))$.

VFE-HW.VerifyCT(mpk, CT):
    1. Parse $mpk = (pars, pk_{vpke}, vk_{sign})$.
    2. If $VPKE.Ver(pars, pk_{vpke}, CT) = \perp$, then output 0. Otherwise, output 1.

VFE-HW.VerifyK(mpk, P, sk_P):
    1. Parse $mpk = (pars, pk_{vpke}, vk_{sign})$, and $sk_P = sig$.
    2. If $SIG.Verify(vk_{sign}, sk_P, P) = 0$, then output 0. Otherwise, output 1.

VFE-HW.Dec$^{HW(\cdot)}$(mpk, hdl, P, sk_P, CT):
    1. Parse $mpk = (pars, pk_{vpke}, vk_{sign})$, $hdl = hdl_{DE}$, $sk_P = sig$.
    2. Call $hdl_{FE}(P) \leftarrow HW.Load(params, Q_{FE}(P))$.
    3. Call $report \leftarrow HW.Run\&Report_{sk_{report}}(hdl_{FE}(P), (\text{"init"}, sig))$.

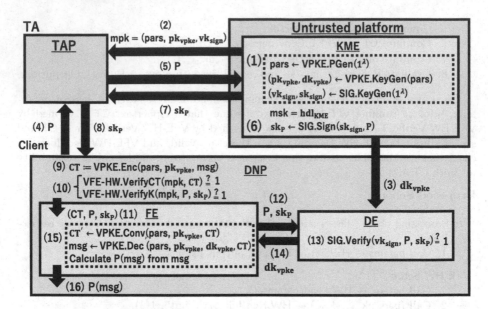

Fig. 1. Protocol flow. Steps (1) and (2) specify VFE-HW.Setup, step (3) specifies VFE-HW.DecSetup, steps (4), (5), (6), (7) and (8) specify VFE-HW.KeyGen, step (9) specifies VFE-HW.Enc, steps (10) and (11) specify VFE-HW.VerifyK and VFE-HW.VerifyCT, and steps (12), (13), (14), (15) and (16) specify VFE-HW.Dec.

4. If $\mathsf{HW.ReportVerify}_{\mathsf{sk}_{\mathsf{report}}}(\mathsf{hdl}_{\mathsf{DE}}, \mathsf{report}) = 0$, then output $\bot$. Otherwise, call $\mathsf{report}_{\mathsf{dk}} \leftarrow \mathsf{HW.Run\&Report}_{\mathsf{sk}_{\mathsf{report}}}(\mathsf{hdl}_{\mathsf{DE}}, (\text{"provision"}, \mathsf{report}, \mathsf{sig}))$.

5. If $\mathsf{HW.ReportVerify}_{\mathsf{sk}_{\mathsf{report}}}(\mathsf{hdl}_{\mathsf{FE}}(\mathsf{P}), \mathsf{report}_{\mathsf{dk}}) = 0$, then output $\bot$. Otherwise, call $\mathsf{out} \leftarrow \mathsf{HW.Run}(\mathsf{hdl}_{\mathsf{P}}, (\text{"run"}, \mathsf{pars}, \mathsf{params}, \mathsf{mpk}, \mathsf{pk}_{\mathsf{la}}, \mathsf{report}_{\mathsf{dk}}, \mathsf{CT}))$, and output out.

Obviously, correctness holds if VPKE, PKE, SIG, and HW are correct.

For clarity, we describe the protocol flow of VFE-HW using Fig. 1, where the gray areas represent the untrusted space of each platform, orange areas represent the trusted space of each platform, and the procedures inside dashed boxes are run within enclaves. For example, the TA manages a Trusted Authority Platform TAP, and setups the KME in the TAP. A client manages a Decryption Node Platform (DNP), and setups a DE in the DNP. The TA generates a public key $\mathsf{pk}_{\mathsf{vpke}}$ and a secret key $\mathsf{dk}_{\mathsf{vpke}}$, as well as a signing key $\mathsf{sk}_{\mathsf{sign}}$ and a verification key $\mathsf{vk}_{\mathsf{sign}}$ as step (1) within KME. Here, mpk generated by the VFE-HW.Setup^{HW} algorithm consists of pars, $\mathsf{pk}_{\mathsf{vpke}}$ and $\mathsf{vk}_{\mathsf{sign}}$ as step (2). Furthermore, msk generated by the VFE-HW.Setup^{HW} algorithm is a handle $\mathsf{hdl}_{\mathsf{KME}}$ used to confirm the KME. Next, the client preserves $\mathsf{dk}_{\mathsf{vpke}}$ into the DE via a remote attestation as step (3). Next, the client gets the secret key sk_{P} of the VFE-HW.KeyGen^{HW} algorithm which KME issues as a signature on a function P via a secure channel as step (4) to (8). Here, let CT be a ciphertext of a plaintext msg under pk using the VFE-HW.Enc algorithm as step (9). If an external encryptor generates CT, it is sent to the client. Note that we omit this procedure in Fig. 1. In the decryption procedure, the client setups a FE parameterized P in the DNP. Then, the client checks the validity of sk_{P} and CT using the VFE-HW.VerifyK and VFE-HW.VerifyCT algorithms respectively as step (10). If sk_P and CT are valid, the client inputs CT, P and sk_P into the FE via hardware invocation as step (11). If the DNP is managed remotely by the client, then a remote attestation is employed in this case. Next, the FE transfers sk_P to the DE via a local attestation as step (12). The validity of sk_P is confirmed by using the SIG.Verify algorithm as step (13). If sk_P is valid, the DE transfers dk_{vpke} to FE via a local attestation as step (14). The FE decrypts CT as step (15) using the aVPKE.Conv and VPKE.Dec' algorithms. Finally, the client obtains P(msg) as step (16).

6 Security Analysis

We provide two proofs to demonstrate that the proposed scheme provides weak verifiability and simulation security.

6.1 Weak Verifiability

In this section, we prove the weak verifiability of VFE-HW. Essencially, we employ the strictly non-trivial public verifiability of VPKE. To do so, we need to guarantee that dk_{vpke} used in the VPKE.Dec algorithm is generated correctly by the VPKE.KeyGen algorithm. We guarantee this using the correctness of HW. Formally, the following theorem holds.

Theorem 2. VFE-HW *is weak verifiable if* VPKE *is strictly non-trivial public verifiable, and* HW *is correct.*

Proof. According to our trusted setup assumption, $VFE-HW.Setup^{HW}$ and $VFE-HW.DecSetup^{HW,KM(\cdot)}$ algorithms were honestly run which means that dk_{vpke} was correctly generated, and sent from the KME to a DE. Moreover, $VFE-HW.VerifyCT(mpk, CT) = 1$ and $VFE-HW.VerifyK(mpk, P, sk_P) = 1$ hold. Now, we need to guarantee that dk_{vpke} is correctly sent from the DE to a FE in the $VFE-HW.Dec^{HW(\cdot)}$ algorithm. This holds with probability $1 - negl(\lambda)$ due to the correctness of HW. Next, by using this dk_{vpke}, $VPKE.Ver(pars, pk_{vpke}, CT) = 1 \Rightarrow VPKE.Dec(pars, pk_{vpke}, dk_{vpke}, CT) \neq \perp$ holds due to the strictly non-trivial public verifiability of VPKE. Thus, decryption result of CT is determined to be unique since the VPKE.Dec algorithm is deterministic algorithm. Let the decryption result denote msg. Then, the VFE-HW.Dec algorithm outputs P(msg) from P and msg.

6.2 Simulation Security

Here, we prove the simulation security of the VFE-HW scheme. We replace the PKE scheme of IRON with a VPKE scheme. In this case, we primarily consider whether the SIM-based security is preserved after the replacement. In other words, an adversary $\mathcal{A}$ can check the validity of ciphertexts and it may use for distinguishing REAL and IDEAL. For example, if the challenge ciphertext is changed as a random number (typically employed to provide key privacy/anonymity in the PKE/IBE context), then the public verifiability helps $\mathcal{A}$ to distinguish REAL and IDEAL, and the proof fails. Fortunately, the security proof of IRON does not employ the step, and hence we can replace the PKE scheme with the VPKE scheme. We describe the security proof as follows.

Theorem 3. VFE-HW *is simulation secure if* VPKE *is IND-CCA secure,* PKE *is IND-CCA secure,* SIG *is EUF-CMA secure, and* HW *is a secure hardware scheme.*

Proof. We construct a simulator $\mathcal{S}$. First, $\mathcal{S}$ needs to simulate the Pre-Processing phase as REAL. $\mathcal{S}$ runs HW.Setup(1^λ) and records (sk_{report}, sk_{quote}). $\mathcal{S}$ measures the designated program Q_{DE}, and stores the program tag $tag_{Q_{DE}}$. Finally, $\mathcal{S}$ creates seven empty lists $\mathcal{L}_K, \mathcal{L}_R, \mathcal{L}_D, \mathcal{L}_{KM}, \mathcal{L}_{DE}, \mathcal{L}_{DE2},$ and $\mathcal{L}_{FE}$.

We use sequences of games $Game_0, \dots, Game_7$ to prove that adversary $\mathcal{A}$ cannot computationally distinguish between REAL and IDEAL as follows.

$Game_0$ $\mathcal{S}$ runs REAL.

$\boxed{Game_1}$ $\mathcal{S}$ runs as $Game_0$ with the following exceptions

- HW.LOAD(params, Q_{DE}): If $\mathcal{A}$ queries this oracle as input params and Q_{DE}, $\mathcal{S}$ responds hdl_{DE} by running the HW.Load(params, Q_{DE}) algorithm, and storing it in $\mathcal{L}_D$.
- HW.LOAD(params, $Q_{FE}(P)$): If $\mathcal{A}$ queries this oracle as input params and $Q_{FE}(P)$, $\mathcal{S}$ responds hdl_P by running the HW.Load(params, $Q_{FE}(P)$) algorithm, and storing it in $\mathcal{L}_K$. If $tag_{Q_{FE}}(P) \notin \mathcal{L}_K$, then $\mathcal{S}$ stores $(0, tag_{Q_{FE}}(P), hdl_{FE}(P))$ in $\mathcal{L}_K$.
- HW.RUN(hdl, in): If $\mathcal{A}$ queries this oracle as input hdl and in, $\mathcal{S}$ responds out by running the HW.Run(hdl, in) algorithm. If vk_{sign}, which is queried by $\mathcal{A}$ as the HW.Run(hdl_{DE}, in = ("init setup", vk_{sign})) algorithm, is not the same as that of mpk, $\mathcal{S}$ removes hdl_{DE} from $\mathcal{L}_D$.
- VFE-HW.KeyGen^{HW}(msk, P): If $\mathcal{A}$ queries to this oracle as input P, $\mathcal{S}$ responds sk_P by running the HW.Run(hdl, in) algorithm as follows. Parse msk = hdl_{KME}. $\mathcal{S}$ computes $tag_{Q_{FE}(P)}$, calls sig $\leftarrow$ HW.Run(hdl_{KME}, ("sign", $tag_{Q_{FE}(P)}$)), and outputs $sk_P := sig$. If $tag_{Q_{FE}(P)}$ already has an entry in $\mathcal{L}_K$, $\mathcal{S}$ creates the first entry 1 (we call "honest-bit" for the first entry in $\mathcal{L}_K$); otherwise, $\mathcal{S}$ adds the tuple $(1, tag_{Q_{FE}(P)}, \{\})$ to $\mathcal{L}_K$.
- VFE-HW.Enc(mpk, msg): If $\mathcal{A}$ queries this encryption algorithm as input msg, $\mathcal{S}$ responds CT by running the VPKE.Enc(pars, pk_{vpke}, msg) algorithm. If msg is a challenge plaintext msg^*, $\mathcal{S}$ responds CT^* by running the algorithm, and stores it in $\mathcal{L}_R$.

$\boxed{Game_2}$ $\mathcal{S}$ runs as $Game_1$ with the following exceptions.

HW.RUN&REPORT(hdl, in): If $\mathcal{A}$ queries this oracle as input hdl = hdl_{DE} and in = ("provision", report, sig), then $\mathcal{S}$ responds $report_{dk}$ by running the HW.Run&Report$_{sk_{report}}$(hdl_{DE}, ("provision", report, sig)) algorithm. If $tag_{Q_{FE}(P)}$ in report is not contained as a component of an honest-bit tuple in $\mathcal{L}_K$, $\mathcal{S}$ outputs $\perp$.

Here, we consider a case where the HW.RUN&REPORT(hdl_{DE}, ("provision", report, sig)) algorithm outputs non $\perp$ even if $tag_{Q_{FE}(P)}$ is not contained as an honest-bit tuple in $\mathcal{L}_K$. If $\mathcal{A}$ can make a query while ensuring this case, we can break the existentially unforgeability for SIG with non-negligible probability. The following Lemma is the same as Lemma C.1 of IRON.

Lemma 1. *If the signature scheme SIG is EUF-CMA secure, then $Game_2$ is indistinguishable from $Game_1$.*

$\boxed{Game_{3.0}}$ $\mathcal{S}$ runs as $Game_2$ with the following exceptions.

1. HW.RUN&QUOTE(hdl, in): If $\mathcal{A}$ queries this oracle as input hdl = hdl_{DE} and in = ("init setup", vk_{sign}), $\mathcal{S}$ responds quote by running the HW.Run&Quote$_{sk_{quote}}$(hdl_{DE}, ("init setup", vk_{sign})) algorithm, and stores out = (sid, pk_{ra}) as a component of quote in $\mathcal{L}_{DE2}$.

2. HW.RUN(hdl, in): If $\mathcal{A}$ queries this oracle as input hdl $=$ hdl$_{KME}$ and in $=$ ("provision", quote, params), $\mathcal{S}$ responds (sid, ct$_{dk}$, σ_{dk}) by running the HW.Run(hdl$_{KME}$, ("provision", quote, params)) algorithm. If (sid, pk$_{ra}$) $\notin \mathcal{L}_{DE2}$, then $\mathcal{S}$ outputs $\perp$.

Here, we consider a case where the HW.RUN(hdl$_{KME}$, ("provision", quote, params)) algorithm outputs non $\perp$ even if (sid, pk$_{ra}$) $\notin \mathcal{L}_{DE2}$. Here, if $\mathcal{A}$ can make a query while ensuring this case, then we can break the remote attestation unforgeability for HW with non-negligible probability. The following Lemma is the same as Lemma C.4 of IRON.

Lemma 2. *If the secure hardware scheme* HW *is REM-ATT-UNF secure, then* Game$_{3.0}$ *is indistinguishable from* Game$_2$.

| Game$_{3.1}$ | $\mathcal{S}$ runs as Game$_{3.0}$ with the following exceptions.

1. HW.RUN&REPORT(hdl, in): If $\mathcal{A}$ queries this oracle as input hdl $=$ hdl$_{FE}$(P) and in $=$ "init", then $\mathcal{S}$ responds report by running the HW.Run&Report$_{sk_{report}}$ (hdl$_{FE}$(P), "init") algorithm, and storing out $=$ (sid, pk$_{la}$) as a component of report in $\mathcal{L}_{FE}$.
2. HW.RUN(hdl, in): If $\mathcal{A}$ queries this oracle as input hdl $=$ hdl$_{DE}$ and in $=$ ("provision", report, sig), $\mathcal{S}$ responds report$_{dk}$ by running the HW.Run(hdl$_{DE}$, ("provision", report, sig)) algorithm. If (sid, pk$_{la}$) $\notin \mathcal{L}_{FE}$, $\mathcal{S}$ outputs $\perp$.

Here, we consider a case where the HW.RUN&REPORT(hdl$_{DE}$, ("provision", report, sig)) algorithm outputs non $\perp$ even if (sid, pk$_{la}$) $\notin \mathcal{L}_{FE}$. If $\mathcal{A}$ can make a query while ensuring this case, we can break the local attestation unforgeability for HW with non-negligible probability. The following Lemma is the same as Lemma C.5 of IRON.

Lemma 3. *If the secure hardware scheme* HW *is LOC-ATT-UNF secure,* Game$_{3.1}$ *is indistinguishable from* Game$_{3.0}$.

| Game$_{4.0}$ | $\mathcal{S}$ runs as Game$_{3.1}$ with the following exceptions.

HW.RUN(hdl, in):
1. If $\mathcal{A}$ queries this oracle as input hdl $=$ hdl$_{KME}$ and in $=$ ("provision", quote, params), $\mathcal{S}$ responds (sid, ct$_{dk}$) by running the HW.Run(hdl$_{KME}$, ("provision", quote, params)) algorithm, and storing it in $\mathcal{L}_{KM}$.
2. If $\mathcal{A}$ queries this oracle as input hdl $=$ hdl$_{DE}$ and in $=$ ("complete setup", sid, ct$_{dk}$, σ_{dk}), $\mathcal{S}$ runs the HW.Run(hdl$_{DE}$, ("complete setup", sid, ct$_{dk}$)) algorithm. If (sid, ct$_{dk}$) $\notin \mathcal{L}_{KM}$, then $\mathcal{S}$ outputs $\perp$.

Here, we consider a case that the HW.RUN(hdl$_{DE}$, ("complete setup", sid, ct$_{dk,\sigma_{dk}}$)) algorithm outputs non $\perp$ even if (sid, ct$_{dk}$) $\notin \mathcal{L}_{KM}$. If $\mathcal{A}$ can make a query while ensuring this case, we can break the existentially unforgeability for SIG with non-negligible probability. The following Lemma is the same as Lemma C.2 of IRON.

Lemma 4. *If the signature scheme* SIG *is EUF-CMA secure,* Game$_{4.0}$ *is indistinguishable from* Game$_{3.1}$.

| Game$_{4.1}$ | $\mathcal{S}$ runs as Game$_{4.0}$ with the following exceptions.

1. HW.RUN&REPORT(hdl, in): If $\mathcal{A}$ queries this oracle as input $\mathsf{hdl} = \mathsf{hdl}_{DE}$ and in $=$ ("provision", report, sig), $\mathcal{S}$ responds report_{dk} by running the HW.Run& $\mathsf{Report}_{sk_{report}}(\mathsf{hdl}_{DE}$, ("provision", report, sig)) algorithm, and storing out $=$ (sid, ct_{key}) as a component of report_{dk} in $\mathcal{L}_{DE}$.

2. HW.RUN(hdl, in): If $\mathcal{A}$ queries this oracle as input $\mathsf{hdl} = \mathsf{hdl}_{FE}(P)$ and in $=$ ("run", $\mathsf{params}, \mathsf{mpk}, \mathsf{pk}_{la}, \mathsf{report}_{dk}, CT)$, $\mathcal{S}$ responds $P(\mathsf{msg})$ by running the HW.Run($\mathsf{hdl}_{FE}(P)$, ("run", $\mathsf{params}, \mathsf{mpk}, \mathsf{pk}_{la}, \mathsf{report}_{dk}, CT$)) algorithm. If $(\mathsf{sid}, \mathsf{ct}_{key})$ $\notin \mathcal{L}_{DE}$, $\mathcal{S}$ outputs $\perp$.

Here, we consider a case where the HW.RUN(hdl_P, ("run", $\mathsf{params}, \mathsf{mpk}, \mathsf{pk}_{la}$, report_{dk}, CT)) algorithm outputs non $\perp$ even if $(\mathsf{sid}, \mathsf{ct}_{key}) \notin \mathcal{L}_{DE}$. If $\mathcal{A}$ can make a query while ensuring this case, we can break the local attestation unforgeability for HW with non-negligible probability. The following Lemma is the same as Lemma C.3 of IRON.

Lemma 5. *If the secure hardware scheme* HW *is LOC-ATT-UNF secure,* $\mathsf{Game}_{4.1}$ *is indistinguishable from* $\mathsf{Game}_{4.0}$.

$\boxed{\mathsf{Game}_5}$ $\mathcal{S}$ runs as $\mathsf{Game}_{4.1}$ with the following exceptions.

HW.RUN(hdl, in): If $\mathcal{A}$ queries this oracle as input $\mathsf{hdl} = \mathsf{hdl}_{FE}(P)$ and in $=$ ("run", $\mathsf{params}, \mathsf{mpk}, \mathsf{pk}_{la}, \mathsf{report}_{dk}, CT$), $\mathcal{S}$ evaluates CT as follows.

- If $CT \notin \mathcal{L}_R$, $\mathcal{S}$ retrieves dk_{vpke} from ct_{key}, and computes $\mathsf{msg} \leftarrow$ VPKE. Dec($\mathsf{pars}, \mathsf{pk}_{vpke}, \mathsf{dk}_{vpke}, CT$). Finally, $\mathcal{S}$ evaluates P on msg, and outputs out $:= P(\mathsf{msg})$
- If $CT \in \mathcal{L}_R$, $\mathcal{S}$ uses the $U^*_{\mathsf{msg}}(P)$ oracle, and responds with $P(\mathsf{msg}^*)$.

$\boxed{\mathsf{Game}_6}$ $\mathcal{S}$ runs as Game_5 with the following exceptions.

KM(quote): If $\mathcal{A}$ queries this oracle as input quote $=$ ($\mathsf{md}_{\mathsf{hdl}_{DE}}$, $\mathsf{tag}_{Q_{DE}}$, in $=$ ("run", vk_{sign}), out $=$ (sid, pk_{ra}), σ), $\mathcal{S}$ runs the HW.Run(hdl_{KME}, ("provision", quote, params)) algorithm, which internally runs $\mathsf{ct}_{dk} \leftarrow$ PKE.Enc($\mathsf{pk}_{ra}, 0^{|\mathsf{dk}_{vpke}|}$), and outputs $(\mathsf{sid}, \mathsf{ct}_{dk,\sigma_{dk}})$.

The following Lemma is the same as Lemma C.6 of IRON.

Lemma 6. *If the public key encryption scheme* PKE *is IND-CCA secure,* Game_6 *is indistinguishable from* Game_5.

$\boxed{\mathsf{Game}_7}$ $\mathcal{S}$ runs as Game_6 with the following exceptions.

VFE-HW.Enc($\mathsf{mpk}, 0^{|\mathsf{msg}^*|}$): If $\mathcal{A}$ queries this algorithm as input msg, $\mathcal{S}$ responds CT by running VPKE.Enc($\mathsf{pars}, \mathsf{pk}_{vpke}, 0^{|\mathsf{msg}|}$). If msg is a challenge plaintext msg^*, $\mathcal{S}$ responds CT^* by running the algorithm, and storing it in $\mathcal{L}_R$.

Here, no step replaces a valid ciphertext with an invalid ciphertext, e.g., a random number; therefore, the public verifiability does not affect the security proof.

Lemma 7. *If the verifiable public key encryption scheme* VPKE *is IND-CCA secure,* Game_7 *is indistinguishable from* Game_6.

Proof. Let $\mathcal{A}$ be an adversary who distinguishes between $Game_6$ and $Game_7$, and let$\mathcal{C}$ be the challenger of IND-CCA security. We construct an algorithm $\mathcal{B}$ that breaks IND-CCA as follows. First, $\mathcal{C}$ runs pars $\leftarrow$ VPKE.PGen(1^λ), then $(pk_{vpke}, dk_{vpke}) \leftarrow$ VPKE.KeyGen(pars), and gives pars and pk_{vpke} to $\mathcal{B}$. $\mathcal{B}$ runs $(sk_{sign}, vk_{sign}) \leftarrow$ SIG.KeyGen(1^λ) and params $\leftarrow$ HW.Setup(1^λ), and gives params and mpk $= (pars, pk_{vpke}, vk_{sign})$ to $\mathcal{A}$.

For key generation query P, $\mathcal{B}$ derives $tag_{Q_{FE}(P)}$ from P, and calls sig $\leftarrow$ HW.Run(hdl_{KME}, ("sign", $tag_{Q_{FE}(P)}$)). Then, $\mathcal{B}$ sends $sk_P := sig$ to $\mathcal{A}$, and stores $tag_{Q_{FE}(P)}$ in $\mathcal{L}_K$.

For run query ($hdl_{FE}(P)$, ("run", params, mpk, pk_{la}, $report_{dk}$, CT)) where $report_{dk}$ is valid and $hdl_{FE}(P) \in \mathcal{L}_K$ with honest-bit, $\mathcal{B}$ forwards CT to $\mathcal{C}$ as a decryption query. $\mathcal{C}$ returns msg by running the VPKE.Dec(pars, pk_{vpke}, dk_{vpke}, CT) algorithm to $\mathcal{B}$. If msg $= \perp$, $\mathcal{B}$ outputs $\perp$; otherwise, $\mathcal{B}$ runs P on msg, and sends P(msg) to $\mathcal{A}$.

In the challenge phase, $\mathcal{A}$ sends (msg^*, $0^{|msg^*|}$) to $\mathcal{B}$. $\mathcal{B}$ sets $msg^* = M_0^*$ and $0^{|msg^*|} = M_1^*$, and sends (M_0^*, M_1^*) to $\mathcal{C}$. $\mathcal{C}$ computes challenge ciphertext $CT^* =$ VPKE.Enc(pars, pk_{vpke}, M_μ^*) where $\mu \in \{0, 1\}$, and sends CT^* to $\mathcal{B}$. $\mathcal{B}$ sends CT^* to $\mathcal{A}$, and stores CT^* in $\mathcal{L}_R$.

For key generation query P, $\mathcal{B}$ derives $tag_{Q_{FE}(P)}$ from P, and calls sig $\leftarrow$ HW.Run(hdl_{KME}, ("sign", $tag_{Q_{FE}(P)}$)). $\mathcal{B}$ sends $sk_P := sig$ to $\mathcal{A}$, and stores $tag_{Q_{FE}(P)}$ in $\mathcal{L}_K$.

For run query ($hdl_{FE}(P)$, ("run", params, mpk, pk_{la}, $report_{dk}$, CT)) where $report_{dk}$ is valid and $hdl_P \in \mathcal{L}_K$ with honest-bit:

- CT $\in \mathcal{L}_R$: $\mathcal{B}$ uses the universal oracle U_{msg}^*(P), and sends P(msg^*) to $\mathcal{A}$.
- CT $\notin \mathcal{L}_R$: $\mathcal{B}$ forwards CT to $\mathcal{C}$ as a decryption query. $\mathcal{C}$ returns msg by running the VPKE.Dec(pars, pk_{vpke}, dk_{vpke}, CT) algorithm to $\mathcal{B}$. If msg $= \perp$, $\mathcal{B}$ outputs $\perp$; otherwise, $\mathcal{B}$ runs P on msg, and sends P(msg) to $\mathcal{A}$.

Finally, $\mathcal{A}$ outputs $\mu' \in \{0, 1\}$. $\mathcal{B}$ outputs μ', and breaks IND-CCA security.

7   Implementation

In this section, we give an implementation result when we employ a cryptographic hash function H as a function P, i.e., the decryption algorithm outputs H(msg). As mentioned before, theoretically the function is not realized in the IND-based VFE scheme [10] due to the collision-resistance of H, and practically the function seems attractive when we compute a hashed value for a sensitive data such as a password. This system can be achieved by IRON, however no verifiability is guaranteed. On the other hand, in our scheme the server can verify the ciphertext, and can delegate the verification to another server as an option.

We measured the average times and standard deviations of the VFE-HW.Enc, VFE-HW.VerifyCT, VFE-HW.VerifyK and VFE-HW.Dec algorithms because we estimate the runtime of the algorithms related to msg for the proposed scheme. Here, except for the VFE-HW.Dec algorithm, all algorithms were run outside enclaves. In the VFE-HW.Dec algorithm, the FE runs the VPKE.Conv and VPKE.Dec' algorithms, and evaluates H on msg. We employ the VPKE scheme [33], ECDSA as SIG, and SHA-256 as H.

The VPKE.Ver algorithm checks whether (part of) the ciphertext is a DDH tuple, we employed symmetric pairings even though asymmetric pairings are desirable for efficient implementation [25]. We used the PBC library [1], which supports the symmetric pairings. We generated parameters for a Type-A curve with 128-bit security, defined over the field $\mathbb{F}_p$ with a 256-bit prime p, where the order is a 1536-bit prime, using a function called pbc_param_init_a_gen. For running the PBC library in enclaves, we employed the PBC for SGX given by Contiu et al. [20]. In our implementation, we set the input-output of enclaves is as an array of unsigned char values regarding a valuable of PBC. We transformed the binary data into an element of elliptic curves using the element_from_bytes function supported by PBC within enclaves.

Our implementation environment includes the CPU: Intel(R) Core(TM) i3-7100U (2.40 GHz), and the libraries openssl 1.0.2g, Intel SGX 1.5 Linux Driver, Intel SGX SDK, Intel SGX PSW, GMP, PBC, and PBC for SGX [20].

Table 2. Implementation results of VFE-HW scheme

Running time (sec)	Average	Standard deviation
VFE-HW.Enc	0.12436	0.00250
VFE-HW.VerifyCT	0.12828	0.00259
VFE-HW.VerifyK	0.00034	0.00005
VFE-HW.Dec	0.06499	0.00163

Table 3. Implementation results of VFE-HW scheme (Invalid ciphertext/secret key)

Running time (sec)	Average	Standard deviation
VFE-HW.VerifyCT (DDH)	0.11828	0.00228
VFE-HW.VerifyCT (OTS)	0.12329	0.00252
VFE-HW.VerifyK (Signature)	0.00034	0.00006

We give our implementation result in Table 2. Compared to the running time of the VFE-HW.Dec algorithm, which was run inside the enclave, those of the VFE-HW.Enc and VFE-HW.VerifyCT algorithms were relatively slow. The reason seems to employ symmetric bilinear groups in our implementation, i.e., the size of the group $\mathbb{G}$ is much larger than that of the case of asymmetric bilinear groups. Thus, proposing a VPKE scheme secure in asymmetric bilinear groups (or without pairings) and re-implementing our VFE-HW scheme seems an interesting future work. Since we focus on verifiability of ciphertexts and secret keys, we also evaluate when VFE-HW.VerifyCT and VFE-HW.VerifyK algorithms output 0 in Table 3. In our implementation, the VFE-HW.VerifyCT algorithm outputs 0 either the DDH test or a verification of One-Time Signature (OTS) [39] fails. The VFE-HW.VerifyK algorithm outputs 0 when a verification of signature fails. Even if the verification process fails when invalid ciphertexts or secret keys are used, the running times are similar to those of valid ciphertexts or secret keys.

8   Conclusion

In this paper, we proposed a SIM-based VFE that supports any functionality. To support any functionality, we employed a hardware-based construction. In addition, we gave a SIM-based VFE construction that employs VPKE, PKE, SIG, and HW. Finally, we give our implementation of proposed VFE-HW scheme for H. Recently, Bhatotia et al. [12] considered a composable security when Trusted Execution Environments (TEEs) including Intel SGX are employed. Considering such a composability in the VFE-HW context is left as a future work. Although we have claimed that the trusted assumption is reasonable in the HW setting, we leave how to remove this assumption without losing the SIM-based security as a future work. In addition, we leave how to construct SIM-based secure VFE without using secure hardware as a future work.

Acknowledgement. This work was supported by the JSPS KAKENHI Grant Numbers JP20K11811, JP20J22324, and JP21K11897. We thank Dr. Rafael Pires for helpful discussion.

A   The Nieto et al. VPKE Scheme

In this appendix, we introduce the Nieto et al. VPKE scheme [[33], Fig. 4] as follows. For the underlying One-Time Signature (OTS) scheme, we employ the discrete-log-based Wee OTS scheme [39], and for the DDH test, we employ symmetric pairings whether $e(g, \pi)$ is the same as $e(c_1, u^t v)$ or not.

VPKE.PGen(1^λ): Choose $(p, e, g, \mathbb{G}, \mathbb{G}_T)$ where $\mathbb{G}$ and $\mathbb{G}_T$ are groups of λ-bit prime order p, $g \in \mathbb{G}$ is a generator, and $e : \mathbb{G} \times \mathbb{G} \to \mathbb{G}_T$ is a bilinear map. Let $H : \mathbb{G} \to \{0,1\}^{\mathsf{poly}(\lambda)}$, $H_{OTS} : \{0,1\}^* \to \{0,1\}^{\mathsf{poly}(\lambda)}$, and TCR $: \mathbb{G} \times \{0,1\} \to \mathbb{Z}_p$ be collision or target collision resistant hash functions where $\mathsf{poly}(\lambda)$ is a polynomial in λ. Output pars $= (p, e, g, \mathbb{G}, \mathbb{G}_T, H, H_{OTS}, TCR)$.

VPKE.KeyGen(pars): Parse pars $= (p, e, g, \mathbb{G}, \mathbb{G}_T, H, H_{OTS}, TCR)$. Choose $x_1 \xleftarrow{\$} \mathbb{Z}_p^*$ and $v \xleftarrow{\$} \mathbb{G}$ and compute $u = g^{x_1}$. Output pk $= (u, v)$ and dk $= x_1$.

VPKE.Enc(pars, pk, msg): Parse pars $= (p, e, g, \mathbb{G}, \mathbb{G}_T, H, H_{OTS}, TCR)$ and pk $= (u, v)$. Choose $s_0, s_1, x_2, r, n \xleftarrow{\$} \mathbb{Z}_p^*$ and compute $u_0 = g^{s_0}$, $u_1 = g^{s_1}$, $c' = g^{x_2}$, $c_1 = g^r$, $t \leftarrow TCR(c_1, (u_0, u_1, c'))$, $K \leftarrow H(u^r)$ and $\pi \leftarrow (u^t v)^r$. Set $c_2 \leftarrow$ msg $\oplus K$ and $c = (c_1, c_2, \pi)$. Compute $w \leftarrow x_2 + n s_0 + s_1(H_{OTS}(c) + n)$. Output CT $\leftarrow (c, (n, w), (u_0, u_1, c'))$.

VPKE.Ver(pars, pk, CT): Parse pars $= (p, e, g, \mathbb{G}, \mathbb{G}_T, H, H_{OTS}, TCR)$, pk $= (u, v)$, CT $= (c, (n, w), (u_0, u_1, c'))$ and $c = (c_1, c_2, \pi)$. Compute $t \leftarrow TCR(c_1, (u_0, u_1, c'))$ and $\pi \leftarrow (u^t v)^r$. If $e(g, \pi) \neq e(c_1, u^t v)$ or $g^w \neq c' u_0^n \cdot u_1^{H_{OTS}(c)+n}$, then output 0. Otherwise, output 1.

VPKE.Conv: Parse pars $= (p, e, g, \mathbb{G}, \mathbb{G}_T, H, H_{OTS}, TCR)$, pk $= (u, v)$, CT $= (c, (n, w), (u_0, u_1, c'))$ and $c = (c_1, c_2, \pi)$. Output CT$' = (c_1, c_2)$.

VPKE.Dec$'$(pars, pk, dk, CT'): Parse pars $= (p, e, g, \mathbb{G}, \mathbb{G}_T, H, H_{OTS}, TCR)$, pk $= (u, v)$, dk $= x_1$ and CT$' = (c_1, c_2)$. Compute $K \leftarrow H(c_1^{x_1})$ and set msg $\leftarrow c_2 \oplus K$. Output msg.

References

1. The PBC (pairing-based cryptography) library. http://crypto.stanford.edu/pbc/
2. Abdalla, M., Bourse, F., Caro, A.D., Pointcheval, D.: Simple functional encryption schemes for inner products. In: PKC, pp. 733–751 (2015)

3. Abdalla, M., Bourse, F., Marival, H., Pointcheval, D., Soleimanian, A., Waldner, H.: Multi-client inner-product functional encryption in the random-oracle model. In: SCN, pp. 525–545 (2020)
4. Abdalla, M., Catalano, D., Gay, R., Ursu, B.: Inner-product functional encryption with fine-grained access control. In: Moriai, S., Wang, H. (eds.) ASIACRYPT 2020. LNCS, vol. 12493, pp. 467–497. Springer, Cham (2020). https://doi.org/10.1007/978-3-030-64840-4_16
5. Abdalla, M., Gong, J., Wee, H.: Functional encryption for attribute-weighted sums from k-Lin. In: Micciancio, D., Ristenpart, T. (eds.) CRYPTO 2020. LNCS, vol. 12170, pp. 685–716. Springer, Cham (2020). https://doi.org/10.1007/978-3-030-56784-2_23
6. Agrawal, S., Gorbunov, S., Vaikuntanathan, V., Wee, H.: Functional encryption: new perspectives and lower bounds. In: Canetti, R., Garay, J.A. (eds.) CRYPTO 2013. LNCS, vol. 8043, pp. 500–518. Springer, Heidelberg (2013). https://doi.org/10.1007/978-3-642-40084-1_28
7. Agrawal, S., Koppula, V., Waters, B.: Impossibility of simulation secure functional encryption even with random oracles. In: Beimel, A., Dziembowski, S. (eds.) TCC 2018. LNCS, vol. 11239, pp. 659–688. Springer, Cham (2018). https://doi.org/10.1007/978-3-030-03807-6_24
8. Agrawal, S., Libert, B., Maitra, M., Titiu, R.: Adaptive simulation security for inner product functional encryption. In: Kiayias, A., Kohlweiss, M., Wallden, P., Zikas, V. (eds.) PKC 2020. LNCS, vol. 12110, pp. 34–64. Springer, Cham (2020). https://doi.org/10.1007/978-3-030-45374-9_2
9. Anati, I., Gueron, S., Johnson, S., Scarlata, V.: Innovative technology for cpu based attestation and sealing. In: HASP (2013)
10. Badrinarayanan, S., Goyal, V., Jain, A., Sahai, A.: Verifiable functional encryption. In: Cheon, J.H., Takagi, T. (eds.) ASIACRYPT 2016. LNCS, vol. 10032, pp. 557–587. Springer, Heidelberg (2016). https://doi.org/10.1007/978-3-662-53890-6_19
11. Barak, B., Pass, R.: On the possibility of one-message weak zero-knowledge. In: Naor, M. (ed.) TCC 2004. LNCS, vol. 2951, pp. 121–132. Springer, Heidelberg (2004). https://doi.org/10.1007/978-3-540-24638-1_7
12. Bhatotia, P., Kohlweiss, M., Martinico, L., Tselekounis, Y.: Steel: composable hardware-based stateful and randomised functional encryption. In: Garay, J.A. (ed.) PKC 2021. LNCS, vol. 12711, pp. 709–736. Springer, Cham (2021). https://doi.org/10.1007/978-3-030-75248-4_25
13. Blum, M., Feldman, P., Micali, S.: Non-interactive zero-knowledge and its applications (extended abstract). In: STOC, pp. 103–112 (1988)
14. Boneh, D., Sahai, A., Waters, B.: Functional encryption: definitions and challenges. In: Ishai, Y. (ed.) TCC 2011. LNCS, vol. 6597, pp. 253–273. Springer, Heidelberg (2011). https://doi.org/10.1007/978-3-642-19571-6_16
15. Boyle, E., Chung, K.-M., Pass, R.: On extractability obfuscation. In: Lindell, Y. (ed.) TCC 2014. LNCS, vol. 8349, pp. 52–73. Springer, Heidelberg (2014). https://doi.org/10.1007/978-3-642-54242-8_3
16. Bulck, J.V., et al.: FORESHADOW: extracting the keys to the intel SGX kingdom with transient out-of-order execution. In: USENIX, pp. 991–1008 (2018)
17. Bulck, J.V., et al.: LVI: hijacking transient execution through microarchitectural load value injection. In: IEEE S&P, pp. 54–72 (2020)
18. De Caro, A., Iovino, V., Jain, A., O'Neill, A., Paneth, O., Persiano, G.: On the achievability of simulation-based security for functional encryption. In: Canetti, R., Garay, J.A. (eds.) CRYPTO 2013. LNCS, vol. 8043, pp. 519–535. Springer, Heidelberg (2013). https://doi.org/10.1007/978-3-642-40084-1_29

19. Chotard, J., Dufour Sans, E., Gay, R., Phan, D.H., Pointcheval, D.: Decentralized multi-client functional encryption for inner product. In: Peyrin, T., Galbraith, S. (eds.) ASIACRYPT 2018. LNCS, vol. 11273, pp. 703–732. Springer, Cham (2018). https://doi.org/10.1007/978-3-030-03329-3_24

20. Contiu, S., Pires, R., Vaucher, S., Pasin, M., Felber, P., Réveillère, L.: IBBE-SGX: cryptographic group access control using trusted execution environments. In: DSN, pp. 207–218 (2018)

21. Damgård, I., Haagh, H., Mercer, R., Nitulescu, A., Orlandi, C., Yakoubov, S.: Stronger security and constructions of multi-designated verifier signatures. In: Pass, R., Pietrzak, K. (eds.) TCC 2020. LNCS, vol. 12551, pp. 229–260. Springer, Cham (2020). https://doi.org/10.1007/978-3-030-64378-2_9

22. Datta, P., Okamoto, T., Tomida, J.: Full-hiding (unbounded) multi-input inner product functional encryption from the k-linear assumption. In: Abdalla, M., Dahab, R. (eds.) PKC 2018. LNCS, vol. 10770, pp. 245–277. Springer, Cham (2018). https://doi.org/10.1007/978-3-319-76581-5_9

23. Dufour-Sans, E., Pointcheval, D.: Unbounded inner-product functional encryption with succinct keys. In: Deng, R.H., Gauthier-Umaña, V., Ochoa, M., Yung, M. (eds.) ACNS 2019. LNCS, vol. 11464, pp. 426–441. Springer, Cham (2019). https://doi.org/10.1007/978-3-030-21568-2_21

24. Fisch, B., Vinayagamurthy, D., Boneh, D., Gorbunov, S.: IRON: functional encryption using intel SGX. In: ACM CCS, pp. 765–782 (2017)

25. Galbraith, S.D., Paterson, K.G., Smart, N.P.: Pairings for cryptographers. In: Discrete Applied Mathematics, pp. 3113–3121 (2008)

26. Garg, S., Gentry, C., Halevi, S., Raykova, M., Sahai, A., Waters, B.: Candidate indistinguishability obfuscation and functional encryption for all circuits. SIAM J. Comput. **45**(3), 882–929 (2016)

27. Garg, S., Gentry, C., Halevi, S., Zhandry, M.: Fully secure attribute based encryption from multilinear maps. IACR Cryptology ePrint Archive 2014:622 (2014)

28. Goldreich, O., Oren, Y.: Definitions and properties of zero-knowledge proof systems. J. Cryptol. **7**(1), 1–32 (1994). https://doi.org/10.1007/BF00195207

29. Goyal, V., Pandey, O., Sahai, A., Waters, B.: Attribute-based encryption for fine-grained access control of encrypted data. In: ACM CCS, pp. 89–98 (2006)

30. Hoekstra, M., Lal, R., Pappachan, P., Phegade, V., Cuvillo, J.D.: Using innovative instructions to create trustworthy software solutions. In: HASP (2013)

31. Johnson, S., Scarlata, V., Rozas, C., Brickell, E., Mckeen, F.: Intel software guard extensions: EPID provisioning and attestation services (2016)

32. McKeen, F., et al.: Innovative instructions and software model for isolated execution. In: HASP 2013 (2013)

33. Nieto, J.M.G., Manulis, M., Poettering, B., Rangasamy, J., Stebila, D.: Publicly verifiable ciphertexts. In: SCN, pp. 393–410 (2012)

34. O'Neill, A.: Definitional issues in functional encryption. IACR Cryptology ePrint Archive 2010:556 (2010)

35. Schwarz, M., et al.: ZombieLoad: cross-privilege-boundary data sampling. In: ACM CCS, pp. 753–768 (2019)

36. Soroush, N., Iovino, V., Rial, A., Rønne, P.B., Ryan, P.Y.A.: Verifiable inner product encryption scheme. In: PKC, pp. 65–94 (2020)

37. Tomida, J., Takashima, K.: Unbounded inner product functional encryption from bilinear maps. In: Peyrin, T., Galbraith, S. (eds.) ASIACRYPT 2018. LNCS, vol. 11273, pp. 609–639. Springer, Cham (2018). https://doi.org/10.1007/978-3-030-03329-3_21

38. Waters, B.: A punctured programming approach to adaptively secure functional encryption. In: Gennaro, R., Robshaw, M. (eds.) CRYPTO 2015. LNCS, vol. 9216, pp. 678–697. Springer, Heidelberg (2015). https://doi.org/10.1007/978-3-662-48000-7_33

39. Wee, H.: Public key encryption against related key attacks. In: PKC, pp. 262–279 (2012)

40. Wee, H.: Attribute-hiding predicate encryption in bilinear groups, revisited. In: Kalai, Y., Reyzin, L. (eds.) TCC 2017. LNCS, vol. 10677, pp. 206–233. Springer, Cham (2017). https://doi.org/10.1007/978-3-319-70500-2_8

Fully Secure Unbounded Zero Inner Product Encryption with Short Ciphertexts and Keys

Subhranil Dutta[✉], Tapas Pal[✉], and Ratna Dutta

Indian Institute of Technology Kharagpur, Kharagpur 721302, West Bengal, India
{subhranildutta,tapas.pal}@iitkgp.ac.in, ratna@maths.iitkgp.ac.in

Abstract. *Inner product encryption* (IPE) generates a secret key for a predicate vector and encrypts a message under an attribute vector such that recovery of the message from a ciphertext requires the vectors to satisfy a linear relation. In the case of *zero IPE* (ZIPE), the relation holds if the inner product between the predicate and attribute vectors is zero. Over the years, several ZIPE schemes have been proposed with numerous applications. However, most of the schemes compute inner products for *bounded* length vectors in the sense that a pre-specified bound on the length of predicate/attribute vectors must be fixed while producing the system parameters. On the other hand, an *unbounded ZIPE* (UZIPE) provides freedom to select the length of vectors at the time of generating keys or producing ciphertexts. The feature of unboundedness expands the applicability of ZIPE in the scenario where the length of vectors varies or is not known in advance. Achieving UZIPE with short secret keys and ciphertexts is the main goal of this paper. More specifically, we present an efficient UZIPE scheme based on *symmetric external Diffie-Hellman assumption* (SXDH) in the standard model. Our UZIPE enjoys short secret keys and ciphertexts which reduce storage and communication costs. Moreover, we prove security in the *adaptively fully attribute-hiding* model meaning that the ciphertexts of our UZIPE hide the payload along with the attribute vector. On the technical side, our work takes inspiration from the unbounded inner product functional encryption (UIPFE) of Tomida and Takashima (ASIACRYPT'18) and modifies their framework to UZIPE with efficiency improvements regarding the sizes of ciphertexts and keys. As UIPFE does not generically imply UZIPE, our scheme goes through several technical modifications in the construction and security analysis over the UIPFE.

Keywords: Inner product encryption · Attribute-hiding · Bilinear maps

1 Introduction

Functional encryption (FE) [3,5,8] is an advanced cryptographic paradigm that is a generalization of plain *public-key encryption* (PKE). The beauty of FE lies in

© Springer Nature Switzerland AG 2021
Q. Huang and Y. Yu (Eds.): ProvSec 2021, LNCS 13059, pp. 241–258, 2021.
https://doi.org/10.1007/978-3-030-90402-9_13

the fact that it unifies almost all modern day cryptographic encryption mechanisms such as *identity-based encryption* (IBE) [2,6,14], *attribute-based encryption* (ABE) [1,5,10,13] and *predicate encryption* (PE) [4,7]. FE produces sophisticated secret-keys sk_f for arbitrary functions f which can be used to decrypt a ciphertext ct_m corresponding to a message m and recover $f(m)$ in contrast to the original message m as in normal PKE. Sahai and Waters [14] formally introduced the notion of ABE which is a specific class of FE that generates secret-keys only for boolean functions. Subsequently, a variety of ABEs has emerged over the years with practical applications. In ABE, a secret-key is associated with a predicate $\boldsymbol{y}$ and a ciphertext corresponds to an attribute $\boldsymbol{x}$ and a message M such that decryption returns M whenever a relation between $\boldsymbol{x}$ and $\boldsymbol{y}$ holds.

Katz, Sahai and Waters [4] initiated the study of *inner product encryption* (IPE) which is a specific class of ABE. In IPE, a ciphertext ct_x encrypts a message M with respect to an attribute vector $\boldsymbol{x}$ and decrypting the ciphertext requires a legitimate secret key sk_y corresponding to a predicate vector $\boldsymbol{y}$ such that a linear relation between $\boldsymbol{x}$ and $\boldsymbol{y}$ holds. In this paper, we consider *zero inner product encryption* (ZIPE) which enables a successful decryption if the inner product $\langle \boldsymbol{x}, \boldsymbol{y} \rangle$ is zero. From the security perspective of ZIPE, *payload-hiding* is a basic requirement where the ciphertext hides only the message M. Katz, Sahai and Waters [4] first introduced a more robust security notion namely *attribute-hiding* (AH) where the ciphertext apart from hiding M does not reveal any information about the attribute $\boldsymbol{x}$. In *weakly attribute-hiding* (WAH), the adversary is restricted to query secret keys sk_y for vectors $\boldsymbol{y}$ such that $\langle \boldsymbol{x}, \boldsymbol{y} \rangle \neq 0$. Therefore, WAH does not allow the adversary to get a functional key that can decrypt the challenge ciphertext. On the other hand, *fully attribute-hiding* (FAH) provides security against more powerful adversaries which can ask polynomially many secret keys sk_y that decrypt the challenge ciphertext.

Unbounded ZIPE. Most of the ZIPEs in the literature suffer from the fact that the size of system parameters depends on the length of attribute/predicate vectors. This is particularly unsuitable in the scenario where the length n of vectors is not known in advance or varies with the application scenarios. A trivial solution for overcoming this problem is to fix a large value of n during the setup and generate the parameters accordingly. But this is not a wise choice as the size of parameters grows at least linearly with n and eventually, the ciphertext size also depends on n although the length of the underlying attribute vector is much smaller than n. Another solution is to construct ZIPE schemes where system parameters do not depend on n and we can choose n according to our requirements during generating keys or encrypting messages. In this paper, our goal is to construct such an *unbounded* ZIPE (UZIPE) scheme with short ciphertexts and secret keys. It is well known that ZIPE schemes can efficiently achieve FE schemes that capture many practical predicates such as polynomial evaluations, disjunction/conjunctions of equality tests, membership tests [3,4]. All these primitives become more applicable and storage efficient when we replace ZIPE with UZIPE. Okamoto and Takashima [10] first proposed a construction of UZIPE in standard model based on decisional linear (DLIN) assumption with

FAH security. However, the ciphertexts and secret keys of the UZIPE [10] are not short and one has to bear a significant efficiency loss when using their UZIPE in the above-mentioned applications.

Our Contribution. In this paper, we propose a construction of the UZIPE scheme with short ciphertexts and secret keys based on the SXDH assumption. Our scheme achieves adaptively FAH security in the standard model. Note that in the adaptive security model, an adversary is allowed to query secret keys at any point of the security experiment. More specifically, our UZIPE acquires more than 50% efficiency gain over the only known UZIPE of [10]. We construct UZIPE in a most natural *permissive* setting described as follows. Let us consider two vectors $x = (x_i)_{i \in I_x}$ and $y = (y_i)_{i \in I_y}$ where I_x, I_y are two index sets corresponding to x, y respectively. In permissive setting, the generalized inner product of y over x is defined by $\sum_{i \in I_y} x_i y_i$ if $I_y \subseteq I_x$.

We use bracket notation to express any group element, i.e., for $\kappa \in \{1, 2, T\}$, $[x]_\kappa$ represents g_κ^x where g_κ is a generator of group G_κ. Here G_1 and G_2 are the source groups and G_T is the target group for a bilinear map $e : G_1 \times G_2 \to G_T$. The starting point of our construction is the recently proposed unbounded IPFE scheme by Tomida and Takashima [15]. It is known that IPFE does not directly imply ZIPE in the public-key setting. Therefore, we carefully modify their scheme [15] as well as the security analysis to achieve a UZIPE with short ciphertexts and keys in FAH security model. In particular, we utilize the dual pairing vector space framework [12] to make the system parameters independent of the vector length. During setup, we consider two dual orthonormal bases $\mathbf{B}$ and $\mathbf{B}^*$ from $\mathbb{Z}_p^{6 \times 6}$ where p is a prime number. Our idea is to perform component wise encryptions of the attribute vector x and bind the components with a common randomness z in such a way that a successful decryption using a secret key corresponding to a predicate vector y requires $\langle x, y \rangle$ to be zero. To encrypt an attribute vector $x = (x_i)_{i \in I_x} \in \mathbb{Z}^{|I_x|}$ along with a message M, encryption algorithm computes $[c_i]_1 = [(\pi_i(1, i), x_i, z, 0, 0)\mathbf{B}]_1$ with uniformly chosen random elements π_i, z from $\mathbb{Z}_p$ for all $i \in I_x$ and $c = M \cdot [z]_T$. For a predicate vector $y = (y_i)_{i \in I_y}$, the trusted authority generates $[k_i]_2 = [(\rho_i(-i, 1), y_i, r_i, 0, 0)\mathbf{B}^*]_2$ where ρ_i and r_i are random elements of $\mathbb{Z}_p$ such that $\sum_{i \in I_y} r_i = 1$. If $\langle x, y \rangle = 0$ then the recipient is able to recover $[z]_T$ by performing pairing operations with $[c_i]_1$ and $[k_i]_2$. However, for security analysis, we need to introduce additional randomness in the original scheme. For more details, we refer to Sect. 3 (scheme) and Sect. 3.1 (security analysis). While comparing with the UZIPE of [10], our UZIPE is more efficient in key size and ciphertext length as we demonstrate in Table 1. For example, the ciphertext of [10] requires $15n + 6$ group elements whereas our ciphertext consists of $6n + 1$ group elements. The secret key sk_y of our UZIPE contains $6n'$ group elements whereas [10] has $15n' + 5$ group elements. In terms of computational cost, our scheme is more efficient than [10]. Our UZIPE scheme requires only $6n$ numbers of pairing operations whereas [10] needs $15n + 1$ numbers of pairing operations during decryption.

Related Work. Katz, Sahai and Waters [4] first built an attribute-hiding ZIPE scheme secure against selective adversaries in the standard model based on

Table 1. Comparison with existing attribute-hiding ZIPE.

Scheme	|mpk|	|msk|	|sk|	|ct|	Assump.	Vector length	Security
[4]	$O(n)|G|$	$O(n^2)\,|G|$	$(2n+1)|G|$	$(2n+1)|G|+|G_T|$	GSD	Bounded	Sel. FAH
[5]	$O(n^2)|G|$	$O(n^2)\,|\mathbb{Z}_p|$	$(2n+1)|G|$	$(2n+3)|G|+|G_T|$	eDDH	Bounded	Adp. WAH
[8]	$O(n^2)|G|$	$O(n^2)\,|G|$	$(3n+2)|G|$	$(3n+2)|G|+|G_T|$	DLIN	Bounded	Adp. WAH
[9]	$O(n^2)|G|$	$O(n^2)\,|\mathbb{Z}_p|$	$(4n+2)|G|$	$(4n+2)|G|+|G_T|$	DLIN	Bounded	Adp. FAH
	$O(n)|G|$	$O(n)|G|$	$11|G|$	$(5n+1)|G|+|G_T|$	DLIN	Bounded	Adp. FAH
[10]	$105|G_1|$	$105|\mathbb{Z}_p|$	$(15n'+5)|G|$	$(15n+5)|G_1|+|G_T|$	DLIN	Unbounded	Adp. FAH
Our work	$24|G_1|$	$24|\mathbb{Z}_p|$	$6n'|G_2|$	$6n|G_1|+|G_T|$	SXDH	Unbounded	Adp. FAH

n, n': length of attribute vectors, predicate vectors respectively and for existing bounded ZIPE scheme $n = n'$; |mpk|, |msk|, |sk|, |ct|: size of master public key, size of master secret key, size of secret key, size of ciphertext respectively; Sel. FAH, Adp. WAH, Adp. FAH: selective fully attribute-hiding, adaptive weak attribute-hiding, adaptive fully attribute-hiding respectively; GSD, eDDH, DLIN, SXDH: general subgroup decisional problem, extended decisional Diffie-Hellman problem, decisional linear assumption and symmetric external Diffie-Hellman respectively; $|G_i|$: size of an element of G_i for $i \in \{1, 2, T\}$ and $|G|$ denotes size of an element of G.

general subgroup decisional assumption. A selective adversary is weaker than an adaptive one in the sense that a selective adversary has to commit to the challenge messages before seeing the public parameters. Lewko et al. [5] proposed the first adaptively secure ZIPE with WAH security based on extended decisional Diffie-Hellman (eDDH) assumption. Okamoto et al. [9] improved this security notion to achieve the first adaptive FAH security for ZIPE based on the DLIN assumption. However, all these constructions of [4,5,8,9,11] can handle only bounded length of vectors until Okamoto and Takashima [10] gave a construction of UZIPE with adaptively FAH security based on the decisional linear (DLIN) assumption in the standard model. Our work describes a more efficient UZIPE which significantly improves storage and communication cost.

2   Preliminaries

Notations: Let λ be the security parameter, 1^λ be its unary encoding and $\mathsf{poly}(\lambda)$ be the set of all polynomial functions. For a prime p, let $\mathbb{Z}_p$ denotes the field $\mathbb{Z}/p\mathbb{Z}$. For a set S, $s \xleftarrow{\mathsf{U}} S$ indicates that s is uniformly chosen from S. If n is a natural number, then $[n]$ defines the set $\{1, 2, \ldots, n\}$. We use a bold upper-case letter e.g., $\mathbf{A}$ to denote a matrix, and a bold lower-case version of the same e.g., $\boldsymbol{a}_i$ letter with subscript i to represent the i-th row of this matrix. Let g_κ be a generator of a cyclic group $\mathbb{G}_\kappa$. For a matrix $\mathbf{A} = (a_{ij}) \in \mathsf{GL}_n(\mathbb{F}_p)$, we define $[\![\mathbf{A}]\!]_\kappa$ as

$$[\![\mathbf{A}]\!]_\kappa = \begin{bmatrix} g_\kappa^{a_{11}} & g_\kappa^{a_{12}} & \cdots & g_\kappa^{a_{1n}} \\ g_\kappa^{a_{21}} & g_\kappa^{a_{22}} & \cdots & g_\kappa^{a_{2n}} \\ \vdots & \cdots & \cdots & \vdots \\ g_\kappa^{a_{n1}} & g_\kappa^{a_{n2}} & \cdots & g_\kappa^{a_{nn}} \end{bmatrix}$$

If $\boldsymbol{a} = (a_1, a_2, \ldots, a_n)$ is an n-tuple vector then $[\![\boldsymbol{a}]\!]_\kappa = (g_\kappa^{a_1}, g_\kappa^{a_2}, \ldots, g_\kappa^{a_n})$. For a field $\mathbb{F}_p$, set $\mathsf{GL}_n(\mathbb{F}_p)$ stands for all $n \times n$ invertible matrices whose elements are in $\mathbb{F}_p$. Let I_m denotes $m \times m$ an identity matrix. For a matrix $\mathbf{B}$, let $\mathbf{B}^T$ signifies the transpose of the matrix $\mathbf{B}$ and $\mathbf{B}^* = (\mathbf{B}^{-1})^T$ is orthonormal dual corresponding the matrix $\mathbf{B}$. For vectors $\boldsymbol{x} = (x_1, x_2, \ldots, x_n) \in \mathbb{Z}^n$ and $\boldsymbol{y} = (y_i)_{i \in S} \in \mathbb{Z}^{|S|}$, the inner product of $\boldsymbol{x}$ and $\boldsymbol{y}$ is defined as $\langle \boldsymbol{x}, \boldsymbol{y} \rangle = \sum_{i \in S} x_i y_i$ if $S \subseteq [n]$. Let $\mathbb{V}$ be a vector space and $\boldsymbol{b}_i \in \mathbb{V}, i \in [n]$. Then $\mathsf{span}\{\boldsymbol{b}_1, \boldsymbol{b}_2 \ldots, \boldsymbol{b}_n\} \subseteq \mathbb{V}$ denotes the subspace generated by $\boldsymbol{b}_1, \boldsymbol{b}_2, \ldots, \boldsymbol{b}_n$. For bases $\mathbf{B} = (\boldsymbol{b}_1, \boldsymbol{b}_2 \ldots, \boldsymbol{b}_N)$, $\mathbf{B}^* = (\boldsymbol{b}_1^*, \boldsymbol{b}_2 \ldots, \boldsymbol{b}_N^*)$ then $(x_1, x_2, \ldots, x_N)\mathbf{B}$ is defined as $\sum_{i=1}^{N} x_i \boldsymbol{b}_i$ and $(y_1, y_2, \ldots, y_N)\mathbf{B}^*$ is defined as $\sum_{i=1}^{N} y_i \boldsymbol{b}_i^*$. A function $\mathsf{negl} : \mathbb{N} \to \mathbb{R}$ is said to be a negligible function if $\mathsf{negl}(\lambda) = \lambda^{-\omega(1)}$. An algorithm A is said to be probabilistic polynomial time (PPT) algorithm if it is modelled as a probabilistic Turing machine that runs in time $\mathsf{poly}(\lambda)$.

2.1 Basic Notions

We discuss the definitions of bilinear group and dual pairing vector space in full version due to page limitation.

Definition 1 *(Symmetric external Diffie–Hellman (SXDH) assumption) [15]: For $\kappa \in \{1, 2\}$ we define the distribution $(D, [t_\beta]_\kappa)$ on a bilinear group $\mathbb{BG} = (p, G_1, G_2, G_T, g_1, g_2, e) \leftarrow \mathcal{G}_{\mathsf{BG.Gen}}(1^\lambda)$ as*

$$D = (\mathbb{BG}, [a]_\kappa = g_\kappa^a, [u]_\kappa = g_\kappa^u) \text{ for } a, u \xleftarrow{\mathsf{U}} \mathbb{Z}_p$$

$$[t_\beta]_\kappa = [au + \beta f]_\kappa = g_\kappa^{au + \beta f} \text{ for } \beta \in \{0, 1\} \text{ and } f \xleftarrow{\mathsf{U}} \mathbb{Z}_p.$$

We say that the SXDH assumption holds if for any PPT adversary $\mathcal{A}$, $\kappa \in \{1, 2\}$,

$$\mathsf{Adv}_{\mathcal{A}}^{\mathsf{SXDH}}(\lambda) = \left| \Pr[\mathcal{A}(D, [t_0]_\kappa) \to 1] - \Pr[\mathcal{A}(D, [t_1]_\kappa) \to 1] \right| \leq \mathsf{negl}(\lambda)$$

Definition 2 *(Unbounded zero inner product encryption (UZIPE)): Unbounded zero inner product encryption $\mathsf{UZIPE} = (\mathsf{Setup}, \mathsf{KeyGen}, \mathsf{Enc}, \mathsf{Dec})$ consists of four PPT algorithms satisfying the following requirements:*

- $\mathsf{Setup}(1^\lambda) \to (\mathsf{msk}, \mathsf{mpk})$: *A trusted authority takes a security parameter λ as input and generates a master public key mpk and a master security key msk. The master public key mpk is made public while the master secret key msk is kept secret to the trusted authority.*

- $\mathsf{KeyGen}(\mathsf{mpk}, \mathsf{msk}, \boldsymbol{y}, I_y) \to \mathsf{sk}_{\boldsymbol{y}}$: *On the input master public key mpk, master secret key msk, a vector $\boldsymbol{y} = (y_i)_{i \in I_y} \in \mathbb{Z}^{|I_y|}$, $I_y \subseteq [s]$, $s = s(\lambda)$ being a polynomial, the trusted authority generates secret key $\mathsf{sk}_{\boldsymbol{y}}$ corresponding to the vector $\boldsymbol{y}$. Here I_y is the index set of $\boldsymbol{y}$.*

- $\mathsf{Enc}(\mathsf{mpk}, \boldsymbol{x}, M) \to \mathsf{ct}_{\boldsymbol{x}}$: *The algorithm is run by an encryptor on input a message M, a master public key mpk and a vector $\boldsymbol{x} = (x_i)_{i \in I_x} \in \mathbb{Z}^{|I_x|}$, $I_x \subseteq [m]$ where $m = m(\lambda)$ is a polynomial. It outputs a ciphertext $\mathsf{ct}_{\boldsymbol{x}}$. Here I_x is the index set of $\boldsymbol{x}$.*

- Dec(mpk, sk_y, ct_x) $\to \alpha$ or $\perp$: *The decryptor uses his secret key sk_y to decrypt the ciphertext ct_x and outputs a decrypted value $\alpha \in \mathbb{Z}$ or a special symbol $\perp$ indicating failure.*

Correctness: *An UZIPE = (Setup, KeyGen, Enc, Dec) scheme is said to be correct if for all (msk, mpk) $\leftarrow$ UZIPE.Setup(1^λ), all vectors $y \in \mathbb{Z}^{|I_y|}$, all decryption keys $\mathsf{sk}_y \leftarrow$ UZIPE.KeyGen(mpk, msk, y, I_y) all messages M, all vectors $x \in \mathbb{Z}^{|I_x|}$, all the ciphertexts $\mathsf{ct}_x \leftarrow$ UZIPE.Enc(mpk, x, M) with $I_y \subseteq I_x$ it holds that $M =$ UZIPE.Dec(mpk, sk_y, ct_x) with overwhelming probability if $\langle x, y \rangle = 0$.*

Definition 3. *(Adaptively fully attribute-hiding security against chosen plaintext attack) [10]: The model for adaptively fully attribute-hiding (FAH) security of UZIPE = (Setup, KeyGen, Enc, Dec) against adversary $\mathcal{A}$ under chosen plaintext attack is described below as a game played between a challenger and $\mathcal{A}$.*

Setup: *The challenger generates (mpk, msk) $\leftarrow$ UZIPE.Setup(1^λ) and sends the master public key mpk to the adversary $\mathcal{A}$.*

Key Query Phase I: *The adversary $\mathcal{A}$ may adaptively make a polynomial number of key queries for vectors $y = (y_i)_{i \in I_y}$ to the challenger. The challenger in turn computes the corresponding key $\mathsf{sk}_y \leftarrow$ UZIPE.KeyGen(mpk, msk, y, I_y) and returns it to $\mathcal{A}$.*

Challenge Query: *The adversary $\mathcal{A}$ submits challenge messages $M^{(0)}, M^{(1)}$, challenge vectors $x^{(0)} = (x_i^{(0)})_{i \in I_{x^{(0)}}}$, $x^{(1)} = (x^{(1)})_{i \in I_{x^{(1)}}}$ with the same index set $I_{x^{(0)}} = I_{x^{(1)}}$ and subject to the following restrictions:*

- *The j-th key query associated to the vector $y^{(j)} = (y_i^{(j)})_{i \in I_{y^{(j)}}}$ in the key query phase must satisfy $\langle y^{(j)}, x^{(0)} \rangle \neq 0$ and $\langle y^{(j)}, x^{(1)} \rangle \neq 0$ for all j.*
- *If the challenge messages are equal i.e., $M^{(0)} = M^{(1)}$, then any j-th key query associated to the vector $y^{(j)} = (y_i^{(j)})_{i \in I_{y^{(j)}}}$ must satisfy $\langle y^{(j)}, x^{(0)} \rangle = \langle y^{(j)}, x^{(1)} \rangle = 0$ for all j.*

The challenger chooses uniformly a bit $b \xleftarrow{\mathsf{U}} \{0,1\}$ and sends the ciphertext $\mathsf{ct}_{x^{(b)}} \leftarrow$ UZIPE.Enc (mpk, $x^{(b)}, M^{(b)}$) to $\mathcal{A}$.

Key Query Phase II: *Key query phase I is repeated with the same aforementioned restrictions for the key query vector y, challenge messages $M^{(0)}, M^{(1)}$ and challenge vectors $(x^{(0)}, x^{(1)})$.*

Guess: *The adversary $\mathcal{A}$ outputs a bit b' and wins if $b = b'$.*
The variable ι is defined as $\iota = 0$ if $M^{(0)} \neq M^{(1)}$ for challenge messages $M^{(0)}$ and $M^{(1)}$ and $\iota = 1$ otherwise. The advantage of $\mathcal{A}$ in this game is defined as

$$\mathsf{Adv}_{\mathcal{A},\mathsf{FAH}}^{\mathsf{UZIPE}}(\lambda) = \left| \Pr[b = b'] - \frac{1}{2} \right|$$

where λ is the security parameter. We say that an UZIPE scheme is adaptively fully attribute-hiding against chosen plaintext attack if all probabilistic polynomial time adversaries $\mathcal{A}$ have at most negligible advantage in the above game.

3   Our UZIPE

Our UZIPE = (Setup, KeyGen, Enc, Dec) scheme describe below.

- Setup(1^λ) $\to$ (msk, mpk): A trusted authority takes a security parameter λ as input and executes the algorithm as follows:
  - Generates a bilinear group $\mathbb{BG} = (p, G_1, G_2, G_T, g_1, g_2, e) \leftarrow \mathcal{G}_{\mathsf{BG.Gen}}(1^\lambda)$ where G_1, G_2 and G_T are the multiplicative groups such that $|G_1| = |G_2| = |G_T| = p$ (prime), g_1, g_2 are the generators of the groups G_1 and G_2 respectively, $e : G_1 \times G_2 \to G_T$ is a bilinear map and $g_T = e(g_1, g_2)$.
  - Generates $\mathsf{params}_V = (p, V, V^*, G_T, A_1, A_2, E) \leftarrow \mathcal{G}_{\mathsf{DPVS.Gen}}(6, \mathbb{BG})$ where $A_1 = (g_1^{e_1}, g_1^{e_2}, \ldots, g_1^{e_6})$ and $A_2 = (g_2^{e_1}, g_2^{e_2}, \ldots, g_2^{e_6})$ are the canonical bases of the vector spaces $V = G_1^6$, $V^* = G_2^6$ respectively with $e_i = (0, \ldots, 0, \overset{i-1}{\overbrace{}} 1, 0, \ldots, 0 \overset{6-i}{\overbrace{}})$ and the mapping $E : V \times V^* \to G_T$ is an extension of the bilinear pairing. Sets $\mathsf{pp} = (p, g_1, g_2, g_T, V, V^*, E)$.
  - Chooses uniformly a matrix $\mathbf{B} \overset{\mathsf{U}}{\leftarrow} \mathsf{GL}_6(\mathbb{Z}_p)$ and computes the master public key mpk and master secret key msk as

$$\mathsf{mpk} = \big(\mathsf{pp}, [\![\boldsymbol{b}_1]\!]_1, [\![\boldsymbol{b}_2]\!]_1, [\![\boldsymbol{b}_3]\!]_1, [\![\boldsymbol{b}_4]\!]_1\big), \quad \mathsf{msk} = (\boldsymbol{b}_1^*, \boldsymbol{b}_2^*, \boldsymbol{b}_3^*, \boldsymbol{b}_4^*).$$

  where $\boldsymbol{b}_i$ is the i-th row of $\mathbf{B}$, $\boldsymbol{b}_i^*$ is i-th row of $\mathbf{B}^* = (\mathbf{B}^{-1})^T$ and $[\![\boldsymbol{b}_i]\!]_1$ represents all components of $\boldsymbol{b}_i$ raise the exponent power of g_1 i.e., if $\boldsymbol{b}_i = (b_{i,1}, b_{i,2}, \ldots, b_{i,6})$ then $[\![\boldsymbol{b}_i]\!]_1 = (g_1^{b_{i,1}}, g_1^{b_{i,2}}, \ldots, g_1^{b_{i,6}})$.
  - Publishes the master public key mpk $= (\mathsf{pp}, [\![\boldsymbol{b}_1]\!]_1, [\![\boldsymbol{b}_2]\!]_1, [\![\boldsymbol{b}_3]\!]_1, [\![\boldsymbol{b}_4]\!]_1)$ and keeps the master secret key msk secret to itself.
- KeyGen(mpk, msk, $\boldsymbol{y}, I_y$) $\to$ sk_y: The trusted authority takes as input the master secret key msk $= (\boldsymbol{b}_1^*, \boldsymbol{b}_2^*, \boldsymbol{b}_3^*, \boldsymbol{b}_4^*)$, master public key mpk $= (\mathsf{pp}, [\![\boldsymbol{b}_1]\!]_1, [\![\boldsymbol{b}_2]\!]_1, [\![\boldsymbol{b}_3]\!]_1, [\![\boldsymbol{b}_4]\!]_1)$ with pp $= (p, g_1, g_2, g_T, V, V^*, E)$ and input vector $\boldsymbol{y} = (y_i)_{i \in I_y} \in \mathbb{Z}^{|I_y|}$ with a non-empty index set $I_y \subseteq [s]$ where $s = s(\lambda)$ is any polynomial. This algorithm performs as follows:
  - Selects $\omega \overset{\mathsf{U}}{\leftarrow} \mathbb{Z}_p$, chooses uniformly $\rho_i, r_i \overset{\mathsf{U}}{\leftarrow} \mathbb{Z}_p$ with $\sum_{i \in I_y} r_i = 1$ for all $i \in I_y$ and defines

$$\boldsymbol{k}_i = (\rho_i(-i, 1), \omega y_i, r_i, 0, 0)\mathbf{B}^* \in \mathbb{Z}_p^6$$

  where $\mathbf{B}^* \in \mathsf{GL}_6(\mathbb{Z}_p)$ has $\boldsymbol{b}_i^*$ as its i-th row.
  - Outputs secret key corresponding to the vector $\boldsymbol{y}$ as $\mathsf{sk}_y = (\boldsymbol{y}, I_y, ([\![\boldsymbol{k}_i]\!]_2)_{i \in I_y})$.
- Enc(mpk, $\boldsymbol{x}, M$) $\to$ ct_x: The algorithm is run by an encryptor with input the master public key mpk $= (\mathsf{pp}, [\![\boldsymbol{b}_1]\!]_1, [\![\boldsymbol{b}_2]\!]_1, [\![\boldsymbol{b}_3]\!]_1, [\![\boldsymbol{b}_4]\!]_1)$ with pp $= (p, g_1, g_2, g_T, V, V^*, E)$ and a vector $\boldsymbol{x} = (x_i)_{i \in I_x} \in \mathbb{Z}^{|I_x|}$ with a non-empty index set $I_x \subseteq [m]$ where $m = m(\lambda)$ is any polynomial and a message $M \in G_T$. It executes the following steps:

– Chooses $\delta, z \xleftarrow{U} \mathbb{Z}_p$, $\pi_i \xleftarrow{U} \mathbb{Z}_p$ for all $i \in I_x$ and computes

$$[\![c_i]\!]_1 = [\![(\pi_i(1,i), \delta x_i, z, 0, 0)\mathbf{B}]\!]_1$$

where $\mathbf{B} \in \mathsf{GL}_6(\mathbb{Z}_p)$ has $\boldsymbol{b}_i$ as its i-th row. Observe that $[\![\boldsymbol{b}_1]\!]_1, [\![\boldsymbol{b}_2]\!]_1$, $[\![\boldsymbol{b}_3]\!]_1, [\![\boldsymbol{b}_4]\!]_1$ are sufficient to compute $[\![c_i]\!]_1$ as $[\![(\pi_i(1,i), \delta x_i, z, 0, 0)\mathbf{B}]\!]_1 = [\![\pi_i \cdot \boldsymbol{b}_1]\!]_1 + [\![i\pi_i \cdot \boldsymbol{b}_2]\!]_1 + [\![\delta x_i \cdot \boldsymbol{b}_3]\!]_1 + [\![z \cdot \boldsymbol{b}_4]\!]_1$ and $[\![\mu \cdot \boldsymbol{b}_i]\!]_1 = \left((g_1^{b_{i,1}})^\mu, (g_1^{b_{i,2,}})^\mu, \ldots, (g_1^{b_{i,6}})^\mu \right)$ using $[\![\boldsymbol{b}_i]\!]_1$ for $i = 1, 2, 3, 4$.

– Computes $c = (g_T)^z \cdot M$.

– Outputs the ciphertext as $\mathsf{ct}_x = (x, ([\![c_i]\!]_1)_{i \in I_x}, c = (g_T)^z \cdot M)$.

• $\mathsf{Dec}(\mathsf{mpk}, \mathsf{sk}_y, \mathsf{ct}_x) \to \alpha$ or $\perp$: The decryptor takes as input the master public key mpk, a ciphertext ct_x for the associated vector x with a non-empty index set $I_x \subseteq [m]$ over $\mathbb{Z}$ and a secret key sk_y corresponding to the vector y with index set $I_y \subseteq [s]$. If $\langle x, y \rangle = 0$ with $I_y \subseteq I_x$ then decryption proceeds by returning $\alpha = c/h$ where $h = \prod_{i \in I_y} E\left([\![c_i]\!]_1, [\![k_i]\!]_2 \right)$. Otherwise, the decryptor returns $\perp$.

Correctness: For our above $\mathsf{UZIPE} = (\mathsf{Setup}, \mathsf{KeyGen}, \mathsf{Enc}, \mathsf{Dec})$ scheme, let the master public key, the master secret key pair be $(\mathsf{mpk}, \mathsf{msk}) \leftarrow \mathsf{UZIPE}.\mathsf{Setup}(1^\lambda)$, the ciphertext be $\mathsf{ct}_x = (x, ([\![c_i]\!]_1)_{i \in I_x}, c = (g_T)^z \cdot M) \leftarrow \mathsf{UZIPE}.\mathsf{Enc}(\mathsf{mpk}, x, M)$ for a vector $x = (x_i)_{i \in [I_x]} \in \mathbb{Z}^{|I_x|}$ encrypting the message M and the secret key be $\mathsf{sk}_y = (y, I_y, ([\![k_i]\!]_2)_{i \in I_y}) \leftarrow \mathsf{UZIPE}.\mathsf{KeyGen}(\mathsf{mpk}, \mathsf{msk}, y, I_y)$ corresponding to a vector $y = (y_i)_{i \in I_y} \in \mathbb{Z}^{|I_y|}$. Then decryption succeeds if $I_y \subseteq I_x$, $\langle x, y \rangle = 0$ as

$$h = \prod_{i \in I_y} E\left([\![c_i]\!]_1, [\![k_i]\!]_2 \right) = e(g_1, g_2)^{\omega\delta \sum_{i \in I_y} x_i y_i + z r_i} = e(g_1, g_2)^{\omega\delta\langle x, y \rangle + z} = (g_T)^z$$

Then compute $c/h = (g_T)^z \cdot M/(g_T)^z = M$.

3.1 Security

Theorem 1. *Assuming the hardness of the SXDH problem, our proposed unbounded zero inner product encryption scheme* $\mathsf{UZIPE} = (\mathsf{Setup}, \mathsf{KeyGen}, \mathsf{Enc}, \mathsf{Dec})$ *is adaptively fully attribute-hiding (FAH) under chosen plaintext attack as per the security model described in Definition 3. More precisely, if there exists a PPT adversary $\mathcal{A}$ that breaks the adaptively FAH security of our proposed* UZIPE *then we can construct a probabilistic machine $\mathcal{B}$ against the SXDH problem such that for any security parameter λ, the advantage*

$$\mathsf{Adv}_{\mathcal{A},\mathsf{FAH}}^{\mathsf{UZIPE}}(\lambda) \leq (5\nu + 3) \cdot \mathsf{Adv}_{\mathcal{B}}^{\mathsf{SXDH}}(\lambda) + (2\nu + 3) \cdot \frac{1}{p} + 2^{-\Omega(\lambda)}$$

where ν is the maximum number of secret key queries.

Proof. Suppose $\mathcal{A}$ be a PPT adversary against the adaptively FAH security of our UZIPE scheme. We construct an algorithm $\mathcal{B}$ for breaking the SXDH assumption that uses $\mathcal{A}$ as subroutine. The proof begins with the real Game 0 and ends with the game where the adversary has advantage zero. Let T_i be the event that $\mathcal{A}$ wins in Game i.

Game 0: In this game, $\mathcal{B}$ plays the role of a challenger for the adaptively FAH security game defined in Definition 3.

– **Setup:** In the first stage, $\mathcal{B}$ generates a master public key, master secret key pair where $\mathsf{mpk} = (\mathsf{pp} = (p, g_1, g_2, g_T, V, V^*, E), [\![b_1]\!]_1, [\![b_2]\!]_1, [\![b_3]\!]_1, [\![b_4]\!]_1)$, $\mathsf{msk} = (b_1^*, b_2^*, b_3^*, b_4^*)$ and sends mpk to $\mathcal{A}$.
– **Key query phase I:** The adversary $\mathcal{A}$ makes a polynomial number of key queries for vectors $\boldsymbol{y} = (y_i)_{i \in I_y}$. The challenger $\mathcal{B}$ in turn computes the corresponding secret key $\mathsf{sk}_{\boldsymbol{y}} = (\boldsymbol{y}, I_{\boldsymbol{y}}, ([\![k_i]\!]_2)_{i \in I_y})$ where

$$k_i = (\rho_i(-i, 1), \omega y_i, r_i, 0, 0)\,\mathbf{B}^* \quad \forall i \in I_y$$

with $\rho_i, \omega, r_i \xleftarrow{\mathsf{U}} \mathbb{Z}_p$ and $\sum_{i \in I_y} r_i = 1$. It returns $\mathsf{sk}_{\boldsymbol{y}}$ to $\mathcal{A}$.
– **Challenge query:** The adversary $\mathcal{A}$ submits challenge messages $M^{(0)}, M^{(1)}$ and challenge vectors $\boldsymbol{x}^{(0)} = (x_i^{(0)})_{i \in I_{x^{(0)}}}$, $\boldsymbol{x}^{(1)} = (x_i^{(1)})_{i \in I_{x^{(1)}}}$ with $I_{x^{(0)}} = I_{x^{(1)}} = I_x$ (say) to $\mathcal{B}$ with the following restrictions:
  • The j-th key query associated to the vector $\boldsymbol{y}^{(j)} = (y_i^{(j)})_{i \in I_{y^{(j)}}}$ in the key query phase must satisfy $\langle \boldsymbol{y}^{(j)}, \boldsymbol{x}^{(0)} \rangle \neq 0$ and $\langle \boldsymbol{y}^{(j)}, \boldsymbol{x}^{(1)} \rangle \neq 0 \; \forall j$.
  • If $M^{(0)} = M^{(1)}$ then the j-th key query associated with the vector $\boldsymbol{y}^{(j)}$ must satisfy $\langle \boldsymbol{y}^{(j)}, \boldsymbol{x}^{(0)} \rangle = \langle \boldsymbol{y}^{(j)}, \boldsymbol{x}^{(1)} \rangle = 0$.

Then $\mathcal{B}$ chooses a random bit $b \xleftarrow{\mathsf{U}} \{0, 1\}$ and computes the challenge ciphertext $\mathsf{ct}_{x^{(b)}} = (\boldsymbol{x}^{(b)}, ([\![c_i]\!]_1)_{i \in I_x}, c) \leftarrow \mathsf{UZIPE.Enc}(\mathsf{mpk}, \boldsymbol{x}^{(b)}, M^{(b)})$ where

$$[\![c_i]\!]_1 = [\![(\pi_i(1, i), \delta x_i^{(b)}, z, 0, 0)\mathbf{B}]\!]_1 \; \forall i \in I_x, \quad c = (g_T)^z \cdot M^{(b)}$$

with $z, \delta \xleftarrow{\mathsf{U}} \mathbb{Z}_p$ and $\pi_i \xleftarrow{\mathsf{U}} \mathbb{Z}_p$ for all $i \in I_x$.
– **Key query phase II:** Key query phase I is repeated with the aforementioned restrictions stated in the challenge query phase.
– **Guess:** Finally, $\mathcal{A}$ outputs a guess bit b'. If $b = b'$, $\mathcal{B}$ outputs $\beta = 1$. A variable ι is defined as $\iota = 0$ if $M^{(0)} \neq M^{(1)}$ for challenge messages $M^{(0)}$ and $M^{(1)}$ and $\iota = 1$ otherwise.

Game 0′: Game 0′ is the same as Game 0 except that $\mathcal{B}$ chooses a bit $t \xleftarrow{\mathsf{U}} \{0, 1\}$ before the setup and the Game 0′ will abort in the challenge query if $t \neq \iota$. The adversary $\mathcal{A}$ will win with probability $\frac{1}{2}$ when the game is aborted and so the advantage of $\mathcal{A}$ in Game 0′ is $|\Pr[T_{0'}] - \frac{1}{2}|$. Therefore, $\mathcal{A}$'s advantage in Game 0′ is half that of Game 0, i.e.,

$$\mathsf{Adv}_{\mathcal{A},\mathsf{Game\ 0'}}^{\mathsf{UZIPE}}(\lambda) = \frac{1}{2} \cdot \mathsf{Adv}_{\mathcal{A},\mathsf{Game\ 0}}^{\mathsf{UZIPE}}(\lambda) = \frac{1}{2} \cdot \mathsf{Adv}_{\mathcal{A},\mathsf{FAH}}^{\mathsf{UZIPE}}(\lambda)$$

Moreover, $\Pr[t = 0] = \frac{1}{2} = \Pr[t = 1]$ as t is uniformly and independently generated

$$\Pr[T_{0'}] = \frac{1}{2} \cdot (\Pr[T_{0'}|t = 0] + \Pr[T_{0'}|t = 1])$$

So, $\mathsf{Adv}_{\mathcal{A},\mathsf{FAH}}^{\mathsf{UZIPE}}(\lambda) = 2\left|\Pr[T_{0'}] - \frac{1}{2}\right| \le \left|\Pr[T_{0'}|t = 0] - \frac{1}{2}\right| + \left|\Pr[T_{0'}|t = 1] - \frac{1}{2}\right|$

The result follows by combining the Lemma 1 and Lemma 2 respectively.

Lemma 1. *Let $T_{0'}$ be the event that a PPT adversary $\mathcal{A}$ wins in Game $0'$ and $t \xleftarrow{U} \{0,1\}$ be the pre-selected random bit chosen by the challenger $\mathcal{B}$ in Game $0'$. Then*

$$\left|\Pr[T_{0'}|t = 0] - \frac{1}{2}\right| \le (2\nu + 2) \cdot \mathsf{Adv}_{\mathcal{B}}^{\mathsf{SXDH}}(\lambda) + \frac{1}{p} + 2^{-\Omega(\lambda)}$$

where ν is the maximum number of secret key queries.

Proof. To prove Lemma 1, we consider $(2\nu + 4)$ many games for $t = 0$ and use notation $\widetilde{\text{Game } i}$ to denote the i-th game which we describe $\widetilde{\text{Game } 0'}$ the same as Game $0'$ in the proof of the Theorem 3.1 where a part framed by a box indicates coefficient which were changed in an experiment from the previous game.

$\widetilde{\text{Game } 0'}$: The game is the same as Game 0 except that a coin $t \xleftarrow{U} \{0,1\}$ is flipped before the setup and the game is aborted in challenge query if $t \ne \iota$. To prove this Lemma, we consider $t = 0$. The challenge ciphertext for the challenge plaintext messages $M^{(0)}, M^{(1)}$ with the vector $\boldsymbol{x}^{(0)} = (x_i^{(0)})_{i \in I_x}, \boldsymbol{x}^{(1)} = (x_i^{(1)})_{i \in I_x}$ is set by $\mathcal{B}$ as $\mathsf{ct}_{\boldsymbol{x}^{(b)}} = (\boldsymbol{x}^{(b)}, (\llbracket c_i \rrbracket_1)_{i \in I_x}, c)$ where $b \xleftarrow{U} \{0,1\}$, $I_x = I_{\boldsymbol{x}^{(0)}} = I_{\boldsymbol{x}^{(1)}}$ and

$$\llbracket c_i \rrbracket_1 = \llbracket (\pi_i(1,i), \delta x_i^{(b)}, z, 0, 0)\mathbf{B} \rrbracket_1 \ \forall i \in I_x, \ c = (g_T)^z \cdot M^{(b)}$$

with $z, \delta, \pi_i \xleftarrow{U} \mathbb{Z}_p$. This ciphertext is called a *normal ciphertext*. In response to the ℓ-th secret key query associated to the vector $\boldsymbol{y}^{(\ell)} = (y_i^{(\ell)})_{i \in I_{\boldsymbol{y}^{(\ell)}}}$ by $\mathcal{A}$, the challenger $\mathcal{B}$ sends $\mathsf{sk}_{\boldsymbol{y}^{(\ell)}} = (\boldsymbol{y}^{(\ell)}, I_{\boldsymbol{y}^{(\ell)}}, \{\llbracket k_i \rrbracket_2\}_{i \in I_{\boldsymbol{y}^{(\ell)}}})$ where

$$\llbracket k_i \rrbracket_2 = \llbracket (\rho_i(-i,1), \omega y_i^{(\ell)}, r_i^{(\ell)}, 0, 0)\mathbf{B}^* \rrbracket_2 \quad \forall i \in I_{\boldsymbol{y}^{(\ell)}}$$

with $\rho_i, \omega, r_i^{(\ell)} \xleftarrow{U} \mathbb{Z}_p$ and $\sum_{i \in I_{\boldsymbol{y}^{(\ell)}}} r_i^{(\ell)} = 1$. This is called a *normal key*.

$\widetilde{\text{Game } 1}$: Same as $\widetilde{\text{Game } 0'}$ except that the challenge ciphertext is

$$\llbracket c_i \rrbracket_1 = \llbracket (\pi_i(1,i), \delta x_i^{(b)}, z, \boxed{\tau x_i^{(b)}}, 0)\mathbf{B} \rrbracket_1 \ \forall i \in I_x, \ c = (g_T)^z \cdot M^{(b)}$$

where $b \xleftarrow{\mathsf{U}} \{0,1\}, \tau \xleftarrow{\mathsf{U}} \mathbb{Z}_p$. All other variables are generated as in $\widetilde{\text{Game } 0'}$.

Game (2-ℓ-1): For $\ell \in [\nu]$, $\widetilde{\text{Game } (2\text{-}\ell\text{-1})}$ is identical as $\widetilde{\text{Game } (2\text{-}(\ell-1)\text{-2})}$ (see the subsequent game) except that the reply of $\mathcal{B}$ to the ℓ-th secret key query for the vector $\boldsymbol{y}^{(\ell)} = (y_i^{(\ell)})_{i \in I_{\boldsymbol{y}}(\ell)}$ is $\mathsf{sk}_{\boldsymbol{y}^{(\ell)}} = (\boldsymbol{y}^{(\ell)}, I_{\boldsymbol{y}^{(\ell)}}, \{[\![\boldsymbol{k}_i]\!]_2\}_{i \in I_{\boldsymbol{y}}(\ell)})$ where

$$[\![\boldsymbol{k}_i]\!]_2 = [\![(\rho_i(-i,1), \omega y_i^{(\ell)}, r_i^{(\ell)}, \boxed{\xi y_i^{(\ell)}}, 0)\mathbf{B}^*]\!]_2 \quad \forall i \in I_{\boldsymbol{y}^{(\ell)}}$$

and $\xi \xleftarrow{\mathsf{U}} \mathbb{Z}_p$. All the other variables $\rho_i, \omega, r_i^{(\ell)}$ are generated by $\mathcal{B}$ as in $\widetilde{\text{Game } (2\text{-}(\ell-1)\text{-2})}$. Note that as mentioned earlier $\widetilde{\text{Game } (2\text{-}0\text{-2})}$ is defined to be $\widetilde{\text{Game } 1}$.

Game (2-ℓ-2): For $\ell \in [\nu]$, $\widetilde{\text{Game } (2\text{-}\ell\text{-2})}$ is the same as $\widetilde{\text{Game } (2\text{-}\ell\text{-1})}$ (defined above) except that reply to $\mathcal{B}$ the ℓ-th secret key query for the associated vector $\boldsymbol{y}^{(\ell)} = (y_i^{(\ell)})_{i \in I_{\boldsymbol{y}}(\ell)}$ is $\mathsf{sk}_{\boldsymbol{y}^{(\ell)}} = (\boldsymbol{y}^{(\ell)}, I_{\boldsymbol{y}^{(\ell)}}, \{[\![\boldsymbol{k}_i]\!]_2\}_{i \in I_{\boldsymbol{y}}(\ell)})$ where

$$[\![\boldsymbol{k}_i]\!]_2 = [\![(\rho_i(-i,1), \omega y_i^{(\ell)}, \boxed{\hat{r}_i^{(\ell)}}, \boxed{r_i'}, 0)\mathbf{B}^*]\!]_2 \quad \forall i \in I_{\boldsymbol{y}^{(\ell)}}$$

$\hat{r}_i^{(\ell)}, r_i' \xleftarrow{\mathsf{U}} \mathbb{Z}_p \ \forall i \in I_{\boldsymbol{y}^{(\ell)}}$. Other variables ρ_i, ω are generated as in $\widetilde{\text{Game}(2\text{-}\ell\text{-1})}$.

Game 3: Same as $\widetilde{\text{Game } (2\text{-}\nu\text{-2})}$ except that the challenge ciphertext is

$$[\![\boldsymbol{c}_i]\!]_1 = [\![(\pi_i(1,i), \delta x_i^{(b)}, \boxed{z'}, \boxed{\mu_i}, 0)\mathbf{B}]\!]_1 \ \forall i \in I_{\boldsymbol{x}} \quad \text{and} \quad c = (g_T)^z \cdot M^{(b)}$$

where $b \xleftarrow{\mathsf{U}} \{0,1\}, z' \xleftarrow{\mathsf{U}} \mathbb{Z}_p$ and $\mu_i \xleftarrow{\mathsf{U}} \mathbb{Z}_p$ for all $i \in I_{\boldsymbol{x}}$. Other variables are generated as in $\widetilde{\text{Game } (2\text{-}\nu\text{-2})}$. This ciphertext is called a *semi randomized ciphertext*.

Game 4: This game is exactly the same as $\widetilde{\text{Game } 3}$ except that the challenge ciphertext set by $\mathcal{B}$ is $\mathsf{ct}_{\boldsymbol{x}^{(b)}} = (\boldsymbol{x}^{(b)}, ([\![\boldsymbol{c}_i]\!]_1)_{i \in I_{\boldsymbol{x}}}, c)$ where

$$[\![\boldsymbol{c}_i]\!]_1 = [\![(\pi_i(1,i), \boxed{0}, z', \mu_i, 0)\mathbf{B}]\!]_1 \ \forall i \in I_{\boldsymbol{x}} \quad \text{and} \quad c = (g_T)^z \cdot M^{(b)}$$

where all the other variables are generated as in $\widetilde{\text{Game } 3}$. This ciphertext is independent from the bit b. This is called a *randomized ciphertext*.

Let S_i be the event that $\mathcal{A}$ wins in $\widetilde{\text{Game } i}$ given $t = 0$. Then $\mathsf{Adv}^{\mathsf{UZIPE}}_{\mathcal{A}, \widetilde{\text{Game } i}}(\lambda) = |\Pr[S_i] - \frac{1}{2}|$. We get $\mathsf{Adv}^{\mathsf{UZIPE}}_{\mathcal{A}, \widetilde{\text{Game } 4}}(\lambda) = 0$ which implies $\Pr[S_4] = \frac{1}{2}$ as the value of b is independent from $\mathcal{A}$'s view in $\widetilde{\text{Game } 4}$. Note that,

$$\left| \Pr[T_{0'}|t=0] - \frac{1}{2} \right| = \mathsf{Adv}^{\mathsf{UZIPE}}_{\mathcal{A},\widetilde{\mathsf{Game}\ 0'}}(\lambda) = \left| \Pr[S_{0'}] - \frac{1}{2} \right| = |\Pr[S_{0'}] - \Pr[S_4]|$$

$$\leq \left| \mathsf{Adv}^{\mathsf{UZIPE}}_{\mathcal{A},\widetilde{\mathsf{Game}\ 0'}}(\lambda) - \mathsf{Adv}^{\mathsf{UZIPE}}_{\mathcal{A},\widetilde{\mathsf{Game}\ 1}}(\lambda) \right| + \sum_{\ell=1}^{\nu} \left| \mathsf{Adv}^{\mathsf{UZIPE}}_{\mathcal{A},\widetilde{\mathsf{Game}\ (2\text{-}(\ell-1)\text{-}2)}}(\lambda) - \mathsf{Adv}^{\mathsf{UZIPE}}_{\mathcal{A},\widetilde{\mathsf{Game}\ (2\text{-}\ell\text{-}1)}}(\lambda) \right|$$

$$+ \sum_{\ell=1}^{\nu} \left| \mathsf{Adv}^{\mathsf{UZIPE}}_{\mathcal{A},\widetilde{\mathsf{Game}\ (2\text{-}\ell\text{-}1)}}(\lambda) - \mathsf{Adv}^{\mathsf{UZIPE}}_{\mathcal{A},\widetilde{\mathsf{Game}\ (2\text{-}\ell\text{-}2)}}(\lambda) \right| + \left| \mathsf{Adv}^{\mathsf{UZIPE}}_{\mathcal{A},\widetilde{\mathsf{Game}\ (2\text{-}\nu\text{-}2)}}(\lambda) - \mathsf{Adv}^{\mathsf{UZIPE}}_{\mathcal{A},\widetilde{\mathsf{Game}\ 3}}(\lambda) \right|$$

$$+ \left| \mathsf{Adv}^{\mathsf{UZIPE}}_{\mathcal{A},\widetilde{\mathsf{Game}\ 3}}(\lambda) - \mathsf{Adv}^{\mathsf{UZIPE}}_{\mathcal{A},\widetilde{\mathsf{Game}\ 4}}(\lambda) \right| + \mathsf{Adv}^{\mathsf{UZIPE}}_{\mathcal{A},\widetilde{\mathsf{Game}\ 4}}(\lambda)$$

Then the result follows from the claim 1 to 5. □

Claim 1: $\left| \mathsf{Adv}^{\mathsf{UZIPE}}_{\mathcal{A},\widetilde{\mathsf{Game}\ 0'}}(\lambda) - \mathsf{Adv}^{\mathsf{UZIPE}}_{\mathcal{A},\widetilde{\mathsf{Game}\ 1}}(\lambda) \right| \leq \mathsf{Adv}^{\mathsf{SXDH}}_{\mathcal{B}}(\lambda) + 2^{-\Omega(\lambda)}$

Proof of Claim 1. We will show the challenger $\mathcal{B}$ can solve the SXDH problem using $\mathcal{A}$ as a subroutine. Let $\mathcal{B}$ obtains an instance $(\mathbb{BG} = (p, G_1, G_2, G_T, g_1, g_2, e), \llbracket a \rrbracket_1 = g_1^a, \llbracket u \rrbracket_1 = g_1^u, \llbracket t_\beta \rrbracket_1 = \llbracket au + \beta f \rrbracket_1 = g_1^{au+\beta f})$ of SXDH problem for $\kappa = 1$ where $a, u, f \xleftarrow{\mathsf{U}} \mathbb{Z}_p, \beta \xleftarrow{\mathsf{U}} \{0,1\}$ and sets $\mathsf{pp} = (p, g_1, g_2, g_T, V, V^*, E)$ as in Game 0 in the proof of Theorem 3.1. Now we will show how $\mathcal{B}$ uses this instances to interpolates between $\widetilde{\mathsf{Game}\ 0'}$ and $\widetilde{\mathsf{Game}\ 1}$. The algorithm $\mathcal{B}$ implicitly defines random orthonormal dual $(\mathbf{B}, \mathbf{B}^*)$ by choosing $\mathbf{D} \xleftarrow{\mathsf{U}} \mathsf{GL}_6(\mathbb{Z}_p)$ and implicitly sets

$$\mathbf{B} = \begin{bmatrix} I_2 & & & \\ & a\ 0\ 1 & \\ & 0\ 1\ 0 & \\ & 1\ 0\ 0 & \\ & & & 1 \end{bmatrix} \mathbf{D}, \quad \mathbf{B}^* = \begin{bmatrix} I_2 & & & \\ & 0\ 0\ 1 & \\ & 0\ 1\ 0 & \\ & 1\ 0\ -a & \\ & & & 1 \end{bmatrix} \mathbf{D}^*$$

where $\mathbf{D}^* = (\mathbf{D}^{-1})^T$ and a is implicitly provided through the SXDH instance. Note that $\llbracket a \rrbracket_1 = g_1^a$ and the algorithm $\mathcal{B}$ can compute $\llbracket \mathbf{B} \rrbracket_1$ using the given SXDH instances and the first four rows of $\llbracket \mathbf{B}^* \rrbracket_2$. Then $\mathcal{B}$ chooses $\eta \xleftarrow{\mathsf{U}} \mathbb{Z}_p$. To simulates the ℓ-th secret key query for $\boldsymbol{y}^{(\ell)} = (y_i^{(\ell)})_{i \in I_{\boldsymbol{y}^{(\ell)}}}$ it responds with the secret key $\mathsf{sk}_{\boldsymbol{y}^{(\ell)}} = (\boldsymbol{y}^{(\ell)}, I_{\boldsymbol{y}^{(\ell)}}, \{\llbracket \boldsymbol{k}_i \rrbracket_2\}_{i \in I_{\boldsymbol{y}^{(\ell)}}})$ where

$$\llbracket \boldsymbol{k}_i \rrbracket_2 = \llbracket (\rho_i(-i, 1), 0, r_i^{(\ell)}, 0, 0)\mathbf{B}^* + y_i^{(\ell)}(0, 0, 0, 0, \eta, 0)\mathbf{D}^* \rrbracket_2$$
$$= \llbracket (\rho_i(-i, 1), \eta y_i^{(\ell)}, r_i^{(\ell)}, 0, 0)\mathbf{B}^* \rrbracket_2 \quad \text{for all } i \in I_{\boldsymbol{y}^{(\ell)}}$$

and $\rho_i, r_i^{(\ell)} \xleftarrow{\mathsf{U}} \mathbb{Z}_p$. Note that, first four rows of $\llbracket \mathbf{B}^* \rrbracket_2$ are utilized by $\mathcal{B}$ to compute $\llbracket \boldsymbol{k}_i \rrbracket_2$ apart from $\mathbf{D}^*$. The challenge ciphertext generated by $\mathcal{B}$ is $\mathsf{ct}_{\boldsymbol{x}^{(b)}} = (\boldsymbol{x}^{(b)}, (\llbracket \boldsymbol{c}_i \rrbracket_1)_{i \in I_{\boldsymbol{x}}}, c)$ where

$$\llbracket \boldsymbol{c}_i \rrbracket_1 = \llbracket (\pi_i(1, i), \delta' x_i^{(b)}, z, 0, 0)\mathbf{B} + x_i^{(b)}(0, 0, t_\beta, 0, u, 0)\mathbf{D} \rrbracket_1$$
$$= \llbracket (\pi_i(1, i), (\delta' + u)x_i^{(b)}, z, \beta f x_i^{(b)}, 0)\mathbf{B} \rrbracket_1 \quad \text{for all } i \in I_{\boldsymbol{x}}$$

where $b \xleftarrow{\mathsf{U}} \{0,1\}$, $\boldsymbol{x}^{(b)} = (x_i^{(b)})_{i \in I_{\boldsymbol{x}^{(b)}}}$, $I_{\boldsymbol{x}^{(0)}} = I_{\boldsymbol{x}^{(1)}} = I_{\boldsymbol{x}}$ and $\delta', z \xleftarrow{\mathsf{U}} \mathbb{Z}_p$, $\pi_i \xleftarrow{\mathsf{U}} \mathbb{Z}_p$ for all $i \in I_{\boldsymbol{x}}$. Here the knowledge of $[\![\boldsymbol{b}_1]\!]_1, [\![\boldsymbol{b}_2]\!]_1, [\![\boldsymbol{b}_3]\!]_1, [\![\boldsymbol{b}_4]\!]_1$ is sufficient to compute $[\![(\pi_i(1, i), \delta' x_i^{(b)}, z, 0, 0)\mathbf{B}]\!]_1 = [\![\pi_i \cdot \boldsymbol{b}_1]\!]_1 + [\![i\pi_i \cdot \boldsymbol{b}_2]\!]_1 + [\![\delta' x_i^{(b)} \cdot \boldsymbol{b}_3]\!]_1 + [\![z \cdot \boldsymbol{b}_4]\!]_1$. Note that, there is no information about $[\![a]\!]_2$. Hence, $\mathcal{B}$ cannot compute $[\![\boldsymbol{b}_5^*]\!]_2$ where $\boldsymbol{b}_5^*$ is the fifth row of $\mathbf{B}^*$ as $\boldsymbol{b}_5^*$ contains the unknown a. However, the above simulation does not require any knowledge of $[\![a]\!]_2 = g_2^a$ as the fifth component of $\boldsymbol{k}_i$ is set as 0 in both Game $0'$ and Game 1. Let us implicitly set $\tau = \beta f, \delta = \delta' + u, \omega = \eta$. Then $\mathcal{A}$'s view simulated by $\mathcal{B}$ is the same as in Game $0'$ if $\beta = 0$ since the fifth component of $[\![\boldsymbol{c}_i]\!]_1$ is 0 and the challenge ciphertext has the same distribution as in Game $0'$. On the other hand, $\mathcal{A}$'s view simulated by $\mathcal{B}$ is identical as in Game 1 if $\beta = 1$ since the fifth components of $\boldsymbol{c}_i$ is $\beta f x_i^{(b)} = \tau x_i^{(b)}$ unless $f = 0$ and the distribution of challenge ciphertext in Game $0'$ is identical with the distribution of Game 1. Thus, $\mathcal{B}$ interpolates between Game $0'$ and Game 1. Thus the claim follows. $\square$

Claim 2: $\left| \mathsf{Adv}^{\mathsf{UZIPE}}_{\mathcal{A}, \mathrm{Game}\ (2\text{-}(\ell-1)\text{-}2)}(\lambda) - \mathsf{Adv}^{\mathsf{UZIPE}}_{\mathcal{A}, \mathrm{Game}\ (2\text{-}\ell\text{-}1)}(\lambda) \right| \leq \mathsf{Adv}^{\mathsf{SXDH}}_{\mathcal{B}}(\lambda) + 2^{-\Omega(\lambda)}$.

Proof of Claim 2. Let $\mathcal{B}$ obtains an instance $(\mathbb{BG} = (p, G_1, G_2, G_T, g_1, g_2, e), [\![a]\!]_2 = g_2^a, [\![u]\!]_2 = g_2^u, [\![t_\beta]\!]_2 = [\![au + \beta f]\!]_2 = g_2^{au+\beta f})$ of SXDH problem for $\kappa = 2$ where $a, u, f \xleftarrow{\mathsf{U}} \mathbb{Z}_p, \beta \xleftarrow{\mathsf{U}} \{0,1\}$ and sets $\mathsf{pp} = (p, g_1, g_2, g_T, V, V^*, E)$ as in the proof of Theorem 3.1. We will show the challenger $\mathcal{B}$ can utilize the instance to interpolates between Game $(2\text{-}(\ell-1)\text{-}2)$ and Game $(2\text{-}\ell\text{-}1)$ the SXDH assumption using $\mathcal{A}$ as a subroutine. The algorithm $\mathcal{B}$ implicitly defines random orthonormal dual $(\mathbf{B}, \mathbf{B}^*)$ by choosing $\mathbf{D} \xleftarrow{\mathsf{U}} \mathsf{GL}_6(\mathbb{Z}_p)$ and implicitly setting

$$\mathbf{B} = \begin{bmatrix} I_2 & & & \\ & 0\ 0\ 1 & \\ & 0\ 1\ 0 & \\ & 1\ 0\ -a & \\ & & & 1 \end{bmatrix} \mathbf{D}, \quad \mathbf{B}^* = \begin{bmatrix} I_2 & & & \\ & a\ 0\ 1 & \\ & 0\ 1\ 0 & \\ & 1\ 0\ 0 & \\ & & & 1 \end{bmatrix} \mathbf{D}^*$$

where $\mathbf{D}^* = (\mathbf{D}^{-1})^T$ and a is implicitly provided through the SXDH instance. Note that $[\![a]\!]_2 = g_2^a$ and the algorithm $\mathcal{B}$ can compute the first four rows $[\![\boldsymbol{b}_1]\!]_1, [\![\boldsymbol{b}_2]\!]_1, [\![\boldsymbol{b}_3]\!]_1, [\![\boldsymbol{b}_4]\!]_1$ of $[\![\mathbf{B}]\!]_1$ and $[\![\mathbf{B}^*]\!]_2$ using the given SXDH instances. Now, the algorithm $\mathcal{B}$ simulates the ℓ-th secret key query for $\boldsymbol{y}^{(\ell)} = (y_i^{(\ell)})_{i \in I_{\boldsymbol{y}^{(\ell)}}}$ by responding with the secret key $\mathsf{sk}_{\boldsymbol{y}^{(\ell)}} = (\boldsymbol{y}^{(\ell)}, I_{\boldsymbol{y}^{(\ell)}}, \{[\![\boldsymbol{k}_i]\!]_2\}_{i \in I_{\boldsymbol{y}^{(\ell)}}})$ where

$$[\![\boldsymbol{k}_i]\!]_2 = [\![(\rho_i(-i, 1), \omega' y_i^{(\ell)}, r_i^{(\ell)}, \xi y_i^{(\ell)}, 0)\mathbf{B}^* + y_i^{(\ell)}(0, 0, t_\beta, 0, u, 0)\mathbf{D}^*]\!]_2$$
$$= [\![(\rho_i(-i, 1), (\omega' + u)y_i^{(\ell)}, r_i^{(\ell)}, \xi y_i^{(\ell)} + \beta f y_i^{(\ell)}, 0)\mathbf{B}^*]\!]_2 \quad \text{for all } i \in I_{\boldsymbol{y}^{(\ell)}}$$

with $\xi, \omega', \xleftarrow{\mathsf{U}} \mathbb{Z}_p, \rho_i, r_i^{(\ell)} \xleftarrow{\mathsf{U}} \mathbb{Z}_p$ for all $i \in I_{\boldsymbol{y}^{(\ell)}}$ such that $\sum_{i \in I_{\boldsymbol{y}^{(\ell)}}} r_i^{(\ell)} = 1$ and $[\![\boldsymbol{b}_1^*]\!]_2, [\![\boldsymbol{b}_2^*]\!]_2, [\![\boldsymbol{b}_3^*]\!]_2, [\![\boldsymbol{b}_4^*]\!]_2$ are utilized to compute $[\![(\rho_i(-i, 1), \omega' y_i^{(\ell)}, r_i^{(\ell)},$

$\xi y_i^{(\ell)}, 0)\mathbf{B}^*]_2 = [-i\rho_i \cdot \boldsymbol{b}_1^*]_2 + [\rho_i \cdot \boldsymbol{b}_2^*]_2 + [\omega' y_i^{(\ell)} \cdot \boldsymbol{b}_3^*]_2 + [r_i^{(\ell)} \cdot \boldsymbol{b}_4^*]_2 + [\xi y_i^{(\ell)} \cdot \boldsymbol{b}_5^*]$. Then $\mathcal{B}$ chooses $\eta', \zeta \xleftarrow{U} \mathbb{Z}_p$. The challenge ciphertext $\mathsf{ct}_{\boldsymbol{x}^{(b)}} = (\boldsymbol{x}^{(b)}, ([\boldsymbol{c}_i]_1)_{i \in I_x}, c)$ is generated by $\mathcal{B}$ by setting

$$[\boldsymbol{c}_i]_1 = [(\pi_i(1, i), 0, z, 0, 0)\mathbf{B} + x_i^{(b)}(0, 0, \zeta, 0, \eta', 0)\mathbf{D}]_1$$
$$= [(\pi_i(1, i), (a\zeta + \eta')x_i^{(b)}, z, \zeta x_i^{(b)}, 0)\mathbf{B}]_1 \quad \text{for all } i \in I_x$$

where $b \xleftarrow{U} \{0, 1\}, \boldsymbol{x}^{(b)} = (x_i^{(b)})_{i \in I_{x^{(b)}}}, I_{x^{(0)}} = I_{x^{(1)}} = I_x$ and $\delta \xleftarrow{U} \mathbb{Z}_p, \pi_i \xleftarrow{U} \mathbb{Z}_p$ for all $i \in I_x$. Here $[\boldsymbol{b}_1]_1, [\boldsymbol{b}_2]_1, [\boldsymbol{b}_4]_1$ are sufficient to compute $[(\pi_i(1, i), 0, z, 0, 0)\mathbf{B}]_1 = [\pi_i \cdot \boldsymbol{b}_1]_1 + [i\pi_i \cdot \boldsymbol{b}_2]_1 + [z \cdot \boldsymbol{b}_4]_1$. Note that, there is no information about $[a]_1$. Hence, $\mathcal{B}$ can not compute $[\boldsymbol{b}_5]_1$ where $\boldsymbol{b}_5$ is the fifth row of $\mathbf{B}$ as $\boldsymbol{b}_5$ contains the unknown a. However the above without any knowledge of $[a]_1 = g_1^a$. Let us implicitly set $\omega = \omega' + u, \delta = a\zeta + \eta', \tau = \zeta, \hat{r}_i^{(\ell)} = r_i^{(\ell)}$ and $r_i' = \xi y_i^{(\ell)} + f y_i^{(\ell)}$ unless $f = 0$. Then $\mathcal{A}$'s view simulated by $\mathcal{B}$ is same as in Game $(2\text{-}(\ell-1)\text{-}2)$ if $\beta = 0$ since the fourth, fifth component of $\boldsymbol{k}_i$ are $r_i^{(\ell)}$ and zero respectively and the secret key has same distribution as in Game $(2\text{-}(\ell-1)\text{-}2)$. On the other hand, $\mathcal{A}$'s view simulated by $\mathcal{B}$ is identical as in Game $(2\text{-}\ell\text{-}1)$ if $\beta = 1$ since the forth, fifth component of $\boldsymbol{k}_i$ are $\hat{r}_i = r_i^{(\ell)}$ and $r_i' = \xi y_i^{(\ell)} + f y_i^{(\ell)}$ respectively and the distribution of the secret key in Game $(2\text{-}(\ell-1)\text{-}2)$ is identical with the distribution of Game $(2\text{-}\ell\text{-}1)$. Thus $\mathcal{B}$ interpolates between the Game $(2\text{-}(\ell-1)\text{-}2)$ and Game $(2\text{-}\ell\text{-}1)$. Thus the claim follows. $\square$

Claim 3: $\left| \mathsf{Adv}_{\mathcal{A}, \text{Game } (2\text{-}\ell\text{-}1)}^{\mathsf{UZIPE}}(\lambda) - \mathsf{Adv}_{\mathcal{A}, \text{Game } (2\text{-}\ell\text{-}2)}^{\mathsf{UZIPE}}(\lambda) \right| \leq \mathsf{Adv}_{\mathcal{B}}^{\mathsf{SXDH}}(\lambda)$

Proof of Claim 3. We will show how the challenger $\mathcal{B}$ utilizes the SXDH instance using $\mathcal{A}$ as a subroutine to interpolates between Game $(2\text{-}\ell\text{-}1)$ and Game $(2\text{-}\ell\text{-}2)$. Given an SXDH instance $(\mathbb{BG} = (p, G_1, G_2, G_T, g_1, g_2, e), [a]_2 = g_2^a, [u]_2 = g_2^u, [t_\beta]_2 = [au + \beta f]_2 = g_2^{au+\beta f})$ of a SXDH problem for $\kappa = 2$ where $a, u, f \xleftarrow{U} \mathbb{Z}_p, \beta \xleftarrow{U} \{0, 1\}$ and sets $\mathsf{pp} = (p, g_1, g_2, g_T, V, V^*, E)$ as in proof of Theorem 3.1. The algorithm $\mathcal{B}$ implicitly defines random orthonormal dual $(\mathbf{B}, \mathbf{B}^*)$ by choosing $\mathbf{D} \xleftarrow{U} \mathsf{GL}_6(\mathbb{Z}_p)$ and implicitly setting

$$\mathbf{B} = \begin{bmatrix} I_3 & & \\ & 1 & 0 & \\ & a & -1 & \\ & & & 1 \end{bmatrix} \mathbf{D}, \quad \mathbf{B}^* = \begin{bmatrix} I_3 & & \\ & 1 & a & \\ & 0 & -1 & \\ & & & 1 \end{bmatrix} \mathbf{D}^*$$

where $\mathbf{D}^* = (\mathbf{D}^{-1})^T$ and a is implicitly provided through the SXDH instance. Note that $[a]_2 = g_2^a$ and the algorithm $\mathcal{B}$ can compute $[\mathbf{B}^*]_2$ using the given SXDH instances and rows of $[\mathbf{B}]_1$ except fifth row. The algorithm $\mathcal{B}$ the ℓ-th secret key query for $\boldsymbol{y}^{(\ell)} = (y_i^{(\ell)})_{i \in I_{y^{(\ell)}}}$ by responding with the secret key $\mathsf{sk}_{\boldsymbol{y}^{(\ell)}} = (\boldsymbol{y}^{(\ell)}, I_{\boldsymbol{y}^{(\ell)}}, \{[\boldsymbol{k}_i]_2\}_{i \in I_{\boldsymbol{y}^{(\ell)}}})$ where

$$\llbracket k_i \rrbracket_2 = \llbracket (\rho_i(-i,1), \omega y_i^{(\ell)}, r_i^{(\ell)}, \xi y_i^{(\ell)}, 0) \mathbf{B}^* + \tilde{r}_i(0,0,0,u,t_\beta,0) \mathbf{D}^* \rrbracket_2$$
$$= \llbracket (\rho_i(-i,1), \omega y_i^{(\ell)}, r_i^{(\ell)} + u\tilde{r}_i, \xi y_i^{(\ell)} - \beta f \tilde{r}_i, 0) \mathbf{B}^* \rrbracket_2 \text{ for all } i \in I_{y^{(\ell)}}$$

with $\rho_i, r_i^{(\ell)}, \tilde{r}_i \xleftarrow{\mathsf{U}} \mathbb{Z}_p$ for all $i \in I_{y^{(\ell)}}$ and $\omega, \xi \xleftarrow{\mathsf{U}} \mathbb{Z}_p$. Choose $\delta', \tau \xleftarrow{\mathsf{U}} \mathbb{Z}_p$. The challenge ciphertext $\mathsf{ct}_{x^{(b)}} = (x^{(b)}, (\llbracket c_i \rrbracket_1)_{i \in I_x}, c)$ is generated by $\mathcal{B}$ by setting

$$\llbracket c_i \rrbracket_1 = \llbracket (\pi_i(1,i), 0, z, 0, 0) \mathbf{B} + x_i^{(b)}(0,0,\delta',0,\tau,0) \mathbf{D} \rrbracket_1$$
$$= \llbracket (\pi_i(1,i), \delta' x_i^{(b)}, z, -\tau x_i^{(b)}, 0) \mathbf{B} \rrbracket_1 \quad \text{for all } i \in I_x$$

where $b \xleftarrow{\mathsf{U}} \{0,1\}, x^{(b)} = (x_i^{(b)})_{i \in I_{x^{(b)}}}, I_{x^{(0)}} = I_{x^{(1)}} = I_x$. Note that $\mathcal{B}$ does not have the fifth row $\llbracket b_5 \rrbracket_1$ of $\llbracket \mathbf{B} \rrbracket_1$ and compute $\llbracket (\pi_i(1,i), 0, z, 0, 0) \mathbf{B} \rrbracket_1 = \llbracket \pi_i \cdot b_1 \rrbracket_1 + \llbracket i\pi_i \cdot b_2 \rrbracket_1 + \llbracket z \cdot b_4 \rrbracket_1$ without $\llbracket b_5 \rrbracket_1$. Let us implicitly set $\hat{r}_i = r_i^{(\ell)} + u\tilde{r}_i$, $r_i' = \xi y_i^{(\ell)} - \beta f \tilde{r}_i, \delta = \delta'$. Then $\mathcal{A}$'s view simulated by $\mathcal{B}$ is the same as in Game (2-ℓ-1) if $\beta = 0$ since the fifth components of k_i is $\xi y_i^{(\ell)}$ and the ciphertext has the same distribution as in Game (2-ℓ-2). On the other hand, $\mathcal{A}$'s view simulated by $\mathcal{B}$ is identical as in Game (2-ℓ-2) if $\beta = 1$ unless $f = 0$, since the fourth, fifth components of $\llbracket k_i \rrbracket_2$ are $r_i^{(\ell)} + u\tilde{r}_i = \hat{r}_i, \xi y_i^{(\ell)} - \beta f \tilde{r}_i = r_i'$ and the distribution of the ciphertext in Game (2-ℓ-1) is identical with that in of Game (2-ℓ-2). Thus, $\mathcal{B}$ interpolates between the Game (2-ℓ-1) and Game (2-ℓ-2). Thus the claim follows. □

Claim 4: $\left| \mathsf{Adv}_{\mathcal{A}, \mathrm{Game} \ (2-\nu-2)}^{\mathsf{UZIPE}}(\lambda) - \mathsf{Adv}_{\mathcal{A}, \mathrm{Game} \ 3}^{\mathsf{UZIPE}}(\lambda) \right| \leq \frac{1}{p}$

Proof of Claim 4. To prove this, we show that the distribution of $\mathsf{pp} = (p, g_1, g_2, g_T, V, V^*, E)$, queried keys $\mathsf{sk}_{y^{(\nu)}} = (y^{(\nu)}, I_{y^{(\nu)}}, \{\llbracket k_i \rrbracket_2\}_{i \in I_{y^{(\nu)}}})$ and challenge ciphertext $\mathsf{ct}_{x^{(b)}} = (x^{(b)}, (\llbracket c_i \rrbracket_1)_{i \in I_x}, c)$ are equivalent in Game (2-ν-2) and Game 3. For this, we define new orthonormal dual basis $(\mathbf{D}, \mathbf{D}^*)$ of V and V^* as follows: generate $\chi \xleftarrow{\mathsf{U}} \mathbb{Z}_p \setminus \{0\}, \eta \xleftarrow{\mathsf{U}} \mathbb{Z}_p$, set $d_4 = \chi b_4 + \eta b_5, d_5^* = \chi b_5^* - \eta b_4^*$ and define

$$\mathbf{D} = (b_1, b_2, b_3, d_4, \chi^{-1} b_5, b_6), \quad \mathbf{D}^* = (b_1^*, b_2^*, b_3^*, \chi^{-1} b_4^*, d_5^*, b_6^*)$$

where b_i and b_i^* are the i-th rows of $\mathbf{B}$ and $\mathbf{B}^*$ respectively used in Game (2-ν-2) and Game 3. We can easily check that $\mathbf{D}$ and $\mathbf{D}^*$ are dual orthonormal and similarly distributed same as $\mathbf{B}$ and $\mathbf{B}^*$. The secret keys component $\llbracket k_i \rrbracket_2$ of $\mathsf{sk}_{y^{(\nu)}}$ and the challenge ciphertext component $\llbracket c_i \rrbracket_1$ of $\mathsf{ct}_{x^{(b)}}$ in Game (2-ν-2) are expressed over the bases $(\mathbf{B}, \mathbf{B}^*)$ and $(\mathbf{D}, \mathbf{D}^*)$ as

$$\llbracket k_i \rrbracket_2 = \llbracket (\rho_i(-i,1), \omega y_i^{(\nu)}, \hat{r}_i, \tilde{r}_i, 0) \mathbf{B}^* \rrbracket_2$$
$$= \llbracket -i\rho_i \cdot b_1^* + \rho_i \cdot b_2^* + \omega y_i^{(\nu)} \cdot b_3^* + (\chi \hat{r}_i + \eta \tilde{r}_i) \cdot (\chi^{-1} b_4^*) + \tilde{r}_i \chi^{-1} \cdot d_5^* \rrbracket_2$$
$$= \llbracket (\rho_i(-i,1), \omega y_i^{(\nu)}, (\chi \hat{r}_i + \eta \tilde{r}_i), \tilde{r}_i \chi^{-1}, 0) \mathbf{D}^* \rrbracket_2$$
$$\text{and} \quad \llbracket c_i \rrbracket_1 = \llbracket (\pi_i(1,i), \delta x_i^{(b)}, z, \tau x_i^{(b)}, 0) \mathbf{B} \rrbracket_1$$

$$= [\![\pi_i \cdot \boldsymbol{b}_1 + i\pi_i \cdot \boldsymbol{b}_2 + \delta x_i^{(b)} \cdot \boldsymbol{b}_3 + \chi^{-1} z \cdot \boldsymbol{d}_4 + (\tau x_i^{(b)} \chi - z\eta) \cdot \chi^{-1} \boldsymbol{b}_5]\!]_1$$
$$= [\![(\pi_i(1,i), \delta x_i^{(b)}, \chi^{-1} z, (\tau x_i^{(b)} \chi - z\eta), 0) \mathbf{D}]\!]_1$$

Let $z' = \chi^{-1} z$ and $\mu_i = \tau x_i^{(b)} \chi - z\eta$. So the $\mathcal{A}$'s view, both $(\mathbf{B}, \mathbf{B}^*)$ and $(\mathbf{D}, \mathbf{D}^*)$ are consistent with master public key mpk as $\chi, \tau, \eta \xleftarrow{\mathsf{U}} \mathbb{Z}_q$ are uniformly, independently distributed except the probability $\frac{1}{p}$ for the case $z = 0$. Therefore, the distribution of ciphertext, secret keys can be expressed as in $\widetilde{\text{Game}}$ (2-ν-2) over the basis $(\mathbf{B}, \mathbf{B}^*)$ and in $\widetilde{\text{Game}}$ 3 over the bases $(\mathbf{D}, \mathbf{D}^*)$. So, $\widetilde{\text{Game}}$ (2-ν-2) can be conceptually changed in $\widetilde{\text{Game}}$ 3. This establishes the claim. $\qquad\square$

Claim 5: $\left| \mathsf{Adv}^{\mathsf{UZIPE}}_{\mathcal{A}, \widetilde{\text{Game}\ 3}}(\lambda) - \mathsf{Adv}^{\mathsf{UZIPE}}_{\mathcal{A}, \widetilde{\text{Game}\ 4}}(\lambda) \right| \leq \mathsf{Adv}^{\mathsf{SXDH}}_{\mathcal{B}}(\lambda)$

Proof of Claim 5. Given an SXDH instance $(\mathbb{BG} = (p, G_1, G_2, G_T, g_1, g_2, e), [\![a]\!]_1 = g_1^a, [\![u]\!]_1 = g_1^u, [\![t_\beta]\!]_1 = [\![au + \beta f]\!]_1 = g_1^{au+\beta f})$ for $\kappa = 1$ where $a, u, f \xleftarrow{\mathsf{U}} \mathbb{Z}_p, \beta \xleftarrow{\mathsf{U}} \{0, 1\}$, the challenger uses $\mathcal{A}$ as a subroutine interpolates the Game 3 and Game 4. Sets $\mathsf{pp} = (p, g_1, g_2, g_T, V, V^*, E)$ as in the proof of Theorem 3.1. The algorithm $\mathcal{B}$ implicitly defines random orthonormal dual $(\mathbf{B}, \mathbf{B}^*)$ by choosing $\mathbf{D} \xleftarrow{\mathsf{U}} \mathsf{GL}_6(\mathbb{Z}_p)$ and

$$\mathbf{B} = \begin{bmatrix} I_2 & & \\ & \begin{matrix} 0 & 0 & 1 \\ -1 & 1 & a \\ 1 & 0 & -a \end{matrix} & \\ & & 1 \end{bmatrix} \mathbf{D}, \quad \mathbf{B}^* = \begin{bmatrix} I_2 & & \\ & \begin{matrix} a & 0 & 1 \\ 0 & 1 & 0 \\ 1 & 1 & 0 \end{matrix} & \\ & & 1 \end{bmatrix} \mathbf{D}^*$$

where $\mathbf{D}^* = (\mathbf{D}^{-1})^T$ and a is implicitly provided through the SXDH instance. Note that $[\![a]\!]_1 = g_1^a$ The algorithm $\mathcal{B}$ can compute $[\![\mathbf{B}]\!]_1$ using the given SXDH instances all rows of $[\![\mathbf{B}^*]\!]_2$ except the third row. Choose $\zeta, \gamma \xleftarrow{\mathsf{U}} \mathbb{Z}_p$. The algorithm simulates ℓ-th secret key query to $\boldsymbol{y}^{(\ell)} = (y_i)_{i \in I_{\boldsymbol{y}^{(\ell)}}}$ by responding with the secret key $\mathsf{sk}_{\boldsymbol{y}^{(\ell)}} = (\boldsymbol{y}^{(\ell)}, I_{\boldsymbol{y}^{(\ell)}}, \{[\![\boldsymbol{k}_i]\!]_2\}_{i \in I_{\boldsymbol{y}^{(\ell)}}})$ where

$$[\![\boldsymbol{k}_i]\!]_2 = [\![(\rho_i(-i, 1), 0, r_i^{(\ell)}, 0, 0) \mathbf{B}^* + y_i^{(\ell)}(0, 0, 0, \gamma, \zeta, 0) \mathbf{D}^*]\!]_2$$
$$= [\![(\rho_i(-i, 1), \zeta y_i^{(\ell)}, (\gamma - a\zeta) y_i^{(\ell)} + r_i^{(\ell)}, -a\zeta y_i^{(\ell)}, 0) \mathbf{B}^*]\!]_2 \quad \text{for all } i \in I_{\boldsymbol{y}^{(\ell)}}$$

with $\rho_i, r_i^{(\ell)}, \xleftarrow{\mathsf{U}} \mathbb{Z}_p$ for all $i \in I_{\boldsymbol{y}^{(\ell)}}$ and $\omega \xleftarrow{\mathsf{U}} \mathbb{Z}_p$. Observe that, $\boldsymbol{b}_1^*, \boldsymbol{b}_2^*, \boldsymbol{b}_4^*$ are sufficient to compute $[\![(\rho_i(-i, 1), 0, r_i^{(\ell)}, 0, 0) \mathbf{B}^*]\!]_2$ as $[\![(\rho_i(-i, 1), 0, r_i^{(\ell)}, 0, 0) \mathbf{B}^*]\!]_2 = [\![-i\rho_i \cdot \boldsymbol{b}_1^*]\!]_2 + [\![\rho_i \cdot \boldsymbol{b}_2^*]\!]_2 + [\![r_i^{(\ell)} \cdot \boldsymbol{b}_4^*]\!]_2$. To generate challenge ciphertext $\mathsf{ct}_{\boldsymbol{x}^{(b)}} = (\boldsymbol{x}^{(b)}, ([\![c_i]\!]_1)_{i \in I_{\boldsymbol{x}}}, c)$, sets the second component as

$$[\![c_i]\!]_1 = [\![(\pi_i(1, i), 0, z', 0, 0) \mathbf{B} + x_i^{(b)}(0, 0, u, 0, -t_\beta, 0) \mathbf{D}]\!]_1$$
$$= [\![(\pi_i(1, i), -\beta f x_i^{(b)}, z', u x_i^{(b)}, 0) \mathbf{B}]\!]_1$$

where $b \xleftarrow{\mathsf{U}} \{0,1\}, \boldsymbol{x}^{(b)} = (x_i^{(b)})_{i \in I_{\boldsymbol{x}^{(b)}}}, I_{\boldsymbol{x}^{(0)}} = I_{\boldsymbol{x}^{(1)}} = I_{\boldsymbol{x}}$ and $z', \pi_i \xleftarrow{\mathsf{U}}$
$\mathbb{Z}_p$ for all $i \in I_{\boldsymbol{x}}$. Here $[\![\boldsymbol{b}_1]\!]_1, [\![\boldsymbol{b}_2]\!]_1, [\![\boldsymbol{b}_3]\!]_1, [\![\boldsymbol{b}_4]\!]_1$ are sufficient to compute
$[\![(\pi_i(1,i), 0, z', 0, 0) \mathbf{B}]\!]_1 = [\![\pi_i \cdot \boldsymbol{b}_1]\!]_1 + [\![i\pi_i \cdot \boldsymbol{b}_2]\!]_1 + [\![z' \cdot \boldsymbol{b}_4]\!]_1$ As there is no information
about $[\![a]\!]_2$, $\mathcal{B}$ cannot compute $[\![\boldsymbol{b}_3^*]\!]_2$, $\boldsymbol{b}_3^*$ being the third row of $[\![\mathbf{B}^*]\!]_2$ that contains the unknown a. However, the above simulation is done without any knowl-
edge of $[\![a]\!]_2$. Let us implicitly set $\delta = -\beta f, \mu_i = ux_i^{(b)}, \hat{r}_i^{(\ell)} = (\gamma - a\zeta)y_i^{(\ell)} + r_i^{(\ell)}$
and $r_i' = -a\zeta y_i^{(\ell)}$. Then $\mathcal{A}$'s view simulated by $\mathcal{B}$ is the same as in Game 3 if
$\beta = 1$ since the third component of $[\![\boldsymbol{c}_i]\!]_1$ is non-zero in Game 3 unless $f = 0$ and
the challenge ciphertext has the same distribution as in Game 3. On the other
hand, $\mathcal{A}$'s view simulated by $\mathcal{B}$ is identical as in Game 4 if $\beta = 0$ since the third
component of $[\![\boldsymbol{c}_i]\!]_1$ is zero and the distribution of secret key in Game 3 is identical with that in Game 4. Thus $\mathcal{B}$ interpolates between Game 3 and Game 4.
and the result follows. $\qquad\square$

Lemma 2. *Let $T_{0'}$ be the event that a PPT adversary $\mathcal{A}$ wins in Game $0'$ and
$t \xleftarrow{\mathsf{U}} \{0,1\}$ be the pre-selected random bit chosen by the challenger $\mathcal{B}$ in Game
$0'$. Then*

$$\left| \Pr[T_{0'} | t = 1] - \frac{1}{2} \right| \leq (3\nu + 1) \cdot \mathsf{Adv}_{\mathcal{B}}^{\mathsf{SXDH}}(\lambda) + (2\nu + 2) \cdot \frac{1}{p} + 2^{-\Omega(\lambda)}$$

where ν is the maximum number of secret key queries.

We discuss the detailed proof of Lemma 2 in the full version.

4   Conclusion

In this paper, we propose a construction of UZIPE based on the SXDH assumption with adaptively FAH security. Mainly, we improve the efficiency in terms of
computation, communication cost of UZIPE over the previous work of [10]. In
particular, our ciphertext and secret key consist of $6n + 1$ and $6n'$ group elements
respectively. In future, it will be interesting to investigate constructions of ABE
or FE for more expressive functionalities with unbounded attributes or messages.

References

1. Bethencourt, J., Sahai, A., Waters, B.: Ciphertext-policy attribute-based encryption. In: 2007 IEEE symposium on security and privacy (SP 2007), pp. 321–334.
IEEE (2007)
2. Boneh, D., Boyen, X.: Secure identity based encryption without random oracles.
In: Franklin, M. (ed.) CRYPTO 2004. LNCS, vol. 3152, pp. 443–459. Springer,
Heidelberg (2004). https://doi.org/10.1007/978-3-540-28628-8_27
3. Boneh, D., Waters, B.: Conjunctive, subset, and range queries on encrypted data.
In: Vadhan, S.P. (ed.) TCC 2007. LNCS, vol. 4392, pp. 535–554. Springer, Heidelberg (2007). https://doi.org/10.1007/978-3-540-70936-7_29

4. Katz, J., Sahai, A., Waters, B.: Predicate encryption supporting disjunctions, polynomial equations, and inner products. In: Smart, N. (ed.) EUROCRYPT 2008. LNCS, vol. 4965, pp. 146–162. Springer, Heidelberg (2008). https://doi.org/10.1007/978-3-540-78967-3_9

5. Lewko, A., Okamoto, T., Sahai, A., Takashima, K., Waters, B.: Fully secure functional encryption: attribute-based encryption and (hierarchical) inner product encryption. In: Gilbert, H. (ed.) EUROCRYPT 2010. LNCS, vol. 6110, pp. 62–91. Springer, Heidelberg (2010). https://doi.org/10.1007/978-3-642-13190-5_4

6. Lewko, A., Waters, B.: Unbounded hibe and attribute-based encryption. Cryptology ePrint Archive, Report 2011/049 (2011). https://eprint.iacr.org/2011/049

7. Okamoto, T., Takashima, K.: Hierarchical predicate encryption for inner-products. In: Matsui, M. (ed.) ASIACRYPT 2009. LNCS, vol. 5912, pp. 214–231. Springer, Heidelberg (2009). https://doi.org/10.1007/978-3-642-10366-7_13

8. Okamoto, T., Takashima, K.: Fully secure functional encryption with general relations from the decisional linear assumption. In: Rabin, T. (ed.) CRYPTO 2010. LNCS, vol. 6223, pp. 191–208. Springer, Heidelberg (2010). https://doi.org/10.1007/978-3-642-14623-7_11

9. Okamoto, T., Takashima, K.: Adaptively attribute-hiding (hierarchical) inner product encryption. In: Pointcheval, D., Johansson, T. (eds.) EUROCRYPT 2012. LNCS, vol. 7237, pp. 591–608. Springer, Heidelberg (2012). https://doi.org/10.1007/978-3-642-29011-4_35

10. Okamoto, T., Takashima, K.: Fully secure unbounded inner-product and attribute-based encryption. In: Wang, X., Sako, K. (eds.) ASIACRYPT 2012. LNCS, vol. 7658, pp. 349–366. Springer, Heidelberg (2012). https://doi.org/10.1007/978-3-642-34961-4_22

11. Okamoto, T., Takashima, K.: Achieving short ciphertexts or short secret-keys for adaptively secure general inner-product encryption. Des. Codes Cryptogr., 725–771 (2015). https://doi.org/10.1007/s10623-015-0131-1

12. Okamoto, T., Takashima, K.: Dual pairing vector spaces and their applications. IEICE Trans. Fund. Electron. Commun. Comput. Sci. **E98.A**(1), 3–15 (2015). https://doi.org/10.1587/transfun.E98.A.3

13. Ostrovsky, R., Sahai, A., Waters, B.: Attribute-based encryption with non-monotonic access structures. In: Proceedings of the 14th ACM Conference on Computer and Communications Security, pp. 195–203 (2007)

14. Sahai, A., Waters, B.: Fuzzy identity-based encryption. In: Cramer, R. (ed.) EUROCRYPT 2005. LNCS, vol. 3494, pp. 457–473. Springer, Heidelberg (2005). https://doi.org/10.1007/11426639_27

15. Tomida, J., Takashima, K.: Unbounded inner product functional encryption from bilinear maps. In: Peyrin, T., Galbraith, S. (eds.) ASIACRYPT 2018. LNCS, vol. 11273, pp. 609–639. Springer, Cham (2018). https://doi.org/10.1007/978-3-030-03329-3_21

Inner-Product Functional Encryption from Random Linear Codes: Trial and Challenges

Zhuoran Zhang[1,2], Zheng Zhang[1,2], and Fangguo Zhang[1,2(✉)]

[1] School of Computer Science and Engineering, Sun Yat-sen University,
Guangzhou 510006, China
isszhfg@mail.sysu.edu.cn
[2] Guangdong Province Key Laboratory of Information Security Technology,
Guangzhou 510006, China

Abstract. Inner-product encryption scheme is an important branch of functional encryption schemes, which has wide applications in modern society. There have existed many inner-product encryption schemes, but as far as we know, no code-based inner-product functional encryption scheme has been proposed. As one of the most popular post-quantum cryptographic techniques, why code-based cryptosystems are seldom applied in these areas raises our concern. In this paper, we build an inner product encryption scheme from random linear codes and prove its security. Unfortunately, our scheme still suffers from the so large parameter size, which indicates that how to build a practical code-based functional encryption scheme remains a challenging problem.

Keywords: Inner-product · Functional encryption · Code-based cryptosystem · Post-quantum cryptosystem

1 Introduction

With the rapid development of information technique, people nowadays pay more and more attention to the protection of personal privacy, especially private data. The traditional encryption schemes can avoid privacy leakage, but how to calculate this encrypted information has become a new problem. Aimed at solving this kind of problems, functional encryption (FE) was first proposed by Sahai and Waters [23] in 2005 and was formalized six years later by Boneh *et al.* [7]. In a nutshell, the decryption key in an FE scheme allows a user to learn a function of the privacy information but not the whole information. More specifically, an FE scheme for functionality $F : K \times X \to \Sigma$ is defined over key space K, plaintext space X and output space Σ. The owner of the master secret key msk associated with master public key mpk can generate a secret key sk_k for every key $k \in K$. This sk_k allows the computation of $F(k,x)$ from a ciphertext of x computed under the master public key mpk. In another word,

© Springer Nature Switzerland AG 2021
Q. Huang and Y. Yu (Eds.): ProvSec 2021, LNCS 13059, pp. 259–276, 2021.
https://doi.org/10.1007/978-3-030-90402-9_14

everyone can encrypt $x \in X$ into a ciphertext Ct via the public key mpk, and $F(k, x)$ is returned by decrypt Ct using secret key sk_k.

The inner-product functionality is one of the most widely studied functionality in FE researches. Imagine that in an interview, different departments may have different requirements. For example, department A prefers employees who are good at mathematics, while department B prefers employees who are good at writing. Then, how to protect the privacy of candidates' course grades and keep the outcome of the interview fair and convincing at the same time? One functional encryption scheme for inner-product may solve it. In order to protect the personal privacy of candidates and ensure that the results are open and transparent, we can apply the inner-product encryption scheme in the following way. Each candidate encrypts his/her course grade $\mathbf{x} = (x_1, x_2, \ldots, x_l)$ into a ciphertext Ct and send it to the HR department. Each department inputs the weight $\mathbf{y} = (y_1, y_2, \ldots, y_l)$ set by itself to extract the secret key sk_y, which can be used to decrypt the weighted mean $\langle \mathbf{x}, \mathbf{y} \rangle = \sum_{i=0}^{l} x_i y_i$.

The early inner-product encryption schemes focused on predicate encryption supporting inner-product predicate [2,11,19,20]. These schemes are different from the FE schemes where they output a message if and only if the inner-product equals 0. The first functional encryption for inner-product was presented by Abdalls et $al.$ [1]. Their schemes are based on DDH assumption or LWE assumption. Later, Some works [6,12] discussed how to generate function-hiding inner-product encryption under the symmetric external Diffie-Hellman assumption. Recently, Katsumata et $al.$ [10] proposed an adaptively secure inner-product encryption from LWE assumption, but their scheme only supports inner-product predicate as well.

Nowadays, with the fast development of quantum computing, cryptosystems whose security relies on traditional hard problems may face efficient attacks. Hence post-quantum cryptosystem which can resist attacks from quantum computing arises public concern. But as we have seen, except for the lattice-based cryptography, or more precisely, LWE assumptions from lattice-based cryptography, other post-quantum cryptography techniques have not been applied into constructing inner-product encryption schemes. As one of the principal available post-quantum cryptographic techniques, code-based cryptosystems present many advantages: it is very fast for both encryption and decryption and the best-known attacks are exponential in the length of the code. However, it requires a large key size to reach a good security level, which makes it hard to be applied in practice. Moreover, compared with lattice-based cryptosystems, code-based cryptosystems seldom be used in constructing cryptographic applications. As far as we are concerned, the difficulty that makes code-based cryptosystem hard to be applied is that they do not have good homomorphic properties. [1] shows a generic construction from public key encryption system with specific structural and homomorphic properties to inner product encryption schemes with s-IND-CPA secure. However, to the best of our knowledge, no such code-based public key encryption system has been proposed.

Our Contributions: In this paper, we propose a code-based inner product functional encryption system. As far as we know, this is the first inner product encryption scheme based on coding theory. Our idea is inspired by the LWE based inner product encryption system [1]. However, we do not follow the generic construction from it because our scheme does not transform from an existed public key encryption system. Moreover, it is difficult to construct a code-based encryption system to satisfy the structural and homomorphic properties mentioned in [1]. Unlike the lattice-based cryptosystems which add an error with a small norm, code-based cryptosystems usually introduce errors with a small weight. Since the non-zero positions of the error vector are randomly chosen, the weight of the errors will be accumulated in the operation on ciphertexts. This proposition also makes code-based public key encryption systems hard to be applied in modern applications such as homomorphic encryption.

In this work, we try to construct a code-based inner product encryption scheme with IND-secure. The master public key and master secret key are indeed the message and ciphertext in a McEliece encryption system. The first part of the ciphertext ct_0 can be viewed as the ciphertext of a random vector $\mathbf{r}$ in the Niederreiter encryption system [17]. This is also a commitment of $\mathbf{r}$. Then this vector $\mathbf{r}$ together with the i-th public key mpk_i are used to cover the i-th coordinate of $\mathbf{x}$. The secret key of vector $\mathbf{y}$ is extracted as the sum of $y_i msk_i$. When it comes to the decryption algorithm, here comes a problem that the noise error can not be totally eliminated. We analyse the distribution of the noise in detail, and find that the decryption failure rate can be reduced by repeating enough times. However, the cost is a very large parameter size.

Organization: The remainder of this paper is organized as follows. In Sect. 2, we recall some preliminaries on coding theory and code-based cryptosystems. In Sect. 3, the definition and security properties of functional encryption are reviewed. In Sect. 4, we present our basic idea of constructing the inner-product encryption scheme and prove its security based on syndrome decoding problem. In Sect. 5, the full scheme which has tolerable decryption failure rate (DFR) is presented and the DFR is analysed in detail to prove the correctness. Lastly, Sect. 6 concludes the paper.

2 Preliminaries

In this section, we present the notions of coding theory that are prerequisite for the following sections as well as basic knowledge about code-based cryptography.

2.1 Notation and Conventions

Let $\mathbb{N}$ denote the set of natural numbers. If $n \in \mathbb{N}$, then $\{0,1\}^n$ denotes the set of n-bit strings, and $\{0,1\}^*$ is the set of all bit strings. We use $\mathbb{F}_q$ denote the finite field of q elements, and then $\mathbb{F}_q^n$ denotes the set of vectors with length n over $\mathbb{F}_q$, $\mathbb{F}_q^{m \times n}$ denotes the set of $m \times n$ matrices over $\mathbb{F}_q$. The Hamming weight of a vector $\mathbf{v}$ is denoted as $\mathsf{wt}(\mathbf{v})$ and all the vectors of length n with Hamming weight w is denoted as S_n^w. If S is a set, we use $x \leftarrow_\$ S$ to denote the assignment to x of an element chosen uniformly at random from S. If $\mathcal{A}$ is an algorithm, then $y \leftarrow \mathcal{A}(x)$ denotes the assignment to y of the input x.

2.2   Linear Codes

We now recall some basic definitions for linear codes.

An $[n,k]_q$ linear error-correcting code $\mathcal{C}$ is a linear subspace of a vector space $\mathbb{F}_q^n$, where $\mathbb{F}_q$ denotes the finite field of q elements, and k denotes the dimension of the subspace. The generator matrix G for a linear code is a $k \times n$ matrix with rank k which defines a linear mapping from $\mathbb{F}_q^k$ (called the message space) to $\mathbb{F}_q^n$. Namely, the code $\mathcal{C}$ is

$$\mathcal{C} = \mathcal{C}(\mathsf{G}) = \{\mathbf{x}\mathsf{G} \mid \mathbf{x} \in \mathbb{F}_q^k\}.$$

If $\mathcal{C}$ is the kernel of a matrix $\mathsf{H} \in \mathbb{F}_q^{(n-k) \times k}$, we call H a parity check matrix of $\mathcal{C}$, i.e.

$$\mathcal{C} = \mathcal{C}^\perp(\mathsf{H}) = \mathrm{Ker}(\mathsf{H}) = \{\mathbf{y} \in \mathbb{F}_q^n \mid \mathsf{H}\mathbf{y} = \mathbf{0}\}.$$

We call a vector in $\mathcal{C}$ a codeword.

Given a codeword $\mathbf{c} = (c_1, c_2, \ldots, c_n) \in \mathbb{F}_q^n$, its Hamming weight $\mathsf{wt}(\mathbf{c})$ is defined to be the number of non-zero coordinates, i.e. $\mathsf{wt}(\mathbf{c}) = |\{i \mid c_i \neq 0, 1 \leq i \leq n\}|$. The distance of two codewords $\mathbf{c}_1, \mathbf{c}_2$, denoted by $d(\mathbf{c}_1, \mathbf{c}_2)$ counts the number of coordinates in which they differ.

If $\mathbf{c}$ is a codeword and $\mathbf{c} + \mathbf{e}$ is the received word, then we call $\mathbf{e}$ the error vector and $\{i | e_i \neq 0\}$ the set of error positions, $\mathsf{wt}(\mathbf{e})$ is the number of errors of the received word. If $\mathbf{r} = \mathbf{c} + \mathbf{e}$ is the received word and the distance from $\mathbf{r}$ to the code $\mathcal{C}$ is t', then there exists a codeword $\mathbf{c}'$ and an error vector $\mathbf{e}'$ such that $\mathbf{r} = \mathbf{c}' + \mathbf{e}'$ and $\mathsf{wt}(\mathbf{e}') = t'$. If the number of errors is at most $(d-1)/2$, then it is sure that $\mathbf{c} = \mathbf{c}'$ and $\mathbf{e} = \mathbf{e}'$. In other words, the nearest codeword to $\mathbf{r}$ is unique when $\mathbf{r}$ has distance at most $(d-1)/2$ to $\mathcal{C}$.

2.3   Hard Problems in Coding Theory

There are many hard problems in coding theory, one of the well-known problems is general decoding problem. Syndrome decoding (SD) problem is a dual variant of general decoding problem, and both of them have been proved to be NP-hard for general linear codes in [5]. Nowadays, most of the code-based cryptosystems are constructed on SD problem or its variant such as rank-SD problem. An instance of computation SD problem is as follows:

Instance 1 (Computation SD Problem). *Given an $(n-k) \times n$ parity check matrix H of code $\mathcal{C}$, a syndrome $\mathbf{s}$, the Computation SD Problem $CSD(n,k,w)$ asks for a vector $\mathbf{x}$, whose weight $\mathsf{wt}(\mathbf{x}) = w$, such that $\mathsf{H}\mathbf{x} = \mathbf{s}$.*

An SD distribution is defined as follows: For positive integers n, k and w, the $SD(n,k,w)$ distribution chooses $\mathsf{H} \leftarrow_\$ \mathbb{F}_q^{(n-k) \times n}$ and $\mathbf{x} \leftarrow_\$ \mathbb{F}_q^n$ such that $\mathsf{wt}(\mathbf{x}) = w$, and outputs $(\mathsf{H}, \mathbf{s} = \mathsf{H}\mathbf{x}^T)$. The security of our inner-product encryption scheme relies on the Decision SD problem. An instance is as follows:

Instance 2 (Decision SD Problem). *Given an* $(n - k) \times n$ *matrix* H *and a vector* $\mathbf{y}$ *with length* $n - k$, *the Decision SD Problem* $DSD(n, k, w)$ *asks to decide with non-negligible advantage whether* $(\mathsf{H}, \mathbf{y})$ *comes from the* $SD(n, k, w)$ *distribution or the uniform distribution over* $\mathbb{F}_q^{(n-k) \times n} \times \mathbb{F}_q^{n-k}$.

3 Functional Encryption

Following Boneh *et al.* [7], we begin by recalling the syntactic definition of functionality. The functionality F describes the functions of a plaintext that can be learned from the ciphertext. Formally, the functionality is defined as follows.

Definition 1 (Functionality [7]). *A functionality F defined over (K, X) is a function $F : K \times X \to \Sigma \cup \{\bot\}$ described as a (deterministic) Turing Machine. The set K is called the key space, the set X is called the plaintext space, the set Σ is the output space and $\bot$ is a special string not contained in Σ.*

A functional encryption scheme for the functionality F enables one to evaluate $F(k, x)$ given the encryption of x and a secret key sk_k for k. The algorithm for evaluation $F(k, x)$ using sk_k is called decrypt. More precisely, a functional encryption scheme is defined as follows.

Definition 2 (Functional Encryption Scheme [7]). *A functional encryption scheme $\mathcal{FE}$ for functionality F is a tuple $\mathcal{FE} = (\mathsf{Setup}, \mathsf{KeyDer}, \mathsf{Encrypt}, \mathsf{Decrypt})$ of four algorithms:*

1. $\mathsf{Setup}(1^\lambda)$ *generates a public and master secret key pair (mpk, msk) for a given security parameter λ.*
2. $\mathsf{KeyDer}(msk, k)$ *on input a master secret key msk and key $k \in K$ outputs secret key sk_k.*
3. $\mathsf{Encrypt}(mpk, x)$ *on input a master public key mpk and message $x \in X$ outputs the ciphertext Ct.*
4. $\mathsf{Decrypt}(mpk, \mathsf{Ct}, \mathsf{sk}_k)$ *outputs $y \in \Sigma \cup \{\bot\}$.*

Correctness. The correctness requirement: for all $(mpk, msk) \leftarrow \mathsf{Setup}(1^\lambda)$, all $k \in K$ and $x \in X$, for $\mathsf{sk}_k \leftarrow \mathsf{KeyDer}(msk, k)$ and $\mathsf{Ct} \leftarrow \mathsf{Encrypt}(mpk, x)$, we have that $\mathsf{Decrypt}(mpk, \mathsf{Ct}, \mathsf{sk}_k) = F(k, m)$ whenever $F(k, m) \neq \bot$, except with negligible probability.

Indistinguishability-Based Security. Our security definition is defined by the game-playing notions. In such games, there exist procedures for initialization and finalization and procedures to respond to adversary oracle queries. A game G is executed with an adversary $\mathcal{A}$ as follows. First, **Initialize** executes and its outputs are the inputs to $\mathcal{A}$. Then $\mathcal{A}$ executes, its oracle queries being answered by the corresponding procedures of G. When $\mathcal{A}$ terminates, its output becomes the input to the **Finalize** procedure. The output of the latter, denoted by $G(\mathcal{A})$, is called the output of the game, and $G(\mathcal{A}) = y$ denotes the event that the output takes a value y. Boolean flags are assumed initialized to false. Here is the formal definition about indistinguishability-based security.

Definition 3 (IND-FE-CPA secure [1]). *For any functional encryption scheme* $\mathcal{FE}$ = (Setup, KeyDer, Encrypt, Decrypt) *for functionality* F *defined over* (K, X), *the security against chosen-plaintext attacks game is defined in Fig. 1. We say that* $\mathcal{FE}$ *is secure against chosen-plaintext attacks (IND-FE-CPA secure) if*

$$|\Pr[\mathsf{Exp}_{\mathcal{FE},\lambda}^{ind-fe-cpa-0}(\mathcal{A}) = 1] - \Pr[\mathsf{Exp}_{\mathcal{FE},\lambda}^{ind-fe-cpa-1}(\mathcal{A}) = 1]| = \mathsf{negl}(\lambda).$$

Moreover, we say $\mathcal{FE}$ *is selective secure against chosen-plaintext attacks (s-IND-FE-CPA secure) when the challenge messages* m_0^* *and* m_1^* *have been chosen before hand.*

Game $\mathsf{Exp}_{\mathcal{FE},\lambda}^{ind-fe-cpa-b}(\mathcal{A})$		Game $\mathsf{Exp}_{\mathcal{FE},\lambda}^{s-ind-fe-cpa-b}(\mathcal{A})$
Initialize(λ)	**LR**(m_0^*, m_1^*)	**Initialize**(λ, m_0^*, m_1^*)
$(mpk, msk) \leftarrow_{\$} \mathsf{Setup}(1^\lambda)$	$\mathsf{Ct}^* \leftarrow_{\$} \mathsf{Encrypt}(mpk, m_b^*)$	$(mpk, msk) \overset{R}{\leftarrow} \mathsf{Setup}(1^\lambda)$
$V \leftarrow \emptyset$	Return Ct^*	$V \leftarrow \emptyset$
Return mpk		Return mpk
	Finalize(b')	
KeyDer(k)	if $\exists k \in V$ such that	
$V \leftarrow V \cup \{k\}$	$F(k, m_0^*) \neq F(k, m_1^*)$	**LR**$()$
$\mathsf{sk}_k \leftarrow_{\$} \mathsf{KeyDer}(msk, k)$	**then return** flase	$\mathsf{Ct}^* \leftarrow_{\$} \mathsf{Encrypt}(mpk, m_b^*)$
Return sk_k	Return $(b' = b)$	Return Ct^*

Fig. 1. Games $\mathsf{Exp}_{\mathcal{FE},\lambda}^{ind-fe-cpa-b}(\mathcal{A})$ and $\mathsf{Exp}_{\mathcal{FE},\lambda}^{s-ind-fe-cpa-b}(\mathcal{A})$ [1]

4   The Basic Idea of Constructing Inner-Product Encryption Scheme

In this section, we describe our inner product encryption scheme by showing the basic idea firstly. Then we prove our basic idea to be IND-FE-CPA secure. In the next section, we will show the full scheme.

4.1   Basic-IPFEc Scheme

Our basic idea is inspired from [1] and we describe it as follows.

- **Setup**$(1^\lambda, l, B)$: First generate the public parameter param = (q, n, k, l, w_1, w_2). Then generate independent vectors $(\mathbf{m}_i)_{i=1}^l \leftarrow_{\$} \mathbb{F}_q^k$, and $(\mathbf{e}_i)_{i=1}^l \leftarrow_{\$} \mathcal{S}_n^{w_1}$. As a result, the master keys are set as $msk = (\mathbf{m}_i)_{i=1}^l$ and $mpk = (\mathbf{m}_i \mathsf{G} + \mathbf{e}_i)_{i=1}^l$.
- **KeyDer**$(msk, \mathbf{y})$: On input master secret key $msk = (\mathbf{m}_i)_{i=1}^l$ and vector $\mathbf{y} = (y_1, \ldots, y_l) \in \mathbb{Z}_p^l$, this algorithm outputs $\mathsf{sk}_y = \sum_{i=1}^l y_i \mathbf{m_i}$.

- **IPEncrypt**$(mpk, \mathbf{x})$: On input master public key mpk and message $\mathbf{x} = (x_1, \ldots, x_l) \in \mathbb{Z}_p^l$, choose a random vector $\mathbf{r} \in \mathcal{S}_n^{w_2}$, and compute $\mathsf{ct}_0 = \mathsf{Gr}$. For each $i \in 1, 2, \ldots, l$, compute $\mathsf{ct}_i = \langle mpk_i, \mathbf{r} \rangle + x_i$. Then the algorithm returns the ciphertext $\mathsf{Ct} = (\mathsf{ct}_0, (\mathsf{ct}_i)_{i \in [l]})$.
- **IPDecrypt**$(mpk, \mathsf{Ct}, \mathsf{sk}_y)$: On input master public key mpk, ciphertext $\mathsf{Ct} = (\mathsf{ct}_0, (\mathsf{ct}_i)_{i=1}^l)$ and secret key sk_y for vector $\mathbf{y}$, compute

$$
R = \sum_{i=1}^{l} y_i \mathsf{ct}_i - \langle \mathsf{sk}_y, \mathsf{ct}_0 \rangle
$$

$$
= \sum_{i=1}^{l} y_i \langle mpk_i, \mathbf{r} \rangle + \sum_{i=1}^{l} y_i x_i - \sum_{i=1}^{l} \langle y_i \mathbf{m}_i, \mathsf{Gr} \rangle
$$

$$
= \langle \mathbf{x}, \mathbf{y} \rangle + \sum_{i=1}^{l} y_i \langle \mathbf{e}, \mathbf{r} \rangle \tag{1}
$$

Note. In the above scheme, we set $\mathbf{e}$ and $\mathbf{r}$ are both random vectors with small weight, such that the corresponding $\mathrm{CSD}(n, k, w_1)$ problem and $\mathrm{CSD}(n, n - k, w_2)$ problem are hard. The probability of $\sum y_i \langle \mathbf{e}, \mathbf{r} \rangle = 0$ will be analysed in the following part. In a nutshell, the probability above is not large enough to support the correctness of the scheme. Thus to ensure the correctness of the scheme, we have to make a transformation inspired by Fiat-Shamir [9]. The full scheme will be present in Sect. 5.1.

4.2 Security Analysis

Now we provide the security results for the basic scheme.

Theorem 1. *If there exists an adversary $\mathcal{A}$ can break the IND-FE-CPA of the Basic-IPFEc scheme with non-negligible probability, then there exists an algorithm $\mathcal{B}$ can solve the Decision SD problem with non-negligible probability.*

Proof. Suppose there exists an adversary $\mathcal{A}$ who can break the IND-FE-CPA of the Basic-IPFEc scheme, then we can build an algorithm $\mathcal{B}$ to solve a Decision SD problem.

When given a $\mathrm{DSD}(n, k, w)$ problem with a parity check matrix H^* and a vector $\mathbf{s}^*$, $\mathcal{B}$ will simulate the oracles $\mathcal{S}_{init}$ and $\mathcal{S}_{LR}$ for the **Initialize** and **LR** step in the IND-FE-CPA game respectively, and then builds a sequence of games as follows:

- $Game^0$: This is the real IND-FE-CPA challenge game which $\mathcal{B}$ encrypts the message $\mathbf{x}_0$, and we describe it as follows.
  - **Initialize**: Input the security parameter 1^λ, output the public parameters $\mathsf{param} = \{q, n, k, l, w_1, w_2\}$ and a matrix G which can be viewed as a generator matrix of a random linear $[n, k]$ code. The **Setup** step also generates the master public key and master secret key as follows:

$$msk = (\mathbf{m}_1, \mathbf{m}_2, \ldots, \mathbf{m}_l);$$
$$mpk = (\mathbf{m}_1 \mathsf{G} + \mathbf{e}_1, \mathbf{m}_2 \mathsf{G} + \mathbf{e}_2, \ldots, \mathbf{m}_l \mathsf{G} + \mathbf{e}_l).$$

This step returns the master public key mpk.

- **KeyDer**: Input a vector $\mathbf{y}$ given by the adversary $\mathcal{A}$, output the secret key $\mathsf{sk}_y = y_1 \mathbf{m}_1 + y_2 \mathbf{m}_2 + \cdots + y_l \mathbf{m}_l$
- **Enc**: Input two challenge messages $\mathbf{x}_0$ and $\mathbf{x}_1$, the challenger first checks whether $\langle \mathbf{x}_0, \mathbf{y} \rangle = \langle \mathbf{x}_1, \mathbf{y} \rangle$ holds for all queried $\mathbf{y}$ in the **KeyDer** queries. If not, return *false*. Else it encrypts $\mathbf{x}^* = \mathbf{x}_1$ into Ct^* as follows:

$$\mathsf{ct}_0^* = \mathsf{G}\mathbf{r};$$
$$\mathsf{ct}_i^* = \langle mpk_i, \mathbf{r} \rangle + x_i^*, \, i \in \{1, 2, \ldots, l\};$$
$$\mathsf{Ct}^* = \left(\mathsf{ct}_0, (\mathsf{ct}_i)_{i=1}^l \right).$$

- **Finalize**: The adversary $\mathcal{A}$ guesses which message $\mathbf{x}_{b'}$ is encrypted, and output b'.

We denote by $\Pr[G_i]$ the probability that $\mathcal{A}$ wins the game i. Then we have $\Pr[G_0] = \Pr[\mathcal{A} \text{ output } 0] = p$.

- *Game*^{1}: In this game, $\mathcal{B}$ simulates the **Initialize** step to answer the mpk queries from $\mathcal{A}$, and other steps remain the same. This simulator uses a list $\Lambda(mpk)$ to store the master key pairs (msk, mpk). We describe the simulator $\mathcal{S}_{init}$ in Fig. 2.

Algorithm 1: Initialize simulator $\mathcal{S}_{init}$

Input: 1^λ.
Output: mpk and param.
1 $\mathsf{G} \leftarrow_\$ \mathbb{F}^{k \times n}$;
2 **for** $i = 1$ *to* l **do**
3 $\quad \mathbf{m}_i \leftarrow_\$ \mathbb{F}^k$;
4 $\quad \mathbf{e}_i \leftarrow_\$ \mathbb{F}^n$;
5 **if** $num == t_1$ **then**
6 $\quad \mathsf{G} = (\mathsf{H}^*)^T$;
7 $msk = (\mathbf{m}_1, \mathbf{m}_2, \ldots, \mathbf{m}_l)$;
8 $mpk = (\mathbf{m}_1 \mathsf{G} + \mathbf{e}_1, \mathbf{m}_2 \mathsf{G} + \mathbf{e}_2, \ldots, \mathbf{m}_l \mathsf{G} + \mathbf{e}_l)$;
9 **Return** (mpk, G);

Algorithm 2: LR simulator $\mathcal{S}_{LR}$

Input: x.
Output: Ct^*.
1 $\mathsf{ct}_0 = \mathbf{s}^*$;
2 **for** $i = 1$ *to* l **do**
3 $\quad a_i = \langle \mathbf{m}_i, \mathbf{s}^* \rangle$;
4 $\quad r_i' \leftarrow \mathcal{D}(\langle \mathbf{e}, \mathbf{r} \rangle)$;
5 $\quad \mathsf{ct}_i = a_i + x_i + r_i'$;
6 $\mathsf{ct}_t = \mathsf{ct}_t + r'$;
7 $\mathsf{Ct}^* = (\mathsf{ct}_0, (\mathsf{ct}_i)_{i=1}^l)$;
8 **Return** Ct^*;

Fig. 2. Simulators $\mathcal{S}_{init}$ and $\mathcal{S}_{LR}$

In the real **Setup** algorithm, the matrix G is sampled uniformly from the full rank $k \times n$ matrix over $\mathbb{F}_q$, and the only difference in $\mathcal{S}_{init}$ is that in the t_1-th query, the matrix is given by a determinant full rank matrix H^*. We emphasis here that this parity check matrix has noting to do with the generator matrix mentioned before. Namely, if this parity check matrix H^* is a $(\hat{n} - \hat{k}) \times \hat{n}$ matrix, then the challenger will set the public parameters as param $= \{\hat{n}, \hat{n} - \hat{k}, q, w_1, w_2\}$. From the view of $\mathcal{A}$, there is no difference between *Game*^{1} and *Game*^{0}. Thus we have $\Pr[S_1] = \Pr[S_0]$.

- $Game^2$: In this game, the challenger modifies the winning condition. This game is conditioned by the adversary making the final distinguish on the t_1-th query to mpk, where $t_1 \leftarrow_\$ \{1, 2, \ldots, q_{init}\}$. In another word, the challenge ciphertext Ct^* is encrypted by the key H^*. Hence we have $\Pr[S_2] = \frac{1}{q_{init}} \Pr[S_1]$.
- $Game^3$: In this game, $\mathcal{B}$ encrypts the message $\mathbf{x}_0$ by the simulator $\mathcal{S}_{LR}$ shows in Fig. 2.

Here $r_i' \leftarrow \mathcal{D}(\langle \mathbf{e}, \mathbf{r} \rangle)$ denotes the distribution of $\langle \mathbf{e}, \mathbf{r} \rangle$. This distribution is analysed in Sect. 5.2.

On one hand, if $(\mathsf{H}, \mathbf{s}^*)$ comes from an $\mathrm{SD}(n, k, w_2)$ distribution, the challenge ciphertext is a well-distributed ciphertext of the message $\mathbf{x}_b$. In more detail, there will exist a vector $\mathbf{r}^* \in \mathcal{S}_n^w$ such that $\mathbf{s}^* = \mathsf{H}^* \mathbf{r}^*$. As a result, we have

$$\mathsf{ct}_0 = \mathbf{s}^* = \mathsf{H}^* \mathbf{r}^*$$

and

$$
\begin{aligned}
\mathsf{ct}_i &= a_i + x_i + r_i' = \langle \mathbf{m}_i, \mathbf{s}^* \rangle + x_i + r_i' \\
&= \langle \mathbf{m}_i, \mathsf{H}^* \mathbf{r}^* \rangle + x_i + r_i' = \langle \mathbf{m}_i \mathsf{H}^*, \mathbf{r}^* \rangle + x_i + r_i' \\
&= \langle mpk_i - \mathbf{e}_i, \mathbf{r}^* \rangle + x_i + r_i' = \langle mpk_i, \mathbf{r}^* \rangle + x_i - \langle \mathbf{e}_i, \mathbf{r}^* \rangle + r_i' \\
&= \langle mpk_i, \mathbf{r}^* \rangle + x_i
\end{aligned}
$$

On the other hand, if $(\mathsf{H}^*, \mathbf{s}^*)$ does not come from an $\mathrm{SD}(n, k, w_2)$ distribution, $\mathcal{A}$ will get the ciphertext $\mathsf{Ct}^* = (\mathsf{ct}_0, (\mathsf{ct})_{i=1}^l)$ and the secret key sk_y for vector $\mathbf{y}$. Then he can run the **Decrypt** algorithm and get

$$
\begin{aligned}
\mathbf{Decrypt}(mpk, \mathsf{Ct}, \mathsf{sk}_y) &= \sum_{i=1}^l y_i \mathsf{ct}_i - \langle \mathsf{sk}_y, \mathsf{ct}_0 \rangle \\
&= \sum_{i=1}^l y_i a_i + \sum_{i=1}^l y_i r_i' + \sum_{i=1}^l x_i y_i - \langle \sum_{i=1}^l y_i \mathbf{m}_i, \mathbf{s}^* \rangle \\
&= \sum_{i=1}^l x_i y_i + \sum_{i=1}^l y_i \langle \mathbf{m}_i, \mathbf{s}^* \rangle + \sum_{i=1}^l y_i \cdot r_i' - \sum_{i=1}^l y_i \langle \mathbf{m}_i, \mathbf{s}^* \rangle \\
&= \sum_{i=1}^l x_i y_i + \sum_{i=1}^l y_i \cdot r_i'.
\end{aligned}
$$

Since $\mathbf{r}'$ is sampled from the same distribution as the real inner production of small weight vectors $\mathbf{e}$ and $\mathbf{r}$, the real ciphertext and the output of simulator have the same distribution.

If $\mathcal{A}$ can distinguish $Game^3$ from $Game^2$, then $\mathcal{B}$ can build an algorithm $\mathcal{D}$ invoke $\mathcal{A}$ by outputting "Syndrome" or "Uniform" if $\mathcal{A}$ outputs "Game 2" or "Game 3" respectively. Since $\mathrm{DSD}(n, k, w_2)$ is a hard problem, i.e. $\Pr[\mathcal{D} \text{ wins}] = \mathsf{negl}(\lambda)$, we have $|\Pr[S_3] - \Pr[S_2]| = \mathsf{negl}(\lambda)$.

- $Game^4$: This game is the same as $Game^3$ except for the encrypted message is $\mathbf{x}_1$. Since $msk = (\mathbf{m}_i)_{i=1}^l$ and each $\mathbf{m}_i$ is sampled uniformly from $\mathbb{F}_q^k$, we have $a_i = \langle \mathbf{m}_i, \mathbf{s}^* \rangle$ is uniformly distribute over $\mathbb{F}_q$. Thus x_i in $\mathsf{ct}_i = a_i + x_i + r_i'$ is well hid by a_i. As a result, $Game^4$ is indistinguishable from $Game^3$, and we have $\Pr[S_4] = \Pr[S_3]$.

- $Game^5$: This game is the same as $Game^2$ except for the encrypted message is $\mathbf{x}_1$. The indistinguishability between $Game^4$ and $Game^5$ is similar as that between $Game^3$ and $Game^2$. Thus we have $|\Pr[S_5] - \Pr[S_4]| = \mathsf{negl}(\lambda)$.
- $Game^6$: This game is the same as $Game^1$ except for the encrypted message is $\mathbf{x}_1$. The indistinguishability between $Game^5$ and $Game^6$ is similar as that between $Game^2$ and $Game^1$. Thus we have $\Pr[S_6] = \frac{1}{q_{init}}\Pr[S_5]$.
- $Game^7$: This game is the same as $Game^0$ except for the encrypted message is $\mathbf{x}_1$, i.e. the real IND-FE-CPA challenge game which encrypts the message $\mathbf{x}_1$. The indistinguishability between $Game^6$ and $Game^7$ is similar as that between $Game^1$ and $Game^0$. Thus we have $\Pr[S_7] = \Pr[S_6]$.

To sum up, we have

$$
\begin{aligned}
Succ_{IPFEc,\lambda}^{ind-fc-cpa-b} &= \Pr[S_7] - \Pr[S_0] = \Pr[S_6] - \Pr[S_1] \\
&= \frac{1}{q_{init}}\Pr[S_5] - \frac{1}{q_{init}}\Pr[S_2] \\
&= (\Pr[S_4] + \mathsf{negl}(\lambda)) - (\Pr[S_3] + \mathsf{negl}(\lambda)) \\
&= \mathsf{negl}(\lambda).
\end{aligned}
$$

$\square$

Note 1. The public key of our basic scheme is actually a ciphertext of the McEliece public key encryption system with the secret key as the corresponding plaintext. Since we choose G as a generator matrix of a random linear code $\mathcal{C}$, there exists no decoding algorithm to $\mathcal{C}$ which is more efficient than the information set decoding (ISD) algorithm. Thus, the most efficient way to break the onewayness from the master public key to the master secret key is the ISD attack. The effect of the ISD attack will be analysed in Sect. 5.3.

Note 2. If an adversary asked $\mathbf{y}$ vectors sufficient times such that they form a basis for $\mathbb{F}_q^l$, then the adversary can recover $\mathbf{x}$ from the ciphertext and wins the security game. Moreover, leakage of the master secret key will happen if there is no limitation to the number of KeyDer Oracle queries. As is said in [1], this has nothing to do with the specific implementation of the functionality, it is something inherent to the functionality itself. Since our basic idea follows the generic construction in [1], this problem does not matter and can be avoided by setting a limitation on the query times.

5 The Full Scheme

In the FE schemes, correctness means that the decryption step will always output the correct result $\langle \mathbf{x}, \mathbf{y} \rangle$ except for a negligible probability. However, as mentioned before, our scheme may return a value with some noise at the decryption step with some probability. A simple idea to solve this problem is to repeat the encryption and decryption step until one value is returned twice. However, in an interactive protocol, online immediate communication may have a high cost. This problem can be solved by using Fiat-Shamir transformation. In more detail, the basic scheme is repeated c times, and the decryption algorithm will return the most frequent occurrence value. In this section, we will present the full scheme at first. Then an analysis of the correctness will be given in detail. The security of the full scheme is discussed at last.

5.1 The Presentation of the Full Scheme

Add c into the parameter list, then our scheme can be described as the following four algorithms.

- **Setup** $(1^\lambda, l)$:
  1. Load the public parameters param $= (q, n, k, 1, w_1, w_2, c)$;
  2. $G \leftarrow_\$ \mathbb{F}_q^{n \times k}$;
  3. **for** $j = 1$ *to* c **do**
  4.   **for** $i = 1$ to l **do**
  5. $msk_j[i] = \mathbf{m}_i \leftarrow_\$ \mathbb{F}_q^k$;
  6. $\mathbf{e}_i \leftarrow_\$ S_n^{w_1} \subset \mathbb{F}_q^n$;
  7. $mpk_j[i] = \mathbf{m}_i G + \mathbf{e}_i$;
  8. $msk = (msk_j)_{j=1}^c$;
  9. $mpk = (mpk_j)_{j=1}^c$;
  10. **Return** (msk, mpk, G);

- **KeyDer** $(msk, \mathbf{y})$:
  1. Load the public parameters param $= (q, n, k, l, w_1, w_2, c)$;
  2. **for** $j = 1$ *to* c **do**
  3. $\mathsf{sk}_{y,j} = 0$;
  4.   **for** $i = 1$ to l **do**
  5. $\mathsf{sk}_{y,j} = \mathsf{sk}_{y,j} + y_i msk_{j,i}$;
  6. $\mathsf{sk}_y = (\mathsf{sk}_{y,j})_{j=1}^c$;
  7. **Return** sk_y;

- **IPEncrypt** $(mpk, \mathbf{x} = (x_1, x_2, \ldots, x_l))$:
  1. Load the public parameters param $= (q, n, k, l, w_1, w_2, c)$;
  2. **for** $j = 1$ *to* c **do**
  3. $\mathsf{r} \leftarrow_\$ S_n^{w_2} \subset \mathbb{F}_q^n$;
  4. $\mathsf{ct}_0 = G\mathsf{r}$;
  5.   **for** $i = 1$ to l **do**
  6. $\mathsf{ct}_i = \langle mpk_j[i], \mathsf{r} \rangle + x_i$;
  7. $\mathsf{Ct}_j = \left(\mathsf{ct}_0, (\mathsf{ct}_i)_{i=1}^l \right)$;
  8. **Return** $\mathsf{Ct}_{i=1}^c$;

- **IPDecrypt** $(\mathsf{Ct}_{i=1}^c, \mathsf{sk}_y, \mathbf{y})$:
  1. Load the public parameters param $= (q, n, k, l, w_1, w_2, c)$;
  2. **for** $i = 1$ *to* c **do**
  3. $R_i = \sum_{j=1}^l y_j \mathsf{Ct}_{i,j} - \langle \mathsf{sk}_{y,j}, \mathsf{Ct}_{j,0} \rangle$;
  4. $\mathbf{a} = \mathbf{0} \in \mathbb{Z}^q$;
  5. **for** $i = 1$ *to* c **do**
  6. $a[R_i] = a[R_i] + 1$;
  7. **Return** index$(\max(\mathbf{a}))$;

5.2   Correctness

The correctness of the scheme ensures that the decryption step will return the correct value of the inner product of $\mathbf{x}$ and $\mathbf{y}$. As we have seen in the basic idea, the probability of $\langle \mathbf{e}, \mathbf{r} \rangle = 0$ is not large enough. In this subsection, we will first calculating the distribution of $\langle \mathbf{e}, \mathbf{r} \rangle$, i.e. $\Pr[\langle \mathbf{e}, \mathbf{r} \rangle = 0]$, then analysing the correctness of the full scheme.

Suppose $\mathsf{wt}(\mathbf{e}) = \mathsf{wt}(\mathbf{r}) = w$ we have

$$\Pr\left[\langle \mathbf{e}, \mathbf{r} \rangle = 0 | \mathsf{wt}(\mathbf{e}) = \mathsf{wt}(\mathbf{r}) = w\right] := 1 - p_1 - p_2 - \cdots - p_w$$

$$= 1 - \Pr[\exists \text{ only one position } i \text{ s.t. } e_i r_i \neq 0]$$

$$-\Pr[\exists \text{ only two positions } i_1, i_2 \text{ s.t. } e_{i_j} r_{i_j} \neq 0 \wedge \sum_j e_{i_j} r_{i_j} \neq 0 \text{ for } j \in \{1,2\}] - \cdots$$

$$-\Pr[\exists \text{ only } w \text{ positions } i_j \text{ s.t. } e_{i_j} r_{i_j} \neq 0 \wedge \sum_j e_{i_j} r_{i_j} \neq 0 \text{ for } j \in \{1,\ldots,w\}]$$

and

$$p_1 = \binom{w}{1} \frac{w}{n} \prod_{j=1}^{w-1} \frac{n-w-(j-1)}{n-j};$$

$$p_2 = \frac{q-1}{q} \binom{w}{2} \frac{w(w-1)}{n(n-1)} \prod_{j=2}^{w-1} \frac{n-w-(j-1)}{n-j};$$

$$\cdots$$

$$p_w = \frac{q-1}{q} \binom{w}{w} \prod_{j=w}^{w-1} \frac{w-j}{n-j}.$$

As a result, we have

$$\Pr[\langle \mathbf{e}, \mathbf{r} \rangle = 0] = 1 - \sum_{i=1}^{w} p_i := \hat{p}$$

In order to guarantee that $\mathsf{wt}(\mathbf{e}) = \mathsf{wt}(\mathbf{r}) = w$ can be selected, we have to set $n = 2k$. Hence the $n \times k$ matrix which is denoted as G in our scheme can be viewed as a generator matrix of a random $[n, k]$ code as well as a parity check matrix of another random $[n, k]$ code. Thus, we have to choose parameters such that $\mathrm{CSD}(n = 2k, k, w)$ is hard.

Lemma 1. *Let $z_1, z_2, \ldots, z_n$ be independent identically distributed random variables with $\Pr[z_i = 0] = p$ and $\Pr[z_i = a \neq 0] = (1-p)/(q-1)$ for $a \in [1, q-1]$. If $Z_n = \sum_{i=1}^{n} z_i$, we have $\Pr[Z_n = 0] = \frac{1}{q} + \frac{q-1}{q}\left(\frac{qp-1}{q-1}\right)^n$.*

Proof.

$$\Pr[Z_1 = 0] = \Pr[z_1 = 0] = p.$$

$$\Pr[Z_n = 0] = \Pr[\sum_{i=1}^{n} z_i = 0] = \sum_{a_n=0}^{q-1} \Pr[\sum_{i=1}^{n-1} z_i = a_n | z_n = -a_n] \Pr[z_n = -a_n]$$

$$= \Pr[\sum_{i=1}^{n-1} z_i = 0 | z_n = 0] \Pr[z_n = 0]$$

$$+ \sum_{a_n=1}^{q-1} \Pr[\sum_{i=1}^{n-1} z_i = a_n | z_n = -a_n] \Pr[z_n = -a_n]$$

$$= p\Pr[\sum_{i=1}^{n-1} z_i = 0] + \frac{1-p}{q-1} \sum_{a_n=1}^{q-1} \Pr[\sum_{i=1}^{n-1} z_i = a_n]$$

$$= p\Pr[Z_{n-1} = 0] + \frac{1-p}{q-1}(1 - \Pr[Z_{n-1} = 0])$$

$$= \frac{1-p}{q-1} + \left(p - \frac{1-p}{q-1}\right) \Pr[Z_{n-1} = 0]$$

$$= \frac{1-p}{q-1} + \frac{qp-1}{q-1}\Pr[Z_{n-1} = 0]. \tag{2}$$

Similarly, for $\Pr[Z_{n-1} = 0]$ we have

$$\Pr[Z_{n-1} = 0] = \Pr[\sum_{i=1}^{n-2} z_i = 0 | z_{n-1} = 0]\Pr[z_{n-1} = 0]$$

$$+ \sum_{a_n=1}^{q-1} \Pr[\sum_{i=1}^{n-2} z_i = a_n | z_{n-1} = -a_n]\Pr[z_{n-1} = -a_n]$$

$$= \frac{1-p}{q-1} + \frac{qp-1}{q-1}\Pr[Z_{n-2} = 0]. \tag{3}$$

Denoting $C = \frac{1-p^*}{q-1}$ and $Q = \frac{qp^*-1}{q-1}$, then from Eq. (2) and Eq. (3) we have

$$\Pr[Z_n = 0] = C + Q\Pr[Z_{n-1} = 0].$$

Then we have

$$\Pr[Z_n = 0] + \frac{C}{Q-1} = Q(\Pr[Z_{n-1} = 0] + \frac{C}{Q-1}).$$

And hence

$$\Pr[Z_n = 0] + \frac{C}{Q-1} = Q^{n-1}\left(\Pr[Z_1 = 0] + \frac{C}{Q-1}\right) = Q^{n-1}\left(p + \frac{C}{Q-1}\right),$$

$$\Pr[Z_n = 0] = Q^{n-1}\left(p + \frac{C}{Q-1}\right) - \frac{C}{Q-1}. \tag{4}$$

Finally, from Eq. (4) we have

$$\Pr[Z_n = 0] = Q^{n-1} \left(p + \frac{C}{Q-1} \right) - \frac{C}{Q-1}$$

$$= \left(\frac{qp-1}{q-1} \right)^{n-1} \left(p - \frac{1}{q} \right) + \frac{1}{q}$$

$$= \frac{1}{q} + \frac{q-1}{q} \left(\frac{qp-1}{q-1} \right)^{n}.$$

□

The following corollary shows the DFR of the simple idea.

Corollary 1. *If* $\mathbf{e}_i, \mathbf{r} \in S_n^w$, *and* y_i *is uniformly distributed over* $[0, q-1]$, *we have* $\Pr[\sum_{i=1}^{l} y_i \langle \mathbf{e}_i, \mathbf{r} \rangle = 0] = \frac{1}{q} + \frac{q-1}{q} \left(\frac{q\hat{p}-1}{q-1} \right)^{l} := \bar{p}.$

In the full scheme, we repeat the basic idea c times, and choose the most frequency occurred value in the decryption algorithm as the final output. The probability of a correct value occurs most frequency can be calculate precisely as follows.

Denote T_i as the number of i duplicate values occurs and T_0 as the number of 0 occurs, and $T_0 + \sum_i iT_i = a$. For example, if $\mathbf{s} = (0, 0, 1, 2, 3, 4, 4, 5, 5, 6, 6, 6)$, then we have $T_0 = 2$ and $T_1, T_2, T_3 = 3, 2, 1$, $T_0 + \sum_i iT_i = 12$. Given a sequence $\mathbf{s} \in \mathbb{F}_q^c$ with length c, each coordinate is independent identical distributed with $\Pr[s_i = 0] = \bar{p}$ and $\Pr[s_i = a \in \mathbb{F}_q^*] = \frac{1-\bar{p}}{q-1}$, we have

$$\Pr[0 \text{ occurs } t \text{ times}] = \binom{c}{t} \bar{p}^t (1 - \bar{p})^{c-t}.$$

Note that our aim is to evaluate the DFR of the full scheme. Obviously, if $t > \lceil c/2 \rceil$, the decryption will return the correct value, and hence we only consider when $t < \lfloor c/2 \rfloor$. If for all $i \geq t$, we have $T_i = 0$, i.e. $T_0 + \sum_{i<t} iT_i = c$, then the decryption will also success. As a result, the DFR can be calculated as follows:

$$\Pr[\text{Decryption fails}] = \Pr[T_0 = t \wedge T_0 + \sum_i iT_i = c \wedge (\exists i > t, T_i > 0)]$$

$$= 1 - \Pr[T_0 = t \wedge t > \lfloor c/2 \rfloor] - \Pr[T_0 = t \wedge T_0 + \sum_{i<t} iT_i = c]$$

$$= 1 - \sum_{t=\lceil c/2 \rceil}^{c} \binom{c}{t} \bar{p}^t (1 - \bar{p})^{c-t} - \Pr[T_0 = t \wedge T_0 + \sum_{i<t} iT_i = c]. \quad (5)$$

For $\Pr[T_0 = t \wedge T_0 + \sum_{i<t} iT_i = c]$, we have

$$\Pr[T_0 = t \wedge T_0 + \sum_{i<t} iT_i = c] = \sum_{t=2}^{\lfloor c/2 \rfloor} \Pr[T_0 = t \wedge T_0 + \sum_{i<t} iT_i = c]$$

$$= \binom{t}{2} p^2 (\frac{1-p}{q-1})^{c-2} \frac{(q-1)!}{(q-1-(c-2))!} + \binom{t}{3} p^3 (\frac{1-p}{q-1})^{c-2}$$

$$\cdot \sum_{T_1} \sum_{T_2} \binom{c-3}{T_1} \frac{(q-1)!}{(q-1-T_1)!} \prod_{i=0}^{T_2} \binom{c-3-T_1-2i}{2} \frac{(q-1-T_1)!}{(q-1-T_1-T_2)!}$$

$$+ \cdots$$

$$= \sum_{t=2}^{\lfloor c/2 \rfloor} \binom{c}{t} \frac{p^t (1-p)^{c-t}(q-1)!}{(q-1)^{c-t}(q-1-(c-t))!} \sum_{T_t,\dots,T_2} \prod_{j=t}^{2} \prod_{i=0}^{T_j} \binom{c-t-\sum_{k=t}^{j+1} T_k}{i}$$

$$:= p. \tag{6}$$

Take p in Eq. (6) into Eq. (5), we have

$$\mathrm{DFR} = 1 - \sum_{t=\lceil c/2 \rceil}^{c} \binom{c}{t} \bar{p}^t (1-\bar{p})^{c-t} - p. \tag{7}$$

However, this Eq. (7) is hard to evaluate because the computational complexity is approximately $\mathcal{O}(c^c)$. Here we use another method to roughly estimate the DFR. We take q much larger than c to ensure that the possibility of a random non-zero value occurs more than 3 times in the decryption algorithm is less enough to omit. Thus we only have to make sure that the 0 occurs more than 4 times in the total c repetitions. Hence we take the DFR as $\sum_{i=0}^{3} \bar{p}^i (1-\bar{p})^{c-i}$.

5.3   Security

The security of the full scheme is very similar to the basic idea, except for that in the full scheme, one basic scheme is repeated many times. As we have proved before in Theorem 1, any PPT adversary can only break the basic scheme in negligible probability. Since the full scheme only repeat the basic scheme limited times, this does not effect on the security property of the inner product encryption scheme. As a result, we give the following theorem.

Theorem 2. *If there exists an adversary $\mathcal{A}$ can break the IND-FE-CPA of our IPFEc scheme with non-negligible probability, then there exists an algorithm $\mathcal{B}$ can solve the Decision SD problem with non-negligible probability.*

For known attacks, given a security parameter λ, we need take two factors into account. The first one is that in the **Setup** algorithm, it is difficult to recover the master secret key msk given a public key mpk. In fact, this procedure is an encryption in McEliece encryption system [16]. The second one is that in the **IPFEncrypt** algorithm, it is difficult to recover the random vector $\mathbf{r}$ given the ciphertext ct_0. And in fact, this procedure is an encryption in Niederreiter encryption system [17]. The security of both cryptosystems are based on the hardness of decoding problem which is known to be hard when the weight of error vector is small or large enough. In a nutshell, for a given parity check matrix $H \in \mathbb{F}_q^{(n-k) \times n}$ or a correspond generator matrix $G \in \mathbb{F}_q^{k \times n}$, the decoding problem is hard [8] if we seek a word e of relative weight $w/n < w_{\text{easy}}^- = \frac{q-1}{q} \frac{r}{n}$ or $w/n > w_{\text{easy}}^+ = 1 - \frac{1}{q} \frac{r}{n}$. Considering the decrypt failure rate, we choose small weight as our parameters in the IPFEc scheme (Fig. 3).

Fig. 3. Asymptotic hardness of decoding

Nowadays, the most effect attack toward these code-based encryption systems is the information set decoding attack. Information set decoding is an approach introduced by Prange [22]. The idea is to find a set of coordinates of a garbled vector which are error-free and such that the restriction of the codes generator matrix to these positions is invertible. Then, the original message can be computed by multiplying the encrypted vector by the inverse of the submatrix. Peters [21] generalised the ISD algorithm over $\mathbb{F}_2$ to $\mathbb{F}_q$, afterwards Niebuhr et al. [18] optimized it and show a lower bound for their ISD algorithm in $\mathbb{F}_q$. [4,14,15] improves the ISD algorithm over $\mathbb{F}_q$ by using the technique of nearest neighbour approach, but there are many limitations in the scope of application of these works. With big q as the size of the finite field, [18] still can be viewed as the most effective ISD attack.

Let n be the length of the code $\mathcal{C}$ over $\mathbb{F}_q$, k be the dimension and $r = n - k$ be the co-dimension. To correct t errors, the lower bound for the expected cost in the binary operation of the algorithm is

$$\text{ISD}(n, k, t, q) = \min_p \frac{1}{\sqrt{q-1}} \cdot \frac{2l \min \left(\binom{n}{t}(q-1)^t, q^r \right)}{\lambda_q \binom{r-l}{t-p} \binom{k+l}{p}(q-1)^t} \cdot \sqrt{\binom{k+l}{p}(q-1)^p} \quad (8)$$

with $l = \log_q \left(K_q \lambda_q \sqrt{\binom{k}{p}(q-1)^{p-1}} \cdot \ln(q)/2 \right)$ and $\lambda_q = 1 - \exp(-1) \approx 0.63$.

In order to resist the ISD attack, we have to take parameters n, k, t, q for security parameter 2^λ such that

$$\text{ISD}(n, k, w, q) > 2^\lambda.$$

Performance. For example, to support inner-product encryption of vector with length $l = 5$ and to reach 2^{80} security, we have to choose $(q, n, k, w, c) = (32771, 8000, 4000, 78, 800)$, which causes a public key size as 50.07 MB and ciphertext size as 5.01 MB. Since we do not need any decode operation, our encryption and decryption algorithms runs fast. With the above parameters, we simulate our full scheme on MAGMA [13]. It shows that the **Setup** and **Key-Der** step can be done within 167s, the **IPEncrypt** algorithm takes 256s, and the **IPDecrypt** algorithm takes 1.79s.

6 Conclusion

In this work, we construct a code based inner product encryption scheme. As far as we know, this is the first code-based FE scheme. The security of our scheme can be reduced to the syndrome decoding problem for random linear codes. Since the basic scheme suffers from an intolerant decrypt fail rate, we use Fiat-Shamir transformation to get the full scheme with correctness property. This costs a very large parameter size but our scheme performs well in the running time. Although our scheme needs a very large parameter size, it is a pioneering trial to construct cryptographic applications from coding theory. For future, how to design more efficient code-based inner product FE schemes and other FE schemes are worthwhile to work on.

Acknowledgements. This work is supported by Guangdong Major Project of Basic and Applied Basic Research (2019B030302008) and the National Natural Science Foundation of China (No. 61972429).

References

1. Abdalla, M., Bourse, F., De Caro, A., Pointcheval, D.: Simple functional encryption schemes for inner products. In: Katz, J. (ed.) PKC 2015. LNCS, vol. 9020, pp. 733–751. Springer, Heidelberg (2015). https://doi.org/10.1007/978-3-662-46447-2_33
2. Agrawal, S., Agrawal, S., Badrinarayanan, S., et al.: Function private functional encryption and property preserving encryption: new de and positive results. Cryptology ePrint Archive, Report 2013/744
3. Albrecht, M., Bernstein, D.J., Chou, T., et al.: Classic McEliece (2020). https://classic.mceliece.org/
4. Becker, A., Joux, A., May, A., Meurer, A.: Decoding random binary linear codes in $2^{n/20}$: how $1 + 1 = 0$ improves information set decoding. In: Pointcheval, D., Johansson, T. (eds.) EUROCRYPT 2012. LNCS, vol. 7237, pp. 520–536. Springer, Heidelberg (2012). https://doi.org/10.1007/978-3-642-29011-4_31
5. Berlekamp, E., McEliece, R., van Tilborg, H.: On the inherent intractability of certain coding problems. IEEE Trans. Inf. Theory **24**(3), 384–386 (1978)
6. Bishop, A., Jain, A., Kowalczyk, L.: Function-hiding inner product encryption. In: Iwata, T., Cheon, J.H. (eds.) ASIACRYPT 2015. LNCS, vol. 9452, pp. 470–491. Springer, Heidelberg (2015). https://doi.org/10.1007/978-3-662-48797-6_20
7. Boneh, D., Sahai, A., Waters, B.: Functional encryption: definitions and challenges. In: Ishai, Y. (ed.) TCC 2011. LNCS, vol. 6597, pp. 253–273. Springer, Heidelberg (2011). https://doi.org/10.1007/978-3-642-19571-6_16
8. Debris-Alazard, T., Sendrier, N., Tillich, J.-P.: Wave: a new family of trapdoor one-way preimage sampleable functions based on codes. In: Galbraith, S.D., Moriai, S. (eds.) ASIACRYPT 2019. LNCS, vol. 11921, pp. 21–51. Springer, Cham (2019). https://doi.org/10.1007/978-3-030-34578-5_2

9. Fiat, A., Shamir, A.: How to prove yourself: practical solutions to identification and signature problems. In: Odlyzko, A.M. (ed.) CRYPTO 1986. LNCS, vol. 263, pp. 186–194. Springer, Heidelberg (1987). https://doi.org/10.1007/3-540-47721-7_12

10. Katsumata, S., Nishimaki, R., Yamada, S., Yamakawa, T.: Adaptively secure inner product encryption from LWE. In: Moriai, S., Wang, H. (eds.) ASIACRYPT 2020. LNCS, vol. 12493, pp. 375–404. Springer, Cham (2020). https://doi.org/10.1007/978-3-030-64840-4_13

11. Katz, J., Sahai, A., Waters, B.: Predicate encryption supporting disjunctions, polynomial equations, and inner products. In: Smart, N. (ed.) EUROCRYPT 2008. LNCS, vol. 4965, pp. 146–162. Springer, Heidelberg (2008). https://doi.org/10.1007/978-3-540-78967-3_9

12. Kim, S., Lewi, K., Mandal, A., Montgomery, H., Roy, A., Wu, D.J.: Function-hiding inner product encryption is practical. In: Catalano, D., De Prisco, R. (eds.) SCN 2018. LNCS, vol. 11035, pp. 544–562. Springer, Cham (2018). https://doi.org/10.1007/978-3-319-98113-0_29

13. MAGMA Computational Algebra System. http://magma.maths.usyd.edu.au/calc/

14. May, A., Ozerov, I.: On computing nearest neighbors with applications to decoding of binary linear codes. In: Oswald, E., Fischlin, M. (eds.) EUROCRYPT 2015. LNCS, vol. 9056, pp. 203–228. Springer, Heidelberg (2015). https://doi.org/10.1007/978-3-662-46800-5_9

15. May, A., Meurer, A., Thomae, E.: Decoding random linear codes in $\tilde{\mathcal{O}}(2^{0.054n})$. In: Lee, D.H., Wang, X. (eds.) ASIACRYPT 2011. LNCS, vol. 7073, pp. 107–124. Springer, Heidelberg (2011). https://doi.org/10.1007/978-3-642-25385-0_6

16. Mceliece, R.J.: A public-key cryptosystem based on algebraic coding theory. DSN Progress Rep. **42**(44), 114–116 (1978)

17. Niederreiter, H.: Knapsack-type cryptosystems and algebraic coding theory. Probl. Contr. Inf. Theory **15**(2), 159–166 (1986)

18. Niebuhr, R., Cayrel, P.L., Bulygin, S., et al.: On lower bounds for information set decoding over FQ. In: SCC 2010, pp. 143–157. Springer

19. Okamoto, T., Takashima, K.: Adaptively attribute-hiding (hierarchical) inner product encryption. IEICE Trans. Fund. Electr. Commun. Comput. Sci. **E99.A**(1), 92–117 (2016)

20. Okamoto, T., Takashima, K.: Fully secure unbounded inner-product and attribute-based encryption. In: Wang, X., Sako, K. (eds.) ASIACRYPT 2012. LNCS, vol. 7658, pp. 349–366. Springer, Heidelberg (2012). https://doi.org/10.1007/978-3-642-34961-4_22

21. Peters, C.: Information-set decoding for linear codes over $\mathbf{F}_q$. In: Sendrier, N. (ed.) PQCrypto 2010. LNCS, vol. 6061, pp. 81–94. Springer, Heidelberg (2010). https://doi.org/10.1007/978-3-642-12929-2_7

22. Prange, E.: The use of information sets in decoding cyclic codes. IRE Trans. Inf. Theory **8**(5), 5–9 (1962)

23. Sahai, A., Waters, B.: Fuzzy identity-based encryption. In: Cramer, R. (ed.) EUROCRYPT 2005. LNCS, vol. 3494, pp. 457–473. Springer, Heidelberg (2005). https://doi.org/10.1007/11426639_27

Digital Signature

A CCA-Full-Anonymous Group Signature with Verifiable Controllable Linkability in the Standard Model

Ru Xiang, Sha Ma$^{(\boxtimes)}$, Qiong Huang, and Ximing Li

College of Mathematics and Informatics, South China Agricultural University,
Guangzhou 510642, China
qhuang@scau.edu.com, liximing@scau.edu.cn

Abstract. Group signatures allow users to anonymously sign messages on behalf of a group. In this paper, we construct a group signature with verifiable controllable linkability in a generic way, where a linking authority (LA) can link two signatures to determine whether they are generated by the same unknown signer or not. Our core building block is a structure-preserving public key encryption with equality test, where public keys, plaintexts, and ciphertexts are all group elements, encryption, decryption, and test algorithms only consist of group and pairing operations. Due to its structure-preserving property, our scheme is easy to combine with non-interactive zero-knowledge proofs on bilinear groups and hence make this combination more efficient than the most CCA-full-anonymous GSS-VCL constructions in the standard model.

Keywords: Group signature · Verifiable controllable linkability ·
CCA-full-anonymity · Standard model · Structure-preserving public
key encryption with equality test

1 Introduction

By providing real-time information about current traffic conditions, collision avoidance assistance, automatic emergency notification or visual enhancement systems, Vehicle Safety Communication (VSC) technology will help drivers make more coordinated and smarter decisions, which improves the national highway system overall safety and efficiency. However, the VSC technology broadcasts information about the current location, speed and heading of the vehicle, which causes malicious entities to track individuals, collect information, and then use the collected information to blackmail them. What is more serious is that this may even threaten the user's personal safety. So the notification message from the vehicle in vehicle adhoc network (VANET) should be anonymous. However, unconditional anonymity may be abused, such as sending false messages, Sybil attacks, and spam. As one of the most common anonymous primitives, people have done a lot of research on group signature schemes (GSS). Compared with the traditional digital signature schemes where signers can be publicly identified,

© Springer Nature Switzerland AG 2021
Q. Huang and Y. Yu (Eds.): ProvSec 2021, LNCS 13059, pp. 279–295, 2021.
https://doi.org/10.1007/978-3-030-90402-9_15

group signature schemes, proposed by Chaum and van Heyst [1], allow users to anonymously sign messages on behalf of a group. The verifiers can determine if a signature has been actually generated by a member in the group, while they cannot determine the specific identity of the signer. The group manager (GM) can open a signature to determine the specific identity of the signer if necessary.

At the same time, considering that a signer may wish to provide a specific verifier with linking capability, his signature is still unlinked to other verifiers. In the traditional GSS [2], the verifier can have this linkability in a very limited way by querying two signatures to the Opener to compare their signer identities. This online linking operation not only puts a serious burden on the Opener, but the whole process is very slow. In order to make a group signature suitable for those real-time applications such as VANET, we construct a group signature with verifiable controllable linkability (GSS-VCL) in the standard model, where a linking authority (LA) can link two signatures to determine whether they are generated by the same unknown signer. This verifiable controllable linkability (VCL) will significantly reduce the burden of the Opener by distributing linking tasks to local verifiers.

Bellare et al. [2] define CCA-full-anonymity, which requires that an adversary can't determine whether a signature is generated by a user in question, even if the adversary has the secret keys of all users. It allows the adversary to query the opening oracle. Boneh et al. [4] relax the requirement of CCA-full-anonymity and define CPA-full-anonymity, where the adversary cannot query the opening oracle. Moreover, some group signature schemes [5] only achieve selfless anonymity, which is a weaker notion than CPA-full-anonymity. It can only resist adversaries who do not have the users' signing keys. If a user's secret key is exposed, the anonymity of the signature associated with the secret key will not be guaranteed.

In some cases, it may be desirable to link different signatures of the same anonymous signer, such as anonymous credentials, electronic voting, and so on. To solve this problem, Blazy et al. [6] propose a generic framework of GSS-VCL. The main idea of this primitive is similar to the group signatures with controllable linkability (GSS-CL) [7,8], where a dedicated linking authority (LA) can link two signatures to determine whether they are produced by the same signer without learning the actual identity of the signer, in other words, the signer is still anonymous. Compared with GSS-CL, GSS-VCL takes untrusted LAs into account, i.e., a LA needs to provide verifiable evidence to prove that its decision is correct. However, the above schemes [7,8] are constructed in the random oracle, and [7] can only achieve CPA-full-anonymity. As we know, it's limited to make a heuristic argument in terms of security in the random oracle and it may be required to achieve CCA-full-anonymity in some applications. Though [6,8]can achieve CCA-full-anonymity using the twin encryption paradigm [9] or Cramer-Shoup encryption [10] that makes their scheme can only use generic zero-knowledge proof technology to prove knowledge of the respective values, which makes their scheme inefficient. Those motivate our work for a new efficient GSS-VCL scheme which can achieve CCA-full-anonymity in the standard model. The core of our VCL technique is a tool to extend an

IND-CPA/IND-CCA secure public key encryption scheme so that the scheme has a feature that allows a designated party to determine whether two messages contained in two ciphertexts are the same value without decrypting the ciphertexts.

1.1 Our Contributions

The contributions of this paper are as follows.

- We construct a group signature with verifiable controllable linkability (GSS-VCL) in the standard model, where a linking authority (LA) can link two signatures to determine whether they are generated by the same unknown signer. Compared with the existing group signature with verifiable controllable linkability [6], since the core building block of our scheme is structure-preserving that makes our scheme easy to combine with non-interactive zero-knowledge proofs for bilinear groups, which may make our GSS-VCL more efficient than [6] when implementing CCA-full-anonymity in the standard model.
- As a core building block of our GSS-VCL, we introduce structure-preserving into public key encryption with equality test scheme and propose structure-preserving public key encryption with equality test (SP-PKEET). A public key encryption with equality test scheme is structure-preserving if the public keys, plaintexts, and ciphertexts are all group elements, and the encryption, decryption, and test algorithms consist of only group and pairing operations.
- We prove the security of SP-PKEET in the standard model. It can achieve S-PRIV1-CCA security against the Type-I adversary who has the trapdoors and IND-CCA security against the Type-II adversary without trapdoors under the DLIN assumption [4].

1.2 Related Work

PKEET. The main idea of the VCL is related to the concept of public-key encryption with equality tests (PKEET) [8,11,12], where a party can determine whether the two ciphertexts contain the same plaintext without decryption. [8] makes use of cryptographic hash functions to achieve security against chosen-ciphertext attacks, these hash functions prevent one from efficiently proving relations between the input and output of the encryption procedure. It is worth mentioning that the above schemes are constructed in the random oracle, which is limited to make a heuristic argument in terms of security. Though [11,12] are constructed in the standard model, they involve encrypting hashes of the messages.

Group Signatures with Opening. In standard group signatures [2,4], given two signatures, the group manager (GM) with the opening key can open them and recover the identities of the signers to determine whether the two signatures are signed by the same signer, but at high costs for privacy: the full identity of the signer will be recovered for each linking request.

Group Signatures Supporting Public Linking. Link-but-not-trace group signatures, first proposed by Nakanishi et al. [13], typically tag the double signer in a way so that signatures from the same signer can be linked easily in the future. In the tracing-by-linking (TbL) group signatures [14], the signer's anonymity cannot be revoked by any combination of authorities. But if a group member signs twice (per event), then its identity can be traced by any member of the public without needing any trapdoor. Subsequently, some group signatures [15] based on basename or pseudonym to achieve linkability are proposed. Since the linking in these schemes are public operations, they cannot achieve CL, let alone VCL.

Convertably Linkable Group Signatures. The convertably linkable group signatures (CL-GSS), first proposed by Garms et al. [16], allow for flexible and selective linkability. All group signatures are associated with pseudonyms, which are unlinkable by default. A converter converts the received pseudonyms into a consistent representation when needed, which means that all pseudonyms from the same user will be converted to the same value. However, this method requires a computational cost that is linearly related to the number of group members to perform the link operation. Besides, this scheme needs to create a new default unlinkable pseudonym for each newly joined member.

Traceable Signatures. Traceable signatures introduced by Kiayias et al. [17] allow tracers to link all group signatures related to a given tracing trapdoor. However, the group signatures generated by other group members are still unlinkable unless the group manager also sends their tracing trapdoors to the tracers. The method requires computational costs linearly related to the number of group members to perform the link operations, which will become impractical for larger groups. In addition, whenever a new member joins a group, the group manager needs to communicate the tracing trapdoors of new members in time.

Group Signatures with Verifier-Local Revocation. Group signatures with verifier-local revocation (GSS-VLR) introduced by Boneh et al. [5] allow the verifiers to determine whether a signature was signed by a member who has been revoked. However, the verifiers must update the revocation list (RL) on every revocation, and the signatures of the revoked members are linkable for all verifiers. Besides that, GSS-VLR [5] can only achieve selfless anonymity.

Group Signatures with Controllable Linkability. Group signatures with controllable linkability (GSS-CL) [7,8] allow a dedicated linking authority (LA) to determine whether the two signatures have been signed by the same signer without learning the actual identity of the signer, in other words, its anonymity remains. However, they can only achieve CPA-full-anonymity in the random oracle, and they do not take untrusted LAs into account.

1.3   Comparison

As shown in Table 1, we give the features comparison of proposed group schemes from implementation of CL or VCL, CCA-full-anonymity, and other functionalities. It can be learnt from the Table 1 that our GSS-VCL is a dynamic group signature in the standard model, which can achieve CCA-full-anonymity, while most existing works can only achieve CPA-full-anonymity [7,8,13,14,16] or self-less anonymity [5] in the random oracle model. The LA in our scheme can efficiently perform the linking operation in a constant time. Since the LA has a single trapdoor, our scheme does not require additional memory requirements to store trapdoors as schemes [5,13,14,16,17], and there is no need for the LA to communicate new users' trapdoors with the group manager when new users join the group.

2 Preliminaries

2.1 Mathematical Preliminaries

Bilinear Map. Let $\mathbb{G}, \mathbb{G}_T$ denote two groups of prime order p. A bilinear map $e : \mathbb{G} \times \mathbb{G} \to \mathbb{G}_T$ satisfies the following properties:

1. Bilinear: For any $U, V \in \mathbb{G}$ and $a, b \in \mathbb{Z}_p^*$, $e\left(U^a, V^b\right) = e\left(U, V\right)^{ab}$;
2. Non-degenerate: If g is a generator of $\mathbb{G}$, then $e(g, g)$ is the generator of $\mathbb{G}_T$;
3. Computable: There exists an efficient algorithm to compute $e(U, V)$ for any $U, V \in \mathbb{G}$.

Table 1. Comparison of concepts regarding their applicability for VCL

Mechanism	CL^a	VCL^b	$U\text{-}Join^c$	$Dy\text{-}G^d$	SM^e	$CCA\text{-}FA^f$	$Link^g$	$Memory^h$
TbL [14]	×	×	✓	✓	×	×	$\mathcal{O}(N)$	$\mathcal{O}(N)$
Link-but-not-trace [13]	×	×	×	✓	×	×	$\mathcal{O}(N)$	$\mathcal{O}(N)$
GSS-UCL [15]	×	×	✓	✓	×	×	$\mathcal{O}(N)$	$\mathcal{O}(N)$
Traceable signatures [17]	✓	×	✓	✓	×	✓	$\mathcal{O}(N)$	$\mathcal{O}(N)$
GSS-VLR [5]	✓	×	✓	×	×	×	$\mathcal{O}(N)$	$\mathcal{O}(N)$
CL-GSS [16]	✓	×	✓	✓	×	×	$\mathcal{O}(N)$	$\mathcal{O}(N)$
GSS-CL [7,8]	✓	×	×	✓	×	×	$\mathcal{O}(1)$	$\mathcal{O}(1)$
Ours	✓	✓	×	✓	✓	✓	$\mathcal{O}(1)$	$\mathcal{O}(1)$

[a] CL denotes implementation of CL.
[b] VCL denotes implementation of VCL.
[c] U-Join denotes the communication overhead (communication of the trapdoors to the LA) each time a new user joins the group or a member leaves a group.
[d] Dy-G denotes dynamic group.
[e] SM denotes standard model.
[f] CCA-FA denotes CCA-full-anonymity.
[g] Link denotes the additional computational overhead for linking.
[h] Memory denotes the additional memory overhead for linking.

Decisional Linear Assumption (DLIN) [4]. Let $\mathbb{G}$ be a group of prime order p. For randomly chosen $g_1, g_2, g_3 \leftarrow \mathbb{G}$ and $r, s, t \leftarrow \mathbb{Z}_q$, the following two distributions are computationally indistinguishable:

$$\left(\mathbb{G}, g_1, g_2, g_3, g_1^r, g_2^s, g_3^t\right) \approx \left(\mathbb{G}, g_1, g_2, g_3, g_1^r, g_2^s, g_3^{r+s}\right)$$

2.2 Sign-Encrypt-Proof Paradigm and Efficient Non-interactive Proofs for Bilinear Groups

Signature-encryption-proof (SEP) paradigm [3] is a typical framework of group signatures, which includes a secure signature scheme $DS = (KeyGen_s, Sign, Verify)$, a public key encryption scheme (at least IND-CPA security) $AE = (KeyGen_e, Enc, Dec)$, and a non-interactive zero-knowledge proof system, which is used to prove that the respective values are well-formed.

Groth and Sahai [18] propose efficient non-interactive witness-indistinguishable (NIWI) proofs and non-interactive zero-knowledge (NIZK) proofs for languages on bilinear groups, which can be described as a series of satisfiable equations, i.e., pairing product equations (PPEs), multi-exponentiation equations, and quadratic equations.

3 Group Signatures with Verifiable Controllable Linkability

A GSS-VCL scheme is specified as a tuple $GS = (GkGen, UkGen, Join, Issue, GSig, GVf, Open, Judge, Link, Judge_{Link})$ of polynomial-time algorithms (following [6]).

- $GkGen\left(1^\lambda\right)$: It takes security parameter 1^λ as input, and outputs a tuple (gpk, mik, mok, mlk). The master issue key mik is provided to the IA for issuing certificates, the master opening key mok is provided to the OA for opening signatures, the master linking key mlk is provided to the LA to link two different signatures. gpk represents the group public key.
- $UkGen\left(1^\lambda\right)$: When a $user_i$ wants to join a group, the $user_i$ should run $UkGen$ algorithm to compute a pair of keys (upk_i, usk_i), representing a personal public key and a private key separately.
- $Join/Issue(user_i : upk_i, usk_i; issuer : gpk, mik, upk_i)$: This is an interactive protocol between a $user_i$ and the $issuer$. On input (upk_i, usk_i), the $user_i$ interacts with the $issuer$ and stores some corresponding secret signing key information in gsk_i. On input gpk, mik, upk_i, the $issuer$ interacts with the $user_i$ and registers the usk_i's public key upk_i in $reg[i]$.
- $GSig\left(gpk, m, gsk_i, upk_i\right)$: It takes the group public key gpk, the master issuing key gsk_i, a message m and the personal public key upk_i as input, and it outputs a signature σ.
- $GVf\left(gpk, m, \sigma\right)$: It takes the group public key gpk, a signature σ, a message m and the personal public key upk_i as input, it verifies whether the signature σ is valid concerning the message m and the gpk, and outputs 1 if the verification succeeds and 0 otherwise.
- $Open\left(gpk, reg[i], m, \sigma, mok\right)$: It takes the group public key gpk, the registration table $reg[i]$, the valid signature σ, the message m and the master opening key mok as input, and it returns the signer i and a publicly verifiable proof τ for the corresponding claim. Otherwise, it claims that no group member generates τ.

- *Judge* $(gpk, m, \sigma, i, upk_i, \tau)$: On input the group public key gpk, the signature σ of the message m, the claimed i of the corresponding signer of σ, and the corresponding public key upk_i, the proof τ that the claimed i is indeed the signer of σ. If the proof τ is valid, it outputs 1 and 0 otherwise.
- *Link* $(gpk, m, \sigma, m', \sigma', mlk)$: It takes the group public key gpk, the master linking key mlk, a signature m with σ, and a signature m' with σ' as input. It verifies whether the two signatures are valid for m and m' by asking the GVf algorithm. If all the signatures are valid for the corresponding messages, it uses the mlk to determine whether σ and σ' are produced by the same unknown signer, and outputs $b \in \{1, 0\}$ and a publicly verifiable proof ρ to prove the validity of the result.
- *Judge*$_{Link}$ $(gpk, m, \sigma, m', \sigma', b, \rho)$: It takes the group public key gpk, a signature m with σ, a signature m' with σ', b and the corresponding ρ as input. If the proof ρ is valid for b, it outputs 1 and 0 otherwise.

A GSS-VCL must satisfy the following security properties. Note that in addition to the correctness, anonymity, non-frameability, and traceability properties defined in the BSZ model, Hwang et al. [7] also define LO-Linkability (Link-Only Linkability), JP-Unforgeability (Judge-Proof Unforgeability), and E-Linkability (Enforced Linkability) to satisfy verifiable controllable linkability (VCL), and then Blazy et al. [6] also add the definition of open soundness and Linking Soundness.

4   Structure Preserving Public Key Encryption with Equality Test

We define the notion of structure-preserving encryption with equality test. The term "structure preserving" is borrowed from a structure preserving digital signature [19]. A signature scheme is structure-preserving if its verification keys, messages, and signatures are group elements and the verification predicate is a conjunction of pairing product equations. In 2011, Camenisch et al. [20] proposed a structure preserving CCA secure encryption scheme. A public key encryption scheme is said to be structure-preserving if (1) its public keys, messages, and ciphertexts consist entirely of elements of a bilinear group, (2) its encryption and decryption algorithms perform only group and bilinear map operations, and (3) it is provably secure against chosen-ciphertext attacks. In the paper, we propose a structure preserving encryption with equality test (SP-PKEET), which can be used as a main building block of the GSS-VCL in the standard model. Compared with [20], we add an authorization algorithm and a test algorithm to realize the equality test function in our SP-PKEET, in which the authorization algorithm and the test algorithm perform only group and bilinear map operations.

4.1 Definition

A structure-preserving public key encryption with equality test (SP-PKEET) cryptosystem consists of the following algorithms $(KeyGen, Enc, Dec, Aut, Test)$:

- $KeyGen\,(1^\lambda)$: It takes the security parameter 1^λ as input and outputs the public key pk and the private key sk.
- $Enc(pk, L, m)$: It takes the public key pk, a message m with a label L as input and outputs a ciphertext C.
- $Dec(sk, L, C)$: It takes the private key sk, a label L and ciphertext C as input. If C is a valid ciphertext, it outputs the message m, Otherwise, it outputs $\perp$.
- $Aut(sk)$: It takes the private key sk as input and outputs a trapdoor td.
- $Test(C_i, C_j, td_i, td_j)$: It takes two ciphertexts C_i, C_j, td_i, td_j for $user_i, user_j$ as input and outputs 1 if messages associated with C_i, C_j are equal. Otherwise it outputs 0.

4.2 Security Models for SP-PKEET

We consider the following two types of adversaries to define the security model for SP-PKEET.

1. Type-I adversary: The adversary can request to issue a trapdoor for the target user and thus can perform equality tests on the challenge ciphertext C_t. This type of adversary aims to decide C_t is the encryption of which message between two candidates.
2. Type-II adversary: The adversary cannot request to issue a trapdoor for the target user and thus cannot perform equality tests on the challenge ciphertext C_t. This type of adversary aims to decide C_t is the encryption of which message between two candidates.

Lu et al. [21] propose the security notion of S-PRIV1-CCA. Below we recall S-PRIV1-CCA security against Type-I adversary $\mathcal{A}_1 = (\mathcal{A}_m, \mathcal{A}_g)$ in SP-PKEET. $\mathcal{A}_m$ and $\mathcal{A}_g$ share neither coins nor state. Assume that the target receiver has index t $(1 \leq t \leq n)$. The game between $\mathcal{A}_1$ and the challenger is as follows:

(1) Setup: The challenger takes a security parameter 1^λ and runs the $KeyGen$ algorithm to generate public/secret key pair (pk_i, sk_i) for $1 \leq i \leq N$. Then, it gives the pk_i to $\mathcal{A}_m$ and $\mathcal{A}_g$.
(2) Phase 1: $\mathcal{A}_m$ is allowed to issue key retrieve queries, decryption queries, and authorization queries for polynomially many times. The constraint is that $\langle t \rangle$ does not appear in key retrieve queries.
   - Key retrieve queries $\langle i \rangle$: The challenger sends sk_i to $\mathcal{A}_m$.
   - Decryption queries $\langle i, C_i \rangle$: The challenger runs Dec algorithm on input $\langle C_i, sk_i \rangle$ to decrypt C_i using sk_i, and sends the output to $\mathcal{A}_m$.
   - Authorization queries $\langle i \rangle$: The challenger runs Aut algorithm on input $\langle i \rangle$ to compute td_i and sends td_i to $\mathcal{A}_m$.

(3) Challenge: The challenger $\mathcal{A}_m$ randomly chooses massage $(m_0, x_0), (m_1, x_1)$ and sends them to the challenger. Then the challenger randomly chooses $b \in \{0, 1\}$ and runs the Enc algorithm to encrypt m_b to get the challenge ciphertext C_t, and it sends the challenge ciphertext C_t to $\mathcal{A}_g$.
(4) Phase 2: $\mathcal{A}_g$ issues queries as in Phase 1. The constraints are that
  - $\langle t \rangle$ cannot be queried to the key retrieve queries.
  - $\langle t, C_t \rangle$ does not appear in the decryption queries.
(5) Guess: $\mathcal{A}_g$ outputs h. If $h = x_1$, then $b' = 1$ else $b' = 0$.

The advantage of $\mathcal{A}_1$ is defined as

$$\mathbf{Adv}_{SP\text{-}PKEET,\mathcal{A}_1}^{S\text{-}PRIV1\text{-}CCA}(\lambda) = \left| \Pr\left[b' = b\right] - \frac{1}{2} \right|.$$

Definition 1. *For any PPT adversary $\mathcal{A}_1$, if its advantage $\mathbf{Adv}_{SP\text{-}PKEET,\mathcal{A}_1}^{S\text{-}PRIV1\text{-}CCA}(\lambda)$ is negligible in the security parameter 1^λ, we say that SP-PKEET is S-PRIV1-CCA secure.*

We define IND-CCA security against Type-II adversary $\mathcal{A}_2$ in SP-PKEET. Assume that the target receiver has index t $(1 \leq t \leq n)$. The game between $\mathcal{A}_2$ and the challenger is as follows.

(1) Setup: The challenger takes a security parameter 1^λ and runs the $KeyGen$ algorithm to generate public/secret key pair (pk_i, sk_i) for $1 \leq i \leq N$. Then, it gives the pk_i to $\mathcal{A}_2$.
(2) Phase 1: $\mathcal{A}_2$ is allowed to issue decryption queries for polynomially many times. The constraints are that $\langle t \rangle$ does not appear in key retrieve queries as well as authorization queries.
  - Key retrieve queries $\langle i \rangle$: The challenger sends sk_i to $\mathcal{A}_2$.
  - Decryption queries $\langle i, C_i \rangle$: The challenger runs Dec algorithm on input $\langle C_i, sk_i \rangle$ to decrypt C_i using sk_i to get m, and sends m to $\mathcal{A}_2$.
  - Authorization queries $\langle i \rangle$: The challenger runs Aut algorithm on input $\langle i \rangle$ to compute td_i and sends td_i to $\mathcal{A}_2$.
(3) Challenge: The adversary $\mathcal{A}_2$ randomly chooses massage $m_0, m_1 \in \mathcal{M}$ and sends them to the challenger. Then the challenger randomly chooses $b \in \{0, 1\}$ and runs the Enc algorithm to encrypt m_b to get the challenge ciphertext C_t, and it sends the challenge ciphertext C_t to $\mathcal{A}_2$.
(4) Phase 2: $\mathcal{A}_2$ issues queries as in Phase 1. The constraints are that $\langle t \rangle$ does not appear in key retrieve queries as well as authorization queries, $\langle t, C_t \rangle$ does not appear in the decryption queries.
(5) Guess: $\mathcal{A}_2$ outputs b' and wins if $b' = b$.
    The advantage of $\mathcal{A}_2$ is defined as

$$\mathbf{Adv}_{SP\text{-}PKEET,\mathcal{A}_2}^{IND\text{-}CCA}(\lambda) = \left| \Pr\left[b' = b\right] - \frac{1}{2} \right|.$$

Definition 2. *For any PPT adversary $\mathcal{A}_2$, if its advantage $\mathbf{Adv}_{SP\text{-}PKEET,\mathcal{A}_2}^{IND\text{-}CCA}(\lambda)$ is negligible in the security parameter 1^λ, we say that SP-PKEET is IND-CCA secure.*

4.3 Construction

We construct an SP-PKEET scheme in a bilinear group based on the DLIN assumption, which is described as follows.

- $KeyGen\,(1^\lambda)$: Choose random group generators $g, g', g_1, g_2, g_3 \in \mathbb{G}$. For randomly chosen $\alpha \leftarrow \mathbb{Z}_q^3$, set $h_1 = g_1^{\alpha_1} g_3^{\alpha_3}, h_2 = g_2^{\alpha_2} g_3^{\alpha_3}$. Then, select $\beta_0, \ldots, \beta_5 \leftarrow \mathbb{Z}_q^3$, and compute $f_{i,1} = g_1^{\beta_{i,1}} g_3^{\beta_{i,3}}, f_{i,2} = g_2^{\beta_{i,2}} g_3^{\beta_{i,3}}$, for $i = 0, \ldots, 5$. Output $pk = (g, g', g_1, g_2, g_3, h_1, h_2, \{f_{i,1}, f_{i,2}\}_{i=0}^5)$ and $sk = (\{\alpha\}, \{\beta_i\}_{i=0}^5)$.
- $Enc(pk, L, m)$: To encrypt a message m with a label L, choose random $r, s \leftarrow \mathbb{Z}_q$ and set $u_1 = g_1^r, u_2 = g_2^s, u_3 = g_3^{r+s}, \quad c = m \cdot h_1^r h_2^s, \quad v = \prod_{i=0}^3 \hat{e}\left(f_{i,1}^r f_{i,2}^s, u_i\right) \cdot \hat{e}\left(f_{4,1}^r f_{4,2}^s, c\right) \cdot \hat{e}\left(f_{5,1}^r f_{5,2}^s, L\right)$, where $u_0 = g$. Output $C = (u_1, u_2, u_3, c, v)$.
- $Dec(sk, L, C)$: Parse C as (u_1, u_2, u_3, c, v). Then check whether

$$v \stackrel{?}{=} \prod_{i=0}^3 \hat{e}\left(u_1^{\beta_{i,1}} u_2^{\beta_{i,2}} u_3^{\beta_{i,3}}, u_i\right) \cdot \hat{e}\left(u_1^{\beta_{4,1}} u_2^{\beta_{4,2}} u_3^{\beta_{4,3}}, c\right) \cdot \hat{e}\left(u_1^{\beta_{5,1}} u_2^{\beta_{5,2}} u_3^{\beta_{5,3}}, L\right),$$

where $u_0 = g$. If the latter is unsuccessful, reject the ciphertext as invalid. Otherwise, output $m = c \cdot (u_1^{\alpha_1} u_2^{\alpha_2} u_3^{\alpha_3})^{-1}$.
- $Aut(sk)$: This algorithm outputs $td = (g'^{\alpha_1}, g'^{\alpha_2}, g'^{\alpha_3})$.
- $Test(C_i, C_j, td_i, td_j)$: This algorithm outputs 1 if

$$e\left(\frac{c_i}{c_j}, g'\right) = \frac{e\left(u_{i,1}, td_{i,1}\right) e\left(u_{i,2}, td_{i,2}\right) e\left(u_{i,3}, td_{i,3}\right)}{e\left(u_{j,1}, td_{j,1}\right) e\left(u_{j,2}, td_{j,2}\right) e\left(u_{j,3}, td_{j,3}\right)},$$

otherwise return 0.

The ciphertext $C \in \mathbb{G}^4 \times \mathbb{G}_T$. With the pairing randomization technique in [22], $v \in \mathbb{G}_T$ can be replaced with six group elements $v_0, \ldots, v_5 \in \mathbb{G}$ for which the equation holds: $v = \prod_{i=0}^3 \hat{e}\left(v_i, u_i\right) \cdot \hat{e}\left(v_4, c\right) \cdot \hat{e}\left(v_5, L\right)$. Therefore, the ciphertext only consists of the elements in $\mathbb{G}$.

Theorem 1. *If DLIN holds, the above SP-PKEET scheme is S-PRIV1-CCA secure against type-I adversary in the standard model.*

Proof. Let $\mathcal{A}_1$ be a PPT adversary who can break the S-PRIV1-CCA security of SP-PKEET. We start with the original S-PRIV1-CCA game and end up with a game where the challenge ciphertext is an encryption of a random message from the message space. Let X_i be the event that the adversary $\mathcal{A}_1$ outputs $b' = b$ in **Game** i.

Game 0. This is the standard S-PRIV1-CCA game.

$$\Pr\left[X_0\right] = \mathbf{Adv}_{SP\text{-}PKEET, \mathcal{A}_1}^{S\text{-}PRIV1\text{-}CCA}(\lambda) + \frac{1}{2}.$$

Game 1. For the tuple $((m_0, x_0), (m_1, x_1), L)$ chosen by the adversary $\mathcal{A}_m$, the challenger computes the challenge ciphertext using the "decryption procedure" as follows: $u_1 = g_1^r, u_2 = g_2^s, u_3 = g_3^{r+s}, c = m \cdot u_1^{\alpha_1} u_2^{\alpha_2} u_3^{\alpha_3}, v = \prod_{i=0}^{3} \hat{e}(u_1^{\beta_{i,1}} u_2^{\beta_{i,2}} u_3^{\beta_{i,3}}, u_i) \cdot \hat{e}(u_1^{\beta_{4,1}} u_2^{\beta_{4,2}} u_3^{\beta_{4,3}}, c) \cdot \hat{e}(u_1^{\beta_{5,1}} u_2^{\beta_{5,2}} u_3^{\beta_{5,3}}, L)$. Since the change is only syntactical, Game 1 is identical to Game 0. We have $\Pr[X_1] = \Pr[X_0]$.

Game 2. The first three parts of the challenge ciphertext are computed as follows: $u_1 = g_1^r, u_2 = g_2^s, u_3 = g_3^t$ where $r, s, t \leftarrow \mathbb{Z}_q$ and $r + s \neq t$, Game 1 and Game 2 are indistinguishable by DLIN assumption. We have $|\Pr[X_2] - \Pr[X_1]| = negl(\lambda)$.

Game 3. Note that in all the games, any decryption queries with correct ciphertext, i.e., a decryption query with random vector DLIN tuple, will produce a unique plaintext. In other words, regardless of the concrete choice of sk matching the pk seen by the adversary, this type of queries will not reveal any information about the sk.

In this game, the decryption queries with "malformed" ciphertext will be rejected. We consider the following two cases into account.

- $(u_1', u_2', u_3', c', L') = (u_1, u_2, u_3, c, L)$. Decryption queries like this will be rejected whether v is equal to v' or not, because the former is the challenge ciphertext and the latter fails in verification predicate trivially.
- $(u_1', u_2', u_3', c', L') \neq (u_1, u_2, u_3, c, L)$. Decryption queries like this will be rejected with overwhelming probability. Denote this by **Lemma** 2.

Since the number of decrypted queries is polynomial, We have $|\Pr[X_3] - \Pr[X_2]| = negl(\lambda)$.

Game 4. The challenge ciphertext is an encryption of a random message from the message space. By **Lemma 1**, Game 4 is identical to Game 3. $\Pr[X_4] = \Pr[X_3]$.

Due to the challenger's choice b is independent from the ciphertext in **Game 4**, We have $\Pr[X_4] = \frac{1}{2}$. Then, by the indistinguishability of the sequence games, $\mathbf{Adv}_{SP\text{-}PKEET,\mathcal{A}_1}^{S\text{-}PRIV1\text{-}CCA}(\lambda) = negl(\lambda)$.

Lemma 1 shows that when computing the challenge ciphertext in Game 4, the one-time pad of the message can be replaced by a random message from the message space. Lemma 2 shows that any decryption query with incorrect ciphertext will be rejected except with negligible probability.

For the proof of the Lemma 1 and Lemma 2, let $g, g', g_1, g_2, g_3 \in \mathbb{G}$ and $u_1 = g_1^r, u_2 = g_2^s, u_3 = g_3^t$ where $r, s, t \leftarrow \mathbb{Z}_q$ and $r + s \neq t$. For convenience, let $g_1 = g^{z_1}, g_2 = g^{z_2}, g_3 = g^{z_3}, g' = g^{z_4}, z_1, z_2, z_3, z_4 \in \mathbb{Z}_q$.

Lemma 1. *For randomly chosen $\alpha_1, \alpha_2, \alpha_3 \leftarrow \mathbb{Z}_q^3$, let $h_1 = g_1^{\alpha_1} g_3^{\alpha_3}, h_2 = g_2^{\alpha_2} g_3^{\alpha_3}, \pi = u_1^{\alpha_1} u_2^{\alpha_2} u_3^{\alpha_3}, td = (td_1, td_2, td_3) = (g'^{\alpha_1}, g'^{\alpha_2}, g'^{\alpha_3})$. Then, it is true that the following distributions are equivalent for a randomly chosen $\phi \leftarrow \mathbb{G}$:*

$$(h_1, h_2, \pi, td) \equiv (h_1, h_2, \phi, td).$$

Proof. *Due to* $h_1 = g^{z_1\alpha_1 + z_3\alpha_3}$, $h_2 = g^{z_2\alpha_2 + z_3\alpha_3}$, $\pi = g^{rz_1\alpha_1 + sz_2\alpha_1 + tz_3\alpha_3}$, $td = (td_1, td_2, td_3) = (g^{z_4\alpha_1}, g^{z_4\alpha_2}, g^{z_4\alpha_3})$, *so for the tuple* (h_1, h_2, π, td) *we have*

$$
\begin{pmatrix}
z_1 & 0 & z_3 \\
0 & z_2 & z_3 \\
z_1 r & z_2 s & z_3 t \\
z_4 & 0 & 0 \\
0 & z_4 & 0 \\
0 & 0 & z_4
\end{pmatrix}
\cdot
\begin{pmatrix}
\alpha_1 \\
\alpha_2 \\
\alpha_3
\end{pmatrix}
=
\begin{pmatrix}
\operatorname{dlog}_g(h_1) \\
\operatorname{dlog}_g(h_2) \\
\operatorname{dlog}_g(\pi) \\
\operatorname{dlog}_g(td_1) \\
\operatorname{dlog}_g(td_2) \\
\operatorname{dlog}_g(td_3)
\end{pmatrix}.
$$

We denote the coefficient matrix by M *and the corresponding augmented matrix by* $\bar{M}$. *The relationship between the rank of matrix* M *and the rank of* $\bar{M}$ *is* $r(M) = r(\bar{M}) = 3$. *Therefore, for any* $\pi \leftarrow \mathbb{G}$, *and fixed* h_1, h_2, td, *there exists a unique solution* x *which yields the tuple* (h_1, h_2, π, td).

Lemma 2. *Let* (u'_1, u'_2, u'_3) *be any tuple where* $u'_1 = g_1^{r'}$, $u'_2 = g_2^{s'}$, $u'_3 = g_3^{t'}$ *and* $r' + s' \neq t'$. *For randomly chosen* $\boldsymbol{\beta}_0, \ldots, \boldsymbol{\beta}_5 \leftarrow \mathbb{Z}_q^3$, *let* $f_{i,1} = g_1^{\beta_{i,1}} g_3^{\beta_{i,3}}$, $f_{i,2} = g_2^{\beta_{i,2}} g_3^{\beta_{i,3}}$, *for* $i = 0, \ldots, 5$. *Let*

$$
v = \prod_{i=0}^{5} \hat{e}\left(u_1^{\beta_{i,1}} u_2^{\beta_{i,2}} u_3^{\beta_{i,3}}, m_i\right), \quad v' = \prod_{i=0}^{5} e\left(u_1^{\beta_{i,1}} u_2^{\beta_{i,2}} u_3^{\beta_{i,3}}, m'_i\right),
$$

where $m_i, m'_i \in \mathbb{G}^5$ *and* $m_0 = m'_0 = g$. *Then, it is true that the following distributions are equivalent for any* m_i *and* m'_i, $m_i \neq m'_i$: $\left(\{f_{i,1}, f_{i,2}\}_{i=0}^{5}, v, v'\right) \equiv \left(\{f_{i,1}, f_{i,2}\}_{i=0}^{5}, v, \varphi\right)$, *where* $\varphi \leftarrow \mathbb{G}$ *is randomly chosen.*

Proof. *For convenience, let* $m_i = g^{w_i}$, $m'_i = g^{w'_i}$. *Then, for the tuple* $\left(\{f_{i,1}, f_{i,2}\}_{i=0}^{5}, v, v'\right)$ *we have a coefficient matrix of* $(\boldsymbol{\beta}_0^{\top}, \ldots, \boldsymbol{\beta}_5^{\top})^{\top}$:

$$
\begin{pmatrix}
z_1 & 0 & z_3 & \cdots & - & - & - \\
0 & z_2 & z_3 & \cdots & - & - & - \\
- & - & - & \cdots & - & - & - \\
- & - & - & \cdots & - & - & - \\
\vdots & \vdots & \vdots & \ddots & \vdots & \vdots & \vdots \\
- & - & - & \cdots & 0 & z_2 & z_3 \\
r' z_1 & s' z_2 & t' z_3 & \cdots & w'_5 r' z_1 & w'_5 s' z_2 & w'_5 t' z_3 \\
r z_1 & s z_2 & t z_3 & \cdots & w_5 r z_1 & w_5 s z_2 & w_5 t z_3
\end{pmatrix}
$$

Since there exists $i(i \geq 1)$, *such that* $m'_i \neq m_i$, *if we choose the sub-matrix consisting of the intersection of the last two rows and rows* 1, 2, $2i + 1$, $2i + 2$ *with columns* 1, 2, 3, $3i + 1$, $3i + 2$, $3i + 3$, *we can get:*

$$\begin{pmatrix} z_1 & 0 & z_3 & - & - & - \\ 0 & z_2 & z_3 & - & - & - \\ - & - & - & z_1 & 0 & z_3 \\ - & - & - & 0 & z_2 & z_3 \\ r'z_1 & s'z_2 & t'z_3 & w_i'r'z_1 & w_i's'z_2 & w_i't'z_3 \\ rz_1 & sz_2 & tz_3 & w_i rz_1 & w_i sz_2 & w_i tz_3 \end{pmatrix},$$

where the absolute value of its determination is $\pm z_1^2 z_2^2 z_3^2 (w_i' - w_i)(t' - r' - s')(t - r - s) \neq 0$. Therefore, the rows of matrix of the corresponding coefficients are linearly independent.

Theorem 2. *If DLIN holds, the above SP-PKEET scheme is IND-CCA secure against type-II adversary in the standard model.*

We omit the proof of Theorem 2 here and show the proof in the full version.

5   A CCA-Full-Anonymous Group Signature with Verifiable Controllable Linkability

5.1   Adding the VCL Property

Group signatures that are Groth-Sahai proofs of knowledge in a symmetric bilinear group based on the SEP paradigm can be generic transformed to support VCL [6]. This transformation replaces the public key encryption scheme used for the identity escrow within a group signature scheme with our SP-PKEET.

5.2   Making Use of SP-PKEET

The core building block of our GSS with verifiable controllable linkability scheme is SP-PKEET. In order to achieve verifiable controllable linkability, the trapdoor td generated by the Aut algorithm is given to the linking authority (LA) as the master linking key mlk. Given two message-signature pairs (m, σ) and (m', σ'), the LA runs the $Link$ algorithm to determine whether the two signatures are generated by the same unknown signer and output a proof related to the result. The secret key sk generated by the Enc algorithm is given to OA as the master opening key mok.

5.3   Our Concrete Instantiation

We will use the group signature scheme on which we base our construction as a black box and simply add SP-PKEET and a proof of consistency to make it a VCL scheme. We require that the group signature is a Groth-Sahai proof of knowledge [18] in a symmetric bilinear group $(p, \mathbb{G}, \mathbb{G}_T, e, g_1)$ and that $user_i$'s verification key contains a component $g_1^{x_i}$, where x_i is $user_i$'s signing key. Suppose the verification key of the group signature scheme v is of the form $v = g_1^x$, where x is the signing key of the group signature scheme that is used as mik in our constrction.

In the setup phase of scheme (when the common reference string for Groth-Sahai proofs is created), we creat $pk_{sp} = (g, g', g_1, g_2, g_3, h_1, h_2, \{f_{i,1}, f_{i,2}\}_{i=0}^5)$, $sk_{sp} = (\{\alpha_i\}_{i=1}^3, \{\beta_i\}_{i=0}^5)$ for our SP-PKEET and add pk_{sp} to the public parameters. The $user_i$'s (holding secret key x_i) membership certificate is defined as $A_i = g_1^{\frac{1}{x+x_i}}$.

When creating a group signature, the $user_i$ must additionally encrypt his certificate A_i and prove that it is well-formed. The certificate is of the form $A_i = g_1^{\frac{1}{x+x_i}}$, so we need to prove that x_i is the same as in the $user_i$ verification key element $w := g_1^{x_i}$. The SP-PKEET encryption of A_i is as follows.

$$u_1 = g_1^r, u_2 = g_2^s, u_3 = g_3^{r+s}, c = A_i \cdot h_1^r h_2^s,$$

$$v = \prod_{i=0}^3 \hat{e}\left(f_{i,1}^r f_{i,2}^s, u_i\right) \cdot \hat{e}\left(f_{4,1}^r f_{4,2}^s, c\right) \cdot \hat{e}\left(f_{5,1}^r f_{5,2}^s, L\right).$$

$C = (u_1, u_2, u_3, c, v)$. To prove well-formedness, we introduce some auxiliary variables $\theta_1 = g_3^s, \theta_2 = g_1^s, \theta_3 = (g_1^x)^r = g_1^{x \cdot r}, \theta_4 = (g_1^{x_i})^r = g_1^{x_i \cdot r}, \theta_5 = (g_1^x)^s = g_1^{x \cdot s}, \theta_6 = (g_1^{x_i})^s = g_1^{x_i \cdot s}$, of which we also prove knowledge in the group signature. Groth-Sahai proofs allow us to prove knowledge of group elements that satisfy pairing-product equations (PPEs). Then the following PPEs assert that $w = g_1^{x_i}$ (the group elements of which we prove knowledge are underlined):

$$e(g_1, \underline{\theta_3}) = e(u_1, g_1^x), e(g_1, \underline{\theta_4}) = e(u_1, \underline{w}), e(g_2, \underline{\theta_5}) = e(u_2, g_1^x),$$

$$e(g_2, \underline{\theta_6}) = e(u_2, \underline{w}), e(g_1, u_3) = e(u_1, g_3)e(g_1, \underline{\theta_1}), e(g_2, \underline{\theta_1}) = e(u_2, g_3),$$

$$e(f_{i,1}^r f_{i,2}^s, g_1) = e(f_{i,1}, u_1)e(f_{i,2}, \underline{\theta_2}), e(\underline{\theta_2}, g_2) = e(g_1, u_2),$$

$$e(c, \underline{w}) = e(A_i, \underline{w})e(h_1, \underline{\theta_3})e(h_1, \underline{\theta_4})e(h_2, \underline{\theta_5})e(h_2, \underline{\theta_6}).$$

In addition to C, we include in the group signature Groth-Sahai proofs for bilinear groups that the above equations are satisfied.

When opening a group signature, OA must decrypt C to get A_i and prove that it is well-formed. The certificate is of the form $A_i = g_1^{\frac{1}{x+x_i}}$, so we need to prove that x_i is the same as in the $user_i$ verification key element $g_1^{x_i}$. Similar to the process above, the following a PPE assert that $w = g_1^{x_i}$ (the group element of which we prove knowledge is underlined): $e(A_i, g_1^x \cdot \underline{w}) = e(g_1, g_1)$. We include in the group signature a Groth-Sahai proof for the bilinear group that the above equation is satisfied.

When linking two group signatures, LA's decision must be proven to be correct. we introduce some auxiliary variables $\theta_8 = g'^{\alpha_1}, \theta_9 = g'^{\alpha_2}, \theta_{10} = g'^{\alpha_3}$, of which we also prove knowledge in the group signature. The following equations should be satisfied (the group elements of which we prove knowledge are underlined):

$$e(h_1, g') = e(g_1, \underline{\theta_8})e(g_3, \underline{\theta_{10}}), e(h_2, g') = e(g_2, \underline{\theta_9})e(g_3, \underline{\theta_{10}}),$$

$$e\left(c \cdot c'^{-1}, g'\right) = e\left(u_1 u_1'^{-1}, \underline{\theta_8}\right) e\left(u_2 u_2'^{-1}, \underline{\theta_9}\right) e\left(u_3 u_3'^{-1}, \underline{\theta_{10}}\right).$$

We include in the group signature Groth-Sahai proofs for the bilinear group that the above equations are satisfied.

5.4 Security Analysis

This transformation will not affect traceability, non-frameability, opening soundness and linking soundness defined in [6,7]. The following theorems show the security properties of our GSS-VCL related to verifiable controllable linkability, the proofs of which are omitted here for brevity.

Theorem 3. *The GSS-VCL has CCA-full-anonymity assume that SP-PKEET has IND-CCA security.*

Theorem 4. *The GSS-VCL has LO-Linkability assume that SP-PKEET has IND-CCA security.*

Theorem 5. *The GSS-VCL has JP-Unforgeability assume that SP-PKEET has S-PRIV1-CCA security.*

Theorem 6. *The GSS-VCL is E-Linkability based on the correctness of SP-PKEET.*

6 Conclusion

In this paper, we construct a group signature with verifiable controllable linkability, where a linking authority (LA) can link two signatures to determine whether they are generated by the same unknown signer, which can achieve CCA-full-anonymity in the standard model. As a core building block of it, we propose a new structure-preserving public key encryption with equality test (SP-PKEET) scheme and prove its security in the standard model, which is independent of interest.

Acknowledgments. We gratefully acknowledge the anonymous reviewers as well as the editor of *ProvSec* for their invaluable comments. This work is supported by Guangdong Basic and Applied Basic Research Foundation [2020A1515010751] and the National Natural Science Foundation of China [61872409].

References

1. Chaum, D., van Heyst, E.: Group signatures. In: Davies, D.W. (ed.) EUROCRYPT 1991. LNCS, vol. 547, pp. 257–265. Springer, Heidelberg (1991). https://doi.org/10.1007/3-540-46416-6_22
2. Bellare, M., Micciancio, D., Warinschi, B.: Foundations of group signatures: formal definitions, simplified requirements, and a construction based on general assumptions. In: Biham, E. (ed.) EUROCRYPT 2003. LNCS, vol. 2656, pp. 614–629. Springer, Heidelberg (2003). https://doi.org/10.1007/3-540-39200-9_38

3. Camenisch, J., Stadler, M.: Efficient group signature schemes for large groups. In: Kaliski, B.S. (ed.) CRYPTO 1997. LNCS, vol. 1294, pp. 410–424. Springer, Heidelberg (1997). https://doi.org/10.1007/BFb0052252

4. Boneh, D., Boyen, X., Shacham, H.: Short group signatures. In: Franklin, M. (ed.) CRYPTO 2004. LNCS, vol. 3152, pp. 41–55. Springer, Heidelberg (2004). https://doi.org/10.1007/978-3-540-28628-8_3

5. Boneh, D., Shacham, H.: Group signatures with verifier-local revocation. In: The 11th ACM Conference on Computer and Communications Security - CCS 2004, pp. 168–177. ACM (2004)

6. Blazy, O., Derler, D., Slamanig, D., Spreitzer, R.: Non-interactive plaintext (in-)equality proofs and group signatures with verifiable controllable linkability. In: Sako, K. (ed.) CT-RSA 2016. LNCS, vol. 9610, pp. 127–143. Springer, Cham (2016). https://doi.org/10.1007/978-3-319-29485-8_8

7. Hwang, J.Y., Lee, S., Chung, B.H., Cho, H.S., Nyang, D.: Group signatures with controllable linkability for dynamic membership. Inf. Sci. **222**, 761–778 (2013)

8. Slamanig, D., Spreitzer, R., Unterluggauer, T.: Adding controllable linkability to pairing-based group signatures for free. In: Chow, S.S.M., Camenisch, J., Hui, L.C.K., Yiu, S.M. (eds.) ISC 2014. LNCS, vol. 8783, pp. 388–400. Springer, Cham (2014). https://doi.org/10.1007/978-3-319-13257-0_23

9. Rackoff, C., Simon, D.R.: Non-interactive zero-knowledge proof of knowledge and chosen ciphertext attack. In: Feigenbaum, J. (ed.) CRYPTO 1991. LNCS, vol. 576, pp. 433–444. Springer, Heidelberg (1992). https://doi.org/10.1007/3-540-46766-1_35

10. Cramer, R., Shoup, V.: A practical public key cryptosystem provably secure against adaptive chosen ciphertext attack. In: Krawczyk, H. (ed.) CRYPTO 1998. LNCS, vol. 1462, pp. 13–25. Springer, Heidelberg (1998). https://doi.org/10.1007/BFb0055717

11. Zhang, K., Chen, J., Lee, H.T., Qian, H., Wang, H.: Efficient public key encryption with equality test in the standard model. Theor. Comput. Sci. **755**, 65–80 (2019)

12. Lee, H.T., Ling, S., Seo, J.H., Wang, H., Youn, T.: Public key encryption with equality test in the standard model. Inf. Sci. **516**, 89–108 (2020)

13. Nakanishi, T., Fujiwara, T., Watanabe, H.: A linkable group signature and its application to secret voting. Trans. Inf. Process. Soc. Jpn. **40**, 3085–3096 (1999)

14. Zhang, L.Y., Li, H.L., Li, Y.N., Yu, Y., Au, M.H., Wang, B.C.: An efficient linkable group signature for payer tracing in anonymous cryptocurrencies. Future Gener. Comput. Syst. **101**, 29–38 (2019)

15. Bernhard, D., Fuchsbauer, G., Ghadafi, E., Smart, N.P., Warinschi, B.: Anonymous attestation with user-controlled linkability. Int. J. Inf. Secur. **12**, 219–249 (2013). https://doi.org/10.1007/s10207-013-0191-z

16. Garms, L., Lehmann, A.: Group signatures with selective linkability. In: Lin, D., Sako, K. (eds.) PKC 2019. LNCS, vol. 11442, pp. 190–220. Springer, Cham (2019). https://doi.org/10.1007/978-3-030-17253-4_7

17. Kiayias, A., Tsiounis, Y., Yung, M.: Traceable signatures. In: Cachin, C., Camenisch, J.L. (eds.) EUROCRYPT 2004. LNCS, vol. 3027, pp. 571–589. Springer, Heidelberg (2004). https://doi.org/10.1007/978-3-540-24676-3_34

18. Groth, J., Sahai, A.: Efficient non-interactive proof systems for bilinear groups. In: Smart, N. (ed.) EUROCRYPT 2008. LNCS, vol. 4965, pp. 415–432. Springer, Heidelberg (2008). https://doi.org/10.1007/978-3-540-78967-3_24

19. Abe, M., Fuchsbauer, G., Groth, J., Haralambiev, K., Ohkubo, M.: Structure-preserving signatures and commitments to group elements. In: Rabin, T. (ed.) CRYPTO 2010. LNCS, vol. 6223, pp. 209–236. Springer, Heidelberg (2010). https://doi.org/10.1007/978-3-642-14623-7_12

20. Camenisch, J., Haralambiev, K., Kohlweiss, M., Lapon, J., Naessens, V.: Structure preserving CCA secure encryption and applications. In: Lee, D.H., Wang, X. (eds.) ASIACRYPT 2011. LNCS, vol. 7073, pp. 89–106. Springer, Heidelberg (2011). https://doi.org/10.1007/978-3-642-25385-0_5

21. Lu, Y., Zhang, R., Lin, D.: Stronger security model for public-key encryption with equality test. In: Abdalla, M., Lange, T. (eds.) Pairing 2012. LNCS, vol. 7708, pp. 65–82. Springer, Heidelberg (2013). https://doi.org/10.1007/978-3-642-36334-4_5

22. Abe, M., Haralambiev, K., Ohkubo, M.: Signing on elements in bilinear groups for modular protocol design. Cryptology ePrint Archive 2010/133 (2010). http://eprint.iacr.org

Cryptanalysis of LRainbow: The Lifted Rainbow Signature Scheme

Vikas Srivastava$^{(\boxtimes)}$ and Sumit Kumar Debnath

Department of Mathematics, National Institute of Technology Jamshedpur,
Jamshedpur, India
{2020rsma011,sdebnath.math}@nitjsr.ac.in

Abstract. Over the last two decades, the field of multivariate public key cryptography (MPKC) has seen tremendous growth and a rich influx of novel ideas. Gradually, MPKC has emerged as a top candidate for the construction of new generation of algorithms that provides resistance to attacks by quantum algorithms. In 2020, Duong et al. [8] put forth a new multivariate-based signature scheme LRainbow. It utilizes the idea of field lifting put forward by Beullens et al. at INDOCRYPT 2017. The essence of the construction is to produce the key pair of Rainbow over a small field and then lift it to the bigger field. Herein, we present the design and analysis of the proposed subfield differential attack (SDA) on LRainbow. We theoretically show that LRainbow does not meet the stipulated security target. In the end, we come up with a possible modification to bypass the threat possessed by SDA on LRainbow. We call this modified version of LRainbow as Prime LRainbow.

Keywords: LRainbow · Post-quantum cryptography · Multivariate public key cryptography · Subfield differential attack · Differential-cryptanalysis

1 Introduction

In 1994, Shor [17] came up with an algorithm that makes it feasible to defeat classical cryptographic schemes like RSA. The security of these classical primitives relies on the traditional and long-established number theoretic hardness assumptions such as prime factorization and discrete logarithm. With the help of Shor's algorithm, almost all of the currently used classical cryptographic designs can be broken in polynomial time. It possesses a grave threat to the security of modern information system. In addition, it rings an alarming bell for the confidentiality and integrity of modern digital communication networks. Recent research has shown that within a few decades large scale quantum computers will become a reality. Even if the exact time of the arrival of big quantum computers can not determined, there is a need of cryptographic building blocks that can

This work is supported by DRDO, India (ERIP/ER/202005001/M/01/1775).

Q. Huang and Y. Yu (Eds.): ProvSec 2021, LNCS 13059, pp. 296–308, 2021.
https://doi.org/10.1007/978-3-030-90402-9_16

provide resistance against this completely new breed of attacks. This emerging threat has led the researchers all around the world to develop the next generation of cryptographic designs and systems that offers resistance against the attack by quantum computers. This new direction of research is also known as post-quantum cryptography.

Although there are several contenders that present themselves as a post-quantum cryptographic candidate, but multivariate public key cryptography (MPKC) still leads the race among the others. It is largely due to the fact that MPKC schemes in general are very fast, robust and needs only minimal computing resources to put-in-use. They are efficient and only mathematical operations they require are modular field multiplications and additions. The theoretical security of MPKC hinge upon the hardness of MQ problem. MQ problem is NP-hard [11], even for small field $GF(2)$.

The work on multivariate-based cryptographic schemes began around the 1980s. Matsumoto and Imai proposed the first scheme [13] that used multivariate polynomials as a public key. Subsequently, a lot of MPKC schemes were developed. This new direction of research has seen a rich and tremendous improvement over the last two decades. The first major breakthrough came when Patarin [16] proposed the so called Unbalanced Oil and Vinegar (UOV) scheme. Even after more than two decades of rigorous cryptanalysis, UOV is still unbroken and secure given a choice of parameters. To fill the loopholes and shortcomings of UOV, Ding et al. [6] presented a new signature scheme called Rainbow which derives its motivation from the UOV. Very recently, Beullens et al. [3] put forward a new kind of construction known as LUOV. LUOV can be thought of as a modified version of UOV. They first generated the UOV scheme over a small field and later lifted it to the bigger field. The authors of [8] later extended this novel idea of field lifting to the Rainbow signature scheme. Ding et al. [5] introduced a novel attack strategy called subfield differential attack (SDA) to completely break the LUOV signature scheme. The attack proposed in [5] does not depend upon the internal machinery of the LUOV signature scheme. It simply uses the *lifted structure* of LUOV.

1.1   Our Contribution

In this paper, we present the design, analysis, and complexity of the subfield differential attack (SDA) [5] on LRainbow. The proposed attack does not depend upon the scheme's internal workflow, and only utilizes the structure of field extension. It makes use of the fact that coefficients of the key pair of LRainbow is contained in a fixed subfield of the bigger field. The idea of SDA attack is very uncomplicated and straightforward, yet it is very powerful and efficient in practice. Given a public polynomial $\mathcal{X}$, we demonstrate the existence of small subfields $\mathcal{L}_2 = \mathbb{F}_{2^d}$ such that for any fixed $\mathbf{w}' \in \mathbb{F}_{2^r}^n$ and $\mathbf{z} \in \mathbb{F}_{2^r}^m$, there is a $\overline{\mathbf{w}} \in \mathcal{L}_2^n$ with $\mathcal{X}(\mathbf{w}' + \overline{\mathbf{w}}) = \mathbf{z}$. By viewing the bigger field $\mathbb{F}_{2^r}$ as the quotient of polynomial ring $\mathcal{L}_2[x]$ over a small subfield $\mathcal{L}_2$, we reduce the complexity of solving the underdetermined system of quadratic equations. We utilize the approach of Thomae and Wolf [18] to convert the resulting system into a determined one.

In the end, we use direct attack techniques to solve the obtained determined system. To illustrate the method of SDA, we pick a explicit set of parameters LRainbow(23, 16, 18) and carry out the attack. We theoretically show via rigorous complexity analysis that LRainbow does not meet the required security target. In response to the proposed attack, we pitch possible modifications to LRainbow. We call our proposed scheme Prime LRainbow, and argue why it is immune from SDA.

2   Preliminaries

In this section, we revisit some of the basic facts about MPKC. The basic objects of multivariate public-key cryptosystem are system of multivariate quadratic polynomial equations over a finite field $\mathbb{F}_q$.

Let $\mathbb{F}_q$ denote the finite field of order q. A multivariate quadratic polynomial in n variables $z_1, \ldots z_n$ is of the form

$$f(\mathbf{z}) = \sum_{i,j} a_{ij} z_i z_j + \sum_i b_i z_i + c$$

with n-tuple $(z_1, \ldots, z_n)$ denoted by $\mathbf{z}$. a_{ij}, b_i and c belongs to the finite field $\mathbb{F}_q$.

The underlying idea and concept behind the design of MPKC is to select a system $\mathcal{W} : \mathbb{F}_q^n \rightarrow \mathbb{F}_q^m$ of m multivariate polynomials of degree two in n variables. We stipulate that this map $\mathcal{W}$, also known as central map, is easily inverted in the sense that finding preimage of y under $\mathcal{W}$ is easy. To obfuscate the structure of $\mathcal{W}$, we pick two affine invertible transformations $\mathcal{C}_1 : \mathbb{F}_q^m \rightarrow \mathbb{F}_q^m$ and $\mathcal{C}_2 : \mathbb{F}_q^n \rightarrow \mathbb{F}_q^n$. To find the public key of the cryptosystem, we move on by taking the composed map $\mathcal{X} = \mathcal{C}_1 \circ \mathcal{W} \circ \mathcal{C}_2 : \mathbb{F}_q^n \rightarrow \mathbb{F}_q^m$. The secret key of the MPKC is a three tuple $(\mathcal{C}_1, \mathcal{W}, \mathcal{C}_2)$.

2.1   Multivariate Signature Scheme

A multivariate signature scheme consists of following algorithms:

$(PK, SK) \leftarrow$ Gen(η): Given a security parameter η, Gen outputs the pair of public key and private key $(\mathcal{X}, \{\mathcal{C}_1, \mathcal{W}, \mathcal{C}_2\})$.

$\sigma \leftarrow$ Sign(msg, SK): To generate the signature for a given message msg $\in \mathbb{F}_q^m$, signer executes recursively $\alpha = \mathcal{C}_1^{-1}(\text{msg}), \beta = \mathcal{W}^{-1}(\alpha)$ and $\sigma = \mathcal{C}_2^{-1}(\beta)$ to get the signature $\sigma \in \mathbb{F}_q^n$

$0/1 \leftarrow$ Verify(σ, PK): Given a signature $\sigma \in \mathbb{F}_q^n$, verifier computes msg$' = \mathcal{X}(\sigma)$. If msg = msg$'$, verifier accepts the signature and outputs 1, otherwise outputs 0 and the signature is rejected.

2.2   Hardness Assumption

The theoretical security of a multivariate scheme relies on MQ problem - a NP hard problem from the field of algebraic geometry. It is mathematically formulated as

Definition 1. *Given a system* $\mathcal{Q} = (q_{(1)}(\phi_1, \ldots, \phi_n), \ldots, q_{(m)}(\phi_1, \ldots, \phi_n))$ *of* m *quadratic equations in variables* $(\phi_1, \ldots, \phi_n)$, *find a n tuple* $(\bar{\phi}_1, \ldots, \bar{\phi}_n)$ *such that*

$$q_{(1)}(\bar{\phi}_1, \ldots, \bar{\phi}_n) = \cdots = q_{(m)}(\bar{\phi}_1, \ldots, \bar{\phi}_n) = 0.$$

All the variables along with coefficients belong to $\mathbb{F}_q$.

2.3 Rainbow Signature Scheme [6]

Rainbow signature scheme, put forwarded by Ding et al. [6], is one of the most stable multivariate signature scheme, and has successfully withstood the cryptanalysis for the last 15 years. The scheme takes its motivation from the Oil-Vinegar signature scheme developed by Patarin. It can also be thought of as a multi-layered version of UOV. Rainbow was also among the three NIST Post-quantum signature finalists, thus proving its mettle as a robust signature scheme. The design of Rainbow is explained below:

Let $\mathcal{K} = \mathbb{F}_q$ and $v_1 < v_2 < \ldots < v_\lambda < v_{\lambda+1} = n$ be a sequence of natural numbers. Set $m = n - v_1$, where m and n are natural numbers. $O_i = \{v_i + 1, \ldots, v_{i+1}\}$ is used to index oil variables and $V_i = \{1, \ldots, v_i\}$ is utilized to enumerate vinegar variables with i ranging from $i = 1 \ldots, \lambda$.

- *Key Generation*: The central map $\mathcal{W}(\mathbf{x}) = (h^{(v_1+1)}(\mathbf{x}), \ldots, h^{(n)}(\mathbf{x})) : \mathcal{K}^n \to \mathcal{K}^m$ consists of $m = n - v_1$ quadratic polynomial $h^{(l)}(\mathbf{x})$ $(l = v_1 + 1, \ldots, n)$ of the form

$$h^{(l)}(\mathbf{x}) = \sum_{i,j \in V_k} \alpha_{ij}^{(l)} \cdot x_i \cdot x_j + \sum_{i \in V_k, j \in O_k} \beta_{ij}^{(l)} \cdot x_i \cdot x_j + \sum_{i \in V_k \cup O_k} \gamma_i^{(l)} \cdot x_i + \delta^{(l)},$$

where $\mathbf{x} = (x_1, \ldots, x_n)$. The coefficients of the polynomials are randomly chosen from the field $\mathcal{K}$. Here, $k \in \{1, \ldots, \lambda\}$ is the only integer such that $l \in O_k$. To obfuscate the underlying structure of $\mathcal{W}$, it is composed with two invertible affine transformations $\mathcal{C}_1 : \mathcal{K}^m \to \mathcal{K}^m$ and $\mathcal{C}_2 : \mathcal{K}^n \to \mathcal{K}^n$ to give the final public key $\mathcal{X} = \mathcal{C}_1 \circ \mathcal{W} \circ \mathcal{C}_2 : \mathcal{K}^n \to \mathcal{K}^m$.

- *Signature Generation*: Given a message $\mathbf{w} \in \mathcal{K}^m$, we generate the signature by successively computing $\mathbf{y} = \mathcal{C}_1^{-1}(\mathbf{w}) \in \mathcal{K}^m$, $\mathbf{x} = \mathcal{W}^{-1}(\mathbf{y}) \in \mathcal{K}^n$ and $\mathbf{z} = \mathcal{C}_2^{-1}(\mathbf{x}) \in \mathcal{K}^n$. Here, $\mathcal{W}^{-1}(\mathbf{y})$ denote the pre-images of $\mathbf{y}$ under the central map $\mathcal{W}$. We can compute the required pre-image by successively inverting each single UOV layer. The procedure is formulated below:

  1: The first layer vinegar variables $x_1, \ldots, x_{v_1}$ are assigned random values from $\mathcal{K}$ and then substituted into the multivariate quadratic polynomials $h^{(l)}$ $(l = v_1 + 1, \ldots, n)$ to obtain a reduced system of multivariate polynomial equations.

  2: Set $k = 1$.

  3: If $k \leq \lambda$, then we will perform the following steps.

  4: Use Gaussian elimination on the polynomials $h^{(l)}$ $(l \in O_k)$ to obtain the values of the variables x_l $(l \in O_k)$.

5: Replace the values of x_l ($l \in O_k$) obtained in the previous step into the polynomials $h^{(l)}$ ($l \in \{v_k + 1, \ldots, n\}$).

6: Increase the value of k by 1 and go to step 3.

If the system of linear equation in step 4 is not consistent, we need to choose another set of values for $x_1, \ldots, x_{v_1}$ and start from the step 1 again. Finally we publish $\mathbf{z} \in \mathcal{K}^n$ as the signature for the message.

- *Signature Verification*: To investigate whether a signature $\mathbf{z} \in \mathcal{K}^n$ is authentic, one may simply verify $\mathbf{w} \stackrel{?}{=} \mathcal{X}(\mathbf{z}) \in \mathcal{K}^m$. If the equality holds true, signature is accepted otherwise rejected.

2.4   LRainbow: Lifting the Field for Rainbow [8]

The authors of [8] employed the idea of field lifting proposed by [3] to Rainbow signature scheme. The fundamental and key difference between Rainbow and LRainbow is as follows. In the Rainbow scheme, there is practically no restriction on the coefficients of key pair. However, in the LRainbow, all the coefficients are from a fixed subfield $\mathcal{L}_1 = \mathbb{F}_{2^t}$.

Herein, we describe briefly the construction of LRainbow. Let $\mathcal{L} = \mathbb{F}_{2^r}$ be a field of order 2^r. Let $\mathcal{L}_1 = \mathbb{F}_{2^t}$ denote the subfield of $\mathcal{L}$ where (with $1 \le t \le r$). We generate the Rainbow key pair over $\mathcal{L}_1$, that is all the coefficients of $\mathcal{C}_1, \mathcal{W}, \mathcal{C}_2$ and thus of $\mathcal{X}$ are chosen from $\mathcal{L}_1$. In the next step, we lift it $\mathcal{L}$ and consider the new scheme as a Rainbow scheme over $\mathcal{L} = \mathbb{F}_{2^r}$. More precisely, the coefficients of the public polynomial $\mathcal{X}$ belongs to the small subfield, but we now view it as an element of $\mathcal{L} = \mathbb{F}_{2^r}$. Thus, message, and signature generation takes place over the extension field. This scheme is known as LRainbow.

3   Proposed Attack on LRainbow

3.1   General Idea of the Attack: A High Level Overview

The beauty of subfield differential attack (SDA) [5] lies in the fact that it does not depend upon the internal machinery of the LRainbow signature scheme. The crucial idea on which SDA builds its foundation is the structure of finite field extension. Let $\mathcal{L} = \mathbb{F}_{2^r}$ and $\mathcal{L}_2 = \mathbb{F}_{2^d}$, where $\mathcal{L}_2$ is a subfield of $\mathcal{L}$. We denote by $\mathcal{X}$ the public polynomial of LRainbow with coefficients of $\mathcal{X}$ taken from a fixed subfield $\mathcal{L}_1 = \mathbb{F}_{2^t}$ of $\mathcal{L}$. Recall:

Theorem 1   [12]. *Let d, r be two positive integers such that d divides r. Let $\mathcal{L} = \mathbb{F}_{2^r}$ be a finite field. Then we may represent $\mathcal{L}$ as a quotient ring*

$$\mathcal{L} = \mathbb{F}_{2^r} \simeq \mathbb{F}_{2^d}[x]/\langle b(x) \rangle = \mathcal{L}_2[x]/\langle b(x) \rangle$$

where $b(x)$ is an irreducible polynomial of degree l that satisfies $r = ld$.

Let us see how the above stated theorem is helpful to us. Suppose $\mathcal{X} : \mathcal{L}^n \to \mathcal{L}^m$ be the public polynomial of the LRainbow scheme having coefficients from a fixed subfield $\mathcal{L}_1 = \mathbb{F}_{2^t}$ of $\mathcal{L}$. Let $\mathbf{z} \in \mathcal{L}^m$ be an arbitrary element. We define the differential as $\mathbf{w}' + \overline{\mathbf{w}}$, where $\mathbf{w}'$ is an arbitrary element chosen from $\mathcal{L}^n$ and $\overline{\mathbf{w}}$ is an indeterminate element in $\mathcal{L}_2^n$. If we compute the public polynomial $\mathcal{X}$ at the differential and set it equal to $\mathbf{z}$, the final expression would have terms like $w'_i w'_j, w'_i \overline{w}_j, \overline{w}_i \overline{w}_j$. The values of w'_i are known and the values of $\overline{w}_i$ are unknown. We know that $\mathcal{L} \simeq \mathcal{L}_2[x]/\langle b(x) \rangle$ so every element of $\mathcal{L}$ can be described by a polynomial expression in variable x. We apply this on both sides of the equation and compare the coefficients of power of x to obtain almost linear equation. A natural question comes to mind now. Given a message $\mathbf{z} = (z_1, \ldots, z_m) \in \mathcal{L}^m$ and an arbitrary element $\mathbf{w}'$ chosen from $\mathcal{L}^n$, can we find a small natural number d such that we have a $\overline{\mathbf{w}} \in \mathcal{L}_2^n = \mathbb{F}_{2^d}^n \subset \mathcal{L}^n$ with $\mathcal{X}(\mathbf{w}' + \overline{\mathbf{w}}) = \mathbf{z}$.

In the next section, we prove that such a small integer d exists.

3.2   Existence of Small Subfields $\mathcal{L}_2$

We fix $\mathbf{w}' \in \mathcal{L}^n$ and define a new polynomial map by $\overline{\mathcal{X}} : \mathcal{L}_2^n \to \mathcal{L}^m$ given by

$$\overline{\mathcal{X}}(\overline{\mathbf{w}}) = \mathcal{X}(\mathbf{w}' + \overline{\mathbf{w}}).$$

We assume that $\overline{\mathcal{X}}$ acts as a random map from $\mathcal{L}_2^n \to \mathcal{L}^m$. We now prove the desired result.

Theorem 2 [7]. *Given $\overline{\mathcal{X}} : \mathcal{L}_2^n \to \mathcal{L}^m$, the probability that $\overline{\mathcal{X}}^{-1}(\mathbf{z}) \neq \emptyset$ is given by $1 - e^{-2^{rm-dn}}$.*

Proof. Fix $\mathbf{w}' \in \mathcal{L}^n$ and consider the function $\overline{\mathcal{X}} : \mathcal{L}_2^n \to \mathcal{L}^m$ given by $\overline{\mathcal{X}}(\overline{\mathbf{w}}) = \mathcal{X}(\mathbf{w}' + \overline{\mathbf{w}})$. We arbitrarily chose an element $\mathbf{z} \in \mathcal{L}^m$ and estimate the probability that there does not exist $\overline{\mathbf{w}} \in \mathcal{L}_2^n$ such that $\overline{\mathcal{X}}(\overline{\mathbf{w}}) = \mathbf{z}$. Since $|\mathcal{L}_2^n| = 2^{dn}$ and $|\mathcal{L}^m| = 2^{rm}$, we find that for any $\overline{\mathbf{w}} \in \mathcal{L}_2^n$, the probability that $\overline{\mathcal{X}}(\overline{\mathbf{w}}) \neq \mathbf{z}$ is $1 - \frac{1}{2^{dn}}$. Since the output of $\overline{\mathcal{X}}$ is random and independent, the needed probability is

$$\left(1 - \frac{1}{2^{dn}}\right)^{2^{rm}} = \left(\left(1 - \frac{1}{2^{dn}}\right)^{2^{dn}}\right)^{2^{rm-dn}}$$

$$\approx e^{-2^{rm-dn}}$$

3.3   Method of Finding $\overline{\mathbf{w}}$ and Forging the Signature

In the previous section, we saw the existence of a small subfield $\mathcal{L}_2$ such that $\overline{\mathbf{w}} \in \mathcal{L}_2^n \subset \mathcal{L}^n$, with $\mathcal{X}(\mathbf{w}' + \overline{\mathbf{w}}) = \mathbf{z}$. We already know that $\mathcal{L} = \mathbb{F}_{2^r} \simeq \mathbb{F}_{2^d}[x]/\langle b(x) \rangle = \mathcal{L}_2[x]/\langle b(x) \rangle$ where $b(x)$ is an irreducible polynomial of degree l with $l = r/d$. Let $\overline{\mathbf{w}} = (\overline{w}_1, \ldots, \overline{w}_n) \in \mathcal{L}_2^n$ be an indeterminate point and $\mathbf{w}' = (w'_1, \ldots, w'_n) \in \mathcal{L}^n$ be a randomly chosen fixed point. Define $\overline{\mathcal{X}}(\overline{\mathbf{w}}) = \mathcal{X}(\overline{\mathbf{w}} + \mathbf{w}')$. k^{th} component of $\overline{\mathcal{X}}(\overline{\mathbf{w}})$ is given by

$$\overline{\mathcal{X}}^{(k)}(\overline{\mathbf{w}}) = \sum_{i=1}^{n} \sum_{j=1}^{n} \alpha_{i,j,k}(\overline{w}_i + w'_i)(\overline{w}_j + w'_j) + \sum_{i=1}^{n} \beta_{i,k}(\overline{w}_i + w'_i) + \gamma_k$$

Expanding, we get

$$\overline{\mathcal{X}}^{(k)}(\overline{\mathbf{w}}) = \sum_{i=1}^{n}\sum_{j=1}^{n}\alpha_{i,j,k}(w'_i\overline{w}_i + w'_j\overline{w}_j + w'_iw'_j) + \sum_{i=1}^{n}\beta_{i,k}(\overline{w}_i + w'_i) + \sum_{i=1}^{n}\alpha_{i,j,k}\overline{w}_i\overline{w}_j + \gamma_k$$

Recall that $\alpha_{i,j,k} \in \mathcal{L}_1$ which in turn implies that coefficients of quadratic term $\overline{w}_i\overline{w}_j$ belongs to a fixed subfield $\mathcal{L}_1$ of $\mathcal{L}$. Second thing to note is that $w'_i \in \mathcal{L}$ are arbitrarily chosen. Thus, the coefficients of the linear $\overline{w}_i$ term consists of all the powers of x upto $l - 1$. Therefore, grouping the various powers of x, helps us to rewrite

$$\overline{\mathcal{X}}(\overline{\mathbf{w}}) = \begin{pmatrix} \overline{\mathcal{X}}^{(1)}(\overline{\mathbf{w}}) = Q_1(\overline{\mathbf{w}}) + \sum_{i=1}^{l-1} L_{i,1}(\overline{\mathbf{w}})x^i \\ \overline{\mathcal{X}}^{(2)}(\overline{\mathbf{w}}) = Q_2(\overline{\mathbf{w}}) + \sum_{i=1}^{l-1} L_{i,2}(\overline{\mathbf{w}})x^i \\ \vdots \\ \overline{\mathcal{X}}^{(m)}(\overline{\mathbf{w}}) = Q_m(\overline{\mathbf{w}}) + \sum_{i=1}^{l-1} L_{i,m}(\overline{\mathbf{w}})x^i \end{pmatrix}$$

Forging: Given a message/document $\mathbf{z} \in \mathcal{L}^m$, we describe the method of creating a forged signature. In the first step we express $\mathbf{z}$ in powers of x. We can write $\mathbf{z} = (z_1, \ldots, z_m)$. Here $z_k = \sum_{i=0}^{l-1} z_{i,k}x^i$ with each $z_{i,k} \in \mathcal{L}_2$. In the next step, we try to obtain the solution set Sol for the system of linear equations

$$\Delta = \{L_{i,k}(\overline{\mathbf{w}}) = z_{i,k} : 1 \le i \le l-1, 1 \le k \le m\}.$$

Δ is nothing but a random system of linear equations therefore it has a very high probability of being a full rank system. To state it in other words, with high probability we can say that the rank of the system is $(l-1)m$ (or n if $(l-1)m \ge n$). Thus, dimension of the solution space is given by

$$\text{dim Sol} = \text{maximum}\{n - (l-1)m, 0\}.$$

In the following, we attempt to extract a solution of the system of m quadratic polynomials over the Sol

$$\mathcal{B} = \{Q_k(\text{Sol}) = z_{0,k} : 1 \le k \le m\}.$$

So our problem reduces to solving $\mathcal{B}$ over Sol. The solution $\overline{\mathbf{w}}$ to $\mathcal{B}$ gives $\overline{\mathcal{X}}(\overline{\mathbf{w}}) = \mathbf{z}$ which implies that $\mathcal{X}(\overline{\mathbf{w}} + \mathbf{w}') = \mathbf{z}$. In this way, we get our desired signature $\overline{\mathbf{w}} + \mathbf{w}'$.

4   Complexity of the Attack

The bulk of the complexity lies in finding a solution to the system of m quadratic equations in $n - (l-1)m$ number of variables. Therefore, to gauge the efficiency and to see how efficacious our proposed attack on LRainbow is, we try to find the complexity of solving the aforementioned system of polynomial equations. We will mathematically express the complexity in terms of number of field multiplication required to successfully carry out the attack. We already know that for a signature scheme we require number of variables to be greater than or equal to number of equations. This is to ensure that $\mathcal{X}^{-1}(\mathbf{z})$ has a pre-image. Thus, public polynomial $\mathcal{X}$ of a signature scheme is essentially a underdetermined system. So our problem reduces to solving a underdetermined system of quadratic polynomials. There are various methods to solve such a system but the most powerful approach is the one proposed by Thomae and Wolf [18]. The underlying idea is the following: In the first step we convert the given underdetermined system (using a linear change of variable) to a determined system. This newly constructed determined system has less equations than the previous underdetermined system. We then employ the direct attack techniques to solve the determined system.

4.1 Preliminaries: Approach by Thomae and Wolf [18]

Theorem 3 (Thomae and Wolf). *It is possible to modify an underdetermined system of m quadratic equations in n variables with $n = \gamma m$ to determined system of $1 + m - \lceil \gamma \rceil$ quadratic equations by a linear change of variable. Moreover, if $\lceil \gamma \rceil$ divides m then the complexity overhead may be additionally brought down to finding a solution to determined system having $m - \lceil \gamma \rceil$ equations.*

We apply the method of Thomae and Wolf and calculate the size of determined system produced. We summarize the result in Table 1. The notation used in the table to represent the system of quadratic equation is the following: number of variables × number of equations. After this step, the complexity of our proposed attack on LRainbow only depends upon the direct attack techniques to solve the obtained determined system.

Table 1. Determined systems to solve after Thomae and Wolf

Security level	Scheme (v_1, o_1, o_2)	Finite field	Original system	New system
100	LRainbow $(23, 16, 18)$	GF(256)	57×34	33×33
128	LRainbow $(28, 21, 23)$	GF(256)	72×44	43×43
192	LRainbow $(44, 32, 36)$	GF(256)	112×68	67×67
256	LRainbow $(61, 46, 48)$	GF(256)	155×94	93×93

4.2 Solving the Determined Systems

One of the best methods available to solve the determined system is so called the hybrid approach [1,2]. In this approach, we first fix the values of some of the variables. As a result of this, we get a new system of quadratic polynomial which is overdetermined in nature. At the end, we preform a direct attack on this newly obtained system. It may be possible that no solution is found after executing these steps. In that case, we repeat the procedure until we obtain a solution of the system.

Number of variables, whose value is fixed, depend on two things: (i) firstly it depends upon the underlying algorithm used (ii) secondly, it relies upon the cardinality of the finite field. For example, if the order of the field is small then more variables needs to be guessed.

There are many algorithms that utilize the hybrid approach to solve a determined system. Out of these, two algorithms are generally considered to be the most effective. First one is family of XL algorithm [4]. It was put forwarded by Courtois et al. and the second one is $F4/F5$ algorithm [9,10] which was developed by Faugère. There are some other algorithms as well which are based on these two. In our case, we will be going with Wiedemann XL algorithm following the works of [19]. It belongs to the family of XL algorithms.

Let us denote by κ the amount of variables that we are guessing beforehand. Let $\mathsf{Deg}_0^{(\kappa)}$ be the estimated degree after fixing the values for those variables. We state below a result in the form of theorem which will help in determining the complexity of our proposed attack.

Theorem 4 [4]. *Let q denote the size of the finite field. Given a determined system of quadratic polynomials having m equations, complexity of executing the XL algorithm in terms of field multiplications can be estimated by:*

$$Complexity_{XL} = \min_{\kappa}\left\{q^{\kappa} \times 3 \times \binom{m - \kappa + \mathsf{Deg}_0^{(\kappa)}}{\mathsf{Deg}_0^{(\kappa)}} \times \binom{m - \kappa}{2}\right\}.$$

Let us explain in brief why we picked the Wiedemann XL out of the family of XL algorithms. It provides parallel compatibility. In addition, it has low and cheaper memory cost and offers efficient computation time. These reasons made us pick out Wiedemann XL out of the other variants of XL [14,15].

4.3   Calculating the Complexity

To illustrate the workflow, we explicitly compute the complexity of our proposed attack on LRainbow. We take $\mathcal{L} = \mathbb{F}_{256}, \mathcal{L}_2 = \mathbb{F}_4, n = 57$, and $m = 34$. The chosen parameter set offers security level of 100 bits. We will be taking the help of Wiedemann XL to carry out the attack. As we saw in the previous subsection, system of quadratic polynomial over the small subfield $\mathcal{L}_2$ has $m = 34$ equations in 57. variables. Using the approach of Thomae and Wolf, we can transform it into a determined system with 33 equations. Recall that κ denote the amount of variables that we are guessing beforehand. Let us take $\kappa = 16$. We find out that degree of regularity $\mathsf{Deg}_0^{(\kappa)}$ by using the below mentioned definition. $\mathsf{Deg}_0^{(\kappa)}$ is defined as the first power of x with a non-positive coefficient in the Taylor series expansion of

$$\frac{(1-x^q)^m(1-x^2)^m}{(1-x)^{m-\kappa+1}(1-x^{2q})^m}.$$

In our case, $q = 4, \kappa = 16, m = 33$. Therefore, we have:

$$\frac{(1-x^q)^m(1-x^2)^m}{(1-x)^{m-\kappa+1}(1-x^{2q})^m} = 1 + 18x + 138x^2 + 546x^3 + 853x^4 - 2088x^5 + \mathcal{O}(x^6)$$

Since the first power of x with a non-positive coefficient is x^5. Thus, $\mathsf{Deg}_0^{(\kappa)} = 5$. Now we have all the data available to compute the complexity. We know that complexity of XL in terms of field multiplications is given by

$$\text{Complexity}_{XL} = \min_{\kappa} \left\{ q^{\kappa} \times 3 \times \binom{m - k + \mathsf{Deg}_0^{(\kappa)}}{\mathsf{Deg}_0^{(\kappa)}} \times \binom{m - k}{2} \right\}.$$

In our case,

$$\text{Complexity}_{XL} = \left\{ 4^{16} \times 3 \times \binom{33 - 16 + 5}{5} \times \binom{33 - 16}{2} \right\}$$

$$= 46146296859328512 \approx 2^{56} < 2^{100}$$

Therefore, we note that LRainbow fails to meet the required security level. We will now show that other security levels are also vulnerable to SDA.

- LRainbow $(28, 21, 23)$

We proceed with $\mathcal{L} = \mathbb{F}_{256}, \mathcal{L}_2 = \mathbb{F}_4, n = 72$, and $m = 44$. The parameter set offers security level of 128 bits. Using the approach of Thomae and Wolf, we obtain an equivalent determined system of 43 equations. With $\kappa = 21, m = 43, q = 4$, the degree of regularity can be calculated as:

$$\frac{(1-x^q)^m(1-x^2)^m}{(1-x)^{m-\kappa+1}(1-x^{2q})^m} = 1 + 23x + 233x^2 + 1311x^3 + 3942x^4 + 1610x^5 - 39242x^6 + \mathcal{O}(x^7)$$

Thus, $\mathsf{Deg}_0^{(\kappa)} = 6$. Complexity of XL in terms of field multiplications is given by

$$\text{Complexity}_{XL} = \left\{ 4^{16} \times 3 \times \binom{43 - 21 + 6}{6} \times \binom{43 - 21}{2} \right\}$$

$$= 1148245589517171425280 \approx 2^{70} < 2^{128}.$$

- LRainbow $(44, 32, 36)$
  We now calculate the attack complexity for parameter set offering security level of 192 bits. We have $\mathcal{L} = \mathbb{F}_{256}, \mathcal{L}_2 = \mathbb{F}_4, n = 112$, and $m = 68$. We reduce

it to an equivalent determined system of 67 equations using the approach of Thomae and Wolf. The degree of regularity can be computed as:

$$\frac{(1-x^q)^m(1-x^2)^m}{(1-x)^{m-\kappa+1}(1-x^{2q})^m} = 1 + 35x + 563x^2 + 5425x^3 + 33749x^4 + 130207x^5$$
$$+ 200079x^6 - 954459x^7 + \mathcal{O}(x^8)$$

where κ was taken to be 33. Thus, $\mathrm{Deg}_0^{(\kappa)} = 7$. Complexity of XL can be estimated using

$$\mathrm{Complexity}_{XL} = \left\{ 4^{16} \times 3 \times \binom{67-33+7}{7} \times \binom{67-33}{2} \right\}$$
$$= 279188557117604370188681084928 0 \approx 2^{102} < 2^{192}.$$

- LRainbow $(61, 46, 48)$
  We will now compute the attack complexity for parameter set $\mathcal{L} = \mathbb{F}_{256}, \mathcal{L}_2 = \mathbb{F}_4, n = 155$, and $m = 94$ offering a security level of 256 bits. Using the approach of Thomae and Wolf, we obtain an equivalent determined system of 93 equations. With $\kappa = 46, m = 93, q = 4$, the degree of regularity can be calculated as:

$$\frac{(1-x^q)^m(1-x^2)^m}{(1-x)^{m-\kappa+1}(1-x^{2q})^m} = 1 + 48x + 1083x^2 + 15136x^3 + 144717x^4 + 977040x^5$$
$$+ 4517233x^6 + 11609664x^7 - 11555130x^8 + \mathcal{O}(x^9)$$

Thus, $\mathrm{Deg}_0^{(\kappa)} = 8$. Complexity of the attack is given by

$$\mathrm{Complexity}_{XL} = \left\{ 4^{16} \times 3 \times \binom{93-46+5}{8} \times \binom{93-46}{2} \right\}$$
$$= 19552360081185998307771217042570267852800 \approx 2^{134} < 2^{256}.$$

5   Response to Attack: Prime LRainbow

To circumvent the proposed SDA, we suggest some modifications in the LRainbow scheme. We call the modified version of LRainbow as Prime LRainbow. We will see how our newly proposed scheme is immune from SDA. Let p be a prime number. We denote by $\mathbb{F}_p$ the finite field with cardinality p. We consider the field extension of the form $\mathbb{F}_{p^r}$ where r is a prime number. This constraint ensures that no intermediate field extension exists. In Prime LRainbow scheme coefficients of public key-secret key pair $(\mathcal{X}, \{\mathcal{C}_1, \mathcal{W}, \mathcal{C}_2\})$ are picked from $\mathbb{F}_p$ and later lifted to the bigger field $\mathbb{F}_{p^r}$. Since there are no intermediate field extensions, Prime LRainbow is immune from SDA. We propose a new parameter set to safeguard the LRainbow from SDA. We point out that these new parameter set for LRainbow should withstand normal attacks on LRainbow (Table 2).

Table 2. Proposed parameter set for LRainbow

Security level	Scheme (v_1, o_1, o_2)	r	p
100	LRainbow $(23, 16, 18)$	7	2
128	LRainbow $(28, 21, 23)$	7	2

6 Conclusion

In this work, we put forward the cryptanalysis of LRainbow through SDA. The SDA only utilizes the structure of field extension. Although the proposed attack works on a very straightforward idea, yet it is very robust when implemented. Through complexity analysis, we theoretically demonstrate that LRainbow does not meet the required security target. In response to the proposed attack, we pitch a possible modification to LRainbow and name the modified version as Prime LRainbow. It makes use of the prime extensions and thus avoids the threat presented by SDA.

References

1. Bettale, L., Faugere, J.-C., Perret, L.: Solving polynomial systems over finite fields. In: Proceedings of the 37th International Symposium on Symbolic and Algebraic Computation - ISSAC 2012. ACM Press (2012)
2. Bettale, L., Faugère, J.-C., Perret, L.: Hybrid approach for solving multivariate systems over finite fields. J. Math. Cryptol. **3**(3), 177–197 (2009)
3. Beullens, W., Preneel, B.: Field lifting for smaller UOV public keys. In: Patra, A., Smart, N.P. (eds.) INDOCRYPT 2017. LNCS, vol. 10698, pp. 227–246. Springer, Cham (2017). https://doi.org/10.1007/978-3-319-71667-1_12
4. Courtois, N., Klimov, A., Patarin, J., Shamir, A.: Efficient algorithms for solving overdefined systems of multivariate polynomial equations. In: Preneel, B. (ed.) EUROCRYPT 2000. LNCS, vol. 1807, pp. 392–407. Springer, Heidelberg (2000). https://doi.org/10.1007/3-540-45539-6_27
5. Ding, J., Deaton, J., Schmidt, K., Vishakha, Zhang, Z.: Cryptanalysis of the lifted unbalanced oil vinegar signature scheme. In: Micciancio, D., Ristenpart, T. (eds.) Advances in Cryptology. CRYPTO 2020. LNCS, vol. 12172., pp. 279–298. Springer, Cham (2020). https://doi.org/10.1007/978-3-030-56877-1_10
6. Ding, J., Schmidt, D.: Rainbow, a new multivariable polynomial signature scheme. In: Ioannidis, J., Keromytis, A., Yung, M. (eds.) ACNS 2005. LNCS, vol. 3531, pp. 164–175. Springer, Heidelberg (2005). https://doi.org/10.1007/11496137_12
7. Ding, J., Zhang, Z., Deaton, J., Schmidt, K., Vishakha, F.: New attacks on lifted unbalanced oil vinegar. In: Second-PQC-Standardization-Conference. NIST (2019)
8. Duong, D.H., Van Luyen, L., Tran, H.T.N.: Choosing subfields for LUOV and lifting fields for rainbow. IET Inf. Secur. **14**(2), 196–201 (2020)
9. Faugere, J.C.: A new efficient algorithm for computing Grobner bases without reduction to zero (f₅). In: Proceedings of the 2002 International Symposium on Symbolic and Algebraic Computation - ISSAC 2002. ACM Press (2002)
10. Faugére, J.-C.: A new efficient algorithm for computing Gröbner bases (f4). J. Pure Appl. Algebra **139**(1), 61–88 (1999)

11. Garey, M.R., Johnson, D.S.: Computers and Intractability: A Guide to the Theory of NP-Completeness (Series of Books in the Mathematical Sciences), 1st edn. W. H. Freeman (1979)
12. Lidl, R., Niederreiter, H.: Finite Fields. Cambridge University Press, Cambridge (1996)
13. Matsumoto, T., Imai, H., et al.: Public quadratic polynomial-tuples for efficient signature-verification and message-encryption. In: Barstow, D. (ed.) EUROCRYPT 1988. LNCS, vol. 330, pp. 419–453. Springer, Heidelberg (1988). https://doi.org/10.1007/3-540-45961-8_39
14. Mohamed, M.S.E., Cabarcas, D., Ding, J., Buchmann, J., Bulygin, S.: MXL_3: an efficient algorithm for computing Gröbner bases of zero-dimensional ideals. In: Lee, D., Hong, S. (eds.) ICISC 2009. LNCS, vol. 5984, pp. 87–100. Springer, Heidelberg (2010). https://doi.org/10.1007/978-3-642-14423-3_7
15. Mohamed, M.S.E., Mohamed, W.S.A.E., Ding, J., Buchmann, J.: *MXL2*: solving polynomial equations over GF(2) using an improved mutant strategy. In: Buchmann, J., Ding, J. (eds.) PQCrypto 2008. LNCS, vol. 5299, pp. 203–215. Springer, Heidelberg (2008). https://doi.org/10.1007/978-3-540-88403-3_14
16. Patarin, J.: The oil and vinegar signature scheme. In: Dagstuhl Workshop on Cryptography, September 1997
17. Shor, P.W.: Polynomial-time algorithms for prime factorization and discrete logarithms on a quantum computer. SIAM Rev. **41**(2), 303–332 (1999)
18. Thomae, E., Wolf, C.: Solving underdetermined systems of multivariate quadratic equations revisited. In: Fischlin, M., Buchmann, J., Manulis, M. (eds.) PKC 2012. LNCS, vol. 7293, pp. 156–171. Springer, Heidelberg (2012). https://doi.org/10.1007/978-3-642-30057-8_10
19. Yeh, J.Y.-C., Cheng, C.-M., Yang, B.-Y.: Operating degrees for XL vs. F_4/F_5 for generic $\mathcal{MQ}$ with number of equations linear in that of variables. In: Fischlin, M., Katzenbeisser, S. (eds.) Number Theory and Cryptography. LNCS, vol. 8260, pp. 19–33. Springer, Heidelberg (2013). https://doi.org/10.1007/978-3-642-42001-6_3

Identification Scheme and Forward-Secure Signature in Identity-Based Setting from Isogenies

Surbhi Shaw[✉] and Ratna Dutta[✉]

Department of Mathematics, Indian Institute of Technology Kharagpur,
Kharagpur 721302, India
surbhi_shaw@iitkgp.ac.in, ratna@maths.iitkgp.ac.in

Abstract. *Identity-based cryptography* (IBC) introduced by Adi Shamir [17] has paved the way for authenticating the public key of a user without the use of certificates. In addition to *identity-based encryption* (IBE), a full-fledged identity-based system would require identity-based authentication, which is where *ID-based identification* (IBID) and *identity-based signature* (IBS) comes into picture. Thus the advent of IBID and IBS renews interest in IBE. Since the discovery of IBC, a number of IBID and IBS were proposed in the literature. The overwhelming majority of them, however, substantially rely on discrete logarithm problem and are thus vulnerable to quantum attacks. As a result, developing a quantum-resistant IBID and IBS is the dire need of the hour.

In this work, we examine the limitations of Peng et al.'s [16] recently proposed IBS from isogenies. We have identified significant flaws in their major building block, which caused their proposed IBS scheme to fall short of the claimed *unforgeability against chosen identity and chosen message attacks* (UF-IBS-CMA) security. On a more positive note, we have proposed a viable fix for their scheme by adopting a framework different from theirs. This prompted us to construct the *first* IBID scheme from isogenies. Furthermore, we provide a formal proof for the *impersonation under passive attacks* (ID-IMP-PA) security of our IBID scheme using rewinding techniques of Multi-Instance Reset lemma [10]. In this work, we have additionally proposed the *first* construction of *forward-secure identity-based signature* (FSIBS) from isogenies.

Keywords: Isogenies · Post-quantum cryptography · ID-based identification · Identity-based signature · Forward-secrecy

1 Introduction

Identity-based cryptography has brought a revolutionary breakthrough to public key cryptography. Identity-based cryptography offers a significant benefit over traditional certificate-based cryptography by eliminating the onerous certificate management mechanism involved in certificate-based cryptography. *ID-based identification* (IBID) is a basic component of identity-based cryptography

© Springer Nature Switzerland AG 2021
Q. Huang and Y. Yu (Eds.): ProvSec 2021, LNCS 13059, pp. 309–326, 2021.
https://doi.org/10.1007/978-3-030-90402-9_17

that was first proposed in 2004 independently by Bellare et al. [3] and Kurosawa et al. [11]. In an IBID scheme, each user sets its identity (e.g. email address) as its public key. The key generator center (KGC) derives the secret key corresponding to user identity employing its master secret key. The user, playing the role of a prover can then identify itself to a verifier holding the associated public key. The notion of *identity-based signature* (IBS) scheme is similar except that instead of identifying itself, the user signs message and the verifier checks the validity of the signature.

With the rapid growth of networks, user authentication is turning out to be progressively significant. In numerous applications, for instance, in wireless sensor network and mobile social network, the battery life of devices is so limited that sophisticated authentication procedures are unacceptably inefficient. This necessitates improving the performance of authentication. Since a digital signature is a key component of authentication, reducing its complexity is apparently the obvious way to address this concern. One way of reducing the complexity of signatures is to use identity-based signatures instead of traditional signatures. Thus, in most of the real-life applications identity-based signatures are more preferred than traditional signature schemes.

Research on identity-based cryptography has been very active in recent years, culminating in a flurry of works on IBID and IBS schemes. These include the Fiat-Shamir IBID and IBS schemes [7], the Guillou-Quisquater IBID and IBS schemes [9], the IBS scheme in Shamir's paper [17] introducing identity-based cryptography, and many more [8,14]. Since then, several excellent proposals for IBS based on pairings appeared [15,23]. These IBS proposals are very efficient for practical applications, however, they all rely heavily on the discrete logarithm problem that is facile for quantum computers. In light of the recent advancement of quantum computer, seeking quantum-resistant IBS seems alarming. This lead to a line of new research on identity-based signature over lattice assumptions [19, 22] and many more.

Contributions. Peng et al. [16] were the first to propose an IBS scheme based on the hardness assumption of isogenies. They defined a family of trapdoor samplable relation $\mathcal{R}$ and exploit it to derive a convertible identification scheme cID. The generic framework underlying their IBS scheme comprises of sequential composition of a set of transforms fs-1-2-S and cSS-2-IBS on cID as shown in Fig. 1(a). The authors of [16] claim that their proposed IBS scheme is *unforgeability against chosen identity and chosen message attacks* (UF-IBS-CMA) secure. In this work we have identified several shortcomings in their IBS scheme which are summarized as follows:

- The family of trapdoor samplable relation $\mathcal{R}$ which lies at the heart of their IBS scheme is incorrect and it fails to meet the fundamental definition.
- Their IBS scheme does not adhere to the generic framework discussed in Fig. 1(a). Moreover, their work is devoid of concrete security proof supporting their claim. As their IBS scheme deviates from the generic framework, we believe that their security argument is jeopardized.

- Their IBS scheme can be viewed as the identity-based version of SeaSign signature [6]. Thus, the Sign and Verify algorithm of their IBS involve rejection sampling which makes their signing and verification time expensive.

We address each of the aforementioned concern in our work. To overcome these barriers, we adopt a different framework than those of [16] depicted in Fig. 1(b). We exploit the identification scheme underlying the signature scheme CSI-FiSh [5] to derive an IBID scheme from isogenies. We provide a comprehensive security analysis using a variant of Reset Lemma given in [10] to prove that our proposed IBID scheme is *impersonation under passive attacks* (ID-IMP-PA) secure. We further construct an isogeny-based IBS from our IBID following the Fiat-Shamir transform paradigm [7]. Our IBS scheme does not involve method of rejection sampling which brings a major improvement to the signing and verification time.

(a)

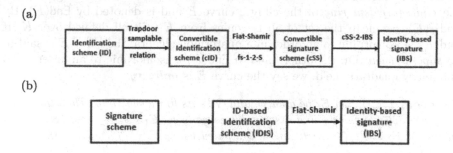

(b)

Fig. 1. (a) Framework for Peng et al.'s IBS scheme. (b) Framework for our IBS scheme.

The main highlight of this work can be summed up as follows:

- *Firstly*, we revisit the IBS scheme of Peng et al. and reveal the flaws in their IBS scheme as well as in their trapdoor samplable relation which is the main building block of their scheme (Sect. 5).
- *Secondly*, we sketch ways to fill the gaps in their IBS scheme by adopting a framework different from theirs. Thus, our IBS scheme turns out to be the first IBS from isogenies achieving UF-IBS-CMA security (see Sect. 6.3).
- As a bi-product, we have also offered the first construction of IBID from isogenies. We have provided an elaborate security argument showing our IBID is ID-IMP-PA secure (see Sect. 6.2).
- *Finally*, we have shown how we can incorporate the forward secrecy property to our IBS by suitably combining our IBS with CSI-FiSh signature and a pseudorandom generator (Sect. 7).

2 Preliminaries

Notation. Let $\lambda \in \mathbb{N}$ denotes the security parameter. A function $\nu(\cdot)$ is negligible if for every integer c, there exists an integer k such that for all $\lambda > k$,

$|\nu(\lambda)| < 1/\lambda^c$. By $s_1||s_2$ we mean concatenation of strings s_1 and s_2. We denote by $[0, I]^n$ the collection of n-tuple integer vectors with co-ordinates $\{0, 1, \ldots, I\}$.

Elliptic Curves, Isogenies and Endomorphsim Ring [18]. Let K be a finite field and $\overline{K}$ be its algebraic closure. An elliptic curve E over K is a non-singular, projective, cubic curve having genus one with a special point O, called the point at infinity. The set of K-rational points of the elliptic curve E form an additive abelian group with O as the identity element. A *Montgomery elliptic curve E* is of the form $E : By^2 = x^3 + Ax^2 + x$ where $B(A^2 - 4) \neq 0$ for some $A, B \in K$. Let E_1 and E_2 be two elliptic curves over a field K. An *isogeny* from E_1 to E_2 is a non-constant morphism $\phi : E_1 \longrightarrow E_2$ over $\overline{K}$ preserving the point at infinity O. The *degree* of the isogeny ϕ, denoted by $\deg(\phi)$ is its degree as a rational map. A non-zero isogeny ϕ is called *separable* if and only if $\deg(\phi) = \#\ker(\phi)$ where $\ker(\phi) = \phi^{-1}(O_{E_2})$. The set of all isogenies from E to itself defined over $\overline{K}$ forms a ring under pointwise addition and composition. This ring is called the *endomorphism ring* of the elliptic curve E and is denoted by $\mathsf{End}(E)$. By $\mathsf{End}_K(E)$, we mean the set of all isogenies from E to itself defined over K. If $\mathsf{End}(E)$ is isomorphic to an order in a quaternion algebra, the curve E is said to be *supersingular*. On the other hand, if $\mathsf{End}(E)$ is isomorphic to an order in an imaginary quadratic field, we say the curve E is *ordinary*.

Theorem 1 [21]. *Let E_1 be a curve and G be its finite subgroup. Then there is a unique elliptic curve E_2 and a separable isogeny $\phi : E_1 \longrightarrow E_2$ with $\ker(\phi) = G$ such that $E_2 \cong E_1/G$ which can be computed using Vélu's formulae* [20].

Ideal Class Group [13]. Let F be a number field, and $\mathcal{O}$ be an order in F. A fractional ideal $\mathfrak{a}$ of $\mathcal{O}$ is a finitely generated $\mathcal{O}$-submodule of F. Let $\mathcal{I}(O)$ be a set of invertible fractional ideals of $\mathcal{O}$. Then $\mathcal{I}(\mathcal{O})$ is an abelian group derived from the multiplication of ideals with the identity $\mathcal{O}$. Let $\mathcal{P}(\mathcal{O})$ be a subgroup of $\mathcal{I}(\mathcal{O})$ defined by $\mathcal{P}(\mathcal{O}) = \{\mathfrak{a}|\mathfrak{a} = \alpha\mathcal{O} \text{ for some } \alpha \in F \setminus \{0\} \}$. The abelian group $\mathsf{Cl}(\mathcal{O})$ defined by $\mathcal{I}(\mathcal{O})/\mathcal{P}(\mathcal{O})$ is called the *ideal class group* of $\mathcal{O}$. An element of $\mathsf{Cl}(\mathcal{O})$ denoted by $[\mathfrak{a}]$ is an equivalence class of $\mathfrak{a}$.

The Class Group Action. Let $\mathsf{Ell}_p(\mathcal{O})$ denote the set of $\mathbb{F}_p$-isomorphic classes of supersingular curves E, whose $\mathbb{F}_p$-endomorphism ring $\mathsf{End}_{\mathbb{F}_p}(E) \cong \mathcal{O} = \mathbb{Z}[\sqrt{-p}]$. The ideal class group $\mathsf{Cl}(\mathcal{O})$ acts freely and transitively on $\mathsf{Ell}_p(\mathcal{O})$. For the curve $E \in \mathsf{Ell}_p(\mathcal{O})$, the *action* $*$ of $[\mathfrak{a}] \in \mathsf{Cl}(\mathcal{O})$ on E is defined as follows:

- Consider all the endomorphisms α in $\mathfrak{a}$.
- Compute the subgroup $E[\mathfrak{a}] = \bigcap_{\alpha \in \mathfrak{a}} \ker(\alpha)$.
- Compute the elliptic curve $E/E[\mathfrak{a}]$ and an isogeny $\phi_\mathfrak{a} : E \longrightarrow E/E[\mathfrak{a}]$ using Velu's formula. (see Theorem 1) and returns the elliptic curve $E/E[\mathfrak{a}]$.

Henceforth, we shall use the notation $[\mathfrak{a}]E$ instead of $[\mathfrak{a}] * E$ to denote the curve $E/E[\mathfrak{a}]$ obtained by the action of $[\mathfrak{a}] \in \mathsf{Cl}(\mathcal{O})$ on the curve $E \in \mathsf{Ell}_p(\mathcal{O})$.

Theorem 2.01 [21]. *Let $\mathcal{O}$ be an order of an imaginary quadratic field $\mathbb{Q}(\sqrt{-p})$ and E be a curve defined over $\mathbb{F}_p$. If $Ell_p(\mathcal{O})$ contains the $\mathbb{F}_p$-isomorphism class of supersingular curves, then the action of $Cl(\mathcal{O})$ on $Ell_p(\mathcal{O})$, defined by*

$$Cl(\mathcal{O}) \times Ell_p(\mathcal{O}) \longrightarrow Ell_p(\mathcal{O})$$
$$([\mathfrak{a}], E) \longrightarrow E/E[\mathfrak{a}]$$

is free and transitive where $\mathfrak{a}$ is an integral ideal of $\mathcal{O}$.

The structure of the class group $Cl(\mathcal{O})$ where $\mathcal{O} = \mathbb{Z}[\sqrt{-p}]$ is computed by Beullens et al. [5] where p is a prime p of the form $p = 4\,l_1 l_2 \dots l_n - 1$, where l_i's are small distinct odd primes with $n = 74$, $l_1 = 3$, $l_{73} = 373$, and $l_{74} = 587$. They have shown that $Cl(\mathcal{O})$ is a cyclic group with generator $\mathfrak{g} = <3, \pi - 1>$ and computer the class number of ideal class group which we denote by N. Thus for simplicity we can consider class group $Cl(\mathcal{O})$ to be $\mathbb{Z}_N$.

We shall use the following notations for the sake of simplicity.

- $[\mathfrak{a}]E$ will be replaced by $[a]E$ for any element $[\mathfrak{a}] \in Cl(\mathcal{O})$ which can be written as $[\mathfrak{g}^a]$ for some $a \in \mathbb{Z}_N$.
- $[\mathfrak{a}][\mathfrak{b}]E$ will be replaced by $[a + b]E$ where $[\mathfrak{a}]$, $[\mathfrak{b}] \in Cl(\mathcal{O})$ and $[\mathfrak{a}]E = [\mathfrak{g}^a]E$, $[\mathfrak{b}]E = [\mathfrak{g}^b]E$ for some $a, b \in \mathbb{Z}_N$.

3   Identity-Based Signature

An identity-based signature scheme is a tuple $IBS = (\text{Setup}, \text{Extract}, \text{Sign}, \text{Verify})$ of four polynomial-time algorithms detailed below:

$\text{Setup}(1^\lambda) \rightarrow (pp_{ibs}, msk)$: This algorithm is run by a KGC that on input 1^λ and returns a public parameter pp_{ibs} and master secret key msk.

$\text{Extract}(pp_{ibs}, msk, id) \rightarrow usk_{id}$: The KGC runs this key extract algorithm on input the public parameter pp_{ibs}, the master secret key msk and user identity id and returns the user secret key usk_{id} for the given identity id.

$\text{Sign}(pp_{ibs}, usk_{id}, m) \rightarrow \sigma$: Taking input the public parameter pp_{ibs}, user secret key usk_{id} and a message m, the signer executes this randomized algorithm and outputs a signature σ on the message m.

$\text{Verify}(pp_{ibs}, id, m, \sigma) \rightarrow \text{Valid/Invalid}$: The verifier runs this deterministic algorithm to verify the validity of signature σ.

Correctness. For all $(pp_{ibs}, msk) \leftarrow \text{Setup}(1^\lambda)$, all $usk_{id} \leftarrow \text{Extract}(pp_{ibs}, msk, id)$, all m and all id, we must have $\text{Verify}(pp_{ibs}, id, m, \text{Sign}(pp_{ibs}, usk_{id}, m)) = 1$.

Definition 3.01 (UF-IBS-CMA). An IBS scheme is said to be secure against *unforgeability against chosen identity and chosen message attacks* (UF-IBS-CMA) if for all PPT adversaries $\mathcal{A}$, there exists a negligible function ϵ such that $\text{Adv}_{IBS, \mathcal{A}}^{\text{UF-IBS-CMA}}(\lambda) = \Pr[\mathcal{A} \text{ wins in } \text{Exp}_{IBS, \mathcal{A}}^{\text{UF-IBS-CMA}}(\lambda)] < \epsilon$, where the experiment $\text{Exp}_{IBS, \mathcal{A}}^{\text{UF-IBS-CMA}}(\lambda)$ described in Fig. 2 formalizes the unforgeability game.

Setup: The challenger C takes input the security parameter 1^λ and generate $(pp_{ibs}, msk) \leftarrow$ Setup(1^λ). It gives the public parameter pp_{ibs} to adversary A while keeps msk secret to itself.

Query Phase: C responds to polynomially many adaptive queries made by A as follows:
- *Oracle* $O_{Extract}(msk, \cdot)$: On receiving queries on a user identity id from A, the challenger C responds with user secret key $usk_{id} \leftarrow$ Extract(pp_{ibs}, msk, id) for the given identity id.
- *Oracle* $O_{Sign}(usk_{id}, \cdot)$: On receiving queries on a message m and a user identity id from the adversary A, the challenger C responds with a signature $\sigma \leftarrow$ Sign(pp_{ibs}, usk_{id}, m) where $usk_{id} \leftarrow$ Extract(pp_{ibs}, msk, id) is the user secret key corresponding to the identity id.

Forgery: A eventually outputs a message m^*, user identity id* and a forge signature σ^*. A wins the game if Verify$(pp_{ibs}, id^*, m^*, \sigma^*) = 1$, with the restriction that id* has not been queried to $O_{Extract}(msk, \cdot)$ and (m^*, id^*) has not been queried to $O_{Sign}(usk_{id}, \cdot)$.

Fig. 2. Experiment $Exp_{IBS, A}^{UF\text{-}IBS\text{-}CMA}(\lambda)$: unforgeability against chosen-message attacks.

4   Peng et al.'s Framework for Achieving IBS from Trapdoor Samplable Relations

Definition 4.01 (Trapdoor Samplable Relations). A family of *trapdoor samplable relations* $\mathcal{F} = (\mathsf{TDG}, \mathsf{Smp}, \mathsf{Inv})$ is a tuple of PPT algorithms satisfying:

$\mathsf{TDG}(1^\lambda) \rightarrow (\langle \mathcal{R} \rangle, \mathsf{td})$: On input 1^λ, the trusted party outputs the description $\langle \mathcal{R} \rangle$ of a relation $\mathcal{R}$ along with its trapdoor information td.

$\mathsf{Smp}(\langle \mathcal{R} \rangle) \rightarrow (x, y)$: On input the description $\langle \mathcal{R} \rangle$ of the relation $\mathcal{R}$, any public entity can run this algorithm and return a uniformly random pair $(x, y) \in \mathcal{R}$.

$\mathsf{Inv}(\langle \mathcal{R} \rangle, \mathsf{td}, y) \rightarrow x$: Taking input the description $\langle \mathcal{R} \rangle$ of a relation $\mathcal{R}$ with domain $\mathsf{Dom}(\mathcal{R})$ and range $\mathsf{Rng}(\mathcal{R})$, the corresponding trapdoor td and an element $y \in \mathsf{Rng}(\mathcal{R})$, the trusted party runs this randomized algorithm and returns a random element $x \in \mathcal{R}^{-1}(y) \subseteq \mathsf{Dom}(\mathcal{R})$ where $\mathsf{Rng}(\mathcal{R}) = \{y : \exists\, x \in \mathsf{Dom}(\mathcal{R}) \text{ such that } (x, y) \in \mathcal{R}\}$ and $\mathcal{R}^{-1}(y) = \{x : (x, y) \in \mathcal{R}\}$.

For every relation $\mathcal{R}$ in the family, $\exists\, h$ such that $|\mathcal{R}^{-1}(y)| = h \,\forall\, y \in \mathsf{Rng}(\mathcal{R})$.

Definition 4.02 (Convertible identification scheme cID). A canonical identification scheme $\mathsf{ID} = (\mathsf{KGen}, \mathsf{Prove} = (\mathsf{Prove}_1, \mathsf{Prove}_2), \mathsf{Verify})$ with challenge set ChSet is said to be *convertible* if the algorithm KGen is supported by a family of trapdoor samplable relations $\mathcal{F} = (\mathsf{TDG}, \mathsf{Smp}, \mathsf{Inv})$ in a manner that the key pair $(\mathsf{pk}, \mathsf{sk})$ output by $\mathsf{KGen}(1^\lambda)$ is generated as follows: $(\langle \mathcal{R} \rangle, \mathsf{td}) \leftarrow \mathsf{TDG}(1^\lambda)$, $(x, y) \leftarrow \mathsf{Smp}(\langle \mathcal{R} \rangle)$, $\mathsf{pk} = (\langle \mathcal{R} \rangle, y)$, $\mathsf{sk} = (\langle \mathcal{R} \rangle, x)$.

One can employ the well-known Fiat-Shamir transform fs-1-2-S [12] to turn a canonical convertible identification scheme cID into a convertible signature scheme cSS = fs-1-2-S(cID). The cSS-2-IBS transform turns the convertible signature scheme cSS into an identity-based signature scheme IBS = cSS-2-IBS(fs-1-2-S(cID)) = (Setup, Extract, Sign, Verify). The four polynomial-time algorithms are explicitly detailed in Fig. 3 where the hash function $G : \{0,1\}^* \rightarrow \mathsf{Rng}(\mathcal{R})$ and $H : \{0,1\}^* \rightarrow \mathsf{ChSet}$ are modelled as random oracles and Dec is a deterministic function of the public parameter and transcript returning 0 or 1.

Theorem 4.03 [3]. *Let* cID *be a canonical convertible identification scheme and* IBS = cSS-2-IBS(fs-1-2-S(cID)) *be an IBS scheme as defined in Fig. 3. If* cID *is* IMP-PA *secure, then* IBS *is* UF-IBS-CMA *secure.*

Setup(1^λ)	Extract(pp, msk, id)
$(\langle \mathcal{R} \rangle, \mathsf{td}) \leftarrow \mathsf{TDG}\ (1^\lambda)$	$y \leftarrow G(\mathsf{id})$
$\mathsf{pp} \leftarrow \langle \mathcal{R} \rangle$	$x \leftarrow \mathsf{Inv}(\langle \mathcal{R} \rangle, \mathsf{td}, y)$
$\mathsf{msk} \leftarrow \mathsf{td}$	$\mathsf{usk}_\mathsf{id} \leftarrow (\langle \mathcal{R} \rangle, x)$
Return (pp, msk)	Return usk_id
Sign(pp, $\mathsf{usk}_\mathsf{id}, m$)	Verify(pp, id, m, σ)
$(w, st) \leftarrow \mathsf{Prove}_1(\mathsf{pp}, \mathsf{usk}_\mathsf{id})$	Parse σ as $w \,\|\, z$
$c \leftarrow H(w \,\|\, m)$	$c \leftarrow H(w \,\|\, m)$
$z \leftarrow \mathsf{Prove}_2(\mathsf{pp}, \mathsf{usk}_\mathsf{id}, w, c, st)$	$d \leftarrow \mathsf{Dec}((\mathsf{pp}, G(\mathsf{id})), w \,\|\, c \,\|\, z)$
Return $\sigma = w \,\|\, z$	Return d

Fig. 3. IBS derived from fs-1-2-S and cSS-2-IBS transform.

5 Flaws in Peng et al.'s Work [16]

Flaws in Trapdoor Samplable Relation. Despite intuitively appealing approach of Peng et al. towards construction of IBS scheme CsiIBS through a family of trapdoor samplable relation, we identify some limitations in their trapdoor samplable relation. (We refer the reader to [16] to recall Peng et al.'s scheme.)

- Their work claims that the relation $\mathcal{R}$ is a trapdoor samplable relation. We identity that their claim is false as their algorithm Smp makes use of the trapdoor $\mathsf{td} = \{\mathsf{s}_i\}_{i=1}^{S_0}$ and thus is not a public algorithm. This should not be the case as a sampling algorithm takes the description $\langle \mathcal{R} \rangle$ of the relation $\mathcal{R}$ as input and not the trapdoor td. Their algorithm Smp and Inv is precisely the same.
- They have incorporated the user identity id in Smp algorithm, which is not a part of input. Furthermore, their inverse algorithm Inv is deterministic. These leads to their proposed relation $\mathcal{R}$ violate the basic requirements of a trapdoor samplable relation given in Definition 4.01.
- No explanation is given in support of the fact that for every relation $\mathcal{R}$ in the family, there is an integer h such that $|\mathcal{R}^{-1}(y)| = h$ for all $y \in \mathsf{Rng}(\mathcal{R})$. The trapdoor samplable relation is the main building block for their IBS scheme. The incorrect construction of trapdoor samplable relation eventually makes their identity-based signature scheme incorrect.

Flaws in IBS Scheme. The scheme CsiIBS = (Setup, Extract, Sign, Verify) of [16] employs the trapdoor samplable relation $\mathcal{F} = (\mathsf{TDG}, \mathsf{Smp}, \mathsf{Inv})$. We identify some limitations of Peng et al.'s IBS scheme below.

- It is noteworthy that even though the sampling algorithm $\mathcal{F}$.Smp is not exploited in CsiIBS of [16], the security proof in their adapted framework gets affected by the incorrect Smp algorithm. As their proposed Smp algorithm makes use of the trapdoor it is no longer a public algorithm. Thus, the real environment cannot be simulated by an entity without the trapdoor.
- The underlying framework behind IBS scheme of [16] is IBS = cSS-2-IBS(fs-1-2-S(cID)) explicitly described in Fig. 3. The Extract algorithm of Fig. 3 involves inversion of the element $y \in \text{Rng}(\mathcal{R})$ which is associated with the user identity id determined as $y = G(\text{id})$ where G is a hash function modelled as random oracle. In contrast, the Extract algorithm of IBS scheme of [16] involves inversion of any random element $y = (\text{id}, \{\mathbf{r}_{i,j}\}_{i=1,j=1}^{T_1,S_1}) \in \text{Rng}(\mathcal{R})$ where $\mathbf{r}_{i,j}$'s are generated randomly from $[-(I_0 + I_1), (I_0 + I_1)]^n$. This deviated from the general framework for IBS obtained from sequential composition of fs-1-2-S and cSS-2-IBS transform.
- The work of [16] claims that their proposed scheme CsiIBS is UF-IBS-CMA secure following Theorem 4.03 of Bellare et al. [3] stated in Sect. 4. However, as pointed out above, their scheme does not fit well in the general framework and thus Theorem 4.03 cannot be employed to conclude the security of their scheme. We believe an independent security proof is necessary to claim the security of their scheme which is missing in their paper.

6   Framework for Our Construction

6.1   ID-Based Identification Scheme

Definition 6.11. An ID-based identification scheme IBID = (Setup, Extract, Identification protocol) consists of polynomial-time algorithms Setup and Extract and an interactive protocol between a prover P and verifier V detailed below:

Setup(1^λ) $\rightarrow$ (pp, msk): On input the security parameter 1^λ, the KGC outputs the public parameter pp and master secret key msk. While pp is made publicly available, msk will be known to the KGC only.

Extract(pp, msk, id) $\rightarrow$ usk$_{\text{id}}$: The KGC executes this randomized algorithm taking input the public parameter pp, its master secret key msk and a user identity id and returns the user secret key usk$_{\text{id}}$.

Identification protocol: The prover P on input (pp, usk$_{\text{id}}$) and the verifier V on input (pp, id) involves in an interactive session with their respective inputs. On completion of an interactive execution of this protocol, V outputs a bit b with $b = 1$ signifying "accept" and $b = 0$ signifying "reject".

Definition 6.12 (ID-IMP-PA). An ID-based identification scheme IBID is $(t, q_\mathcal{I}, \epsilon)$-secure against *impersonation under passive attacks* (ID-IMP-PA) if for any passive impersonator $\mathcal{I}$ who runs in time t and makes at most $q_\mathcal{I}$ key extract queries, there exists a negligible function ϵ such that for any security parameter λ, $\mathsf{Adv}_{\mathsf{IBID}, \mathcal{I}}^{\mathsf{ID\text{-}IMP\text{-}PA}}(\lambda) = \Pr[\mathcal{I}\text{ can impersonate in } \mathsf{Exp}_{\mathsf{IBID}, \mathcal{I}}^{\mathsf{ID\text{-}IMP\text{-}PA}}(\lambda)] < \epsilon$ where the experiment $\mathsf{Exp}_{\mathsf{IBID}, \mathcal{I}}^{\mathsf{ID\text{-}IMP\text{-}PA}}(\lambda)$ in described in Fig. 4.

Setup: The challenger $\mathcal{C}$ takes input the security parameter 1^λ and generates the keys $(\mathsf{pp}, \mathsf{msk}) \leftarrow$ $\mathsf{Setup}(1^\lambda)$. It gives pp to the impersonator $\mathcal{I}$ while keeps msk secret to itself.

Phase 1: The challenger $\mathcal{C}$ responds to polynomial many adaptive queries made by the impersonator $\mathcal{I}$ in the following manner:
  – *Oracle* $\mathcal{O}_{\mathsf{Extract}}(\mathsf{msk}, \cdot)$: On receiving query on a user identity $\mathsf{id} \in \{0,1\}^*$ from $\mathcal{I}$, the challenger $\mathcal{C}$ responds with user secret key $\mathsf{usk}_{\mathsf{id}} \leftarrow \mathsf{Extract}(\mathsf{pp}, \mathsf{msk}, \mathsf{id})$ for the given identity id.
  – *Oracle* $\mathcal{O}_{\mathsf{Trans}}(\cdot)$: On receiving a transcript query on an identity id from $\mathcal{I}$, the challenger $\mathcal{C}$ responds with a transcript.
  Without loss of generality, we may assume that $\mathcal{I}$ will not query the same id in the transcript query that has been issued to the extract oracle.

Phase 2:
  – The impersonator $\mathcal{I}$ eventually outputs a challenge identity id^* on which it wishes to be impersonate whereby acting as a cheating prover trying to convince the verifier.
  – The impersonator $\mathcal{I}$ can still issue some polynomial many extract and transcript queries in **Phase 2**, subject to the restriction that no queries on the challenge identity id^* is allowed.

Fig. 4. Experiment $\mathsf{Exp}_{\mathsf{IBID}, \mathcal{A}}^{\mathsf{ID\text{-}IMP\text{-}PA}}(\lambda)$: impersonation under passive attack.

6.2 Canonical ID-Based Identification Scheme from Isogenies

The algorithms Setup and Extract are executed by the KGC and are presented in Algorithm 1 and Algorithm 2 respectively. The Identification protocol described in Fig. 5 is an interactive session between the prover P with input $(\mathsf{pp}, \mathsf{usk}_{\mathsf{id}})$ and the verifier V with input $(\mathsf{pp}, \mathsf{id})$.

Algorithm 1: $\mathsf{Setup}(1^\lambda) \rightarrow (\mathsf{pp}, \mathsf{msk})$

1 Choose a prime p of the form $p = 4\, l_1 l_2 \ldots l_n - 1$ where l_i's are small distinct odd primes with $n = 74$, $l_1 = 3$, $l_{73} = 373$ and $l_{74} = 587$.
2 Select the base elliptic curve $E_0 : y^2 = x^3 + x \in \mathsf{Ell}_p(\mathcal{O})$ over $\mathbb{F}_p$ with $\mathcal{O} = \mathbb{Z}[\sqrt{-p}]$.
3 Set the generator of the ideal class group $\mathcal{G} = \mathsf{Cl}(\mathcal{O})$ to be $\mathfrak{g} = \,<3, \pi - 1>$ with class number N.
4 Select the integers $T_1, T_2, S_0 = 2^{\eta_0} - 1$ and $S_1 = 2^{\eta_1} - 1$ where η_0, η_1 are integers and $T_1 < S_0$, $T_2 < S_1$.
5 Sample a cryptographic hash function $H : \{0,1\}^* \rightarrow [0, S_0]^{T_1 S_1}$.
6 **for** $i = 1$ **to** S_0 **do**
7   $\quad\quad s_i \xleftarrow{\$} \mathbb{Z}_N$
8   $\quad\quad E_i = [s_i] E_0$
9 **end for**
10 Return $\mathsf{pp} = \{p, E_0, \mathfrak{g}, N, T_1, T_2, S_0, S_1, H, \{E_i\}_{i=1}^{S_0}\}$ and $\mathsf{msk} = \{s_i\}_{i=1}^{S_0}$

Algorithm 2: Extract(pp, msk, id) → uskid

---

1 $s_0 \leftarrow 0$
2 **for** $i = 1$ **to** T_1 **do**
3   **for** $j = 1$ **to** S_1 **do**
4          $r_{i,j} \xleftarrow{\$} \mathbb{Z}_N$
5          $R_{i,j} = [r_{i,j}]E_0$
6   **end for**
7 **end for**
8 $\mathbf{u} \leftarrow H(\text{id} \,\|\, \{R_{i,j}\}_{i=1,j=1}^{T_1,S_1})$
9 Parse $\mathbf{u}$ as $\{u_i \in [0, S_0]\}_{i=1}^{T_1 S_1}$
10 **for** $i = 1$ **to** T_1 **do**
11   **for** $j = 1$ **to** S_1 **do**
12         $x_{i,j} = r_{i,j} - s_{u_i} \pmod{N}$
13   **end for**
14 **end for**
15 Return uskid $= (\mathbf{u} = \{u_i\}_{i=1}^{T_1 S_1}, \mathbf{x} = \{x_{i,j}\}_{i=1,j=1}^{T_1,S_1})$

Correctness. To prove the correctness of our IBID we show that $K_{i,j} = K'_{i,j}$ for all $i = 1, \ldots, T_1$ and $j = 1, \ldots T_2$. For the case when $v_{i,j} \neq 0$, we have $K'_{i,j} = [z_{i,j}]X_{i,v_{i,j}} = [k_{i,j} - x_{i,v_{i,j}} + x_{i,v_{i,j}}]E_{u_i} = K_{i,j}$ On the other hand, when $v_{i,j} = 0$, then $z_{i,j} = k_{i,j}$ as $x_{i,0}$ is set to 0. Thus, $K'_{i,j} = [z_{i,j}]E_{u_i} = [k_{i,j}]E_{u_i} = K_{i,j}$.

Theorem 6.21. *The above ID-based identification scheme IBID is $(t, q_\mathcal{I}, \epsilon)$-secure against impersonation under passive attack as per Definition 6.12 if H is a collision-resistant hash function and the signature scheme CSI-FiSh [5] is (t', q_S, ϵ')-secure against existential unforgeability under adaptive chosen message attack where*

$$t' \approx 2Dt, \quad q_I = q_S, \quad \epsilon \leq 1 - (1 - \sqrt{\epsilon'})^{\frac{1}{D}} + \frac{1}{(S_1 + 1)^{T_1 T_2}}.$$

Here D is the number of parallel execution of reset instances.

Proof. Let $\mathcal{I}$ be an impersonator who $(t, q_\mathcal{I}, \epsilon)$-breaks the isogeny based IBID scheme. We will use the impersonator $\mathcal{I}$ in the experiment $\mathsf{Exp}_{\mathsf{IBID}, \mathcal{I}}^{\mathsf{ID\text{-}IMP\text{-}PA}}(\lambda)$ described in Definition 6.12 as a subroutine to construct a forger $\mathcal{F}$ that breaks the UF-CMA security of CSI-FiSh. The forger $\mathcal{F}$ will interact with $\mathcal{I}$ playing the role of the challenger in the experiment $\mathsf{Exp}_{\mathsf{IBID}, \mathcal{I}}^{\mathsf{ID\text{-}IMP\text{-}PA}}(\lambda)$.

In the experiment $\mathsf{Exp}_{\mathsf{CSI\text{-}FiSh}, \mathcal{F}}^{\mathsf{UF\text{-}CMA}}(\lambda)$ described in [5], the challenger generates $\mathsf{pp}_{sgn} = (p, \mathfrak{g}, E_0, N, H : \{0,1\}^* \to [0, S_0]^{T_1 S_1}, S_0, T_1, S_1) \leftarrow \mathsf{CSI\text{-}FiSh.Setup}(1^\lambda)$. It then generates the signing key $\mathsf{sk} = \{s_i\}_{i=1}^{S_0}$ and verification key $\mathsf{vk} = \{E_i\}_{i=1}^{S_0}$ where $E_i = [s_i]E_0$ by executing the algorithm CSI-FiSh.KeyGen and sends $\mathsf{pp}_{sgn}, \mathsf{vk}$ to the forger $\mathcal{F}$. The forger $\mathcal{F}$ is also allowed to access oracles $\mathcal{O}_{\mathsf{CSI\text{-}FiSh.Sign}}(\mathsf{sk}, \cdot)$ where $\mathsf{sk} = \{s_i\}_{i=1}^{S_0}$.

Setup: In the setup phase, $\mathcal{F}$ samples integer T_2, sets the public parameter $\mathsf{pp} = \{p, \mathfrak{g}, E_0, N, S_0, S_1, T_1, T_2, H, \{E_i\}_{i=1}^{S_0}\}$ and sends it to $\mathcal{I}$.

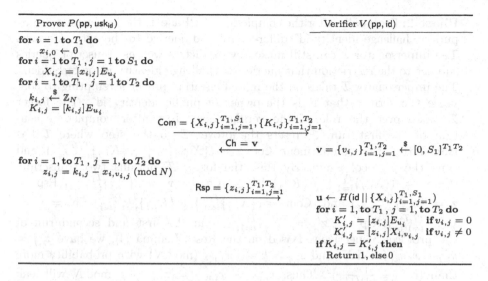

Fig. 5. Identification protocol between the prover P and verifier V.

Phase 1: In this phase the impersonator $\mathcal{I}$ makes polynomial many adaptive key extract and transcript queries.

Extract queries: On receiving an extraction query on a user identity id $\in \{0,1\}^*$, $\mathcal{F}$ issues a query on id to its own signature oracle $\mathcal{O}_{\mathsf{CSI\text{-}FiSh.Sign}}(\mathsf{sk}, \cdot)$ where $\mathsf{sk} = \{s_i\}_{i=1}^{S_0}$. The forger $\mathcal{F}$ returns the signature $(\mathbf{u}, \mathbf{x} = \{x_{i,j}\}_{i=1,j=1}^{T_1,S_1})$ obtained from its own signature oracle to $\mathcal{I}$ as the user secret key $\mathsf{usk_{id}}$ corresponding to the identity id. Thus, we have $q_I = q_S$.

Transcript queries: If the impersonator $\mathcal{I}$ issues a transcript query on id, the forger $\mathcal{F}$ performs the following steps:

- Sample $x_{i,j} \xleftarrow{\$} \mathbb{Z}_N$ for $i = 1, \ldots, T_1, j = 1, \ldots, S_1$.
- Set $x_{i,0} \leftarrow 0$ for $i = 1, \ldots, T_1$.
- Sample $\mathbf{u} = \{u_i\}_{i=1}^{T_1 S_1} \xleftarrow{\$} [0, S_0]^{T_1 S_1}$.
- Compute the curves $X_{i,j} = [x_{i,j}]E_{u_i}$ for $i = 1, \ldots, T_1, j = 1, \ldots, S_1$.
- Sample a response $z_{i,j} \xleftarrow{\$} \mathbb{Z}_N$ for $i = 1, \ldots T_1, j = 1, \ldots, T_2$.
- Sample a challenge string $\mathbf{v} = \{v_{i,j}\}_{i=1,j=1}^{T_1,T_2} \xleftarrow{\$} [0, S_1]^{T_1 T_2}$
- For $i = 1, \ldots T_1, j = 1, \ldots, T_2$ compute the curves

$$K_{i,j} = \begin{cases} [z_{i,j}]X_{i,v_{i,j}} & \text{if } v_{i,j} \neq 0 \\ [z_{i,j}]E_{u_i} & \text{if } v_{i,j} = 0 \end{cases}$$

- Return the transcript which comprises of the commitment $(\{X_{i,j}\}_{i=1,j=1}^{T_1,S_1}, \{K_{i,j}\}_{i=1,j=1}^{T_1,T_2})$, challenge $\mathbf{v} = \{v_{i,j}\}_{i=1,j=1}^{T_1,T_2}$ and response $\mathbf{z} = \{z_{i,j}\}_{i=1,j=1}^{T_1,T_2}$ corresponding to the identity id.

Phase 2: Eventually after the completion of **Phase 1**, the impersonator outputs a challenge identity id^* different from id queried to the extract oracle. The impersonator $\mathcal{I}$ can still make key extract as well as transcript queries subject to the restriction that queries on challenge identity id^* is forbidden. The impersonator $\mathcal{I}$ takes on the role of cheating prover attempting to convince the verifier that it is the owner of public identity id^*. The forger $\mathcal{F}$ takes over the role of the verifier now. Just after complete execution of the first run, $\mathcal{F}$ resets the prover $\mathcal{I}$ to the step where $\mathcal{I}$ has transmitted the commitment $\mathsf{Com} = (\{X_{i,j}\}_{i=1,j=1}^{T_1,S_1}, \{K_{i,j}\}_{i=1,j=1}^{T_1,T_2})$ and runs the protocol again. By this, the forger $\mathcal{F}$ obtains two transcripts $(\mathsf{Com} = (\{X_{i,j}\}_{i=1,j=1}^{T_1,S_1}, \{K_{i,j}\}_{i=1,j=1}^{T_1,T_2}), \mathsf{Ch} = \mathbf{v} = \{v_{i,j}\}_{i=1,j=1}^{T_1,T_2}, \mathsf{Rsp} = \mathbf{z} = \{z_{i,j}\}_{i=1,j=1}^{T_1,T_2})$ and $(\mathsf{Com} = (\{X_{i,j}\}_{i=1,j=1}^{T_1,S_1}, \{K_{i,j}\}_{i=1,j=1}^{T_1,T_2}), \mathsf{Ch}' = \mathbf{v}' = \{v'_{i,j}\}_{i=1,j=1}^{T_1,T_2}, \mathsf{Rsp}' = \mathbf{z}' = \{z'_{i,j}\}_{i=1,j=1}^{T_1,T_2})$ in the first and second run of the protocol respectively. Based on the Reset Lemma [4], we have $z_{i,j} = k_{i,j} - x_{i,v_{i,j}} \pmod{N}$ and $z'_{i,j} = k_{i,j} - x_{i,v'_{i,j}} \pmod{N}$ with probability more than $(\epsilon - \frac{1}{(S_1+1)^{T_1 T_2}})^2$. Thus, $x_{i,v'_{i,j}} - x_{i,v_{i,j}} = z_{i,j} - z'_{i,j} \bmod N$ will leak information of $\{x_{i,j}\}_{i=1,j=1}^{T_1,S_1}$. Following Multi-Instance Reset Lemma [10], we rewind D parallel instances of Reset Lemma which reveals enough information to extract $\{x_{i,j}\}_{i=1,j=1}^{T_1,S_1}$ with probability more than $(1 - (1 - \epsilon + \frac{1}{(S_1+1)^{T_1 T_2}})^D)^2$. Thus $\epsilon' \geq (1 - (1 - \epsilon + \frac{1}{(S_1+1)^{T_1 T_2}})^D)^2$, which in turn implies $\epsilon \leq 1 - (1 - \sqrt{\epsilon'})^{\frac{1}{D}} + \frac{1}{(S_1+1)^{T_1 T_2}}$. Furthermore, it also extracts $\mathbf{u}$ by computing $H(\text{id}^* \| \{X_{i,j}\}_{i=1,j=1}^{T_1,S_1})$.

Finally, the forger $\mathcal{F}$ submits the message-signature pair $(\text{id}^*, (\mathbf{u} = \{u_i\}_{i=1}^{T_1 S_1}, \mathbf{x} = \{x_{i,j}\}_{i=1,j=1}^{T_1,S_1}))$ as its forgery to its own challenger. Note that as the challenged identity id^* has never been queried by $\mathcal{I}$ to the extract oracle, id^* has never been queried to the sign oracle as well. The validity of the signature follows immediately from the validity of the transcripts. The running time t' of $\mathcal{F}$ is that of Reset algorithm, which thereby implies $t' \approx 2Dt$. $\square$

6.3   Identity-Based Signature Scheme from Isogenies

In this section, we apply the well-known strategy Fiat Shamir with aborts [12] to our $\mathsf{IBID} = (\mathsf{Setup}, \mathsf{Extract}, \mathsf{Identification~protocol})$ described in Sect. 6.2 to obtain our identity-based signature scheme $\mathsf{IBS} = (\mathsf{Setup}, \mathsf{Extract}, \mathsf{Sign}, \mathsf{Verify})$.

$\mathsf{Setup}(1^\lambda) \to (\mathsf{pp}_{ibs}, \mathsf{msk})$: This algorithm is the same as Setup algorithm of our IBID scheme. Additionally, the KGC samples $H' : \{0,1\}^* \to [0, S_1]^{T_1 T_2}$ and sets $\mathsf{pp}_{ibs} = \{p, E_0, \mathfrak{g}, N, T_1, T_2, S_0, S_1, H, H', \{E_i\}_{i=1}^{S_0}\}$ and $\mathsf{msk} = \{s_i\}_{i=1}^{S_0}$.

$\mathsf{Extract}(\mathsf{pp}_{ibs}, \mathsf{msk}, \mathsf{id}) \to \mathsf{usk}_{\mathsf{id}}$: This algorithm is identical to $\mathsf{Extract}$ algorithm of our IBID scheme.

Algorithm 3:	Algorithm 4:
$\mathsf{Sign}(\mathsf{pp}_{ibs}, \mathsf{usk_{id}}, m) \rightarrow \sigma$	$\mathsf{Verify}(\mathsf{pp}_{ibs}, \mathsf{id}, m, \sigma) \rightarrow \mathsf{Valid/Invalid}$

1 for $i = 1$ to T_1 do	1 Retrieve $\mathbf{u} = H(\mathsf{id} \,\|\, \{X_{i,j}\}_{i=1,j=1}^{T_1,S_1})$
2 $\quad$ Set $x_{i,0} \leftarrow 0$	2 Parse $\mathbf{v}$ as $\{v_{i,j}\}_{i=1,j=1}^{T_1,T_2}$
3 end for	3 for $i = 1$ to T_1 do
4 for $i = 1$ to T_1 do	4 $\quad$ for $j = 1$ to T_2 do
5 $\quad$ for $j = 1$ to S_1 do	5 $\quad\quad$ if $v_{i,j} = 0$ then
6 $\quad\quad$ $X_{i,j} = [x_{i,j}]E_{u_i}$	6 $\quad\quad\quad$ $K'_{i,j} = [z_{i,j}]E_{u_i}$
7 $\quad$ end for	7 $\quad\quad$ else
8 end for	8 $\quad\quad\quad$ $K'_{i,j} = [z_{i,j}]X_{i,v_{i,j}}$
9 for $i = 1$ to T_1 do	9 $\quad\quad$ end if
10 $\quad$ for $j = 1$ to T_2 do	10 $\quad$ end for
11 $\quad\quad$ $k_{i,j} \xleftarrow{\$} \mathbb{Z}_N$	11 end for
12 $\quad\quad$ $K_{i,j} = [k_{i,j}]E_{u_i}$	12 $\mathbf{v} \leftarrow H'(m \,\|\, \{K'_{i,j}\}_{i=1,j=1}^{T_1,T_2})$
13 $\quad$ end for	13 if $v' \neq v$ then
14 end for	14 $\quad$ Invalid
15 $\mathbf{v} \leftarrow H'(m \,\|\, \{K_{i,j}\}_{i=1,j=1}^{T_1,T_2})$	15 end if
16 Parse $\mathbf{v}$ as $\{v_{i,j} \in [0, S_1]\}_{i=1,j=1}^{T_1,T_2}$	16 Return Valid
17 for $i = 1$ to T_1 do	
18 $\quad$ for $j = 1$ to T_2 do	
19 $\quad\quad$ $z_{i,j} = k_{i,j} - x_{i,v_{i,j}} \pmod{N}$	
20 $\quad$ end for	
21 end for	
22 $\sigma \leftarrow (\{z_{i,j}\}_{i=1,j=1}^{T_1,T_2}, \{X_{i,j}\}_{i=1,j=1}^{T_1,S_1}, \mathbf{v})$	
23 Return σ	

Correctness. The correctness of our IBS follows immediately from the correctness of our canonical ID-based identification scheme IBID from isogenies.

From Theorem 6.21 and Lemma 3.5 of [1] we arrive at the following theorem:

Theorem 6.31. *Let* IBID *be the ID-based identification scheme from isogenies described in Sect. 6.2 and* IBS *be an identity-based signature from isogenies presented in Sect. 6.3. Let* $\mathcal{A}$ *be an adversary that breaks the* UF-IBS-CMA *security of* IBS, *then we can construct an impersonator* $\mathcal{I}$ *breaking the* IMP-PA *security of* IBID.

7 Our Construction of Forward-Secure Identity-Based Signature

In this section we describe our construction of forward-secure identity-based signature FSIBS using the IBS scheme presented in Sect. 6.3.

$\mathsf{Setup}(1^\lambda) \rightarrow (\mathsf{pp}_{fs}, \mathsf{msk})$: The KGC runs the algorithm IBS.Setup on input 1^λ to generate $\mathsf{pp}_{ibs} = \{p, E_0, \mathfrak{g}, N, T_1, T_2, S_0, S_1, H, H', \{E_i\}_{i=1}^{S_0}\}$ and $\mathsf{msk} = \{s_i\}_{i=1}^{S_0}$.

- Sample a hash function $\widetilde{H} : \{0,1\}^* \rightarrow [0, S_0]^{T_1}$.
- Sample a forward-secure pseudo-random generator FSPRG $G : \{0,1\}^d \rightarrow \{0,1\}^e$ where $d < e$ with $e_L + e_R = e$, integer $e_L > 0$ and integer $e_R > 0$ and a pseudo-random function $f : \{0,1\}^{e_L} \rightarrow \mathbb{Z}_N^{S_0}$.

- Run IBS.Setup to generate $pp_{ibs} = \{p, E_0, \mathfrak{g}, N, T_1, T_2, S_0, S_1, H, H',$
  $\{E_i\}_{i=1}^{S_0}\}$.
- Return $pp_{fs} = \{pp_{ibs}, \widetilde{H}, G, f,\}$ and $msk = \{s_i\}_{i=1}^{S_0}$.

Extract(pp_{fs}, msk, id) $\rightarrow$ usk_{id}: On input the public parameter pp_{fs}, the master secret key $msk = \{s_i\}_{i=1}^{S_0}$ and the identity $id = \mathcal{ID} \| \mathcal{T_{ID}}$ where $\mathcal{ID}$ is the user's identifier information and $\mathcal{T_{ID}}$ is the pre-specified number of time periods over which the signing key is generated, the KGC runs this algorithm and outputs the secret key usk_{id} for the given identity id in the following manner:

- Set $s_0 \leftarrow 0$.
- Sample integer vectors $r_{i,j} \xleftarrow{\$} \mathbb{Z}_N$ and compute the curves $R_{i,j} = [r_{i,j}]E_0$
  for $i = 1, \ldots, T_1, j = 1, \ldots, S_1$
- Compute $\mathbf{u} = (u_1, \ldots, u_{T_1 S_1}) = H(id \| \{R_{i,j}\}_{i=1,j=1}^{T_1,S_1})$
- Compute $x_{i,j} = r_{i,j} - s_{u_i} \pmod{N}$ for $i = 1, \ldots, T_1, j = 1, \ldots, S_1$.
- Return $usk_{id} = (\mathbf{u}, \{x_{i,j}\}_{i=1,j=1}^{T_1,S_1})$.

Initialize(pp_{fs}, id, usk_{id}) $\rightarrow$ ($SK_{id,0}$, aux_{id}): The signer on input pp_{fs}, user identity $id = \mathcal{ID} \| \mathcal{T_{ID}}$ and its secret key $usk_{id} = (\mathbf{u}, \{x_{i,j}\}_{i=1,j=1}^{T_1,S_1})$ generates its initial signing key $SK_{id,0}$ and some auxiliary information aux_{id} in the following manner:

- Select a random seed $\beta_0 \in \{0,1\}^d$ for the pseudo-random generator G.
- for $l = 1, \ldots, \mathcal{T_{ID}}$ do
  - Compute $(\alpha_l, \beta_l) \leftarrow G(\beta_{l-1})$.
  - Compute $f(\alpha_l) = (a_1^{(l)}, \ldots, a_{S_0}^{(l)})$.
  - Run CSI-FiSh.KeyGen algorithm of CSI-FiSh with the public parameter $pp_{sgn} = (p, \mathfrak{g}, N, E_0, \widetilde{H}, S_0, T_1)$ extracted from pp_{fs} to generate signing-verification key pair (sk_l, vk_l).
    * Compute the curves $A_i^{(l)} = [a_i^{(l)}]E_0$ for $i = 1, \ldots, S_0$.
    * Set the signing key $sk_l = \{a_i^{(l)}\}_{i=1}^{S_0}$ and verification key $vk_l = \{A_i^{(l)}\}_{i=1}^{S_0}$.
  - Run IBS.Sign algorithm (see Algorithm 3) on input the public parameter $pp_{ibs} = \{p, E_0, \mathfrak{g}, N, T_1, T_2, S_0, S_1, H, H', \{E_i\}_{i=1}^{S_0}\}$, user secret key $usk_{id} = (\mathbf{u}, \{x_{i,j}\}_{i=1,j=1}^{T_1,S_1})$ to generate a signature σ_l on $id \| l \| vk_l$.
    * Set $x_{i,0} \leftarrow 0$ for $i = 1, \ldots, T_1$.
    * Compute the curves $X_{i,j} = [x_{i,j}]E_{u_i}$ for $i = 1, \ldots, T_1, j = 1, \ldots, S_1$ where $\mathbf{u} = (u_1, \ldots, u_{T_1 S_1})$ is extracted from usk_{id}.
    * Sample the integer vector $k_{i,j}^{(l)} \xleftarrow{\$} \mathbb{Z}_N$ and compute the curves $K_{i,j}^{(l)} = [k_{i,j}]E_{u_i}$ for $i = 1, \ldots, T_1, j = 1, \ldots, T_2$.
    * Compute $\mathbf{v}^{(l)} = (v_{1,1}^{(l)}, \ldots, v_{T_1,T_2}^{(l)}) = H'(id \| l \| \{A_i^{(l)}\}_{i=1}^{S_0} \| \{K_{i,j}^{(l)}\}_{i=1,j=1}^{T_1,T_2})$.
    * Compute $z_{i,j}^{(l)} = k_{i,j}^{(l)} - x_{i,v_{i,j}^{(l)}} \bmod N$ for $i = 1, \ldots, T_1, j = 1, \ldots, T_2$.
    * Set $\sigma_l = (\{z_{i,j}^{(l)}\}_{i=1,j=1}^{T_1,T_2}, \{X_{i,j}\}_{i=1,j=1}^{T_1,S_1}, \mathbf{v}^{(l)})$.
  - Set the auxiliary information $aux_{id,l} = (id, l, vk_l, \sigma_l)$.

- Save $\mathsf{aux_{id}} = (\{\mathsf{aux_{id},}{}_l\}_{l=1}^{\mathcal{T}_{\mathcal{ID}}})$ not necessarily in a secure storage..
- Erase $\mathsf{usk_{id}}, \mathsf{sk}_l, \alpha_l, \beta_l$ for $l = 1, \ldots, \mathcal{T}_{\mathcal{ID}}$.
- Set $\mathsf{SK_{id,\,0}} = \beta_0$ and keep it secret.

$\mathsf{Update}(\mathsf{pp}_{fs}, \mathsf{id}, t, \mathsf{aux_{id}}, \mathsf{SK_{id,\,t-1}}) \rightarrow \mathsf{SK_{id,\,t}}$: The signer executes this algorithm on input the public parameter pp_{fs}, user identity $\mathsf{id} = \mathcal{ID} \,\|\, \mathcal{T}_{\mathcal{ID}}$, an index of the current time period $t < \mathcal{T}_{\mathcal{ID}}$, the auxiliary information $\mathsf{aux_{id}}$ and the signing key $\mathsf{SK_{id,\,t-1}}$ corresponding to previous time period and generates signing key $\mathsf{SK_{id,\,t}}$ for the current time period t by following the steps detailed below:

- If $t = 1$, parse $\mathsf{SK_{id,\,t-1}}$ into β_{t-1}. Otherwise, parse $\mathsf{SK_{id,\,t-1}}$ into $(\mathsf{sk}_{t-1}, \beta_{t-1})$.
- Compute $(\alpha_t, \beta_t) \leftarrow G(\beta_{t-1})$.
- Compute $f(\alpha_l) = (a_1^{(l)}, \ldots, a_{S_0}^{(l)})$ and retrieve the curves $A_i^{(t)} = [a_i^{(t)}]E_0$ for $i = 1, \ldots, S_0$.
- Set the signing key $\mathsf{sk}_t = \{a_i^{(t)}\}_{i=1}^{S_0}$ and verification key $\mathsf{vk}_t = \{A_i^{(t)}\}_{i=1}^{S_0}$.
- Retrieve $\mathsf{aux_{id,\,t}}$ from $\mathsf{aux_{id}}$ and parse it to (M_1, M_2, M_3, M_4). Check if $M_1 = \mathsf{id}$, $M_2 = t$ and $M_3 = \mathsf{vk}_t$. If any of these test fails, abort. If the checks succeed, run the IBS.Verify algorithm to check the validity of the signature $M_4 = (\{z_{i,j}^{(t)}\}_{i=1,j=1}^{T_1,T_2}, \{X_{i,j}\}_{i=1,j=1}^{T_1,S_1}, \mathbf{v}^{(t)})$ on the message $\mathsf{id} \,\|\, t \,\|\, \mathsf{vk}_t$.
  - Retrieve $\mathbf{u} = H(\mathsf{id} \,\|\, \{X_{i,j}\}_{i=1,j=1}^{T_1,S_1})$.
  - Extract $\mathbf{v}^{(t)}$ from M_4 and parse it as $\{v_{i,j}^{(t)}\}_{i=1,j=1}^{T_1,T_2}$.
  - for $i = 1, \ldots, T_1$, $j = 1, \ldots, T_2$, if $v_{i,j}^{(l)} = 0$ then compute $\bar{K}_{i,j}^{(t)} = [z_{i,j}^{(t)}]E_{u_i}$ else compute $\bar{K}_{i,j}^{(t)} = [z_{i,j}^{(t)}]X_{i,v_{i,j}^{(t)}}$.
  - Compute $\bar{\mathbf{v}}^{(t)} = H'(\mathsf{id} \,\|\, t \,\|\, \mathsf{vk}_t \,\|\, \{\bar{K}_{i,j}^{(t)}\}_{i=1,j=1}^{T_1,T_2})$.
  - If $\bar{\mathbf{v}}^{(t)} \neq \mathbf{v}^{(t)}$ return Invalid else return Valid.
- Abort if the verification fails and continue otherwise.
- Set $\mathsf{SK_{id,\,t}} = (\mathsf{sk}_t, \beta_t)$. Save $\mathsf{SK_{id,\,t}}$ in a secure storage and erase $\mathsf{SK_{id,\,t-1}}$.

$\mathsf{Sign}(\mathsf{pp}_{fs}, t, \mathsf{id}, \mathsf{aux_{id}}, \mathsf{SK_{id,\,t}}, m) \rightarrow \gamma$: Taking input the public parameter pp_{fs}, an index of time period t, user identity id, the auxiliary information $\mathsf{aux_{id}}$, the signing key $\mathsf{SK_{id,\,t}} = (\mathsf{sk}_t, \beta_t)$ associated with time period t and a message, the signer runs this algorithm to generate a signature γ on m associated with id and t. It executes the following steps:

- Retrieve the current values of $\mathsf{aux_{id,\,t}}$ from $\mathsf{aux_{id}}$ and $\mathsf{SK_{id,\,t}}$.
- Parse $\mathsf{SK_{id,\,t}}$ into (sk_t, β_t).
- Compute the CSI-FiSh signature ρ_t on input the public parameter $\mathsf{pp}_{sgn} = (p, \mathfrak{g}, N, E_0, \tilde{H}, S_0, T_1)$, the message m and the signing key $\mathsf{sk}_t = \{a_i^{(t)}\}_{i=1}^{S_0}$.
  - Sets $a_0^{(t)} \leftarrow 0$.
  - Samples $b_i^{(t)} \xleftarrow{\$} \mathbb{Z}_N$ and compute $B_i^{(t)} = [b_i^{(t)}]E_0$ for $i = 1, \ldots, T_1$.
  - Computes the challenge bits $\mathbf{c}^{(t)} = (c_1^{(t)}, \ldots, c_{T_1}^{(t)}) = \tilde{H}(m \,\| \{B_i^{(t)}\}_{i=1}^{S_0})$.
  - Computes the response $y_i^{(t)} = b_i^{(t)} - a_{c_i^{(t)}}^{(t)} \pmod{N}$ for $i = 1, \ldots, T_1$.

- Sets the signature $\rho_t = (\{c_i^{(t)}\}_{i=1}^{T_1}, \{y_i^{(t)}\}_{i=1}^{T_1})$.
  - Sets the signature $\gamma = (\mathsf{aux}_{\mathsf{id},\,t}, \rho_t)$

$\mathsf{Verify}(\mathsf{pp}_{fs}, \mathsf{id}, t, m, \gamma) \rightarrow \mathsf{Valid}/\mathsf{Invalid}$: On input the public parameter pp_{fs}, user identity id, an index of current time period t, a message and a signature $\gamma = (\mathsf{aux}_{\mathsf{id},\,t}, \rho_t)$, the verifier runs this algorithm in the following manner:

- Parse $\mathsf{aux}_{\mathsf{id},\,t}$ to (M_1, M_2, M_3, M_4).
- Check if $M_1 = \mathsf{id}$ and $M_2 = t$.
- Run the IBS.Verify algorithm (see Algorithm 4) with input the public parameter $\mathsf{pp}_{ibs} = \{p, E_0, \mathfrak{g}, N, T_1, T_2, S_0, S_1, H, H', \{E_i\}_{i=1}^{S_0}\}$, user identity id, the message $\mathsf{id} \,\|\, t \,\|\, M_3$ and the signature M_4 to verify the signature.
- Run the algorithm CSI-FiSH.Verify to verify the validity of the signature ρ_t on the message m under the verification key M_3.
  - Parse $\rho_t = (\{c_i^{(t)}\}_{i=1}^{T_1}, \{y_i^{(t)}\}_{i=1}^{T_1})$.
  - Compute the elliptic curves $B_i^{(t)} = [y_i^{(t)}]A_{c_i^{(t)}}$ for $i = 1, \ldots, T_1$.
  - Compute $\bar{\mathbf{c}}^{(t)} = (\bar{c}_1^{(t)}, \ldots, \bar{c}_{T_1}^{(t)}) = \widetilde{H}(m \,\|\, \{B_i^{(t)}\}_{i=1}^{S_0})$
  - If $\mathbf{c}^{(t)} = \bar{\mathbf{c}}^{(t)}$ then returns Valid, else returns Invalid.
- If all the above tests succeed, return Valid, else return Invalid.

Correctness. The correctness of our FSIBS scheme follows immediately from the correctness of CSI-FiSh signature and correctness of our IBS scheme.

Theorem 7.01. *If the underlying signature scheme CSI-FiSh, identity-based signature IBS and forward-secure pseudorandom generator G are UF-CMA, UF-IBS-CMA and ROR secure respectively, then our scheme FSIBS is UF-FSIBS-CMA secure following the security model of [2].*

References

1. Abdalla, M., An, J.H., Bellare, M., Namprempre, C.: From identification to signatures via the Fiat-Shamir transform: minimizing assumptions for security and forward-security. In: Knudsen, L.R. (ed.) EUROCRYPT 2002. LNCS, vol. 2332, pp. 418–433. Springer, Heidelberg (2002). https://doi.org/10.1007/3-540-46035-7_28
2. Al Ebri, N., Baek, J., Shoufan, A., Vu, Q.H., ETISALAT British Telecom Innovation Center: Forward-secure identity-based signature: new generic constructions and their applications. J. Wirel. Mob. Netw. Ubiquit. Comput. Dependable Appl. **4**(1), 32–54 (2013)
3. Bellare, M., Namprempre, C., Neven, G.: Security proofs for identity-based identification and signature schemes. J. Cryptol. **22**(1), 1–61 (2009). https://doi.org/10.1007/s00145-008-9028-8
4. Bellare, M., Palacio, A.: GQ and Schnorr identification schemes: proofs of security against impersonation under active and concurrent attacks. In: Yung, M. (ed.) CRYPTO 2002. LNCS, vol. 2442, pp. 162–177. Springer, Heidelberg (2002). https://doi.org/10.1007/3-540-45708-9_11

5. Beullens, W., Kleinjung, T., Vercauteren, F.: CSI-FiSh: efficient isogeny based signatures through class group computations. In: Galbraith, S.D., Moriai, S. (eds.) ASIACRYPT 2019. LNCS, vol. 11921, pp. 227–247. Springer, Cham (2019). https://doi.org/10.1007/978-3-030-34578-5_9
6. De Feo, L., Galbraith, S.D.: SeaSign: compact isogeny signatures from class group actions. In: Ishai, Y., Rijmen, V. (eds.) EUROCRYPT 2019. LNCS, vol. 11478, pp. 759–789. Springer, Cham (2019). https://doi.org/10.1007/978-3-030-17659-4_26
7. Fiat, A., Shamir, A.: How to prove yourself: practical solutions to identification and signature problems. In: Odlyzko, A.M. (ed.) CRYPTO 1986. LNCS, vol. 263, pp. 186–194. Springer, Heidelberg (1987). https://doi.org/10.1007/3-540-47721-7_12
8. Girault, M.: An identity-based identification scheme based on discrete logarithms modulo a composite number. In: Damgård, I.B. (ed.) EUROCRYPT 1990. LNCS, vol. 473, pp. 481–486. Springer, Heidelberg (1991). https://doi.org/10.1007/3-540-46877-3_44
9. Guillou, L.C., Quisquater, J.-J.: A "paradoxical" indentity-based signature scheme resulting from zero-knowledge. In: Goldwasser, S. (ed.) CRYPTO 1988. LNCS, vol. 403, pp. 216–231. Springer, New York (1990). https://doi.org/10.1007/0-387-34799-2_16
10. Kiltz, E., Masny, D., Pan, J.: Optimal security proofs for signatures from identification schemes. In: Robshaw, M., Katz, J. (eds.) CRYPTO 2016. LNCS, vol. 9815, pp. 33–61. Springer, Heidelberg (2016). https://doi.org/10.1007/978-3-662-53008-5_2
11. Kurosawa, K., Heng, S.-H.: From digital signature to ID-based identification/signature. In: Bao, F., Deng, R., Zhou, J. (eds.) PKC 2004. LNCS, vol. 2947, pp. 248–261. Springer, Heidelberg (2004). https://doi.org/10.1007/978-3-540-24632-9_18
12. Lyubashevsky, V.: Fiat-Shamir with aborts: applications to lattice and factoring-based signatures. In: Matsui, M. (ed.) ASIACRYPT 2009. LNCS, vol. 5912, pp. 598–616. Springer, Heidelberg (2009). https://doi.org/10.1007/978-3-642-10366-7_35
13. Moriya, T., Onuki, H., Takagi, T.: SiGamal: a supersingular isogeny-based PKE and its application to a PRF. In: Moriai, S., Wang, H. (eds.) ASIACRYPT 2020. LNCS, vol. 12492, pp. 551–580. Springer, Cham (2020). https://doi.org/10.1007/978-3-030-64834-3_19
14. Okamoto, T.: Provably secure and practical identification schemes and corresponding signature schemes. In: Brickell, E.F. (ed.) CRYPTO 1992. LNCS, vol. 740, pp. 31–53. Springer, Heidelberg (1993). https://doi.org/10.1007/3-540-48071-4_3
15. Paterson, K.G.: ID-based signatures from pairings on elliptic curves. Electron. Lett. 38(18), 1025–1026 (2002)
16. Peng, C., Chen, J., Zhou, L., Choo, K.-K.R., He, D.: CsiIBS: a post-quantum identity-based signature scheme based on isogenies. J. Inf. Secur. Appl. 54, 102504 (2020)
17. Shamir, A.: Identity-based cryptosystems and signature schemes. In: Blakley, G.R., Chaum, D. (eds.) CRYPTO 1984. LNCS, vol. 196, pp. 47–53. Springer, Heidelberg (1985). https://doi.org/10.1007/3-540-39568-7_5
18. Silverman, J.H.: The Arithmetic of Elliptic Curves, vol. 106. Springer, New York (2009). https://doi.org/10.1007/978-0-387-09494-6
19. Tian, M., Huang, L.: Efficient identity-based signature from lattices. In: Cuppens-Boulahia, N., Cuppens, F., Jajodia, S., Abou El Kalam, A., Sans, T. (eds.) SEC 2014. IAICT, vol. 428, pp. 321–329. Springer, Heidelberg (2014). https://doi.org/10.1007/978-3-642-55415-5_26

20. Vélu, J.: Isogénies entre courbes elliptiques. CR Acad. Sci. Paris, Séries A **273**, 305–347 (1971)
21. Waterhouse, W.C.: Abelian varieties over finite fields. In: Annales scientifiques de l'École Normale Supérieure, vol. 2, pp. 521–560 (1969)
22. Xie, J., Yu-pu, H., Gao, J., Gao, W.: Efficient identity-based signature over NTRU lattice. Front. Inf. Technol. Electron. Eng. **17**(2), 135–142 (2016). https://doi.org/10.1631/FITEE.1500197
23. Yi, X.: An identity-based signature scheme from the Weil pairing. IEEE Commun. Lett. **7**(2), 76–78 (2003)

Linearly Homomorphic Signatures
with Designated Combiner

Chengjun Lin[1,2], Rui Xue[1,2], and Xinyi Huang[3(✉)]

[1] State Key Laboratory of Information Security, Institute of Information Engineering, Chinese Academy of Sciences, Beijing 100093, China
[2] School of Cyber Security, University of Chinese Academy of Sciences, Beijing 100049, China
{linchengjun,xuerui}@iie.ac.cn
[3] Fujian Provincial Key Laboratory of Network Security and Cryptology, College of Computer and Cyber Security, Fujian Normal University, Fuzhou 350117, China
xyhuang@fjnu.edu.cn

Abstract. Linearly homomorphic signatures provide authenticity services for a series of scenarios such as network coding routing mechanisms and verifiable computation mechanisms. However, most of the present constructions are publicly combinable and verifiable. Motivated by the problem proposed by Rivest, we introduce the concept of designated combiner into linearly homomorphic signatures. In the new notion, the verification procedure remains public, nevertheless, the homomorphic operation is infeasible for other entities except the one designated by the signer (we call it the designated combiner). In addition, we present a specific construction with provable security in the random oracle model.

Keywords: Linearly homomorphic signatures · Designated combiner · Publicly verifiable · Random oracle model

1 Introduction

The aim of digital signatures [16] is to provide authenticity, integrity and non-repudiation of the signed message. Among these properties, authenticity is used to guarantee the source and the content of the signed message; integrity is in order to prevent an adversary from modifying the signed message, or from injecting a malicious message unsigned by the signer; non-repudiation means that the signer cannot deny the message signed by she previously. Informally, a digital signature scheme consists of three algorithms (KeyGen, Sign, Verify). The signer who wishes to send some messages in an authenticated way begins by generating her private/public key pair (sk, pk) using the KeyGen algorithm. When she wants to send a message m to others, she runs the Sign algorithm that takes as input a message m and private key sk, and outputs a signature σ. Upon receiving the pair (m, σ), any entity with the signer's public key pk can check whether σ is a valid signature on message m or not. This is completed by running the Verify algorithm.

© Springer Nature Switzerland AG 2021
Q. Huang and Y. Yu (Eds.): ProvSec 2021, LNCS 13059, pp. 327–345, 2021.
https://doi.org/10.1007/978-3-030-90402-9_18

Although digital signatures are widely used, some extra properties should be added to satisfy the requirements in specific scenarios. As a class of special digital signatures, homomorphic signatures [20] have an additional algorithm called `Combine`, which allows any entity with the signer's public key to compute on the signed message in a honest and homomorphic way.

Both digital signatures [16] and homomorphic signatures [20] require existential unforgeability under adaptively chosen-message attacks. The difference lies in the type of the unforgeability they require: the former requires that the adversary must be unable to produce even one signature on a message unsigned by the signer, while the latter captures the ability to combine the signed data by any entity, i.e., a derived signature obtained in honest and homomorphic way is not a forgery. More precisely, a signer has a dataset $\{m_i\}_{i=1}^n$ and produce corresponding signature σ_i for each message m_i. Any entity, without the knowledge of the signer's private key, can compute $m = f(m_1, \ldots, m_n)$ together with a valid signature σ on it. There are two key features in the above primitive: first, the homomorphic operation over authenticated data is feasible for any entity, even though they don't have the signer's private key; second, any entity can verify the validity of σ, and this procedure does not need original messages $\{m_i\}_{i=1}^n$. Because of these attractive properties, much attention has been paid to homomorphic signatures, and there are various types of homomorphic signatures according to different computations they support. These include linearly homomorphic signatures [9], homomorphic signatures for polynomial functions [7], fully homomorphic signatures [10], transitive signatures [6], redactable signatures [20] and so on.

As a special type of homomorphic signatures, linearly homomorphic signatures (LHS) [9,26] allow any entity to homomorphically evaluate linear functions over the signed data (usually a vector group). In a LHS scheme $\mathcal{LHS} = $ (`KeyGen, Sign, Combine, Verify`), more specifically, the message space usually is a vector subspace, and `Combine` allows for public computation for linear functions over the signed data (we call this property public combinability). `Verify`, run by any entity with the signer's public key, can tell whether a message is valid or not (we call this property public verifiability). Note that a message is valid if it came directly from the signer or was linearly derived from the signer's original dataset. LHS were originally used to prevent pollution attacks in the network coding routing mechanisms [9], and enjoy desirable applications in proofs of storage [3] and cloud computing area [21] such as verifiable computation mechanisms [1,5]. Besides, LHS can improve the robustness for lager-scale system [9,19].

In the verifiable computation mechanisms [1], the signer who has a set of data $m_1, m_2, \ldots, m_n \in \mathbb{F}_p$ wants to delegate computations over this dataset to a cloud server. However, there always exist some servers who would not perform computation honestly. In this scenario, we can use LHS to establish verifiable computation mechanisms. First of all, the signer extends each data m_k to the vector $(m_k \mid \mathbf{e}_k) \in \mathbb{F}_p^{n+1}$, and then computes signatures on each vector $(m_k \mid \mathbf{e}_k)$. Next, all (m_k, k) and the corresponding signature σ_k are transmitted to the server by the signer. Then, the server can carry any linear computation f over the original dataset and accordingly derive a signature σ for the computation result $m = f(m_1, m_2, \ldots, m_n)$. The signature σ can assure the recipient that the value m is indeed equal to $f(m_1, m_2, \ldots, m_n)$.

However, there exist two problems in the above framework if the signer wants the server to be the only entity who can combine the signatures: first, the signer needs a reliable channel for transmitting the data/signature pair (m_k, σ_k) to the server. Otherwise, any entity who intercepts these pairs can also serve as the combiner because existing LHS schemes are publicly combinable; second, any verifier who receives the pairs (m, σ) derived by the server can simply calculate a signature on any linear function over m.

Recently, Lin *et al.* [22] defined a framework for linearly homomorphic signatures with designated entities (LHSDE): only the designated combiner can produce signatures on linearly-combined signed vectors, and only the designated verifier would be convinced about the validity of those signatures. The motivation of [22] is raised by Rivest in [24], namely, how to design a transitive signature scheme such that only one entity called the designated combiner is able to derive the edge signature $\sigma(A, C)$ from the edge signatures $\sigma(A, B)$ and $\sigma(B, C)$. Both transitive signatures and linearly homomorphic signatures are special cases of homomorphic signatures, so Lin *et al.* study a similar problem in the setting of the latter. Although the works of Lin *et al.* [22] can solve the above two problems, linearly homomorphic signatures with designated combiner (LHSDC) with public verifiability have not yet appeared in the literature, and the reason why [22] does not achieve public verifiability would be detailed in the Sect. 1.1.

There are two reasons for making the syntax of LHSDC publicly verifiable. The first issue of introducing the designated verifier is the loss of non-repudiation property which is indispensable in many scenarios. Second, LHSDC is more efficient than LHSDE in aspects like public key distribution, management, and revocation, etc. So it is worth spending a bit more time on this research line.

1.1 Contributions

Our Results. A major concern in this work is to prevent the non-authorized entities from combining the certified data. To do so, we first introduce a new notion called linearly homomorphic signatures with designated combiner (LHSDC). Both of LHSDC and LHS are publicly verifiable, but the main difference lies in that the combiner in the former is designated by the signer and only he/she can perform the Combine algorithm, while the latter are publicly combinable. Then, we present the formal definition of LHSDC as well as its security requirements including two types of unforgeability. Finally, we use the idea of IBS (Identity-Based Signatures) to design a concrete LHSDC scheme satisfying two types of unforgeability in the random oracle model, assuming that the co-CDH and the CDH problems are hard, respectively.

Overview of Techniques. Our starting point is a LHS scheme such as [9] and a message is a vector $\mathbf{v} \in \mathbb{F}_p^N$. Recall that, in a LHS scheme, the signer has a dataset $\{\mathbf{v}_i\}_{i=1}^n$ and uses private key to generate signature σ_i for each message $\mathbf{v}_i$. Any entity who knows the public key that acts as both verification and combination key can perform two tasks: verify signatures sent by the signer or derived by upstream combiners; carry any linear function f over the received messages $\{\mathbf{x}_i\}_{i=1}^k$ (either the origin messages issued by the signer or the evaluated messages output by the upstream combiner) and derive a new signature σ on the result $f(\mathbf{x}_1, \ldots, \mathbf{x}_k)$.

We now focus on the reason of introducing the concept of the designated verifier in [22], and show that making linearly homomorphic signatures with designated combiner (LHSDC) publicly verifiable is not trivial. As discussed earlier, the goal of [22] is to design a homomorphic signature scheme such that only one entity, called the designated combiner, can combine the signatures.

To this end, the signer multiplies each σ_i by a hash h_i and denotes the product by the designated signature $\widehat{\sigma}_i$. Note that issuing σ_i without multiplying it by h_i would completely result in public combinability, and so the function of h_i is somehow to mask the value of σ_i. Only the entity designated by the signer can unmask the designated signature $\widehat{\sigma}_i$, and obtain exact value σ_i. Then, the combiner can run nearly the same `Combine` algorithm as in LHS, and derive a value $\sigma_\mathbf{v}$ on a linear function result $\mathbf{v}$.

Unfortunately, it is insecure to directly consider the value $\sigma_\mathbf{v}$ as the signature on message $\mathbf{v}$. Since linearly homomorphic signatures enjoy public combinability and there is no masking on the derived value $\sigma_\mathbf{v}$, any entity who receives the pair $(\mathbf{v}, \sigma_\mathbf{v})$ can simply apply a linear function $f(\mathbf{x}_1, \ldots, \mathbf{x}_k) = k\mathbf{x}_1$ over the message $\mathbf{v}$, and derive a valid signature $\sigma_{k\mathbf{v}}$ on message $k\mathbf{v}$, resulting that the role of the designated combiner is replaced by an non-authorized entity.

The solution in [22] is to apply the notion of designated verifier put forward by Steinfeld et al. [25] into LHS. The general idea behind this notion is that the signer uses verifier's public key to transform standard signatures into a new signature (usually a pairing of standard signature and verifier's public key) designated to verifier. Similarly, the combiner in LHS uses verifier's public key to transform evaluated signatures into a new signature designated to verifier. Accordingly, only the designated verifier can be convinced about the validity of signature σ.

Our approach for removing the designated verifier from LHSDE is to use the idea of IBS. In the IBS, TA (Trust Authority) uses both her private key and the user identity to generate the user's private key. Analogously, the signer in the LHSDC uses both her private key and the combiner's public key to generate the signatures on the vector subspace V. Then, the signatures can be seen as a witness of the combiner, which is used to generate a convincing proof of the statement that the combiner has a valid signature on the linearly-derived vector.

1.2   Related Work

The concept of homomorphic signatures dates back to Desmedt [15] while the formal definition was gave by Johnson et al. [20]. Since then, various types of homomorphic signatures with different homomorphic operations have been proposed (please refer to the work of Traverso, Demirel, and Buchmann [26]).

Linearly homomorphic signatures, an important part of homomorphic signatures, allow any entity (without the signer's secret key) to linearly combine the signed messages and derive a valid signature on the combined-message. In particular, the derived signature is indistinguishable with the corresponding signature signed by the signer. The initial motivation is to establish the authentication mechanism in network coding and to prevent pollution attacks [9,13]. In the following study, linearly homomorphic signatures have also be used as an important building block for proofs of storage [2,3] and verifiable computation mechanisms [1], because they allow for linear computations on the signed data. The work of Boneh et al. [9], providing a practical framework and capturing the security model for such schemes, can be seen as the milestone of linearly homomorphic signatures. In fact, the messages are viewed as a linear vector subspace over a prime field, and message encoding can be seen as a linear computation over the authentication vectors with some integer coefficients in [9]. Since then, many different LHS schemes have been proposed, and we divide them into two groups: security proof relies on random oracle model or standard model.

Random Oracle Model. Gennaro et al. [17] proposed the first LHS scheme based on the RSA assumption. In their scheme, modulo a large integer $N = pq$ (p,q are two safe primes) directly yields both the homomorphic properties and the ability to work with small coefficients, which improves the computation of the combiners and reduces the communication overhead for moderate-size networks. The scheme [8] proposed by Boneh and Freeman is the first such construction authenticating vectors over binary fields $\mathbb{F}_2$, and its security relies on a variant version of the SIS problem called k-SIS. Further improvement was given by the same authors [7]; that led to a new proposed lattice-based LHS scheme whose vector defined over a finite field $\mathbb{F}_p$ with small prime p, and its security relies on a standard problem SIS. Wang et al. [27] improve the efficiency and the security of the scheme proposed in [8].

Standard Model. Attrapadung and Libert [4] put forth the first LHS scheme with provable security in the standard model. Their scheme works over the bilinear group of the composite order, and each signature includes three 1024-bit group elements. Subsequently, Attrapadung, Libert, and Peters [5] use $e(g,g)^\alpha$ instead of g^α as one part of the public key to improve the efficiency of the above scheme. In order to further improve the efficiency of LHS in the standard model, Catalano, Fiore, and Warinschi [12] present two new such schemes, and the security relies on q-SDH assumption and S-RSA assumption, respectively. Chen, Lei, and Qi [14] design the first lattice-based LHS scheme in the standard model. Catalano, Fiore, and Nizzardo [11] introduce a private version of programmable hash functions (called asymmetric programmable hash functions) to construct the first LHS scheme whose public key is sub-linear in both the vector dimension and the dataset size.

Organization of the Paper. We begin in Sect. 2 with some background material on LHSDC including the definition and the security. Section 3.1 introduces the complexity assumption needed in our scheme. In Sect. 3.2, we construct a concrete LHSDC scheme. The last section concludes the paper.

2 Definitions and Preliminaries

We assume that every document is associated with an identifier id chosen by the signer. Every entity uses identifiers to recognise packets of the same document.

2.1 The Properly Augmented Basis Vectors

Let p be a large prime. In a LHS scheme [9], a document is viewed as an ordered sequence of n-dimensional vectors $\overline{\mathbf{v}}_1, \ldots, \overline{\mathbf{v}}_m \in \mathbb{F}_p^n$. In order to allow the downstream entities to derive the linear combination coefficients from a combined-vector, the signer creates the properly augmented basis vectors $\mathbf{v}_1, \ldots, \mathbf{v}_m$, where

$$\mathbf{v}_i = (-\overline{\mathbf{v}}_i-, \underbrace{0, \ldots, 0, 1, 0, \ldots, 0}_{i}) \in \mathbb{F}_p^N \text{ for each } i \in \{1, \ldots, m\}, \text{ and } N = n + m.$$

In fact, the augmented vector $\mathbf{v}_i$ is the concatenation of vector $\overline{\mathbf{v}}_i$ and the i'th m-dimensional unit vector. Upon receiving vector $\mathbf{v}$, any entity can easily derive the coefficients, which are the posterior m coordinates of the vector $\mathbf{v}$.

2.2 Syntax of LHSDC

Here, we keep the designated combiner exactly the same as [22], but introduce two key modifications in the definition itself:

1. We now consider that every entity can verify the message combined by the combiner, whereas in [22] this is not publicly known and the designated verifier was introduced.
2. Because LHSDC satisfy public verifiability, so the Simulation algorithm introduced in [22] is no longer needed.

Definition 1. *A linearly homomorphic signature scheme with designated combiner is a tuple of the following probabilistic polynomial-time (PPT) algorithms* $\mathcal{LHSDC} = (\text{Setup}, \text{KeyGen}, \text{Sign}, \text{DVerify}, \text{Combine}, \text{Verify})$.

- $cp \leftarrow \text{Setup}(1^k, N)$ is the Setup algorithm which, takes as input a security parameter k and a positive integer N (the dimension of a vector being signed), outputs the common parameter cp.
- $(pk, sk) \leftarrow \text{KeyGen}(cp)$ is the KeyGen algorithm. The signer (the combiner designated by the signer) runs it to generate a public key PK_A (PK_B) and the corresponding private key SK_A (SK_B).
- $\widehat{\sigma} \leftarrow \text{Sign}(SK_A, PK_B, id, m, \mathbf{v})$ is the Sign algorithm which, takes as input a private key SK_A (of the signer), a public key PK_B (of the combiner), an identifier id randomly chosen from the set $\mathcal{I} = \{0, 1\}^k$, a positive integer $m < N$ (the dimension of vector subspace), and a vector $\mathbf{v} \in \mathbb{F}_p^N$, outputs a designated signature $\widehat{\sigma}$ on the vector $\mathbf{v}$.

- 1 or 0 ← DVerify(PK_A, SK_B, id, m, $\mathbf{v}$, $\widehat{\sigma}$) is the DVerify algorithm which, takes as input a public key PK_A, a private key SK_B, an identifier id, a positive integer $m < N$, a vector $\mathbf{v} \in \mathbb{F}_p^N$, and a designated signature $\widehat{\sigma}$, outputs 1 (accept) or 0 (reject).
- $(\mathbf{v}, \sigma)$ ← Combine(PK_A, SK_B, id, $\{(\mathbf{v}_k, \widehat{\sigma}_k)\}_{k=1}^l$) is the Combine algorithm which, takes as input a public key PK_A, a private key SK_B, an identifier id, and l pairs of $\{(\mathbf{v}_k, \widehat{\sigma}_k)\}_{k=1}^l$, outputs a vector/signature pair $(\mathbf{v}, \sigma)$.
- 1 or 0 ← Verify(PK_A, id, m, $\mathbf{v}$, σ) is the Verify algorithm which, takes as input a public key PK_A, an identifier id, a positive integer $m < N$, a vector $\mathbf{v} \in \mathbb{F}_p^N$, and a signature σ, outputs 1 (accept) or 0 (reject).

Except for the above six algorithms, the following obvious properties should be satisfied in any LHSDC scheme.

- **Correctness of the Sign algorithm.** $\forall\, id \in \mathcal{I}$ and $\forall\, \mathbf{v} \in \mathbb{F}_p^N$, if $\widehat{\sigma} \leftarrow$ Sign(SK_A, PK_B, id, m, $\mathbf{v}$), then

$$\text{DVerify}(PK_A, SK_B, id, m, \mathbf{v}, \widehat{\sigma}) = 1.$$

- **Correctness of the Combine algorithm.** $\forall\, id \in \mathcal{I}$ and any set of pairs $\{(\mathbf{v}_k, \widehat{\sigma}_k)\}_{k=1}^l$, if DVerify($PK_A$, SK_B, id, m, $\mathbf{v}_k$, $\widehat{\sigma}_k$) = 1 for all $k \in \{1, \ldots, l\}$, then

$$\text{Verify}(PK_A, id, m, \mathbf{v}, \sigma) = 1,$$

where $(\mathbf{v}, \sigma) \leftarrow$ Combine(PK_A, SK_B, id, $\{(\mathbf{v}_k, \widehat{\sigma}_k)\}_{k=1}^l$).

2.3   Security

A successful attack means that an adversary can achieve one of the following two targets. First, he either creates a valid signature on a non-zero vector belonged to a new vector subspace (unsigned by the signer previously), or injects a malicious vector (can not be expressed as a linear combination of the bases of the corresponding vector subspace) into an existing vector subspace (has been signed by signer). Second, he is capable of combining the designated signatures signed by the signer, which means that the role of the designated combiner has been replaced by the adversary. From the above we have the impression of what is considered a "break" of the LHSDC schemes, and below two types of unforgeability will be introduced.

UF$_1$: Type 1 Unforgeability. UF$_1$ requires that no efficient adversary have the ability to forge a signature on a non-zero vector belonged to a new vector subspace or on a malicious vector. It is intuitive that no entity has more knowledge than the designated combiner. Therefore, we only need to define UF$_1$ against the malicious designated combiner, and the formal definition will be characterized by the following game between an adversary $\mathcal{A}$ and a challenger $\mathcal{C}$.

Definition 2 (UF$_1$). *We say that a LHSDC scheme satisfies UF$_1$ if no PPT adversary $\mathcal{A}$ has non-negligible success probability with respect to the security parameter k in the following game:*

– Setup$_1$. Given a positive integer N, $\mathcal{C}$ runs Setup($1^k, N$) to obtain the common parameter cp, and then generates the signer's key pair (SK_A, PK_A) using the algorithm KeyGen(cp). The pair (cp, PK_A) is sent to $\mathcal{A}$. As response, $\mathcal{A}$ sends the designated combiner's public key PK_B to $\mathcal{C}$.

– Query$_1$. Proceeding adaptively, $\mathcal{A}$ specifies a sequence of vector subspaces $V_i \subset \mathbb{F}_p^N$. For each i, $\mathcal{C}$.

　1. Chooses an identifier $id_i \in \mathcal{I}$ uniformly at random and then generates a designated signature $\widehat{\sigma}_i$ on V_i.

　2. Sends the pair $(id_i, \widehat{\sigma}_i)$ to $\mathcal{A}$.

– Output$_1$. Finally, $\mathcal{A}$ outputs an identifier id^*, a non-zero vector $\mathbf{v}^* \in \mathbb{F}_p^N$, and a signature σ^*.

The adversary $\mathcal{A}$ wins if Verify($PK_A, id^*, m, \mathbf{v}^*, \sigma^*$) = 1, and either $id^* \neq id_i$ for any i (Type 1.1 forgery, which means that $\mathcal{A}$ succeeds in creating a valid signature on a non-zero vector belonged to a new vector space) or $id^* = id_i$ for some i but $\mathbf{v}^* \notin V_i$ (Type 1.2 forgery, which means that $\mathcal{A}$ has injected some malicious vectors into an existing vector subspace). The success probability of $\mathcal{A}$ is defined as $Succ_{\mathcal{A},\mathcal{S}}^{UF_1}$.

UF$_2$: Type 2 Unforgeability. UF$_2$ requires that no entity except the signer is able to pretend to be the designated combiner, namely, the operation of combining the designated signatures is infeasible for other entities except the signer or the designated combiner. Next, we use the following game between an adversary $\mathcal{A}$ and a challenger $\mathcal{C}$ to define Type 2 Unforgeability.

Definition 3 (UF$_2$). *We say that a LHSDC scheme satisfies UF$_2$ if no PPT adversary $\mathcal{A}$ has non-negligible success probability with respect to the security parameter k in the following game:*

– Setup$_2$. Given a positive integer N, $\mathcal{C}$ runs Setup($1^k, N$) to obtain the common parameter cp, and then generates the signer's key pair (SK_A, PK_A) and the designated combiner's key pair (SK_B, PK_B) using the algorithm KeyGen(cp) two times. The tuple (cp, PK_A, PK_B) is sent to $\mathcal{A}$.

– Sign Query$_2$. Proceeding adaptively, $\mathcal{A}$ specifies a sequence of vector subspaces $V_i \subset \mathbb{F}_p^N$. For each i, $\mathcal{C}$.

　1. Uses the properly augmented basis vectors $\mathbf{v}_{i1}, \ldots, \mathbf{v}_{im} \in \mathbb{F}_p^N$ to describe V_i;

　2. Chooses an identifier $id_i \in \mathcal{I}$ uniformly at random;

　3. For all $j \in \{1, \ldots, m\}$, runs Sign($SK_A, PK_B, id_i, m, \mathbf{v}_{ij}$) to generate the designated signature $\widehat{\sigma}_{ij}$ on the vector $\mathbf{v}_{ij}$, and sets $\widehat{\sigma}_i = (\widehat{\sigma}_{i1}, \ldots, \widehat{\sigma}_{im})$ as the designated signature on the vector subspace V_i;

　4. Sends the pair $(id_i, \widehat{\sigma}_i)$ to $\mathcal{A}$.

– Combine Query$_2$. Proceeding adaptively, $\mathcal{C}$ is given $(id_i, \{(\mathbf{v}_{ik}, \widehat{\sigma}_{ik}, \beta_k)\}_{k=1}^l)$ which is specified by $\mathcal{A}$, and runs Combine($PK_A, SK_B, id_i, \{(\mathbf{v}_{ik}, \widehat{\sigma}_{ik})\}_{k=1}^l$) to generate a vector/signature pair $(\mathbf{v}, \sigma)$, where $\mathbf{v} = \sum_{k=1}^l \beta_k \mathbf{v}_{ik}$.

– Output$_2$. The adversary $\mathcal{A}$ outputs an identifier id^*, a vector $\mathbf{v}^* \in \mathbb{F}_p^N$, and a signature σ^*.

The adversary wins if $\mathtt{Verify}(PK_A, id^*, m, \mathbf{v}^*, \sigma^*) = 1$, where $id^* = id_i$ for some i and $\mathbf{0} \neq \mathbf{v}^* \in V_i$ (Type 2 forgery, which means that $\mathcal{A}$ successfully pretends to be the designated combiner). Clearly, $\mathbf{v}^*$ should not be a vector that have been queried to the combine oracles. Besides, we define the success probability of $\mathcal{A}$ as $Succ_{\mathcal{A},\mathcal{S}}^{UF_2}$.

Definition 4. *We say that a LHSDC scheme is unforgeable against adaptively chosen-message attacks if, for any PPT adversary $\mathcal{A}$, both $Succ_{\mathcal{A},\mathcal{S}}^{UF_1}$ and $Succ_{\mathcal{A},\mathcal{S}}^{UF_2}$ are negligible with the security parameter k.*

The next lemma shows the forking lemma [23], which is used to obtain two valid signatures on the same message from an adversary that queries the same random oracle.

Lemma 1 [23]. *Let S be a signature scheme, k be a security parameter, and $\mathcal{A}$ be a probabilistic polynomial-time adversary who makes at most q queries of random oracle. If within the time bound t_A the adversary $\mathcal{A}$ outputs a valid signature (r, h, σ) on message m with probability $Succ_{\mathcal{A},\mathcal{S}}^{UF} \geq 7q/2^k$, then within the time bound $t_B \leq 16qt_A/Succ_{\mathcal{A},\mathcal{S}}^{UF}$ he, with probability $\varepsilon \geq 1/9$, will outputs two valid signatures (r, h, σ) and (r, h', σ') on the same message m such that $h \neq h'$.*

3   Our Design of LHSDC

Based on the network coding signature scheme proposed by Boneh *et al.* [9] and the idea of the IBS [18], we construct a concrete and secure LHSDC scheme whose two types of unforgeability rely on co-CDH and CDH assumptions, respectively.

3.1   Bilinear Groups and Complexity Assumptions

Definition 5. *Let p be a large prime, $\mathbb{G}_1$, $\mathbb{G}_2$ and $\mathbb{G}_T$ be three cyclically multiplicative groups of the same order p, and $e : \mathbb{G}_1 \times \mathbb{G}_2 \to \mathbb{G}_T$ be a bilinear map. A tuple of $(\mathbb{G}_1, \mathbb{G}_2, \mathbb{G}_T, e, \varphi)$ is defined as a bilinear group tuple which has the following properties:*

1. Computability: $\forall\, g \in \mathbb{G}_1$ and $\forall\, h \in \mathbb{G}_2$, $e(g, h)$ can be efficiently calculated.
2. Bilinearity: $\forall\, a, b \in \mathbb{Z}_p$, $\forall\, g \in \mathbb{G}_1$, and $\forall\, h \in \mathbb{G}_2$, we have $e(g^a, h^b) = e(g, h)^{ab} = e(g^b, h^a)$.
3. Non-degeneracy: Assuming g and h are the generators of group $\mathbb{G}_1$ and $\mathbb{G}_2$, respectively, then $e(g, h)$ is a generator of group $\mathbb{G}_T$, i.e., $e(g, h) \neq 1_{\mathbb{G}_T}$.
4. $\varphi : \mathbb{G}_2 \to \mathbb{G}_1$ is an efficient, computable isomorphism.

Definition 6 (co-CDH Problem). *Given three randomly chosen elements $g_1 \in \mathbb{G}_1$ and $g_2, g_2^a \in \mathbb{G}_2$ for some unknown $a \in \mathbb{Z}_p$, calculate $g_1^a \in \mathbb{G}_1$.*

Let $Adv_{\mathcal{A},(\mathbb{G}_1,\mathbb{G}_2)}^{co-CDH} = \Pr[g_1^a \leftarrow \mathcal{A}(g_1, g_2, g_2^a)]$ be the probability of a PPT adversary solving the co-CDH problem. We say that the co-CDH problem is hard in $(\mathbb{G}_1, \mathbb{G}_2)$ if no PPT adversary has non-negligible probability $Adv_{\mathcal{A},(\mathbb{G}_1,\mathbb{G}_2)}^{co-CDH}$.

Definition 7 (CDH Problem). *Given three randomly chosen elements* $g_1, g_1^a,$ $g_1^b \in \mathbb{G}_1$ *for some unknown* $a, b \in \mathbb{Z}_p$, *calculate* g_1^{ab}.

Let $Adv_{\mathcal{A},(\mathbb{G}_1,\mathbb{G}_2)}^{CDH} = \Pr[g_1^{ab} \leftarrow \mathcal{A}(g_1, g_1^a, g_1^b)]$ be the probability of a PPT adversary solving the CDH problem. We say that the CDH problem is hard in $(\mathbb{G}_1, \mathbb{G}_2)$ if no PPT adversary has non-negligible probability $Adv_{\mathcal{A},(\mathbb{G}_1,\mathbb{G}_2)}^{CDH}$.

3.2 Our LHSDC Scheme

This subsection describes our signature scheme that enjoys two characteristics: (1) the combination operation can only be implemented by the entities designated by the signer; (2) the message-signature pairs output by the combiner are publicly verifiable.

- Setup($1^k, N$). Take as input a security parameter k and an integer $N > 0$:
  1. Let $\mathcal{G} = (\mathbb{G}_1, \mathbb{G}_2, \mathbb{G}_T, e, \varphi)$ be a bilinear group as in Definition 5.
  2. Choose generators $g_1, g_2, \ldots, g_N \xleftarrow{R} \mathbb{G}_1 \setminus \{1\}$, and $h \xleftarrow{R} \mathbb{G}_2 \setminus \{1\}$.
  3. Choose four hash functions $H_1 : \{0,1\}^* \to \mathbb{G}_1$, $H_2 : \mathbb{F}_p^N \to \mathbb{G}_1$, $H_3 : \mathbb{G}_T \to \mathbb{G}_1$, and $H : \mathbb{F}_p^N \times \mathbb{G}_T \to \mathbb{F}_p$.
  4. Output the common parameter $cp = (\mathcal{G}, p, \{H_j\}_{j=1}^3, H, h, \{g_i\}_{i=1}^N)$.
- KeyGen(cp). The signer (combiner) chooses $\alpha_A \xleftarrow{R} \mathbb{F}_p$ ($\alpha_B \xleftarrow{R} \mathbb{F}_p$), and then calculates $u_A = h^{\alpha_A}$ ($u_B = h^{\alpha_B}$). The signer's (combiner's) public key is $PK_A = u_A$ ($PK_B = u_B$) and private key is $SK_A = \alpha_A$ ($SK_B = \alpha_B$).
- Sign($SK_A, PK_B, id, m, \mathbf{v}$). Take as input a private key SK_A (of the signer), a public key PK_B (of the combiner), an identifier $id \xleftarrow{R} \{0,1\}^k$, a positive integer $m < N$, and a vector $\mathbf{v} \in \mathbb{F}_p^N$. Output a designated signature

$$\hat{\sigma} = \left(\prod_{i=1}^m H_1(id, i)^{v_{n+i}} \prod_{j=1}^n g_j^{v_j} \right)^{\alpha_A} H_3(e(H_2(\mathbf{v}), u_B)^{\alpha_A}).$$

- DVerify($PK_A, SK_B, id, m, \hat{\sigma}, \mathbf{v}$). Take as input a public key PK_A (of the signer), a private key SK_B (of the combiner), an identifier id, a positive integer $m < N$, a designated signature $\hat{\sigma}$ and a vector $\mathbf{v}$:
  1. Define $\gamma_1(PK_A, \hat{\sigma}) \overset{\text{def}}{=} e(\hat{\sigma}, h)$ and

  $$\gamma_2(SK_B, PK_A, id, m, \mathbf{v}) \overset{\text{def}}{=}$$
  $$e(\prod_{i=1}^m H_1(id, i)^{v_{n+i}} \prod_{j=1}^n g_j^{v_j}, u_A) e(H_3(e(H_2(\mathbf{v}), u_A)^{\alpha_B}), h).$$

  2. Output 1 (accept) if $\gamma_1(PK_A, \hat{\sigma}) = \gamma_2(SK_B, PK_A, id, m, \mathbf{v})$; otherwise, output 0 (reject).
- Combine($PK_A, SK_B, id, \{(\mathbf{v}_k, \hat{\sigma}_k)\}_{k=1}^l$). Take as input a public key PK_A (of the signer), a private key SK_B (of the combiner), an identifier id, and l pairs of $\{(\mathbf{v}_k, \hat{\sigma}_k)\}_{k=1}^l$, where $\mathbf{v}_k = (v_{k,1}, \ldots, v_{k,N})$:

1. Calculate $\mathbf{v} = \sum_{k=1}^{l} \beta_k \mathbf{v}_k = (v_1, \ldots, v_N)$ ($\beta_1, \ldots, \beta_l \in \mathbb{F}_p$ are chosen by the combiner) and then further calculate

$$\sigma_{\mathbf{v}} = \prod_{k=1}^{l} (\widehat{\sigma}_k \cdot [H_3(e(H_2(\mathbf{v}_k), u_A)^{\alpha_B})]^{-1})^{\beta_k}.$$

2. Choose $c \xleftarrow{R} \mathbb{F}_p$ and compute $R = e(g, h)^c$, $S = H(\mathbf{v}, R)$, and $T = \sigma_{\mathbf{v}}^S \cdot g^c$.
3. Output a vector $\mathbf{v}$ and a signature $\sigma = (S, T)$.

- Verify($PK_A, id, m, \mathbf{v}, \sigma$). Take as input a public key PK_A (of the signer), an identifier id, a positive integer $m < N$, a vector $\mathbf{v} \in \mathbb{F}_p^N$, and a signature σ. Then, calculate $\sigma_{\mathbf{v}}' = \prod_{k=1}^{m} H_1(id, i)^{v_{n+i}} \prod_{j=1}^{n} g_j^{v_j}$ and $R' = e(T, h)e(\sigma_{\mathbf{v}}', (h^{\alpha_A})^{-1})^S$. Output 1 if $S = H(\mathbf{v}, R')$; otherwise, output 0.

- **Correctness of the Sign algorithm.** $\forall\, id$ and $\forall\, \mathbf{v} \in \mathbb{F}_p^N$, if $\widehat{\sigma} \leftarrow \text{Sign}(SK_A, PK_B, id, m, \mathbf{v})$ then

$$\gamma_1(PK_A, \widehat{\sigma}) = e(\widehat{\sigma}, h)$$

$$= e\left(\left(\prod_{i=1}^{m} H_1(id, i)^{v_{n+i}} \prod_{j=1}^{n} g_j^{v_j}\right)^{\alpha_A} H_3\left(e(H_2(\mathbf{v}), u_B)^{\alpha_A}\right), h\right)$$

$$= \gamma_2(SK_B, PK_A, id, m, \mathbf{v}).$$

- **Correctness of the Combine algorithm.** $\forall\, id$ and $\forall\, \{(\mathbf{v}_k, \widehat{\sigma}_k)\}_{k=1}^{l}$, if it holds that DVerify($PK_A, SK_B, id, m, \widehat{\sigma}_k, \mathbf{v}_k$) $= 1$ for all k, and if $\mathbf{v} = \sum_{k=1}^{l} \beta_k \mathbf{v}_k$ and $\sigma = (S, T)$ are output by the Combine algorithm. Then we have

$$H(\mathbf{v}, R') = H(\mathbf{v}, e(T, h)e(\sigma_{\mathbf{v}}', (h^{\alpha_A})^{-1})^S)$$

$$= H(\mathbf{v}, e(\sigma_{\mathbf{v}}^S \cdot g^c, h)e(\sigma_{\mathbf{v}}', (h^{\alpha_A})^{-1})^S)$$

$$= H(\mathbf{v}, e(\sigma_{\mathbf{v}}^S, h)e(g^c, h)e(\sigma_{\mathbf{v}}^{-S}, h))$$

$$= H(\mathbf{v}, e(g, h)^c) = S.$$

Efficiency. If G is a group, we denote the length of one element in the group G by $\|G\|$. The computational cost of one exponent operation, pairing operation, map-to-point operation, inverse operation, and multiply operation are denoted by T_E, T_P, T_H, T_I and T_M, respectively. The formal analysis please see the Table 1. In Table 2, we give a rough comparison of the existing LHS schemes. For simplicity, the dimension of the signed vector that has not been augmented (the augmented vector) is set to be n. We omit hash functions in the public key.

3.3 Security Proof

Given an adversary that breaks the signature scheme, in UF_1, we construct a challenger that simulates the signature scheme, the hash functions, and solves the co-CDH problem in $(\mathbb{G}_1, \mathbb{G}_2)$. Similarly, we show a challenger can solve a complexity problem in UF_2 if there exists a successful adversary, except that the CDH problem is used instead of the co-CDH problem.

Table 1. Efficiency analysis

Algorithm	Signature Length	Computational Cost
Sign	$1\|\mathbb{G}\|$	$(n+2)T_E + 1T_P + 3T_H + (n+1)T_M$
DVerify		$(n+1)T_E + 3T_P + 3T_H + (n+1)T_M$
Combine	$1\|\mathbb{Z}_p\| + 1\|\mathbb{G}\|$	$(m+3)T_E + 1T_P + 1T_H + mT_I + 2mT_M$
Verify		$(N+1)T_E + 2T_P + (m+1)T_H + 1T_I + NT_M$

Table 2. Comparison to the existing linearly homomorphic signatures

Schemes	Public key	Signature	Model	Ass.	DC	DV
[9]	$(n+2)\|\mathbb{G}\|$	$1\|\mathbb{G}\|$	ROM	co-CDH	No	
[17]	$n\|QR_{N'}\|$	$1\|\mathbb{Z}_{N'}^*\|$	ROM	RSA		
[8]	$1\|\mathbb{Z}_{2q}^{n \times h}\|$	Short vector	ROM	k-SIS		
[7]	$1\|\mathbb{Z}\| + 1\|\mathbb{Z}_q^{n \times h}\|$	Short vector	ROM	SIS		
[4]	$(N+4)\|\mathbb{G}\| + 1\|\mathbb{G}_T\|$	$3\|\mathbb{G}\|$	Standard	DHP		
[5]	$(N+3)\|\mathbb{G}\|$	$2\|\mathbb{G}\|$	Standard	DHP		
[12]	$(N+4)\|\mathbb{G}\|$	$1\|\mathbb{G}\| + 1\|\mathbb{Z}_p\|$	Standard	S-RSA, q-SDH		
[14]	$1\|\mathbb{Z}\| + (k+1)\|\mathbb{Z}_q^{n \times h}\| + m\|\mathbb{Z}_p^h\|$	Short vector	Standard	SIS		
[11]	$2(\sqrt{n} + \sqrt{m} + 1)\|\mathbb{G}\|$	$4\|\mathbb{G}\|$	Standard	DHP		
[22]	$(n+2)\|\mathbb{G}\|$	$1\|\mathbb{G}\|$ (in Sig), $1\|\mathbb{G}_T\|$ (in Com)	ROM	co-BDH, GBDH	Yes	
Our	$(n+2)\|\mathbb{G}\|$	$1\|\mathbb{G}\|$ (in Sig), $1\|\mathbb{Z}_p\| + 1\|\mathbb{G}\|$ (in Com)	ROM	co-CDH, CDH	Yes	No

Theorem 1. *Let $\mathcal{S}$ be the LHSDC scheme described above. Then $\mathcal{S}$ satisfies UF_1 in the random oracle model assuming that the co-CDH problem is infeasible.*

In particular, let $\mathcal{A}$ be a ppt adversary as in Definition 2, and q_s, q_{h_1} be the number of signature queries, hash H_1 queries made by $\mathcal{A}$, respectively. Then there exists a ppt algorithm $\mathcal{B}$ that solves co-CDH problem, such that $Adv_{\mathcal{B},(\mathbb{G}_1,\mathbb{G}_2)}^{co-CDH} \geq Succ_{\mathcal{A},\mathcal{S}}^{UF_1} - \frac{q_s(q_s+q_{h_1})+1}{2^k}$.

The proof is in Appendix 5.

Theorem 2. *Let $\mathcal{S}$ be the LHSDC scheme described above. Then $\mathcal{S}$ satisfies UF_2 in the random oracle model assuming that the CDH problem is infeasible.*

In particular, suppose that $\mathcal{A}$ is a ppt adversary as in Definition 3, and he/she makes at most q queries of hash H and combine oracle. If $\mathcal{A}$ breaks UF_2, within the time bound $t_{\mathcal{A}}$, with success probability $Succ_{\mathcal{A},\mathcal{S}}^{UF_2} \geq \frac{14q^2}{2^k}$. Then, there exists a ppt algorithm $\mathcal{B}$ that, with probability $Adv_{\mathcal{B},(\mathbb{G}_1,\mathbb{G}_2)}^{CDH} \geq \frac{1}{9} - \frac{1}{p}$, solves CDH problem, in expected time $t_{\mathcal{B}} \leq \frac{16qt_{\mathcal{A}}}{Succ_{\mathcal{A},\mathcal{S}}^{UF_2}}$.

The proof is in Appendix 6.

4   Conclusion

This paper introduces the notion of the designated combiner into linearly homomorphic signatures and formally depicts the framework of LHSDC and its security model including two types of unforgeability. In the new framework, the operation of the Combine algorithm is no longer public, but open to the entities designated by the signer, while every entity can verify the validity of the signatures output by the designated combiner. Starting from formal definition, we construct a concrete and secure LHSDC design, whose two types of unforgeability rely on the co-CDH assumption and CDH assumption, respectively, showing that our design is feasible.

Acknowledgements. This work was supported by National Natural Science Foundation of China (Grant Number 61772514, 61822202, 62172096), and Beijing Municipal Science & Technology Commission (Project Number: Z191100007119006).

5   Proof of Theorem 1

Proof (Adapted from [9]). As mentioned above, we assume that $\mathcal{A}$ is an adversary that breaks the UF_1 with success probability $Succ_{\mathcal{A},\mathcal{S}}^{UF_1}$, and our goal is to construct an algorithm $\mathcal{B}$ that solves co-CDH problem in $(\mathbb{G}_1, \mathbb{G}_2)$: given a bilinear group tuple $\mathcal{G} = (\mathbb{G}_1, \mathbb{G}_2, \mathbb{G}_T, e, \varphi)$, and $g \in \mathbb{G}_1$, $h, u \in \mathbb{G}_2$ with $u = h^{\alpha_A}$ for an unknown integer $\alpha_A \in \mathbb{F}_p^*$, output an element $\omega \in \mathbb{G}_1$ such that $\omega = g^{\alpha_A}$.

In the first place, two lists H_1-List and H_2-List were maintained by $\mathcal{B}$ to record H_1 queries and H_2 queries. H_1-List consists of tuples $(id, i, H_1(id, i))$, and H_2-List consists of pairs $(\mathbf{v}, H_2(\mathbf{v}))$. While the other hash functions H_3, H are viewed as two ordinary hash functions in this proof.

Setup. $\mathcal{B}$ chooses a positive integer N, then

1. Chooses $s_j, t_j \xleftarrow{R} \mathbb{F}_p$, and sets $g_j = g^{s_j} \varphi(h)^{t_j}$ for $j \in [N]$. Chooses $a \xleftarrow{R} \mathbb{F}_p^*$ and calculates $u_A = u^a$. Let $PK_A = u_A$, and $cp = (\mathcal{G}, p, H_3, H, h, \{g_j\}_{j=1}^N)$.
2. Sends the pair (cp, PK_A) to $\mathcal{A}$.

As response, $\mathcal{A}$ sends the designated combiner's public key $PK_B = u_B$ to $\mathcal{B}$.

H$_1$ Queries. When $\mathcal{A}$ requests the value of $H_1(id, i)$, $\mathcal{B}$:

1. If there exists a tuple $(id, i, H_1(id, i))$ in the H_1-List, returns $H_1(id, i)$.
2. Otherwise, randomly chooses $\varsigma_i, \tau_i \xleftarrow{R} \mathbb{F}_p$ and sets $H_1(id, i) = g^{\varsigma_i} \varphi(h)^{\tau_i}$. The new tuple $(id, i, H_1(id, i))$ is added into the H_1-List. $\mathcal{B}$ returns $H_1(id, i)$ to $\mathcal{A}$.

H$_2$ Queries. When $\mathcal{A}$ requests the value of $H_2(\mathbf{v})$, $\mathcal{B}$:

1. If there exists a tuple $(\mathbf{v}, H_2(\mathbf{v}))$ in the H_2-List, returns $H_2(\mathbf{v})$.

2. Otherwise, randomly chooses $k \xleftarrow{R} \mathbb{F}_p$ and sets $H_2(\mathbf{v}) = \varphi(h)^k$. The new pair $(\mathbf{v}, H_2(\mathbf{v}))$ is added into the H_2-List and $H_2(\mathbf{v})$ is sent to $\mathcal{A}$.

Sign Queries. When $\mathcal{A}$ requests the designated signature on the vector subspace $V \subset \mathbb{F}_p^N$ represented by the augmented vectors $\mathbf{v}_1, \ldots, \mathbf{v}_m \in \mathbb{F}_p^N$, $\mathcal{B}$:

1. Chooses an identifier $id \xleftarrow{R} \{0,1\}^k$. If there exists a tuple $(id, \cdot, \cdot)$ in the H_1-List, then this simulation is aborted.
2. For any $i \in [m]$, calculates $\varsigma_i = -\sum_{j=1}^{n} s_j v_{ij}$, and sets $\mathbf{s} = (s_1, \ldots, s_n, \varsigma_1, \ldots, \varsigma_m)$. $\mathcal{B}$ chooses $\tau_1, \ldots, \tau_m \in \mathbb{F}_p$, and sets $\mathbf{t} = (t_1, \ldots, t_n, \tau_1, \ldots, \tau_m)$.
3. For any $i \in [m]$, calculates $H_1(id, i) = g^{\varsigma_i} \varphi(h)^{\tau_i}$ and $H_2(\mathbf{v}_i)$ is calculated as in the H_2 queries.
4. Calculates $\widehat{\sigma}_i = \varphi(u_A)^{\mathbf{v}_i \cdot \mathbf{t}} \cdot H_3(e(\varphi(u_A), u_B)^{k_i})$ for every $i \in \{1, \ldots, m\}$.
5. Returns id and the designated signature $\widehat{\sigma} = (\widehat{\sigma}_1, \ldots, \widehat{\sigma}_m)$.

Output. If $\mathcal{B}$ does not abort, and a successful adversary $\mathcal{A}$ outputs an identifier id^*, a signature σ^*, and a nonzero vector $\mathbf{v}^*$, $\mathcal{B}$:

1. If there is no tuple $(id^*, \cdot, \cdot)$ appeared on the signature queries, calculates the value of $H_1(id^*, i)$ for all $i \in \{1, \ldots, m\}$ as in H_1 queries, and sets $\mathbf{s} = (s_1, \ldots, s_n, \varsigma_1, \ldots, \varsigma_m)$ and $\mathbf{t} = (t_1, \ldots, t_n, \tau_1, \ldots, \tau_m)$.
2. If there exists a tuple $(id^*, \cdot, \cdot)$ appeared on the signature queries, we obtain directly the two vectors $\mathbf{s}$ and $\mathbf{t}$ from the corresponding signature query.
3. Calculates $\omega = (\frac{(\frac{T}{g^c})^{\frac{1}{s}}}{\varphi(u_A)^{(\mathbf{t} \cdot \mathbf{v}^*)}})^{\frac{1}{a(\mathbf{s} \cdot \mathbf{v}^*)}}$, and outputs ω finally.

The random oracles H_1, H_2, and the **Setup** algorithm have been correctly simulated by $\mathcal{B}$, because all of the hash values and $\{g_j\}_{j=1}^{N}$ are uniformly random in the group $\mathbb{G}_1$. Next, we show that if the simulator does not abort, $\mathcal{B}$ will correctly simulate the **Sign** algorithm. In fact, setting the public key PK_A and hash queries as above, we have

$$
\left(\prod_{i=1}^{m} H_1(id, i)^{v_{i,n+i}} \prod_{j=1}^{n} g_j^{v_{ij}} \right)^{\alpha_A a} H_3(e(H_2(\mathbf{v}_i), u_B)^{\alpha_A a})
$$

$$
= \left(\prod_{i=1}^{m} (g^{\varsigma_i} \varphi(h)^{\tau_i})^{v_{i,n+i}} \prod_{j=1}^{n} (g^{s_j} \varphi(h)^{t_j})^{v_{ij}} \right)^{\alpha_A a} H_3(e(\varphi(h)^{\alpha_A a}, u_B)^{k_i}) \tag{1}
$$

$$
= \varphi(u_A)^{\mathbf{v}_i \cdot \mathbf{t}} H_3(e(\varphi(u_A), u_B)^{k_i})
$$

for $i = 1, \ldots, m$. From the construction of $\mathbf{s}$ in signature queries, we have $\mathbf{s} \cdot \mathbf{v}_i = 0$ for any i (i.e., $\mathbf{s} \in V^{\perp}$), which follows that the last two formulas in (1) are equal. Thus, the **Sign** algorithm has been correctly simulated by $\mathcal{B}$.

Right now, we show the probability that $\mathcal{B}$ aborts the simulation is negligible. Such abort situation includes the following two aspects:

- $\mathcal{B}$ chooses the same identifier id in two different signature queries. This probability is at most $\frac{q_s \cdot q_s}{2^k}$.

- $\mathcal{B}$ chooses an identifier in a signature query while there exists a tuple $(id, \cdot, \cdot)$ already in the H_1 queries. This probability is at most $\frac{q_s \cdot q_{h_1}}{2^k}$.

Assume that the simulator does not abort and the adversary $\mathcal{A}$ finally outputs a signature σ^*, an identifier id^*, and a nonzero vector $\mathbf{v}^*$ such that $\mathtt{Verify}(PK_A, id^*, m, \mathbf{v}^*, \sigma^*) = 1$, where $\sigma^* = (S, T)$, $S = H(\mathbf{v}^*, R)$, and $R = e(g, h)^c$ for an integer $c \in \mathbb{F}_p$ chosen by $\mathcal{A}$, we have

$$
\begin{aligned}
R' &= e(T, h)e(\sigma_{\mathbf{v}^*}', (u_A)^{-1})^S \\
&= e(\sigma_{\mathbf{v}^*}^S \cdot g^c, h)e\left(\left(\prod_{i=1}^{m} H_1(id, i)^{v_{n+i}^*} \prod_{j=1}^{n} g_j^{v_j^*}\right)^{-a\alpha_A}, h\right)^S \\
&= e(g, h)^c e(\sigma_{\mathbf{v}^*}, h)^S e\left(\left(\prod_{i=1}^{m}(g^{\varsigma_i}\varphi(h)^{\tau_i})^{v_{n+i}^*} \prod_{j=1}^{n}(g^{s_j}\varphi(h)^{t_j})^{v_j^*}\right)^{-a\alpha_A}, h\right)^S \\
&= e(g, h)^c e(\sigma_{\mathbf{v}^*}, h)^S e(g^{-a\alpha_A(\mathbf{s}\cdot\mathbf{v}^*)}\varphi(u_A)^{-(\mathbf{t}\cdot\mathbf{v}^*)}, h)^S \\
&= e(g, h)^c = R,
\end{aligned}
$$

which means that $\sigma_{\mathbf{v}^*} = \left(\frac{T}{g^c}\right)^{\frac{1}{S}} = g^{a\alpha_A(\mathbf{s}\cdot\mathbf{v}^*)}\varphi(u_A)^{(\mathbf{t}\cdot\mathbf{v}^*)}$.

Therefore, $\omega = \left(\frac{(\frac{T}{g^c})^{\frac{1}{S}}}{\varphi(u_A)^{(\mathbf{t}\cdot\mathbf{v}^*)}}\right)^{\frac{1}{a(\mathbf{s}\cdot\mathbf{v}^*)}} = g^{\alpha_A}$ if $\mathbf{s} \cdot \mathbf{v}^* \neq 0$. The probability of $\mathbf{s} \cdot \mathbf{v}^* = 0$ is showed in the following:

1. There is no tuple $(id^*, \cdot, \cdot)$ in the signature queries which means that $(id^*, \sigma^*, \mathbf{v}^*)$ is a type 1.1 forgery. The knowledge about ς_i for this id^* can be acquired by $\mathcal{A}$ is only the value of $H_1(id^*, i)$ (i.e., the functions of ς_i). We also have all coordinates of the vector $\mathbf{s}$ are uniform in $\mathbb{F}_p$ and leak no information to $\mathcal{A}$, and have the fact that $\mathbf{v}^*$ is a nonzero vector, then $\mathbf{s} \cdot \mathbf{v}^*$ is uniform in $\mathbb{F}_p$, implying that the probability of $\mathbf{s} \cdot \mathbf{v}^* = 0$ is $\frac{1}{p}$ and hence is at most $\frac{1}{2^k}$.

2. There exists a tuple $(id^*, \cdot, \cdot)$ in the signature queries, and $\mathbf{v}^* \notin V$ (assuming id^* is the identifier of the vector subspace V) which means that $(id^*, \sigma^*, \mathbf{v}^*)$ is a type 1.2 forgery. Just like above case, $s_1, \ldots, s_N$ are uniformly distributed in $\mathbb{F}_p$ and leak no information to $\mathcal{A}$, which follows that the vector $\mathbf{s}$ is uniformly distributed in $V^\perp$. Assuming that $(\mathbf{y}_1, \ldots, \mathbf{y}_n)$ is a basis of space $V^\perp$, and let $\mathbf{s} = \sum_{i=1}^{n} x_i \mathbf{y}_i$. Based on the fact that $\mathbf{s}$ is uniformly distributed in $V^\perp$, we have all x_i are uniformly distributed in $\mathbb{F}_p$. Because $\mathbf{v}^* \notin V$, so there must be some $j \in \{1, \ldots, n\}$ such that $\mathbf{v}^* \cdot \mathbf{y}_j \neq 0$, which follows that $\mathbf{s} \cdot \mathbf{v}^* = \sum_{i=1}^{n} x_i(\mathbf{y}_i \cdot \mathbf{v}^*)$ is uniform in $\mathbb{F}_p$, i.e., the probability of $\mathbf{s} \cdot \mathbf{v}^* = 0$ also is $\frac{1}{p}$ and hence is at most $\frac{1}{2^k}$.

In conclusion, $\mathcal{B}$ can output $\omega = g^{\alpha_A}$ with success probability

$$
Adv_{\mathcal{B},(\mathbb{G}_1,\mathbb{G}_2)}^{co-CDH} \geq Succ_{\mathcal{A},\mathcal{S}}^{UF_1} - \frac{q_s(q_s + q_{h_1}) + 1}{2^k}.
$$

This completes the proof of Theorem 1. $\square$

6   Proof of Theorem 2

Proof (Adapted from [18]). We assume that $\mathcal{A}$ is an adversary that breaks the UF$_2$ with success probability $Succ_{\mathcal{A},\mathcal{S}}^{UF_2}$, and our goal is to construct an algorithm $\mathcal{B}$ that solves CDH problem in $(\mathbb{G}_1, \mathbb{G}_2)$: given a bilinear group tuple $\mathcal{G} = (\mathbb{G}_1, \mathbb{G}_2, \mathbb{G}_T, e, \varphi)$, and a tuple of $(\varphi(h), \varphi(u), g)$, where $\varphi(h), \varphi(u), g \in \mathbb{G}_1$, and $h, u \in \mathbb{G}_2$ with $u = h^{\alpha_A}$, outputs an element $\omega \in \mathbb{G}_1$ such that $\omega = g^{\alpha_A}$. Note that H_2, H_3 are viewed as an ordinary hash function in this proof.

Setup. $\mathcal{B}$ chooses a positive integer N, then

1. Chooses $k_j \xleftarrow{R} \mathbb{F}_p$, and sets $g_j = \varphi(h)^{k_j}$ for $j \in [N]$, $cp = (\mathcal{G}, p, H_2, H_3, h, \{g_j\}_{j=1}^N)$ and sets the signer's public key as $PK_A = u_A$.
2. Chooses $\alpha_B \xleftarrow{R} \mathbb{F}_p^*$ and calculates $u_B = h^{\alpha_B}$, and then sets the designated secret/public key pair as (α_B, u_B). $\mathcal{B}$ sends cp, PK_A, and PK_B to $\mathcal{A}$.

H_1 Queries. When $\mathcal{A}$ requests the value of $H_1(id, i)$, $\mathcal{B}$:

1. If (id, i) has already been defined, directly returns $H_1(id, i)$ to $\mathcal{A}$.
2. Otherwise, sets $H_1(id, i) = \varphi(h)^{\tau_{li}}$ where $\tau_l = (\tau_{l1}, \ldots, \tau_{lN}) \in \mathbb{F}_p^N$ and $\tau = (\tau_l)_{l=1,2,\ldots}$ constitutes a random tape. $\mathcal{B}$ returns the tuple $(id, i, H_1(id, i))$.

Sign Queries. When $\mathcal{A}$ requests the designated signature on the vector subspace $V_l \subset \mathbb{F}_p^N$ represented by the augmented vectors $\mathbf{v}_1, \ldots, \mathbf{v}_m \in \mathbb{F}_p^N$, $\mathcal{B}$:

1. Chooses a random identifier id_l.
2. For any $i \in [m]$, calculates $H_1(id_l, i)$ as in the H_1 queries, and then sets

$$\mathbf{s}_{li} = (k_1, \ldots, k_n, \overbrace{0, \ldots, 0, \tau_{li}, 0, \ldots, 0}^{m}).$$
$$\underset{i}{}$$

3. For any basis vector $\mathbf{v}_i = (v_{i1}, \ldots, v_{iN})$ and $i \in [m]$, calculates $\widehat{\sigma}_{li} = \varphi(u_A)^{\mathbf{s}_{li} \cdot \mathbf{v}_i} \cdot H_3(e(H_2(\mathbf{v}_i), u_A)^{\alpha_B})$.
4. Returns id_l, and the designated signature $\widehat{\sigma}_l = (\sigma_{l1}, \ldots, \sigma_{lm})$.

H Queries. When $\mathcal{A}$ requests the value of $H(\mathbf{v}, R)$, $\mathcal{B}$:

1. If $(\mathbf{v}, R)$ has already been defined, returns $H(\mathbf{v}, R)$ to $\mathcal{A}$.
2. Otherwise, takes a random $S_j \in \mathbb{F}_p^*$ successively from a random tape $\varsigma = (S_j)_{j=1,2,\ldots}$, and sets $H(\mathbf{v}, R) = S_j$.

Combine Queries. When $\mathcal{A}$ submits $(id, \{(\mathbf{v}_k, \widehat{\sigma}_k, \beta_k)\}_{k=1}^l)$ to the combine oracle. $\mathcal{B}$ checks whether the identifier id already appears in the sign queries, and if so, further checks whether $\widehat{\sigma}_k$ is the valid signature on the vector $\mathbf{v}_k$ for all $k = 1, \ldots, l$. If both of the above two conditions are met, $\mathcal{B}$:

1. Calculates $\mathbf{v} = \sum_{k=1}^l \beta_k \mathbf{v}_k = (v_1, \ldots, v_N)$ and $\sigma_{\mathbf{v}_k} = \widehat{\sigma}_k \cdot (H_3(e(H_2(\mathbf{v}_k), u_A)^{\alpha_B}))^{-1}$ for all $k \in [l]$.

2. Calculates $\sigma_{\mathbf{v}} = \prod_{k=1}^{l} \sigma_{\mathbf{v}_k}^{\beta_k}$.
3. Chooses a random $T \in \mathbb{G}_1^*$, and a random integer $S \in \mathbb{F}_p^*$ which are successively taken from the random tapes η and ς, respectively.
4. Computes $R = \frac{e(T,h)}{e(\sigma_{\mathbf{v}},h)^S}$. We remark that the procedure fails if $H(\mathbf{v}, R)$ has already been defined. Because R is random, the probability of failure during the q_2 hash H and combine queries is at most $2q_2^2/2^k$.

Since $\mathcal{A}$ can break UF$_2$ with success probability $Succ_{\mathcal{A},\mathcal{S}}^{UF_2}$ within time t_A, and the failure probability of this simulation is at most $2q_2^2/2^k$, $\mathcal{A}$, within time t_A, can output a valid signature (R, S, T) on vector $\mathbf{v}$ with probability at least $Succ_{\mathcal{A},\mathcal{S}}^{UF_2} - 2q^2/2^k \geq \frac{Succ_{\mathcal{A},\mathcal{S}}^{UF_2}}{2} \geq \frac{7q}{2^k}$ in the simulation.

We assume that the vector $\mathbf{v}$ belongs to the vector subspace V_β labeled as an identifier id_β. Then, we replay the attack with the same η, ς, and $\tau = (\tau)_{l=1,2,\ldots}$ unchange for $l < \beta$ and randomly chosen for $l > \beta$. For $l = \beta$ and all $i \in [m]$ (m is the dimension of the vector subspace V_β), we randomly choose $\lambda_i \in \mathbb{F}_p^*$ and set $H_1(id_\beta, i) = g^{\lambda_i}$. Note that $\mathcal{A}$ now can not query the combine oracle for the identifier id_β, because $\mathcal{B}$ is unable to answer.

Using the forking lemma technique of [23] to control the values of the hashs H_1 and H, we obtain, with probability at least $1/9$, two valid signatures (R, S_1, T_1) and (R, S_2, T_2) on the vector $\mathbf{v} \in V_\beta$ after at most $2/Succ_{\mathcal{A},\mathcal{S}}^{UF_2} + 14q/Succ_{\mathcal{A},\mathcal{S}}^{UF_2} \leq 16q/Succ_{\mathcal{A},\mathcal{S}}^{UF_2}$ repetitions of the above attack.

We now observe that $H_1(id_\beta, i) = g^{\lambda_{1i}} \neq g^{\lambda_{2i}} = H_1'(id_\beta, i)$ for all $i = 1, \ldots, m$. We set $\mathbf{k} = (k_1, \ldots, k_n)$, $\lambda_t = (\lambda_{t1}, \ldots, \lambda_{tm})$ for $t = 1, 2$, $\mathbf{v}_1 = (v_1, \ldots, v_n)$, and $\mathbf{v}_2 = (v_{n+1}, \ldots, v_{n+m})$ such that $\mathbf{v} = (\mathbf{v}_1 \| \mathbf{v}_2)$, and then compute $\rho_1 = \prod_{i=1}^{m} H_1(id_\beta, i)^{v_{n+i}} \prod_{j=1}^{n} g_j^{v_j} = g^{\lambda_1 \cdot \mathbf{v}_2} \varphi(h)^{\mathbf{k} \cdot \mathbf{v}_1}$ and $\rho_2 = \prod_{i=1}^{m} H_1'(id_\beta, i)^{v_{n+i}} \prod_{j=1}^{n} g_j^{v_j} = g^{\lambda_2 \cdot \mathbf{v}_2} \varphi(h)^{\mathbf{k} \cdot \mathbf{v}_1}$.

Let $\sigma_1 = (S_1, T_1)$, and $\sigma_2 = (S_2, T_2)$. From $\mathtt{Verify}(PK_A, id_\beta, m, \mathbf{v}, \sigma_t) = 1$ for $t = 1, 2$, we have

$$e(T_1, h) = e(\rho_1, u_A)^{S_1} R, \tag{2}$$

and

$$e(T_2, h) = e(\rho_2, u_A)^{S_2} R. \tag{3}$$

By dividing the Eq. 2 from the Eq. 3, we obtain the equation

$$e\left(\frac{T_1}{T_2}, h\right) = e\left(\frac{\rho_1}{\rho_2}, u_A\right)^{S_1 - S_2}$$
$$= e\left(g^{\lambda_1 \cdot \mathbf{v}_2 - \lambda_2 \cdot \mathbf{v}_2}, h^{\alpha_A}\right)^{S_1 - S_2} \tag{4}$$
$$= e\left(g^{(\lambda_1 - \lambda_2) \cdot \mathbf{v}_2 \alpha_A (S_1 - S_2)}, h\right).$$

Since the value of $(\lambda_1 - \lambda_2) \cdot \mathbf{v}_2 (S_1 - S_2)$ is random in $\mathbb{F}_p$, the probability of $(\lambda_1 - \lambda_2) \cdot \mathbf{v}_2 (S_1 - S_2) = 0$ is at most $1/p$. Hence $g^{\alpha_A} = (T_1/T_2)^{((S_1 - S_2)(\lambda_1 - \lambda_2) \cdot \mathbf{v}_2)^{-1}}$ so that $\mathcal{B}$ solves the CDH problem in time $t_B \leq \frac{16qt_A}{Succ_{\mathcal{A},\mathcal{S}}^{UF_2}}$ with probability $Adv_{\mathcal{B},(\mathbb{G}_1,\mathbb{G}_2)}^{CDH} \geq \frac{1}{9} - \frac{1}{p}$. This completes the proof of Theorem 2. $\qquad\square$

References

1. Ahn, J.H., Boneh, D., Camenisch, J., Hohenberger, S., Shelat, A., Waters, B.: Computing on authenticated data. In: Cramer, R. (ed.) TCC 2012. LNCS, vol. 7194, pp. 1–20. Springer, Heidelberg (2012). https://doi.org/10.1007/978-3-642-28914-9_1

2. Ateniese, G., et al.: Provable data possession at untrusted stores. In: Ning, P., di Vimercati, S.D.C., Syverson, P.F. (eds.) Proceedings of the 2007 ACM Conference on Computer and Communications Security, CCS 2007, Alexandria, Virginia, USA, 28–31 October 2007, pp. 598–609. ACM (2007)

3. Ateniese, G., Kamara, S., Katz, J.: Proofs of storage from homomorphic identification protocols. In: Matsui, M. (ed.) ASIACRYPT 2009. LNCS, vol. 5912, pp. 319–333. Springer, Heidelberg (2009). https://doi.org/10.1007/978-3-642-10366-7_19

4. Attrapadung, N., Libert, B.: Homomorphic network coding signatures in the standard model. In: Catalano, D., Fazio, N., Gennaro, R., Nicolosi, A. (eds.) PKC 2011. LNCS, vol. 6571, pp. 17–34. Springer, Heidelberg (2011). https://doi.org/10.1007/978-3-642-19379-8_2

5. Attrapadung, N., Libert, B., Peters, T.: Computing on authenticated data: new privacy definitions and constructions. In: Wang, X., Sako, K. (eds.) ASIACRYPT 2012. LNCS, vol. 7658, pp. 367–385. Springer, Heidelberg (2012). https://doi.org/10.1007/978-3-642-34961-4_23

6. Bellare, M., Neven, G.: Transitive signatures based on factoring and RSA. In: Zheng, Y. (ed.) ASIACRYPT 2002. LNCS, vol. 2501, pp. 397–414. Springer, Heidelberg (2002). https://doi.org/10.1007/3-540-36178-2_25

7. Boneh, D., Freeman, D.M.: Homomorphic signatures for polynomial functions. In: Paterson, K.G. (ed.) EUROCRYPT 2011. LNCS, vol. 6632, pp. 149–168. Springer, Heidelberg (2011). https://doi.org/10.1007/978-3-642-20465-4_10

8. Boneh, D., Freeman, D.M.: Linearly homomorphic signatures over binary fields and new tools for lattice-based signatures. In: Catalano, D., Fazio, N., Gennaro, R., Nicolosi, A. (eds.) PKC 2011. LNCS, vol. 6571, pp. 1–16. Springer, Heidelberg (2011). https://doi.org/10.1007/978-3-642-19379-8_1

9. Boneh, D., Freeman, D., Katz, J., Waters, B.: Signing a linear subspace: signature schemes for network coding. In: Jarecki, S., Tsudik, G. (eds.) PKC 2009. LNCS, vol. 5443, pp. 68–87. Springer, Heidelberg (2009). https://doi.org/10.1007/978-3-642-00468-1_5

10. Boyen, X., Fan, X., Shi, E.: Adaptively secure fully homomorphic signatures based on lattices. IACR Cryptol. ePrint Arch. **2014**, 916 (2014)

11. Catalano, D., Fiore, D., Nizzardo, L.: Programmable hash functions go private: constructions and applications to (homomorphic) signatures with shorter public keys. In: Gennaro, R., Robshaw, M. (eds.) CRYPTO 2015. LNCS, vol. 9216, pp. 254–274. Springer, Heidelberg (2015). https://doi.org/10.1007/978-3-662-48000-7_13

12. Catalano, D., Fiore, D., Warinschi, B.: Efficient Network coding signatures in the standard model. In: Fischlin, M., Buchmann, J., Manulis, M. (eds.) PKC 2012. LNCS, vol. 7293, pp. 680–696. Springer, Heidelberg (2012). https://doi.org/10.1007/978-3-642-30057-8_40

13. Charles, D.X., Jain, K., Lauter, K.E.: Signatures for network coding. IJICoT **1**(1), 3–14 (2009)

14. Chen, W., Lei, H., Qi, K.: Lattice-based linearly homomorphic signatures in the standard model. Theor. Comput. Sci. **634**, 47–54 (2016)
15. Desmedt, Y.: Computer security by redefining what a computer is. In: Michael, J.B., Ashby, V., Meadows, C.A. (eds.) Proceedings on the 1992–1993 Workshop on New Security Paradigms, 22–24 September 1992 and 3–5 August 1993, Little Compton, RI, USA, pp. 160–166. ACM (1993)
16. Diffie, W., Hellman, M.E.: New directions in cryptography. IEEE Trans. Inf. Theory **22**(6), 644–654 (1976)
17. Gennaro, R., Katz, J., Krawczyk, H., Rabin, T.: Secure network coding over the integers. In: Nguyen, P.Q., Pointcheval, D. (eds.) PKC 2010. LNCS, vol. 6056, pp. 142–160. Springer, Heidelberg (2010). https://doi.org/10.1007/978-3-642-13013-7_9
18. Hess, F.: Efficient identity based signature schemes based on pairings. In: Nyberg, K., Heys, H. (eds.) SAC 2002. LNCS, vol. 2595, pp. 310–324. Springer, Heidelberg (2003). https://doi.org/10.1007/3-540-36492-7_20
19. Huang, X., Xiang, Y., Bertino, E., Zhou, J., Xu, L.: Robust multi-factor authentication for fragile communications. IEEE Trans. Dependable Secure Comput. **11**(6), 568–581 (2014)
20. Johnson, R., Molnar, D., Song, D., Wagner, D.: Homomorphic signature schemes. In: Preneel, B. (ed.) CT-RSA 2002. LNCS, vol. 2271, pp. 244–262. Springer, Heidelberg (2002). https://doi.org/10.1007/3-540-45760-7_17
21. Li, J., et al.: Secure distributed deduplication systems with improved reliability. IEEE Trans. Comput. **64**(12), 3569–3579 (2015)
22. Lin, C.-J., Huang, X., Li, S., Wu, W., Yang, S.-J.: Linearly homomorphic signatures with designated entities. In: Liu, J.K., Samarati, P. (eds.) ISPEC 2017. LNCS, vol. 10701, pp. 375–390. Springer, Cham (2017). https://doi.org/10.1007/978-3-319-72359-4_22
23. Pointcheval, D., Stern, J.: Security arguments for digital signatures and blind signatures. J. Cryptol. **13**(3), 361–396 (2000)
24. Rivest, R.L.: Two signature schemes. Talk at Cambridge University, October 2000. http://people.csail.mit.edu/rivest/pubs/Riv00.slides.pdf
25. Steinfeld, R., Bull, L., Wang, H., Pieprzyk, J.: Universal designated-verifier signatures. In: Laih, C.-S. (ed.) ASIACRYPT 2003. LNCS, vol. 2894, pp. 523–542. Springer, Heidelberg (2003). https://doi.org/10.1007/978-3-540-40061-5_33
26. Traverso, G., Demirel, D., Buchmann, J.A.: Homomorphic Signature Schemes - A Survey. BRIEFSCOMPUTER, Springer, Heidelberg (2016). https://doi.org/10.1007/978-3-319-32115-8
27. Wang, F., Hu, Y., Wang, B.: Lattice-based linearly homomorphic signature scheme over binary field. Sci. China Inf. Sci. **56**(11), 1–9 (2013)

Efficient Attribute-Based Signature for Monotone Predicates

Jixin Zhang[1], Jiageng Chen[1(✉)], and Weizhi Meng[2]

[1] Central China Normal University, Luoyu Road 152, Wuhan, China
chinkako@gmail.com
[2] Technical University of Denmark, 2800 Kgs. Lyngby, Denmark

Abstract. By using attribute based signature (ABS), users can sign messages and prove that their attributes conform to the ones published by the designated attribute authority through certain verification policies. In the verification process, the identity and attributes of the signer will not be disclosed, which makes ABS scheme a convenient tool for applications requiring privacy preserving authentication and other role-based security applications.

However, previous ABSs suffer from efficiency issues related to the monotone or more expressive predicates. In this work, we propose a general construction to reduce the size of the signature, and give an instantiation based on SDH assumption in random oracle model. To achieve it, we apply a new approach to implement the monotonic access structure control so that we can reduce the cost of the signatures to be close to the number of attributes used by the signer instead of the number of attributes involved in the signature.

Keywords: Attribute-based signatures · Monotone · Efficiency

1 Introduction

Attribute-based signatures (ABS), introduced in the seminal work of Maji et al. [22], provides a privacy-preserving mechanism for authenticating messages. In ABS each user is granted from the authority a personal signature key, which represents the user's attributes. If the attributes satisfy a specified predicate policy, the corresponding user can use the signature key to sign messages under the predicate. Thus, ABS can be seen as a generalization of group and ring signatures, in which case identities are viewed as attributes and policies are designed by containing the disjunction over the corresponding attributes. The basic security requirements of ABS are anonymity and unforgeability. Informally, a user is anonymous if the user's signature does not reveal his/her identity and the attributes used in the signature. Unforgeability requires that no user can forge any attribute that he/she does not own to sign messages under a predicate whose attribute is not satisfied. In the centralized setting, there would be a single central authority issuing and managing attributes. In order to be more flexible, Maji also proposed the setting of multiple attribute authorities, which allows users to

© Springer Nature Switzerland AG 2021
Q. Huang and Y. Yu (Eds.): ProvSec 2021, LNCS 13059, pp. 346–362, 2021.
https://doi.org/10.1007/978-3-030-90402-9_19

obtain attributes from different attribute authorities that may not trust each other.

Related Work. ABS is different from ring signature and group signature because it supports expressive predicates. In general, signing polices can have various levels of flexibilities which can be demonstrated by threshold policies [8,14,17], monotone boolean predicates [10,15,21], non monotone access structure [24,26,27] and generalized circuits [9,11,28–30]. It has been shown that more restrictive policies allow for more efficient constructions. Except for the threshold policies, the cost of all the other schemes need to be at least in the linear relationship with the number of predicate attributes. For example, for monotone predicates ABSs, they mainly rely on the monotone span programs [18], which is defined as a matrix to achieve the requirements of predicates. In other words, only when the signer proves that he (by obtaining the private key) has a vector authenticated by the attribute authority, the product of which to the predicate matrix is a special vector (generally this vector has one 1 and the rest is 0). However, the predicate matrix size defined by the monotone span programs is linearly related to the number of properties involved in the predicates (see Sect. 2.6). In order to achieve anonymity, a signer has to generate a proof for all the attributes in the prediction matrix regardless of whether or not he possesses. This indicates that there exists a lower bound in the size of the signature and our main contribution is to make an improvement over the issue.

[21,22,24] proposed ABS schemes supporting multiple attribute authorities (MA-ABS). However, although there is no centralized authority, the central authority is required for implementing trusted setup in those multi-authority schemes. Thus, Okamoto and Takashima proposed in [23] the first fully decentralized structure that does not require trusted setup, which they called decentralized multi-authority attribute-based signature (DMA-ABS). Then the scheme was further improved in [27].

Traceability is added to the standard ABS scheme by Escala et al. [12]. Their scheme is in the single attribute authority setting and provably secure in random oracle model (ROM). Then El Kaafarani et al. [10] proposed decentralized traceable attribute-based signatures (DTABS) and its security model, which is enhanced by Ghadafi [15].

Our Contribution. In this paper, we address the efficiency of the MA-ABS with monotone predicates. Although full security of non-monotonic predicates can be achieved by using the dual pairing vector spaces [24,25] technology, they are complicated and difficult to be used for further adjusting. Thus we focus on monotonic predicate, which has also been widely applied in many applications. A novel approach is proposed to achieve access control, which help us to improve the overall efficiency. From a high level, we divide the monotonic access structure into multiple OR relation attribute sets, and then do membership proof for the AND relation attribute sets in all access structures. In this way, we are no longer limited by the order of magnitude of the access structure matrix, so that we can achieve the $O(\bar{P})$ signature size. Here, $O(\bar{P})$ indicates the maximum number of the AND relation attributes, and is far less then the

Table 1. Comparison

Scheme	Signature size	Number of attribute authority	Predicate	Security model
[24]	$O(|P|)$	One	Non-Monotone	Standard
[21]	$O(|P|)$	Many	Monotone	Generic group
[16]	$O(|P|)$	One	Monotone	Standard
[23]	$O(|P|)$	Many	Non-Monotone	Random oracle
Ours	$O(|\bar{P}|)$	Many	Monotone	Random oracle

number of attributes in predicate $|P|$ in non-extreme cases. In the worst case scenario, they are equivalent to each other. In order to use efficient ZK proof, we give a general construction and an instantiation in the RO model. Table 1 shows the comparison with other related works regarding the signature size, number of attribute authorities, predicate and security models. Except for [23], none of listed previous schemes work in DMA setting.

Organization. In the second Section, we define some basic assumptions and building block. We introduce our definition and security model in Sect. 3. In Sect. 4 and 5, we introduce our generic structure and prove its security, and a corresponding instantiation is given in Sect. 6. We conclude our result in Sect. 7.

2   Preliminaries

In this section, we give definitions of mathematical assumptions, and introduce cryptographic tools which are applied in our scheme. Denote $r \xleftarrow{R} R$ be an element r picked uniformly at random from a set R. A function $f : \mathbb{Z}_{\geq 1} \to \mathbb{R}$ is negligible if for all $c \in \mathbb{R}_{>0}$ there exists $n_0 \in \mathbb{Z}_{\geq 1}$ such that for all integers $n \geq n_0$, we have $|f(n)| < 1/n^c$. We say PPT to be the probabilistic polynomial time.

2.1   Mathematical Assumptions

Bilinear Pairings. Let $\mathbb{G}$ and $\mathbb{G}_T$ be two cyclic groups of prime order p, and g be a generator of $\mathbb{G}$. A function $e : \mathbb{G} \times \mathbb{G} \to \mathbb{G}_T$ is a bilinear maps if the following properties hold:

- Bilinearity: $e(A^x, B^y) = e(A, B)^{xy}$ for all $A, B \in \mathbb{G}$ and $x, y \in \mathbb{Z}_p$.
- Non-degeneracy: $e(g, g) \neq 1$, where 1 is the identity of $\mathbb{G}_T$.
- Efficient computability: there exists an algorithm that can efficiently compute $e(A, B)$ for all $A, B \in \mathbb{G}$.

The q-Strong Diffie-Hellman (SDH) assumption [5]. Let $g \xleftarrow{R} \mathbb{G}$ and $\gamma \xleftarrow{R} \mathbb{Z}_p^*$. The q-SDH holds in $\mathbb{G}$ if given $(g, g^\gamma, g^{\gamma^2}, ..., g^{\gamma^q})$, all PPT algorithms can find a pair $(g^{1/(\gamma+e)}, e) \in \mathbb{G} \times \mathbb{Z}_p$ with at most negligible advantage.

2.2   Digital Signature Schemes

A digital signature for a message space $\mathcal{M}$ is a tuple of polynomial-time algorithms $\mathsf{DS} := (\mathsf{KeyGen}, \mathsf{Sign}, \mathsf{Verify})$ defined as follows:

- $\mathsf{KeyGen}(\lambda)$ takes as input the security parameter λ and outputs a pair of verification/signing keys (vk, sk).
- $\mathsf{Sign}(sk, M)$ takes as input a signing key sk and a message $M \in \mathcal{M}$, and outputs a signature σ.
- $\mathsf{Verify}(vk, M, \sigma)$ takes as input a verification key vk, a message $M \in \mathcal{M}$ and a signature σ, and outputs 1 if σ is a valid signature on M, otherwise 0.

Definition 1 (Correctness). *A signature scheme* DS *is correct if for all* $\lambda \in \mathbb{N}$,

$$\Pr \left[\begin{array}{l} (vk, sk) \leftarrow \mathsf{KeyGen}(\lambda); \\ M \xleftarrow{R} \mathcal{M}; \\ \sigma \leftarrow \mathsf{Sign}(sk, M) \end{array} : \mathsf{Verfy}(vk, M, \sigma) = 1 \right] = 1.$$

Definition 2 (Existential Unforgeability). *A signature scheme* DS *is Existentially Unforgeable against adaptive Chosen Message Attack (EUF-CMA) if for all* $\lambda \in \mathbb{N}$ *for all PPT adversaries* $\mathcal{D}$,

$$\Pr \left[\begin{array}{l} (vk, sk) \leftarrow \mathsf{GenKey}(\lambda); M^* \notin Q_{Sign} \wedge \\ (\sigma^*, M^*) \leftarrow \mathcal{D}^{\mathsf{Sign}(sk, \cdot)} \; \mathsf{Verfy}(vk, M^*, \sigma^*) = 1 \end{array} \right] \leq neg(\lambda),$$

where Q_{Sign} *is the set of messages queried to* Sign.

2.3   Signature of Knowledge

Signature of Knowledge [7] (SoK) generalize digital signatures by replacing the verification key with an instance in a language in NP. If one has an instance of a witness, he can sign a message, otherwise not. The signature of knowledge is closely related to the simulated-extractable Non-interactive zero-knowledge (NIZK) parameters. A large number of previous literatures have used the connection between SoKs and NIZK proofs.

A SoK protocol for relation $\mathcal{R}$ over message space $\mathcal{M}$ comprises of a triple of polynomial-time algorithms $(\mathsf{Gen}, \mathsf{Sign}, \mathsf{Verify})$ with the following syntax:

- $\mathsf{Gen}(\mathcal{R})$ takes as input a relation $\mathcal{R}$ and outputs public parameters pp.
- $\mathsf{Sign}(pp, x, w, M)$ takes as input the public parameters pp, a pair $(x, w) \in \mathcal{R}$ and a message $M \in \mathcal{M}$, and outputs a signature σ.
- $\mathsf{Verify}(pp, x, M, \sigma)$ takes as input the public parameters pp, a statement x, a message M and a signature σ, and outputs 1 if σ is a valid SoK, otherwise 0.

Definition 3 (SimExt Security of SoK). *A SoK protocol* $(\mathsf{Gen}, \mathsf{Sign}, \mathsf{Verify})$ *for a relation* $\mathcal{R}$ *has SimExt Security if for all* $\lambda \in \mathbb{N}$ *if it satisfies the correct, simulatable and extractable properties:*
   Correctness: For all pair $(x, w) \in \mathcal{R}$ *and all message* $M \in \mathcal{M}$, *it holds that*

$$\Pr\left[\begin{array}{l} pp \leftarrow \mathsf{Gen}(\mathcal{R}); \\ \sigma \leftarrow \mathsf{Sign}(pp, x, w, M) \end{array} : \mathsf{Verify}(pp, x, M, \sigma) = 1\right] = 1.$$

Simulatability: *There exists a polynomial-time simulator* $\mathsf{Sim} = (\mathsf{SimGen},$ $\mathsf{SimSign})$, *such that for any PPT adversary* $\mathcal{D}$, *it holds that*

$$\left|\Pr\left[(pp_0, \tau) \leftarrow \mathsf{SimGen}(\mathcal{R}); b \leftarrow \mathcal{D}^{\mathsf{SimSign}(pp, \cdot, \tau, \cdot)} : b = 1\right]\right.$$

$$\left.-\Pr\left[pp_1 \leftarrow \mathsf{Gen}(\mathcal{R}); b \leftarrow \mathcal{D}^{\mathsf{Sign}(pp, \cdot, \cdot, \cdot)} : b = 1\right]\right| \leq neg(\lambda),$$

where τ *is the trapdoor information used by* Sim *to simulate a signature of* Sign *without using the witness* w.

Extraction: *If* Sim *exists, there also exists a polynomial-time extractor* Ext, *such that for any PPT adversary* $\mathcal{D}$, *it holds that*

$$\Pr\left[\begin{array}{ll} (pp, \tau) \leftarrow \mathsf{SimGen}(\mathcal{R}); & (x, w) \notin \mathcal{R} \wedge \\ (x, M, \sigma) \leftarrow \mathcal{D}^{\mathsf{SimSign}(pp, \cdot, \tau, \cdot)}; & (x, M) \notin Q \wedge \\ w \leftarrow \mathsf{Ext}(pp, \tau, M, x, \sigma) & \mathsf{Verify}(pp, x, M, \sigma) \end{array}\right] \leq neg(\lambda),$$

where Q *is the set of all queries* (x, M) *to* $\mathsf{SimSign}$.

The concept of SoK imitates a digital signature with unforgeability; even if one sees many signatures on any message in any instance, one cannot create a new signature without knowing the witness of the instance.

2.4 Commitment Schemes Without Hiding

We need a homomorphic commitment scheme in our protocol. A cryptographic commitment scheme should satisfy hiding, i.e. the commitment does not tell any information about the committed value, and should be binding, i.e. the commitment can only be opened as the value when it is committed. A commitment scheme is a pair of polynomial-time algorithms $(\mathsf{Com.Gen}, \mathsf{Com})$ which are defined as follows:

- $\mathsf{Com.Gen}(\lambda)$ takes as input the security parameter λ and outputs a commitment key ck, which specify a message space $\mathcal{M}$, a randomness space $\mathcal{R}$ and a commitment space $\mathcal{C}$.
- $\mathsf{Com}_{ck}(m; r)$ takes as input a commitment key ck, a message $m \in \mathcal{M}$ and a randomness $r \in \mathcal{R}$, and outputs a commitment $c \in \mathcal{C}$.

Informally, a commitment scheme Com_{ck} is homomorphic if for a commitment key ck, messages a, b, and random coins r, s, it holds that $\mathsf{Com}_{ck}(a; r)\mathsf{Com}_{ck}(b; s) = \mathsf{Com}_{ck}(a + b; r + s)$. We also require that it can commit to n elements in $\mathbb{Z}_p$ at the same time; in other words, given n elements $(a_1, ..., a_n) \in \mathbb{Z}_p^n$, we can compute a single commitment $c = \mathsf{Com}_{ck}(a_1, ..., a_n; r) \in \mathbb{G}$. In our scheme, we focus on the extent Pedersen commitment scheme. Specifically, $(g, g_1, ..., g_n) \xleftarrow{R} \mathsf{Com.Gen}(\lambda, N)$, $\mathsf{Com}_{ck}(a_1, ..., a_n; r) = g^r g_1^{a_1} ... g_n^{a_n}$. In addition, we only rely on the binding property but not the hiding property, so the randomizer r and the parameter g will thus be removed.

2.5 Accumulators with One-Way Domain

The accumulator [4] accumulates multiple values into a single value, and for each accumulated value, there is a witness to prove that it has been indeed accumulated.

An accumulator is a tuple of four PPT algorithms (Gen, Eval, Wit, Verf) defined as follows:

- Gen(λ) takes as input the security parameter λ and outputs a description *desc*, which possibly includes some auxiliary information.
- Eval(*desc*, X) takes as input the description *desc* and a source set $X \subseteq \mathcal{X}_\lambda$, and outputs an accumulated value v.
- Wit(*desc*, X, x) takes as input the description *desc* and a source set X and an element $x \in X$, and outputs a witness w for the element x being in X.
- Verf(*desc*, v, x, w) takes as input the description *desc*, an accumulated value v, an element x and a witness w, outputs 1 if x is an element accumulated in v, otherwise 0.

Definition 4. *An accumulator is called accumulator with one-way domain [2, 31], if for any security parameter $\lambda \in \mathbb{N}$, it holds that:*

Quasi-Commutativity: *For all description desc $\leftarrow$ Gen(λ), it holds that*

$$\text{Eval}(desc, (x_1, x_2)) = \text{Eval}(desc, (x_2, x_1)).$$

Collision-Resistance: *For any PPT adversary $\mathcal{D}$, it holds that*

$$\Pr \begin{bmatrix} desc \leftarrow \text{Gen}(\lambda); & X \subset \mathcal{X}_\lambda \wedge \\ (x, X, w) \leftarrow \mathcal{D}(desc); & : x \in \mathcal{X}_\lambda \backslash X \wedge \\ v \leftarrow \text{Eval}(desc, X) & \text{Verf}(desc, v, x, w) \end{bmatrix} \leq neg(\lambda).$$

One-Way Domain: *Let $\{\mathcal{Y}_\lambda\}$, $\mathcal{R}_\lambda$ be two sequences of families of sets associated with $\mathcal{X}_\lambda$, such that $\mathcal{R}_\lambda$ is an efficiently verifiable, samplable relation over $\mathcal{Y}_\lambda \times \mathcal{X}_\lambda$, for any PPT adversary $\mathcal{D}$, it holds that*

$$\Pr [(y, x) \leftarrow \text{Sample}(\lambda); y' \leftarrow \mathcal{D}(x) : (y', x) \in \mathcal{R}_\lambda] \leq neg(\lambda),$$

where Sample is the efficient sampling algorithm over $\mathcal{R}_\lambda$.

2.6 Monotone Span Program and Linear Secret Sharing Scheme

The main purpose of this section is to introduce the size of Monotone Span Program (MSP) predicate matrix and the computational cost of its use. Karchmer and Wigderson introduced the equivalence of MSP and linear secret sharing scheme (LSSS). The construction and use of LSSS matrix is similar to that of MSP matrix.

Both LSSS matrix and MSP matrix are rarely described in detail in non-special research papers. And special research articles may be expensive for readers who only want to know the relevant content. We recommend that readers refer to appendix G of the full version [20] of Lewko and Waters' article published in EUROCRYPT 2011 [19] or Section 3.1 of [3].

3 Syntax and Security

Let $P(\mathcal{A}) = 1$ denote the attribute set $\mathcal{A}$ satisfying the predicate P. A monotonic predicate can be divided into multiple OR relations of attribute sets of AND relations, such as "$A \wedge (B \vee C \vee D) = (A \wedge B) \vee (A \wedge C) \vee (A \wedge D)$". We define the maximum length of the AND relation in the predicate P as n_P and the size of the (OR-connected) AND relation set as $n_{\mathcal{A}}$, so in the previous example, $n_P = 2$ and $n_{\mathcal{A}} = 3$.

To express clearly, we use the syntax of [10, 15] and make a little adjustment. We do not use additional ID for each attribute authority to distinguish them but use attributes as subscripts to directly index the public and private keys of attribute authorities. It should be noted that attribute public and private keys with different subscripts can be the same key as long as these attributes belong to the same attribute authority.

An Attribute-Based Signature in multi-authority setting (MA-ABS) scheme consists of the following five algorithms.

- GSetup(λ, N): this algorithm takes as inputs a security parameter $\lambda \in \mathbb{N}$ and a maximum length of the AND relation in all predicates $N \in \mathsf{poly}(\lambda)$ and $N \geq n_P$, and outputs the global public parameter pp. For simplicity, all the following algorithms take as implicit input the public parameters pp.
- ASetup(): when a peer wants to be an attribute authority or an attribute authority wants to add its attributes, it runs the algorithm with pp as input to produce its own public and secret key pair, APK, ASK for granting its own attributes.
- GetAtt(ASK_a, id, a): a signer with identity id obtains secret key $sk_{id,a}$ for attribute a from attribute authorities through this algorithm. The algorithm takes as input attribute secret key ASK_a, id and an attribute $a \in \mathbb{A}$, outputs $sk_{id,a}$.
- Sign($\{APK_a\}_{a \in P}, \{sk_{id,a}\}_{a \in \mathcal{A}}, P, M$):   given   attribute   public   keys $\{APK_a\}_{a \in P}$, secret keys $\{sk_{i,a}\}_{a \in \mathcal{A}}$ with a predicate P such that $P(\mathcal{A}) = 1$ and a message M, this algorithm outputs a signature σ.
- Verify($\{APK_a\}_{a \in P}, \sigma, P, M$): given attribute public keys $\{APK_a\}_{a \in P}$, a signature σ, a predicate P and a message M, this algorithm outputs either 0 or 1.

Definition 5 (Correctness). *A MA-ABS scheme is correct if for any security parameter* $\lambda \in \mathbb{N}$, $pp \leftarrow$ GSetup(λ), *purported* (APK, ASK), *attribute set* $\mathcal{A} \subset \mathbb{A}$, *purported identity* id, *secret key* $sk_{id,a} \leftarrow$ GetAtt(ASK_a, id, a) *for any* $a \in \mathcal{A}$, *message* M, *claim-predicates* P *such that* $P(\mathcal{A}) = 1$ *and any* $\sigma \leftarrow$ Sign($\{APK_a\}_{a \in P}, \{sk_{id,a}\}_{a \in \mathcal{A}}, P, M$), *we have* Verify($\{APK_a\}_{a \in P}$, $\sigma, P, M) = 1$.

Similar to most of the schemes in the multi-authority setting, we assume that all attributes are prefixed with attribute authority, such as "University XXX||Professor", to avoid the problem of attribute duplication between different attribute authorities. We also assume that there is a collision resistant hash function that can map attributes to the appropriate fields. This will not be reflected in the following description.

3.1 Security

The security properties required by a MA-ABS scheme are: anonymity, unforgeability. In the following we define the oracles required by the security experiment. The following global lists are maintained by environment: HUL is the honest user list; BUL is the list of compromised users whose secret keys are revealed to the adversary; HAL is the list of honest attribute authorities; CAL is the list of corrupted attribute authorities whose key is chosen by the adversary; BAL is the list of compromised attribute authority whose secret key is learned by the adversary; SL is the list of signatures from Sign oracle; CL is the list of the challenge signatures from Ch oracle.

The details of the following oracles are given in Fig. 1.

- AddU(id, a) adds an honest user id with an attribute a.
- RevU(id, a) reveals secret keys of an honest user id with an attribute a.
- AddA(a) adds an honest attribute authority with an attribute $a \in \mathbb{A}$.
- CrptA(a) adds a corrupted attribute authority with attribute $a \in \mathbb{A}$. The adversary can generate the attribute key $\{APK_a, ASK_a\}$ dishonestly.
- RevA(a) reveals an honest attribute authority with attribute $a \in \mathbb{A}$. The adversary learns the secret keys ASK_a.
- Sign$(id, M, \mathcal{A}, P)$ returns a signature σ on M using attributes $\mathcal{A}$ belonging to user id where $P(\mathcal{A}) = 1$.
- Ch$(b, (id_0, \mathcal{A}_0), (id_1, \mathcal{A}_1), M, P)$ is a challenge oracle for anonymity. It takes two user and secret key pairs $(id_0, \mathcal{A}_0), (id_1, \mathcal{A}_1)$ such that $P(\mathcal{A}_0) = P(\mathcal{A}_1) = 1$, and returns a signature on M using $\mathcal{A}_b$ for a bit b.

We require MA-ABS to be anonymous and unforgeable. The security requirements are defined by the security games in Fig. 2.

In the following game, unless otherwise specified, adversaries are given the ability to add attributes to users, learn user attribute secrets, add authority attributes, learn authority attribute secrets and query a signature. The details of the security requirements are as follows:

(Full) Anonymity. This security property requires that a signature does not reveal any information about the identity of the user nor the set of attributes used in the signature even if the adversary knows the signer's secret keys.

In this game, querying for a signature is not necessary because adversaries are allowed to represent all users. In the challenge phase, adversary selects a message M, a predicate P as well as two pairs $((id_0, \mathcal{A}_0), (id_1, \mathcal{A}_1))$ consisting of a user and attributes used to sign, and $P(\mathcal{A}_b) = 1$ for $b \in \{0, 1\}$.

Formally, a MA-ABS is fully anonymous if all PPT adversaries $\mathcal{D}$ have negligible advantage in

$$\mathbf{Adv}^{anon}(\mathcal{D}) := |\mathrm{Pr}[\mathbf{Exp}_{\mathcal{D}}^{anon}(\lambda) = b] - 1/2|.$$

AddU(id, a)

- If $(id, a) \in$ HUL then return $\bot$.
- if $a \notin$ HAL then return $\bot$.
- $(sk_{id,a}) \leftarrow$ GetAtt(ASK_a, id, a).
- HUL $\leftarrow$ HUL $\cup \{(id, a)\}$.

RevU(id, a)

- If $(id, a) \notin$ HUL $\setminus$ BUL then return $\bot$.
- BUL $\leftarrow$ BUL $\cup \{(id, a)\}$.
- return $sk_{id,a}$.

Sign$(id, M, \mathcal{A}, P)$

- If $\exists a \in \mathcal{A}$ s.t. $(id, a) \notin$ HUL then return $\bot$.
- If $P(\mathcal{A}) = 0$ return $\bot$.
- $\sigma \leftarrow$ Sign$(\{APK_a\}_{a \in P}, \{sk_{id,a}\}_{a \in \mathcal{A}}, P, M)$.
- SL $\leftarrow$ SL $\cup \{\sigma, M, P\}$.
- return σ.

AddA(a)

- If $a \in$ HAL $\cup$ CAL then return $\bot$.
- $(APK_a, ASK_a) \leftarrow$ ASetup().
- HAL $\leftarrow$ HAL $\cup \{a\}$.

CrptA(a)

- If $a \in$ HAL $\cup$ CAL then return $\bot$.
- CAL $\leftarrow$ CAL $\cup \{a\}$.

RevA(a)

- If $a \notin$ HAL $\setminus$ BAL then return $\bot$.
- BAL $\leftarrow$ BAL $\cup \{a\}$.
- return (APK_a, ASK_a).

Ch$(b, (id_0, \mathcal{A}_0), (id_1, \mathcal{A}_1), M, P)$

- If for any $b \in \{0, 1\}$, $P(\mathcal{A}_b) = 0$ or $\exists a \in \mathcal{A}_b$ s.t. $(id_b, a) \notin$ HUL then return $\bot$.
- $\sigma_b \leftarrow$ Sign$(\{APK_a\}_{a \in P}, \{sk_{id_b,a}\}_{a \in \mathcal{A}_b}, P, M)$.
- CL $\leftarrow$ CL $\cup (M, \sigma_b, P)$.
- return σ_b.

Fig. 1. Oracles used in the security games for MA-ABS

Experiment $\mathbf{Exp}_{\mathcal{D}}^{anon}(\lambda)$

- $pp \leftarrow$ GSetup(λ).
- HUL, BUL, HAL, BAL, CAL, CL $:= \emptyset$.
- $b \xleftarrow{R} \{0, 1\}$.
- $b' \leftarrow \mathcal{D}$(play :AddU$(\cdot)$, RevU$(\cdot)$, AddA$(\cdot)$, CrptA$(\cdot)$, RevA$(\cdot)$, Ch$(b, (\cdot, \cdot), (\cdot, \cdot), \cdot, \cdot))$.
- return b'.

Experiment $\mathbf{Exp}_{\mathcal{D}}^{unfo}(\lambda)$

- $pp \leftarrow$ GSetup(λ).
- HUL, BUL, HAL, BAL, CAL, SL $:= \emptyset$.
- $(\sigma^*, M^*, P^*) \leftarrow \mathcal{D}$(play : AddU$(\cdot)$, RevU$(\cdot)$, AddA$(\cdot)$, CrptA$(\cdot)$, RevA$(\cdot)$, Sign$(\cdot, \cdot, \cdot, \cdot))$.
- If Verify$(\{APK_a\}_{a \in P}, \sigma, P, M) = 0$ then return 0.
- If $\exists \mathcal{A}^*$ s.t. $\{id^*, a\}_{a \in \mathcal{A}} \subset$ BUL and $\exists \mathcal{A} \subset$ BAL $\cup$ CAL satisfying $P^*(\mathcal{A}^* \cup \mathcal{A}) = 1$ then return 0.
- If $(\cdot, M^*, P^*) \in$ SL return 0, otherwise return 1.

Fig. 2. Security experiments for MA-ABS

Unforgeability. This security states that no valid signature can be generated without secret keys required by the predicate.

In this game, the collusion attacks is considered. Users cannot combine their secret keys to complete a signature with attributes required by the signature predicate that are not owned by them respectively. In the end, to win the game, the adversary needs to output a valid signature σ^* on M^* with predicate P^* such that (M^*, P^*) is never queried to Sign oracle and the attributes controlled by the adversary don't satisfy the predicate.

Formally, a MA-ABS is unforgeable if all PPT adversaries $\mathcal{D}$ have negligible advantage in

$$\mathbf{Adv}^{unfo}(\mathcal{D}) := \left| \Pr[\mathbf{Exp}_{\mathcal{D}}^{unfo}(\lambda) = 1] \right|.$$

4 Construction

In this section, we present a MA-ABS protocol under our new framework. Specifically, our scenario is based on an EUF-CMA digital signature DS, a signature of knowledge SoK, a homomorphic commitment scheme Com and accumulator with one-way domain ACC.

Before presenting the details, we first give an intuition of our protocol. When a signer wants to prove her attributes satisfying a predicate P, she first parses predicate as multiple OR relations of attribute sets of AND relations, again $(A \wedge B) \vee (A \wedge C) \vee (A \wedge D)$. Thanks to the commitment scheme, we can commit every attribute set of AND relation (recall $n_P = 2$) to an element with binding. Using the accumulator ACC, the Signer accumulates every commitment element and gets a witness for one of elements she want to prove. We define the accumulation as ACC.Eval($desc$, Com(P)), which will be used in the following construction. Then she can sign a message by using SoK with the knowledge of attributes. Thus, the witness of SoK is linearly dependent on the maximum size of the attribute sets of AND relations in P.

For the worst case, such as $P = (X_1 \vee Y_1) \wedge \cdots \wedge (X_n \vee Y_n)$, we have $n_p = n$ so $O(\bar{P})$ and $O(P)$ are the same.

4.1 Protocol Description

The GSetup algorithm generates a public parameter pp_s for the SoK, a commitment key ck for the homomorphic commitment scheme and a description $desc$ for accumulator with one-way domain, and outputs global public parameter $pp = (\lambda, pp_s, ck, desc)$.

When a new attribute authority joins the system, it runs the ASetup algorithm by running DS.KeyGen to generate public/private key pair for granting its own attributes.

When a member user id wants to get a new attribute a, she informs her ID to the corresponding attribute authority. The attribute authority runs DS.Sign algorithm for id with the attribute a, and returns a signature $\sigma_{id,a}$ to id.

GSetup(λ, N):

- $pp_s \leftarrow$ SoK.Gen($\mathcal{R}$), ck $\leftarrow$ Com.Gen(λ, N), $desc \leftarrow$ ACC.Gen(λ).
- $pp := (\lambda, pp_s, ck, desc)$, return pp.

ASetup():

- $(\mathcal{APK}, \mathcal{ASK}) \leftarrow$ DS.KeyGen(λ), return $(\mathcal{APK}, \mathcal{ASK})$.

GetAtt(ASK_a, id, a):

- $\sigma_{id,a} \leftarrow$ DS.Sign($ASK_a, (id, a)$), return $\sigma_{id,a}$.

Sign($\{APK_a\}_{a \in P}, \{\sigma_{id,a}\}_{a \in \mathcal{A}}, P, M$):

- $v \leftarrow$ ACC.Eval($desc$, Com$_{ck}(P)$),
  $w_\mathcal{A} \leftarrow$ ACC.Wit($desc$, Com$_{ck}(P)$, Com$_{ck}(\mathcal{A})$).
- $x := (P, \{APK_a\}_{a \in P}, v)$, $w := (\mathcal{A}, w_\mathcal{A}, \{\sigma_{id,a}\}_{a \in \mathcal{A}}, id)$.
- $\sigma \leftarrow$ SoK.Sign(pp, x, w, M), return σ.

Verify($\{APK_a\}_{a \in P}, \sigma, P, M$):

- $v \leftarrow$ ACC.Eval($desc$, Com$_{ck}(P)$).
- $x := (P, \{APK_a\}_{a \in P}, v)$.
- output SoK.Verify(pp, x, M, σ).

Fig. 3. Construction

To sign a message M w.r.t. a signing policy P, the user id computes an accumulation value v for attributes in P as previously mentioned in the intuition. For the convenience of expression, we use Com$_{ck}(P)$ to represent the commitment set of AND connected attributes in the disjunctive paradigm of P. Note that this step can be achieved by anyone and same result can be achieved. She also generates a witness $w_\mathcal{A}$, where $\mathcal{A}$ is a committed element i.e. $P(\mathcal{A}) = 1$. With the knowledge of $a \in \mathcal{A}$ granted by attribute authorities, she signs M by SoK.Sign and outputs the signature as the MA-ABS signature.

To verify the signature, one verifies σ with message M and predicate P.

The construction is in Fig. 3, whereas the relation associated with the SoK is as follows: If $x := (P, \{APK_a\}_{a \in P}, v)$, $w := (\mathcal{A}, w_\mathcal{A}, \{\sigma_{id,a}\}_{a \in \mathcal{A}}, id)$, Let

$$\mathcal{R}(x, w) \Leftrightarrow \text{ACC.Verf}(desc, v, \text{Com}_{ck}(\mathcal{A}), w_\mathcal{A}) = 1$$
$$\text{and } \{\text{DS.Verify}(APK_a, (id, a), \sigma_{id,a}) = 1\}_{a \in \mathcal{A}}$$

5   Proof of Theorems

5.1   Proof of Anonymity

Theorem 1. *The construction in Fig. 3 is anonymous if* SoK *is a SimExt-secure signature of knowledge.*

The advantage of any anonymity adversary is at most

$$\mathbf{Adv}^{anon}(\mathcal{D}) \leq \mathbf{Adv}_{\mathcal{B}}^{\text{Sim}}(\lambda).$$

Proof. The proof is straightforward. Due to the SimExt security of SoK, there exist a Sim can sign any signature without using any witness. Thus, the signatures signed by Sim don't include any information. Formally, if there exists an adversary $\mathcal{D}$ breaking anonymity, we can construct adversaries: $\mathcal{B}$ against the simulatability of the SoK. First, in GSetup, SoK.SimGen is replaced SoK.Gen. Then with the trapdoor td, $\mathcal{B}$ can respond all signing queries without using any attribute key. Last, if $\mathcal{D}$ wins her game, $\mathcal{B}$ outputs 1. So $\mathcal{B}$ has the same advantage of $\mathcal{D}$.

5.2   Proof of Unforgeability

Theorem 2. *The construction in Fig. 3 is unforgeable if* DS *is EUF-CMA,* SoK *is a SimExt-secure signature of knowledge,* Com *is binding and* ACC *is an accumulator with one-way domain.*

The advantage of any unforgeability adversary is at most

$$\mathbf{Adv}^{unfo}(\mathcal{D}) \leq \mathbf{Adv}_{\mathcal{B}_1}^{\text{Ext}}(\lambda) + \mathbf{Adv}_{\mathcal{B}_2}^{\text{EUF}}(\lambda) + \mathbf{Adv}_{\mathcal{B}_3}^{\text{Binding}}(\lambda) + \mathbf{Adv}_{\mathcal{B}_4}^{\text{CR}}(\lambda).$$

Proof. We show that if there exists an adversary $\mathcal{D}$ breaking unforgeability, we can construct adversaries: $\mathcal{B}_1$ against the SimExt security of SoK, $\mathcal{B}_2$ against the EUF-CMA of the digital signature DS, $\mathcal{B}_3$ against the binding property of the commitment scheme Com and $\mathcal{B}_4$ against the collision-resistance of the accumulator ACC. We start by replacing the SoK.Gen setting with SoK.SimGen, which ensures that the adversary cannot achieve misidentification attacks by faking proofs for false statements. Otherwise, there is an adversary $\mathcal{B}_1$ who can break the SimExt security of SoK. Depending on the Ext, we can extract $(\mathcal{A}^*, w_{\mathcal{A}}^*, \{\sigma_{id,a}^*\}_{a \in \mathcal{A}}, id^*)$ from the adversary's output (σ^*, M^*, P^*), then we distinguish the following cases:

Case 1: There exist an attribute certificate σ_{id,a^*}^* in $\{\sigma_{id,a}^*\}_{a \in \mathcal{A}}$ that is never signed by its attribute authority and the attribute authority is honest. If this happens, there is an adversary $\mathcal{B}_2$ breaking the EUF-CMA security of DS. $\mathcal{B}_2$ gets APK^* from his game and sets up remaining himself and he set APK^* as an honest attribute authority public key. He runs $\mathcal{D}$ like real challenger of $\mathcal{D}$, expect for RevA oracle and AddU oracle. For RevA oracle, if $\mathcal{D}$ queries APK^*, $\mathcal{B}_2$ aborts. For responding AddU oracle for attribute a belong to APK^*, $\mathcal{B}_2$ sign

(id, a) by querying his sign oracle of his attack game. Finally, $\mathcal{D}$ outputs its forgery. $\mathcal{B}_2$ uses Ext to get a forgery σ^*_{id,a^*}, which is never queried through AddU oracle and a belongs to an honest organization, otherwise it would not be the case. If $a^* \notin APK^*$, $\mathcal{B}_2$ aborts, otherwise return $(id, a^*, \sigma^*_{id,a^*})$ directly. The loss probability is $\frac{1}{k(\lambda)}$, where $k(\lambda)$ is a polynomial in λ representing an upper bound on the number of honest attribute. We have $\Pr[\text{Case 1}] \leq \mathbf{Adv}^{\text{EUF-CMA}}_{DS,\mathcal{B}_2}(\lambda)$.

Case 2: The adversary $\mathcal{D}$ finds an unbound instance for $\text{Com}_{ck}(\mathcal{A}^*) = \text{Com}_{ck}(\mathcal{A})$. If this happens, there is an adversary $\mathcal{B}_3$ breaking the binding property of commitment scheme. $\mathcal{B}_3$ gets ck from his game and sets up remaining himself. He runs $\mathcal{D}$ like real challenger of $\mathcal{D}$, because he can generate all secret keys. Finally, $\mathcal{D}$ outputs its forgery. $\mathcal{B}_3$ uses Ext to get a forgery $(\mathcal{A}^*, \{\sigma^*_{id,a}\}_{a \in \mathcal{A}})$, where $\mathcal{A}^* \neq \mathcal{A}$. Then $\mathcal{B}_3$ returns $(\mathcal{A}, \mathcal{A}^*)$. We have $\Pr[\text{Case 2}] \leq \mathbf{Adv}^{\text{binding}}_{com,\mathcal{B}_3}(\lambda)$.

Case 3: The adversary $\mathcal{D}$ finds a collision instance for $\text{ACC.Verf}(desc, v^*, \mathcal{A}^*, w^*_{\mathcal{A}}) = \text{ACC.Verf}(desc, v^*, \mathcal{A}, w^*_{\mathcal{A}}) = 1$, where $v^* = \text{ACC.Eval}(desc, \text{Com}(P^*))$. If this happens, there is an adversary $\mathcal{B}_4$ breaking the collision-resistance property of accumulator scheme. $\mathcal{B}_4$ gets $desc$ from his game and sets up remaining himself. He runs $\mathcal{D}$ like real challenger of $\mathcal{D}$. Finally, $\mathcal{D}$ outputs its forgery. $\mathcal{B}_4$ uses Ext to get a forgery $(\mathcal{A}^*, w^*_{\mathcal{A}}, \{\sigma^*_{id,a}\}_{a \in \mathcal{A}})$, where $P^*(\mathcal{A}^*) = 1$ and $P^*(\mathcal{A}) = 0$. Then $\mathcal{B}_4$ returns $(\text{Com}_{ck}(\mathcal{A}), \text{Com}_{ck}(P^*), w^*_{\mathcal{A}})$. Then we have $\Pr[\text{Case 3}] \leq \mathbf{Adv}_{CR,\mathcal{B}_4}(\lambda)$.
This all cases concludes the proof.

6 An Instantiation

Our instantiation of homomorphic commitment scheme is constructed based on the de-random extent Pedersen commitment Com with $ck = (g_1, ..., g_N)$. If $n_{\mathcal{A}} < n_p$, we set the rest of attribute as 0. The EUF-CMA digital signature uses a variant BBS group signature [1] for signing two message in $\mathbb{Z}_p$. We give an instantiation of DS, SoK and ACC as follows.

Digital Signature. As shown in [1], the algorithms of which are described as follows:

- DS.KeyGen(λ): Randomly chooses $\gamma \in \mathbb{Z}_p$ and outputs $pk = g^\gamma$, $sk = \gamma$.
- DS.Sign(sk, M_1, M_2): On input $(M_1, M_2) \in \mathbb{Z}_p^2$, chooses random numbers e and s in $\mathbb{Z}_p$. Computes $A = (\hat{g}_1 \hat{g}_1^{M_1} \hat{g}_2^{M_2} \hat{g}_3^s)^{\frac{1}{e+\gamma}}$, and outputs (A, e, s).
- DS.Verify(pk, M_1, M_2, σ): check if $e(A, pk g^e) = e(\hat{g}_1 \hat{g}_1^{M_1} \hat{g}_2^{M_2} \hat{g}_3^s, g)$.

Accumulator with one-way domain. We use the accumulator for DDH groups [2], the algorithms of which are described as follows:

- ACC.Gen(λ): generates cyclic groups $\mathbb{G}_1 = \langle g_0 \rangle$ and $\mathbb{G}_2$ of prime order q, a bilinear pairing $e_0 : \mathbb{G}_1 \times \mathbb{G}_1 \to \mathbb{G}_2$. The domain of accumulatable elements is $\mathbb{G} = \langle g \rangle$, which is a cyclic group of prime order p such that $\mathbb{G} \subset \mathbb{Z}_q^*$. The auxiliary information α is randomly chosen from $\mathbb{Z}_q^*$ Output the description $desc = (\mathbb{G}_1, \mathbb{G}_2, \mathbb{G}, e_0, g_0, g_0^\alpha, ..., g_0^{\alpha^n})$.

- ACC.Eval($desc, X$): computes the accumulated value v for X by evaluating $\prod_{i=0}^{n}(g_0^{\alpha^i})^{u_i}$ with public information $g_0^{\alpha^i}$, where u_i is the coefficient of the polynomial $\prod_{x \in X}(x + \alpha)$.
- ACC.Wit($desc, x_s, X$): for $x_s \in X$, it computes the witness as $w_s = \prod_{i=0}^{n-1}(g_0^{\alpha^i})^{u_i}$, where u_i is the coefficient of the polynomial $\prod_{i=0, i \neq s}^{n}(x + \alpha)$.
- ACC.Verf($desc, v, x_s, w_s$): verifies $e_0(w_s, g_0^{x_s}g_0^{\alpha}) = e(v, g_0)$.

The one-way relation for our ACC is defined as $R_p = \{(y, x) \in \mathbb{Z}_p \times \mathbb{G} : x = h^y\}$.

Remark 1. Due to the property of the accumulator, we will need the trusted setup, which can be partially relieved by using MPC technique. In addition, for some application, this is reasonable and can be accepted.

As to the SoK associated with our protocol, it can be obtained from a generalized interactive zero-knowledge protocol by using the Fiat-Shamir paradigm [13]. In the following, we present more details on the zero-knowledge protocol. Let g_0, h_0 be generators of $\mathbb{G}_1$ and $g, h, g_1, ..., g_N$ be generators of $\mathbb{G}$ and $G \in \mathbb{Z}_q^*$. An interactive zero-knowledge protocol is described as follows:

$$PoK : \Big\{ (\mathcal{A}, w_{\mathcal{A}}, \{\sigma_{id,a} = (A_a, e_a, s_a)\}_{a \in \mathcal{A}}, id)) : e_0(w_{\mathcal{A}}, g_0^{\mathsf{Com}_{ck}(\mathcal{A})}g_0^{\alpha}) = e((v, g_0))$$
$$\wedge \mathsf{Com}_{ck}(\mathcal{A}) = \{g_i^a\}_{i \in [n_p], a \in \mathcal{A} \cup \{0\}} \wedge \{e(A_a, k_a g^{e_a}) = e(\hat{g}_1 \hat{g}_1^{id} \hat{g}_2^a \hat{g}_3^{s_a}, g)\}_{a \in \mathcal{A}} \Big\}$$

To instantiate this protocol, we further treat it as the composition of the following sub-protocols:

$$PoK_1 : \Big\{ (d, r) : C = g_0^d h_0^r \Big\}$$
$$PoK_2 : \Big\{ (\mathsf{Com}_{ck}(\mathcal{A}), r, id) : C = g_0^{\mathsf{Com}_{ck}(\mathcal{A})}h_0^r \wedge$$
$$\{e(A_a, k_a g^{e_a}) = e(\hat{g}_1 \hat{g}_1^{id} \hat{g}_2^a \hat{g}_3^{s_a}, g)\}_{a \in \mathcal{A}} \Big\}$$
$$PoK_3 : \Big\{ (d, r, w_{\mathcal{A}}) : C = g_0^d h_0^r \wedge e_0(w_{\mathcal{A}}, g_0^{\mathsf{Com}_{ck}(\mathcal{A})}g_0^{\alpha}) = e((v, g_0)) \Big\}$$

The instantiation of PoK_1 is a standard DL problem. For the instantiation of PoK_2, it makes use of the zero-knowledge proof-of-knowledge of double discrete logarithms [6] and proof of knowledge of the signature [1]. Regarding the instantiation of PoK_3, by using the similar technique in [2], a prover with knowledge of $(d, r, w_{\mathcal{A}})$ can compute this protocol by first computing quantities $w_1 = g_0^{f_1} h_0^{f_2}$, $w_2 = w_{\mathcal{A}} h_0^{f_1}$ for some random $f_1, f_2 \in \mathbb{Z}_q$, and then perform the following proof-of-knowledge protocol:

$$PoK_3' : \Big\{ (f_1, f_2, d, r, t_1, t_2) : C = g_0^d h_0^r \wedge w_1 = g_0^{f_1} h_0^{f_2} \wedge w_1^d = g_0^{t_1} h_0^{t_2} \wedge$$
$$\frac{e_0(w_2, g_0^{\alpha})}{e_0(v, g_0)} = e_0(w_2, g_0)^{-d} e_0(h_0, g_0)^{t_1} e_0(h_0, g_0^{\alpha})^{f_1} \Big\}$$

Our instantiation is secure based on SDH assumption in the RO model, the signature consist of $(\lambda + 5)|\mathbb{G}_1| + 1|\mathbb{G}_2| + ((n_P + 3)\lambda + 6)|\mathbb{Z}_p| + (n_P + 2)\lambda|\mathbb{Z}_q|$, where n_P is the maximum length of the AND relation and λ is the length of element in $\mathbb{Z}_p$.

7 Conclusion

We propose a general and efficient construction of MA-ABS. In order to avoid the linear increasing of the signature size caused by the access control matrix, we develop a new method to implement monotone access structure control. We also give an instantiation based on the SDH assumption. Although our results require the trusted setup, we point out that this is all due to the use of accumulators, and other components can be replaced with non-trusted installations. Therefore, our scheme directly benefits from the development of membership proof and accumulator, which have been widely studied recently. This also makes our framework more advantageous than the traditional frameworks.

References

1. Au, M.H., Susilo, W., Mu, Y.: Constant-size dynamic k-TAA. In: De Prisco, R., Yung, M. (eds.) SCN 2006. LNCS, vol. 4116, pp. 111–125. Springer, Heidelberg (2006). https://doi.org/10.1007/11832072_8
2. Au, M.H., Tsang, P.P., Susilo, W., Mu, Y.: Dynamic universal accumulators for DDH groups and their application to attribute-based anonymous credential systems. In: Fischlin, M. (ed.) CT-RSA 2009. LNCS, vol. 5473, pp. 295–308. Springer, Heidelberg (2009). https://doi.org/10.1007/978-3-642-00862-7_20
3. Balu, A., Kuppusamy, K.: An expressive and provably secure ciphertext-policy attribute-based encryption. Inf. Sci. **276**, 354–362 (2014)
4. Benaloh, J., de Mare, M.: One-way accumulators: a decentralized alternative to digital signatures. In: Helleseth, T. (ed.) EUROCRYPT 1993. LNCS, vol. 765, pp. 274–285. Springer, Heidelberg (1994). https://doi.org/10.1007/3-540-48285-7_24
5. Boneh, D., Boyen, X., Shacham, H.: Short group signatures. In: Franklin, M. (ed.) CRYPTO 2004. LNCS, vol. 3152, pp. 41–55. Springer, Heidelberg (2004). https://doi.org/10.1007/978-3-540-28628-8_3
6. Camenisch, J., Stadler, M.: Efficient group signature schemes for large groups. In: Kaliski, B.S. (ed.) CRYPTO 1997. LNCS, vol. 1294, pp. 410–424. Springer, Heidelberg (1997). https://doi.org/10.1007/BFb0052252
7. Chase, M., Lysyanskaya, A.: On signatures of knowledge. In: Dwork, C. (ed.) CRYPTO 2006. LNCS, vol. 4117, pp. 78–96. Springer, Heidelberg (2006). https://doi.org/10.1007/11818175_5
8. Chen, C., et al.: Fully secure attribute-based systems with short ciphertexts/signatures and threshold access structures. In: Dawson, E. (ed.) CT-RSA 2013. LNCS, vol. 7779, pp. 50–67. Springer, Heidelberg (2013). https://doi.org/10.1007/978-3-642-36095-4_4
9. Datta, P., Okamoto, T., Takashima, K.: Efficient attribute-based signatures for unbounded arithmetic branching programs. In: Lin, D., Sako, K. (eds.) PKC 2019. LNCS, vol. 11442, pp. 127–158. Springer, Cham (2019). https://doi.org/10.1007/978-3-030-17253-4_5
10. El Kaafarani, A., Ghadafi, E., Khader, D.: Decentralized traceable attribute-based signatures. In: Benaloh, J. (ed.) CT-RSA 2014. LNCS, vol. 8366, pp. 327–348. Springer, Cham (2014). https://doi.org/10.1007/978-3-319-04852-9_17
11. El Kaafarani, A., Katsumata, S.: Attribute-based signatures for unbounded circuits in the ROM and efficient instantiations from lattices. In: PKC 2018, vol. 10770, pp. 89–119 (2018)

12. Escala, A., Herranz, J., Morillo, P.: Revocable attribute-based signatures with adaptive security in the standard model. In: Nitaj, A., Pointcheval, D. (eds.) AFRICACRYPT 2011. LNCS, vol. 6737, pp. 224–241. Springer, Heidelberg (2011). https://doi.org/10.1007/978-3-642-21969-6_14

13. Fiat, A., Shamir, A.: How to prove yourself: practical solutions to identification and signature problems. In: Odlyzko, A.M. (ed.) CRYPTO 1986. LNCS, vol. 263, pp. 186–194. Springer, Heidelberg (1987). https://doi.org/10.1007/3-540-47721-7_12

14. Gagné, M., Narayan, S., Safavi-Naini, R.: Short pairing-efficient threshold-attribute-based signature. In: Abdalla, M., Lange, T. (eds.) Pairing 2012. LNCS, vol. 7708, pp. 295–313. Springer, Heidelberg (2013). https://doi.org/10.1007/978-3-642-36334-4_19

15. Ghadafi, E.: Stronger security notions for decentralized traceable attribute-based signatures and more efficient constructions. In: Nyberg, K. (ed.) CT-RSA 2015. LNCS, vol. 9048, pp. 391–409. Springer, Cham (2015). https://doi.org/10.1007/978-3-319-16715-2_21

16. Gu, K., Jia, W., Wang, G., Wen, S.: Efficient and secure attribute-based signature for monotone predicates. Acta Informatica 54(5), 521–541 (2016). https://doi.org/10.1007/s00236-016-0270-5

17. Herranz, J., Laguillaumie, F., Libert, B., Ràfols, C.: Short attribute-based signatures for threshold predicates. In: Dunkelman, O. (ed.) CT-RSA 2012. LNCS, vol. 7178, pp. 51–67. Springer, Heidelberg (2012). https://doi.org/10.1007/978-3-642-27954-6_4

18. Karchmer, M., Wigderson, A.: On span programs. In: Proceedings of the Eigth Annual Structure in Complexity Theory Conference, pp. 102–111. IEEE Computer Society (1993)

19. Lewko, A., Waters, B.: Decentralizing attribute-based encryption. In: Paterson, K.G. (ed.) EUROCRYPT 2011. LNCS, vol. 6632, pp. 568–588. Springer, Heidelberg (2011). https://doi.org/10.1007/978-3-642-20465-4_31

20. Lewko, A.B., Waters, B.: Decentralizing attribute-based encryption. IACR Cryptol. ePrint Arch. 2010, 351 (2010). http://eprint.iacr.org/2010/351

21. Maji, H.K., Prabhakaran, M., Rosulek, M.: Attribute-based signatures. In: Kiayias, A. (ed.) CT-RSA 2011. LNCS, vol. 6558, pp. 376–392. Springer, Heidelberg (2011). https://doi.org/10.1007/978-3-642-19074-2_24

22. Maji, H.K., Prabhakaran, M., Rosulek, M.: Attribute-based signatures: achieving attribute-privacy and collusion-resistance. IACR Cryptol. ePrint Arch. 2008, 328 (2008)

23. Okamoto, T., Takashima, K.: Decentralized attribute-based signatures. In: Kurosawa, K., Hanaoka, G. (eds.) PKC 2013. LNCS, vol. 7778, pp. 125–142. Springer, Heidelberg (2013). https://doi.org/10.1007/978-3-642-36362-7_9

24. Okamoto, T., Takashima, K.: Efficient attribute-based signatures for non-monotone predicates in the standard model. In: Catalano, D., Fazio, N., Gennaro, R., Nicolosi, A. (eds.) PKC 2011. LNCS, vol. 6571, pp. 35–52. Springer, Heidelberg (2011). https://doi.org/10.1007/978-3-642-19379-8_3

25. Okamoto, T., Takashima, K.: Fully secure functional encryption with general relations from the decisional linear assumption. In: Rabin, T. (ed.) CRYPTO 2010. LNCS, vol. 6223, pp. 191–208. Springer, Heidelberg (2010). https://doi.org/10.1007/978-3-642-14623-7_11

26. Okamoto, T., Takashima, K.: Efficient attribute-based signatures for non-monotone predicates in the standard model. IEEE Trans. Cloud Comput. 2(4), 409–421 (2014)

27. Okamoto, T., Takashima, K.: Decentralized attribute-based encryption and signatures. IEICE Trans. Fundam. Electron. Commun. Comput. Sci. **103-A**(1), 41–73 (2020)

28. Sakai, Y., Attrapadung, N., Hanaoka, G.: Attribute-based signatures for circuits from bilinear map. In: Cheng, C.-M., Chung, K.-M., Persiano, G., Yang, B.-Y. (eds.) PKC 2016. LNCS, vol. 9614, pp. 283–300. Springer, Heidelberg (2016). https://doi.org/10.1007/978-3-662-49384-7_11

29. Sakai, Y., Attrapadung, N., Hanaoka, G.: Practical attribute-based signature schemes for circuits from bilinear map. IET Inf. Secur. **12**(3), 184–193 (2018)

30. Sakai, Y., Katsumata, S., Attrapadung, N., Hanaoka, G.: Attribute-based signatures for unbounded languages from standard assumptions. In: Peyrin, T., Galbraith, S. (eds.) ASIACRYPT 2018. LNCS, vol. 11273, pp. 493–522. Springer, Cham (2018). https://doi.org/10.1007/978-3-030-03329-3_17

31. Sun, S.-F., Au, M.H., Liu, J.K., Yuen, T.H.: RingCT 2.0: a compact accumulator-based (linkable ring signature) protocol for blockchain cryptocurrency Monero. In: Foley, S.N., Gollmann, D., Snekkenes, E. (eds.) ESORICS 2017. LNCS, vol. 10493, pp. 456–474. Springer, Cham (2017). https://doi.org/10.1007/978-3-319-66399-9_25

Practical Security Protocols

Spatial Steganalysis Based on Gradient-Based Neural Architecture Search

Xiaoqing Deng[1] , Weiqi Luo[2](✉) , and Yanmei Fang[2]

[1] Guangdong Key Laboratory of Information Security Technology,
Sun Yat-sen University, Guangzhou, China
dengxq6@mail2.sysu.edu.cn
[2] School of Computer Science and Engineering, Sun Yat-sen University,
Guangzhou, China
{luoweiqi,fangym}@mail.sysu.edu.cn

Abstract. Most existing steganalytic networks are designed empirically, which probably limits their performances. Neural architecture search (NAS) is a technology that can automatically find the optimal network architecture in the search space without excessive manual intervention. In this paper, we introduce a gradient-based NAS method called PC-DARTS in steganalysis. We firstly define the overall network architecture, and the search spaces of the corresponding cells in the network. We then use softmax over all candidate operations to construct an over-parameterized network. By updating the parameters of such a network based on gradient descent, the optimal operations, i.e., the high-pass filters in pre-processing module and operations in feature extraction module, can be obtained. Experimental results show that the resulting steganalytic network via NAS can achieve competitive performance with some advanced well-designed steganalytic networks, while the searching time is relatively short.

Keywords: Steganalysis · Deep learning · Neural architecture search

1 Introduction

Steganalysis is a technology used to detect the presence of the secret information embedded by steganography, which can effectively monitor the use of steganography. The existing steganalytic methods can be divided into two types, i.e. conventional methods based on handcrafted features and deep learning-based methods. The representative of conventional methods is SRM (Spatial Rich Model) [7], which firstly uses different high-pass filters to get image residuals, and achieves steganalytic statistics of the residuals. Several adaptive steganalytic methods such as [19] and maxSRM [4] can further improve the detection performances by using the embedding property of steganography. The deep learning-based method was first proposed in 2014 by Tan et al. [18]. In 2017, Ye et al. [22]

© Springer Nature Switzerland AG 2021
Q. Huang and Y. Yu (Eds.): ProvSec 2021, LNCS 13059, pp. 365–375, 2021.
https://doi.org/10.1007/978-3-030-90402-9_20

proposed a convolutional neural network called YeNet which initializes the first convolutional layer with 30 spam high-pass filters used in SRM and applies a new truncated linear unit. The detection performance of YeNet firstly exceeds SRM. In 2019, Boroumand et al. [3] proposed a deep residual network called SRNet which achieves satisfactory performance in both spatial and JPEG domains.

Though the modern steganalytic methods based on deep learning have achieved greater performances than conventional methods, they are usually constructed empirically after lots of trials. For instance, the operations and hyperparameters in each layer, the layer numbers used in network. It is quite time-consuming or impossible to try all candidates to achieve the best one. Recently, a technique called Neural Architecture Search (NAS) is proposed to automatically search for the optimal network architecture in a predefined search space. According to the search strategy [6], the existing NAS methods can be divided into 5 types, namely, based on random search [12], Bayesian optimization [16], evolutionary algorithm [17], reinforcement learning [23], and gradient [20]. In [21], Yang et al. first introduce NAS based on reinforcement learning in JPEG steganalysis, and show that it outperforms some advanced networks in JPEG domain. However, this method [21] is quite time-consuming. Even the image is as small as 128×128, it takes 15 days to search for the optimal network on a server with 3 NVIDIA TITAN Xp 1080 GPUs.

Among the 5 types of search strategies in NAS, the first 4 types treat architecture search as a black-box optimization problem in a discrete space, which usually require huge computing resources for evaluation [15]. In contrast, the gradient-based search strategy relaxes the discrete search space into continuous space, and uses gradient descent for optimization, which is more efficient. Thus we first introduce a novel gradient-based method called PC-DARTS [20] in spatial steganalysis. In our method, a pre-processing cell is firstly employed to search an optimal set of high-pass filters to enhance the signal of steganographic artifacts. And then several cells to be searched are stacked manually for feature extraction. The classification part is fixed to output the probability of classification. By using a softmax function, all possible high-pass filters and cell architectures are combined together to get an over-parameterized network. Finally, we optimize this network by gradient descent, and get the corresponding optimal network architecture. The experimental results show that the proposed method is very promising in spatial steganalysis.

The rest of the paper is organized as follows. Section 2 describes the proposed method. Section 3 shows the experimental results and discussions. Finally, the concluding remarks of this paper and future works are given in Sect. 4.

2   Proposed Method

Like most related steganalytic works, the proposed network architecture includes three modules, that is, pre-processing, feature extraction and the classification, as shown in Fig. 1. The classification module here is fixed, which consists of a global covariance pooling layer [13,14], a fully-connected layer and a softmax

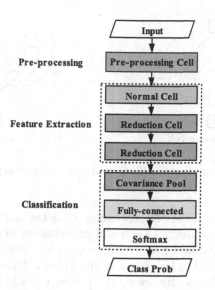

Fig. 1. The architecture of the search network.

function. In the following two subsections, we will define the search spaces of cells in pre-processing and feature extraction modules separately. Finally, we will describe the search process to determine the cells.

2.1   Search Space in Pre-processing Module

To enhance the signal-to-noise ratio of the input image, most steganalytic networks such as [5,22] usually employ 30 linear high-pass filters proposed in SRM [7] to get image residuals in pre-processing module. However, some selected filters are probably redundant. In our method, we use 30 SRM filters like most steganalytic networks as the search space F, and aim to search an optimal subset in the pre-processing module. To this end, we define the pre-processing cell in Fig. 2(a). As shown in Fig. 2(a), the input node is an image, the output node represents image feature maps, each dashed line denotes a candidate filter $f_i \in F, i = 1, 2, \ldots, 30$, which is followed by a TLU (Truncated Linear Unit) [22]. The threshold of the TLU is set as 5, which has a better performance than other settings like 1, 3 or no threshold according to our experiments. The result of each dashed line (denoted as r_i) is defined as follows:

$$r_i(input) = \frac{exp(\alpha^{f_i})}{\sum_{f_i' \in F} exp(\alpha^{f_i'})} \cdot TLU(f_i(input)), \tag{1}$$

where α^{f_i} is the weight of the filter f_i, which is randomly initialized, and then would be updated according to the loss on training set by using gradient descent during search process.

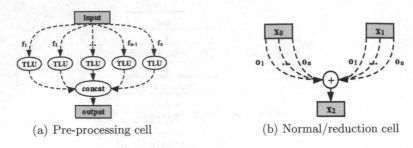

(a) Pre-processing cell   (b) Normal/reduction cell

Fig. 2. The architecture of cells to be searched.

Finally, the output of the pre-processing cell is the concatenation of all $r_i, i = 1, 2, \ldots, 30$. We have conducted a series of experiments to determine the number of filters to be reserved and found that keeping 16 filters has the improvement of 0.3% to 1% compared to keeping 8 or all of them. Therefore, when the search process is finished, the 16 filters with the largest α^{f_i} will be reserved.

2.2 Search Space in Feature Extraction Module

As shown in Fig. 1, feature extraction module is composed of a normal cell followed by two reduction cells. The architecture of normal/reduction cell is shown in Fig. 2(b), which can be regarded as a directed acyclic graph with three nodes. Node x_0 and x_1 denote the feature maps, which are the outputs of previous cells; node x_2 is output of the cell; the dashed lines represent the candidate operations. Note that the architecture and the search space of two types of cells are the same, except that the stride of operations is 1 for normal cell, while it becomes 2 for reduction cell. In addition, the cells of the same type share the same architecture parameters. The channel number of normal cell is 64, while the channel numbers of two reduction cells are 128 and 256 respectively.

The candidate operation set O employed in the proposed feature extraction module includes 7 elements, i.e., $O = \{3 \times 3$ convolution, 5×5 convolution, 3×3 separable convolution, 3×3 max-pooling, 3×3 average-pooling, skip-connection, no operation$\}$. In DARTS [15], they relax the selection of a specific operation to a softmax calculation over all candidate operations in search space O as follows:

$$y(x_j) = \sum_{o_i \in O} \frac{exp(\alpha_j^{o_i})}{\sum_{o_i' \in O} exp(\alpha_j^{o_i'})} \cdot o_i(x_j), \tag{2}$$

where $y(x_j)$ denotes the result of $x_j, j = 0, 1$ after passing all candidate operations in dashed lines connected to it; $\alpha_j^{o_i}$ is the weight of the operation o_i in dashed line connected to x_j.

However, it requires huge memory to store the corresponding outputs of 7 candidate operations in each node during the training stage. To overcome this, we employ PC-DARTS [20] to select partial channels instead of all channels of

each input node for operation mixture (i.e. Eq. 2) while the unselected channels
are directly copied to the output, that is,

$$y^{PC}(x_j) = \sum_{o_i \in O} \frac{exp(\alpha_j^{o_i})}{\sum_{o_i' \in O} exp(\alpha_j^{o_i'})} \cdot o_i(S_j \times x_j) + (1 - S_j) \times x_j, \qquad (3)$$

where $y^{PC}(x_j)$ is the result of $x_j, j = 0, 1$ after passing all candidate operations
in dashed lines connected to it with partial channel connections; S_j is a vector of
the same length as the channels number of x_j called channel sampling mask on
input $x_j, j = 0, 1$. The element of S_j is set as 1 when the channel is selected, and
set as 0 when the channel is unselected. In our method, the first half elements
of the S_j are set as 1 while the remaining are 0. Moreover, in order to mitigate
the fluctuation caused by partial channel connections, an edge normalization is
adopted as follows,

$$x_2^{PC} = \sum_{j=0}^{1} \frac{exp(\beta_j)}{\sum_{j'=0}^{j'=1} exp(\beta_{j'})} \cdot y^{PC}(x_j), \qquad (4)$$

where β_j is the weight on the lines connected to node x_j. It means that the
output of the cell i.e., x_2 with partial channel connections, i.e., x_2^{PC}, is the
weighted sum of two input node after passing candidate operations.

During the search process, both parameters $\alpha_j^{o_i}$ and β_j are randomly initialized, and then updated according to the loss function using gradient descent.
When the search process is finished, the operation o_i with the largest $\alpha_j^{o_i}$ value
among dashed lines connected to x_j is preserved to be the optimal operation to
construct the cells, which means that only one line with the largest $\alpha_j^{o_i}$ connected
to each input node will be preserved in the normal/reduction cells.

2.3 Search Process

After defining the overall network architecture, the basic cell architecture, and
the search space of each cell, we can obtain an over-parameterized network
Net_{op}, which covers all candidate filters and operations. Searching the optimal steganalytic network from Net_{op} is then converted to determine the filters
and operations in cells via training Net_{op}. According to the search space of
each cell, the total number of networks that can be searched is 349,159,842,675
($= C_{30}^{16} \times 7 \times 7 \times 7 \times 7$, in which, C_{30}^{16} represents the number of choices of selecting
16 filters from 30 filters in pre-processing module, and two 7×7 represent the
number of choices of two kinds of cells, namely the normal cell and reduction
cell). The search algorithm is illustrated in Algorithm 1.

Firstly, we create an over-parameterized network Net_{op} according to the
network architecture in Fig. 1, two cell architectures in Fig. 2. Then in the first
B epochs, we first update the network parameters w like weights of convolutional
kernels according to the cross entropy loss on a half of training set i.e. $\mathcal{L}_{train1}$,
while the architecture parameters like α (including α^{o_i} and α^{f_i}) and β are fixed.
After B epochs, the architecture parameters and the network parameters will be

---

Algorithm 1. Search Process Based on Gradient Descent

Input: Search space O and F, Training epochs T, Begin epoch B
Output: Optimal architectures of cells
    Create an over-parameterized network Net_{op}
    for $t = 1, 2, ..., T$ **do**
        if $t \geq B$ **then**
            Update architecture parameters α, β by descending $\nabla_{\alpha,\beta}\mathcal{L}_{train2}$
        end if
        Update network parameters w by descending $\nabla_w\mathcal{L}_{train1}$
    end for
    Obtain optimal architecture of cells according to α

---

updated in turns according to the cross entropy loss on another half of training set i.e. $\mathcal{L}_{train2}$ and $\mathcal{L}_{train1}$, respectively. After T epochs, we can obtain the optimal architecture of cells i.e. pre-processing cell, normal/reduction cell by preserving the candidate operations with largest α.

3   Experimental Results

We conduct experiments on the datasets BOSSBase [1] and BOWS2 [2]. Each dataset contains 10,000 grayscale images of size 512×512. The images are first resized to 256×256 by "imresize" with default setting in MATLAB. As data partitioning in existing works, such as YeNet [22], SRNet [3], and method [21], the training set includes 4,000 images from BOSSBase and 10,000 images from BOWS2. The validation set contains 1,000 images from BOSSBase. The remaining 5,000 images from BOSSBase are used for test.

In the search stage, we set $T = 70$, $B = 35$. We use SGD optimizer with momentum of 0.9 and weight decay of 3×10^{-5} to optimize the network parameters. The initial learning rate is 0.5 and decays following cosine schedule. The Adam [10] optimizer with a fixed learning rate of 6×10^{-3} is used to optimize the architecture parameters. The momentum and weight decay of Adam are $(0.5, 0.999)$ and 10^{-3} respectively. The batch size is 16 (i.e., 8 cover-stego pairs). After the search stage, we determine the 16 high-pass filters used in the pre-processing cell and the operations in normal/reduction cells based on the architecture parameters that perform best on the train2. Then the obtained optimal network will be trained from scratch. In this training stage, the whole training set is used. The batch size is 32 (i.e., 16 cover-stego pairs). And we use SGD optimizer with the momentum of 0.9 and weight decay of 3×10^{-5}. The initial learning rate is 0.2 and is divided by 10 at epoch 80, 140, 180. Note that we have provided the source code of the proposed method online[1], so that readers can repeat our results easily.

---

[1] Codes available at: https://github.com/DXQer/Spatial-Steganalysis-Based-on-Gradient-Based-Neural-Architecture-Search.

3.1 Analysis on the Resulting Steganalytic Network

In our experiments, the search process is performed on S-UNIWARD at payload 0.4 bpp. Totally, it takes only 15 h to train the over-parameterized network on a server with 4 GeForce RTX 2080 Ti GPUs. Thus, the proposed method is much more efficient than the steganalytic method [21] based on NAS via reinforcement learning[2]. Table 1 shows the 16 resulting high-pass filters in the pre-processing cell, and Fig. 3 shows the operations in the normal and reduction cells. Note that the reduction cell can be regarded as a residual cell, since it contains a skip connection. Finally, the resulting steganalytic network is illustrated in Fig. 4. From Fig. 4, we observe that this network contains 8 parameter layers, including a 1×1 convolutional layers inside each cell for input pre-processing.

Table 1. The 16 selected linear high-pass filters.

1st Order	Original version and its $90°$, $180°$, $225°$, $270°$ and $315°$ rotation versions
2nd Order	Original version and its $45°$ rotation version
3rd Order	Original version and its $90°$ and $180°$ rotation versions
EDGE 3×3	Original version and its $90°$ and $270°$ rotation versions
SQUARE 3×3	Original version
SQUARE 5×5	Original version

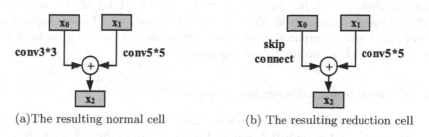

(a)The resulting normal cell   (b) The resulting reduction cell

Fig. 3. The operations used in the normal and reduction cells.

We make a comparison of the parameters employed in YeNet, SRNet and the resulting network with our method. We observe that among three networks, YeNet has the least amount of parameters with the number is 0.1 M. Although the number of parameter layers of our network is the least among three models, the number of channels in each layer is large, such as 64, 128, 256 while the maximum number of channels in YeNet is only 32. Therefore, the number of

---

[2] Note that the image database is exactly the same for both methods. Our method employ bigger images of size 256×256, while the method use smaller images of size 128×128.

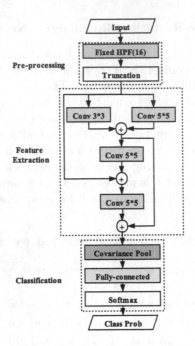

Fig. 4. The resulting steganalytic network.

parameters of the obtained network is 2.4 M which is much larger than that of YeNet. SRNet has the largest amount of parameters of 4.8 M, which is about twice as large as our network. As for the training time, YeNet needs around 36 h to train and SRNet requires more than 72 h, while the resulting network only takes around 15 h according to our experiments.

3.2 Comparison on Detection Accuracy

Three typical steganographic methods, including S-UNIWARD [9], HILL [11] and WOW [8], at payloads 0.2 bpp and 0.4 bpp are evaluated separately. We compare the resulting network architecture searched on S-UNIWARD 0.4 bpp with two advanced steganalytic networks i.e. YeNet [22] and SRNet [3]. To get convincing results, we repeat the experiments twice on different dataset partition, and show the average results in the following. And for a fair comparison, all networks are evaluated under the same condition.

The comparative results are shown in Table 2. From Table 2, we observe that our detection accuracies are higher than YeNet in all cases. When compared with SRNet, the detection accuracy of the proposed network is competitive. For example, when detecting WOW for payload of 0.4 bpp, the detection accuracy of the proposed network achieves 91.40% which is 0.74% higher than SRNet. In other cases, the detection performance of the proposed network is slightly worse than SRNet, but the distance between SRNet and our network is less than 0.57%.

Table 2. Comparison on detection accuracies (%).

Steganalytic network	S-UNIWARD		HILL		WOW	
	0.2	0.4	0.2	0.4	0.2	0.4
YeNet	77.84	87.47	74.63	83.63	82.46	89.95
SRNet	79.64	89.74	75.67	85.33	83.75	90.66
Proposed	79.52	89.57	75.44	84.76	83.66	91.40

Note that another related NAS steganalytic method via reinforcement learning [21] is for JPEG domain while the proposed method is for spatial domain, the corresponding detection accuracy comparison is not given in this paper.

4 Conclusion

In this paper, we first introduce the gradient-based neural architecture search (NAS) in spatial steganalysis, and provide experimental results to show that the resulting network is competitive with the advanced manually designed networks, while our searching time (around 15 h) is significantly shorter than the related NAS steganalytic method via reinforcement learning [21] (around 15 d for smaller images).

This is our preliminary attempt to get steganalytic network via gradient-based network architecture search. Limited by our computing resources, the proposed network architecture in Fig. 1 and the cell architectures in Fig. 2 are relatively simple. The search spaces of filters and operations are small too. Thus there is great room for improvement. In addition, there are still some artificially designed parts in our method, such as the way of cells stacking, and the number of nodes in cells, which would limit the scope of architecture search. Therefore, how to make the search stage more automatically is worth further considering.

Acknowledgements. This work was supported in part by the National Natural Science Foundation of China under Grant 61972430, in part by the Natural Science Foundation of Guangdong under Grant 2019A1515011549.

References

1. Bas, P., Filler, T., Pevný, T.: Break our steganographic system: the ins and outs of organizing BOSS. In: Filler, T., Pevný, T., Craver, S., Ker, A. (eds.) IH 2011. LNCS, vol. 6958, pp. 59–70. Springer, Heidelberg (2011). https://doi.org/10.1007/978-3-642-24178-9_5
2. Bas, P., Furon, T.: Bows2 (2007). http://bows2.ec-lille.fr
3. Boroumand, M., Chen, M., Fridrich, J.: Deep residual network for steganalysis of digital images. IEEE Trans. Inf. Forensics Secur. **14**(5), 1181–1193 (2019). https://doi.org/10.1109/TIFS.2018.2871749

4. Denemark, T., Sedighi, V., Holub, V., Cogranne, R., Fridrich, J.: Selection-channel-aware rich model for steganalysis of digital images. In: IEEE International Workshop on Information Forensics and Security, pp. 48–53. IEEE, Atlanta (2014). https://doi.org/10.1109/WIFS.2014.7084302

5. Deng, X., Chen, B., Luo, W., Luo, D.: Fast and effective global covariance pooling network for image steganalysis. In: ACM Workshop on Information Hiding and Multimedia Security, pp. 230–234. ACM, Paris (2019). https://doi.org/10.1145/3335203.3335739

6. Elsken, T., Metzen, J.H., Hutter, F.: Neural architecture search: a survey. J. Mach. Learn. Res. **20**(55), 1–21 (2019)

7. Fridrich, J., Kodovsky, J.: Rich models for steganalysis of digital images. IEEE Trans. Inf. Forensics Secur. **7**(3), 868–882 (2012). https://doi.org/10.1109/TIFS.2012.2190402

8. Holub, V., Fridrich, J.: Designing steganographic distortion using directional filters. In: IEEE International Workshop on Information Forensics and Security, pp. 234–239. IEEE, Costa Adeje (2012). https://doi.org/10.1109/WIFS.2012.6412655

9. Holub, V., Fridrich, J., Denemark, T.: Universal distortion function for steganography in an arbitrary domain. EURASIP J. Inf. Secur. **2014**(1), 1–13 (2014). https://doi.org/10.1186/1687-417X-2014-1

10. Kingma, D.P., Ba, J.: Adam: A method for stochastic optimization. In: International Conference for Learning Representations, San Diego (2015)

11. Li, B., Wang, M., Huang, J., Li, X.: A new cost function for spatial image steganography. In: IEEE International Conference on Image Processing, pp. 4206–4210. IEEE, Paris (2014). https://doi.org/10.1109/ICIP.2014.7025854

12. Li, L., Talwalkar, A.: Random search and reproducibility for neural architecture search. In: Proceedings of the Thirty-Fifth Conference on Uncertainty in Artificial Intelligence, vol. 115, pp. 367–377. AUAI Press, Tel Aviv (2019)

13. Li, P., Xie, J., Wang, Q., Gao, Z.: Towards faster training of global covariance pooling networks by iterative matrix square root normalization. In: IEEE Conference on Computer Vision and Pattern Recognition, pp. 947–955. IEEE Computer Society, Salt Lake City (2018). https://doi.org/10.1109/CVPR.2018.00105

14. Li, P., Xie, J., Wang, Q., Zuo, W.: Is second-order information helpful for large-scale visual recognition? In: IEEE International Conference on Computer Vision, pp. 2089–2097. IEEE Computer Society, Venice (2017). https://doi.org/10.1109/ICCV.2017.228

15. Liu, H., Simonyan, K., Yang, Y.: DARTS: Differentiable architecture search. In: International Conference on Learning Representations. New Orleans, LA, USA (2019). https://openreview.net/forum?id=S1eYHoC5FX

16. Mendoza, H., Klein, A., Feurer, M., Springenberg, J.T., Hutter, F.: Towards automatically-tuned neural networks. In: Proceedings of the Workshop on Automatic Machine Learning, vol. 64, pp. 58–65. New York City (2016)

17. Real, E., Aggarwal, A., Huang, Y., Le, Q.V.: Regularized evolution for image classifier architecture search. In: AAAI Conference on Artificial Intelligence, pp. 4780–4789. AAAI Press, Honolulu(2019). https://doi.org/10.1609/aaai.v33i01.33014780

18. Tan, S., Li, B.: Stacked convolutional auto-encoders for steganalysis of digital images. In: Signal and Information Processing Association Annual Summit and Conference, pp. 1–4. IEEE, Siem Reap (2014). https://doi.org/10.1109/APSIPA.2014.7041565

19. Tang, W., Li, H., Luo, W., Huang, J.: Adaptive steganalysis against WOW embedding algorithm. In: ACM workshop on Information Hiding and Multimedia Security, pp. 91–96. ACM, Salzburg (2014). https://doi.org/10.1145/2600918.2600935

20. Xu, Y., et al.: PC-DARTS: Partial channel connections for memory-efficient architecture search. In: International Conference on Learning Representations. Addis Ababa, Ethiopia (2020). https://openreview.net/forum?id=BJlS634tPr
21. Yang, J., Lu, B., Xiao, L., Kang, X., Shi, Y.: Reinforcement learning aided network architecture generation for JPEG image steganalysis. In: ACM Workshop on Information Hiding and Multimedia Security, pp. 23–32. ACM, New York (2020). https://doi.org/10.1145/3369412.3395060
22. Ye, J., Ni, J., Yi, Y.: Deep learning hierarchical representations for image steganalysis. IEEE Trans. Inf. Forensics Secur. **12**(11), 2545–2557 (2017). https://doi.org/10.1109/TIFS.2017.2710946
23. Zoph, B., Le, Q.: Neural architecture search with reinforcement learning. In: International Conference on Learning Representations. Toulon, France (2017). https://openreview.net/forum?id=r1Ue8Hcxg

Turn-Based Communication Channels

Carlo Brunetta[1]([✉]), Mario Larangeira[2,3], Bei Liang[4], Aikaterini Mitrokotsa[1,5], and Keisuke Tanaka[2]

[1] Chalmers University of Technology, Gothenburg, Sweden
brunetta@chalmers.se
[2] Department of Mathematical and Computing Science, School of Computing, Tokyo Institute of Technology, Tokyo, Japan
keisuke@is.titech.ac.jp
[3] IOHK, Tokyo, Japan
mario.larangeira@iohk.io
[4] Yanqi Lake Beijing Institute of Mathematical Sciences and Applications, Beijing, China
lbei@bimsa.cn
[5] School of Computer Science, University of St. Gallen, St. Gallen, Switzerland
aikaterini.mitrokotsa@unisg.ch

Abstract. We introduce the concept of turn-based communication channel between two mutually distrustful parties with communication consistency, *i.e.* both parties have the same message history, and happens in sets of exchanged messages across a limited number of turns. Our construction leverages on *timed primitives*. Namely, we consider a Δ-delay hash function definition and use it to establish *turns* in the channel. Concretely, we introduce the one-way turn-based communication scheme and the two-way turn-based communication protocol and provide a concrete instantiation that achieves communication consistency.

Keywords: Time puzzle · Delay · Hash function · Consistency

1 Introduction

Communication channels are the core mediums allowing different parties to build dialogues. They can either be *physical* or *abstract*, *e.g.* electromagnetic wave propagation or a key exchange protocol that allows to *establish a secure communication channel*. Either the case, channels achieve different properties which can be related to the medium, *e.g.* reliability, energy efficiency, bandwidth, or based on the *"content"*, *e.g.* confidentiality, privacy or other.

A fundamental and highly desirable property of a channel is *consistency*, *i.e.* different parties exchange messages which cannot be modified or repudiated in the future once the communication is over. In other words, whenever a message is shared, it is permanently fixed in the transcription. An example of a protocol that allows such a property is the *public bulletin board* which allows

A full version of this paper can be found at https://eprint.iacr.org/2021/1126.

© Springer Nature Switzerland AG 2021
Q. Huang and Y. Yu (Eds.): ProvSec 2021, LNCS 13059, pp. 376–392, 2021.
https://doi.org/10.1007/978-3-030-90402-9_21

any party to publish any information on the *"board"*, while receiving a *"proof"* that guarantees the *integrity* that the information is indeed *published*. Recently, blockchains, or public ledgers [4,15], have emerged as complex protocols that allow the instantiation of a public bulletin board, without relying on a central authority. Their security relies on a specially purposed *consensus protocol*, which often requires assumptions of game-theoretic nature, *e.g.* the *proof-of-work* consensus protocol implies that an adversary does not have more than 51% of the available computing power at its disposal. Bulletin boards based on consensus protocols, albeit practical, suffer from significant delays when persisting entries. Notably, blockchain-based systems, typically suffer from scalability issues without a clear solution yet. Consequently, for time critical systems, blockchain-based bulletin boards may not be a useful alternative. An emerging technology, autonomous driving, illustrates the challenge between time-critical systems and blockchains. Autonomous driving in a real-world environment is a notoriously hard task because of the high number of variables that must be taken into account. Moreover, in such systems, communication between cars is a viable design approach. Different systems must communicate and coherently agree on their action plans. Let us consider a simplified example where a car is overtaking another one. The one taking the action and surrounding cars must securely execute their algorithms while communicating to each other. All the communication between the cars should be timely available and guaranteed to be correct, *i.e.* could not be changed a posteriori, for audit purposes. The transcript of the whole communication could be used later, or even in court, for legal issues. A straightforward approach is to let vehicles be equipped with cryptographic primitives, such as digital signatures. Despite its feasibility, the aid of public key cryptography may not be an option for some devices, in particular, resource restricted ones. Besides, it may require the use of Public Key Infrastructure (PKI) which may be, again, prohibitive for some systems. One of the most basic building blocks in cryptographic literature are *hash functions*. They are used to guarantee data integrity and are widely employed in the computer science discipline in numerous applications. A natural question is whether such a building block would allow the construction of a *pair-wise communication channel*, avoiding the somewhat heavier cryptographic primitives earlier cited. An application relying only on hash functions could be significantly *"easier"*, since it would not be aided by public key cryptography schemes with PKI, typically more *"complex"* than their private key cryptography counterpart. Furthermore, it could also sidestep the early mentioned limitations of blockchain based protocols, yet providing a consistent and timely communication channel between two users. More succinctly, we investigate the question: *is it possible to design a consistent channel between two parties **without** using blockchain's assumptions **nor** public key infrastructure?*

Concept's Overview. All the communication is held over *time* which allows to *order* events during communication, *e.g.* message exchange. Commonly, our daily interaction is held over **continuous communication channels** in which the communicating parties can communicate at *any* point in time. Our main idea relies on providing a **turn-based communication channel** (TBCC) that forces the two parties to communicate in a *limited* amount of distinct *turns* separated by a Δ time interval. The parties' interaction is slowed down by the necessity of *waiting for the next turn*, contrary to the almost-instantaneous reply ability of continuous channels. To do so, we assume the existence of functions that *"computationally"* create time delays and are used to extend the hash function definition and introduce the Δ-delay hash function, which paves the way to the construction of **time-lock puzzles** in the spirit of Mahmoody *et al.* [17], *i.e.* a primitive that allows Alice P_A to generate a puzzle-solution pair (y, π), send the puzzle y to Bob P_B that spends a time Δ to compute the solution π. Concretely, Δ is the turn interval in our TBCC construction. The novel feature provided by TBCC is that P_A knows the solution π in advance and can use it to *"commit"* to a message m. By releasing m and the puzzle y, P_B must invest Δ amount of time in computing π *before being able* to verify the validity of m. The early described *timed-commitment* is the stepping stone of our first construction for a **one-way turn-based scheme** that allows the communication of blocks of messages in turns in a single direction, *e.g.* from P_A to P_B. We show that if the one-way turn-based scheme is correct and tamper resistant, *i.e.* the adversary is unable to modify the past communication and/or the correctness of the exchanged messages, intuitively this yields to **communication consistency**, *i.e.* both parties have the same view of the exchanged messages even if the adversary delays/tampers any message. We define the **two-way** TBCC **protocol** as a *"two one-way scheme"* which allows a simpler extension of the properties to the protocol, *i.e.* correctness, tamper resistance, sequentiality and consistency. Additionally, we introduce the concept of **turn synchronisation**, *i.e.* the two communicating parties must always agree in which *shared* turn they are communicating. The protocol provides a **recovery procedure** that allows the communicating parties to fix the last-turn messages in case of a communication error or an adversarial tamper.

Related Work. *Blockchains and Bulletin Boards.* The blockchain is commonly used in a distributed environment, where cryptographic primitives and game theoretical assumptions create a distributed database, where consistency comes for the orderly generation of blocks added to the structure. There are many examples of either *using* blockchains as a building block with new primitives, *e.g.* public verifiable proofs [20], or applying existing cryptographic primitives into blockchains and achieve new functionalities [7,14], or the theoretical aspects related to the consensus mechanism or the blockchains' theoretical model [10].

Time and Cryptographic Primitives. Cryptography and timing are long time distinct aspects that are commonly not considered together. Rivest *et al.* [19] described the possibility of using time to create a *cryptographic time-capsule*, *i.e.* a ciphertext that will be possible to decrypt after a specified amount of time. Their work defines the concept of *time-lock puzzles*, where timing is achieved by cleverly tweaking the security parameters of some secure cryptographic primitives. Boneh *et al.* [8] presented the concept of timed commitments, *i.e.* a commitment scheme in which at any point, by investing an amount of effort, it is possible to correctly decommit into the original message. The main conceptual difference with respect to previous works is that, in this work, timing properties are achieved by forcing the algorithm to compute a naturally sequential mathematical problem. From a different perspective, Mahmoody *et al.* [17] defined time-lock puzzles by just assuming the existence of timed primitives. In the last years, many community efforts have been devoted to introduce *verifiable delay functions* (VDFs), *i.e.* to compute a timed function and be able to verify the correct computation of it. There are multiple instantiations of this primitive in the literature, *e.g.* Lenstra *et al.*'s random zoo [16], a construction using randomized encoding by Bitansky *et al.* [5] or Alwen-Tackmann's theoretical consideration regarding *moderately hard functions* [1]. The VDF's formal definition is given by Boneh *et al.* [6], subsequent papers provide additional properties for these time related primitives such as Malavolta-Thyagarajan's homomorphic time-puzzles [18] or the *down-to-earth* VDF instantiation by Wesolowski [21].

Timing Model. Perhaps the closest set of works to our study deals with the Timing Model as introduced by Dwork *et al.* [9], and used by Kalai *et al.* [11]. While they do present similarities to our work, *e.g.* the idea of *"individual clock"*, they also present significant differences. For instance, while in [9,11] every party in the real execution is equipped with a *"clock tape"*, extending the Interactive Turing Machine (ITM) with clocks, in our model the parties are regular ITMs, that perform computations in order to realize a *"single clock"*. Additionally, our work also shares similarities with Azar *et al.* [2] work on *ordered MPC*, which studies delays and ordered messages in the context of MPC. Our framework is positioned between both models as it focuses on turns equipped with a message validating mechanism, which is a different approach. Recently, a concurrent work by Baum *et al.* [3] formalizes the security of time-lock puzzles in the UC framework. They introduce the *UC with Relative Time* (RUC), which allows modelling relative delays in communication and sequential computation without requiring parties to keep track of a clock, in contrast to Katz *et al.*'s [13] approach which models a *"central clock"* that all parties have access. The main contribution introduces a *semi-synchronous* message transmission functionality in which the adversary is aware of a delay Δ used to schedule the message exchanges, while the honest parties are not aware. In their work, composable time-puzzle realizes such novel functionality, and yields UC secure fair coin flips and two party computation achieving the notion of *output independent abort*. They focused on composable primitives and rely on a constrained environment, *i.e.* it has to signal the adversary and activate every party at least once. Another theoretical difference is the focus of the order and turns but not in relative delays as in [3]. Baum *et al.* state as future work a possible extension to their transmission model in which all the parties have a *local clock* that would allow to always terminate any protocol.

2   Preliminaries

We denote vectors with bold font, *e.g.* v, and $\Pr[E]$ the probability of the event E. Let $\{0,1\}^*$ be the binary strings space of arbitrary length, $\mathbb{N}$ the natural numbers, $\mathbb{R}$ the real numbers and $\mathbb{R}_+$ the positive ones. Let $[a, b] \subseteq \mathbb{N}$ denote intervals between a and b and $x \leftarrow_\$ X$ the random uniform sampling in the set X. Let $\mathsf{negl}(\lambda)$ denote a negligible function in λ, *i.e.* $\mathsf{negl}(\lambda) = O(\lambda^{-c})$ for every constant $c > 0$. We omit λ whenever obvious by the context.

Definition 1 (One-Way Hash Function [12]). *Let $n \in \mathbb{N}$. The function* $\mathsf{H} : \{0, 1\}^* \rightarrow \{0, 1\}^n$ *is a* **one-way hash function** *if it satisfies the properties:*

- **Preimage resistance:** *for any* $x \leftarrow_\$ \{0, 1\}^*$ *and* $y := \mathsf{H}(x)$, *for any PPT adversary $\mathcal{A}$ that, on input y, outputs x', it holds that* $\Pr[\mathsf{H}(x') = y] < \mathsf{negl}$;
- **2nd Preimage resistance:** *for any* $x \leftarrow_\$ \{0, 1\}^*$, $y := \mathsf{H}(x)$, *for any PPT adversary $\mathcal{A}$ that, on input x, outputs $x' \neq x$, it holds* $\Pr[\mathsf{H}(x') = y] < \mathsf{negl}$;

Complexity and Time. Let time be modelled as the positive real numbers $\mathbb{R}_+$. At the core of our construction, we must assume the existence of a measure $\mu(\cdot)$ that plays the role of a *"bridge"* between *complexity and timing*. In a nutshell, we want to provide an axioms model that allows to consider algorithms with same computation time whenever executed by different devices. Formally,

Assumption 1. *Given a model of computation $\mathcal{M}$, there exists a measure $\mu(\cdot)$ that takes as input an $\mathcal{M}$-computable function f with input x and outputs the amount of time $\mu(\mathsf{f}, x) \in \mathbb{R}_+$ necessary to compute $\mathsf{f}(x)$ in the model $\mathcal{M}$. If $\mathsf{f}^*(x)$ is a* probabilistic *function with input x and internal randomness r, then there exists $\mathsf{f}(x; r)$ deterministic function that executes $\mathsf{f}^*(x)$ with fixed randomness r.*

Another required assumption is the existence of a function family $\mathcal{F}$ whose functions always output the results after the same amount of time. Formally,

Assumption 2. *Given a model of computation $\mathcal{M}$ and associated $\mu(\cdot)$, there exists a function family $\mathcal{F}$ such that for any function $\mathsf{f} \in \mathcal{F}$, for any inputs x, x', f is* input-independent *with computing time $\mu(\mathsf{f})$, i.e. $\mu(\mathsf{f}) = \mu(\mathsf{f}, x) = \mu(\mathsf{f}, x')$.*

Through the remaining of this work, we consider timing as the output of $\mu(\cdot)$ applied on input-independent functions. Whenever not specified, a *hard* problem is a problem of which solution, computed via f, has *large* computation time $\mu(\mathsf{f})$.

The *timed* one-way hash function extends the hash's properties of Definition 1.

Definition 2. *Let $n \in \mathbb{N}$. The function $_\Delta\mathsf{H} : \{0, 1\}^* \rightarrow \{0, 1\}^n$ is a Δ-delay one-way hash function if it is input-independent as described in Assumption 2 and, in addition to the properties of Definition 1, the following property also holds:*

- **Δ-Delay:** *for any PPT adversary $\mathcal{A}$ that takes an input x and outputs y which runs in time $\mu(\mathcal{A}, x) < \Delta = \mu(_\Delta\mathsf{H})$, it holds that* $\Pr[y = {}_\Delta\mathsf{H}(x)] < \mathsf{negl}$.

Observe that, in order for the Δ-delay's property to make sense, the length of x might be limited, *e.g.* the size of x must be polynomial. We omit such detail and always consider delay hash functions with the appropriate input space size.

Define the **time-lock puzzle** (TLP) as a *generate-solve* algorithm pair in which time plays a design/security aspect. Our definition is inspired by Azar *et al.* [2] and, more specifically, we consider the construction presented by Mahmoody *et al.*'s [17] in the random oracle (RO) model. The provided TLP generates $m{+}1$ *sequential* puzzles, *i.e.* a list of **partial puzzle** y_i of which **partial solution** π_i is necessary in order to solve the next partial puzzle y_{i+1}.

Definition 3. *Let* $m \in \mathbb{N}$, *security parameter* λ *and* $\Delta \in \mathbb{R}_+$ *be the desired time delay. Let* $_\Delta\mathsf{H} : \{0,1\}^* \to \{0,1\}^n$ *be a* Δ-*delay hash function for some* $n \in \mathbb{N}$. *Let* $(\mathsf{GenPuz}, \mathsf{SolPuz})$ *define a* $(m\Delta)$ **time-lock puzzle** *($m\Delta$-TLP) as:*

- $\mathsf{GenPuz}(\lambda, (m, \Delta)) \to (\boldsymbol{y}, \boldsymbol{\pi})$: *the generation algorithm randomly samples* $m + 1$ *bit-strings* $x_i \in \{0,1\}^n$ *and it computes the hash* $_\Delta\mathsf{H}(x_i)$ *for* $i \in [0, m]$. *The algorithm outputs the list of partial puzzles and partial solutions:*

$$(\boldsymbol{y}, \boldsymbol{\pi}) := \Big((x_0, {_\Delta\mathsf{H}}(x_0) \oplus x_1, \ldots, {_\Delta\mathsf{H}}(x_{m-1}) \oplus x_m), (x_0, x_1, \ldots, x_m) \Big);$$

- $\mathsf{SolPuz}(\boldsymbol{y}, k, (\pi_0, \ldots, \pi_{k-1})) \to \pi_k$: *the algorithm parses the puzzle* $\boldsymbol{y}$ *into* $(y_0, y_1, \cdots, y_m)$, $k \in [1, m]$ *and the known partial solutions* $(\pi_0, \ldots, \pi_{k-1})$. *It then outputs the partial solution* $\pi_k := y_k \oplus {_\Delta\mathsf{H}}(\pi_{k-1})$ *where* $\pi_0 := y_0$.

The following three properties must hold:

- *Correctness: for every delay* Δ, *security parameter* λ *and* $m, n \in \mathbb{N}$, *for every puzzle* $(\boldsymbol{y}, \boldsymbol{\pi}) \leftarrow \mathsf{GenPuz}(\lambda, (m, \Delta))$, *for every* $k \in [1, m]$, *it holds that* $\Pr[\mathsf{SolPuz}(\boldsymbol{y}, k, (\pi_0, \ldots, \pi_{k-1})) = \pi_k] = 1$;
- *Timing: for every delay* Δ, *security parameter* λ *and values* $m, n \in \mathbb{N}$, *for every puzzle* $(\boldsymbol{y}, \boldsymbol{\pi}) \leftarrow \mathsf{GenPuz}(\lambda, (m, \Delta))$, *for every* $k \in [1, m]$ *it holds that* $\mu(\mathsf{SolPuz}) = \Delta$ *and generating the puzzle is faster than solving it, i.e.* $\mu(\mathsf{GenPuz}) \leq m \cdot \mu(\mathsf{SolPuz})$;
- *Locking: for every delay* Δ, *security parameter* λ *and values* $m, n \in \mathbb{N}$, *for every puzzle* $(\boldsymbol{y}, \boldsymbol{\pi}) \leftarrow \mathsf{GenPuz}(\lambda, (m, \Delta))$, *for every* $k \in [1, m]$ *and adversary* $\mathcal{A}$ *that solves the* k-*th partial puzzle, i.e.* $\mathcal{A}(y, k, (\pi_0, \ldots, \pi_{k-1})) = \pi_k$, *it holds that* $\mu(\mathcal{A}) < \Delta$ *with only negligible probability.*

The $(m\Delta)$-TLP describes a sequence of sequential puzzles that must be solved one at a time. The timing property guarantees that the SolPuz algorithm requires a specific Δ amount of time to be executed and that generating the whole puzzle takes less time than solving all the m puzzles. The locking property guarantees that any adversary $\mathcal{A}$ is unable to solve the partial puzzle in less time than Δ which implies, intuitively, that SolPuz is the *most optimised* algorithm for solving the partial puzzle y_i. If a better solving algorithm SolPuz' exists with solving time $\Delta' < \Delta$, then $(\mathsf{GenPuz}, \mathsf{SolPuz}')$ is a $(m\Delta')$-TLP while $(\mathsf{GenPuz}, \mathsf{SolPuz})$ cannot satisfy the locking property.

3   Instantiating the Turn Based Communication Channel

In this section, we discuss the core concepts of **timed disclosure**, **turns block** and **communication consistency**, later used to fully instantiate one and two-way TBCC, from a time-lock puzzle based on a Δ-delay hash function.

Timed Disclosure and Message Block. Consider a Δ-delay hash function and the related time-lock puzzle (y, π) as defined in Definition 3. Alice generates and publishes the puzzle y. On receiving y, Bob starts solving it. Within the amount of time Δ, only Alice knows the solution π, which allows her to produce an efficient digest $\xi = H(m, \pi)$ for any message m that she wants to communicate with Bob. At this stage, Bob is unable to compute the same digest because he does not know π. The *"timed disclosure"* is achieved whenever Bob finds the solution π which enables him to accept or reject the previously received message by verifying the correctness of the digest ξ. *Timing is key* for the security of the disclosure: Alice must use the knowledge **before** it is disclosed and, on the other hand, Bob should reject anything that uses such secret **after** the disclosure. Differently, **only** after Δ time, Bob can check which are the correct messages that are binded to the specific solution π and can collect them into a **turn block**. Whenever we consider that Alice can publish a sequential time-lock puzzle in which one partial solution π_i is the *starting point* for the next partial puzzle y_{i+1}, Bob must filter and accept the received messages into a block every Δ amount of time therefore creating the concept of **turns** and relative message blocks. This **turn point-of-view** is possible because of the *sequential timed disclosure* that can be seen as a *"clock that ticks"* every Δ amount of time. This means that the communication is *one-way*, from Alice to Bob. Alice does *not see* the turn because all the partial solutions are known to her and therefore she is able to generate any possible message-digest pair at any time, see Fig. 1.

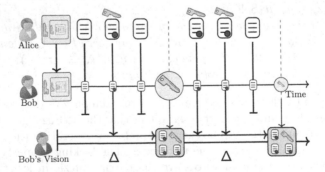

Fig. 1. One-way channel scheme representation. Alice shares a time-lock puzzle with Bob and then sends messages of which some are correctly binded with the next puzzle's partial solution. With that solution, Bob is able to filter out the correct messages. Since this is done every Δ time, in Bob's eyes is as if he is receiving messages in turns.

Block of Messages and Communication Consistency. The next step is to create a *two-way* communication between Alice and Bob by allowing them to instantiate two independent one-way TBCC channels between each other, *i.e.* by exchanging time-lock puzzles and communicating message-digest pairs that are accepted and personally saved in blocks. These blocks are not stored in a trusted third party service but Alice and Bob have their own local copy of the exchanged message history and this means that it is required to provide a procedure to guarantee **consistency** between the copies. Consider our communicating Alice and Bob to be in the i-th turn, *i.e.* at the end of the turn they will create the i-th block. Naively, to achieve consistency of all blocks, every message, of the current block, should be bound to the *previous and future block*. For the *previous block*, they include a digest h_{i-1} of the previous block in every message they share in order to correctly verify that both have the same previous block vision. When the i-th turn ends, they separately create their own block-vision which could be different. When they enter the $(i+1)$-th turn, they will have to share the previous block digest h_i and they will see that the values are different. They will therefore start a **recovery phase** by publishing the content of the i-th block. At this point in time, the message's digest ξ_i can be tampered by anyone since the partial solution π_i is publicly known. For this reason, for every message we define a second digest σ_i that binds such message with the *next turn/future block* solution π_{i+1}. This procedure allows every party to understand *"who is cheating"* or *"where the errors are"*. In this way it is possible to abort the communication at any point in time, whenever a malicious party hijacks the channel. All the parties are thus forced to honestly participate if they want to maintain the channel up.

Timing Simplification and Further Development. For the sake of simplicity, we consider the underlying Δ-delay hash function $_\Delta H$ to have an exact computation timing, *i.e.* every device computing $_\Delta H$ takes exactly $\mu\left(_\Delta H\right) = \Delta$ time. A realistic assumption consider that devices (P_A, P_B) has *similar/comparable* computation times $\left(\mu\left(_\Delta H\right)_{P_A}, \mu\left(_\Delta H\right)_{P_B}\right)$ which means that the difference $\left|\mu\left(_\Delta H\right)_{P_A} - \mu\left(_\Delta H\right)_{P_B}\right|$ must be less (or equal) a designed value ϵ. In this realistic context, the turn-timing provided by the puzzle y is uncertain, *i.e.* the turn length is a value contained in the interval $\Delta - \epsilon < \mu\left(_\Delta H\right)_{P_A} < \Delta + \epsilon$.

Our simplification allows to develop the general TBCC framework and we leave as open questions the technique necessary for achieving a more realistic timing assumption and a more profound security analysis that handles active adversaries and protocol's composition weaknesses.

3.1 One-Way TBCC Definition

In this section, we define the turn-based one-way channel from Alice to Bob. A *"channel"* is any collection of parameters that allows to participate into the communication, *e.g.* whenever a list of parameters is published, anyone can use them to correctly parse future messages shared using them.

Definition 4. *The **one-way channel scheme** is defined with the PPT algorithms* (setup, send, ext, turntoken, valid-ver, tamper-ver) *as:*

- setup$(\lambda, \Delta, n) \rightarrow (\mathcal{C}, \mathcal{C}_{priv})$: *to setup the communication channel, P_A parses the security parameter λ, the delay Δ and the number of turns n The setup algorithm outputs the public and private channels $(\mathcal{C}, \mathcal{C}_{priv})$;*
- send$(\mathcal{C}_{priv}, m, v, t) \rightarrow (\xi, \text{aux})$: *the send-message algorithm takes in input the private channel information $\mathcal{C}_{priv}$, a message m with validity $v \in \{0,1\}$ and the turn $t < n$. The algorithm outputs the message correctness proof ξ and the channel auxiliary information aux.*
- turntoken$(\mathcal{C}, t, \{x_0, \ldots, x_{t-1}\}) \rightarrow x_t$: *this algorithm is executed at the beginning of turn t. The algorithm parses the channel $\mathcal{C}$, the current turn t and the set of previously computed turn tokens $\{x_0, \ldots, x_{t-1}\}$, after Δ amount of time, the algorithm outputs the turn token x_t.*
- valid-ver$(\mathcal{C}, t, m, \xi, x_t) \rightarrow \{0,1\}$: *at the end of the t-th turn, the validity verification takes as input a message m and its proof ξ and the turn token x_t. The algorithm outputs the validity v for the sent message m with proof ξ;*
- tamper-ver$(\mathcal{C}, t, M_{t-1}, m, \text{aux}, \xi) \rightarrow \{0,1\}$: *during the t-th turn, the tamper-verification algorithm takes in input the public channel $\mathcal{C}$, the current turn t, the ordered block of messages M_{t-1} which is the list of valid messages for the turn $t-1$, a sent message m with proof ξ and auxiliary information aux. The algorithm verifies if the sent message m correctly relates to the previously sent messages contained in the block M_{t-1}, thus outputting 1 when this is achieved, otherwise 0.*
- ext$(\mathcal{C}, \mathcal{C}_{priv}, t) \rightarrow x_t$: *the extraction algorithm takes as input the public channel $\mathcal{C}$, the private channel $\mathcal{C}_{priv}$ and a turn $t \leq n$ and outputs the turn token x_t, without investing any multiple of Δ time;*
- backward-ver$(\mathcal{C}, t, M_{t-1}, l) \rightarrow \{0,1\}$: *the recovery algorithm takes as input the public channel $\mathcal{C}$, the current turn t, the previous ordered block M_{t-1} of $b_{t-1} = |M_{t-1}|$ valid messages m_i and an index $l \in [1, b_{t-1}]$. The algorithm outputs if the l-th message m^* in the block M_{t-1} is a correct message for the block M_{t-1} at the end of turn t.*

Let us explain how to generate a communication channel from Alice P_A to Bob P_B. First, P_A executes setup for an agreed delay Δ and amount of turns n, and obtains the channels $(\mathcal{C}, \mathcal{C}_{priv})$, *e.g.* the public channel $\mathcal{C}$ can consist of P_A's public key and public parameters while the private channel $\mathcal{C}_{priv}$ contains P_A's private key. The knowledge of $\mathcal{C}_{priv}$ allows P_A to quickly compute each turn token x_t *directly* as ext$(\mathcal{C}, \mathcal{C}_{priv}, t)$ while P_B must *sequentially* compute them as turntoken$(\mathcal{C}, t, \{x_0, \ldots, x_{t-1}\})$ and obtain them every Δ amount of time, similarly to a periodic scheduling process. Whenever P_A sends the message m in a turn t, she executes send for a *valid* message in the t *turn* and sends to P_B the tuple (m, ξ, aux). P_B can execute valid-ver$(\mathcal{C}, t, m, \xi, x_t)$ and verify the message validity only whenever P_B obtains the turn token x_t, computable only after $t \cdot \Delta$ amount of time. This allows P_A to communicate several messages of which P_B cannot immediately verify the validity of m but it has to wait for turntoken to output the specific turn token x_t thus creating the view of turns of the channel.

Message Validity. The sender's inputs are the validity value v, a bit which indicates if the message is considered valid or not, along with the message m

itself and the choice of turn t. Only when the turn t ends, the receiver can verify the validity of the message via the valid-ver algorithm and the turn token x_t.

Definition 5 (Channel Correctness/Message Validity). *Assume a turn* $t \leq n$ *in a* n-*turn channel generated by the algorithms of Definition 4, then for all message/validity pairs* m *and* v, *the channel is said to be correct if*

$$\Pr\left[\text{valid-ver}(\mathcal{C}, t, m, \xi, x_t) \neq v \,\middle|\, \begin{array}{l} \text{setup}(\lambda, \Delta, n) \to (\mathcal{C}, \mathcal{C}_{priv}); \\ \text{send}(\mathcal{C}_{priv}, m, v, t) \to (\xi, \text{aux}); \\ \text{ext}(\mathcal{C}, \mathcal{C}_{priv}, t) \to x_t; \end{array}\right] \leq \text{negl}(\lambda),$$

with probability computed over the random coins of setup, send, ext *and* valid-ver.

Sequentiality and Turn Definition. The turns of the channel rely on the time necessary to compute the token values x_t via turntoken, defined in the channel $\mathcal{C}$ during the general setup. Each computed turn-tokens x_t, allows the receiver to verify the validity and consistency of all received messages during the turn t, crucially, only at the end of the turn after the expected delay time Δ.

Definition 6 (Sequentiality). *The channel is* Δ-*sequential if for any turn* t, *for any PPT adversary* $\mathcal{A}$ *running in time* $\mu(\mathcal{A}) < \Delta$, *the adversary wins the game* $\text{Game}_{seq}^{\mathcal{A},\Delta}(\lambda, t, n)$ *of Algorithm 1, with negligible advantage, namely,*

$$\left|\Pr[\text{Game}_{seq}^{\mathcal{A},\Delta}(\lambda, t, n) = 1] - \frac{1}{2}\right| \leq \text{negl}(\lambda).$$

Algorithm 1. Sequentiality Game $\text{Game}_{seq}^{\mathcal{A},\Delta}(\lambda, t, n)$ for the adversary $\mathcal{A}$

1: Execute $\text{setup}(\lambda, \Delta, n) \to (\mathcal{C}, \mathcal{C}_{priv})$;
2: Choose a random message m and validity $v \leftarrow \{0, 1\}$.
3: Execute $\text{ext}(\mathcal{C}, \mathcal{C}_{priv}, i) \to x_i$ for $i \in [1, t-1]$ and $\text{send}(\mathcal{C}_{priv}, m, v, t) \to (\xi, \text{aux})$
4: $v^* \leftarrow \mathcal{A}(\mathcal{C}, t, m, \xi, \text{aux}, \{x_i\}_{i=1}^{t-1})$
5: Execute $\text{ext}(\mathcal{C}, \mathcal{C}_{priv}, t) \to x_t$
6: If $\text{valid-ver}(\mathcal{C}, t, m, \xi, x_t) = v^*$, output 1. Otherwise, 0

Last Turn Tamper Resistance. Given any $t \leq n$ of a TBCC with public setup information $\mathcal{C}$, define the block M_{t-1} as the set of all j_{t-1} messages in the turn $t-1$ with respective auxiliary information $\text{aux}_1, \ldots, \text{aux}_{j_{t-1}}$ and sent proof $\xi_1, \ldots, \xi_{j_{t-1}}$. The algorithm $\text{tamper-ver}(\mathcal{C}, t, M_{t-1}, m, \text{aux}, \xi)$ checks, for any correctly computed message $(m, \text{aux}, \xi) \in M_t$, if it correctly relates to the previous turn block M_{t-1} by spotting whenever this connection is tampered.

Definition 7 (Last Turn Tamper Resistance). *During the turn* $t \leq n$ *of a channel* $\mathcal{C}$ *between two honest parties with correct message blocks* M_i *for each turn* $1 \leq i < t$, $\mathcal{C}$ *is tamper resistant, if for any PPT adversary* $\mathcal{A}$, *it holds*

$$\Pr\left[\begin{array}{l} \text{tamper-ver}(\mathcal{C}, t, M^*_{t-1}, m^*, \text{aux}^*, \xi^*) = 1| \\ (M^*_{t-1}, m^*, \text{aux}^*, \xi^*) \leftarrow \mathcal{A}(\mathcal{C}, t, M_1, \ldots, M_{t-1}) \end{array}\right] \leq \text{negl}(\lambda)$$

such that $M^*_{t-1} \neq M_{t-1}$ *and* tamper-ver$(\mathcal{C}, t, M_{t-1}, m^*, aux^*, \xi^*) = 1$. *The probability is computed over the random coins of* $\mathcal{A}$ *and algorithm* tamper-ver.

Communication Consistency. For any turn $t \leq n$ of a one-way channel $\mathcal{C}$, the channel is *consistent until turn* $t-1$ whenever the *valid* messages view between the parties is the same during the turn t, *i.e.* an adversary **must not** be able to force a wrong message history, regardless if it is the sender or the receiver.

Definition 8 (Consistency). *During turn* $t \leq n$ *of a one-way TBCC channel* $\mathcal{C}$ *between two parties with correct message blocks* M_i *for each turn* $1 \leq i < t$, *the channel is* **consistent until turn** $t-1$, *if for any PPT adversary* $\mathcal{A}$, *it holds*

$$\Pr\left[\text{tamper-ver}(\mathcal{C}, t, M^*_{t-1}, m^*, aux^*, \xi^*) = 1 \mid \right.$$
$$\left. (M^*_{t-1}, m^*, aux^*, \xi^*) \leftarrow \mathcal{A}(\mathcal{C}, t, M_1, \ldots, M_{t-1}) \right] \leq \text{negl}(\lambda)$$

such that $M^*_{t-1} \neq M_{t-1}$, tamper-ver$(\mathcal{C}, t, M_{t-1}, m^*, aux^*, \xi^*) = 1$ *and for all the messages of the tampered block, along with auxiliary information and proof, i.e.* $(m^*_{j_i}, aux^*_{j_i}, \xi^*_{j_i}) \in M^*_{t-1}$, *it holds* valid-ver$(\mathcal{C}, t - 1, m^*_{j_i}, \xi^*_{j_i}, x_{t-1}) = 1$ *The probability is computed over the random coins of* $\mathcal{A}$, tamper-ver *and* valid-ver.

One-Way Channel Instantiation. Let $\Delta \in \mathbb{R}_+$ be a time-delay and $n \in \mathbb{N}$ a maximal turn number, both chosen by Alice, denoted with P_A. Let H and $_\Delta$H be respectively regular and Δ-delay hash functions. Let (GenPuz, SolPuz) be the $(n\Delta)$-TLP of Definition 3 based on $_\Delta$H.

Construction 1. *Let* λ *be the security parameter,* $n \in \mathbb{N}$ *number of turns, a sender* P_A *and a receiver* P_B. *Instantiate the one-way channel scheme with the PPT algorithms* (setup, send, ext, turntoken, valid-ver, tamper-ver) *defined as:*

- setup$(\lambda, \Delta, n) \rightarrow (\mathcal{C}, \mathcal{C}_{priv})$: *to setup the communication channel,* P_A *parses the security parameter* λ, *the delay* Δ *and the number of turns* n *and executes* GenPuz$(\lambda, (n, \Delta))$ *as defined in Definition 3 and obtains the* n *turn puzzle with solution* $(\boldsymbol{y}, \boldsymbol{\pi})$. *Output* $(\mathcal{C}, \mathcal{C}_{priv})$ *as* $(\boldsymbol{y}, \boldsymbol{\pi})$;
- send$(\mathcal{C}_{priv}, m, v, t) \rightarrow (\xi, aux)$: *to send a message* m *with validity* v *in the turn* $t < n$, P_A *parses the private channel information* $\mathcal{C}_{priv} = \boldsymbol{\pi}$, *and compute* $h_{t-1} := H(M_{t-1}, m, \pi_{t-1})$, $\xi := H(m, \pi_t)$ *and* $\sigma := H(m, \xi, \pi_{t+1})$ *where* M_{t-1} *is the ordered list of valid messages in the turn* $(t-1)$, *together with validity proof and auxiliary information. The sending algorithm outputs, if* $v = 1$, *the message correctness proof* ξ *and the channel auxiliary information* aux $=$ (h_{t-1}, σ), *otherwise random values* (ξ, aux) *different from the correct ones.*
- turntoken$(\mathcal{C}, t, \{x_0, \ldots, x_{t-1}\}) \rightarrow x_t$: *this algorithm is executed by the receiver* P_B *at the beginning of turn* t. *It parses the channel* $\mathcal{C} = \boldsymbol{y}$ *and continually executes* SolPuz$(\boldsymbol{y})$ *by considering that every* $\pi_i := x_i$ *for the* t *partial solution. After* Δ *amount of time, the output of the algorithm is* $x_t := \pi_t$.

- valid-ver$(\mathcal{C}, \mathsf{t}, \mathsf{m}, \xi, x_\mathsf{t}) \rightarrow \{0,1\}$: *at the end of the* t-*th turn, the validity verification takes as input a message* m *and its proof* ξ *and the turn token* $x_\mathsf{t} = \pi_\mathsf{t}$. *Output 1 if the equality* $H(\mathsf{m}, \pi_\mathsf{t}) \stackrel{?}{=} \xi$ *holds. Otherwise, 0;*
- tamper-ver$(\mathcal{C}, \mathsf{t}, \mathsf{M}_{\mathsf{t}-1}, \mathsf{m}, \mathsf{aux}, \xi) \rightarrow \{0,1\}$: *during the* t-*th turn, the receiver* P_B *verify the correctness of the ordered* (t − 1)-*th block* $\mathsf{M}_{\mathsf{t}-1}$ *which contains the previously valid ordered messages* $\{m_i\}_{i=1}^{j_{t-1}}$ *for some* $j_{t-1} \in \mathbb{N}$, *by parsing the auxiliary information as* $\mathsf{aux} = (\mathsf{h}_{\mathsf{t}-1}, \sigma)$ *and outputs the result of the equality verification* $H(\mathsf{M}_{\mathsf{t}-1}, \mathsf{m}, \pi_{\mathsf{t}-1}) \stackrel{?}{=} \mathsf{h}_{\mathsf{t}-1}$.
- ext$(\mathcal{C}, \mathcal{C}_{priv}, \mathsf{t}) \rightarrow x_\mathsf{t}$: *the extraction algorithm takes as input the public channel* $\mathcal{C}$, *the private channel* $\mathcal{C}_{priv} = \pi$ *and a turn* $\mathsf{t} \leq n$ *and outputs* $x_\mathsf{t} = \pi_\mathsf{t}$;
- backward-ver$(\mathcal{C}, \mathsf{t}, \mathsf{M}_{\mathsf{t}-1}, l) \rightarrow \{0,1\}$: *the algorithm takes as input the public channel* $\mathcal{C}$, *the current turn* t, *the previous ordered block* $\mathsf{M}_{\mathsf{t}-1}$, *of accepted message* m_i *for* $i \in [1, j_{t-1}]$, *and an index* l *such that* m^* *is the* l-*th message in the block* $\mathsf{m}^* = m_l \in \mathsf{M}_{\mathsf{t}-1}$ *with auxiliary information* $\mathsf{aux}^* = \mathsf{aux}_l = (\mathsf{h}_{\mathsf{t}-2}^*, \sigma^*)$. backward-ver *computes* $\xi^* = H(\mathsf{m}^*, \pi_{\mathsf{t}-1})$ *and outputs if* $H(\mathsf{m}^*, \xi^*, \pi_\mathsf{t}) \stackrel{?}{=} \sigma^*$. *The* backward-ver *algorithm verifies at the end of turn* t *if the message* m^* *is a correct message for the block* $\mathsf{M}_{\mathsf{t}-1}$.

Proposition 1. *The proposed one-way channel instantiation of Construction 1 achieves channel correctness as stated in Definition 5, sequentiality as stated in Definition 6 and last turn tamper resistance as stated in Definition 7. Furthermore, it holds that consistency* $\leftrightarrow$ *last turn tamper resistant and correctness.*

Two-Way TBCC Protocol Instantiation. We instantiate a two-way TBCC and explain how to correctly realise the *recovery procedure, i.e.* a procedure executed between the parties that allows them to force the communication's correctness and coherence. Consider the parties P_A and P_B and let both independently setup the consistent one-way channel of Construction 1 which casts them both as receiver and sender into two independent channels each. Both parties can send a message to the other one in the channel they created. Concurrently, each party tracks its local turn, receive and check messages by *(1)* continuously executing turntoken and *(2)* keeping of the previously generated turn tokens x_i for $i \leq \mathsf{t}$

Protocol 1 (The Two-Way TBCC Protocol). *Given two parties* P_A *and* P_B, *an integer value* n *and real non-zero value* Δ, *define the (Two-Way) TBCC across* n *turns with delay* Δ *with the procedures:*

- **Setup:** *on input the security parameter* λ, P_A *(respectively* P_B) *executes* setup(λ, Δ, n), *obtains* $(\mathcal{C}_A, \mathcal{C}_{A,priv})$, *and sends* $\mathcal{C}_A$ *to* P_B, *which replies with* $\mathcal{C}_B$. P_A *outputs the two-way* TBCC *channel information* $(\mathcal{C}_A, \mathcal{C}_B)$, *along with its respective private information* $\mathcal{C}_{priv}$ *and* P_A *performs* turntoken$(\mathcal{C}_B, 1, x_{B,0})$;
- **Local Turn (analogously for** P_B**):** *on receiving a call to this procedure,* P_A *returns the current local turn* t *corresponding to the last computed* $x_{P_B, \mathsf{t}}$;

- **Send Message (analogously for P_B):** *on a given local turn* t, *when* P_A *receives the input* (m, v), *it executes* send$(\mathcal{C}_{A,priv}, \mathsf{m}, v, \mathsf{t}) \rightarrow (\xi, \mathsf{aux})$ *where the previous block digest is computed as* $\mathsf{h}_{t-1} := \mathsf{H}(\mathsf{M}_{t-1}, \mathsf{m}, \pi_{t-1}^{P_A}, \pi_{t-1}^{P_B})$, *and sends* $(\mathsf{m}, \xi, \mathsf{aux})$ *to* P_B;

- **Reveal Validity (analogously for P_A):** *at the end of the local turn* t, *i.e. when the algorithm* turntoken$(\mathcal{C}_A, \mathsf{t}, \{x_{A,0}, \dots, x_{A,t-1}\})$ *outputs the token* $x_{A,t}$, P_B *executes* valid-ver$(\mathcal{C}_A, \mathsf{t}, m_i, \xi_i, x_{A,t}) \rightarrow v_i$, *and outputs the block of both the parties valid messages* $\mathsf{M}_t = \{(m_i, \xi_i, \mathsf{aux}_i)\}_i$ *along with the turn token* t *whenever* $v_i = 1$. *Furthermore, for all the messages* m_i, tamper-ver$(\mathcal{C}_A, \mathsf{t}, \mathsf{M}_{t-1}, m_i, \mathsf{aux}_i, \xi_i)$ *is executed and if any result is* 0, *abort the communication. If* $\mathsf{t} + 1 > n$, *then output* CLOSE *and stop. Otherwise, execute* turntoken$(\mathcal{C}_A, \mathsf{t} + 1, \{x_{A,0}, \dots, x_{A,t}\})$.

The TBCC protocol naturally extends the one-way properties of correctness and tamper resistance to the two-way channel.

Turn Synchronization and Consistency. When considering the two-way protocol by instantiating two one-way turn based schemes, an additional problem that naturally arises is *turn synchronization between the parties*. Consider the parties P_A and P_B communicating using Protocol 1 which depends on the specific one-way channels $\mathcal{C}_A$ and $\mathcal{C}_B$. The specific channel turn is identified by the input of the algorithm turntoken which are, *almost surely*, never synchronized, *i.e.* the outputs are disclosed in different moments. This timing difference creates a problem in which a message m might be seen in turn t by P_A and in turn (t + 1) by P_B. We capture this idea by formalizing the *turn synchronization* property.

Definition 9 (Turn Synchronization). *Let P_A and P_B be parties communicating over the two-way* TBCC. *The* TBCC *channel* $(\mathcal{C}_A, \mathcal{C}_B)$ *is* **turn-consistent** *if both players have a **unique and equal** way to decide in which turn the message* m *belongs even then the **local turns** of the two parties are different.*

The TBCC without turn synchronization cannot achieve communication consistency since the parties might disagree in which block M the message m belongs, making it unlikely to create an unique communication history. We prove that if we have a sequential one-way scheme, then there exists a natural way to achieve turn-consistency by cleverly letting the parties **avoid communicating**.

Proposition 2. *Let P_A and P_B be parties communicating via the two-way* TBCC *protocol, constructed from a sequential one-way scheme as in Definition 6. The strategy of (i) dropping communicated messages during de-synchronization, i.e. the local turn between the parties is different; and (ii) globally advance the turn whenever both parties have the same local turn; allows turn-consistency as in Definition 9.*

Recovery Procedure. We consider the existence of a *recovery procedure* that should be executed whenever a party spots a possible communication tamper and, instead of directly aborting the protocol, the two parties try to find a common correct message block. In other words, the algorithm tamper-ver from Construction 1 takes as input the last block views M_{P_A} and M_{P_B} that the two parties have and either outputs a commonly agreeable block M or aborts.

Definition 10 (Recovery). *Define the recovery procedure for Protocol 1 as the procedure executed during turn* $t \leq n$ *by* P_A *(resp.* P_B*) whenever the tamper verification* tamper-ver$(\mathcal{C}, t, M_{t-1}, m, aux, \xi)$ *is equal* 0 *and defined as:*

– **Recovery**: *P_A sends its view M_{t-1}^A to P_B from whom it receives the view M_{t-1}^B which is a ordered list of messages $\{m_i\}_{i=1}^{j_{t-1}}$ and, additionally, for every message the received auxiliary information σ. After identifying the set of indexes I where the views differ, for each index $l \in I$, if the message m_l is a message from P_B, then P_A executes* backward-ver$(\mathcal{C}_B, t, M_{t-1}^B, l)$*, otherwise P_B will compute* backward-ver$(\mathcal{C}_A, t, M_{t-1}^A, l)$*. Either the case, if the result is 1, both parties are forced to use the message m_l resolving the discrepancy and saving the result into the same resolved block M_{t-1}. Otherwise, if there exists an index for which the result is 0, the communication is aborted.*

The spirit of the TBCC is *"if anything seems wrong, abort!"*. This forces the parties to behave honestly otherwise nothing can be achieved, meaning there can never exist **two** different correct views. During the recovery procedure, the communication is paused and completely verified and fixed before continuing and, if necessary, aborted because it is unrecoverable. The receiver must promptly alert the sender if h_{i-1} is wrong and, if it is the case, only the receiver can force the sender to adopt a specific message m_i by exhibiting the received proof σ_i, only computable by the sender. Formally, suppose P_A and P_B are correctly communicating until the i-th turn, *i.e.* all the blocks until M_{i-1} are consistent. P_A sends $\left(h_{i-1}^A, m_i^A, \xi_i^A, \sigma_i^A\right)$ and P_B does the same with the message m_i^B. Let us suppose that the values $\{\xi_i^A, \xi_i^B\}$ are correct otherwise the messages will be discarded by valid-ver. Thus the correct next block is $M_i = \{m_i^A, m_i^B\}$. Whenever the turn $(i+1)$ starts, P_B and P_A must share the block digests h_i^A and h_i^B and suppose they are not equal. The recovery procedure is executed and P_B will publish the block-view $\{m_i^A, m_i^B\}$, respectively P_A must do the same, and there must be at least a different message pair, *w.l.o.g.* suppose it is message m_i^A and m^{A*}. Since this is the message that Alice sent, in the recovery, we will just consider Bob's view m^{A*} with received auxiliary information σ^{A*} which Bob cannot correctly forge by assumption, *i.e.* he cannot produce a correct valid pair. Therefore P_B can only publish what P_A sent **or** abort the communication. Regardless of P_B's maliciousness, he is unable to modify P_A's messages and therefore the procedure continues only if σ^{A*} is correctly computed by P_A. In the case that P_B's message m_i^B is different, P_A's vision is considered. If P_B is honest, the previous discussion applies for Alice. Otherwise, P_B might try to force the acceptance of a different pair (m^{B*}, σ^{B*}). Since his vision during recovery is not considered, he must have sent the tampered values (m^{B*}, σ^{B*}) *before* but if this is the case, either Alice is presenting the tampered pair (m^{B*}, σ^{B*}), which makes the pair not longer a tamper, since it is correctly received by Alice and not later modified, or by sending an incorrect pair that will lead to aborting the communication.

4   Collectively Flipping Coins over the **TBCC**

In this section, we sketch a protocol that allows two parties to *collectively flip a coin* The provided coin-flip solution is *simplistic* and it has the main goal of showing the TBCC's expressiveness/potentiality. The underlying idea is that two parties, communicating over a TBCC's instance, are able to *jointly* flip a coin by both time-committing to some randomness which is later revealed and used to compute the coin result. By repeatedly flipping coins, the results produce a random string which is guaranteed to be consistent since communicated over TBCC. Let us formalise of the protocol between Alice P_A and Bob P_B, defined by a set of choices Σ and a set of rules that uniquely determine the *result* between any two choices, denoted with the function $\phi(\cdot, \cdot)$. The protocol is defined as:

1. P_A and P_B set up the two-way TBCC protocol of Protocol 1 and obtain the public channel $\mathcal{C} = (\mathcal{C}_{P_A}, \mathcal{C}_{P_B})$;
2. In the current turn, P_A selects its choice $a \in \Sigma$ and sends on $\mathcal{C}$ as a valid message, *i.e.* P_A execute the sending procedure with the message $(a, 1)$. For each other choice $a^* \in \Sigma$, P_A sends the non-valid message $(a^*, 0)$. Respectively, P_B sends his valid and invalid messages;
3. At the end of the turn, P_A computes the validity of P_B's received messages and obtains b. Respectively for P_B;
4. Both the parties compute $\phi(a, b)$ and, if necessary, repeat the game. If the channel loses consistency, *i.e.* one of the party tries to tamper the results, the communication is aborted;
5. The random string is obtained by concatenating several consecutive results of the consistent channel.

The *"commit-decommit"* phase created by the turn token is key to allow a fair-play since, for example, if P_A knows P_B's choice b in advance, she can select a winning choice a^*. Furthermore, ϕ must be defined even in the case of one party not participating in the round or it tries to cheat by proposing multiple choices. We are now left to define the choice's set Σ and the rule's map $\phi(\cdot, \cdot)$. Σ contains the choices head and tail, respectively 1 and 0 and, additionally, a special element x that represents any non-correct choice, *i.e.* a party does not correctly participate in the game. Define the map ϕ as $\phi(a, b) = a \oplus b$, *i.e.* the xor between the inputs where the special element is mapped as $\phi(x, a) = \phi(a, x) = a$ for each $a \in \Sigma$ and we consider a special state X used to denote that both player wrongly participated in the flipping, *i.e.* $\phi(x, x) = X$. In a nutshell, $\phi(a, b)$ computes the xor of both the parties inputs whenever they are correctly participating in the coin-flip. Complementary, if both the parties wrongly flip the coin, $\phi(x, x)$ returns that the coin is in a *"draw position"* with *"no winner"*. Whenever a party, *e.g.* P_A, wrongly participates in the protocol, $\phi(x, b)$ awards the other party P_B for correctly behaving and let P_B's choice be the final result. This forces the parties to correctly behave to avoid the other party highly influence the coin-flip. For example, suppose that P_A selects 1 as her first choice and sends to P_B the TBCC messages $(1, 1)$ and $(0, 0)$ during the current turn. By the sequentiality property,

P_B is unable to discover *"which message is the valid one"* and therefore has no advantage and must therefore provide his own choice, *w.l.o.g.* let P_B choose 0. At the end of the turn, the valid messages are maintained thus the block will contain P_A's message 1 and P_B's one 0. Both the parties can now compute $\phi(1,0) = 1$ and acknowledge that the coin flip is 1. The TBCC protocol guarantees communication coherence which implies that, whenever repeating the game, both the parties **must** accept the previous communication transcription. In other words, *while* communicating over C, P_A and P_B cannot modify the output of the different rounds played. This means that if the result is 1, in the next round P_B cannot pretend a different outcome and must accept it if he wants to participate in the next round. The game output's transcript can be seen as a random string between P_A and P_B which cannot be tampered with by a malicious adversary. Additionally, every time the adversary is caught tampering or deny the communication, the whole protocol is terminated making it impossible for the adversary to gain any relevant advantage.

Observe that our protocol **does not** approximate a *public coin flip* protocol since, in our protocol the parties *actively collaborate* to sample a random string.

Acknowledgements. This work was partially supported by the Swedish Research Council (Vetenskapsrådet) through the grant PRECIS (621-2014-4845), National Nature Science Foundation of China (No. 61972124), Zhejiang Provincial Natural Science Foundation of China (No. LY19F020019) and STINT grant (2017-7444).

References

1. Alwen, J., Tackmann, B.: Moderately hard functions: definition, instantiations, and applications. In: TCC (2017). https://doi.org/10.1007/978-3-319-70500-2_17
2. Azar, P.D., Goldwasser, S., Park, S.: How to incentivize data-driven collaboration among competing parties. In: ITCS (2016). https://doi.org/10.1145/2840728.2840758
3. Baum, C., David, B., Dowsley, R., Nielsen, J.B., Oechsner, S.: TARDIS: time and relative delays in simulation. Technical Report 537 (2020)
4. Bentov, I., Gabizon, A., Mizrahi, A.: Cryptocurrencies without proof of work. In: FC (2016). https://doi.org/10.1007/978-3-662-53357-4_10
5. Bitansky, N., Goldwasser, S., Jain, A., Paneth, O., Vaikuntanathan, V., Waters, B.: Time-lock puzzles from randomized encodings. In: ITCS (2016). https://doi.org/10.1145/2840728.2840745
6. Boneh, D., Bonneau, J., Bünz, B., Fisch, B.: Verifiable delay functions. In: CRYPTO, vol. 10991 (2018). https://doi.org/10.1007/978-3-319-96884-1_25
7. Boneh, D., Bünz, B., Fisch, B.: Batching techniques for accumulators with applications to IOPs and stateless blockchains. In: CRYPTO (2019). https://doi.org/10.1007/978-3-030-26948-7_20
8. Boneh, D., Naor, M.: Timed commitments. In: CRYPTO (2000)
9. Dwork, C., Naor, M., Sahai, A.: Concurrent zero-knowledge. J. ACM **51**(6) (2004). https://doi.org/10.1145/1039488.1039489
10. Garay, J., Kiayias, A., Leonardos, N.: The bitcoin backbone protocol: analysis and applications. https://doi.org/10.1007/978-3-662-46803-6_10

11. Kalai, Y.T., Lindell, Y., Prabhakaran, M.: Concurrent composition of secure protocols in the timing model. J. Cryptol. **20**(4), 431–492 (2007). https://doi.org/10.1007/s00145-007-0567-1
12. Katz, J., Lindell, Y.: Introduction to modern cryptography (2014)
13. Katz, J., Maurer, U., Tackmann, B., Zikas, V.: Universally composable synchronous computation. In: TCC. https://doi.org/10.1007/978-3-642-36594-2_27
14. Katz, J., Miller, A., Shi, E.: Pseudonymous broadcast and secure computation from cryptographic puzzles. Cryptology ePrint Archive, Report 2014/857 (2014). https://eprint.iacr.org/2014/857
15. Kiayias, A., Russell, A., David, B., Oliynykov, R.: Ouroboros: a provably secure proof-of-stake blockchain protocol. In: CRYPTO, vol. 10401 (2017). https://doi.org/10.1007/978-3-319-63688-7_12
16. Lenstra, A.K., Wesolowski, B.: A random zoo: sloth, unicorn, and trx. Cryptology ePrint Archive, Report 2015/366 (2015). https://eprint.iacr.org/2015/366
17. Mahmoody, M., Moran, T., Vadhan, S.: Time-lock puzzles in the random oracle model. In: CRYPTO (2011). https://doi.org/10.1007/978-3-642-22792-9_3
18. Malavolta, G., Thyagarajan, S.A.K.: Homomorphic time-lock puzzles and applications. In: CRYPTO (2019). https://doi.org/10.1007/978-3-030-26948-7_22
19. Rivest, R.L., Shamir, A., Wagner, D.A.: Time-lock puzzles and timed-release crypto. Technical report, Massachusetts Institute of Technology (1996)
20. Scafuro, A., Siniscalchi, L., Visconti, I.: Publicly verifiable proofs from blockchains. In: PKC (2019). https://doi.org/10.1007/978-3-030-17253-4_13
21. Wesolowski, B.: Efficient verifiable delay functions. In: EUROCRYPT (2019). https://doi.org/10.1007/978-3-030-17659-4_13

Author Index

Printed in the United States
by Baker & Taylor Publisher Services

Printed in the United States
by Baker & Taylor Publisher Services